VW
GOLF/JETTA/CABRIOLET
1990-93 REPAIR MANUAL

President, Chilton Enterprises   David S. Loewith

Senior Vice President   Ronald A. Hoxter
Publisher & Editor-In-Chief   Kerry A. Freeman, S.A.E.
Managing Editors   Peter M. Conti, Jr., W. Calvin Settle, Jr., S.A.E.
Assistant Managing Editor   Nick D'Andrea
Senior Editors   Debra Gaffney, Ken Grabowski, A.S.E., S.A.E.
Michael L. Grady, Richard J. Rivele, S.A.E.
Richard T. Smith, Jim Taylor
Ron Webb
Project Managers   Martin J. Gunther, Jeffrey M. Hoffman
Director of Manufacturing   Mike D'Imperio
Editor   Jacques Gordon

CHILTON BOOK COMPANY

ONE OF THE **DIVERSIFIED PUBLISHING COMPANIES,**
A PART OF **CAPITAL CITIES/ABC, INC.**

Manufactured in USA
© 1993 Chilton Book Company
Chilton Way, Radnor, PA 19089
ISBN 0-8019-8429-7
Library of Congress Catalog Card No. 92-054889
1234567890 2109876543

Contents

1 ROUTINE MAINTENANCE

1-2 HOW TO USE THIS BOOK
1-6 MODEL IDENTIFICATION
1-6 SERIAL NUMBER IDENTIFICATION
1-9 ROUTINE MAINTENANCE
1-20 FLUIDS AND LUBRICANTS
1-28 JACKING

2 ENGINE PERFORMANCE AND TUNE-UP

2-2 SPECIFICATIONS CHARTS
2-3 FIRING ORDERS
2-4 ELECTRONIC IGNITION
2-10 VALVE LASH
2-10 IDLE SPEED

3 ENGINE AND ENGINE REBUILDING

3-2 ENGINE ELECTRICAL
3-7 ENGINE MECHANICAL
3-40 EXHAUST SYSTEM

4 EMISSION CONTROLS

4-2 AIR POLLUTION
4-3 EXHAUST EMISSIONS
4-6 VOLKSWAGEN EMISSION CONTROLS
4-10 ELECTRONIC ENGINE CONTROLS
4-23 DIAGNOSTIC CODES DATA
4-31 VACUUM DIAGRAMS

5 FUEL SYSTEM

5-2 CIS-E MOTRONIC FUEL INJECTION SYSTEM
5-7 DIGIFANT FUEL INJECTION SYSTEM
5-10 DIESEL FUEL SYSTEM
5-13 FUEL TANK

6 ELECTRICAL CHASSIS

6-9 AIR BAG
6-15 AIR CONDITIONING
6-18 CRUISE CONTROL
6-21 WINDSHIELD WIPERS
6-25 LIGHTING
6-26 CIRCUIT PROTECTION
6-27 WIRING DIAGRAMS

Contents

7-2 MANUAL TRANSAXLE
7-12 CLUTCH
7-14 AUTOMATIC TRANSAXLE

DRIVE TRAIN 7

8-2 SUSPENSION AND STEERING
8-9 STEERING
8-2 FRONT SUSPENSION
8-8 REAR SUSPENSION

SUSPENSION AND STEERING 8

9-2 BRAKE OPERATING SYSTEM
9-5 FRONT DISC BRAKES
9-9 REAR DRUM BRAKES
9-11 REAR DISC BRAKES
9-14 PARKING BRAKE
9-14 ANTI-LOCK BRAKE SYSTEM

BRAKES 9

10-2 EXTERIOR
10-8 INTERIOR

BODY AND TRIM 10

10-15 GLOSSARY

GLOSSARY

10-21 MASTER INDEX

MASTER INDEX

SAFETY NOTICE

Proper service and repair procedures are vitatl to the safe, reliable operation of all motor vehicles, as well as the personal safety of those performing repairs. This manual outlines procedures for servicing and repairing vehicles using safe, effective methods. The procedures contain many NOTES, CAUTIONS, and WARNINGS which should be followed along with standard procedures to eliminate the possibility of personal injury or improper service which could damage the vehicle or compromise its safety.

It is important to note that the repair procedures and techniques, tools and parts for servicing motor vehicles, as well as the skill and experience of the individual performing the work vary widely. It is not possible to anticipate all of the conceivable ways or conditions under which vehicles may be serviced, or to provide cautions as to all of the possible hazards that may result. Standard and accepted safety precautions and equipment should be used when handling toxic or flammable fluids, and safety goggles or other protection should be used during cutting, grinding, chiseling, prying,or any other process that can cause material removal or projectiles.

Some procedures require the use of tools specially designed for a specific purpose. Before substituting another tool or procedure, you must be completely satisfied that neither your personal safety, nor the performance of the vehicle will be endangered.

Although information in this manual is based on industry sources and is complete as possible at the time of publication, the possibility exists that some car manufacturers made later changes which could not be included here. While striving for total accuracy, Chilton Book Company cannot assume responsibility for any errors, changes or omissions that may occur in the compilation of this data.

PART NUMBERS

Part numbers listed in this reference are not recommendation by Chilton for any product by brand name. They are references that can be used with interchange manuals and aftermarket supplier catalogs to locate each brand supplier's discrete part number.

SPECIAL TOOLS

Special tools are recommended by the vehicle manufacturer to perform their specific job. Use has been kept to a minimum, but where absolutely necessary, they are referred to in the text by the part number of the tool manufacturer. These tools can be purchased, under the appropriate part number, from your Honda dealer or regional distributor, or an equivalent tool can be purchased locally from a tool supplier or parts outlet. Before substituting any tool for the one recommended, read the SAFETY NOTICE at the top of this page.

ACKNOWLEDGMENTS

The Chilton Book Company expresses appreciation to the Volkswagen of America, Inc. for their generous assistance.

FLUIDS AND LUBRICANTS
  AUTOMATIC TRANSAXLE 1-23
  BODY LUBRICATION 1-26
  CHASSIS GREASING 1-25
  CLUTCH MASTER CYLINDER 1-25
  COOLING SYSTEM 1-24
  DIFFERENTIAL 1-24
  ENGINE OIL
   RECOMMENDATIONS 1-21
  FLUID DISPOSAL 1-20
  FUEL REQUIREMENTS 1-20
  MANUAL TRANSAXLE 1-23
  MASTER CYLINDER 1-25
  POWER STEERING PUMP 1-25
  REAR WHEEL BEARINGS 1-26
  STEERING GEAR 1-25
HISTORY 1-6
HOW TO USE THIS BOOK 1-2
JACKING 1-28
MODEL IDENTIFICATION 1-6
PUSH-STARTING AND TOWING 1-28
ROUTINE MAINTENANCE
  AIR CLEANER 1-9
  AIR CONDITIONING SYSTEM 1-16
  BATTERY 1-12

BELTS 1-15
  CRANKCASE VENTILATION
   SYSTEM 1-11
  EVAPORATIVE CANISTER 1-12
  FUEL FILTER 1-10
  FUEL/WATER SEPARATOR 1-11
  HOSES 1-16
  SERVICE INTERVALS 1-9
  TIRES AND WHEELS 1-19
  WINDSHIELD WIPERS 1-19
SERIAL NUMBER IDENTIFICATION
  ENGINE 1-8
  TRANSAXLE 1-8
  VEHICLE 1-6
SERVICING YOUR VEHICLE SAFELY
  DO'S 1-5
  DON'TS 1-5
TOOLS AND EQUIPMENT
  SPECIAL TOOLS 1-3
TRAILER TOWING
  ENGINE COOLING 1-27
  HITCH WEIGHT 1-27
  TRAILER WEIGHT 1-27
  WIRING 1-27

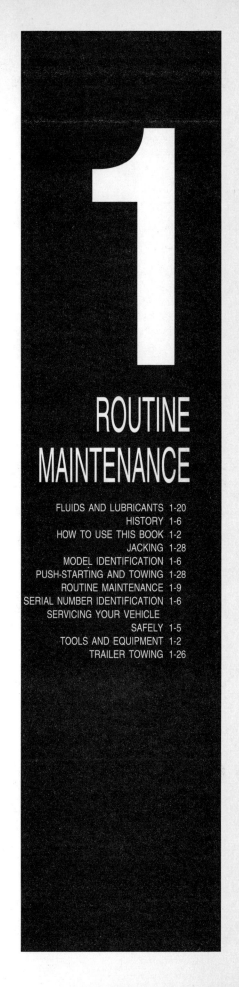

1
ROUTINE MAINTENANCE

FLUIDS AND LUBRICANTS 1-20
HISTORY 1-6
HOW TO USE THIS BOOK 1-2
JACKING 1-28
MODEL IDENTIFICATION 1-6
PUSH-STARTING AND TOWING 1-28
ROUTINE MAINTENANCE 1-9
SERIAL NUMBER IDENTIFICATION 1-6
SERVICING YOUR VEHICLE
SAFELY 1-5
TOOLS AND EQUIPMENT 1-2
TRAILER TOWING 1-26

HOW TO USE THIS BOOK

Chilton's Total Car Care for Golf, Jetta and Cabriolet is intended to help you learn more about your car and save you money on its upkeep and operation.

The first two sections will be the most used, since they contain basic maintenance procedures and tune-up information. Later sections deal with the more complex systems of your car. Systems from the engine through the brakes are covered to the extent that the average do-it-yourselfer can perform seemingly difficult operations with confidence. It will give you detailed instructions to help you change your own brake pads and shoes, replace plugs, and do many more jobs that will save you-money and help you avoid expensive problems.

This book can also be used as a reference for owners who want to understand their car and/or their mechanics better. Before undertaking any repair, read through the entire procedure. This will give you the overall view of what tools and supplies will be required. Read ahead and plan ahead. When overhauling a defective part is not considered practical, we tell you how to remove the part and how to install a new or rebuilt part. Rebuilt parts of excellent quality are, in many cases, readily available. These generally carry a guarantee similar to that of a new part. Since the price of these parts is usually much lower than that of a new part and the quality is often comparable, the option to purchase a rebuilt part should never be overlooked. When working on your car, remember that whenever the left side of the car or engine is referred to, it is meant to specify the driver's side. Conversely, the right side refers to the passenger's side.

Safety is always the most important rule. Constantly be aware of the dangers involved in working on or underneath any automobile and always take the proper precautions. (See the section on 'Servicing your Vehicle Safely' and the SAFETY NOTICE on the acknowledgment page.)

Pay attention to the instructions provided. There are 3 common mistakes in mechanical work:

1. Incorrect order of assembly, disassembly or adjustment. When taking something apart or putting it together, doing things in the wrong order often just costs you extra time, however it can break something. Read the entire procedure before beginning disassembly. Do everything in the order in which the instructions say you should do it, even if you can't immediately see a reason for it. When you're taking apart something that is very complex, you might want to make a drawing or take a picture of how it looks when assembled in order to make sure you get everything back in its proper position. We will supply exploded views whenever possible. When making adjustments, especially tune-up adjustments, do them in order. Occasionally one adjustment affects another and you cannot expect satisfactory results unless each adjustment is made only when it cannot be changed by any other.

2. Overtorquing (or undertorquing). While it is more common for overtorquing to cause damage, undertorquing can cause a fastener to vibrate loose causing serious damage. Especially when dealing with aluminum parts, pay attention to torque specifications and utilize a torque wrench in assembly. If a torque figure is not available, remember that if you are using the right tool to do the job, you will probably not have to strain yourself to get a fastener tight enough. The pitch of most threads is so slight that the tension you put on the wrench will be multiplied many, many times in actual force on what you are tightening. A good example of how critical torque is can be seen in the case of spark plug installation, especially when you are putting the plug into an aluminum cylinder head. Too little torque can fail to crush the gasket, causing leakage of combustion gases and consequent loss of power and overheating of the plug and engine parts. Too much torque can damage the threads or distort the plug, whi ch changes the spark gap. There are many commercial products available for ensuring that fasteners won't come loose, even if they are not torqued just right (a very common brand is Loktite). If you're worried about getting something together tight enough to hold, but loose enough to avoid mechanical damage during assembly, one of these product might offer substantial insurance. Read the label on the package and make sure the product is compatible with the materials, fluids, etc. involved before choosing one.

3. Crossthreading. This occurs when a part such as a bolt is screwed into a nut or casting at the wrong angle and forced. Crossthreading is more likely to occur if access is difficult. It helps to clean and lubricate fasteners, and to start threading with the part to be installed going straight in. Start the bolt, spark plug, etc. with your fingers. If you encounter resistance, unscrew the part and start over again, don't force it or resist a change in angle. Don't put a wrench on the part until it's been turned a couple of times by hand. If you suddenly encounter resistance, and the part has not seated fully, don't force it. Take it back out and make sure it's clean and threading properly. Always take your time and be patient; once you have some experience, working on your car can become an enjoyable hobby.

TOOLS AND EQUIPMENT

▶ **See Figures 1 and 2**

The last thing you want to do is to rush out and buy an enormous set of tools on the theory that you may need one of them some day. The best approach is to proceed slowly, gathering together a set of those tools that are used most frequently. Don't be misled by the low cost of bargain tools. It is far better to spend the extra money and use quality, name brand tools than to mangle your knuckles when one of your bargain sockets cracks and looses its grip. Some tools are guaranteed for life (that's right, life) which means you buy them once and only once, unless you lose them. Forged wrenches, 12 point sockets and fine tooth ratchets are far preferable than their less expensive counterparts.

Begin accumulating those tools that are used most frequently: Those associated with routine maintenance and tune-up. In addition to the usual assortment of pliers and screwdrivers, you should have the following tools for routine maintenance jobs:

1. Metric wrenches and sockets to at least 22mm. Combination open end/box end wrenches are the best buy and there are some applications that require deep sockets.

2. Metric allen wrenches: not necessarily a full set but make sure it includes 5, 6, 8, 10, 12 and 17mm. These are available as sockets that can be used with a torque wrench.

3. Jackstands for safety and support.

4. Oil filter wrench.

5. Oil filler spout or funnel.

6. A low flat pan for draining Oil.

7. A supply of rags for cleaning up the unavoidable spill when changing a Volkswagen oil filter.

The second set of tools is for tune-ups. While the tools involved here are slightly more sophisticated, they need not be outrageously expensive. There are several inexpensive tach/dwell meters on the market that are every bit as good as the expensive professional model. Just be sure that it goes to at least 1,500 rpm on the tach scale and that it can be used on 4, 6 or 8 cylinder engines. Basic tune-up equipment should include:

8. Tach/dwell meter.

9. Spark plug wrench.

10. An inductive type DC timing light that works from the car's battery.

11. A set of flat feeler gauges.

12. A set of round wire spark plug gauges.

In addition to these basic tools there are a few other tools and gauges you may find useful but don't go out and buy them until you need them. These include:

13. A compression gauge. The screw in type is slower to use but it eliminates the possibility of a faulty reading due to escaping pressure.

14. A manifold vacuum gauge.

15. A test light.

16. A fuel pressure test gauge with the appropriate fittings. Especially on CIS fuel systems, being able to read the fuel system pressure is essential to repair and troubleshooting.

As a final note, you will probably find a torque wrench necessary for all but the most basic work. There are four types of torque wrenches available: deflecting beam type, dial indicator, click type and digital. The beam and dial indicator models are perfectly adequate, although the click type and digital models are generally more precise and easier to use. No matter what type of torque wrench you purchase, have it calibrated periodically to ensure accuracy.

Special Tools

Some repair procedures in this book call for the use of special factory tools. Although every effort is made to explain the repair job using your regular set of tools, sometimes the use of a special tool cannot be avoided. Most of these tools are available at parts stores or can be ordered, however the special diagnostic equipment used by dealers is usually not available and an equivalent substitute is often difficult to find.

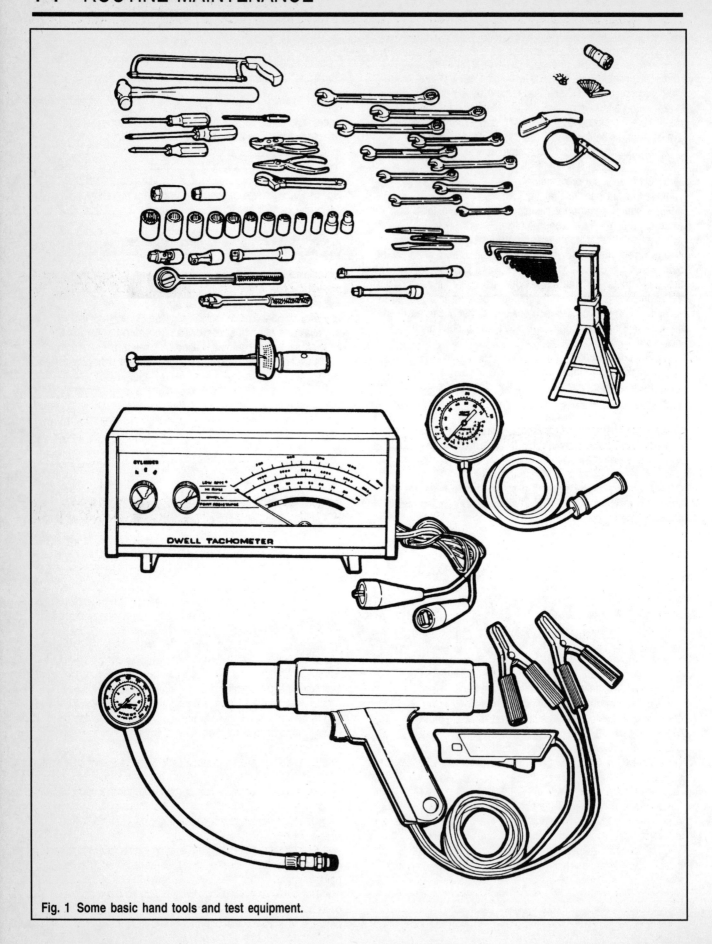

Fig. 1 Some basic hand tools and test equipment.

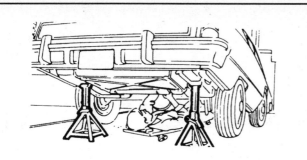

Fig. 2 Always use jack stands when working under a car.

SERVICING YOUR VEHICLE SAFELY

It is virtually impossible to anticipate all of the hazards involved with automotive maintenance and service, but care and common sense will prevent most accidents.

The rules of safety for mechanics range from 'don't smoke around gasoline,' to 'use the proper tool for the job.' The trick to avoiding injuries is to develop safe work habits and take every possible precaution.

Do's

• Do keep a fire extinguisher and first aid kit within easy reach.

• Do wear safety glasses or goggles when cutting, drilling, grinding or prying. If you wear glasses for the sake of vision, then they should be made of hardened glass that can serve also as safety glasses, or wear safety goggles over your regular glasses.

• Do shield your eyes whenever you work around the battery. Batteries contain sulfuric acid; in case of contact with the eyes or skin, flush the area with water or a mixture of water and baking soda and get medical attention immediately.

• Do use safety stands for all under-car service. Jacks are for raising vehicles; safety stands are for making sure the vehicle stays raised until you want it to come down. Whenever the vehicle is raised, block the wheels remaining on the ground and set the parking brake.

• Do use adequate ventilation when working with any chemicals. Asbestos dust resulting from brake lining wear can cause cancer.

• Do disconnect the negative battery cable when working on the electrical system. On most vehicles, the radio is equipped with a theft protection feature. Make sure the security is available before disconnecting the battery.

• Do follow manufacturer's directions whenever working with potentially hazardous materials. Both brake fluid and antifreeze are poisonous if taken internally.

• Do properly maintain your tools. Loose hammerheads, mushroomed punches and chisels, frayed or poorly grounded electrical cords, excessively worn screwdrivers, spread wrenches (open end), cracked sockets, slipping ratchets, or faulty droplight sockets can cause accidents.

• Do use the proper size and type of tool for the job being done.

• Do, when pulling or pushing a wrench, adjust your stance to prevent a fall. Hold the wrench with an open hand when pushing to avoid smashed knuckles.

• Do be sure that adjustable wrenches are tightly adjusted on the nut or bolt and the fixed jaw is doing the work.

• Do select a wrench or socket that fits the nut or bolt. The wrench or socket should sit straight, not cocked.

• Do strike squarely with a hammer to avoid glancing blows.

• Do set the parking brake and block the drive wheels if the work requires that the engine be running.

• Do properly dispose of used engine oil and coolant at a recycling center.

Don'ts

• Don't run an engine in a garage or anywhere else without proper ventilation EVER! Carbon monoxide is poisonous; it is absorbed by the body 400 times faster than oxygen; it takes a long time to leave the human body and you can build up a deadly supply of it in your system by simply breathing in a little every day. YOU may not realize you are slowly poisoning yourself. Always use power vents, windows, fans or open the garage doors.

• Don't work around moving parts while wearing a necktie or other loose clothing. Short sleeves are much safer than long, loose sleeves. Hard-toed shoes with neoprene soles protect your toes and give a better grip on slippery surfaces. Jewelry such as rings, necklaces and watches or large belt buckles are not safe working around a car. Long hair should be secured under a hat or cap.

• Don't use pockets for toolboxes. A fall or bump can drive a screwdriver deep into your body. Even a wiping cloth hanging from the back pocket can wrap around a spinning shaft or fan.

• Don't smoke when working around gasoline, cleaning solvent or other flammable material.

• Don't smoke when working around the battery. Batteries give off explosive hydrogen gas at some level even when not being charged.

• Don't use gasoline to wash your hands; there are excellent soaps available. Even unleaded gasoline contains benzene, a known carcinogen, which is absorbed through the skin. Gasoline also removes all the natural oils from the skin so that bone dry hands will suck up oil and grease.

• Don't service the air conditioning system unless you are equipped with the necessary tools and training. The refrigerant, R-12, is extremely cold and when exposed to the air, will instantly freeze any surface it comes in contact with, including your eyes. Whenever possible R-12 should be drained using the proper recycling equipment. Although the refrigerant is normally non-toxic, R-12 becomes a deadly poisonous gas in the presence of an open flame. One good whiff of the vapors from burning refrigerant can be fatal.

HISTORY

Volkswagen first began production of the Golf in 1974 as the replacement for the Type I, better known as the Beetle. The Golf came to this country in 1975 as the Rabbit and was also the platform used for both generations of the Scirocco. All Cabriolet models are still based on the original Golf/Rabbit chassis. The second generation Golf chassis went into production for the 1985 model year and is the platform used up through 1992 for all Golf and Jetta models. For 1993, there is a third generation chassis with a new 2 liter 8-valve engine.

MODEL IDENTIFICATION

Volkswagen's official Vehicle Identification Label is mounted somewhere in the luggage compartment, usually on the rear panel or under the carpet. It is separate from the federal VIN plate required on all vehicles. The label includes the VIN, a model code, engine and transaxle codes, paint and interior codes and option code numbers. Since the manufacturer sometimes makes production changes in mid-model year, this information is often the most useful when locating parts.

SERIAL NUMBER IDENTIFICATION

Vehicle

▶ See Figure 3

All models have the standard 17 digit VIN plate on the left side of the dashboard, visible through the windshield. On Golf and Jetta, a second plate is on the top of the cowling behind the engine. On Cabriolet, the VIN also appears on the model identification plate in the luggage compartment.

The VIN number will show information on where the vehicle was manufactured, body style, engine type, passenger restraint system, vehicle model, model year and the sequential serial number. This information can be helpful when locating parts or specifications.

Fig. 3 Standard VIN can be seen through the lower left corner of the windshield.

VIN explained: (Example shown only)

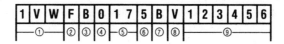

Position	Digits	Description	Code	
①	1–3	Manufacturer's Identification	1VW WVW 3VM	Passenger Car, U.S. Production Passenger Car, European Production Mexican Production
②	4	Line and Body Type (Varies by body style, models and manufacturer's location) • only code examples shown	B C D F G R T	Golf 2-Door Golf GT, Jetta—2-Door GTI 2-Door 4-Door (Golf, USA Jetta) Golf GT 4-Door, Jetta 4-Door Jetta Carat 4-Door Jetta GLI-16V 4-Door
③	5	Engine		
④	6	Passenger Restraint System	0 2 9 or 1	Active Restraint System Passive w/Lap Belt Passive Restraint System
⑤	7–8	Model	1G 16 17	Golf/GTI-16V, Jetta GL, Carat Jetta Golf
⑥	9	Check Digit (no significance for mechanic)	0 through 9 or X for 10	
⑦	10	Model Year	L M N P	1990 1991 1992 1993
⑧	11	Manufacturing Plant	E H K V W M	Emdern Hannover Oenabrueck Westmoreland Wolfsburg Mexico
⑨	12–17	Sequential Production Number	000 001 through 999 999	

| W | V | W | F | B | 0 | 1 | 5 | 5 | F | K | 1 | 2 | 3 | 4 | 5 | 6 |

Position	Digits	Description	Code	
①	1–3	Manufacturer's Identification	WVW	Passenger Car, European Production
②	4	Line and Body Type	A	Sedan 2-Door
③	5	Engine		
④	6	Passenger Restraint System	0	Active Restraint System
			9	Passive Restraint System
⑤	7–8	Model	15	Cabriolet
⑥	9	Check Digit (no significance for mechanic)	0 through 9 or X for 10	
⑦	10	Model Year	L	1990
			M	1991
			N	1992
			P	1993
⑧	11	Manufacturing Plant	K	Oenabrueck
⑨	12–17	Sequential Production Number	000 001 through 999 999	

Engine

▶ See Figure 4

On all models, the engine number is stamped into the block near the crankcase breather or upper coolant hose fitting. The first 2 digits are the engine code and will be the most useful description of the engine when locating specifications or ordering parts. Although engines share many components, the code indicates differences in engine management systems, emissions specifications, compression ratios, power ratings and other details. The engine code also appears in large type on the model identification label in the luggage compartment.

Transaxle

▶ See Figure 5

The transaxle is identified by a letter code that is stamped into the case near the top of the bellhousing. The first two or three digits are the transaxle code and the remaining numbers are the build date: day, month and year. The letter code indicates details about the transaxle such as the engine it goes with and the gear ratios. This code should also appear on the model identification label in the luggage compartment.

On automatic transaxles, the letter code also describes the valve body and torque converter. When obtaining parts or components for repairing an automatic transaxle, these codes must match.

On all units, a three digit type number is stamped into the housing near the final drive output flange to identify the

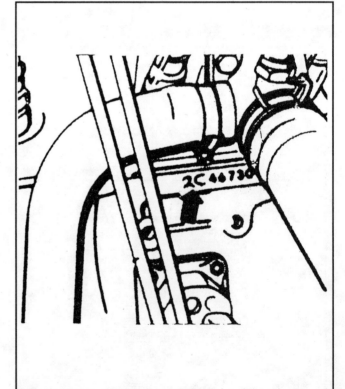

Fig. 4 The first 2 digits of the engine number are the engine ode

housing. Manual transaxles are type 020, automatic transaxles are type 010.

ROUTINE MAINTENANCE

Volkswagen specifies 3 maintenance intervals with a different level of service at each interval. These maintenance intervals are for normal vehicle service. Under severe vehicle service conditions, the same service levels can be used but maintenance should be performed twice as often. Severe service is described as extremely low temperatures, constant dusty or sandy conditions, or probably worst or all, repeated short trips where the engine never fully warms-up.

Service Intervals

7500 MILE SERVICE

1. Change oil and filter
2. Check all fluid levels
3. Drain diesel water separator

15,000 MILE SERVICE

1. Change oil and filter
2. Check all fluid levels
3. Drain diesel water separator
4. Check for exhaust or vacuum leaks
5. Check idle speed, adjust as required
6. Check on-board diagnostic program

30,000 MILE SERVICE

1. Change oil and filter
2. Check all fluid levels
3. Drain diesel water separator
4. Change diesel fuel filter
5. Check for exhaust or vacuum leaks
6. Check idle speed, adjust as required
7. Check on-board diagnostic program
8. Check transaxle for leaks
9. Check brake pad and shoe wear, replace as required
10. Check half-shaft and steering rack boots
11. Check ball joint and tie rod end dust seals
12. Check seats and seat belts for wear and freedom of movement
13. Clean and lubricate sun roof track

60,000 MILE SERVICE

Same as 30,000 mile service plus replace the oxygen sensor.

EVERY 2 YEARS

Change the brake fluid regardless of the mileage. Also check the condition of the engine coolant, change as required.

Air Cleaner

▶ **See Figure 6**

A restrictive, dirty air cleaner filter will cause a reduction in fuel economy and performance and an increase in emissions. The air filter should be replaced according to the maintenance interval chart in this Section, or more often in dusty conditions.

On gasoline engines with CIS-E fuel injection, the air cleaner is mounted directly under the fuel distributor/air flow sensor assembly. When changing the filter on these engines, the lower portion of the air cleaner housing stays in place and the distributor/sensor assembly is lifted up away from the housing. It is not necessary to disconnect any fuel lines or wires.

On diesel engines, the air cleaner housing is mounted directly to the intake manifold for noise control and ease of maintenance.

REMOVAL & INSTALLATION

1. On models with CIS-E fuel injection, loosen the hose clamps to remove the rubber boot from the top of the air flow sensor.
2. On Digifant engines, loosen the clamp and remove the air duct from the air filter housing.
3. Unsnap the cover retaining clips, starting with the hardest ones to reach. The last clip released will be difficult to unsnap, so it should be the easiest to reach.

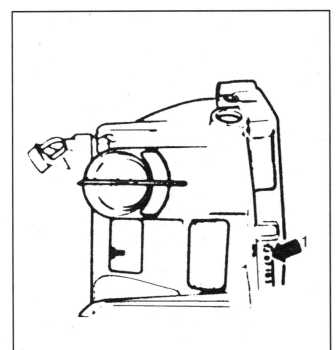

Fig. 5 The transaxle code and date or manufacture are stamped on the bell housing; automatic transaxle shown.

4. On Digifant engines, lift the cover off and remove the air filter element. If the air flow sensor is mounted to the cover, it's not necessary to disconnect the wires.

5. On CIS-E engines, lift the fuel distributor/air flow sensor assembly enough to remove the filter element.

6. With the paper side down, drop the element just a few inches repeatedly on a flat surface to shake out any loose dirt, then examine the element. On CIS-E engines, there may be fuel stains on the element. Dry stains are not a problem but if the element is wet with fuel, the fuel distributor is leaking. Section 5 describes how to pressure test the system.

7. Wipe out the housing and install the new element. Make sure the rubber seal fits properly into the groove in the housing.

8. Replace the cover and secure the clips, starting with the least accessible clip.

9. When installing the boot on the CIS-E air flow sensor, make sure the boot is fully seated all the way around the lip before tightening the clamp.

Fuel Filter

REMOVAL & INSTALLATION

▶ **See Figures 7, 8 and 9**

Gasoline Engine

The fuel filter removes particulate matter from the fuel system which might clog the fuel distributor block or fuel injectors. Unless other wise specified, all gasoline vehicles covered by this book are equipped with 'life time' fuel filters. According to the manufacturer, unless the fuel system is damaged or contaminated, the filter is large enough to handle all normal fuel filtering requirements for the life of the engine. However changing this filter more often than recommended can ease the load on the fuel pump, especially on higher mileage vehicles.

The fuel filter is under the car next to the fuel pump reservoir and looks like a large, metal container. Arrows point the direction of fuel flow through the filter. Banjo type fittings

with copper gaskets connect the fuel lines to the filter. Always replace these gaskets any time the fittings are loosened.

❋❋CAUTION

Never smoke when working around gasoline! Avoid all sources of sparks or ignition. Gasoline vapors are EXTREMELY volatile! This procedure will cause a small fuel spill. Make sure the work area is well ventilated and take appropriate fire safety precautions.

1. Raise and safely support the rear of the vehicle. Have a pan ready to catch the fuel that will run out of the reservoir.

2. Have a rag handy and wear safety glasses when loosening the fittings. The system may be under pressure and fuel will be sprayed.

3. Hold the filter with a 19mm or 22mm wrench and loosen the fittings with a 17mm wrench. Have the catch pan ready.

➡**Always use a back-up wrench to hold the filter or the fuel lines may be damaged.**

4. Disconnect the fuel lines, loosen the mounting bracket and remove the filter.

5. Install the new filter but do not tighten the mounting bracket yet.

6. Make sure all fittings and sealing surfaces are clean. Install the banjo bolts with new copper gaskets and torque to 14 ft. lbs. (20 Nm).

Diesel Engine

The fuel filter is located in the engine compartment on the right side shock tower. If the filter cannot be easily reached with an oil filter wrench, the best way to do the job is to remove the filter mounting base.

1. Open the fuel filler cap to relieve any pressure that may be in the tank. If the front of the vehicle is facing down hill, raise and safely support the front end to prevent fuel flowing from the open lines.

2. Open the vent bolt and remove both fuel lines from the filter. Some fuel will spill when the lines are removed.

3. Remove the 2 bolts that hold the base to the shock tower and remove the base and filter together.

4. Carefully clamp the base in a vise. Be sure the jaws of the vise do not contact the fuel line gasket surface.

5. Use an oil filter wrench to loosen the filter. Have a drain pan ready to catch the fuel and remove the filter.

Fig. 6 Lift the fuel distributor/air flow sensor assembly enough to remove the air filter element.

Fig. 7 Always use a back-up wrench to hold the fuel filter when loosening or tightening the fittings.

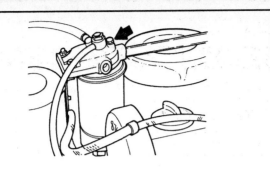

Fig. 8 Some diesel fuel filter bases may not have the vent bolt

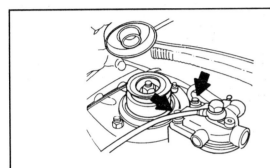

Fig. 9 It may be easier to remove the filter base to remove the filter.

6. If new fuel is available, fill the new filter almost to the top with clean diesel fuel. It doesn't take much to stop a diesel injection pump, so don't use the fuel drained from the old filter.

7. Thread the new filter onto the base and make it only hand tight, just like an oil filter.

8. Install the filter and base assembly onto the shock tower and torque the nuts to 18 ft. lbs. (25 Nm).

9. Use new copper gaskets to connect the fuel lines to the filter base and torque the banjo bolts to 14 ft. lbs. (20 Nm). Be careful not to over-tighten these fittings or the copper washers will split.

10. Start the engine. It probably won't start right away but keep cranking. Accelerate it a few times to clear the air bubbles and check for fuel leaks.

11. If the engine won't start or run properly but it was OK before, see Section 5 for instructions on bleeding the diesel fuel system.

Fuel/Water Separator

DRAINING WATER

Diesel Engine

Although diesel fuel and water do not readily mix, fuel does tend to entrap moisture from the air each time it is moved from one container to another. Eventually every diesel fuel system collects enough water to become a potential hazard. Fortunately, when it's allowed to settle out, the water will

always drop to the bottom of the tank or filter housing. Some diesel fuel filters are equipped with a water drain; a bolt or petcock at the bottom of the housing. All ECO Diesel models sold in North America are equipped with a water separator, located in front of the fuel tank under the right side of the vehicle. It's purpose is to allow water to settle from the fuel right at the tank and to alert the driver when draining is required. When the water level in the separator reaches a certain point, a sensor turns on the glow plug indicator light on the dashboard, causing it to blink continuously.

AT THE WATER SEPARATOR

▶ See Figure 10

1. Raise and safely support the vehicle. Remove the fuel filler cap.

2. At the separator, connect a hose from the separator drain to a catch pan.

3. Open the drain valve (3 turns) and drain the separator until a steady stream of fuel flows from the separator, then close the valve. Don't forget to install the filler cap.

AT THE FILTER

1. If the filter is equipped with a water drain at the bottom, place a pan under the drain to catch the water and fuel.

2. If equipped, loosen the vent bolt on the filter base. If there is no vent, loosen the return line at the pump, the line not connected to the filter.

3. Loosen the bolt or valve. When fuel flows in a clean stream, close the drain and tighten the vent or return line.

Crankcase Ventilation System

▶ See Figures 11 and 12

To send oil fumes and crankcase blow-by gasses into the engine for burning, all engines are equipped with some type of crankcase breather control valve. Volkswagen uses two different types; one is a simple restrictor and the other is a spring loaded diaphragm.

On 16V engines, a breather is mounted to the side of the engine block near the oil cooler. The breather contains a baffle plate that allows the oil to condense out of the blow-by gasses and drain back to the engine. The large hose connects to the air cleaner so filtered air can be drawn in as required. The small hose connecting to the intake manifold has a built-in restrictor orifice, creating a controlled vacuum leak to the intake manifold. When the throttle opening is small and

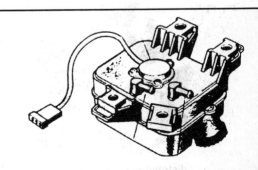

Fig. 10 The water separator includes a sensor that flashes the glow plug light when draining is required

manifold vacuum is high, crankcase oil fumes are drawn directly into the intake manifold. When the throttle opening is large and manifold vacuum low, some of the oil fumes flow through the large hose to the air cleaner.

On engines equipped with diaphragm control valves, the valve is mounted in the top of the cylinder head cover and connects to the intake manifold. The spring and diaphragm maintain a constant balance against manifold vacuum, keeping blow-by vapor flow at a constant percentage of the total intake air volume. Another hose connecting to the air cleaner allows filtered air into the engine as required.

On both systems, there is no service required other than to check for vacuum leaks.

Evaporative Canister

SERVICING

▶ **See Figures 13 and 14**

All vehicles with gasoline engines are equipped with some form of fuel vapor control device. The evaporative emission control system prevents the escape of raw fuel vapors (unburned hydrocarbons, or HC) into the atmosphere. On Volkswagens, a carbon (charcoal) canister is used to store fuel

Fig. 11 The crankcase breather is mounted directly on the block near the oil cooler.

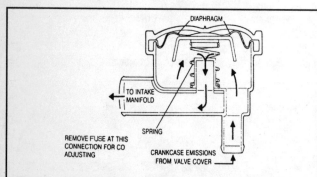

Fig. 12 The diaphragm valve is mounted on top of the cylinder head cover.

tank vapors that accumulate when the engine is not running. When the engine is running, the vapors in the canister are carried to the intake manifold by allowing fresh air into the bottom of the canister. The canister is located in the inner fender below the air cleaner. On vehicles with a Digifant engine management system, the canister is purged when a vacuum actuated valve is opened during normal driving. The vacuum signal comes from the throttle body, while the purge air flows directly to the intake manifold.

On vehicles with CIS-E fuel injection, the carbon canister is isolated from the intake manifold by a solenoid valve and a frequency valve. The solenoid valve is **ON** or open whenever the engine is running. The frequency valve is cycled open and closed by the Motronic control unit to control flow rate depending on coolant temperature and engine speed/load conditions.

Other components of the system include an unvented fuel filler cap, fuel tank expansion chamber and one or more check valves to prevent liquid fuel from entering the canister. On most models, the purge hose must be disconnected at the canister when checking or adjusting air/fuel mixture. Make sure the orifice is still connected to the hose to the intake manifold.

The system does not require any service under normal conditions other than to check for leaks. Check the hoses visually for cracks, breaks, and disconnections. Also check the seal on the gas tank filler cap. Replace the cap if the is split. If any hoses are in need of replacement, use only hoses marked EVAP, available from your local automotive supply store. If you suspect a problem with the purge valve or any other component, see Section 5 for information on testing the system.

Battery

GENERAL MAINTENANCE

✳✳CAUTION

Battery electrolyte contains sulfuric acid. If you should splash any on your skin or in your eyes, flush the affected area with plenty of clear water. If it lands in your eyes, get medical help immediately.

Unless the vehicle is equipped with a maintenance-free battery, maintenance consists of checking the battery electrolyte level and specific gravity at regular intervals and keeping the battery and terminals clean. Two tools which will facilitate battery maintenance are a hydrometer and a terminal cleaning brush. These are inexpensive and widely available at automotive parts stores.

Keep the top of the battery clean, as a film of dirt can sometimes completely discharge a battery that is not used for long periods. A solution of baking soda and water may be used for cleaning, but be careful to flush this off with clear water. DO NOT let any of the solution into the filler holes.

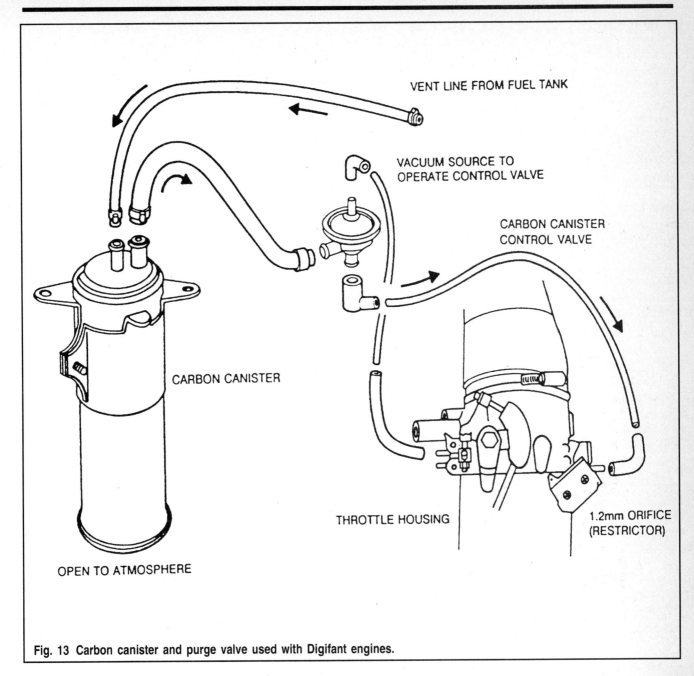

VENT LINE FROM FUEL TANK

VACUUM SOURCE TO
OPERATE CONTROL VALVE

CARBON CANISTER
CONTROL VALVE

CARBON CANISTER

OPEN TO ATMOSPHERE

THROTTLE HOUSING

1.2mm ORIFICE
(RESTRICTOR)

Fig. 13 Carbon canister and purge valve used with Digifant engines.

Baking soda neutralizes battery acid and will de-activate a battery cell.

❊❊CAUTION

The chemical action in batteries generates hydrogen gas. A spark can cause the battery to explode and splash acid. To avoid serious personal injury, be sure there is proper ventilation and take appropriate fire safety precautions when connecting, disconnecting, or charging a battery or when using jumper cables.

FLUID LEVEL INSPECTION

Except Maintenance Free Battery

Check the battery electrolyte level at least once a month, or more often in hot weather or during periods of extended car operation. The level can be checked through the case on translucent polypropylene batteries. The cell caps must be removed on other models. The electrolyte level should be at the split ring inside each cell, or about 1/2 inch above the level of the plates if there is no ring. If overfilled, the electrolyte will boil out when the battery is being charged by the alternator and cause corrosion or acid damage. Ideally, only distilled water should be used, but this is not critical. Tap water contains minerals that can accelerate battery aging. If water is added in freezing weather, the car should be driven

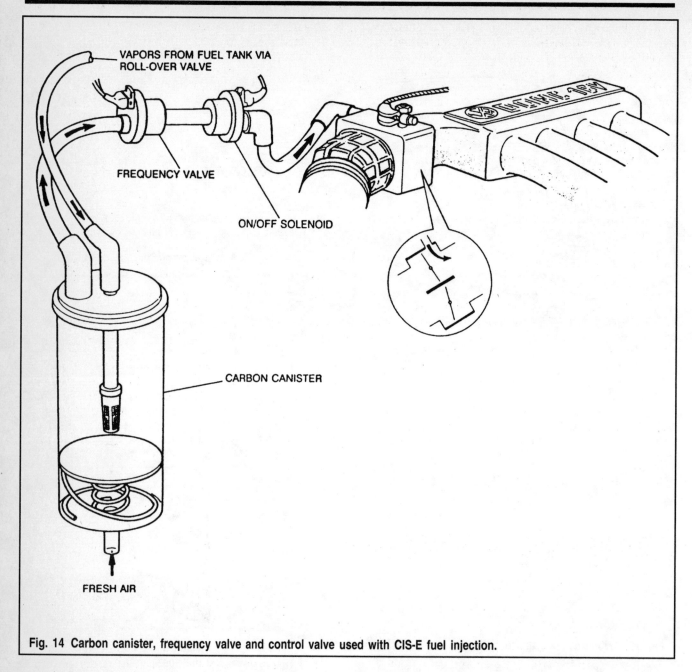

VAPORS FROM FUEL TANK VIA
ROLL-OVER VALVE

FREQUENCY VALVE

ON/OFF SOLENOID

CARBON CANISTER

FRESH AIR

Fig. 14 Carbon canister, frequency valve and control valve used with CIS-E fuel injection.

several miles to allow the water to mix with the electrolyte. Otherwise, the battery could freeze.

TESTING SPECIFIC GRAVITY

Except Maintenance Free Battery

At least once a year, check the specific gravity of the battery. Specific gravity of any fluid is measured with a hydrometer (water has a gravity of 1.000). The specific gravity of the electrolyte in a fully charged battery at room temperature will normally be between 1.270 and 1.200. However even more important is that the readings for each cell are the same. If one or more cells varies by more than 0.500, the battery will soon no longer accept or hold a charge.

If the readings are all low but fairly close, the battery should hold a charge.

The hydrometer used for batteries looks like a large eye dropper with a float inside. Battery electrolyte is sucked into the hydrometer until the float is fully lifted from its seat but not touching the top. The specific gravity is then read by noting the level of the electrolyte on the float.

CABLES AND CLAMPS

Any time the terminals appear corroded, they should be cleaned. Volkswagen uses steel cable ends that can be easily removed without special tools, just a 10mm wrench.

Clean the cable clamps and the battery terminal with a wire brush, until all corrosion, grease, etc. is removed and the metal is shiny. It is especially important to clean the inside of the clamp thoroughly, since a small deposit of foreign material or oxidation there will prevent a sound electrical connection and inhibit either starting or charging.

As long as the cables are disconnected, it's a good idea to remove the battery to clean the battery tray and all metal underneath. Rust should be wire brushed away, and the area should be cleaned with a water and baking soda solution to neutralize any acid deposits. Don't forget to clean the holddown clamp and bolt. When everything is dry again, paint the battery tray and holddown. There are special corrosion resistant spray paints available for battery trays and terminals.

When the battery is installed, be careful not to over-tighten the holddown or the battery could be cracked. After the clamps and terminals are clean, examine the clamping bolts. They can be replaced separately if need be. Loosen the bolts enough to allow the clamps to fit easily onto the battery posts. Tighten the clamps securely but do not distort them. Give the clamps and terminals a thin external coat of the same spray paint or grease after installation, to retard corrosion. Check the cables at the same time that the terminals are cleaned. If the cable insulation is cracked or broken, or if the ends are frayed, the cable should be replaced with a new cable of the same length and gauge.

REPLACEMENT

When it becomes necessary to replace the battery, select a battery with a rating equal to or greater than the battery originally installed. Deterioration, embrittlement and just plain aging of the battery cables, starter motor, and associated wires makes the battery's job harder in successive years. The slow increase in electrical resistance over time makes it prudent to install a new battery with a greater capacity than the old.

Belts

CHECKING TENSION AND ADJUSTMENT

▶ **See Figures 15, 16, 17 and 18**

The belt tension on most driven components is adjusted by moving the component (alternator, power steering pump etc.) within the range of a slotted or toothed bracket(s). Some brackets use a sliding toothed rack mechanism turned by a gear bolt which moves the alternator side-to-side to adjust the belt tension. With this configuration, no prying tools are required. Before adjusting the belt tension on any engine, look at the alternator mounting and determine what kind of bracket is used. Adjust the belt tension using the proper procedure outlined below. Check the belt tension every 3 months or 3,000 miles.

To check belt tension, push in on the drive belt about midway between the crankshaft pulley and the driven component. If the belt is less than 1000mm (39.4 inches) long, it should deflect 2-5mm (0.80-0.120 inches). For longer belts, it should deflect 10-15mm (0.40-0.060 inches). Belt size is

usually printed on the back side of the belt. If it can't be read, it's probably time to replace it.

1. Loosen the adjustment nut and bolt in the slotted bracket. Slightly loosen the pivot bolt.

2. Some components such as the air conditioner compressor may be mounted with a long threaded bolt to make adjustment easy and precise. Loosen the adjuster locknut and turn the threaded adjustment bolt in or out to gain correct tension.

3. On some models, the alternator is equipped with a rack (**A**) and pinion (**B**) adjusting bracket. Loosen the adjusting bolt and bolt **C** and turn the adjuster **B** as required to obtain the proper belt tension.

4. If there are no special the adjusting bolts, pull (don't pry) the component outward to increase tension. Push inward to reduce tension.

5. Torque the pivot and lock nuts and bolts to 26 ft. lbs. (35 Nm) and check the belt tension again. Readjust if necessary.

REPLACEMENT

Belt replacement requires the loosening of the mounting and adjustment bolts as described in belt adjustment. Relax tension on the belt until removal from the pulleys is possible. Remove old belt and install new one in the reverse order. Adjust belt tension. Some models have a front engine mount installed through the air conditioner compressor belt circle. Support the engine and remove the mount prior to belt removal and installation.

Fig. 15 Loosen the pivot bolt and the adjustment bolt at the slotted bracket and pull the alternator to tighten the belt.

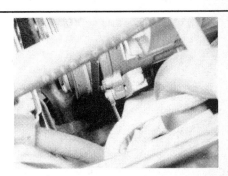

Fig. 16 Loosen the adjuster locknut. The adjustment bolt is to the right.

Fig. 17 Turn the adjustment bolt clockwise to tighten the belt.

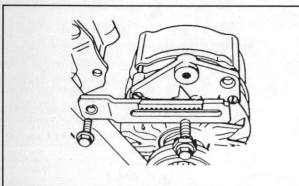

Fig. 18 Rack and pinion type adjusting bracket

Hoses

REMOVAL & INSTALLATION

✳✳CAUTION

Disconnect the radiator cooling fan when changing hoses. If the engine is warm, the cooling fan could operate even if the ignition switch is off.

1. Make sure the engine is not hot and loosen the coolant reservoir cap.

2. Place a large pan under the lower radiator hose and disconnect the hose from the radiator. It makes a mess but it's the only way to drain the system.

3. Loosen the clamps on the hose and remove the hose by cutting it or twisting it to break its grip on the flange. Note the position of the clamps on the hose before removing them. Often installing the clamp in a different position makes it impossible to reach the screw.

4. Clean all hose connections and slip the clamps onto the new hose.

5. When installing the new hose, don't overtighten the clamps or the hose may be cut. Position the hose clamps so that the end of the clamp is about 6mm (1/4 in.) from the end of the hose.

6. After the new hose is installed and the cooling system is refilled (See Cooling System, below), run the engine up to operating temperature and check for coolant leaks.

Air Conditioning System

SAFETY WARNINGS

✳✳CAUTION

Do not discharge the refrigerant from the air conditioning system into the atmosphere.

The R-12 refrigerant used in all models is a chlorofluorocarbon that destroys the earth's ozone layer in the upper atmosphere. Ozone filters out harmful radiation from the sun. In most states, it is against the law to discharge an air conditioning system into the atmosphere and air conditioning service that involves R-12 can only be legally performed by certified technicians. Make sure the proper recovery equipment is available before servicing the air conditioning system. Volkswagen recommends the Kent-Moore ACR3 recovery/recycling unit or an equivalent system.

• Always wear eye protection when working with R-12.

• Make sure R-12 does not come in contact with skin or eyes.

• If contact occurs, flush with cool water for 15 minutes and seek medical attention.

• Avoid breathing fumes when using flame-type leak detectors. R-12 becomes a poisonous gas when in contact with open flame.

• Avoid contact with a charged refrigeration system, even when working on another part of the air conditioning system or vehicle. If a heavy tool comes into contact with a section of tubing or a heat exchanger, it can easily cause the relatively soft material to rupture.

• When it is necessary to apply force to a fitting which contains refrigerant, as when checking that all system couplings are securely tightened, use a wrench on both parts of the fitting involved. This will avoid twisting the tubing.

• Avoid applying heat to any refrigerant line or storage vessel. Never allow a refrigerant storage container to sit out in the sun, or near any other source of heat, such as a radiator.

• Always keep refrigerant can fittings capped when not in use. Avoid sudden shock to the can which might occur from dropping it, or from banging a heavy tool against it. Never carry a can in the passenger compartment of a car.

• Always completely discharge the system before painting the vehicle (if the paint is to be baked on), or before welding anywhere near the refrigerant lines.

SYSTEM INSPECTION

Even if you are not properly equipped to service an air conditioning system, there are some simple things to check that may avoid expensive problems later. The most important aspect of air conditioning service is the maintenance of a full charge of refrigerant in the system. A refrigeration system cannot function properly if a significant percentage of the charge is lost. The refrigerant also carries the lubricating oil for the entire system. This means that even if there is enough of a charge for the system to provide effective cooling, there may not be enough oil to properly protect the system.

Leaks in the air conditioning system usually occur at the compressor shaft seals. The compressor is the major moving part and is subjected to engine vibrations, temperature extremes and great pressure differentials. The greatest damage to these seals occurs when the system is not used for long periods. When the compressor is finally turned on, the rubber seals are stiff and dry and can easily form tiny cracks. The seals leak slowly at first but eventually system pressure drops enough for the low pressure safety switch to prevent compressor operation.

One way Volkswagen prolongs compressor seal life is to make the compressor run any time the defroster is in use. This not only assures that the compressor will be run throughout the year, it also makes the defroster very effective by drying the air being blown at the windshield. Since the system is in use all year long, it is important that a full charge be maintained at all times. Fortunately no special equipment is required to inspect the condition of the system and to check the refrigerant level.

Engine Cooling System

Under extreme conditions, it may take as much as 10 horsepower to run the air conditioner compressor. If the engine is required to work that much harder, the cooling system must be up to the job. Make sure the water pump belt is properly adjusted and that there are no leaks in the system. Pressure test the system and the reservoir cap if possible. Just as important is the condition of the antifreeze.

In order to prevent heater core freeze-up during air conditioner operation, it is necessary to maintain permanent type antifreeze protection of +15°F (-9°C) or lower. Protection to -15°F (-26°C) is ideal since this protection also supplies sufficient corrosion inhibitors for the engine cooling system. Make sure the antifreeze is not in use longer than recommended by the manufacturer (usually 2-3 years).

Condenser

The condenser is in front of the engine's radiator. Any obstruction of or damage to the condenser will restrict the air flow that carries away the heat. If many of the fins are crushed or if they are clogged with bugs or dirt, it will take a long time to cool off the inside of the car. Blowing compressed air through the fins from behind the radiator will usually also clean the condenser. If the front of the car is fitted with a bra or other type of bug screen, air conditioner efficiency is usually somewhat decreased.

Condensation Drain Tube

This molded tube drains out the water that condenses from the air into the evaporator housing inside the vehicle. The tube usually exits into the engine compartment through the firewall. If this tube is obstructed, the evaporator housing will fill with water and eventually the air conditioner vents will emit fog or a fine mist when the air conditioner is running. Another sign of a clogged drain tube is a bad odor when using the air conditioner. This is caused by bacteria growth in the water

sitting in the evaporator housing. There are some products available to deal with this problem but they aren't easy to find in auto parts stores.

REFRIGERANT LEVEL CHECK

▶ **See Figure 19**

You can safely make a few simple checks to determine if your air conditioning system needs service. The tests work best if the temperature is warm, about 70°F (21°C).

➡**This test is for the factory installed air conditioning system only. Aftermarket air conditioner testing procedures may be different. If in doubt, contact the manufacturer of your particular unit.**

1. Place the automatic transmission in Park or the manual transmission in Neutral. Set the parking brake.
2. Run the engine at a fast idle, about 2500 rpm.
3. Set the air conditioning controls for maximum cold and the highest fan speed.
4. Locate the sight glass and wipe it clean. The sight glass is located either in the high pressure tube between the high pressure service valve and the receiver drier or on top of the receiver drier itself.
5. If you see foam or lots of bubbles, the system is low on refrigerant and should be recharged. There is probably a leak in the system but it may not be serious enough to require repairs at this point.
6. If there are no bubbles in the sight glass and air coming from the vents is warm, the charge is very low and the system needs a full service. If there are few or no bubbles and the vent air is cold, the charge is OK.
7. Have an assistant in the car turn the fan control on and off to operate the compressor clutch. Watch the sight glass.
8. If bubbles appear when the clutch is disengaged and disappear when it is engaged, the system is properly charged. If the refrigerant takes more than 45 seconds to bubble when the clutch is disengaged, the system is overcharged. This usually causes poor cooling at low speeds.

GAUGE SETS

Most of the service work performed in air conditioning requires the use of a set of two gauges, one for the high

Fig. 19 The sight glass should have little or no air bubbles when the system is operating with the correct charge.

(head) pressure side of the system, the other for the low (suction) side. The low side gauge records both pressure and vacuum. Vacuum readings are calibrated from 0 to 30 in.Hg and the pressure graduations read from 0 to no less than 60 psi. The high side gauge measures pressure from 0 to at least 600 psi. Both gauges are threaded into a manifold that contains two hand shut-off valves. Proper manipulation of these valves the use of appropriate service equipment allows the user to perform the following services:

1. Read high and low side pressures.
2. Remove air, moisture, and contaminated refrigerant.
3. Purge the system of refrigerant.
4. Charge the system with refrigerant and the correct amount of oil.

The manifold valves are designed so that they have no direct effect on gauge readings but provide precise flow control of refrigerant through the manifold. During all testing and hook-up operations, the valves are kept closed to avoid disturbing the refrigeration system. The valves are opened only to read pressures, to purge the system or to charge it.

DISCHARGING THE SYSTEM

▶ **See Figures 20 and 21**

✳✳CAUTION

Do not discharge the refrigerant from the air conditioning system into the atmosphere.

The R-12 refrigerant used in all models is a chlorofluorocarbon that destroys the earth's ozone layer in the upper atmosphere. Ozone filters out harmful radiation from the sun. In most states, it is against the law to discharge an air conditioning system into the atmosphere. In some states, air conditioning service can only be legally performed by certified technicians at properly equipped shops. Make sure the proper recovery/recyling equipment is available before servicing the air conditioning system. Volkswagen recommends the Kent-Moore ACR3 recovery/recycling unit or an equivalent system.

1. Check for any special instructions on the recovery equipment. If they are different from what is shown here, follow those instructions.
2. Connect the center hose of the gauge manifold set to the recovery unit.
3. Remove the caps from the service valves or clean the valves if the caps are missing.
4. Make sure both gauge set manifold valves are closed. Connect the low pressure hose of the recovery equipment to the low pressure service valve. The return line with this valve is the line without the sight glass.
5. Connect the high pressure hose to the high pressure service valve.
6. Slowly open both valves and allow the system to discharge into the recovery equipment.
7. When the system is fully discharged, close the valves and remove the hoses.
8. Be sure to install the caps again. All fittings must remain closed as much as possible to avoid moisture getting into the system. Disconnect the wire to the compressor clutch to avoid accidently running the compressor.

EVACUATING THE SYSTEM

1. With the manifold gauges connected and the system discharged, close both valves and connect the center service hose to the inlet fitting of the vacuum pump.
2. Turn both manifold valves to the wide open position.
3. Start the pump and note the low side gauge reading.
4. Operate the pump for a minimum of 30 minutes after the lowest observed gauge reading.
5. Close the valves, stop the pump and note the low side gauge reading. The needle should remain stationary at the point at which the pump was turned off. If the needle starts to drop and does not stop, there is a leak and the system will not hold a charge.
6. If the needle remains stationary for 3 to 5 minutes, open the manifold valves and run the pump for at least 30 minutes more.
7. Close both valves and stop the pump. The system is now ready for charging.

CHARGING THE SYSTEM

If the proper recovery/recyling equipment has been used to discharge the system, follow the instructions with that equipment for charging the system. The procedure shown here is for charging the system with individual cans of R-12. Be sure to read and follow the safety precautions outlined at the beginning of the air conditioning section.

1. With the valves closed, connect the center hose of the manifold set to the refrigerant can opener valve.

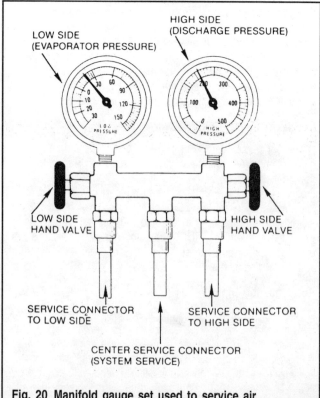

Fig. 20 Manifold gauge set used to service air conditioning systems

2. Make sure the can opener valve is unscrewed (the needle is raised) and connect the valve to the can. Open the can by screwing the valve in to puncture the can with the needle.

3. Momentarily loosen the center hose fitting at the pressure gauge, allowing refrigerant to purge the hose of air.

4. Open the low side gauge set valve and the can valve.

5. Start the engine and turn the air conditioner to the maximum cooling mode. The compressor will operate and pull refrigerant gas into the system. If more than one can of refrigerant is needed, close the can valve and gauge set low side valve when the can is empty and connect a new can to the opener. The frost line on the outside of the can will indicate how much is left.

6. When the system is fully charged, system pressures will depend on ambient temperature, as shown on the chart. The lower broken line is where the fan should change from low speed to high speed. The upper broken line is where the fan should change back to low speed.

7. When the charging process has been completed, close the valves and run the system for at least five minutes to allow it to normalize.

8. Check the pressures again and if all is correct, remove the hoses. Screw the covers onto both service valves.

LEAK TESTING

If you don't have the proper service equipment, you can still partially leak check the system. With the engine not running, look at each connection in the system for signs of oil leakage. This will appear as an accumulation of dirt where everything else is clean, or may even be wet with oil. Check for signs of leaking at the clutch end of the compressor; streaks radiating out from the center of the shaft. If there is enough of a charge for the compressor to run, apply a soapy water solution to each connection one at a time with the system operating (don't try to check the compressor this way). If you are adding refrigerant, use R-12 with a dye included. Any leaks will show up quickly.

Windshield Wipers

▶ **See Figure 22**

For maximum effectiveness and longest wiper blade life, the windshield and wiper blades should be kept clean. Dirt, tree

sap, road tar and so on will cause streaking, smearing and shorten blade life. It is advisable to clean the windshield carefully with a commercial glass cleaner and paper towels at least once a week. Wipe off the rubber blades with the wet paper towel afterwards. Examine the wiper blades occasionally. If they look cracked, broken or torn, they should be replaced immediately. Replacement intervals will vary with usage, although ozone deterioration usually limits blade life to about one year or less. If the wiper pattern is smeared or streaked, or if the blade chatters across the glass, the blade should be replaced. If that does not fix the problem, the spring in the wiper arm may be weak or the arm may be bent. See Section 6 for more information.

All Volkswagens are equipped at the factory with Bosch windshield wiper arms and blades. When replacing the blades, it is worth the extra few dollars to stay with Bosch blades. Not only are they the easiest to install, but they also have some unique design features that help them remain effective right up to the end of their service life.

REMOVAL & INSTALLATION

1. Pull the blade away from the windshield and swing the arm all the way up until it locks in place.

2. Pivot the blade so it is perpendicular to the arm.

3. At the looped end of the arm, squeeze the plastic retainer that fits into the loop and push the whole blade assembly towards the other end of the arm.

4. Move the blade so it can be slid off the arm without engaging the retainer. The small shaft in the blade arm is not centered in the open space. Note the orientation of this shaft so the new blade can be installed the same way.

5. Slide the new blade onto the arm, move it so the retainer will fit into the loop and click the blade into place.

Tires and Wheels

TIRE ROTATION

To equalize tire wear and increase the mileage you obtain from your tires, rotate them every 7500 miles. All Volkswagens are designed for radial tires. Radial tires should be rotated by moving the front tires to the rear and the rear tires to the front. Do not move them from side to side unless absolutely

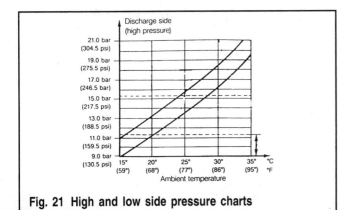

Fig. 21 High and low side pressure charts

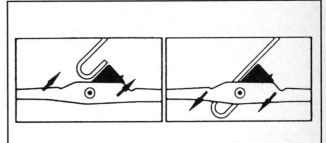

Fig. 22 **Note the orientation of the shaft in the blade arm when removing the old blade**

necessary, or unless the tire is near the end of its life anyway. Radial tires tend to distort slightly and take a set in the direction of rotation. If a tire is moved from one side to the other and turns the opposite direction, the ride and handling will be affected and the tire may wear faster.

TIRE DESIGN

When buying new tires, they should always be replaced in sets of two or four. Always install the same type of tire on all four wheels. Mixing of different types (radial, bias-belted, fiberglass belted) can be hazardous because vehicle handling becomes inconsistent.

Conventional bias tires are constructed so that the cords run bead to bead at an angle. Alternate plies run at an opposite angle. This type of construction gives rigidity to both the tread and the side wall and is good for carrying heavy loads.

Bias belted tires are similar in construction to conventional bias ply tires. Belts run at an angle and also at a 90° angle to the bead, as in radial tires. Tread life is improved considerably over the conventional bias tire and the side wall remains fairly rigid.

On radial tires, instead of the cords and belts being at an angle of 90° to each other, they are all parallel and at an angle of 90° to the bead. The cords wrap directly across the carcass of the tire to make the shortest line from bead to bead. This gives the tread a great deal of rigidity and the side wall a great deal of flexibility. With this construction, it is easier for the tread to stay flat on the road when the car is turning and tire side loads are high. These tires also tend to be rounder and have less rolling resistance. Dry and wet road handling are greatly improved over bias or belted tires. This type of construction accounts for the characteristic bulge associated with radial tires because the side walls are relatively unsupported. This makes proper inflation pressure so important to tire life and performance.

STORAGE

Store the tires at the proper inflation pressure if they are mounted on wheels. Keep them in a cool dry place, laid on their sides. If the tires are stored in the garage or basement, do not let them stand on a concrete floor. Set them on strips of wood.

INFLATION PRESSURE

Tire inflation is the most ignored item of auto maintenance, and one of the most important. Buy a tire pressure gauge and keep it in the glovebox of your car. Service station air gauges are generally either not working or inaccurate and should not be relied upon. Also, using the same gauge all the time increases the accuracy of your pressure readings. The tire pressures recommended for your car are usually found on the left door post and in the owner's manual. If you are driving on replacement tires of a different type, follow the inflation recommendations of the tire manufacturer. Never exceed the maximum pressure shown on the tire sidewall. Always check tire pressure when the tires are cool because air pressure increases with heat. Readings can change as much as 4-6 psi depending on tire temperature. For every 10° rise (or drop) in tire temperature, there is a difference of 1 psi. This explains why tires loose pressure when the weather turns colder.

Excess heat generated while driving on an underinflated tire causes serious damage to the structure of the tire. For long highway drives, inflating the tires to within 3-4 psi (cold pressure) of the maximum allowed will increase fuel mileage and tire life.

TREAD DEPTH

All tires have 7 built-in tread wear indicator bars that show up as 13mm (1/2 inch) wide smooth bands across the tire when 1.5mm (1/16 inch) of tread remains. The appearance of tread wear indicators means that the tires should be replaced. In fact, many states have laws prohibiting the use of tires with less than 1.5mm (1/16 inch) tread. You can check your own tread depth with an inexpensive gauge or by using a Lincoln head penny. Slip the Lincoln penny into several tread grooves. If you can see the top of Lincoln's head in 2 adjacent grooves, the tires have less than 1.5mm (1/16 inch) tread left and should be replaced. You can measure snow tires in the same manner by using the tails side of the Lincoln penny. If you can see the top of the Lincoln memorial, it's time to replace the snow tires.

FLUIDS AND LUBRICANTS

Fluid Disposal

Used fluids such as engine oil, transmission fluid, antifreeze and brake fluid are considered hazardous waste and must be disposed of properly. Before draining any fluids, check with local authorities. Most states have a recycling program in effect, and many service stations and parts stores accept waste fluids for recycling as long as they are not mixed.

Fuel Requirements

GASOLINE ENGINES

All vehicles sold in the U.S. with gasoline engines are designed to operate on lead-free fuel. The minimum octane ratings required by Volkswagen sometimes vary with where the vehicle was intended for sale and use (high altitude). Octane requirements are listed on the inside of the fuel filler door or on the door jamb. Use of leaded gasoline or certain additives will poison the catalytic converter and in some cases, possibly damage fuel injectors. Volkswagen recommends occasional use of Autobahn Gasoline Additive, VW part no. ZVW 246 001, for keeping injectors clean.

DIESEL ENGINES

The Volkswagen diesel engine is designed to run on Diesel Fuel No. 2. Since diesel fuel is generally available, supply is not usually a problem, though it is wise to check in advance. Several diesel station guides are available from fuel companies and are normally sold at diesel fuel stations. Some U. S. States and Canadian provinces require purchasers of diesel fuel to obtain a special permit to buy diesel fuel. Check with your local VW dealer or fuel supplier for regulations in your area.

There is a difference between the refinement levels of Diesel fuel and home heating oil. While you may get away with running your diesel on home heating oil for a while, inevitably you will fill your tank with a batch of oil that will leave you stranded. Even though they don't mix, Diesel fuel tends to attract water. This is another reason to stick to mainstream suppliers when filling the tank. Also, never allow diesel fuel to come in contact with any rubber hoses or other parts. It attacks the rubber and causes it to become soft and unstable.

Engine Oil Recommendations

GASOLINE ENGINES

▶ **See Figures 23 and 24**

The SAE (Society of Automotive Engineers) grade number indicates the viscosity of the engine oil, and thus its ability to lubricate at a given temperature. The lower the SAE grade number, the lighter the oil. The lower the viscosity, the easier it is to crank the engine in cold weather. Oil viscosities should be chosen from those oils recommended for the lowest anticipated temperatures during the oil change interval. Multi-viscosity oils (10W-30, 20W-50, etc.) offer the important advantage of being adaptable to temperature extremes. They allow easy starting at low temperatures, yet give good protection at high speeds and engine temperatures. This is a decided advantage in changeable climates or in long distance touring. The API (American Petroleum Institute) designation indicates the classification of engine oil for use under given operating conditions. Only oils designated for use Service SF or SG should be used. Oils of the SF or SG type perform a variety of functions inside the engi ne in addition to the basic function as a lubricant. Through a balanced system of metallic detergents and polymeric dispersants, the oil prevents the formation of high and low temperature deposits, and also keeps sludge and dirt particles in suspension. Acids, particularly sulfuric acid, as well as other by-products of combustion, are neutralized. Both the SAE grade number and the API designation can be found somewhere on the container.

➡**Non-detergent or straight mineral oils must never be used.**

Oil must be selected with regard to the anticipated temperatures during the period before the next oil change. Using the chart, select the oil viscosity prior to the next oil change for the lowest expected temperature and you will be assured of easy cold starting and sufficient engine protection.

DIESEL ENGINES

Engine oils should be selected from the accompanying chart. The SAE viscosity number should be chosen for the lowest anticipated temperature at which the engine will be required to start, not for the temperature at the time the oil is changed. Use only oils designated by the API (American Petroleum Institute) for service 'CC' or 'CD'. The letters should appear somewhere on the oil can for example 'SF/CC' or 'SG/CD'. This indicates that the oil provides protection from rust, corrosion and high temperature deposits in diesel engines in moderate to severe service.

CHECKING ENGINE OIL LEVEL

▶ **See Figure 25**

Engine oil level should be checked weekly. Always check the oil with the car on level ground and after the engine has been shut off for about five minutes. The oil dipstick is either located on the front side of engine or on the driver's side near the fuel pump.

1. Remove the dipstick and wipe it clean.
2. Reinsert the dipstick.

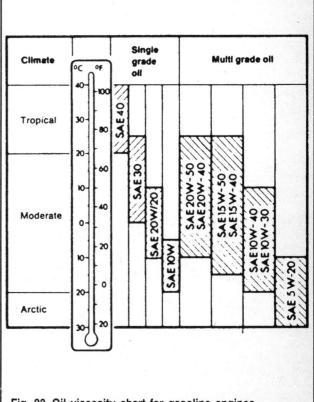

Fig. 23 Oil viscosity chart for gasoline engines

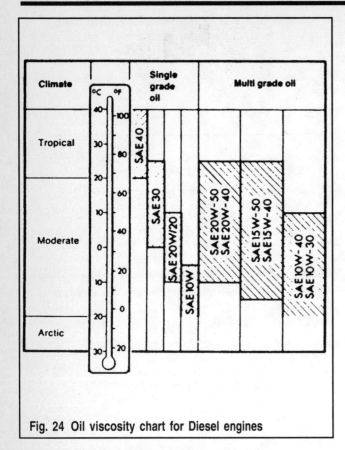

Fig. 24 Oil viscosity chart for Diesel engines

3. Remove the dipstick again. The oil level should be between the two marks. On the flat rod type dipstick, the level between the **MIN** and **MAX** marks is approximately 0.75L (0.79 quart).

4. Add oil through the capped opening on the top of the valve cover. Wipe up any spilled oil.

OIL AND FILTER CHANGE

▶ See Figure 26

Change the oil according to the maintenance interval chart in this Section. This interval is only for average driving. Change the oil and filter more frequently if your car is being used under dusty conditions or mostly stop and go city traffic, where acid and sludge buildup is a problem. When draining the oil, warm oil will flow easier and more contaminants will be

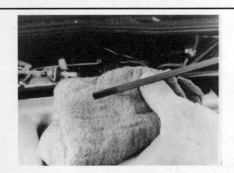

Fig. 25 Only add oil if the level is at or below the lower mark.

removed. Dispose of use oil in accordance with state or local regulations.

➡**Always change the oil and filter at the same time on diesel and gasoline engines.**

1. Run the engine until it reaches the normal operating temperature.
2. Raise and safely support the front of the car on jack stands.
3. Slide a drain pan under the oil pan drain plug.
4. Loosen the drain plug with a socket or box wrench, and then remove it by hand. Push in lightly on the plug as you turn it out, so that no oil escapes until the plug is completely removed.
5. While the oil is draining, check the condition of the copper gasket on the plug. If it looks split or badly deformed, replace it to avoid an oil leak.
6. After the oil is drained, install the plug and torque it to 22 ft. lbs.
7. The filter is located on the front of the engine block. Reach in and turn the filter off counterclockwise. If it's tight use a filter strap wrench.
8. Carefully lower the filter from it's mounting, direct the filter into the oil pan and drain it before disposal.
9. Clean the oil filter seating area with a clean rag. This is important to avoid a leak.
10. Lightly oil the rubber seal on the new filter and spin it on to the base. When the seal contacts the sealing surface, give it an additional 1/2 to 3/4 turn. Tightening the filter more than this will not improve sealing, but just make it harder to remove the next time.

Fig. 26 When removing the oil filter, do not remove the nut that holds the oil cooler onto the same base mount.

11. Refill the engine with 4 quarts of new oil. The empty containers can be used to return the used oil for recycling.

12. Run the engine and check for leaks.

Manual Transaxle

➡**Volkswagen strongly suggests that manual transmission maintenance be left to qualified dealers.**

FLUID RECOMMENDATIONS

All manual transmissions use SAE 80W hypoid oil, API service GL-4, Mil-L-2105. The hypoid type is an important specification. The transaxle holds about 2 U.S. quarts. Under normal service, changing the oil in a manual transaxle is not really required since there are no combustion by-products to contaminate the oil. A large magnet is fitted in the bottom of the case to attract any gear shavings. If the transmission has been abused or used most of its life for towing, an oil change may be in order. The most important thing is to make sure the level is correct, not low or over full.

LEVEL CHECK

1. Raise and safely support the front of the vehicle on jackstands.

2. Position a drain container under the oil filler plug.

3. Remove the oil filler plug. If the transmission is over full, allow the oil to drain from the filler plug opening until it stops.

4. Make sure the fluid level is even with the edge of the hole. If the level is low, add oil as required.

5. Install and tighten the plug.

DRAIN AND REFILL

▶ **See Figure 27**

1. Raise and safely support the front of the car on jackstands.

2. Slide drain pan under the transaxle.

3. Remove the filler plug and then the drain plug.

4. When the oil has been completely drained, install the drain plug. Tighten to 18 ft. lbs.

5. Refill the gearbox up to the level of the filler plug with about 2 quarts of new 80W hypoid gear oil.

6. Install and tighten the filler plug.

Automatic Transaxle

FLUID RECOMMENDATIONS

Dexron®II ATF is used in automatic transaxles. The transaxle holds 3.2 U.S. quarts when changing fluid or 6.3 quarts when refilling a dry (rebuilt) unit. VW recommends that the automatic transmission fluid be replaced every 30,000

Fig. 27 Removing the drain plug on a manual transaxle final drive is the same for an automatic.

miles, or 20,000 miles if you use your car for frequent trailer towing, mountain driving, or other severe service.

➡**The automatic transmission fluid used in later VW's is different in both chemical composition and color from previous models.**

The old fluid which was red in color has been replaced with a red/brown fluid. The new ATF changes to black/brown after a short time in the transaxle. Don't be alarmed by this color change, as it has no effect on the quality and lubricating characteristics of the fluid. The new Dexron®II can be intermixed without any adverse affects.

The final drive section of the automatic transaxle uses 90W hypoid gear oil, API service GL-5, Mil-I-2105B. The final drive unit requires no attention other than an occasional level check.

LEVEL CHECK

➡**DO NOT over fill an automatic transmission. Pressure is generated inside the case and over filling will cause fluid leaks.**

In addition to the **MIN** and **MAX** marks on the dipstick, there is a **20°** mark at the very bottom of the dipstck. The difference between the **MIN** and **MAX** marks is 0.24 qts. When cold, fill the transaxle to the **20°** mark. Warm up the engine to normal operating temperature and check the level again. It should be between the MIN and MAX marks. If not, add fluid as required.

1. Make sure the engine and transaxle are warm. Drive it around the block if necessary.

2. With the selector lever in **P**, remove the dipstick, wipe it clean, reinsert it, and withdraw it again.

3. The fluid level should be within the two marks. Top up with Dextron®II automatic transmission fluid. Bear in mind that the difference between the two marks is less than one pint. Use a long-necked funnel to add the fluid.

DRAIN AND REFILL

The only way to drain the automatic transaxle fluid is to remove the pan. There is no drain plug. The transaxle fluid does not lubricate the differential, which uses regular hypoid gear oil and is changed separately.

PAN AND FILTER SERVICE

1. Purchase the required amount of automatic transmission fluid Dexron®II and a pan gasket. Often the gasket is only available in a kit with the strainer gaskets or even a new strainer.

2. Slide a drain pan under the transaxle. Jack up the front of the car and support it safely on stands.

3. Remove the two rear pan bolts and loosen the two front pan bolts to drain the fluid.

4. Once the oil is drained from the pan, remove the remaining bolts and lower the pan.

5. Discard the old gasket and clean the pan with solvent. Make sure the gasket surface on the pan and the transaxle are clean, dry and free of all old gasket material.

6. Remove the bolt to remove the strainer and clean it. If the strainer is damaged, replace it.

7. Install the oil strainer with a new gasket and torque the bolt to 35 inch lbs. (4 Nm).

8. Fit the gasket onto the pan. Usually the gasket does not require any type of sealing compound to form an effective seal. Sometimes a sealer is necessary to hold the gasket in place while installing the pan. Be sure to glue the gasket to the pan, not to the transaxle.

9. Fit the pan into place and start all the bolts. Torque them in a crisscross pattern to 15 ft.lbs. (20 Nm).

10. Using a long-necked funnel, refill the transaxle with 3.2 quarts of fluid. Run the engine to check for leaks and to check the level.

Differential

➡**This pertains to vehicles with an automatic transaxle only.**

FLUID RECOMMENDATIONS

Use gear oil with API classification GL-5. Viscosity should be
- SAE 90 _ above 30°F (-1°C)
- SAE 85W _ above 0°F (-18°C)
- SAE 80W _ below -30°F° (-34°C)

LEVEL CHECK

Make sure the vehicle is on level ground. Next to the output flange of the transasxle, remove the filler plug. The oil should be even with the lower edge of the filler hole. Add or drain oil as required. The final drive is filled for life and does not require oil changes.

Cooling System

FLUID RECOMMENDATIONS

All VW's are filled with a mixture of water and special phosphate-free antifreeze at the factory. The antifreeze has corrosion inhibitors that prevent frost, the formation of chalk and also raise the boiling point of the water. Volkswagen recommends using VW phosphate free antifreeze/coolant part number ZVW237 when replacing or adding coolant. Most brand name antifreeze manufacturers recommend a 50/50 antifreeze-to-water mixture for maximum protection from freezing and overheating. A hydrometer is available at most parts stores that checks the specific gravity of the coolant, much like a battery hydrometer. Don't use a battery hydrometer though, it's not calibrated for coolant and it would no longer be usable for batteries. When deciding on the antifreeze/water mixture for refilling or adding to the system, follow the manufacturer's instructions on the container.

LEVEL CHECK

▶ **See Figure 28**

The coolant reservoir/expansion tank is translucent and if the reservoir is clean, it can be checked without removing the cap. The reservoir has low and high level marks. The coolant must be between the two marks when the engine is cold and slightly above the high mark at normal operating temperature. When removing the threaded pressure cap from the reservoir, loosen the cap slightly first. If the coolant begins to boil, tighten the cap again and wait for the engine to cool down.

Some models are equipped with a coolant warning light on the dash that flashes until the coolant is filled to the normal level.

DRAIN AND REFILL

▶ **See Figure 29**

The thermostat must be removed to drain the coolant. Before draining the coolant, purchase a new thermostat O-ring.

❄**CAUTION**

Never attempt to drain the coolant from a hot engine. This is a messy job and there is no way to drain the coolant without getting it on your hands.

1. Raise and safely support the front of the vehicle on jackstands.

Fig. 28 The coolant reservoir top is threaded and some have a connector for the coolant level warning light.

2. Place a large drain pan under the engine and loosen the thermostat housing bolts. When they are both loose and the housing is pulled slightly away from the water pump assembly, coolant will start to flow.

3. When the coolant stops flowing, there may still be some in the radiator or in the cylinder block, depending on where the thermostat is stuck in place. Keep the drain pan in place and remove the thermostat housing from the water pump assembly. It's not necessary to disconnect the lower radiator hose.

4. Remove the thermostat and the reservoir cap to drain the rest of the coolant.

To refill:

5. Clean and dry the thermostat housing and the rubber O-ring. Examine the O-ring for cracks or damage and replace as necessary.

6. Install the thermostat into the water pump housing on the engine, then fit the O-ring into place.

7. Install the thermostat housing and tighten the bolts evenly. Torque the bolts to 87 inch lbs. (10 Nm). Do not overtorque these bolts or the housing may break.

8. Loosen the upper radiator hose and begin filling the system through the coolant reservoir. Loosening the upper hose will allow the air to escape and speed the processes.

9. When the system will not take any more coolant, tighten the hose and start the engine. Watch for leaks and add more coolant as required. Don't run the engine too long with the reservoir cap removed or it will boil over.

FLUSHING AND CLEANING THE SYSTEM

The cooling system should be drained and refilled with new coolant at least every 30,000 miles or 24 months. Other than this service, Volkswagen does not recommend any special cooling system flushing. If you decide to do so, use a system flush made for use with aluminum cooling system components and follow the instructions on the package.

Master Cylinder

FLUID RECOMMENDATIONS

Use a good quality brake fluid that meets or exceeds DOT 3 or DOT 4 specifications. Never try to re-use brake fluid.

Fig. 29 Remove the thermostat housing to drain the coolant: 16V engine shown.

LEVEL CHECK

The brake fluid reservoir is located on the left side of the engine compartment at the firewall. Fluid level can be checked visually without removing the cap on this translucent unit. Brake fluid level will decrease slowly as the brake pads wear thinner. If the level is close to the MIN line, check the brake pads and shoes for wear before adding brake fluid. Also check the hydraulic clutch system (if equipped) for fluid leaks. If necessary, top up with a brand name hydraulic fluid which bears the DOT 3 or DOT 4 marking. This information will be printed on the container.

Clutch Master Cylinder

FLUID RECOMMENDATIONS

The hydraulic clutch uses fluid from the brake fluid reservoir. Use only new brake fluid that meets or exceeds DOT 3 or DOT 4 specifications.

Power Steering Pump

FLUID RECOMMENDATIONS

Use Dexron®II ATF when adding fluid to the power steering reservoir.

LEVEL CHECK

The reservoir for the power assisted steering is usually located at the rear of the engine compartment on the firewall. The fluid level should be checked at regular intervals. With the engine running, the fluid level should be between the 'MAX' and 'MIN' marks on the outside of the reservoir. If fluid is added, make sure the filler cap is secured.

Steering Gear

The rack and pinion steering gear is filled with lubricant and sealed at the factory. If you notice any leaks, the rack assembly must be repaired or replaced.

Chassis Greasing

These vehicles require no chassis greasing and are not equipped with grease nipples. Check the axle shaft and steering rack boots and the tie rod and ball joint rubber boots occasionally for leaking or cracking. At the same time, squirt a few drops of oil on the parking brake equalizer (point where cables V-off to the rear brakes). The front wheel bearings are sealed units and cannot be greased. Front wheel bearing replacement is described in Section 8.

Body Lubrication

Periodic lubrication will prevent squeaky, hard-to-open doors and lids. About every three months, pry the plastic caps off the door hinges and squirt in enough oil to fill the chambers. Press the plug back into the hinge after filling. Lightly oil the door check pivots. Finally, spray graphite lock lubricant onto your key and insert it into the door lock a few times.

Rear Wheel Bearings

REMOVAL, PACKING & INSTALLATION

▶ **See Figures 30 and 31**

1. Raise and safely support the vehicle and remove the rear wheels.
2. On drum brakes, insert a small pry tool through a wheel bolt hole and push up on the spring tensioned adjusting wedge to slacken the rear brake adjustment.
3. On disc brakes, remove the bolts to remove the caliper. Hang the caliper from the spring with wire, do not let it hang by the hydraulic hose.
4. Pry off the grease cap, remove cotter pin, locking ring, axle nut and thrust washer. Carefully remove the bearing without dropping it.
5. Remove the brake drum or disc and pry the bearing seal out of the hub. The seal will be destroyed but be careful not to pry on the bearing.
6. Remove the bearing and clean all parts in solvent. Examine the bearings and inner races for wear or damage. If bearings must be replaced, see Section 8.
7. Pack the bearings with new axle bearing grease. If the grease is suitable for use with disc brakes, it's good for all applications.
8. Install the inner bearing and a new wheel seal. Use the old seal or a flat bar across the new seal as an installation tool. The new seal must be driven in straight and seated on the hub.
9. Pack about 1 oz. of grease into the hub and fit the drum or disc onto the axle.
10. Pack the outer bearing with grease and fit the bearing, thrust washer and nut onto the axle. Adjust bearing pre-load and install the locking ring, cotter pin and grease cap.
11. Install the brake caliper, if removed.

ADJUSTMENT

1. Tighten the bearing nut while turning the drum or disc. Torque the nut to 87 inch lbs. (10 Nm) to seat the bearing, then loosen it again.

2. When tightening adjusting nut again, move the thrust washer side to side with a screwdriver. The thrust washer must still be movable with light effort when adjustment is complete.
3. When installing the locking ring, keep trying different positions of the ring on the nut until the cotter pin goes into the hole. Don't turn the nut to align the locking ring with the hole in the axle. Use a new cotter pin.

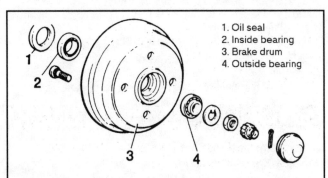

1. Oil seal
2. Inside bearing
3. Brake drum
4. Outside bearing

Fig. 30 Rear wheel bearing assembly on disc and drum brakes.

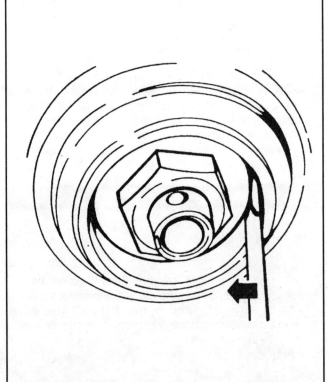

Fig. 31 Wheel bearing adjustment is correct if the thrust washer still moves.

TRAILER TOWING

Factory trailer towing packages are available for most vehicles. However, if you are installing a trailer hitch and wiring on your car, there are a few things that you ought to know.

Trailer Weight

Trailer weight is the first, and most important, factor in determining whether or not your vehicle is suitable for towing the trailer you have in mind. The horsepower-to-weight ratio should be calculated. The basic standard is a ratio of 35:1. That is, 35 pounds of GVW for every horsepower. To calculate this ratio, multiply you engine's rated horsepower by 35, then subtract the weight of the vehicle, including passengers and luggage. The resulting figure is the ideal maximum trailer weight that you can tow. One point to consider: a numerically higher axle ratio can offset what appears to be a low trailer weight. If the weight of the trailer that you have in mind is somewhat higher than the weight you just calculated, you might consider changing your final drive ratio to compensate.

Hitch Weight

There are three kinds of hitches: bumper mounted, frame mounted, and load equalizing. Bumper mounted hitches are those which attach solely to the vehicle's bumper. Many states prohibit towing with this type of hitch, when it attaches to the vehicle's stock bumper, since it subjects the bumper to stresses for which it was not designed. Aftermarket rear step bumpers, designed for trailer towing, are acceptable for use with bumper mounted hitches. Frame mounted hitches can be of the type which bolts to two or more points on the frame, plus the bumper, or just to several points on the frame. Frame mounted hitches can also be of the tongue type, for Class I towing, or, of the receiver type, for classes II and III. Volkswagens should not be used for towing anything with a Class II or class III rating, as maximum towing capacity for these cars is limited to 1000 lbs. gross weight. Load equalizing hitches are usually used for large trailers. Most equalizing hitches are welded in place and use equalizing bars and chains to level the vehicle after the trailer is hooked up. The bolt-on hitches are the most common, since they are relatively easy to install. Check the gross weight rating of your trailer. Tongue weight is usually figured as 10% of gross trailer weight. Therefore, a trailer with a maximum gross weight of 2,000 lb. will have a maximum tongue weight of 200 lb. Class I trailers fall into this category. Class II trailers are those with a gross weight rating of 2,000-3,500 lb., while Class III trailers fall into the 3,500- 6,000 lb. category. Class IV trailers are those over 6,000 lb. and are for use with fifth wheel trucks, only. When you've determined the hitch that you'll need, follow the manufacturer's installation instructions, exactly, especially when it comes to fastener torques. The hitch will be subjected to a lot of stress and good hitches come with hardened bolts. Never substitute an inferior bolt for a hardened bolt.

Wiring

Wiring the car for towing is fairly easy. There are a number of good wiring kits available and these should be used, rather than trying to design your own. All trailers will need brake lights and turn signals as well as tail lights and side marker lights. Most states require extra marker lights for overwide trailers. Also, most states have recently required backup lights for trailers, and most trailer manufacturers have been building trailers with back-up lights for several years. Additionally, some Class I, most Class II and just about all Class III trailers will have electric brakes. Add to this number an accessories wire, to operate trailer internal equipment or to charge the trailer's battery, and you can have as many as seven wires in the harness. Determine the equipment on your trailer and buy the wiring kit necessary. The kit will contain all the wires needed, plus a plug adapter set which included the female plug, mounted on the bumper or hitch, and the male plug, wired into, or plugged in to the trailer harness. When installing the kit, follow the manufacturer's instructions. The color coding of the wires is standard throughout the industry. One point to note: some domestic vehicles, and most imported vehicles, have separate turn signals. On most domestic vehicles, the brake lights and rear turn signals operate with the same bulb. For those vehicles with separate turn signals, you can purchase an isolation unit so that the brake lights won't blink whenever the turn signals are operated, or, you can go to your local electronics supply house and buy four diodes to wire in series with the brake and turn signal bulbs. Diodes will isolate the brake and turn signals. The choice is yours. The isolation units are simple and quick to install, but far more expensive than the diodes. The diodes, however, require more work to install properly, since they require the cutting of each bulb's wire and soldering in place of the diode. One, final point, the best kits are those with a spring loaded cover on the vehicle mounted socket. This cover prevents dirt and moisture from corroding the terminals. Never let the vehicle socket hang loosely; always mount it securely to the bumper or hitch.

Engine Cooling

One of the most common, if not THE most common, problems associated with trailer towing is engine overheating. With factory installed trailer towing packages, a heavy duty cooling system is usually included. Heavy duty cooling systems are available as optional equipment on most vehicles, with or without a trailer package. If you have one of these extra capacity systems, you shouldn't have any overheating problems. If you have a standard cooling system, without an expansion tank, you'll definitely need to get an aftermarket expansion tank kit, preferably one with at least a 2 quart capacity. These kits are easily installed on the radiator's overflow hose, and come with a pressure cap designed for expansion tanks. Through the dealer parts network, Volkswagen offers cooling and lubrication system modifications designed for towing.

PUSH-STARTING AND TOWING

✳✳CAUTION

Pushing or towing in an attempt to start a catalytic converter equipped car can cause raw gasoline to enter the converter and cause major damage.

If your car is equipped with a manual transaxle, it may be push-started in an extreme emergency. It should be recognized that there is the possibility of damaging bumpers and/or fenders of both cars. Make sure that the bumpers of both cars are evenly matched. Depress the clutch pedal, select Second or Third gear, and switch the ignition On. When the car reaches a speed of approximately 10 or 15 mph, release the clutch to start the engine. DO NOT ATTEMPT TO PUSH-START AN AUTOMATIC TRANSMISSION EQUIPPED MODEL.

Both manual and automatic models may be flat-towed short distances, but be aware that this is not legal in some states.

Attach tow lines to the towing eye on the front suspension or the left or right bumper bracket at the rear. Automatic equipped cars must be towed in Neutral no farther than 30 miles and no faster than 30 mph, unless the front wheels are off the ground. If you plan on towing a trailer, don't exceed the manufacturer's recommended towing weight for your VW. Towing a trailer with an automatic equipped car places an extra load on the transmission and a few items should be made note of here. Make doubly sure that the transmission fluid is at the correct level. Change the fluid more frequently if you're doing much trailer hauling. Start out in 1 or 2 and use the lower ranges when climbing hills. Aftermarket transmission coolers are available which greatly ease the load on your automatic and one should be considered if you often pull a trailer.

JACKING

▶ **See Figure 32**

Your car is equipped with a single post, crank handle jack which fits the jacking points behind the front wheel and in front of the rear wheel. These are marked with triangular sections of the body stamping. Never use the tire changing jack for anything other than that. If you intend to use this book to perform your own maintenance, a good pair of scissors or a small hydraulic jack and two sturdy jackstands would be a wise purchase. Always chock the wheels when changing a tire or working beneath the car. It cannot be overemphasized. **CLIMBING UNDER A CAR SUPPORTED BY JUST THE JACK IS EXTREMELY DANGEROUS!**

A jack can be safely placed just forward of or behind the same jacking points used by the tire changing jack. Place the jack on the rocker panel or on the seam, not inside the seem on the floor pan. The seam may crush but it won't effect the strength of the body. Lift the car there and fit the jackstand at the normal jacking point.

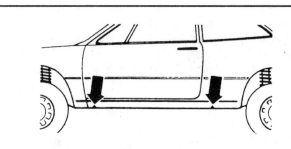

Fig. 32 Jacking points are small triangular marks in the rocker panel. Jack on the rocker panel or on the seem, not inside the seam.

ENGINE IDENTIFICATION

Year	Model	Engine Displacement Liters (cc)	Engine Series (ID/VIN)	Fuel System	No. of Cylinders	Engine Type
1990	Jetta GL	1.8 (1780)	RV	Digifant	4	SOHC
	Jetta GLi 16V	2.0 (1984)	9A	CIS-E	4	DOHC
	Jetta Carat	1.8 (1780)	PF ①	Digifant II	4	SOHC
	Golf GL	1.8 (1780)	RV	Digifant	4	SOHC
	GTI	1.8 (1780)	PF	Digifant II	4	SOHC
	GTI 16V	2.0 (1984)	9A	CIS-E	4	DOHC
	Cabriolet	1.8 (1780)	2H	Digifant II	4	SOHC
1991	Jetta GL	1.8 (1780)	RV	Digifant	4	SOHC
	Jetta GLi 16V	2.0 (1984)	9A	CIS-E	4	DOHC
	Jetta Carat	1.8 (1780)	PF ①	Digifant II	4	SOHC
	Jetta ECO Diesel	1.6 (1588)	1V	Bosch VE	4	Turbo
	Golf GL	1.8 (1780)	RV	Digifant	4	SOHC
	GTI	1.8 (1780)	PF	Digifant II	4	SOHC
	GTI 16V	2.0 (1984)	9A	CIS-E	4	DOHC
	Cabriolet	1.8 (1780)	2H	Digifant II	4	SOHC
1992-93	Jetta GL	1.8 (1780)	RV	Digifant	4	SOHC
	Jetta GLi 16V	2.0 (1984)	9A	CIS-E	4	DOHC
	Jetta Carat	1.8 (1780)	PF ①	Digifant II	4	SOHC
	Jetta ECO Diesel	1.6 (1588)	1V	Bosch VE	4	Turbo
	Golf GL	1.8 (1780)	RV	Digifant	4	SOHC
	GTI	1.8 (1780)	PF	Digifant II	4	SOHC
	GTI 16V	2.0 (1984)	9A	CIS-E	4	DOHC
	Cabriolet	1.8 (1780)	2H	Digifant II	4	SOHC

SOHC—Single Overhead Camshaft
DOHC—Double Overhead Camshaft
Turbo—Turbocharged
① California—RV engine

CAPACITIES

Year	Model	Engine ID/VIN	Engine Displacement Liters (cc)	Engine Crankcase with Filter	Transmission (pts.)		Fuel Tank (gal.)	Cooling System (qts.)
					5-Spd	Auto.		
1990	Jetta GL	RV	1.8 (1780)	4.3	4.2	6.4	14.5	7.3
	Jetta GLi	9A	2.0 (1984)	4.3	4.2	—	14.5	7.3
	Jetta Carat	PF	1.8 (1780)	4.3	4.2	6.4	14.5	7.3
	Golf GL	RV	1.8 (1780)	4.3	4.2	—	14.5	7.3
	GTI	PF	1.8 (1780)	4.3	4.2	—	14.5	7.3
	GTI 16V	9A	2.0 (1984)	4.3	4.2	—	14.5	7.3
	Cabriolet	2H	1.8 (1780)	4.3	4.2	—	13.8	7.3
1991	Jetta GL	RV	1.8 (1780)	4.3	4.2	—	14.5	7.3
	Jetta GLi	9A	2.0 (1984)	4.3	4.2	—	14.5	7.3
	Jetta Carat	PF	1.8 (1780)	4.3	4.2	—	14.5	7.3
	Golf GL	RV	1.8 (1780)	4.3	4.2	—	14.5	7.3
	GTI	PF	1.8 (1780)	4.3	4.2	—	14.5	7.3
	GTI 16V	9A	2.0 (1984)	4.3	4.2	—	14.5	7.3
	Cabriolet	2H	1.8 (1780)	4.3	4.2	—	13.8	7.3
	Jetta ECO Diesel	1V	1.6 (1588)	4.3	4.2	—	13.7	7.3
1992–93	Jetta GL	RV	1.8 (1780)	4.3	4.2	—	14.5	7.3
	Jetta GLi	9A	2.0 (1984)	4.3	4.2	—	14.5	7.3
	Jetta Carat	PF	1.8 (1780)	4.3	4.2	—	14.5	7.3
	Golf GL	RV	1.8 (1780)	4.3	4.2	—	14.5	7.3
	GTI	PF	1.8 (1780)	4.3	4.2	—	14.5	7.3
	GTI 16V	9A	2.0 (1984)	4.3	4.2	—	14.5	7.3
	Cabriolet	2H	1.8 (1780)	4.3	4.2	—	13.8	7.3
	Jetta ECO Diesel	1V	1.6 (1588)	4.3	4.2	—	13.7	7.3

DIESEL ENGINE TUNE-UP
PROCEDURES
DIESEL INJECTION TIMING 2-12
FUEL SYSTEM SERVICE
  PRECAUTIONS 2-11
IDLE SPEED 2-12
ELECTRONIC IGNITION
DESCRIPTION AND OPERATION 2-4
DIAGNOSIS AND TESTING 2-4
FIRING ORDERS 2-3
GASOLINE ENGINE TUNE-UP
PROCEDURES
SPARK PLUG WIRES 2-3

SPARK PLUGS 2-2
IDLE SPEED AND AIR/FUEL MIXTURE
GENERAL INFORMATION 2-10
IGNITION TIMING
IGNITION TIMING 2-9
TIMING MARK LOCATIONS 2-8
SPECIFICATIONS CHARTS
DIESEL ENGINE TUNE-UP
  SPECIFICATIONS 2-11
GASOLINE ENGINE TUNE-UP
  SPECIFICATIONS 2-2
VALVE LASH 2-10

2

ENGINE PERFORMANCE AND TUNE-UP

DIESEL ENGINE TUNE-UP
  PROCEDURES 2-11
ELECTRONIC IGNITION 2-4
FIRING ORDERS 2-3
GASOLINE ENGINE TUNE-UP
  PROCEDURES 2-2
IDLE SPEED AND AIR/FUEL
  MIXTURE 2-10
IGNITION TIMING 2-8
SPECIFICATIONS CHARTS 2-2
VALVE LASH 2-10

GASOLINE ENGINE TUNE-UP PROCEDURES

GASOLINE ENGINE TUNE-UP SPECIFICATIONS

Year	Engine ID/VIN	Engine Displacement Liters (cc)	Spark Plugs Gap (in.)	Ignition Timing (deg.) MT	Ignition Timing (deg.) AT	Fuel Pump (psi) ③	Idle Speed (rpm) MT	Idle Speed (rpm) AT	Valve Clearance In.	Valve Clearance Ex.
1990	RV	1.8 (1780)	0.028	6①	6①	36	800–900	800–900	Hyd.	Hyd.
	9A	2.0 (1984)	0.032	6②	6②	88–96	800–900	800–900	Hyd.	Hyd.
	PF	1.8 (1780)	0.032	6①	6①	36	800–900	800–900	Hyd.	Hyd.
	2H	1.8 (1780)	0.032	6①	6①	36	850–1000	850–1000	Hyd.	Hyd.
1991	RV	1.8 (1780)	0.028	6①	6①	36	800–900	800–900	Hyd.	Hyd.
	9A	2.0 (1984)	0.032	6②	6②	88–96	800–900	800–900	Hyd.	Hyd.
	PF	1.8 (1780)	0.032	6①	6①	36	800–900	800–900	Hyd.	Hyd.
	2H	1.8 (1780)	0.032	6①	6①	36	800–1000	800–1000	Hyd.	Hyd.
1992–93	RV	1.8 (1780)	0.028	6①	6①	36	800–900	800–900	Hyd.	Hyd.
	9A	2.0 (1984)	0.032	6②	6②	88–96	800–900	800–900	Hyd.	Hyd.
	PF	1.8 (1780)	0.032	6①	6①	36	800–900	800–900	Hyd.	Hyd.
	2H	1.8 (1780)	0.032	6①	6①	36	800–1000	800–1000	Hyd.	Hyd.

NOTE: The lowest cylinder pressure should be within 75% of the highest cylinder pressure reading. For example, if the highest cylinder is 134 psi, the lowest should be 101. Engine should be at normal operating temperature with throttle valve in the wide open position.

The underhood specifications sticker often reflects tune-up specification changes in production. Sticker figures must be used if they disagree with those in this chart.

Hyd.—Hydraulic
① At 2250 rpm.
② At idle speed.
③ Fuel system pressure at idle.

Volkswagen calls for a major vehicle service every 30,000 miles. In addition to things such as lubricating door hinges and checking brakes and suspension, the service includes the following engine related items:
1. Change oil and filter
2. Change air filter
3. Change spark plugs
4. Change diesel fuel filter
5. Check belts, including timing belt; adjust or replace as required

Spark Plugs

SELECTION

On many models, Volkswagen installs Bosch Platinum spark plugs at the factory. These have a center electrode made of platinum wire that is completely sheathed in porcelain. The grounding electrode usually does not wear away as on standard spark plugs and it's hard to tell when they are worn. Even though they tend to be more expensive, these and other platinum spark plugs are designed to last at least 30,000 miles. If less expensive standard spark plugs are being installed, keep in mind that they will not last as long.

When removing the spark plugs, examine each one carefully. If one plug has a deposit or a different color from the others, it can indicate a problem with the injector or ignition wire for that cylinder, or possibly a more serious mechanical problem. If they all have a dark fluffy deposit, look for fuel injection or oil consumption problems. Since VW fuel injection systems are so precise, changing the spark plug heat range to keep the plugs clean will only mask the real problem.

REMOVAL & INSTALLATION

▶ See Figure 1

1. On 16-valve engines, pull straight up on the plastic loop attached to one of the spark plug wires. Remove the loop and use it to pull off the remaining wires.
2. On 8-valve engines, disconnect the plug wires by grasping the boot or metal shield, don't pull on the wire. Mark the cylinder number on the boot and, if compressed air is available, blow any dirt off the cylinder head where the spark plugs seat.
3. Remove the plugs with a standard ¹³/₁₆ (21.6mm) spark plug socket and extension. Examine each spark plug as describes above.
4. If the same plugs are to be installed again, check and adjust the gap if necessary.
5. When installing a steel spark plug into an aluminum cylinder head, many experienced technicians apply just a drop of oil to the threads on the spark plug. This can help prevent the two dissimilar metals from seizing together, which would damage the head next time the plugs are removed. Make sure no oil gets on the electrode or porcelain.

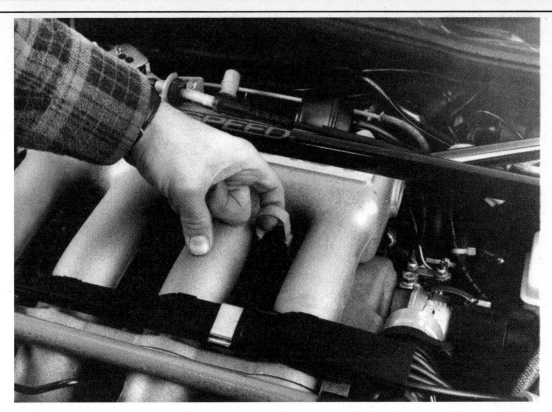

Fig. 1 Remove the loop and use it to disconnect each plug wire

6. Torque the spark plugs to 15 ft. lbs. (20 Nm). Do not over tighten or the threads in the head will be damaged.

7. Reconnect the wires in the correct order.

Spark Plug Wires

REMOVAL & INSTALLATION

If the wires are being replaced, remove one wire and match the length with the new wire. Install the new wire before removing the next old one. If the wires are to be reinstalled, remove them one at a time from the distributor cap before disconnecting them from the spark plugs. As each wire is removed from the distributor cap, mark the cylinder number on the boot and on the cap.

FIRING ORDERS

▶ See Figure 2

➡ To avoid confusion, remove the wires one at a time and identify them for correct installation.

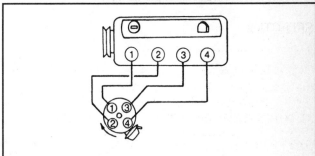

Fig. 2 1.8L and 2.0L Engines
Engine Firing Order:1 — 3 — 4 — 2
Distributor Rotation: Clockwise

ELECTRONIC IGNITION

Description and Operation

▶ **See Figures 3, 4, 5 and 6**

Volkswagen uses two different engine management systems: CIS-E Motronic and Digifant. The Motronic system uses a fuel distributor and mechanical fuel injectors. The Digifant system uses electric fuel injectors. Both systems use a single Electronic Control Unit (ECU) to control all the fuel injection and ignition functions. The ignition system consists of a distributor with a Hall Effect sender, an ignition coil, knock sensors, an ignition switch and the battery. Mechanical timing advance mechanisms are no longer used. Timing advance and retard functions are completely controlled by the ECU, although there is a basic setting.

The ECU is equipped with an internal voltage regulator (operating voltage — 8 volts) to prevent voltage fluctuations when different vehicle components are switched on. On CIS-E engines, the control unit also includes a manifold pressure sensor, so there is a vacuum line from the manifold to the control unit. The ECU is located in the cowling above the fire wall in the engine compartment. If the cover is removed for testing, be sure it is properly replaced and the seal is correctly installed. Even though the unit is sealed and weather resistant, the connectors must be protected.

Diagnosis and Testing

HALL SENDER

The Hall sender replaces the breaker points found in earlier ignition systems. It consists of a permanent magnet, a semi conductor chip and a metal trigger wheel. The chip is supplied with voltage and generates a return signal. As the distributor turns, the trigger wheel rotates in the air gap between the magnet and the chip. As the windows in the wheel pass through the gap, the magnetic field changes, causing the return signal from the chip to rise and fall. The ECU reads these signal changes to calculate ignition timing, crankshaft position and engine speed. Any distortion of the trigger wheel will adversely effect performance of the system.

Digifant System

1. Unplug the Hall sender connector from the distributor, turn the ignition switch **ON** and check for a minimum of 9 volts between the 2 outside terminals of the connector. This voltage comes from the ECU.

2. Turn the ignition **OFF** and push the connector boot back so the wire terminals can be reached with the wiring connected. Reconnect the Hall sender wiring and disconnect the fuel injector wiring to prevent the engine from starting.

3. Connect an LED test light between the center terminal and either of the outer terminals. When the starter is operated

Fig. 3 The engine management system ECU is under the cover in the cowl

Fig. 4 If removed, make sure the cover and seal are properly installed

the LED should flicker, indicating a signal voltage is being generated by the Hall sender.

Motronic System

1. Unplug the connector from the power output stage on the ignition coil. Connect an LED test light between the center and an outer terminal of the connector.

2. When the starter is operated, the LED should flicker indicating a signal voltage is being generated by the Hall sender. If not, try the other outer terminal on the connector.

3. If there is still no signal, unplug the Hall sender connector from the distributor, turn the ignition switch **ON** and check for a minimum of 9 volts between the 2 outside terminals.

4. Turn the ignition **OFF** and move the rubber boot away from the Hall sender connector. Plug the connector into the distributor and connect the test LED between the center wire terminal and the battery positive post. When the starter is activated, the LED should flash. If not, either the Hall sender or the ECU is faulty.

IGNITION CONTROL UNIT

▶ See Figure 7

This unit is used on the Digifant system to turn the primary circuit of the ignition coil on and off. It is mounted to a heat sink bracket on or near the ECU. When replacing the unit, make sure it is clean and there is good contact between the unit and bracket.

1. Unplug the control unit connector and turn the ignition **ON**. Check for 12 volts between terminals **2** and **4** on the ignition control unit connector.

2. Turn the ignition **OFF** and check for continuity between terminal **1** on the connector and terminal **1** on the ignition coil.

3. Connect the voltmeter to terminals **1** and **15** on the ignition coil. Turn the ignition **ON** and ground terminal **12** of the control unit connector. There should be about 2 volts for 1-2 seconds, then the voltage should drop off to 0 volts. If not, the control unit is faulty.

POWER OUTPUT STAGE

▶ See Figure 8

This unit is used on the Motronic system and on California models with the Digifant system. It is a solid state switch mounted on the coil bracket used to turn the primary circuit of the ignition coil on and off. If the unit is replaced, pay close attention to how it is mounted onto the bracket. Its ability to remove heat is important.

1. Unplug the connector from the output stage and connect a voltmeter to terminals **2** and **3**. With the ignition switch **ON**, there should be 12 volts.

2. Connect a test LED to the same terminals and operate the starter. The LED should flicker, indicating the Hall sender signal is reaching the power output stage.

3. Turn the ignition **OFF**, connect the output stage wiring and disconnect the Hall sender plug from the distributor.

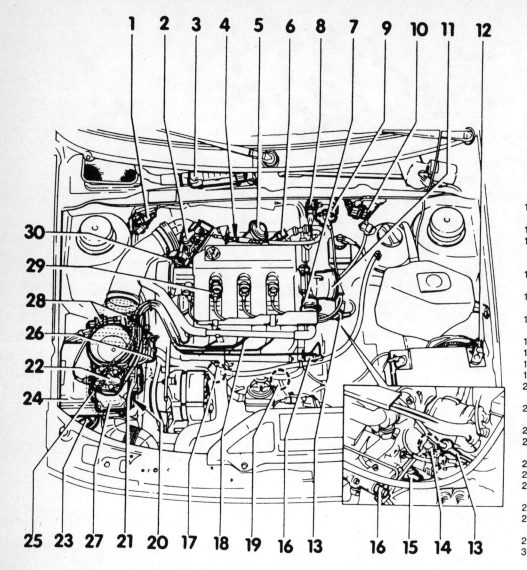

1. Oxygen sensor harness connector on right engine mount
2. Throttle body
3. Control module
4. Intake air temperature sensor—California only
5. EGR valve—California only
6. Exhaust tap
7. Idle stabilizer valve
8. Ignition coil power output stage
9. Ignition coil
10. 6-pin wiring harness connector
11. Distributor
12. EGR vacuum amplifier—California only
13. Ignition timing sensor or plug wire 4
14. EGR vacuum valve—California only
15. Coolant temperature sensor
16. Cold start valve
17. Knock sensor I
18. Fuel injector
19. Knock sensor II
20. Heated air intake control door
21. Differential pressure regulator
22. Fuel distributor
23. Charcoal canister below air cleaner
24. Air filter
25. Potentiometer
26. Fuel pressure regulator
27. Air flow sensor
28. Charcoal canister solenoid valves
29. Spark plug
30. Throttle switch harness connectors

Fig. 5 Motronic engine management system

4. Connect the voltmeter across both coil primary circuit terminals and turn the ignition switch **ON**. Connect a jumper wire to the center terminal of the Hall sender connector and briefly ground the wire. There should be about 2 volts for 1-2 seconds, then the voltage should drop off to 0 volts. If the voltage does not drop, the power output stage or the ECU is faulty.

KNOCK SENSOR

The knock sensor is a Pizieo electric chip that generates a voltage under impact. It is bolted directly to the engine block and is sensitive to the vibration frequency generated by detonation in the cylinders. When the ECU receives a voltage signal from the knock sensor, it will retard ignition timing as required to stop the knock, then gradually advance it again.

The only test of the sensor is with an ohmmeter. There should be 0 ohms across the sensor terminals. If there is any other reading or if there is physical damage to the sensor or wiring, it must be replaced. Installation position and torque are critical to proper function of the sensor. Torque the mounting bolt to 15-18 ft. lbs. (20-25 Nm) and make sure no hoses or other wires touch the sensor.

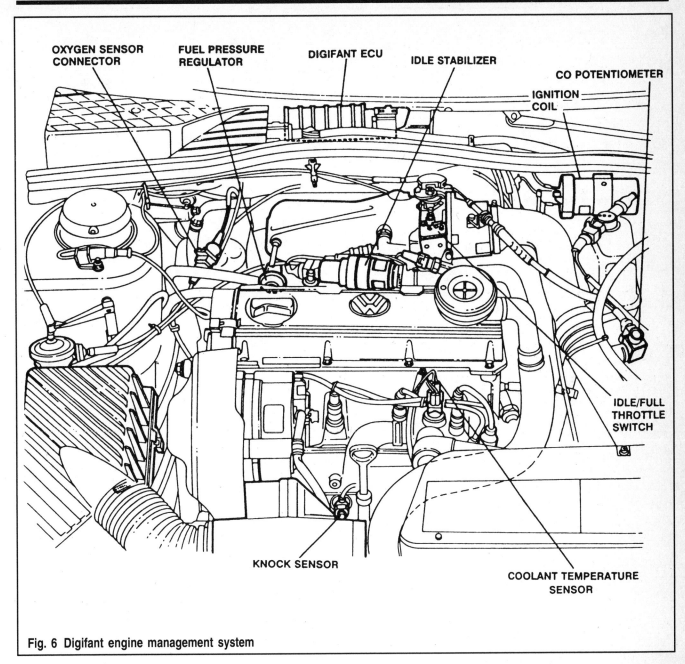

OXYGEN SENSOR CONNECTOR

FUEL PRESSURE REGULATOR

DIGIFANT ECU

IDLE STABILIZER

CO POTENTIOMETER

IGNITION COIL

IDLE/FULL THROTTLE SWITCH

KNOCK SENSOR

COOLANT TEMPERATURE SENSOR

Fig. 6 Digifant engine management system

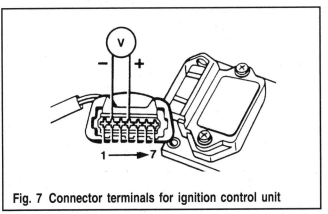

Fig. 7 Connector terminals for ignition control unit

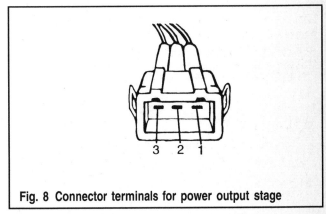

Fig. 8 Connector terminals for power output stage

IGNITION COIL

▶ See Figure 9

Digifant System

EXCEPT CALIFORNIA MODELS

1. For coils with a green label:
   a. Make sure the ignition switch is **OFF** and disconnect all wiring from the coil. Primary circuit resistance across terminals **1** and **15** should be 0.5-0.7 ohms.
   b. Secondary resistance between terminals **15** and **4** should be 2400-3500 ohms.
2. For coils with a gray label:
   a. Make sure the ignition switch is **OFF** and disconnect all wiring from the coil. Primary circuit resistance across terminals **1** and **15** should be 0.6-0.8 ohms.
   b. Secondary resistance between terminals **15** and **4** should be 6900-8500 ohms.

CALIFORNIA MODELS

1. Make sure the ignition switch is **OFF** and disconnect all wiring from the coil. Primary circuit resistance across terminals **1** and **15** should be 0.5-0.7 ohms.
2. Secondary resistance between terminal **15** and the coil output terminal should be 3000-4000 ohms.

Motronic System

1. Make sure the ignition switch is **OFF** and disconnect all wiring from the coil. Primary circuit resistance across terminals **1** and **15** should be 0.6-0.8 ohms.
2. Secondary resistance between terminals **15** and **4** should be 6500-8500 ohms.

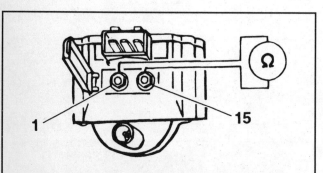

Fig. 9 Check primary circuit resistance across terminals 1 and 15 on all coils, California Digifant coil shown

DISTRIBUTOR CAP AND ROTOR

The distributor cap has a shield for radio interference suppression. Special ignition wires with suppressors are also used. These are the only suppression equipment on the vehicle, so replacement ignition wires should be the same type. On some vehicles with the Motronic system, an ignition reference sensor is attached to the No. 4 plug wire. The ECU uses the input from this sensor when calculating the timing retard required to stop the engine knock.

➡**To maintain exact timing control, the rotor is glued to the distributor shaft and cannot be removed without destroying it.**

To remove the rotor, carefully break it up with pliers to avoid damage to the shaft. Do not hit it with a hammer. Be sure to remove all old adhesive and use the glue that comes with the new part to install the new rotor.

1. Remove the distributor cap and use a mirror to read the number on the under side of the end, near the part number. The rotor should be type R1.
2. Touch the probes of an ohmmeter to the center and the end of the rotor conductor. The resistance should be 600-1400 ohms.
3. If the rotor appears burnt or worn at the center pole or on the end, replace it even if the resistance is correct. The distributor cap should be replaced any time the rotor is replaced.

IGNITION WIRES

Motronic

1. The resistance of the coil-to-distributor wire should be 1600-2400 ohms.
2. The resistance of the spark plug wires should be 4800-7200 ohms.

Digifant

1. The wires are separate from the radio interference suppressing connectors on the distributor cap end. When the connector is removed (unscrewed) the wire should have no resistance.
2. Measure the resistance of the wire connectors at the distributor cap and both connectors on the coil wire; there should be 600-1400 ohms.
3. The spark plug connectors should have 4000-6000 ohms.

IGNITION TIMING

Timing Mark Locations

▶ See Figures 10, 11, 12 and 13

The timing mark is on the flywheel and can be viewed through a window in the bellhousing on the transmission. On some models the plastic cover has a cap that can be pulled out. It's easier to see the marks if the cover is removed completely by unscrewing it with a 27mm Allen wrench.

Two marks appear on the flywheel: Top Dead Center (TDC) of No. 1 cylinder is indicated with a '0'. The only other machined mark on the flywheel is the correct timing mark for that engine. On some flywheels the mark is a machined groove, on others it will appear as a raised lug.

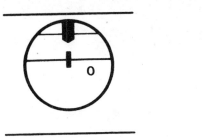

Fig. 10 The timing mark is on the flywheel

Ignition Timing

ADJUSTMENT

➡ **This is a basic timing adjustment procedure. Ignition timing and idle speed must both be checked at the same time.**

1. Run the engine to normal operating temperature, making sure the radiator fan runs at least once.

2. Stop the engine and connect a tachometer to the coil and a timing light to NO. 1 spark plug wire.

❊❊CAUTION

Do not allow terminal 1 of the ignition coil to be grounded or the ECU will be permanently damaged.

3. On Digifant engines, disconnect the blue coolant temperature sensor.
4. With the ignition **ON** but the engine not running, verify that the idle stabilizer valve hums or buzzes.
5. Start the engine and make sure all electrical equipment is turned **OFF** and that idle speed is correct.
6. Shine the timing light at the marks on the flywheel. If adjustment is required, loosen the distributor clamp bolt and

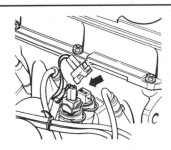

Fig. 12 On Digifant engines, disconnect the blue coolant temperature sensor to check ignition timing and air/fuel mixture

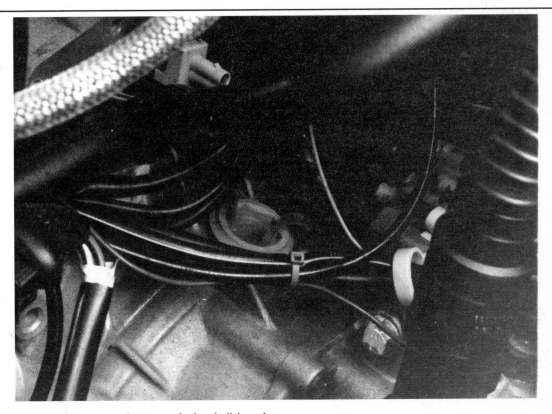

Fig. 11 Timing mark cover on the transmission bell housing

rotate the distributor as needed to align the correct timing marks.

VALVE LASH

All gasoline engines are fitted with hydraulic valve lifters. No adjustment is required or possible.

IDLE SPEED AND AIR/FUEL MIXTURE

General Information

On all Volkswagens, ignition timing, idle speed and air/fuel mixture must all be checked together in that order. These are all controlled with the Motronic or Digifant engine management computer. The ECU operates the idle air stabilizer valve to control idle speed. On 16V engines, this valve is below the end of the spark plug wire tray. On other engines, it is mounted on top of the valve cover.

INSPECTION PROCEDURE

Idle Speed

Idle speed cannot be adjusted but some problems that may cause an incorrect idle speed can be diagnosed quickly. If the engine runs properly but idle speed is not correct, inspect the following:

1. Make sure the engine is at operating temperature and all accessories are **OFF**.
2. Stop the engine and turn the ignition switch **ON**. The idle air valve should buzz or vibrate gently when touched.
3. If there is no activity at the valve, make sure the throttle and the idle position switch on the throttle body are closed.
4. Unplug the idle air valve connector and check for voltage across the terminals. It probably won't be battery voltage and may not be stable but there should be something measurable. If there is no voltage, the wiring between the valve and the ECU may be faulty.
5. Check for vacuum leaks, especially the duct between the air flow meter and the throttle body.

7. On Digifant engines, briefly raise the engine speed to 3000 rpm 3 times, then check idle speed and timing again.

Idle Mixture

The air/fuel mixture is controlled by the ECU and measured by sampling the exhaust with a CO meter. If this equipment is not available, no checking or adjustment is possible. Since adjusting the mixture is not part of a normal tune-up, the adjusting screw is protected with a tamper-proof plug. If the air/fuel ratio is obviously incorrect (lean miss, sooty spark plugs and tail pipe), or if the CO measurement is out of specification, look for other problems such as a vacuum leak, bad sensor, loose connection, etc. and correct any faults before deciding to adjusting the mixture.

1. With the engine at normal operating temperature, make sure the ignition timing and idle speed are correct. Stop the engine.
2. Disconnect the crank case breather hose and move it so only fresh air can enter. On Digifant engines, disconnect the blue coolant temperature sensor.
3. Insert the CO meter probe into the CO test point at the back of the engine compartment, a metal tube with a blue cap. Make sure the probe is a tight fit and will not draw in outside air.
4. Start the engine and turn **OFF** all lights and accessories. If any fuel injection lines have been disconnected, rev the engine to 3000 rpm, 2-3 times to clear any air from the system.
5. On all engines, the CO reading should be 0.2-1.2%. On Digifant engines, the reading should increase linearly at higher altitudes, up to about 2.2-3.7% at 5000 feet altitude.
6. If the CO reading is not correct, see Section 5 for complete instructions on troubleshooting the fuel system.

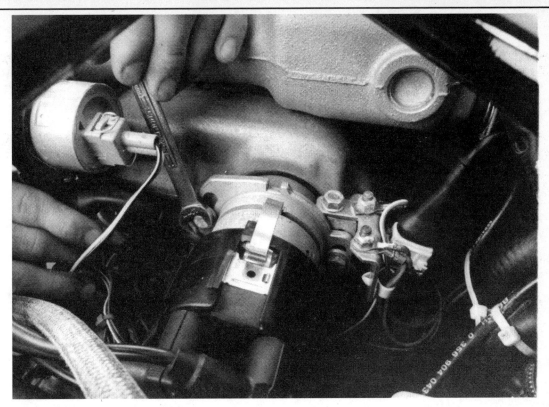

Fig. 13 The distributor on 16V engines has two hold-down bolts

DIESEL ENGINE TUNE-UP PROCEDURES

DIESEL ENGINE TUNE-UP SPECIFICATIONS

Year	Engine ID/VIN	Engine Displacement Liters (cc)	Valve Clearance ① Intake (in.)	Exhaust (in.)	Intake Valve Opens (deg.)	Injection Pump Setting (deg.)	Injection Nozzle Pressure (psi) New	Used	Idle Speed (rpm)	Cranking Compression Pressure (psi)
1991	1V	1.6 (1588)	0.008–0.012	0.016–0.020	NA	Align Marks	NA	NA	800–850	406 min.
1992	1V	1.6 (1588)	Hyd.	Hyd.	NA	Align Marks	NA	NA	800–850	406 min.
1993	1V	1.6 (1588)	Hyd.	Hyd.	NA	Align Marks	NA	NA	800–850	406 min.

Hyd.—Hydraulic
NA—Not available
① Engine warm.

In the 1991 model year, Volkswagen introduced the ECO Diesel engine in the Jetta. This is a standard diesel engine with hydraulic valve lifters, a turbo charger and a catalytic converter. The turbo charger provides only about 6 psi boost but about a 40 percent increase in air flowing through the engine. This provides a modest power increase, but the objective is to greatly improve the engine's emissions performance. Since the system is designed for improved emissions rather than power, there is no fuel enrichment device on the injection pump.

The only tune-up procedures for diesel engines is to change the fuel filter, drain the water separator and check idle speed. If the injection pump or timing belt have been removed, pump timing must also be adjusted. See Section 1 for filter and water separator service.

Fuel System Service Precautions

• Do not allow fuel spray or fuel vapors to come into contact with a heating element or open flame. Do not smoke while working on the fuel system.
• Always relieve the fuel system pressure prior to disconnecting any fitting or fuel line connection.
• To control fuel spray when relieving system pressure, place a shop towel around the fitting prior to loosening to catch the spray. Ensure that all fuel spillage is quickly wiped

up and that all fuel soaked rags are deposited into a proper fire safety container.

• Always keep a dry chemical (Class B) fire extinguisher near the work area.

• Always use a backup wrench when loosening and tightening fuel line fittings. Always follow the proper torque specifications.

• Do not re-use fuel system gaskets and O-rings, replace with new ones. Do not substitute fuel hose where fuel pipe is installed.

• Cleanliness is absolutely essential. Clean all fittings before opening them and maintain a dust free work area while the system is open.

• Place removed parts on a clean surface and cover with paper or plastic to keep them clean. Do not cover with rags that can leave fuzz on the parts.

Diesel Injection Timing

ADJUSTMENT

1. Turn the engine to TDC of No. 1 cylinder.
2. Be sure the manual cold start control is pushed in all the way and the pump lever is on the low idle stop.
3. Remove the center plug on the pump head and install the adapter tool VW-2066 or equivalent, and a dial indicator. Preload the dial indicator to 2.5mm.
4. Slowly turn the engine counterclockwise until the dial gauge stops moving, then zero the dial indicator. If the dial indicator is properly preloaded, this is the bottom of the pump stroke.
5. Turn the engine clockwise until the TDC mark on the flywheel aligns with the pointer on the bell housing.
6. The dial indicator should read 0.93-1.07mm for the ECO Diesel engine.
7. If adjustment is required, remove the timing belt cover and loosen the pump mounting bolts without turning the engine.
8. Turn the pump body until the dial indicator reads 1.00mm.
9. Torque the mounting bolts to 18 ft. lbs. (25 Nm) and turn the engine backwards about 1 turn. Turn the engine forwards to TDC of No. 1 cylinder and recheck the dial indicator reading.

10. When the correct setting is reached on the dial indicator, reinstall the belt cover and the center plug on the pump. Use a new copper gasket.

Idle Speed

ADJUSTMENT

▶ **See Figure 14**

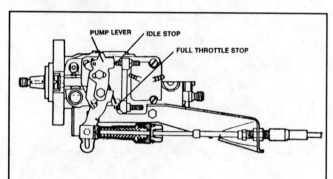

Fig. 14 Low and high idle stop screws on a diesel injection pump

Diesel engines have both an idle speed and a maximum speed adjustment. The maximum speed adjustment is a high idle speed that prevents the engine from over-revving when the control lever is in the full speed position but there is no load on the engine. No increase in power is available through this adjustment. The adjusters are located side by side on top of the injection pump. The screw closest to the engine is the low-idle adjustment, the outer screw is the high-idle adjustment.

1. If the vehicle has no tachometer, connect a suitable diesel engine tachometer as per the manufacturer's instructions.
2. Run the engine to normal operating temperature.
3. If equipped, make sure the manual cold start knob or idle boost is pushed in all the way.
4. Loosen the locknut and set the low idle to 820-880 rpm, or at a speed where there is no vibration.
5. When tightening the locknut, apply a thread sealer to prevent the screw from vibrating loose.
6. Advance the control lever (throttle) to full speed. The high idle speed is 5300-5400 rpm. Adjust as needed and secure the locknut with sealer.

ENGINE ELECTRICAL
ALTERNATOR 3-6
BATTERY 3-6
DIESEL GLOW PLUGS 3-5
DISTRIBUTOR 3-4
DISTRIBUTOR CAP AND ROTOR 3-4
HALL SENDER 3-2
IGNITION COIL 3-2
IGNITION SYSTEM
  PRECAUTIONS 3-2
STARTER 3-7
VOLTAGE REGULATOR 3-6
ENGINE MECHANICAL
CAMSHAFT (VALVE) COVER 3-18
CAMSHAFT(S) AND BEARINGS 3-31
CRANKSHAFT AND MAIN
  BEARINGS 3-38
CYLINDER HEAD 3-22
DESCRIPTION 3-7
ENGINE 3-14
ENGINE MOUNTS 3-18
ENGINE OVERHAUL TIPS 3-8
EXHAUST MANIFOLD 3-19
FLYWHEEL 3-40
INSPECTION TECHNIQUES 3-8
INTAKE MANIFOLD 3-18
INTERMEDIATE SHAFT 3-33

MAIN OIL SEALS 3-38
OIL COOLER 3-20
OIL PAN 3-28
OIL PUMP 3-29
OVERHAUL TIPS 3-8
PISTONS AND CONNECTING
  RODS 3-33
RADIATOR AND FAN 3-20
REPAIRING DAMAGED THREADS 3-8
THERMOSTAT 3-18
TIMING BELT 3-29
TIMING BELT COVER 3-29
TIMING SPROCKETS 3-31
TOOLS 3-8
TURBOCHARGER 3-20
VALVE GUIDES 3-28
VALVE LIFTERS 3-28
VALVE SEATS 3-28
VALVE SPRINGS 3-27
VALVE STEM SEALS 3-27
VALVES 3-26
WATER PUMP 3-20
EXHAUST SYSTEM
EXHAUST PIPE 3-41
GENERAL DESCRIPTION 3-40
REAR SECTION 3-43

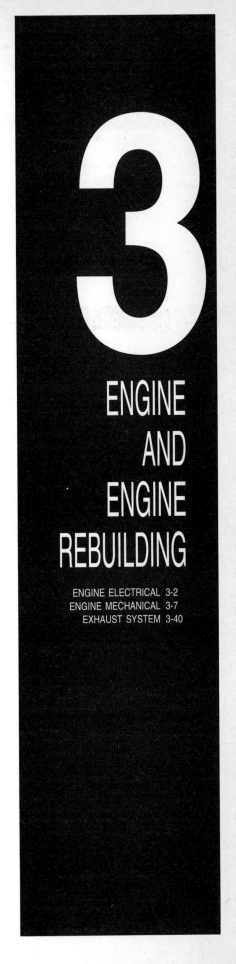

3

ENGINE AND ENGINE REBUILDING

ENGINE ELECTRICAL 3-2
ENGINE MECHANICAL 3-7
EXHAUST SYSTEM 3-40

ENGINE ELECTRICAL

Ignition System Precautions

1. Make sure the ignition switch is **OFF** before connecting or disconnecting any wiring or test equipment.

2. When cranking the engine without starting, as for a compression test, disconnect the high tension coil wire from distributor and ground it to the engine block or head.

3. DO NOT install a standard ignition coil in the system.

4. DO NOT connect a condenser/suppressor or powered test light to the negative terminal (1) of the ignition coil.

5. DO NOT connect any 12-volt test instruments to the positive terminal (15) of the ignition coil. The electronic control unit will be permanently damaged.

6. When boost-starting, DO NOT connect a quick-charger for more than 1 minute, nor exceed 16.5 volts with the booster.

Ignition Coil

TESTING

▶ **See Figures 1, 2 and 3**

Digifant System

EXCEPT CALIFORNIA MODELS

1. For coils with a green label:

   a. Make sure the ignition switch is **OFF** and disconnect all wiring from the coil. Primary circuit resistance across terminals **1** and **15** should be 0.5-0.7 ohms.

   b. Secondary resistance between terminals **15** and **4** should be 2400-3500 ohms.

2. For coils with a gray label:

   a. Make sure the ignition switch is **OFF** and disconnect all wiring from the coil. Primary circuit resistance across terminals **1** and **15** should be 0.6-0.8 ohms.

   b. Secondary resistance between terminals **15** and **4** should be 6900-8500 ohms.

CALIFORNIA MODELS

1. Make sure the ignition switch is **OFF** and disconnect all wiring from the coil. Primary circuit resistance across terminals **1** and **15** should be 0.5-0.7 ohms.

2. Secondary resistance between terminal **15** and the coil output terminal should be 3000-4000 ohms.

Motronic System

1. Make sure the ignition switch is **OFF** and disconnect all wiring from the coil. Primary circuit resistance across terminals **1** and **15** should be 0.6-0.8 ohms.

2. Secondary resistance between terminals **15** and **4** should be 6500-8500 ohms.

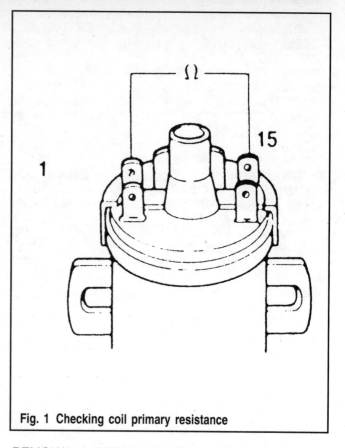

Fig. 1 Checking coil primary resistance

REMOVAL & INSTALLATION

1. Tag and disconnect all the wires from the coil.

2. Disconnect the engine ground strap from the coil, if installed. On CIS-E Motronic coils, unplug the harness connector from the power stage module on the side of the coil.

3. Using a flat blade screwdriver, loosen the adjusting screw which secures the coil inside the clamp.

4. Remove the coil from the vehicle.

5. Installation is the reverse of removal.

Hall Sender

REMOVAL & INSTALLATION

▶ **See Figures 4 and 5**

A procedure for testing the Hall effect sender in the distributor appears in Section 2. The sender can be removed with the distributor still on the engine but most technicians remove the distributor first. This minimizes the chance of loosing parts and installing the distributor correctly is simple.

1. Make sure the ignition switch is **OFF** and remove the distributor cap and suppression shield. It is not necessary to remove the spark plug wires from the cap.

2. Remove the rotor and dust shield. On 16V engines, the rotor is glued onto the distributor and must be broken apart

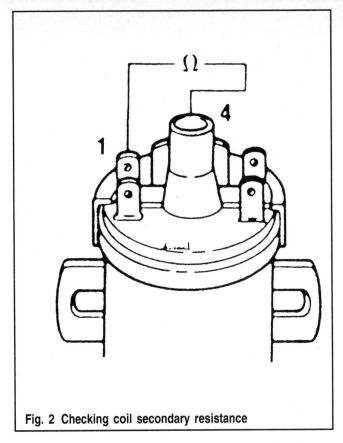

Fig. 2 Checking coil secondary resistance

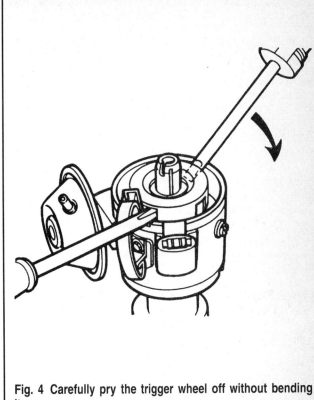

Fig. 4 Carefully pry the trigger wheel off without bending it

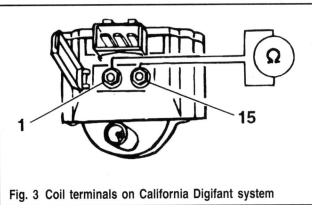

Fig. 3 Coil terminals on California Digifant system

with pliers to remove it. Carefully crush the lower portion, remove the rotor and clean off all the old adhesive.

3. On 8 valve engines, remove the snapring holding the trigger wheel in place.

4. Pry the trigger wheel off carefully as shown. Be careful not to lose the locating pin that indexes the wheel to the shaft and DO NOT distort the trigger wheel.

5. Unplug the Hall sender connector and remove the screw(s) to remove the sender from the base plate.

To install:

6. Install the new Hall sender and use a magnetic screw driver to start the screw.

7. When fitting the trigger wheel into place, make sure the locating pin and wheel are correctly aligned on the shaft. On 8 valve engines, install the snapring.

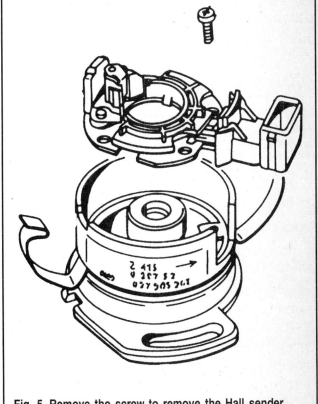

Fig. 5 Remove the screw to remove the Hall sender

8. Install the dust shield and rotor. On 16V engines, use an instant adhesive when installing the rotor.

9. Install the cap and suppressor shield. Run the engine to check ignition timing.

Distributor

REMOVAL & INSTALLATION

▶ **See Figures 6 and 7**

1. Unsnap the clips and remove the distributor cap and suppressor shield. Disconnect the Hall sensor wiring. It is not necessary to disconnect the spark plug wires from the cap.

2. At the front crankshaft pulley bolt, turn the engine to Top Dead Center (TDC) on No. 1 piston. It's easier to turn the engine with the spark plugs removed. Timing mark illustrations appear in Section 2.

3. The rotor should point to the NO. 1 mark on the distributor housing. If not, turn the engine one full turn to align the mark.

4. Make a chalk or paint mark on the engine where the rotor points to the rim of the distributor.

5. On 8 valve engines, remove the bolt, lift off the hold down flange and lift the distributor straight out of the engine.

6. On 16V engines, remove the 2 bolts and pull the distributor straight out of the cylinder head. Note which holes the bolts came from to make sure the timing can be adjusted correctly.

To install:

7. Check the condition of the O-ring on the distributor housing, replace it if necessary.

➡**NOTE the drive at the bottom of the distributor shaft. The lug is offset to one side.**

8. If the engine has not been turned with the distributor out:

   a. Align the rotor with the mark on the rim of the distributor.

   b. Carefully fit the distributor into place and gently push while turning the rotor side-to-side. The lugs will drop into place on the drive shaft or camshaft (16V engine).

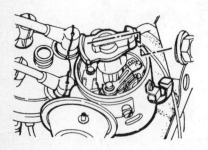

Fig. 6 Align the rotor with the mark on the rim of the distributor

Fig. 7 The slot is parallel with the crankshaft when the timing mark on the flywheel is at TDC

9. If the engine has been rotated while the distributor was out:

   a. Turn the crankshaft so that the No. 1 piston is on its compression stroke and the timing marks on the flywheel are aligned.

   b. On 8 valve engines, the drive slot must be parallel with the crankshaft. This can be turned with a screw driver if necessary.

   c. On 16V engines, look into the mounting hole and note the position of the slot in the crankshaft.

   d. Turn the distributor so that the rotor points to the mark on the rim of the housing.

   e. Install the distributor, making sure the drive lugs engage the slot. On 8 valve engines, the distributor may turn as it is pushed down all the way.

10. Make sure the mark on the distributor aligns with the mark you make on the block or head and install the hold down flange or bolts.

11. Install the cap, connect the wires and check ignition timing.

Distributor Cap and Rotor

TESTING

The distributor cap has a shield for radio interference suppression. Special ignition wires with suppressors are also used. These are the only suppression equipment on the vehicle, so replacement ignition wires should be the same type. On some vehicles with the Motronic system, an ignition reference sensor is attached to the No. 4 plug wire. The ECU uses the input from this sensor when calculating the timing retard required to stop the engine knock.

➡**To maintain exact timing control, the rotor is glued to the distributor shaft and cannot be removed without destroying it.**

To remove the rotor, carefully break it up with pliers to avoid damage to the shaft. Do not hit it with a hammer. Be sure to remove all old adhesive and use the glue that comes with the new part to install the new rotor.

1. Remove the distributor cap and use a mirror to read the number on the under side of the end, near the part number. The rotor should be type R1.

2. Touch the probes of an ohmmeter to the center and the end of the rotor conductor. The resistance should be 600-1400 ohms.

3. If the rotor appears burnt or worn at the center pole or on the end, replace it even if the resistance is correct. The distributor cap should be replaced any time the rotor is replaced.

IGNITION WIRES

Motronic

1. The resistance of the coil-to-distributor wire should be 1600-2400 ohms.

2. The resistance of the spark plug wires should be 4800-7200 ohms.

Digifant

1. The wires are separate from the radio interference suppressing connectors on the distributor cap end. When the connector is removed (unscrewed) the wire should have no resistance.

2. Measure the resistance of the wire connectors at the distributor cap and both connectors on the coil wire; there should be 600-1400 ohms.

3. The spark plug connectors should have 4000-6000 ohms.

Diesel Glow Plugs

TESTING

A common cause of glow plug failure is worn glow plug tips. This may be due to a leaking injector in the related cylinder. If you find that you are constantly replacing glow plugs and have eliminated all other possible faults, check the fuel injector(s) for damage or have the injectors pressure and leak tested by a diesel injector repair shop.

1. Disconnect the engine temperature sensor.

2. Connect a test light between No. 4 cylinder glow plug and ground. The glow plugs are connected by a flat, coated busbar, located near the bottom of the cylinder head.

3. Turn the ignition key **ON**; the test light should light, then go out after 10-15 seconds.

4. If there is no voltage, possible problems include a blown fuse, the glow plug relay or the wiring. See Section 5 to test the glow plug control system.

5. To test each plug individually, disconnect the wire and remove the busbar from the glow plugs.

6. Connect an ohmmeter to each glow plug connection or use a test light. Each plug must have continuity to ground. The engine will probably start with one defective glow plug, but it will smoke an run roughly until warmed up.

REMOVAL & INSTALLATION

▶ **See Figures 8 and 9**

1. Remove the busbar connecting the glow plugs and determine which plugs need replacement.

2. Remove the defective plugs.

3. When installing new plugs, torque to 22 ft. lbs. (30 Nm).

➡**Diesel glow plugs have an air gap much like a spark plug to prevent overheating of the plug. Over-torquing the glow plug will close the gap and cause the plug to burn out.**

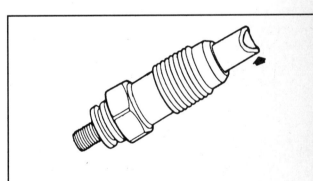

Fig. 8 Glow plug damaged by heat: over-torquing will close the air gap and cause over heating

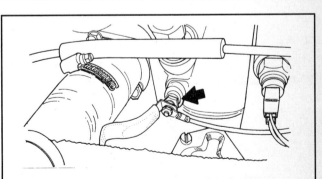

Fig. 9 Remove the busbar to test the glow plugs individually

Alternator

All Volkswagens are equipped with either a Bosch or Motorola alternator. The voltage regulator is mounted on the back of the alternator housing and includes the brushes. No adjustments are possible but the regulator can be replace separately.

ALTERNATOR PRECAUTIONS

- Always disconnect the battery cables when removing or disconnecting the alternator.
- Disconnect the battery cables before using a fast charger. The charger has a tendency to force current 'backwards' through the diodes and burn them out.
- Never disconnect the battery cables or alternator while the engine is running.
- Do not attempt to polarize an alternator.
- Never reverse battery connections. Do not connect the battery in series with another without disconnecting it from the charging system.
- When jump starting from another vehicle, try to avoid running the other car's engine. Do not allow alternators from two different charging systems to be running and connected with jumper cables.
- Do not ground the alternator output terminal.
- Disconnect the battery cables before using an electric arc welder on the car.

REMOVAL & INSTALLATION

Before purchasing a replacement alternator, read the specification plate on the housing. The number 14V will appear to indicate maximum voltage rating. On the same line will be two more digits followed by the letter **A**. This is the maximum amperage output. Be sure to purchase an alternator with the same rating. The regulator can be replaced without removing the alternator.

1. Disconnect the negative battery cable.
2. Disconnect the wiring from the alternator.
3. Loosen the bolts and remove the belt from the alternator pulley.
4. Remove the mounting bolts and remove the alternator.
5. Installation is the reverse of removal. Adjust the belt tension and torque the bolts to 20 ft. lbs. (25 Nm).

Voltage Regulator

The voltage regulator is attached to the rear of the alternator and includes the brushes. Since no adjustment can be performed on the regulator, it is serviced by replacement.

1. It is not necessary to disconnect any wiring. Remove the mounting screws and remove the regulator.
2. Measure the free length of the brushes. If they are less than about 5mm (7/332 inches), the regulator must be replaced. New brushes are 13mm (½ inch) long.

3. Install the new regulator and tighten the screws.

Battery

REMOVAL & INSTALLATION

▶ **See Figure 10**

✳✳CAUTION

Battery electrolyte (acid) is highly corrosive and can damage both you and the paint work. Be careful when lifting the battery in and out of the engine compartment.

1. Disconnect the battery cables, negative cable first.
2. Remove the bolt and retaining plate.
3. If equipped, disconnect the small electrical lead for the computer sensor.
4. Lift the battery carefully out of the tray.
5. Clean all corrosion deposits from the battery tray and the retaining plate with a baking soda and water solution to neutralize the acid.
6. When dry, spray the tray and retaining plate with rust preventive paint.
7. Install the battery in reverse order of removal. Polish the inside of the cables and coat them with grease or silicone compound after installation.

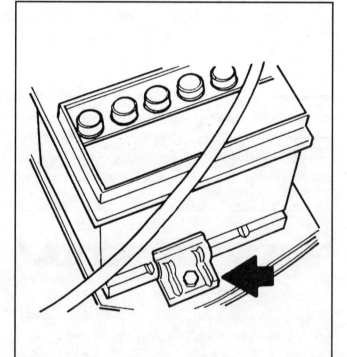

Fig. 10 Battery retaining clamp fits into the groove in the case

Starter

TESTING

✳✳CAUTION

Make sure the vehicle is not in gear and block the wheels from turning. You will be standing in front of or lying under the vehicle to test the starter. Wear safety glasses and make sure there are no fuel leaks. This procedure may produce sparks.

1. Make sure the battery and all connections are in good condition.
2. Disconnect the small wire from terminal 50 on the solenoid.
3. With the ignition switch **OFF**, briefly touch a jumper wire from the solenoid terminal to the large battery wire on the starter. The starter should operate.
4. If the starter turns slowly or not at all, the starter is faulty.
5. If the starter runs at normal speed, the problem is between the ignition switch and starter terminal 50. This could include the wiring, the neutral safety switch on the automatic transaxle or the seat belt interlock system on 1992 Jetta. These are covered in Sections 7 and 10 respectively.

REMOVAL & INSTALLATION

1. Disconnect the battery ground cable.
2. Raise and safely support the front of the vehicle with jackstands.

3. If necessary, label the small wires before disconnecting them.
4. Disconnect the large cable, which is the positive battery cable, from the solenoid.
5. Remove the top bolt first, then remove the bottom bolt while supporting the weight of the starter.
6. Pull the starter straight out.
7. On vehicles with a manual transaxle, there is a bushing where the starter shaft fits into the bellhousing. If the shaft or bushing are worn or if the starter has been jamming, the bushing should be replaced. There is a special bushing removal tool available but a small inside bearing removal tool is usually sufficient.
   To install:
8. If the bushing was removed, carefully drive the new bushing in until it is flush with the case.
9. Lift the starter into place and install the top bolt first. Torque the bolts to 43 ft. lbs. (58 Nm).
10. Connect the wires. Be careful not to over tighten the battery cable connection. The metal is soft and the threads will strip easily.

SOLENOID REPLACEMENT

1. Remove the starter.
2. Remove the nut which secures the connector strip on the end of the solenoid.
3. Take out the two retaining screws on the mounting bracket and withdraw the solenoid after it has been unhooked from the operating lever.
4. Installation is the reverse of removal. In order to facilitate engagement of the lever, the pinion should be pulled out as far as possible when inserting the solenoid.

ENGINE MECHANICAL

Description

GASOLINE ENGINES

The engine in all models is a water cooled inline 4-cylinder with a cast iron block and an aluminum alloy cylinder head. The crankshaft is supported in five plain main bearings and the center bearing includes a 4-piece thrust bearing. The forged steel connecting rods are equipped with plain bearings at the big end and coated steel bushings at the small end. The full floating wrist pins are held in place in the pistons with circlips. The pistons are fitted with two compression rings and a 1-piece oil control ring. The oil pump is mounted below the crankshaft and driven by the intermediate shaft. The 16 valve 2.0 liter block has additional oil passages and spray nozzles for cooling the under side of the pistons. On 8 valve 1.8 liter engines, the oil pump drive shaft includes an extension that engages the drive lugs on the distributor.

The intermediate shaft and the camshaft are driven by a steel-reinforced toothed belt. The overhead camshaft acts directly on the valves through hydraulic lifters for quiet, maintenance free operation. The valves move in alloy guides that can be replaced when worn. The bearing surfaces for the camshafts and lifters are machined directly into the cylinder head and cannot be serviced.

On 16V engines, there are two overhead camshafts that operate 2 intake valves and 2 exhaust valves per cylinder. The exhaust camshaft is driven by the belt and the intake camshaft is driven by a chain connecting the two camshafts. The 4-valve per cylinder design allows a central spark plug location for a more controlled and symmetrical combustion. This allows a higher compression ratio for more power and cleaner combustion with the same fuel consumption. The intake and exhaust manifolds are on opposite sides of the cylinder head to improve the engine's ability to 'breathe' over the entire rpm range.

DIESEL ENGINE

Aside from the obvious external features, there are several internal differences between the ECODiesel engine block and the standard 8 valve engine block it is based on. The cylinders have a smaller bore providing a total piston displacement of only 1.6 liters. There are also additional oil passages and spray nozzles for cooling the under side of the pistons. Even though this engine operates at a compression ratio of about 23:1, the special pistons are designed to do this using only two compression rings for reduced friction losses.

The cylinder head has spherical pre-combustion chambers made of steel set into the lower surface of the head. The fuel injector projects into the pre-chamber and combustion begins there almost at the very beginning of the injection cycle. The burning fuel/air mixture is given a swirl pattern by the chamber's shape. The swirl promotes more complete combustion as the process continues in the main combustion chamber. Using the swirl chamber has other advantages: it reduces the peak load which the force of combustion would normally exert on pistons, rods, bearings and crankshaft, enabling VW to use many standard components. Aside from the pre-chambers, the cylinder head is quite similar to the gasoline engine. The valve train is the same single overhead camshaft with hydraulic lifters

Engine Overhaul Tips

Most engine overhaul procedures are fairly standard. In addition to specific parts replacement procedures and complete specifications for your individual engine, this chapter also is a guide to accepted rebuilding procedures. Examples of standard rebuilding practice are shown and should be used along with specific details concerning your particular engine.

Competent and accurate machine shop services are a must any time an engine is rebuilt. Procedures requiring close tolerance measurements should be performed by a competent machine shop, and are provided so that you will be familiar with the procedures necessary to perform a successful overhaul.

In most instances it is more profitable for the do-it-yourself mechanic to remove, clean and inspect the component, buy the necessary parts and deliver these to a shop for actual machine work. On the other hand, much of the final assembly of the new and machined components is well within the scope of the do-it-yourself mechanic.

Tools

The tools required for an engine overhaul or parts replacement will depend on the depth of your involvement. With a few exceptions, they will be the normal hand tools found in a mechanic's tool kit (see Chapter 1). More in-depth work will require any or all of the following:

- A dial indicator (reading in thousandths) mounted on a universal base
- Micrometers and telescope gauges
- Jaw and screw-type pullers
- Scraper
- Valve spring compressor
- Ring groove cleaner
- Piston ring expander and compressor

- Ridge reamer
- Cylinder hone or glaze breaker
- Plastigage®
- Engine stand

Use of most of these tools is illustrated in this chapter. Many can be rented for a one-time use from a local parts jobber or tool supply house specializing in automotive work. Occasionally, the use of special tools is called for. See the information on Special Tools and Safety Notice in the front of this book before substituting another tool.

Inspection Techniques

Procedures and specifications are given in this chapter for inspecting, cleaning and assessing the wear limits of most major components. Other procedures such as Magnaflux® and Zyglo® can be used to locate material flaws and stress cracks. Magnaflux® is a magnetic process applicable only to ferrous materials. The Zyglo® process coats the material with a fluorescent dye penetrant and can be used on any material. Checks for suspected surface cracks can be more readily made using spot check dye. The dye is sprayed onto the suspected area, wiped off and the area sprayed with a developer. Cracks will show up brightly.

Overhaul Tips

Aluminum has become extremely popular for use in engines, due to its low weight. Observe the following precautions when handling aluminum parts:
- Never hot tank aluminum parts (the caustic hot-tank solution will eat the aluminum.
- Remove all aluminum parts (identification tag, etc.) from engine parts prior to cleaning in a hot tank.
- Always coat threads lightly with engine oil or anti-seize compounds before installation, to prevent seizure.
- Never over-torque bolts or spark plugs especially in aluminum threads. Stripped threads in any component can be repaired using any of several commercial repair kits (Heli-Coil®, Microdot®, Keenserts®, etc.).

When assembling the engine, prelube all power-pack components (pistons, bearings, bearing caps, thrust washers, etc.) to provide lubrication at initial start-up. There are many products specifically formulated for this purpose, but clean engine oil is sufficient. When permanent installation of bolts or nuts is desired, threads should be cleaned and coated with Loctite® or other similar, commercial thread locking compound. When used properly, fasteners will not vibrate loose but can still be removed with tools.

Repairing Damaged Threads

▶ See Figures 11, 12, 13, 14 and 15

Several methods of repairing damaged threads are available. HeliCoil® (shown here), Keenserts® and Microdot® are among the most widely used. All involve basically the same principle — drilling out stripped threads, tapping the hole and installing a prewound insert — making welding, plugging and oversize fasteners unnecessary.

When buying a kit, two types of thread repair inserts are available: a standard type for most English and metric thread sizes and a spark plug type to fit most spark plug port sizes. Consult the individual manufacturer's catalog at your parts store to determine exact applications. Typical thread repair kits will contain a selection of prewound threaded inserts, a tap matching the outside diameter threads of the insert and an installation tool. Spark plug inserts usually differ because they require a tap equipped with pilot threads and a combined reamer/tap section. Most manufacturers also package the inserts separately so you only need to buy the tools once.

Obviously any broken or damaged bolts or studs must be removed before repairing the threads. This is often the hardest part of the job. The easiest solution is to have the machinist do it when the block or head is in the machine shop. If this is not an option, there are several stud extracting tools available. The material, location and accessibility of the broken stud will influence which tool you should use. Even if the stud is not rusted or seized, penetrating oil almost always makes the job easier.

CHECKING ENGINE COMPRESSION

▶ **See Figures 16 and 17**

A noticeable lack of engine power, excessive oil consumption and/or poor fuel mileage measured over an extended period are all indicators of internal engine wear. Worn piston rings, scored or worn cylinder bores, blown head gaskets, sticking or burnt valves and worn valve seats can all

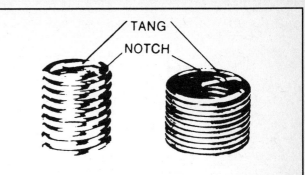

Fig. 12 Standard thread repair insert (left) and spark plug thread insert (right)

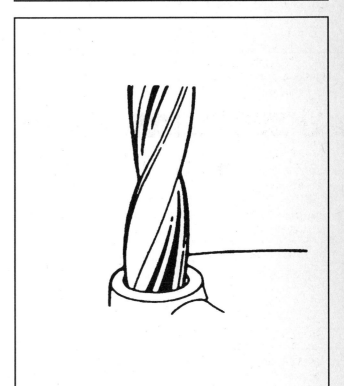

Fig. 13 Drill out the damaged threads all the way through the hole or to the bottom of a blind hole with the correct drill

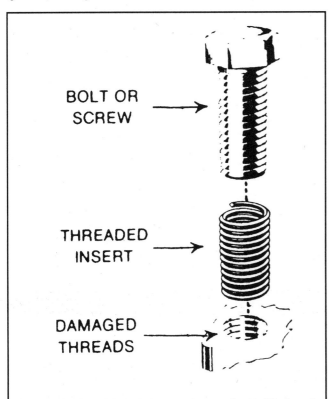

Fig. 11 Damaged bolt holes can be repaired with thread repair inserts

effect engine compression and will show up in a compression test.

This test will provide useful information only if the battery and starter are in good condition and capable of turning the engine at normal cranking speed. As mentioned in the 'Tools and Equipment' section of Chapter 1, a screw-in type compression gauge is more accurate and the job can be done with only one person.

Gasoline Engines

1. Warm up the engine to normal operating temperature.
2. Remove the spark plugs. Note their color and location for later diagnosis.

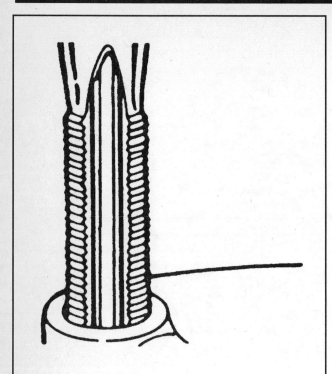

Fig. 14 Tap the new threads for the insert with the tap supplied in the kit. Oil the tap and back it out frequently to prevent clogging

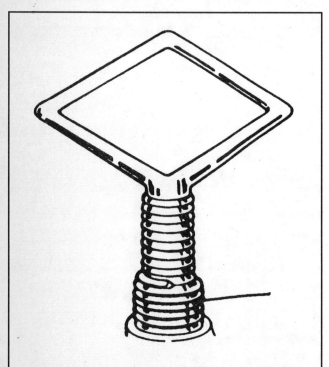

Fig. 15 Screw the threaded insert onto the installation tool until the tang engages the slot. Screw the insert into the tapped hole until it is 1/4-1/2 turn below the top of the hole. Break off the tang

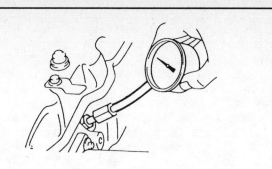

Fig. 16 Screw-in type gasoline engine compression gauge

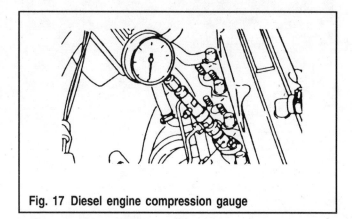

Fig. 17 Diesel engine compression gauge

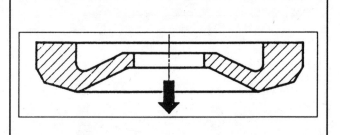

Fig. 18 Install the injector heat shield with the concave side facing away from the nozzle tip

3. On engines with CIS-E fuel injection, disconnect the air duct boot from the throttle body. Disconnect the wiring from the power output stage of the coil and the Hall sender. This will prevent operation of both ignition and fuel injection systems.

4. On engines with Digifant fuel injection, disconnect the ignition control unit and the Hall sender. This will prevent operation of both ignition and fuel injection systems.

5. Screw the compression gauge into the No. 1 spark plug hole until the fitting is snug.

6. Inside the car, depress the accelerator pedal to open the throttle fully and operate the starter continuously for about 3 seconds.

7. Record the compression gauge reading, release the pressure and test the remaining cylinders. Be sure to write down each reading.

8. On new engines, compression will be 145-189 psi (10-13 BAR). Compression must be no less than 109 psi (7.5 BAR) on any cylinder. The maximum difference between cylinders must be no more than 44 psi (3 BAR).

9. If a cylinder is unusually low, a 'wet test' may isolate the problem. Put about a tablespoon of clean engine oil into the cylinder through the spark plug hole and test that cylinder again.

10. Interpret the test results:

   a. If the compression comes up when oil is added, the rings and/or cylinder bore are worn.

   b. If compression in any two adjacent cylinders is low, and if the addition of oil doesn't help the compression, there is leakage past the head gasket indicating a warped head.

   c. If there is little or no change when oil is added, there is probably a leaking valve or head gasket or even a cracked cylinder head. Look for oil in the coolant, coolant in the oil, signs of coolant in the exhaust system or one spark plug with a significantly different color from the others.

   d. If all cylinders are low but within the allowable spread, repeat the test with oil in all cylinders. It will probably increase, indicating worn rings.

11. Any time the compression test shows a big difference between cylinders, a cylinder leak-down test can provide more information. This requires a special tool with a gauge and fittings to apply air pressure to the cylinder. The rate of cylinder leakage can determine the extent of wear or damage but the only way to really know what's wrong is to remove the cylinder head.

Diesel Engines

▶ See Figure 18

Under each injector is a washer to protect the injector tip from heat and form a good seal. These can be used only one time. Have new heat shield washers on hand before removing the injectors.

1. Carefully remove all the injection lines from the pump and the injectors. Use a back-up wrench when loosening the lines from the pump.

2. Cap all the fittings to prevent dirt from getting into the pump or injectors.

3. Remove the injector leak-off tubes and remove the injectors. Remove the heat shield washers under each injector.

4. Disconnect the fuel shut-off solenoid wire from the injection pump so fuel will not squirt out of the pump during the test.

5. Screw the compression gauge into the No. 1 injector hole until the fitting is snug.

6. Inside the car, operate the starter continuously for about 3 seconds.

7. Record the compression gauge reading, release the pressure and test the remaining cylinders. Be sure to write down each reading.

8. On new engines, compression will be 493 psi (34 BAR). Compression must be no less than 412 psi (28 BAR) on any cylinder. The maximum difference between cylinders must be no more than 73 psi (5 BAR).

✳✳CAUTION

Do not add oil to a cylinder when checking diesel engine compression. The compression generates enough heat to ignite the oil in the cylinder.

9. Except for the added-oil compression test, interpreting compression test results for diesel engines is the same as for gasoline engines.

10. When the test is completed, install the injectors with new heat shields. Make sure the heat shield is installed properly as shown and torque the injectors to 51 ft. lbs. (70 Nm).

11. Remove the protective caps and install the injection lines and injector leak-off tubes. Use a back-up wrench to tighten the lines at the pump and torque them 18 ft. lbs. (25 Nm).

➡**Do not over tighten the injector line nuts. The line flare will split and the fittings will leak.**

12. Reconnect the shut-off solenoid and run the engine. It will be difficult to start and will run roughly at first, but manually bleeding the air from the lines is not necessary.

GENERAL ENGINE SPECIFICATIONS

Year	Engine ID/VIN	Engine Displacement Liters (cc)	Fuel System Type	Net Horsepower @ rpm	Net Torque @ rpm (ft. lbs.)	Bore × Stroke (in.)	Com- pression Ratio	Oil Pressure @ rpm
1990	RV	1.8 (1780)	Digifant	100 @ 5400	109 @ 3800	3.19 × 3.40	10.0:1	28 @ 2000
	9A	2.0 (1984)	CIS-E	134 @ 5800	133 @ 4400	3.25 × 3.65	10.8:1	28 @ 2000
	PF	1.8 (1780)	Digifant	105 @ 5400	114 @ 3800	3.19 × 3.40	10.0:1	28 @ 2000
	2H	1.8 (1780)	Digifant	94 @ 5500	100 @ 3000	3.19 × 3.40	8.5:1	28 @ 2000
1991	RV	1.8 (1780)	Digifant	100 @ 5400	109 @ 3800	3.19 × 3.40	10.0:1	28 @ 2000
	9A	2.0 (1984)	CIS-E	134 @ 5800	133 @ 4400	3.25 × 3.65	10.8:1	28 @ 2000
	PF	1.8 (1780)	Digifant	105 @ 5400	114 @ 3800	3.19 × 3.40	10.0:1	28 @ 2000
	2H	1.8 (1780)	Digifant	94 @ 5500	100 @ 3000	3.19 × 3.40	8.5:1	28 @ 2000
	1V	1.6 (1588)	Bosch VE	52 @ 4800	71 @ 2000	3.01 × 3.40	23.0:1	28 @ 2000
1992-93	RV	1.8 (1780)	Digifant	100 @ 5400	109 @ 3800	3.19 × 3.40	10.0:1	28 @ 2000
	9A	2.0 (1984)	CIS-E	134 @ 5800	133 @ 4400	3.25 × 3.65	10.8:1	28 @ 2000
	PF	1.8 (1780)	Digifant	105 @ 5400	114 @ 3800	3.19 × 3.40	10.0:1	28 @ 2000
	2H	1.8 (1780)	Digifant	94 @ 5500	100 @ 3000	3.19 × 3.40	8.5:1	28 @ 2000
	1V	1.6 (1588)	Bosch VE	52 @ 4800	71 @ 2000	3.01 × 3.40	23.0:1	28 @ 2000

NOTE: Horsepower and torque are SAE net figures. They are measured at the rear of the transmission with all accessories installed and operating. Since the figures vary when a given engine is installed in different models, some are representative rather than exact.

VALVE SPECIFICATIONS

Year	Engine ID/VIN	Engine Displacement Liters (cc)	Seat Angle (deg.)	Face Angle (deg.)	Spring Test Pressure (lbs. @ in.)	Spring Installed Height (in.)	Stem-to-Guide Clearance (in.)① Intake	Exhaust	Stem Diameter (in.) Intake	Exhaust
1990	RV	1.8 (1780)	45	45	NA	NA	0.039	0.051	0.314	0.313
	9A	2.0 (1984)	45	45	NA	NA	0.039	0.051	0.314	0.313
	PF	1.8 (1780)	45	45	NA	NA	0.039	0.051	0.314	0.313
	2H	1.8 (1780)	45	45	NA	NA	0.039	0.051	0.314	0.313
1991	RV	1.8 (1780)	45	45	NA	NA	0.039	0.051	0.314	0.313
	9A	2.0 (1984)	45	45	NA	NA	0.039	0.051	0.314	0.313
	PF	1.8 (1780)	45	45	NA	NA	0.039	0.051	0.314	0.313
	2H	1.8 (1780)	45	45	NA	NA	0.039	0.051	0.314	0.313
	1V	1.6 (1588)	45	45	NA	NA	0.051	0.051	0.314	0.313
1992-93	RV	1.8 (1780)	45	45	NA	NA	0.039	0.051	0.314	0.313
	9A	2.0 (1984)	45	45	NA	NA	0.039	0.051	0.314	0.313
	PF	1.8 (1780)	45	45	NA	NA	0.039	0.051	0.314	0.313
	2H	1.8 (1780)	45	45	NA	NA	0.039	0.051	0.314	0.313
	1V	1.6 (1588)	45	45	NA	NA	0.051	0.051	0.314	0.313

① Values listed are maximum wear limit. Measure with dial indicator touching valve face, valve stem end flush with guide.

CRANKSHAFT AND CONNECTING ROD SPECIFICATIONS

All measurements are given in inches.

Year	Engine ID/VIN	Engine Displacement Liters (cc)	Crankshaft Main Brg. Journal Dia.	Crankshaft Main Brg. Oil Clearance	Crankshaft Shaft End-play	Crankshaft Thrust on No.	Connecting Rod Journal Diameter	Connecting Rod Oil ① Clearance	Connecting Rod Side ① Clearance
1990	RV	1.8 (1780)	2.126	0.001–0.003	0.003–0.007	3	1.881	0.005	0.015
	9A	2.0 (1984)	2.126	0.001–0.003	0.003–0.007	3	1.881	0.005	0.015
	PF	1.8 (1780)	2.126	0.001–0.003	0.003–0.007	3	1.881	0.005	0.015
	2H	1.8 (1780)	2.126	0.001–0.003	0.003–0.007	3	1.881	0.005	0.015
1991	RV	1.8 (1780)	2.126	0.001–0.003	0.003–0.007	3	1.881	0.005	0.015
	9A	2.0 (1984)	2.126	0.001–0.003	0.003–0.007	3	1.881	0.005	0.015
	PF	1.8 (1780)	2.126	0.001–0.003	0.003–0.007	3	1.881	0.005	0.015
	2H	1.8 (1780)	2.126	0.001–0.003	0.003–0.007	3	1.881	0.005	0.015
	1V	1.6 (1588)	2.126	0.001–0.003	0.003–0.007	3	1.881	0.005	0.015
1992-93	RV	1.8 (1780)	2.126	0.001–0.003	0.003–0.007	3	1.881	0.005	0.015
	9A	2.0 (1984)	2.126	0.001–0.003	0.003–0.007	3	1.881	0.005	0.015
	PF	1.8 (1780)	2.126	0.001–0.003	0.003–0.007	3	1.881	0.005	0.015
	2H	1.8 (1780)	2.126	0.001–0.003	0.003–0.007	3	1.881	0.005	0.015
	1V	1.6 (1588)	2.126	0.001–0.003	0.003–0.007	3	1.881	0.005	0.015

① Maximum clearances

TORQUE SPECIFICATIONS

All readings in ft. lbs.

Year	Engine ID/VIN	Engine Displacement Liters (cc)	Cylinder Head Bolts	Main Bearing Bolts	Rod Bearing Bolts	Crankshaft Damper Bolts	Flywheel Bolts	Manifold Intake	Manifold Exhaust	Spark Plugs	Lug Nut
1990	RV	1.8 (1780)	①	47	22②	③	④	18	18	14	81
	9A	2.0 (1984)	①	47	22②	③	74	15	18	14	81
	PF	1.8 (1780)	①	47	22②	③	④	18	18	14	81
	2H	1.8 (1780)	①	47	22②	③	④	18	18	14	81
1991	RV	1.8 (1780)	①	47	22②	③	④	18	18	14	81
	9A	2.0 (1984)	①	47	22②	③	74	15	18	14	81
	PF	1.8 (1780)	①	47	22②	③	④	18	18	14	81
	2H	1.8 (1780)	①	47	22②	③	④	18	18	14	81
	1V	1.6 (1588)	①⑤	47	33②	253	④	18	18	—	81
1992-93	RV	1.8 (1780)	①	47	22②	③	④	18	18	14	81
	9A	2.0 (1984)	①	47	22②	③	74	15	18	14	81
	PF	1.8 (1780)	①	47	22②	③	④	18	18	14	81
	2H	1.8 (1780)	①	47	22②	③	④	18	18	14	81
	1V	1.6 (1588)	①⑤	47	33②	253	④	18	18	—	81

① With 12 point bolt head—in 2 steps to 43 ft. lbs., then additional ½ turn: Do not retorque. With 6 point bolt head—in 2 steps to 54 ft. lbs., warm engine and torque to 61 ft. lbs. Retorque at 1000 miles.

② Torque stretch-type bolts one time only to specification plus ¼ turn.
③ 66 ft. lbs. plus ½ turn.
④ Manual trans.—14 ft. lbs. Automatic—72 ft. lbs.
⑤ Use new bolts.

Engine

REMOVAL & INSTALLATION

▶ See Figures 19, 21, 22, 23, 20 and 24

Gasoline Engine

The engine and transmission are lifted from the vehicle as an assembly and separated afterwards. Some of the front body work must be removed but removing the hood is not necessary unless it interferes with the lifting equipment. Some components can be removed without disconnecting hydraulic or coolant hoses. Cover the front fenders so components can be hung over them. Before beginning the job, make sure you have some way of labeling the wires, lines and hoses so they can be reconnected correctly. On the 8 valve engines, special tools are required to remove and install the exhaust pipe-to-manifold spring clamps, VW tool numbers 3140/1 and 3140/2. These may be available at larger parts stores.

✳✳CAUTION

Fuel lines may be pressurized. Make sure the work area is well ventilated and take appropriate fire and personal safety precautions.

1. Disconnect the battery cables and remove the battery.

2. Relieve the fuel system pressure:
   a. Open the fuel filler cap to relieve tank pressure.
   b. On CIS-E fuel injection, loosen the cold start injector line to relieve the fuel system pressure.
   c. On Digifant fuel injection, loosen the pressure test port fitting at the end of the fuel rail that supplies the injectors.
3. Remove the air intake duct between the air cleaner and the throttle body.
4. Disconnect the accelerator cable from the throttle and remove the cable housing from the bracket.
5. Remove the radiator cap and set the heater temperature control to maximum. Place a pan under the thermostat housing and remove the thermostat flange to drain the coolant.
6. If equipped with air conditioning, remove the air conditioner compressor and the condenser without disconnecting the coolant lines and secure them out of the way.
7. Remove the upper radiator hose and disconnect the wiring from the radiator fan motor and switches. Remove the upper mounting brackets and lift out the radiator and fan as an assembly.
8. On Golf and Jetta, the front body section must be removed:
   a. Disconnect the headlight electrical connectors and the hood release cable from the hood latch assembly.
   b. Remove the lower valance and the front grille.
   c. Remove the front apron.
9. Begin disconnecting electrical connections and vacuum lines, carefully labeling each one. Don't forget ground connections that are screwed to the body.

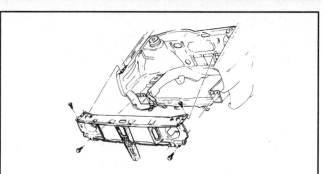

Fig. 19 On Golf and Jetta, remove the grille, valance and front apron to remove the engine

10. Remove the power steering pump and reservoir without disconnecting the hydraulic lines and secure them out of the way.

11. On engines with CIS-E fuel injection, the fuel system can be removed as a unit.

a. Without disconnecting the lines, carefully pry the injectors from their holes and protect them with caps. A little silicone spray can ease removal.

b. Remove the cold start injector, tape all the injector lines together and set them aside.

c. Disconnect the wiring and the fuel supply line from the fuel distributor. Plug the fuel inlet to keep dirt out of the fuel distributor.

d. Disconnect the fuel return line from the pressure regulator.

e. Remove the bolts or clips required to change the air filter and lift the air flow sensor and fuel system out of the vehicle.

12. On engines with Digifant fuel injection, disconnect the fuel supply line from the pressure regulator and the fuel return line from the fuel rail. Disconnect the plug on the end of the injector wiring harness.

13. If equipped with an automatic transaxle, place the selector lever in the **P** position and disconnect the shifter cable at the transaxle. Remove the speedometer cable from the transaxle and plug the hole in the case.

14. If equipped with a manual transaxle, remove the 2 rods with the plastic socket ends and unbolt the remaining linkage from the transaxle case as required. Disconnect the clutch cable, lift it from the case and set it aside.

15. Disconnect the wiring from the starter and the back-up light switch and disconnect the ground cable from the

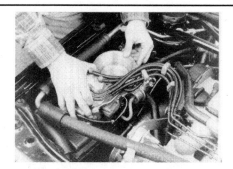

Fig. 20 The CIS-E fuel system can be removed without disconnecting the injector lines

transaxle. Remove the speedometer cable from the transaxle and plug the hole in the case.

16. If not already done, raise and safely support the vehicle on jack stands. Unbolt the halfshafts from the flanges and hang them from the body with wire. DO NOT let the halfshafts hang by the outer CV joint or the joint may fall apart.

17. Unbolt the exhaust pipe from the manifold or remove the spring clamps holding the exhaust pipe to the manifold and lower the pipe.

✳✳CAUTION

If the exhaust pipe is secured to the manifold with spring clamps, use the proper tools and procedures for removal and installation. The springs are under heavy tension and can cause serious injury if mishandled.

18. To remove the spring clamps:

a. Push the pipe to one side to expand the opposite clamp. Insert a wedge into the expanded clamp.

b. Push the pipe to the other side and insert a wedge into the clamp.

c. Push the pipe the other way again to expand the clamp further. It should be possible to grab the wedge with locking pliers and pry the clamp off the pipe flange.

d. Leave the wedges in the clamps and put them in a box so they won't be disturbed and fly apart.

19. Attach a suitable chain sling to the lifting eyes. On 16V engines, a rigid sling must be used. Remove the idle stabilizer valve and upper intake manifold and attach engine sling tool VW-2024A or equivalent, to the engine.

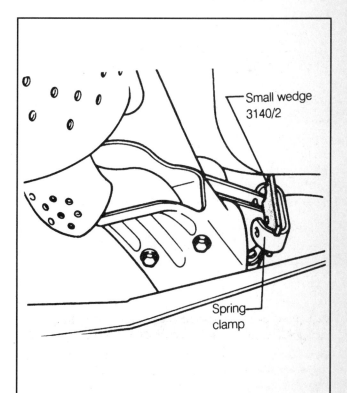

Small wedge
3140/2

Spring clamp

Fig. 21 Push the pipe to one side and install the wedge tool into the opposite clamp

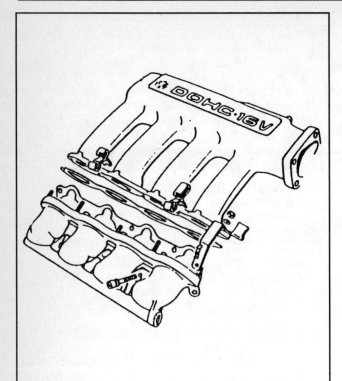

Fig. 22 On 16V engine, remove the upper intake manifold to install the sling tool

Fig. 23 Sling tool installed for removing 16V engine/transaxle assembly

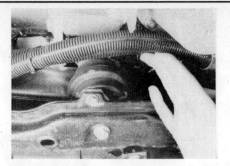

Fig. 24 The front engine mount is hydraulic and must be properly positioned before tightening the bolts

20. Check to make sure everything is disconnected, then unbolt the mounts. Remove the starter first and the front mount with it.

21. With all mounts unbolted, slightly lower the engine/transaxle assembly and tilt it towards the transaxle side. Then carefully lift the assembly from the vehicle. See Section 7 for information on separating the engine and transaxle.

To install:

22. See Section 7 for information on assembling the engine and transaxle. Make sure all mount brackets are securely bolted to the engine/transaxle. Fit the assembly into the engine bay and install the mounts, starting at the rear. Start all nuts and bolts that secure the mounts to the body but don't tighten them yet.

23. With all mounts installed and the engine safely in the vehicle, allow some slack in the lifting equipment. With the vehicle safely supported, shake the engine/transaxle as a unit to settle it in the mounts. Torque all mounting bolts, starting at the rear and working forward. Torque to 33 ft. lbs. (41 Nm) for 10mm bolts or 54 ft. lbs. (73 Nm) for 12mm bolts.

24. Install the starter and torque the bolts to 33 ft. lbs. (45 Nm).

25. Connect the halfshafts to the flanges and torque the bolts to 33 ft. lbs. (45 Nm).

26. Connect the exhaust pipe. On 16V engines, use new self locking nuts to secure the flange and torque the nuts to 30 ft. lbs. (40 Nm).

27. Connect the shift linkage and the clutch cable. Adjust the clutch and shift linkage as required.

28. Install the fuel system components and connect the lines.

29. On Golf and Jetta, install the front apron and connect the wiring.

30. Install the air conditioning compressor and/or power steering pump, if equipped. Install and adjust the drive belts.

31. Install the radiator, fan and heater hoses. Use a new O-ring on the thermostat and torque the thermostat housing bolts to 7 ft. lbs. (10 Nm).

32. Connect all remaining wiring and vacuum hoses. Check carefully to make sure all components are correctly installed and connected.

33. Fill and bleed the cooling system. Check the adjustment of the accelerator cable.

Diesel Engine

The engine and transmission are lifted from the vehicle as an assembly and separated afterwards. Some of the front body work must be removed but removing the hood is not necessary unless it interferes with the lifting equipment. Some components can be removed without disconnecting hydraulic or coolant hoses. Cover the front fenders so components can be hung over them. Before beginning the job, make sure you have some way of labeling the wires, lines and hoses so they can be reconnected correctly. Special tools are required to remove and install the exhaust pipe-to-manifold spring clamps, VW tool numbers 3140/1 and 3140/2. These may be available at larger parts stores.

1. Remove the battery.
2. Turn the heater temperature control to maximum. Remove the radiator cap and the radiator hose at the thermostat housing and drain the cooling system. Remove the thermostat flange.
3. Disconnect the wiring from the radiator fan motor and the thermo-switch. Remove the upper radiator mounting brackets and lift the radiator and fan out of the vehicle.
4. Remove the fuel filter and base. Cap the fuel line connections to prevent leakage.
5. Disconnect the brake booster hose from the vacuum pump.
6. Remove the alternator.
7. Disconnect the wiring to the fuel shut-off solenoid, the glow plugs, the oil pressure switch and the coolant temperature sensor.
8. Disconnect the heater and the expansion tank hoses.
9. At the injection pump, disconnect the accelerator cable and the cold start cable.
10. Disconnect the fuel supply and the return lines from the injection pump. Plug the openings in the pump and cap the ends of the lines to prevent the entry of dirt into the system.
11. If equipped with air conditioning, the injection pump must be removed to remove the compressor. See Section 5 for instructions on removing the pump. To remove the compressor:
    a. Remove the air conditioning belt tensioner, water pump pulley and drive belt.
    b. Disconnect the wiring from the compressor and the pressure switches.
    c. Remove the condenser and compressor together without disconnecting the coolant hoses.
    d. Secure the compressor and condenser out of the way. Do not let them hang by the coolant hoses.
12. The front body section must be removed:
    a. Disconnect the headlight electrical connectors and the hood release cable from the hood latch assembly.
    b. Remove the lower valance and the front grille.
    c. Remove the front apron
13. If equipped with power steering, remove the pump without disconnecting the hydraulic hoses. Secure the pump out of the way, do not let it hang by the hoses.
14. Disconnect the wiring from the starter, back-up light switch and the transaxle mount ground wire.
15. If equipped with a manual transaxle, disconnect the clutch cable and shift linkage.

16. If equipped with an automatic transaxle, place the selector lever in the **P** position and disconnect the shifter cable at the transaxle.
17. Remove the speedometer cable from the transaxle and plug the hole in the case.
18. If not already done, raise and safely support the vehicle on jack stands. Unbolt the halfshafts from the flanges and hang them from the body with wire. DO NOT let the halfshafts hang by the outer CV joint or the joint may fall apart.

✳✳CAUTION

The exhaust pipe is secured to the manifold with spring clamps. Use the proper tools and procedures for removal and installation. The springs are under heavy tension and can cause serious injury if mishandled.

19. To remove the exhaust pipe spring clamps:
    a. Push the pipe to one side to expand the opposite clamp. Insert a wedge into the expanded clamp.
    b. Push the pipe to the other side and insert a wedge into the clamp.
    c. Push the pipe the other way again to expand the clamp further. It should be possible to grab the wedge with locking pliers and pry the clamp off the pipe flange.
    d. Leave the wedges in the clamps and put them in a box so they won't be disturbed and fly apart.
20. Check carefully to make sure all necessary wiring, hoses and linkages have been disconnected. Attach a chain yoke and a hoist to the engine, then lift it slightly.
21. Unbolt the engine mounts, tilt the assembly down at the transaxle side and carefully lift the engine and transaxle out. See Section 7 for information on separating the engine and transaxle.

To install:
22. See Section 7 for information on assembling the engine and transaxle. Make sure all mount brackets are securely bolted to the engine/transaxle. Fit the assembly into the engine bay and install the mounts, starting at the rear. Start all nuts and bolts that secure the mounts to the body but don't tighten them yet.
23. With all mounts installed and the engine safely in the vehicle, allow some slack in the lifting equipment. With the vehicle safely supported, shake the engine/transaxle as a unit to settle it in the mounts. Torque all mounting bolts, starting at the rear and working forward. Torque to 33 ft. lbs. (41 Nm) for 10mm bolts or 54 ft. lbs. (73 Nm) for 12mm bolts.
24. Install the starter and torque the bolts to 33 ft. lbs. (45 Nm).
25. Connect the halfshafts to the flanges and torque the bolts to 33 ft. lbs. (45 Nm).
26. Connect the exhaust pipe.
27. Connect the shift linkage and the clutch cable. Adjust the clutch and shift linkage as required.
28. Install the front apron and connect the wiring.
29. Install the air conditioner compressor and condenser.
30. Install the fuel injection pump as described in Section 5.
31. Install the power steering pump. Install and adjust all accessory drive belts.
32. Install the radiator, fan and heater hoses. Use a new O-ring on the thermostat and torque the thermostat housing bolts to 7 ft. lbs. (10 Nm).

33. Install the remaining components and connect all remaining wiring and vacuum hoses. Check carefully to make sure all components are correctly installed and connected.

34. Fill and bleed the cooling system. Check the adjustment of the accelerator cable.

Engine Mounts

ADJUSTMENT

If there is excessive engine vibration, an engine alignment procedure may cure the problem. Loosen all the bolts that go into the rubber mounts. Do not loosen engine or body mounting brackets. With the vehicle safely supported, shake the engine/transaxle as a unit to settle it in the mounts. Retorque all mounting bolts, starting at the rear and working forward. If engine vibration is not reduced, check for torn rubber mounts. The mount at the timing belt end usually fails first.

Camshaft (Valve) Cover

REMOVAL & INSTALLATION

Except 16V Engine

1. Disconnect the throttle cable and move it out of the way.
2. Use an Allen socket to remove the nut at the front of the upper camshaft belt cover.
3. Remove the nuts and lift the cover from the engine.
4. Installation is the reverse of removal. Use a new gasket without using any additional sealer. Torque the nuts to 87 inch lbs. (10 Nm).

16V Engine

1. Remove the spark plug wires and the intake air duct.
2. Disconnect the wiring and vacuum lines from the throttle body.
3. Remove the support bracket and the 5 nuts to remove the upper intake manifold.
4. Remove the bolts to remove the camshaft cover.
5. Installation is the reverse of removal. Use a new gasket without using any additional sealer. Torque the cover bolts to 87 inch lbs. (10 Nm) and the manifold nuts to 15 ft. lbs. (20 Nm).

Thermostat

REMOVAL & INSTALLATION

▶ **See Figure 25**

1. The thermostat is in the bottom of the water pump housing and the lower radiator hose connects to the thermostat housing. Place a large drain pan under the thermostat housing.
2. Loosen one bolt at a time until coolant begins to flow.
3. Remove the radiator cap and drain the cooling system.
4. Remove both bolts and remove the thermostat. It's not necessary to disconnect the radiator hose.
5. To install, place the thermostat into the water pump housing, then install the new O-ring. Install the housing and torque the bolts to 7 ft. lbs. (10 Nm).

Intake Manifold

REMOVAL & INSTALLATION

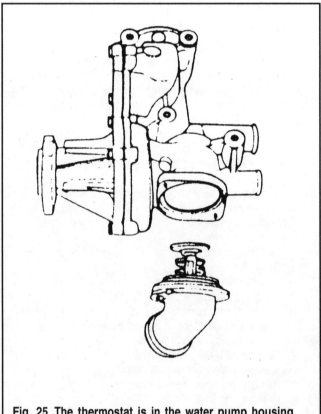

Fig. 25 The thermostat is in the water pump housing

Gasoline Engines

8 VALVE ENGINE

1. Disconnect the negative battery cable and remove the air duct from the throttle body .
2. Disconnect the accelerator cable and the wiring from the throttle switches.
3. Remove the idle stabilizer valve and disconnect the wiring from the fuel injector harness. Disconnect the fuel supply and return lines.
4. Remove the 2 bolts to remove the fuel rail and injectors as an assembly.
5. Label and disconnect the vacuum hoses and any remaining wiring as required.
6. Remove the bolts and remove the manifold from the cylinder head.

To install:

7. Use a new gasket and fit the manifold into place. Torque the bolts to 18 ft. lbs. (25 Nm).
8. Install the fuel injector assembly.
9. Connect fuel system hoses and vacuum lines.
10. Connect the wiring and throttle cable. Install the air duct and battery.
11. Run the engine to check idle speed and ignition timing.

16 VALVE ENGINE

1. Disconnect the negative battery cable and remove the air duct from the throttle body.
2. Disconnect the accelerator cable and the wiring from the throttle switches. Disconnect any vacuum lines at the throttle body.
3. Remove the idle stabilizer valve and disconnect the spark plug wires. On California models, disconnect the vacuum line and wiring from the EGR valve.
4. Remove the bolts to remove the upper intake manifold.
5. To remove the lower intake manifold, pull the injectors straight out and put caps on the tips to protect them. Do not disconnect the lines.
6. Remove the nuts and remove the manifold.

To install:

7. Use a new gasket and fit the manifold into place. Torque the bolts to 18 ft. lbs. (25 Nm). Install the fuel injectors.
8. Use a new gasket and install the upper intake manifold. Torque the bolts to 15 ft. lbs. (20 Nm).
9. Connect the wiring and vacuum lines.
10. Install the idle stabilizer valve.
11. Connect the throttle cable. Install the air duct and battery.
12. Run the engine to check idle speed and ignition timing.

Diesel Engine

1. Disconnect the hose and wiring from the blow-off valve.
2. Disconnect the air inlet hose.
3. Remove the bolts to remove the intake manifold.
4. Installation is the reverse of removal. Use a new gasket and torque the bolts to 18 ft. lbs. (25 Nm).

Exhaust Manifold

REMOVAL & INSTALLATION

▶ **See Figure 26**

Gasoline Engine

➡**On 8 valve engines, two spring clamps are used to hold the exhaust pipe to the manifold. A special wedge tool kit, part no. 3140 is required for removal and installation.**

1. Unplug the oxygen sensor connector. If equipped, remove any heat shields or the EGR tube.
2. To expand the spring clamp, push the exhaust pipe to one side and insert the longer starter wedge into the clamp all the way up to the shoulder.
3. Push the pipe to the other side and install a wedge into the opposite clamp. Continue to work the pipe side to side while pushing the wedges into the clamps. The wedge must be inserted all the way to its shoulder.
4. Push the pipe to one side again, grasp the opposite clamp and wedge with locking pliers and remove them together. Do not remove the wedge if the same clamp is to be installed again.
5. Remove the nuts to remove the exhaust manifold.
6. To remove the wedge from the clamp, set the clamp in the partially open jaws of a vise. Carefully drive the long starter wedge in to spread the clamp further (there will be 2 wedges in the clamp).
7. Turn the clamp over and carefully drive the short wedge out, then the longer wedge.

✳✳CAUTION

The wedges will be forced out with considerable force and could cause serious injury. Position the clamp so the wedge will fly into a container.

To install:

8. Use a new gasket and self-locking nuts and install the manifold. Torque the nuts to 18 ft. lbs. (20 Nm).
9. If new clamps are to be used, set the clamp on the vise and use the starter wedge to spread it far enough to install the short wedge. Remove the starting wedge.

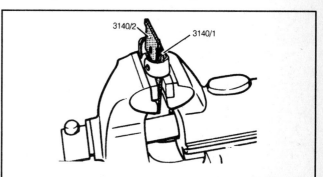

Fig. 26 Use the longer starting wedge to remove the shorter wedge

10. Fit the pipe and gasket into place. Tilt the pipe to one side to install the clamp, then push it to the other side to install the other clamp.

11. Push the pipe side-to-side as necessary to expand the clamps enough to remove the wedges.

Turbocharger

REMOVAL & INSTALLATION

▶ See Figure 27

Diesel Engine

1. Disconnect the negative battery cable. If equipped with an automatic transaxle, remove the starter.

2. Remove the nuts to disconnect the exhaust outlet pipe from the turbocharger outlet. If it's necessary to separate the exhaust pipe from the outlet pipe, follow the procedure is described in exhaust manifold removal for gasoline engines before removing the outlet pipe.

3. Clean the oil supply fitting on the top of the turbocharger and remove the supply line and bracket.

4. Remove the inlet air duct.

5. Under the vehicle, remove the oil return line and the turbocharger mounting bracket.

6. Still underneath, remove the turbo-to-manifold bolts and lift the turbocharger out from the top. The exhaust manifold can be removed after removing the EGR valve.

To install:

7. If removed, install the exhaust manifold with a new gasket and torque the bolts to 18 ft. lbs. (25 Nm).

8. Use a new gasket and fit the turbocharger to the manifold. Coat the bolt threads with anti-seize and torque the turbocharger bolts to 33 ft. lbs. (45 Nm) and the bracket nuts to 18 ft. lbs. (25 Nm).

9. Use a new gasket and connect the oil return line. Torque the bolts to 22 ft. lbs. (30 Nm).

10. Use a new gasket and connect the outlet pipe. Torque the nuts to 18 ft. lbs. (25 Nm).

11. Connect the oil supply line, install the EGR valve.

Radiator and Fan

REMOVAL & INSTALLATION

▶ See Figures 28 and 29

1. Disconnect the wiring from the cooling fan and remove the thermostat housing to drain the cooling system.

2. If the air conditioning coolant hose runs above the radiator, remove the shroud mounting bolts and move the fan and shroud assembly away from the radiator.

3. Disconnect the radiator hoses and the overflow hose.

4. Remove the upper brackets bolts and lift the radiator out. If the air conditioning hose does not interfere, the shroud and fan can be removed with the radiator.

5. Installation is the reverse of removal. After filling the cooling system, run the engine until the fan runs once and check the coolant level again.

Oil Cooler

REMOVAL & INSTALLATION

1. Remove the thermostat to drain the cooling system.
2. Remove the oil filter.
3. Disconnect the hoses from the cooler.
4. Remove the nut holding the cooler to the oil filter base and remove the cooler.
5. Installation is the reverse of removal. Connect the coolant hoses before tightening the nut.

Water Pump

REMOVAL & INSTALLATION

▶ See Figure 30

1. Disconnect the negative battery cable and remove the thermostat to drain the cooling system.

2. Loosen the bolts holding the pulley to the coolant pump, remove the accessory drive belts, then remove the pulley. Note carefully which side of the pulley faces out.

3. Remove the nut and T-bolt securing the timing belt cover to the coolant pump.

4. It is not necessary to remove the coolant pump housing just to replace the pump. When removing the pump-to-housing bolts, note where the different length bolts are located.

5. Turn the pump slightly and lift it out of the pump housing. If necessary, tap around the edges of the pump with a rubber mallet to loosen it. Do not pry the pump out or the gasket surface will be damaged.

To install

6. Clean the pump housing gasket surface to remove all traces of the gasket material.

7. Place the new pump gasket onto the pump and install them into the housing. Make sure all the gasket bolt holes are aligned properly with the holes in the housing before installing the remaining bolts. Torque the bolts to 7 ft. lbs. (10 Nm).

8. Install the pulley and torque the bolts to 15 ft. lbs. (20 Nm). It may be easier to torque the pulley bolts after the accessory drive belts are installed.

9. Install the camshaft cover bolt and not. Install the accessory drive belts adjust the belt tension.

10. Install the thermostat and fill the cooling system. Run the engine until the fan runs once and check the coolant level again.

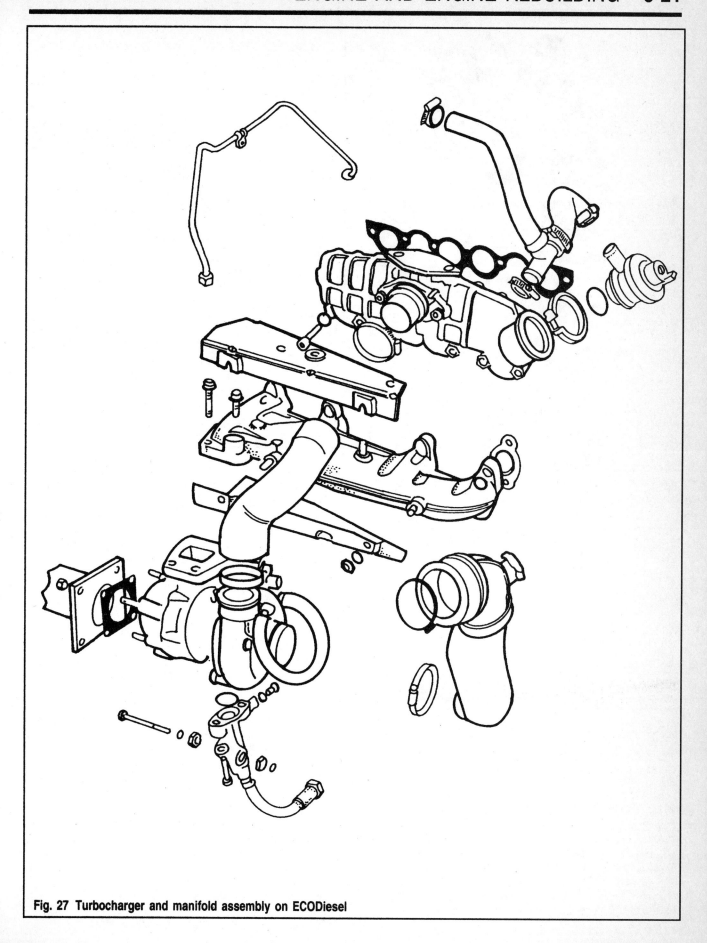

Fig. 27 Turbocharger and manifold assembly on ECODiesel

Fig. 28 If the air conditioner hose interferes, remove the fan shroud to remove the radiator

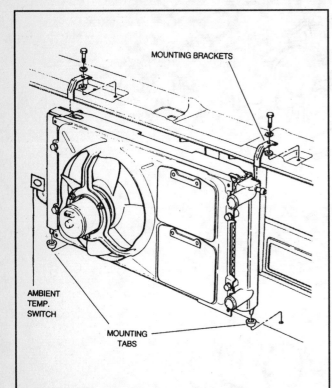

Fig. 29 Remove the upper brackets and lift the radiator out

Cylinder Head

REMOVAL & INSTALLATION

▶ **See Figures 31, 32 and 33**

Gasoline Engine

Special tools are required for removing and installing the clamps; VW3140/1 and /2 or equivalent. This is a set of different sized wedges for spreading the spring clamps in steps. The installed spring clamp has considerable tension and could cause damage or injury if not properly removed. Clamps

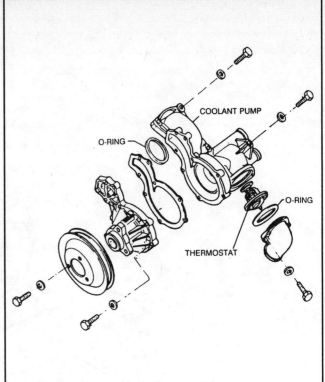

Fig. 30 Coolant pump can be removed without removing the housing

with wedges installed are also under high tension and should be handled carefully.

1. Disconnect the negative battery cable and remove the battery.

2. Open the radiator cap and remove the thermostat housing to drain the cooling system.

3. Disconnect the throttle cable. Label and disconnect all wiring and vacuum lines from the intake manifold. On the 16V engine, remove the upper half of the intake manifold.

4. On vehicles with CIS-E fuel injection, remove the injectors and the cold start valve without disconnecting the fuel lines and cap them. Secure all the lines aside.

5. On vehicles with Digifant fuel injection, the injectors and fuel rail assembly may be left on the head. Disconnect the fuel supply and return lines and the wiring connector for the injectors.

6. Disconnect the radiator and heater hoses.

7. Disconnect and label wiring for oil pressure and temperature sensors.

8. Disconnect the wiring for the oxygen sensor.

9. Remove the distributor cap and wires. On 16V engines, remove the distributor with the cap and wires as an assembly.

10. Disconnect the exhaust pipe from the exhaust manifold. If the pipe is secured to the manifold with spring clamps:

    a. Push the exhaust pipe to one side and insert the longer starter wedge into the opposite clamp.

    b. Push the pipe to the other side and install a wedge into the opposite clamp. Continue to work the pipe side to side while pushing the wedges into the clamps. The wedge must be inserted all the way to its shoulder.

    c. Push the pipe to one side again, grasp the opposite clamp and wedge at the same time with locking pliers and remove them together. Leave the wedge in the clamp if it is going to be reinstalled.

❄❄CAUTION

If the wedge shoots out of the spring clamp, it can travel all the way across the shop and cause serious personal injury. Place the clamps with wedges installed in a box until needed again.

11. Remove the EGR pipe from the exhaust manifold, if equipped.

12. Remove the accessory drive belts and any accessory that is bolted to the head.

13. Turn the engine to TDC of No. 1 cylinder, if possible, and remove the cylinder head cover, timing belt cover and the timing belt.

14. Loosen the cylinder head bolts in the reverse order of the tightening sequence.

15. Remove the bolts and lift the head straight off.

To install:

16. Before reinstalling the head, check the flatness of the head in both width and length, then diagonally from each corner. Maximum allowable warp is 0.004 inches (0.01mm).

17. Make sure the sealing surfaces are clean and free of old gasket material. Install the new cylinder head gasket with the word TOP or OPEN facing upward; do not use any sealing compound.

18. Carefully fit the head in place and install the bolts in positions 8 and 10 in the torque sequence. These holes are smaller and will properly locate the gasket and cylinder head.

19. Install the remaining bolts. Torque the bolts in sequence in 3 steps: 29 ft. lbs. (39 Nm), 44 ft. lbs. (60 Nm) and an additional ½ turn. Two quarter turns are allowed.

20. Install the camshaft drive belt and adjust the tension.

21. Connect the exhaust pipe to the manifold.

   a. On 16V engines, use new gaskets and self-locking nuts and torque to 18 ft. lbs. (25 Nm).

   b. On 8 valve engines, push the pipe to one side and install the clamp. Push the pipe the other way to install the other clamp and continue to work the pipe side to side to remove the wedges.

22. Connect the EGR pipe, if equipped.

23. Install the fuel injection equipment and connect the wiring.

24. On 16V engines, install the upper intake manifold.

25. Install the ignition system components.

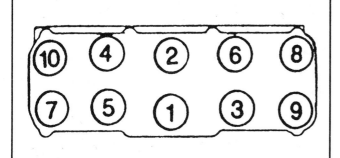

Fig. 31 Cylinder head bolt torque sequence

26. Connect the throttle cable and all wiring and vacuum lines.

27. Connect the cooling system hoses and install the thermostat with a new O-ring. Torque the housing bolts to 7 ft. lbs. (10 Nm). Refill the cooling system.

28. Install the accessory drive belts and adjust the tension.

29. When everything has been properly installed and connected, be sure to change the oil and filter before starting the engine.

Diesel Engine

Special tools are required for removing and installing the clamps; VW3140/1 and /2 or equivalent. This is a set of different sized wedges for spreading the spring clamps in steps. The installed spring clamp has considerable tension and could cause damage or injury if not properly removed. Clamps with wedges installed are also under high tension and should be handled carefully.

➡**The cylinder head bolts on diesel engines are stretch bolts and must be replaced when removed.**

1. Disconnect the battery ground cable.

2. Remove the thermostat and drain the cooling system.

3. Remove the fuel injection lines from the injectors and the pump as an assembly. Put the lines where they'll stay clean and protect the injector and pump fittings with caps.

4. Disconnect the radiator and heater hoses.

5. Disconnect all vacuum and electrical connections and carefully label them for installation.

6. Remove the turbocharger.

7. Remove the cylinder head cover and camshaft drive belt cover.

8. Turn the engine to TDC of No. 1 cylinder, if possible, and remove the camshaft drive belt.

9. Remove the head bolts in the reverse order of the installation torque sequence and lift the head out of the vehicle. The torque sequence is the same as for gasoline engines.

To install:

10. Check the cylinder head for warping: Maximum allowable is 0.004 inch (0.01mm). The cylinder head cannot be resurfaced.

11. On these engines, the pistons actually project above the deck of the block and the cylinder head gasket thickness is used to adjust piston-to-valve clearance. If the crank shaft and pistons are not to be removed, examine the old head gasket to see how many notches are on the edge near the oil return hole, between No. 2 and 3 cylinders. Use a gasket with the same number of notches. If the pistons were removed or if the old gasket is not available, the piston height (pop up) must be measured to select the proper head gasket. Use a dial indicator or caliper to obtain the measurement:

   0.026-0.034 inches (0.66-0.86mm) — 1 notch
   0.034-0.035 inches (0.87-0.90mm) — 2 notches
   0.036-0.040 inches (0.91-1.02mm) — 3 notches

12. Install the new cylinder head gasket with the word TOP or OPEN facing upward. Do not use any sealing compound.

13. Turn the crankshaft to TDC of No. 1 cylinder, then back about ¼ turn to bring all pistons about even.

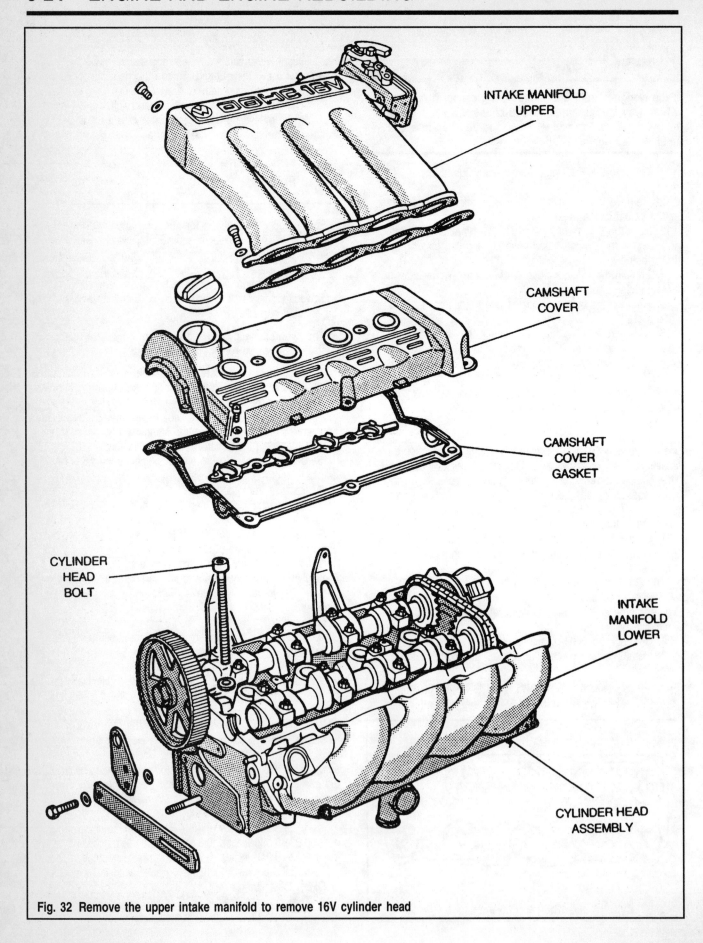

INTAKE MANIFOLD
UPPER

CAMSHAFT
COVER

CAMSHAFT
COVER
GASKET

CYLINDER
HEAD
BOLT

INTAKE
MANIFOLD
LOWER

CYLINDER HEAD
ASSEMBLY

Fig. 32 Remove the upper intake manifold to remove 16V cylinder head

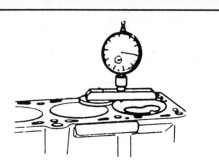

Fig. 33 Piston pop-up must be measured to select a diesel head gasket

14. Carefully lower the head on and install new head bolts into No. 8 and 10 positions first. These holes are smaller and will properly locate the gasket and cylinder head.

15. Install the remaining bolts and torque in the proper sequence in 3 steps: 29 ft. lbs. (40 Nm), 44 ft. lbs. (60 Nm), then a full ½ turn more. Two quarter turns are allowed.

16. Install the timing belt and set injection pump and valve timing.

17. Install the turbocharger and connect the exhaust pipe.

18. Install the fuel injector lines and torque to 18 ft. lbs. (25 Nm). Be careful not to over torque the line nuts or the flare will split and leak.

19. Installation of the remaining parts is the reverse of removal, be sure to change the oil and filter. Install the camshaft drive belt and set injection pump timing.

20. After the engine has be run about 1000 miles, the cylinder head bolts must be re-torqued. Remove the cylinder head cover and turn each head bolt, in sequence, an additional ¼ turn in 1 movement. This can be done on a cold or warm engine.

CLEANING AND INSPECTION

▶ **See Figures 34 and 35**

1. Remove the manifolds and all other items that can be unbolted or unscrewed.

2. Place the head on wooden blocks and remove the camshaft, cam followers and end seals.

➡**Keep the cam followers and bearing shells in order. Tag them so they can be installed in the same location.**

3. Working in a clean area, use spray solvent or brush cleaning solvent on the cylinder head top, sides and combustion chamber surfaces to remove any grease, dirt or oil, and help soften carbon deposits. After cleaning with solvent, wash the head with hot water and wipe dry.

4. Turn the head so the combustion chambers are facing up.

5. Before removing any carbon, examine the chambers and valve faces for obvious damage such as burnt valves or cracks. If one chamber is very clean, this usually indicates a coolant leak into that cylinder.

6. Mount a rotary wire carbon cleaning brush in an electric drill and clean the combustion chambers and valve heads. Be careful not to remove any aluminum or make deep scratches

that may look like cracks. A complete inspection of the cylinder head (combustion chambers, valves, guides etc.) can be done after the valves and springs are removed.

7. To check the head for warping:

a. Place a straight edge along the length of the head and attempt to slip a 0.004 inch (0.01mm) feeler gauge between them. Move the gauge the full length of the head and look for high or low spots.

b. Move the straight edge diagonally across the head and use the feeler gauge again.

c. If the head is warped more than allowed, use thicker feeler gages to determine how much and record the results. This information is needed to determine how much material to remove during resurfacing.

RESURFACING

If the cylinder head is warped more than 0.004 inches (0.01mm), it must be resurfaced. Diesel cylinder heads cannot be resurfaced because the relationship between the pre-chambers, injectors and head surface would be changed. If warped beyond specifications, diesel cylinder heads must be replaced.

To determine how much material can be removed from the cylinder head, measure the thickness of the head between the valve cover and head gasket surfaces. On 8 valve engines, the minimum cylinder head height is 5.22 inches (132.6mm). On 16V engines, minimum head height is 4.650 inches (118.1mm). Measure this dimension at several different points

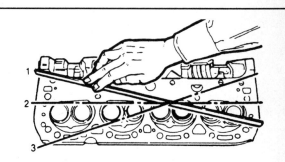

Fig. 34 Use a straight edge and feeler gauges to measure warping

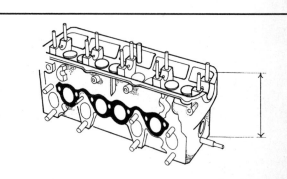

Fig. 35 Measure cylinder head thickness between gasket surfaces

to determine the average thickness. These measurements are often best left for the machinist.

Valves

REMOVAL & INSTALLATION

1. Loosen each cam bearing nut about 1 turn at a time to prevent bending the camshaft. Remove the bearing caps and lift off the camshaft. Remove the lifters and keep them upside down to prevent leak-down. Lifters MUST be reinstalled in their original location.

2. Block the head on wooden supports in a position that permits use of the type of valve spring removing tool you are going to use. VW uses tool VW 541, although you should be able to perform the job with several other available removers, the locking C-clamp type is popular.

3. Compress the valve springs and remove the stem locks and retainers. Remove the valve springs. Keep the parts and each valve separate and in order for reinstallation. It is important that the valves are installed back in their same location. Remove the lower valve spring seats and valve stem oil seals. Remove the valves, keep them in order in case the identification marking wears off.

4. Clean valve faces, tips and combustion chambers with a rotary wire brush or bench grinder wire wheel. Do not wire brush the valve stems, take care not to damage the valve seats. Remove the carbon, do not just burnish. If a stubborn carbon deposit is encountered, use a blunt drift to break the carbon loose. Again use caution around the valve seat.

5. Inspect the valves and guides as described later. Measure valve guide clearance.

6. If a water leak is suspected, or the valve seats, guides or valves need machine work, take the head and parts to the machine shop. Now is also a good time to have the head super cleaned in a cold parts cleaner, the machine shop can handle the job. However, never allow the aluminum head to be hot tanked, this will damage the head and make replacement necessary.

7. After all machine work has been done and all the new parts are on hand, install the valves with new oil seals.

8. When installing the camshaft, tighten the nuts 1 turn at a time to draw the camshaft down evenly against the valve springs.

INSPECTION

▶ See Figure 36

Check the sealing face of the valves and seats. They may be uneven and worn but there must be a distinct ring around the valve showing where it sealed against the seat. If there is any gap or signs of burning, the valve must be replaced and the seat reground.

To check the valve guides, place a new valve the guide with the end of the stem flush with the camshaft end of the guide. Set a dial indicator against the valve head and rock the valve side-to-side. If the free-play is more than 0.039 inches (1.0mm) on gasoline engines or 0.051 inches (1.3mm) on diesel

engines, the guides should be replaced. The guides are pressed out from the camshaft side of the head.

REFACING VALVES

On all engines, machining the intake valves is not recommended, they should only be hand-lapped. See the chart for information on valve face angles and dimensions. To hand lap the valves:

1. Invert the cylinder head, lightly lubricate the valve stem and install the valves in the head as numbered.

2. Moisten the suction cup on the lapping tool and attach to the valve head.

3. Slightly raise the valve from the seat and apply a small amount of valve grinding compound to the seat.

4. Rotate the lapping tool and valve between the palms of your hands while gently pushing the valve into the seat. Lift the tool often and turn the valve to a new position to prevent grooving.

5. Continue until a smooth polished surface is evident on the valve and valve seat. Remove the valve from the head and clean away all traces of lapping compound, especially from the guide.

❋❋CAUTION

The exhaust valves in the 16V engine are sodium filled and must not be machined. Improper handling or disposal can cause serious personal injury. To dispose of sodium filled valves:

Fig. 36 Measure valve guide clearance with the valve stem flush with the guide

6. Wear protective gloves and goggles. Sodium reacts violently with water; make sure the work area is dry.

7. Clamp the valve in a vise and saw the head off with a hack saw. Do not use power tools.

8. Throw the valve pieces into a bucket of water and stand back. When the reaction is done, the valves can be safely thrown away.

Valve Stem Seals

REPLACEMENT

▶ **See Figure 37**

Cylinder Head Removed

1. With the valve springs removed, hold the valve in place and slip the protector sleeve over the valve stem.
2. Lightly oil the seal and fit it over the protector sleeve.
3. Push the seal into place with the installation tool.
4. Install the valve springs.

Cylinder Head Installed

This procedure requires an air adaptor fitting that threads into a spark plug hole. Also required is the special valve spring tool, VW part no. 541.

1. Remove the camshaft.

2. Remove the spark plug and make sure the piston is at the bottom of the stroke.

3. Install an air adaptor fitting into the spark plug hole and apply 85 psi (6 BAR) of air pressure to the cylinder.

4. Install the valve spring tools onto the cylinder head and press down on the handle. The upper seat should move down on the stem so the keepers can be removed.

5. With the valve springs removed, hold the valve in place and slip the protector sleeve over the valve stem.

6. Lightly oil the seal and fit it over the protector sleeve.

7. Push the seal into place with the installation tool.

8. Install the valve springs, upper seat and keepers.

Valve Springs

REMOVAL & INSTALLATION

▶ **See Figure 38**

1. Remove the camshaft.
2. If the cylinder head is still on the engine:

   a. Remove the spark plug and make sure the piston is at the bottom of the stroke.

   b. Install an air adaptor fitting into the spark plug hole and apply 85 psi (6 BAR) of air pressure to the cylinder.

3. Install the valve spring compressor tools onto the cylinder head and press down on the handle. The upper seat should move down on the stem so the keepers can be removed with a magnet.

4. Installation is the reverse of removal.

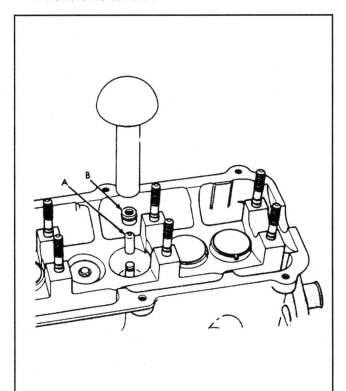

Fig. 37 Protector sleeve (A) eases valve stem seal (B) installation with push-on tool

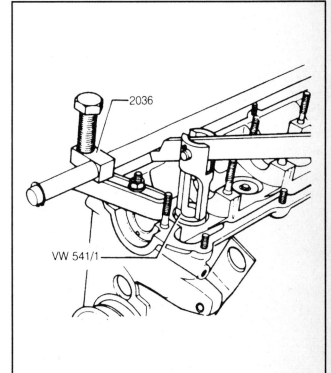

Fig. 38 Tool for removing valve springs with the cylinder head on or off the engine

INSPECTION

Free length, installed height and force specifications are not available from Volkswagen. If the free length of the spring varies more than $1/16$ inches (1.5mm) from side to side, the pair of springs must be replaced.

Valve Seats

RECONDITIONING

▶ See Figure 39

Valve seats cannot be replaced but can be refaced with either grinding stones or cutting tools. There is a limit to how much material can be removed. If the seat is cut too deeply, the hydraulic lifter will not function properly. To determine how much the seat can be cut:

1. Insert the valve and make sure it is flat against the seat.
2. Place a straight edge across the valve cover gasket surface.
3. Measure the distance from the straight edge to the valve stem.
4. Check the table shown below. The final measurement after cutting the valve seat must be no less than the dimension shown.

Fig. 39 Measure from the valve stem to the gasket surface

Engine	Intake	Exhaust
8 Valve Gas	1.331 in. (33.8 mm)	1.343 in. (34.1 mm)
16 Valve	1.354 in. (34.4 mm)	1.366 in. (34.7 mm)
Diesel	1.409 in. (35.8 mm)	1.421 in. (36.1 mm)

Fig. 40 Valve seat dimensions chart

Valve Guides

REMOVAL & INSTALLATION

Worn valve guides should be replaced by the automotive machine shop. The job requires a press and special cutting or reaming tools. In some cases a worn valve guide can be knurled which is a process where metal is displaced and raised, thereby reducing clearance. Consult the machine shop for their advice.

Valve Lifters

The hydraulic lifters can be removed once the camshaft is removed. Lifters should be kept upside down when not in their bore to prevent oil loss. The lifter must be returned to the same bore. They cannot be repaired or rebuilt.

Oil Pan

REMOVAL & INSTALLATION

1. Raise and safely support the vehicle on jack stands and drain the oil.

2. Loosen and remove the socket or Allen head oil pan retaining bolts.

3. Lower the pan from the car. If it is stuck, tap the sides with a mallet. Do not pry against the gasket surfaces.

4. Clean all the gasket surfaces and apply a thin bead of silicone sealant to the block.

5. Fit the new gasket to the pan use two bolts to hold the gasket in place while fitting the pan to the engine.

6. Install all the bolts and tighten them in a crisscross pattern. Torque the hex headed bolts to 15 ft. lbs. (20 Nm) or Allen head bolts to 7 ft. lbs. (10 Nm).

7. Refill the engine with oil. Start the engine and check for leaks.

Oil Pump

REMOVAL

1. Remove the oil pan.

2. Remove the two mounting bolts that hold the pump to the block and lower the pump. One bolt is longer than the other.

INSPECTION

▶ **See Figures 41 and 42**

1. With the oil pump on the bench and the bottom cover removed, insert a feeler gauge between the gear teeth. A new pump will have 0.002 inch (0.05mm) clearance, the wear limit is 0.008 inches (0.20mm).

2. Place a straight edge across the gears and the pump housing. Use a feeler gauge to measure the distance between the gears and the straight edge. The axial play of the gears should be no more than 0.004 inches (0.15mm).

3. The pressure relief valve is in the lower housing. Note position of the piston when removing.

4. Service parts for VW oil pumps are not available. If the measurements do not meet specification, replace the pump.

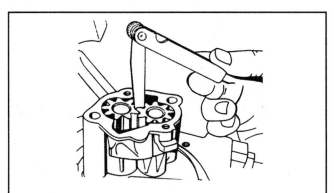

Fig. 41 Checking pump gear backlash

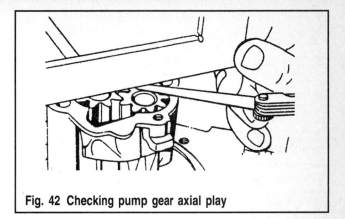

Fig. 42 Checking pump gear axial play

INSTALLATION

Installation is the reverse of removal. Use a new gasket and torque the bolts to 15 ft. lbs. (20 Nm).

Timing Belt Cover

REMOVAL & INSTALLATION

1. Remove the accessory drive belts.

2. To remove the crankshaft accessory drive pulley, hold the center crankshaft sprocket bolt with a socket and loosen the pulley bolts.

3. The cover is now accessible. It comes off in 2 pieces, remove the upper half first. Take note of any special spacers or other hardware.

4. Installation is the reverse of removal.

Timing Belt

Timing belts are designed to last 60,000-75,000 miles. If the vehicle has been stored for long periods (2 years or more), the belt should be changed before returning the vehicle to service.

REMOVAL & INSTALLATION

▶ **See Figures 43, 44, 45, 46, 47 and 48**

➡ **Do not turn the engine or camshaft with the timing belt removed. The pistons will contact the valves and cause internal engine damage.**

Gasoline Engines

1. Disconnect the negative battery cable and remove the accessory drive belts, crankshaft pulley and the timing belt cover(s).

2. Temporarily reinstall the crankshaft pulley bolt and turn the crankshaft to TDC of No. 1 piston. The mark on the camshaft sprocket should be aligned with the mark on the inner timing belt cover or the edge of the cylinder head.

3. With the distributor cap removed, the rotor should be pointing toward the No. 1 mark on the rim of the distributor housing. On 8 valve engines, the notch on the crankshaft pulley should align with the dot on the intermediate shaft sprocket.

4. Loosen the locknut on the tensioner pulley and turn the tensioner counterclockwise to relieve the tension on the timing belt.

5. Slide the timing belt from the sprockets.

To install:

6. Check the alignment of the timing marks. On 16V engines, the mark on the tooth should align with the mark on the rear belt cover.

7. Install the new timing belt and tension the belt so it can be twisted 90 degrees at the middle of it's longest section, between the camshaft and intermediate sprockets.

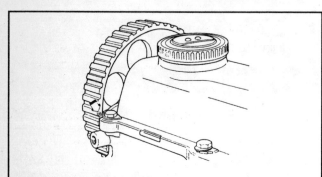

Fig. 43 Align the camshaft sprocket mark with the edge of the cylinder head

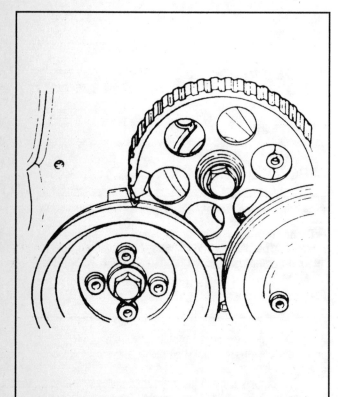

Fig. 44 On 8-valve engines, align the mark on the intermediate pulley

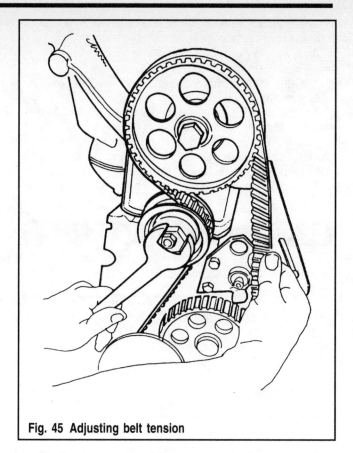

Fig. 45 Adjusting belt tension

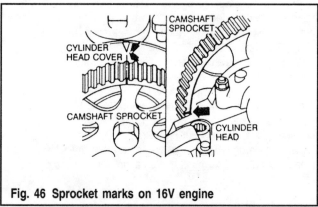

Fig. 46 Sprocket marks on 16V engine

8. Recheck the alignment of the timing marks and, if correct, turn the engine 2 full revolutions to return to TDC of No. 1 piston. Recheck belt tension and timing marks. Readjust as required. Torque the tensioner nut to 33 ft. lbs. (45 Nm).

9. Install the belt cover and accessory drive belts.

10. If the belt is too tight, there will be a growling noise that rises and falls with engine speed.

Diesel Engines

Some special tools are required. A flat bar, VW tool no. 2065A, is used to secure the camshaft in position. A pin, VW tool no. 2064, is used to fix the pump position while the timing belt is removed. The camshaft and pump work against spring pressure and will move out of position when the timing belt is removed. It is not difficult to find substitutes but do not remove the timing belt without these tools.

➡ **Do not turn the engine or camshaft with the timing belt removed. The pistons will contact the valves and cause internal engine damage.**

1. Disconnect the negative battery cable and remove the accessory drive belts, crankshaft pulley and the timing belt cover(s). Remove the camshaft cover and rubber plug at the back end of the camshaft.

2. Temporarily reinstall the crankshaft pulley bolt and turn the crankshaft to TDC of No. 1 piston. The mark on the camshaft sprocket should be aligned with the mark on the inner timing belt cover or the edge of the cylinder head.

3. With the engine at TDC, insert the bar into the slot at the back of the camshaft. The bar rests on the cylinder head to will hold the camshaft in position.

4. Insert the pin into the injection pump drive sprocket to hold the pump in position.

5. Loosen the locknut on the tensioner pulley and turn the tensioner counterclockwise to relieve the tension on the timing belt. Slide the timing belt from the sprockets.

To install:

6. Install the new timing belt and adjust the tension so the belt can be twisted 45 degrees at a point between the camshaft and pump sprockets. Torque the tensioner nut to 33 ft. (45 Nm).

7. Remove the holding tools.

8. Turn the engine 2 full revolutions to return to TDC of No. 1 piston. Recheck belt tension and timing mark alignment, readjust as required.

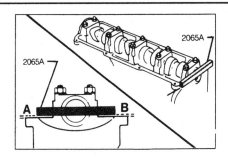

Fig. 47 Holding bar at back end of diesel engine camshaft

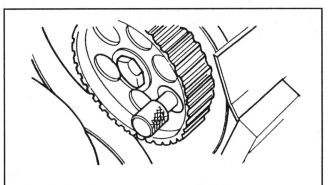

Fig. 48 Pin holding pump sprocket in place

9. Install the belt cover and accessory drive belts.

10. If the belt is too tight, there will be a growling noise that rises and falls with engine speed.

Timing Sprockets

REMOVAL & INSTALLATION

➡ **NOTE The 12 point crankshaft sprocket bolt is meant to be used one time only and must be replaced when removed.**

1. Remove the timing belt covers and the timing belt. The crankshaft sprocket should slide off easily when the center bolt is removed. Don't lose the Woodruff key.

2. Remove the cylinder head cover.

3. Use a wrench to hold the camshaft on the flat section and remove the sprocket retaining bolt.

4. Gently pry or tap the sprocket off the shaft with a soft mallet. If the sprocket will not easily slide off the shaft, use a gear puller. Do not hammer on the sprocket or damage to the sprocket or bearings could occur.

✳✳ CAUTION

On 16 valve engines, make sure the camshaft sprockets are installed so that the curved portion of the sprocket key faces the surface of the engine block. If the sprocket is installed incorrectly, the timing will be advanced and cause the valves to hit the pistons.

5. Installation is the reverse of removal. On crankshaft sprocket bolts, oil the threads before installing the bolt. Torque the bolts as follows:

   a. Camshaft sprocket on 8 valve gasoline engines — 59 ft. lbs. (80 Nm).

   b. Camshaft sprocket on 16V engines — 48 ft. lbs. (65 Nm).

   c. Camshaft sprocket on diesel engines — 33 ft. lbs. (45 Nm)

   d. Crankshaft sprocket 6 sided bolt — 137 ft. lbs. (180 Nm).

   e. Crankshaft sprocket 12 sided bolt — 66 ft. lbs. (90 Nm) plus ½ turn.

6. Install the timing belt, check valve timing, adjust the belt tension, and install the covers.

Camshaft(s) and Bearings

REMOVAL & INSTALLATION

▶ **See Figures 49, 50, 51 and 52**

8 Valve Engine

1. Disconnect the negative battery cable. Remove the timing belt cover(s), the timing belt, cylinder head cover and the camshaft sprocket.

2. Number the bearing caps from front to back. If the cap does not already have one, scribe an arrow pointing towards the front of the engine. The caps are offset and must be installed correctly. Factory numbers on the caps are not always on the same side.

3. Remove the front and rear bearing caps. Loosen the remaining bearing cap nuts a little at a time to avoid bending the camshaft. Start from the outside caps near the ends of the head and work toward the center.

4. Remove the bearing caps and the camshaft.

To install:

5. Install a new oil seal and end plug in the cylinder head. Lubricate the camshaft bearing journals and lobes and set the camshaft in place.

6. Install the bearing caps in the correct position with the arrow pointing towards the front of the engine. Tighten the cap

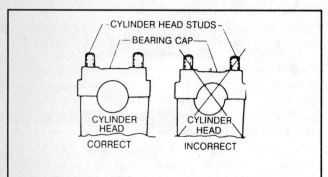

Fig. 50 Check carefully to make sure caps are installed correctly

nuts diagonally and in several steps until they are torqued to 15 ft. lbs. (20 Nm). Do not over torque. Camshaft shaft end-play should be about 0.006 inches (0.15mm).

7. Install the drive sprocket and timing belt. Wait at least ½ hour after installing camshaft shaft before starting the engine to allow the lifters to leak down.

16V Engines

1. Remove the timing belt cover.

2. Remove the upper intake manifold and cylinder head cover.

3. Turn the engine to TDC on cylinder No. 1, then slacken and remove the timing belt and camshaft sprocket.

4. With a felt marker only, matchmark the timing chain to the camshafts for reinstallation.

5. Remove the camshaft chain.

6. On the intake camshaft, remove bearing caps No. 5 and 7 and the chain end cap. Then loosen bearing caps No. 6 and 8 alternately and diagonally.

7. On the exhaust camshaft, remove bearing caps No. 1 and 3 and the end caps. Then loosen bearing caps No. 2 and 4 alternately and diagonally.

8. Remove the remaining bearing cap bolts and remove the camshafts.

To install:

9. Lubricate the camshaft bearing journals and lobes and set the camshafts in place. Install the camshaft drive chain so

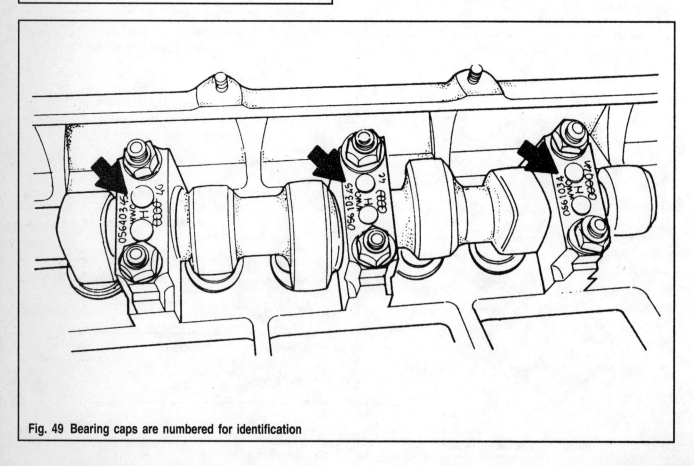

Fig. 49 Bearing caps are numbered for identification

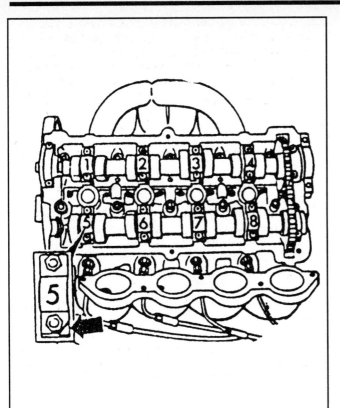

Fig. 51 Camshaft bearing locations on 16V engine

Fig. 52 Sprocket alignment marks with engine at TDC

the marks on the chain sprockets are matched at the base of the cylinder head, directly across from each other.

➡**When installing the bearing caps, make sure the notch points towards the intake side of the head.**

10. On the intake camshaft, install and torque bearing caps No. 6 and 8 alternately and diagonally to 11 ft. lbs. (15 Nm).

11. Install and torque the remaining intake camshaft bearing caps.

12. On the exhaust camshaft, torque bearing caps No. 2 and 4 alternately and diagonally to 11 ft. lbs. (15 Nm).

13. Install and torque the remaining exhaust camshaft bearing caps. Camshaft shaft end play on both camshafts should be about 0.006 inches (0.15mm).

14. Install the drive sprocket and timing belt.

15. Install remaining parts in reverse order of removal. Wait at least ½ hour after installing camshaft shafts before starting the engine to allow the hydraulic lifters to leak down.

INSPECTION

Degrease the camshaft using a safe solvent. Visually inspect the cam lobes and bearing journals for excessive wear. If a lobe is questionable or a bearing journal scored, the camshaft should be replaced. Check the lobes and journals with a micrometer. Measure the lobes from nose to heel. If all intake or all exhaust lobes do not measure the same, replace the camshaft. If the lobes and journals appear intact, place the front and rear journals in V-blocks. Position a dial indicator on the center journal and rotate the camshaft. If deviation exceeds 0.01mm (0.0004 inches) replace the camshaft.

Intermediate Shaft

REMOVAL & INSTALLATION

1. Remove timing belt cover(s), timing belt and intermediate shaft drive sprocket.

2. On 8 valve gasoline engines, remove distributor.

3. Remove the mounting flange retaining bolts. Reinstall sprocket bolt and remove the flange and shaft by pulling on the sprocket bolt.

4. Remove flange from the intermediate shaft and install new oil seal.

5. Install in reverse order of removal. Lubricate the oil seal lips. When installing the mounting flange be sure the oil return hole is at the bottom. Tighten the flange mounting bolts to 18 ft. lbs.

Pistons and Connecting Rods

REMOVAL & INSTALLATION

▶ **See Figures 53, 54, 55 and 56**

1. If the engine is still in the vehicle, the pistons and rods can be removed without removing the crankshaft. Remove the cylinder head and oil pan.

2. Turn the crankshaft until the piston to be removed is at the bottom of its travel.

3. Matchmark the connecting rod and cap on the same side to indicate the cylinder number and so they can be reassembled the same way.

4. Mark the top of the piston to indicate the cylinder number and the front of the crankshaft.

5. Place a rag down the cylinder bore on the head of the piston to be removed. Remove the cylinder top ridge and carbon deposits with a ridge reamer, following the instructions of the reamer's manufacturer.

➡**Do not cut too deeply or remove more than 0.15mm (0.006 inches) from the ring travel area when removing the ridge.**

6. Remove the rag and metal cuttings from the cylinder bore. Remove the connecting rod cap and bearing insert.

7. Push the connecting rod up the bore slightly and remove the upper bearing insert.

8. Push the connecting rod and piston assembly up and out of the cylinder with a hammer handle. It helps to have someone at the top of the engine to catch the piston.

To install

→**Connecting rod bolts with a round head containing six notches are stretch type bolts and cannot be reused. The bolts must be replaced when the connecting rod is disassembled.**

9. After the piston and connecting rod have been cleaned, inspected and prepared for installation, use new oil to lubricate the piston, rings, cylinder walls and crankshaft journal.

10. Lubricate the upper rod bearing saddle and fit the new bearing into place.

11. Install a piston ring compressor over the rings and top of the piston. Before tightening the ring compressor, be sure the ring gaps are staggered 60° apart.

12. Lower the piston and rod assembly into the cylinder bore with the arrow on the piston head facing the front of the engine. When the ring compressor contacts the top of the engine block, check to make sure the connecting rod is properly aligned with the crankshaft journal. Use a wooden hammer handle to tap the piston into the bore.

→**NOTE: If unusual resistance is encountered when starting the piston into the cylinder bore, the piston may be cocked or a ring has slipped out of the compressor and is caught at the top of the cylinder. Remove the piston and reinstall compressor. Forcing the piston in will break the rings.**

13. Carefully guide the connecting rod down the cylinder bore and over the crankshaft journal, taking care not to score the wall or crankshaft.

14. Fit the lower bearing insert into the bearing cap. Lubricate the insert and mount the cap on the rod with matchmarks aligned.

15. Install rod nuts and torque carefully to 22 ft. lbs. (30 Nm). This is not the final torque.

16. Lubricate the cylinder wall and turn the crankshaft to make sure the rod bearing is properly installed. If the crankshaft will not turn, remove the bearing cap and check bearing alignment.

17. When your are sure the rod bearings are properly fitted, tighten the bearing cap nuts an additional 1/4 turn. If equipped, install the oil spray nozzle.

18. Install remaining piston and rod assemblies. Turn the crankshaft each time so the crank journal of the piston being installed is at the bottom of travel.

CLEANING AND INSPECTION

After removing the piston and rod assemblies from the engine, clamp the connecting rod into a vise with the lower edge of the piston just resting on the vise jaws. Use a ring expanding tool and remove the piston rings from the piston.

Save the top compression ring and tag with cylinder location number. The old ring can be used later to check the cylinder bore for wear. Clean the top of the piston with a dull scraper or wire wheel. Use care not to gouge the piston when removing the carbon deposits. Clean the ring grooves using an appropriate groove cleaning tool. A broken piston ring can be used if a groove cleaner is not available. Once again, use care not to cut too deeply or gouge the ring seat. After all the pistons have had the rings removed and grooves cleaned, soak them in safe solvent. Do not use a caustic solvent on the pistons.

After the pistons have been cleaned and wiped dry inspect them for scuffing, scoring, cracks, pitting or excessive ring groove wear. If wear is evident, the piston must be replaced. Hold the connecting rod in one hand, grasp the piston in the other hand and twist the piston and rod in opposite directions. If excessive clearance (looseness) is detected, the piston pin, connecting rod bushing or piston and rod may require replacement. The automotive machine shop can handle the job for you. If you are not sure of the extent of wear present or what component needs replacing, take the assemblies to the machine shop and have them checked.

Make sure the piston, connecting rod and rod cap are marked with the number of the cylinder the assembly came from. Remove the piston from the connecting rod by inserting a small blunt drift in the small cutout provided on each side of the piston at the piston pin ends. Pry upward on the circlip to compress, and remove both circlips. Use a blunt drift slightly smaller than the diameter of the piston pin to gently drive the pin out. If resistance is encountered when removing the piston pin, submerge the pistons in hot water of 140°F to expand the metal and then carefully drive the pin out. Inspect the piston pin, connecting rod bushing and piston pin bore for galling, scoring or excessive wear. If wear is evident, consult the machine shop for advice as to what repair is necessary.

Measure, or have the machine shop measure the piston with a micrometer. Turn the piston upside down and take a measurement at a point 16mm (⁵⁄₈ inches) below the lower edge of the piston, 90° away from the piston pin holes. This information will be used to determine piston-to-cylinder wall clearance.

CYLINDER BORE

Measure the cylinder bore at three places to see if the cylinder is still round and straight. Measurements should be taken at a number of places in each cylinder: at the top, middle and bottom at two points at each location: that is, at a point 90° from the crankshaft, as well as a point parallel to the crankshaft. The difference between the greatest measurement of the cylinder wall and the diameter measurement of the is the piston clearance. If the difference is greater than 0.0028 inches (0.03mm), the clearance is too great and the cylinders should be machined to accept the next oversize piston. If any one cylinder is more than 0.0016 inches (0.04mm) out of round, all cylinders should be bored out to the next oversize. The machine shop or dealer parts department can provide information about what piston sizes are available.

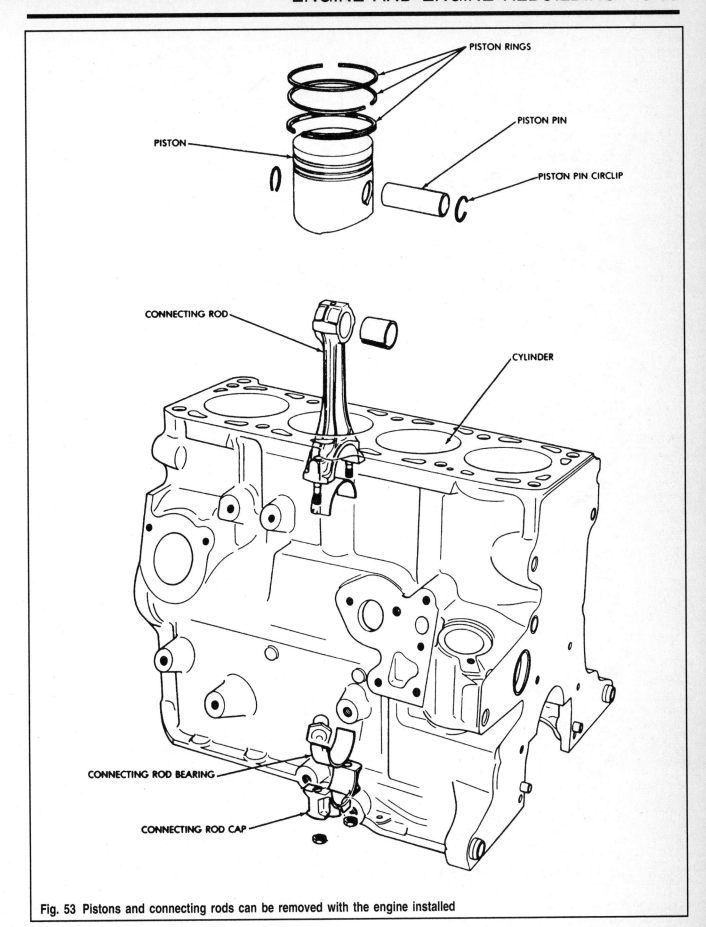

Fig. 53 Pistons and connecting rods can be removed with the engine installed

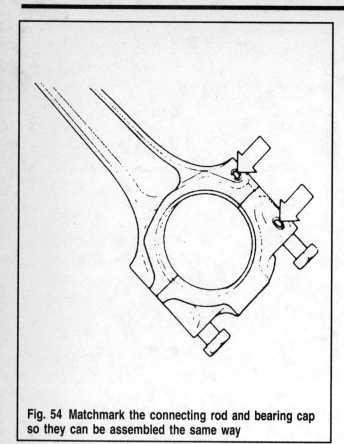

Fig. 54 Matchmark the connecting rod and bearing cap so they can be assembled the same way

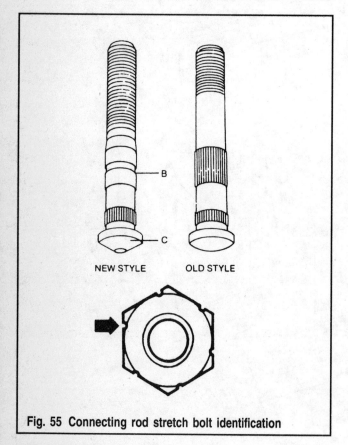

NEW STYLE   OLD STYLE

Fig. 55 Connecting rod stretch bolt identification

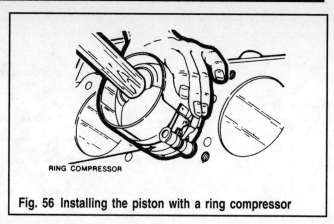

RING COMPRESSOR

Fig. 56 Installing the piston with a ring compressor

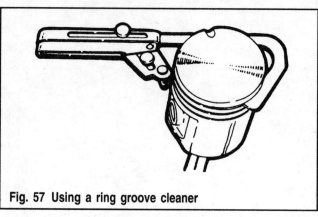

Fig. 57 Using a ring groove cleaner

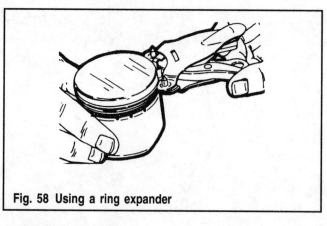

Fig. 58 Using a ring expander

CYLINDER HONING

Honing or deglazing the cylinder walls helps new piston rings seat faster for oil control. Refer to the instruction sheet packaged with the new rings that will be installed for the manufacturer's recommendation. If no special instructions are given, chuck a flexible drive hone into a power drill, lubricate the stones and insert into cylinder. Start the hone and move it up and down in the cylinder at a rate that will produce a 60° crosshatch pattern. Take care not to extend the hone below cylinder bore, or to withdraw it from the bore when operating. You're not trying to remove material, just create a pattern in the metal. After developing the pattern, wash the cylinder with a detergent and water solution to remove abrasive dust. Dry the cylinder wall and wipe it several times with a clan rag soaked in engine oil.

PISTON RINGS

▶ **See Figures 57, 58, 59, 60 and 61**

After the cylinder bore has been finish honed, or determined to be in satisfactory condition, ring end gap clearance can be checked. Compress the piston rings to be used in each cylinder, one at a time, into that cylinder. Press the ring down the bore to a point about 25mm (1 inch) below the top with an inverted piston. Measure the distance between the two ends (ring gap) of the ring with feeler gauges and compare to specifications. Pull the ring from the cylinder and file the ends with a fine file to gain required clearance, if necessary. Roll the outside of the ring around the piston groove it will be installed in to check for burrs or unremoved carbon deposits. Dress the groove with a fine file if necessary. Hold the ring in the groove and measure between top of ring and groove with a set of feeler gauges to check side clearance. If clearance is excessive, a new piston may be required or, in some cases, a spacer can be installed. Consult the machine shop for their advice.

Install the piston rings on the piston starting with the lower oil control ring. Always refer to the ring manufacturer's instruction sheet for guidance. Be sure, when installing a three piece expander type oil ring, that the ends of the expander are butted together and do not overlap. Hold the butted edges together and install the lower rail first. Install with the ring gap about 19mm (¾ inches) away from the butted point of the expander. Install the upper rail on the opposite side, 3/4 away from the butted point of the expander. Use a ring expander and install the compression rings, lower ring first. Most compression rings will have a top mark of some kind, be sure the mark is facing up.

Before installing the piston ring compressor, be sure the piston ring gaps are staggered 60 degrees apart from each other. The gaps should be at three equal spacings, never in a straight line. Avoid installing the rings with their ends in line with the piston pin bosses and the thrust direction. Always refer to the ring manufacturer's instruction sheet for guidance.

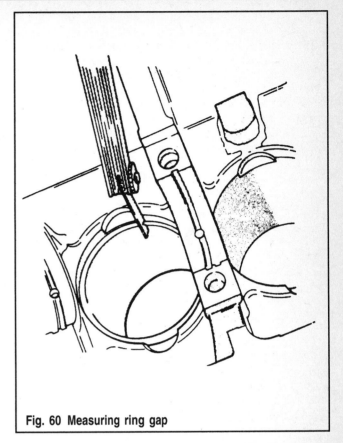

Fig. 60 Measuring ring gap

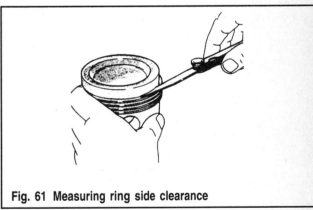

Fig. 61 Measuring ring side clearance

DIESEL PISTONS

▶ **See Figure 62**

On diesel engines, the top of the piston actually protrudes above the top of the cylinder deck when the piston is at TDC. This piston 'pop-up' must be measured before installing the cylinder head.

A spacer (VW385/17) and bar with dial indicator (VW 382/7) are necessary, and should be set up as shown to measure the maximum amount of piston projection above the deck height. To measure the piston height of particular cylinder, bring the piston up so that the top of the piston is dead flush with the surface of the block. Mount the indicator and spacer onto the cylinder deck. Slide the indicator over and zero the indicator stylus on the top of the piston. Now, slowly (very slowly) rotate

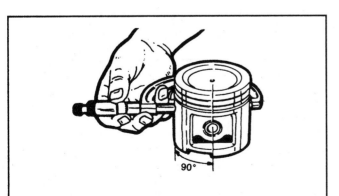

Fig. 59 Measure the piston 90° from the wrist pin

the crankshaft until a deflection is read on the indicator. This is a very tricky reading, because you have to catch the indicator deflection before the piston starts on the downward travel. Take several readings per cylinder to get an average.

After piston height has been determined, a head gasket of suitable thickness must be used. Head gasket thickness is coded by the number of notches located on the edge and by a part number on the gasket near the notches. If the same parts are being used over again, install a new gasket with the same number of notches as the one removed. The following table shows the piston height with it's corresponding notch number:

- 0.65-0.85mm (0.026-0.034 inches) 1 notch
- 0.70-0.90mm (0.027-0.035 inches) 2 notches
- 0.90-1.00mm (0.036-0.040 inches) 3 notches

Main Oil Seals

REMOVAL & INSTALLATION

▶ **See Figures 63 and 64**

The front crankshaft oil seal can be pried out and a new seal installed after the pulley and drive sprocket have been removed. The rear main oil seal is located in a housing on the rear of the cylinder block. To replace the seal, the engine and transaxle must be separated. The transaxle can be removed without removing the engine.

1. Remove the transaxle and flywheel.
2. Using a screwdriver or VW seal remover tool, very carefully pry or pull the old seal out of the support ring.

3. Lightly oil the replacement seal and then press it into place using a VW seal installation tool, canister top or other circular piece of flat metal. Be careful not to damage the seal or score the crankshaft.

4. Install the flywheel and transmission.

Crankshaft and Main Bearings

REMOVAL & INSTALLATION

▶ **See Figure 65**

1. Remove the engine from the vehicle and remove the cylinder head.

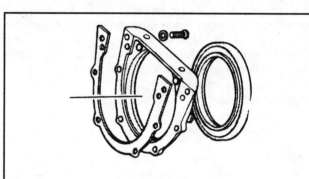

Fig. 63 If the engine is out of the vehicle, remove the seal carrier to change the rear main seal

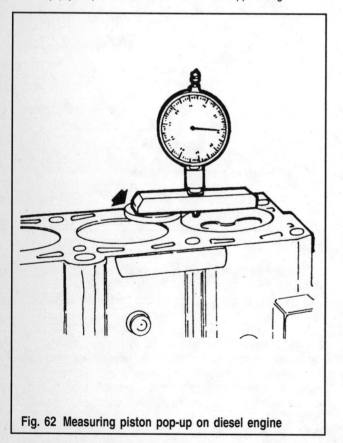

Fig. 62 Measuring piston pop-up on diesel engine

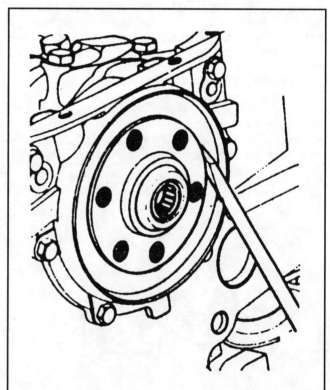

Fig. 64 Carefully pry out the old seal without damaging the crankshaft

2. Remove the oil pan, oil pump, flywheel and the front and rear main seals.

3. Remove the piston and rod assemblies.

4. If not already identified, mark the main bearing caps for location and direction. They must face the same direction when installed.

5. Loosen all the bolts and remove the main bearing caps.

6. Remove the crankshaft and bearing inserts. Clean and inspect the engine block. If this is a high mileage engine, a machine shop should check the main bearing bore alignment.

To install

7. After all parts are fully prepared for assembly and the bearing oil clearance has been checked, lubricate the upper main bearing inserts with new engine oil and fit them into the engine block.

8. If the engine uses a 6-piece center bearing, install the upper thrust bearing washers.

9. Lubricate the bearing inserts and the crankshaft journals. Slowly and carefully lower the crankshaft into position.

10. Lubricate and fit the bearing inserts into the bearing caps and set the caps into place. Don't forget the thrust washers on the center bearing.

11. Start all the bolts and torque them in 3 steps to 48 ft. lbs. (65 Nm). Turn the crankshaft between each step to make sure there is no binding.

BEARING OIL CLEARANCE

▶ **See Figure 66**

The procedure described here assumes the engine is out of the vehicle. The oil clearance can be checked with the engine installed to help determine main bearing and crankshaft

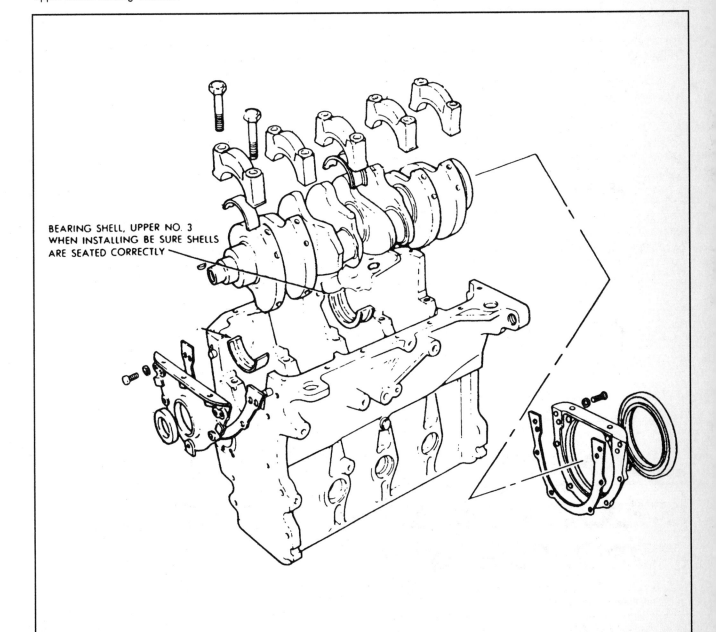

BEARING SHELL, UPPER NO. 3
WHEN INSTALLING BE SURE SHELLS
ARE SEATED CORRECTLY

Fig. 65 Crankshaft and main oil seal carrier assemblies

condition. Follow the same procedure but remove only one main bearing cap at a time.

1. With the upper bearing inserts and the crankshaft installed, wipe the oil from the main journal on the crankshaft so it is dry.

2. Lay a piece of Plastigage® on the crankshaft and install the bearing cap with the bearing. Make sure the bearing is dry and torque the cap bolts to 48 ft. lbs. (65 Nm).

3. Remove the bolts and cap. The Plastigage® may not stick to the crankshaft so don't drop it when removing the cap.

4. Use the gauge and conversion table printed on the package to determine the bearing clearance.

CRANKSHAFT END-PLAY/CONNECTING ROD SIDE PLAY

Place a pry bar between a main bearing cap and crankshaft casting taking care not to damage any journals. Pry backward and forward and measure the distance between the thrust bearing and crankshaft with a feeler gauge. Compare reading with specifications. If too great a clearance is determined, a larger thrust bearing or crank machining may be required. Consult an automotive machine shop for their advice.

Connecting rod clearance between the rod and crank throw casting can be checked with a feeler gauge. Pry the rod carefully to one side as far as possible and measure the distance on the other side of the rod.

CRANKSHAFT REPAIRS

If a journal is damaged on the crankshaft, repair is possible by having the crankshaft machined to a standard undersize. In most cases, however, since the crankshaft must be removed

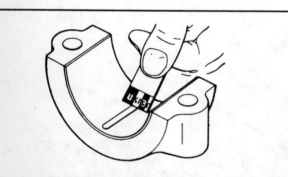

Fig. 66 Using Plastigage® to check main bearing oil clearance

from the engine, some thought should be given to replacing the damaged crankshaft with a reground shaft kit. A reground crankshaft kit contains the necessary main and rod bearings for installation. The shaft has been ground and polished to undersize specifications and will usually hold up well if installed correctly.

Flywheel

REMOVAL & INSTALLATION

▶ See Figure 67

➡The flywheel bolts are stretch bolts and cannot be used again once they have been removed. Make sure new bolts are on hand before removing the flywheel.

1. On automatic transaxles, mark the flywheel so it can be installed with the same face towards the transaxle.

2. The flywheel bolts are secured with a thread locking compound and will be difficult to remove. Use VW tool 558 or an equivalent locking tool to hold the flywheel from turning.

3. Remove the bolts and remove the flywheel. Clean the thread locking compound out of the bolt holes in the crankshaft with a tap.

4. Before installing the automatic transaxle flywheel:
   a. Temporarily install the flywheel with only 2 bolts.
   b. Use a depth caliper to measure the distance between the outer face of the ring gear and the cylinder block.
   c. The distance must be 1.20-1.28 inches (30.6-32.0mm). Remove the flywheel and change the shims as required.

5. Install the flywheel and apply a thread locking compound to the bolts. Torque the bolts in the sequence shown to 22 ft. lbs. (30 Nm). After tightening all the bolts, tighten them an additional 1/4 turn in the same sequence.

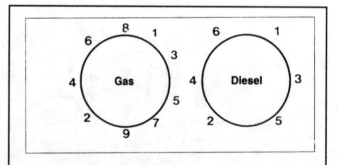

Fig. 67 Flywheel torque sequence is the same for manual or automatic transaxle

EXHAUST SYSTEM

General Description

In addition to the normal assortment of pipes and mufflers, the exhaust system includes the catalytic converter. On 8 valve gasoline and diesel engines, the converter and a heat shield are welded onto the front exhaust pipe. On gasoline engines, there is also a tube upstream of the converter leading to the

engine compartment. The tube is used to sample the exhaust gas to read carbon dioxide (CO) content for testing and adjusting air/fuel mixture. Also on or just upstream of the converter is a threaded fitting for the oxygen sensor. More information about these components is included in Section 4.

The system is suspended by pre-formed rubber rings to limit noise transmission into the body and to allow movement. The rings hook onto tabs welded onto the pipes and the body. This makes proper alignment of the tabs critical when installing new exhaust system components. Misalignment of components or a loose heat shield is the most common cause of rattles and frequent rubber hanger failure. Periodic maintenance of the exhaust system is not required. However, if the vehicle is raised for other service, it is advisable to check the general condition of the entire system, especially the rubber hangers.

Exhaust Pipe

REMOVAL & INSTALLATION

▶ **See Figures 68 and 69**

8 Valve Engine

❋❋CAUTION

On 8 valve engines, the exhaust pipe is secured to the manifold with spring clamps. Do not attempt to remove or install the clamps without the correct tools or serious personal injury could result. Do not work on the exhaust system of a vehicle that is still warm. The catalytic converter operates at temperatures in excess of 950°F and takes time to cool down.

On the 8 valve engines, special tools are required to remove and install the exhaust pipe-to-manifold spring clamps, VW tool numbers 3140/1 and 3140/2.

1. Disconnect the oxygen sensor wiring.
2. Push the pipe to one side to expand the opposite clamp. Insert the starter wedge into the expanded clamp.
3. Push the pipe to the other side and insert a wedge into the clamp.
4. Push the pipe the other way again to expand the clamp further. It should be possible to grab the wedge with locking pliers and pry the clamp off the pipe flange.
5. Leave the wedges in the clamps and put them in a box so they won't be disturbed and fly apart.
6. To remove the wedge from the clamp, set the clamp in the partially open jaws of a vise. Carefully drive the long starter wedge in to spread the clamp further (there will be 2 wedges in the clamp).
7. Turn the clamp over and carefully drive the short wedge out, then the longer wedge.

❋❋CAUTION

The wedges will be forced out with considerable force and could cause serious injury. Position the clamp so the wedge will fly into a container.

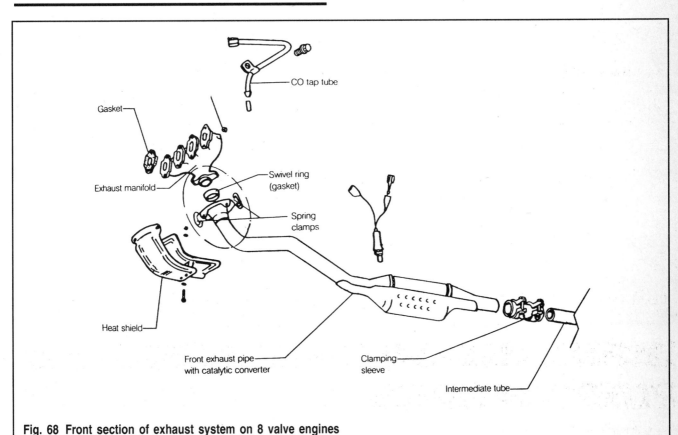

Fig. 68 Front section of exhaust system on 8 valve engines

To install:

8. If new clamps are to be used, set the clamp on the vise and use the starter wedge to spread it far enough to install the short wedge. Remove the starting wedge.

9. Fit the pipe and gasket into place. Tilt the pipe to one side to install the clamp, then push it to the other side to install the other clamp.

10. Push the pipe side-to-side as necessary to expand the clamps enough to remove the wedges.

16 Valve Engine

1. Disconnect the oxygen sensor wiring and remove the heat shield.

2. Disconnect the catalytic converter from the exhaust pipe.

3. Remove the nuts to remove the pipe from the manifold.

4. Installation is the reverse of removal. Use new gaskets and self-locking nuts. Torque the pipe-to-manifold nuts to 30 ft. lbs. (40 Nm) and the pipe-to-catalytic converter nuts to 18 ft. lbs. (25 Nm).

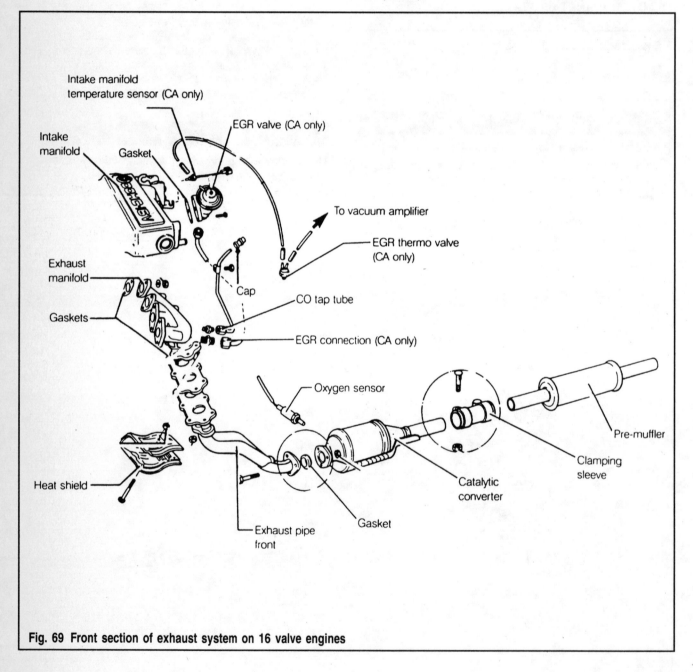

Fig. 69 Front section of exhaust system on 16 valve engines

Rear Section

REMOVAL & INSTALLATION

▶ **See Figures 70 and 71**

To remove the rubber rings, support the exhaust system and pry the rings from the hangers on the body. When installing the system, leave all bolts and nuts loose until the rings are installed and all parts are properly aligned, then tighten the clamps from front to rear.

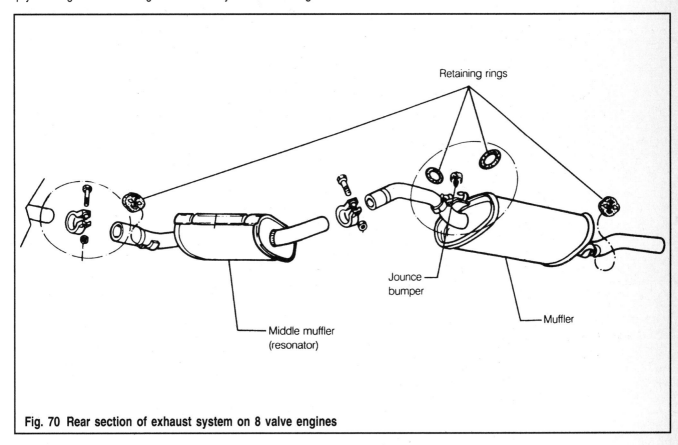

Fig. 70 Rear section of exhaust system on 8 valve engines

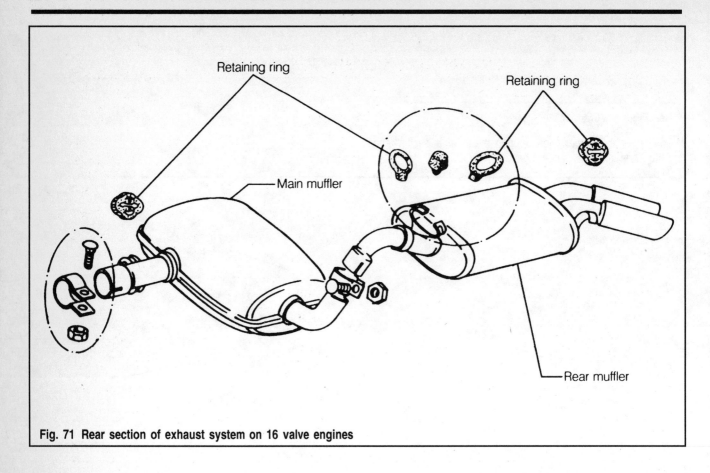

Fig. 71 Rear section of exhaust system on 16 valve engines

ENGINE MECHANICAL SPECIFICATIONS

Component	US	Metric
Cylinder Block		
Maximum Deck Warpage:	0.004 in.	0.01mm
Cylinder Bore		
Standard Diameter		
1.8L Engine:	3.1894 in.	81.01mm
2.0L Engine:	3.2484 in.	82.48mm
Diesel Engine:	3.0122 in.	76.51mm
First Oversize		
1.8L Engine:	3.1992 in.	81.26mm
2.0L Engine:	none	
Diesel Engine:	3.0220 in.	76.76mm
Second Oversize		
1.8L Engine:	3.2091in.	81.51mm
2.0L Engine:	none	
Diesel Engine:	3.0319 in.	77.01mm
Third Oversize		
Diesel Engine:	3.0516 in.	77.51mm
Cylinder Head		
Maximum Warpage:	0.004 in.	0.01mm
Minimum Cylinder Head Thickness		
1.8L Engine:	5.221 in.	132.6mm
2.0L Engine:	4.650 in.	118.1mm
Diesel Engine:	cannot be machined	
Intake Valve		
Stem Diameter		
8 valve engine:	0.3138 in.	7.97mm
16 valve engine:	0.2744 in.	6.97mm
Length		
8 valve gas engine:	3.583 in.	91.00mm
16 valve engine:	3.760 in.	95.50mm
Diesel engine (hydraulic lifters):	3.740 in.	95.00mm
Exhaust Valve		
Stem Diameter		
8 valve engine:	0.3130 in.	7.95mm
16 valve engine:	0.2732 in.	6.94mm
Length		
8 valve engine:	3.575 in.	90.80mm
16 valve engine:	3.846 in.	98.20mm
Diesel engine (hydraulic lifters)	3.740 in.	95mm
Valve Guide Wear		
(Measure with new valve)		
Gasoline engine		
Intake:	0.039 in.	1.0mm
Exhaust:	0.059 in.	1.3mm
Diesel engine		
Intake and Exhaust:	0.059 in.	1.3mm
Valve seat angle:	45°	
Valve Springs (Diesel)		
Outer spring free length:	1.46 in.	37mm
Inner spring free length:	1.28 in.	32.5mm
Camshaft		
Maximum axial play		
8 valve engine:	0.0059 in.	0.15mm
Maximum runout		
Deisel engine:	0.0004 in.	0.01mm
Maximum bearing clearance		
(Plastigage ®):	0.0043 in.	0.11mm

ENGINE MECHANICAL SPECIFICATIONS

Component	US	Metric
Pistons:		
Standard diameter		
1.8L Engine:	3.1894 in.	81.01mm
2.0L Engine:	3.2482 in.	82.51mm
Diesel engine:	3.0122 in.	76.51mm
First oversize		
1.8L Engine:	3.1980 in.	1.23mm
Diesel Engine:	3.0209 in.	76.73mm
Second oversize		
1.8L Engine:	3.2079 in.	81.48mm
Diesel Engine:	3.0307 in.	76.98mm
Third oversize		
Diesel Engine:	3.0504 in.	77.48mm
Piston–to–cylinder clearance		
New parts:	0.0012 in.	0.03mm
Wear limit:	0.003 in.	0.08mm
Piston ring side clearance		
Gasoline Engine:	0.0008–0.0019 in.	0.02–0.05mm
Diesel Engine:		
Top ring:	0.0024–0.0035 in.	0.06–0.09mm
Second ring:	0.0020–0.0031 in.	0.05–0.08mm
Oil ring:	0.0012–0.0024 in.	0.03–0.06mm
Piston ring end gap		
Compression ring		
New:	0.0118–0.0177 in.	0.30–0.45mm
Limit:	0.039 in.	1.0mm
Oil ring		
New:	0.0098–0.0177 in.	0.25–0.45mm
Limit:	0.039 in.	1.0mm
Piston pop–up for Diesel cylinder head gasket selection:		
Hydraulic lifters		
1 notch:	0.0260–0.0339 in.	0.66–0.86mm
2 notches:	0.0343–0.0354 in.	0.87–0.90mm
3 notches:	0.0358–0.0402 in.	0.91–1.02mm
Crankshaft		
Main journal diameter		
1.6L and 1.8L engine		
New:	2.1243–2.1251 in.	53.958–53.978mm
First undersize:	2.1145–2.1153 in.	53.708–53.728mm
Second undersize:	2.1046–2.1054 in.	53.458–53.478mm
Third undersize:	2.0948–2.0956 in.	53.208–53.228mm
2.0L engine		
New:	2.1251–2.1276 in.	53.978–54.042mm
First undersize:	2.1153–2.1178 in.	53.728–53.795mm
Second undersize:	2.1054–2.1079 in.	53.478–53.542mm
Third undersize:	53.228–53.292 in.	2.0956–2.0981mm
Main bearing clearance (Plastigage®)		
New:	0.0012–0.0031 in.	0.03–0.08mm
Limit:	0.0067 in.	0.17mm
Crankshaft end play		
New:	0.0028–0.0067 in.	0.07–0.17mm
Limit		
Gasoline:	0.0098 in.	0.25mm
Diesel:	0.0146 in.	0.37mm

ENGINE MECHANICAL SPECIFICATIONS

Component	US	Metric
Rod journal diameter		
New:	1.8802–1.8810 in.	47.758–47.778mm
First undersize:	1.8704–1.8712 in.	47.508–47.528mm
Second undersize:	1.8606–1.8613 in.	47.258–47.278mm
Third undersize:	1.8507–1.8515 in.	47.008–47.028mm
Rod bearing clearance		
(Plastigage®)		
Limit:	0.0047 in.	0.12mm
Connecting rod end play:	0.0145 in.	0.37mm
Oil pump gears		
Backlash:	0.002–0.008 in.	0.05–0.20mm
End play limit:	0.006 in.	0.15mm
Pressure @ 2000 engine rpm (warm):	28 psi	2.0 BAR

TORQUE SPECIFICATIONS

Component	US	Metric
Alternator bolts:	20 ft. lbs.	25 Nm
Camshaft sprocket		
8 valve gasoline engine:	59 ft. lbs.	80 Nm
16V engine:	48 ft. lbs.	65 Nm
diesel engine:	33 ft. lbs.	45 Nm
Camshaft bearing caps		
8 valve engine:	15 ft. lbs.	20 Nm
16 valve engine:	11 ft. lbs.	15 Nm
Connecting rod nuts:	22 ft. lbs. plus 1/4 turn	30 Nm plus 1/4 turn
Crankshaft sprocket		
6 sided bolt:	137 ft. lbs.	180 Nm
12 sided bolt:	66 ft. lbs.plus ½ turn	90 Nm plus ½ turn
Cylinder head bolts		
Step 1:	29 ft. lbs.	39 Nm
Step 2:	44 ft. lbs.	60 Nm
Step 3:	an additional ½ turn	
Diesel injectors:	51 ft. lbs.	70 Nm
Diesel injection line nuts:	18 ft. lbs.	25 Nm
Engine mounts		
10mm bolts:	33 ft. lbs.	41 Nm
12mm bolts:	54 ft. lbs.	73 Nm
Exhaust manifold:	18 ft. lbs.	20 Nm
Exhaust pipe–to–manifold:	30 ft. lbs.	40 Nm
Flywheel bolts:	22 ft. lbs. plus 1/4 turn	30 Nm plus 1/4 turn
Halfshaft flange bolts:	33 ft. lbs.	45 Nm
Intake manifold		
Upper:	15 ft. lbs.	20 Nm
Lower:	18 ft. lbs.	25 Nm
Main bearing cap bolts:	48 ft. lbs.	65 Nm
Oil pan		
Hex head bolts:	15 ft. lbs.	20 Nm
Allen head bolts:	7 ft. lbs.	10 Nm
Oil pump:	15 ft. lbs.	20 Nm
Spark plugs:	22 ft. lbs.	30 Nm
Starter:	43 ft. lbs.	58 Nm
Thermostat housing:	7 ft. lbs.	10 Nm
Timing belt tensioner:	33 ft. lbs.	45 Nm
Turbocharger–to–manifold:	33 ft. lbs.	45 Nm
Turbocharger oil line:	22 ft. lbs.	30 Nm
Turbocharger outlet pipe:	18 ft. lbs.	25 Nm
Valve cover:	87 inch lbs.	10 Nm
Water pump bolts:	7 ft. lbs.	10 Nm
Water pump pulley:	15 ft. lbs.	20 Nm

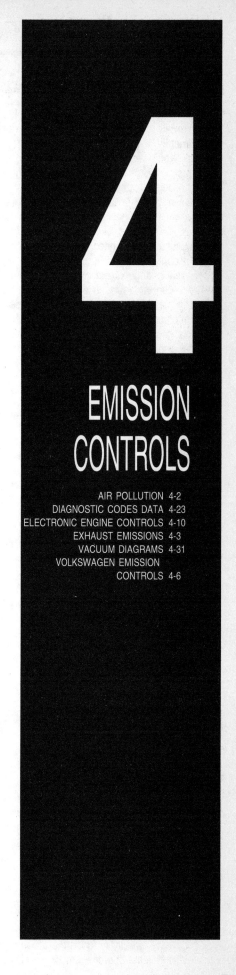

AIR POLLUTION
  AUTOMOTIVE POLLUTANTS 4-2
  INDUSTRIAL POLLUTION 4-2
  INTERNAL COMBUSTION ENGINE
    POLLUTANTS 4-3
  NATURAL POLLUTANTS 4-2
  TEMPERATURE INVERSION 4-2
DIAGNOSTIC CODES DATA
  GENERAL INFORMATION 4-23
  SELF-DIAGNOSTICS 4-24
ELECTRONIC ENGINE CONTROLS
  DIGIFANT SYSTEM 4-18
  MOTRONIC SYSTEM 4-10
EXHAUST EMISSIONS
  COMPOSITION OF THE EXHAUST
    GASES 4-3

OTHER AUTOMOBILE EMISSION
  SOURCES 4-5
VACUUM DIAGRAMS 4-31
VOLKSWAGEN EMISSION CONTROLS
  CATALYTIC CONVERTER 4-9
  CRANKCASE VENTILATION
    SYSTEM 4-6
  EVAPORATIVE EMISSION
    CONTROLS 4-6
  EXHAUST GAS RECIRCULATION
    SYSTEM 4-9
  GENERAL INFORMATION 4-6
  OXYGEN SENSOR 4-10

4

EMISSION CONTROLS

AIR POLLUTION 4-2
DIAGNOSTIC CODES DATA 4-23
ELECTRONIC ENGINE CONTROLS 4-10
EXHAUST EMISSIONS 4-3
VACUUM DIAGRAMS 4-31
VOLKSWAGEN EMISSION
CONTROLS 4-6

AIR POLLUTION

The earth's atmosphere, at or near sea level, consists of 78% nitrogen, 21% oxygen and 1% other gases, approximately. If it were possible to remain in this state, 100% clean air would result. However, many varied causes allow other gases and particulates to mix with the clean air, causing the air to become unclean or polluted.

Certain of these pollutants are visible while others are invisible, with each having the capability of causing distress to the eyes, ears, throat, skin and respiratory system. Should these pollutants be concentrated in a specific area and under the right conditions, death could result due to the displacement or chemical change of the oxygen content in the air. These pollutants can cause much damage to the environment and to the many man made objects that are exposed to the elements.

To better understand the causes of air pollution, the pollutants can be categorized into 3 separate types, natural, industrial and automotive.

Natural Pollutants

Natural pollution has been present on earth before man appeared and is still a factor to be considered when discussing air pollution, although it causes only a small percentage of the present overall pollution problem existing in our country. It is the direct result of decaying organic matter, wind born smoke and particulates from such natural events as plains and forest fires (ignited by heat or lightning), volcanic ash, sand and dust which can spread over a large area of the countryside.

Such a phenomenon of natural pollution has been recent volcanic eruptions, with the resulting plume of smoke, steam and volcanic ash blotting out the sun's rays as it spreads and rises higher into the atmosphere, where the upper air currents catch and carry the smoke and ash, while condensing the steam back into water vapor. As the water vapor, smoke and ash traveled on their journey, the smoke dissipates into the atmosphere while the ash and moisture settle back to earth in a trail hundred of miles long. In many cases, lives are lost and millions of dollars of property damage result, and ironically, man can only stand by and watch it happen.

Industrial Pollution

Industrial pollution is caused primarily by industrial processes, the burning of coal, oil and natural gas, which in turn produces smoke and fumes. Because the burning fuels contain much sulfur, the principal ingredients of smoke and fumes are sulfur dioxide (SO_2) and particulate matter. This type of pollutant occurs most severely during still, damp and cool weather, such as at night. Even in its less severe form, this pollutant is not confined to just cities. Because of air movements, the pollutants move for miles over the surrounding countryside, leaving in its path a barren and unhealthy environment for all living things.

Working with Federal, State and Local mandated rules, regulations and by carefully monitoring the emissions, industries have greatly reduced the amount of pollutant emitted from their industrial sources, striving to obtain an acceptable level. Because of the mandated industrial emission clean up, many land areas and streams in and around the cities that were formerly barren of vegetation and life, have now begun to move back in the direction of nature's intended balance.

Automotive Pollutants

The third major source of air pollution is the automotive emissions. The emissions from the internal combustion engine were not an appreciable problem years ago because of the small number of registered vehicles and the nation's small highway system. However, during the early 1950's, the trend of the American people was to move from the cities to the surrounding suburbs. This caused an immediate problem in the transportation areas because the majority of the suburbs were not afforded mass transit conveniences. This lack of transportation created an attractive market for the automobile manufacturers, which resulted in a dramatic increase in the number of vehicles produced and sold, along with a marked increase in highway construction between cities and the suburbs. Multi-vehicle families emerged with much emphasis placed on the individual vehicle per family member. As the increase in vehicle ownership and usage occurred, so did the pollutant levels in and around the cities, as the suburbanites drove daily to their businesses and employment in the city and its fringe area, returning at the end of the day to their homes in the suburbs.

It was noted that a fog and smoke type haze was being formed and at times, remained in suspension over the cities and did not quickly dissipate. At first this 'smog', derived from the words 'smoke' and 'fog', was thought to result from industrial pollution but it was determined that the automobile emissions were largely to blame. It was discovered that as normal automobile emissions were exposed to sunlight for a period of time, complex chemical reactions would take place.

It was found the smog was a photo chemical layer and was developed when certain oxides of nitrogen (NOx) and unburned hydrocarbons (HC) from the automobile emissions were exposed to sunlight and was more severe when the smog would remain stagnant over an area in which a warm layer of air would settle over the top of a cooler air mass at ground level, trapping and holding the automobile emissions, instead of the emissions being dispersed and diluted through normal air flows. This type of air stagnation was given the name 'Temperature Inversion'.

Temperature Inversion

In normal weather situations, the surface air is warmed by the heat radiating from the earth's surface and the sun's rays and will rise upward, into the atmosphere, to be cooled through a convection type heat expands with the cooler upper air. As the warm air rises, the surface pollutants are carried upward and dissipated into the atmosphere.

When a temperature inversion occurs, we find the higher air is no longer cooler but warmer than the surface air, causing the cooler surface air to become trapped and unable to move. This warm air blanket can extend from above ground level to a few hundred or even a few thousand feet into the air. As the surface air is trapped, so are the pollutants, causing a severe smog condition. Should this stagnant air mass extend to a few thousand feet high, enough air movement with the inversion takes place to allow the smog layer to rise above ground level but the pollutants still cannot dissipate. This inversion can remain for days over an area, with only the smog level rising or lowering from ground level to a few hundred feet high. Meanwhile, the pollutant levels increases, causing eye irritation, respirator problems, reduced visibility, plant damage and in some cases, cancer type diseases.

This inversion phenomenon was first noted in the Los Angeles, California area. The city lies in a basin type of terrain and during certain weather conditions, a cold air mass is held in the basin while a warmer air mass covers it like a lid.

Because this type of condition was first documented as prevalent in the Los Angeles area, this type of smog was named Los Angeles Smog, although it occurs in other areas where a large concentration of automobiles are used and the air remains stagnant for any length of time.

Internal Combustion Engine Pollutants

Consider the internal combustion engine as a machine in which raw materials must be placed so a finished product comes out. As in any machine operation, a certain amount of wasted material is formed. When we relate this to the internal combustion engine, we find that by putting in air and fuel, we obtain power from this mixture during the combustion process to drive the vehicle. The by-product or waste of this power is, in part, heat and exhaust gases with which we must concern ourselves.

EXHAUST EMISSIONS

Composition Of The Exhaust Gases

The exhaust gases emitted into the atmosphere are a combination of burned and unburned fuel. To understand the exhaust emission and its composition review some basic chemistry.

When the air/fuel mixture is introduced into the engine, we are mixing air, composed of nitrogen (78%), oxygen (21%) and other gases (1%) with the fuel, which is 100% hydrocarbons (HC), in a semi-controlled ratio. As the combustion process is accomplished, power is produced to move the vehicle while the heat of combustion is transferred to the cooling system. The exhaust gases are then composed of nitrogen, a diatomic gas (N_2), the same as was introduced in the engine, carbon dioxide (CO_2), the same gas that is used in beverage carbonation and water vapor (H_2O). The nitrogen (N_2), for the most part passes through the engine unchanged, while the oxygen (O2) reacts (burns) with the hydrocarbons (HC) and produces the carbon dioxide (CO_2) and the water vapors (H_2O). If this chemical process would be the only process to take place, the exhaust emissions would be harmless. However, during the combustion process, other pollutants are formed and are considered dangerous. These pollutants are carbon monoxide (CO), hydrocarbons (HC), oxides of nitrogen (NOx) oxides of sulfur (SOx) and engine particulates.

HEAT TRANSFER

The heat from the combustion process can rise to over 4000°F (2204°C). The dissipation of this heat is controlled by a ram air effect, the use of cooling fans to cause air flow and having a liquid coolant solution surrounding the combustion area and transferring the heat of combustion through the cylinder walls and into the coolant. The coolant is then directed to a thin-finned, multi-tubed radiator, from which the excess heat is transferred to the outside air by 1 or all of the 3 heat transfer methods, conduction, convection or radiation.

The cooling of the combustion area is an important part in the control of exhaust emissions. To understand the behavior of the combustion and transfer of its heat, consider the air/fuel charge. It is ignited and the flame front burns progressively across the combustion chamber until the burning charge reaches the cylinder walls. Some of the fuel in contact with the walls is not hot enough to burn, thereby snuffing out or Quenching the combustion process. This leaves unburned fuel in the combustion chamber. This unburned fuel is then forced out of the cylinder along with the exhaust gases and into the exhaust system.

Many attempts have been made to minimize the amount of unburned fuel in the combustion chambers due to the snuffing out or 'Quenching', by increasing the coolant temperature and lessening the contact area of the coolant around the combustion area. Design limitations within the combustion chambers prevent the complete burning of the air/fuel charge, so a certain amount of the unburned fuel is still expelled into the exhaust system, regardless of modifications to the engine.

Lead (Pb), is considered 1 of the particulates and is present in the exhaust gases whenever leaded fuels are used. Lead (Pb) does not dissipate easily. Levels can be high along roadways when it is emitted from vehicles and can pose a health threat. Since the increased usage of unleaded gasoline and the phasing out of leaded gasoline for fuel, this pollutant is gradually diminishing. While not considered a major threat lead is still considered a dangerous pollutant.

HYDROCARBONS

Hydrocarbons (HC) are essentially unburned fuel that have not been successfully burned during the combustion process or have escaped into the atmosphere through fuel evaporation. The main sources of incomplete combustion are rich air/fuel mixtures, low engine temperatures and improper spark timing. The main sources of hydrocarbon emission through fuel evaporation come from the vehicle's fuel tank and carburetor bowl.

To reduce combustion hydrocarbon emission, engine modifications were made to minimize dead space and surface area in the combustion chamber. In addition the air/fuel mixture was made more lean through improved fuel injection and by the addition of external controls to aid in further combustion of the hydrocarbons outside the engine. The installation of a catalytic converter, a unit that is able to burn traces of hydrocarbons without affecting the internal combustion process or fuel economy.

To control hydrocarbon emissions through fuel evaporation, modifications were made to the fuel tank to allow storage of the fuel vapors during periods of engine shut-down, and at specific times during engine operation, to purge and burn these same vapors by blending them with the air/fuel mixture.

CARBON MONOXIDE

Carbon monoxide is formed when not enough oxygen is present during the combustion process to convert carbon (C) to carbon dioxide (CO_2). An increase in the carbon monoxide (CO) emission is normally accompanied by an increase in the hydrocarbon (HC) emission because of the lack of oxygen to completely burn all of the fuel mixture.

Carbon monoxide (CO) also increases the rate at which the photo chemical smog is formed by speeding up the conversion of nitric oxide (NO) to nitrogen dioxide (NO_2). To accomplish this, carbon monoxide (CO) combines with oxygen (O_2) and nitrogen dioxide (NO_2) to produce carbon dioxide (CO_2) and nitrogen dioxide (NO_2). ($CO + O_2 + NO = CO_2 + NO_2$).

The dangers of carbon monoxide, which is an odorless, colorless toxic gas are many. When carbon monoxide is inhaled into the lungs and passed into the blood stream, oxygen is replaced by the carbon monoxide in the red blood cells, causing a reduction in the amount of oxygen being supplied to the many parts of the body. This lack of oxygen causes headaches, lack of coordination, reduced mental alertness and should the carbon monoxide concentration be high enough, death could result.

NITROGEN

Normally, nitrogen is an inert gas. When heated to approximately 2500°F (1371°C) through the combustion process, this gas becomes active and causes an increase in the nitric oxide (NOx) emission.

Oxides of nitrogen (NOx) are composed of approximately 97-98% nitric oxide (NO_2). Nitric oxide is a colorless gas but when it is passed into the atmosphere, it combines with oxygen and forms nitrogen dioxide (NO_2). The nitrogen dioxide then combines with chemically active hydrocarbons (HC) and when in the presence of sunlight, causes the formation of photo chemical smog.

OZONE

To further complicate matters, some of the nitrogen dioxide (NO_2) is broken apart by the sunlight to form nitric oxide and oxygen. ($NO_2 + sunlight = NO + O$). This single atom of oxygen then combines with diatomic (meaning 2 atoms) oxygen (O_2) to form ozone (O_3). Ozone is 1 of the smells associated with smog. It has a pungent and offensive odor, irritates the eyes and lung tissues, affects the growth of plant life and causes rapid deterioration of rubber products. Ozone

can be formed by sunlight as well as electrical discharge into the air.

The most common discharge area on the automobile engine is the secondary ignition electrical system, especially when inferior quality spark plug cables are used. As the surge of high voltage is routed through the secondary cable, the circuit builds up an electrical field around the wire, acting upon the oxygen in the surrounding air to form the ozone. The faint glow along the cable with the engine running that may be visible on a dark night, is called the 'corona discharge.' It is the result of the electrical field passing from a high along the cable, to a low in the surrounding air, which forms the ozone gas. The combination of corona and ozone has been a major cause of cable deterioration. Recently, different types and better quality insulating materials have lengthened the life of the electrical cables.

Although ozone at ground level can be harmful, ozone is beneficial to the earth's inhabitants. By having a concentrated ozone layer called the 'ozonosphere', between 10 and 20 miles (16-32km) up in the atmosphere much of the ultra violet radiation from the sun's rays are absorbed and screened. If this ozone layer were not present, much of the earth's surface would be burned, dried and unfit for human life.

There is much discussion concerning the ozone layer and its density. A feeling exists that this protective layer of ozone is slowly diminishing and corrective action must be directed to this problem. Much experimenting is presently being conducted to determine if a problem exists and if so, the short and long term effects of the problem and how it can be remedied.

OXIDES OF SULFUR

Oxides of sulfur (SOx) were initially ignored in the exhaust system emissions, since the sulfur content of gasoline as a fuel is less than $\frac{1}{10}$ of 1%. Because of this small amount, it was felt that it contributed very little to the overall pollution problem. However, because of the difficulty in solving the sulfur emissions in industrial pollutions and the introduction of catalytic converter to the automobile exhaust systems, a change was mandated. The automobile exhaust system, when equipped with a catalytic converter, changes the sulfur dioxide (SO_2) into the sulfur trioxide (SO_3).

When this combines with water vapors (H_2O), a sulfuric acid mist (H_2SO_4) is formed and is a very difficult pollutant to handle and is extremely corrosive. This sulfuric acid mist that is formed, is the same mist that rises from the vents of an automobile storage battery when an active chemical reaction takes place within the battery cells.

When a large concentration of vehicles equipped with catalytic converters are operating in an area, this acid mist will rise and be distributed over a large ground area causing land, plant, crop, paints and building damage.

PARTICULATE MATTER

A certain amount of particulate matter is present in the burning of any fuel, with carbon constituting the largest percentage of the particulates. In gasoline, the remaining percentage of particulates is the burned remains of the various other compounds used in its manufacture. When a gasoline engine is in good internal condition, the particulate emissions are low but as the engine wears internally, the particulate emissions increase. By visually inspecting the tail pipe emissions, a determination can be made as to where an engine defect may exist. An engine with light gray smoke emitting from the tail pipe normally indicates an increase in the oil consumption through burning due to internal engine wear. Black smoke would indicate a defective fuel delivery system, causing the engine to operate in a rich mode. Regardless of the color of the smoke, the internal part of the engine or the fuel delivery system should be repaired to a 'like new' condition to prevent excess particulate emissions.

Diesel and turbine engines emit a darkened plume of smoke from the exhaust system because of the type of fuel used. Emission control regulations are mandated for this type of emission and more stringent measures are being used to prevent excess emission of the particulate matter. Electronic components are being introduced to control the injection of the fuel at precisely the proper time of piston travel, to achieve the optimum in fuel ignition and fuel usage. Other particulate after-burning components are being tested to achieve a cleaner particular emission.

Good grades of engine lubricating oils should be used, meeting the manufacturers specification. 'Cut-rate' oils can contribute to the particulate emission problem because of their low 'flash' or ignition temperature point. Such oils burn prematurely during the combustion process causing emissions of particulate matter.

The cooling system is an important factor in the reduction of particulate matter. With the cooling system operating at a temperature specified by the manufacturer, the optimum of combustion will occur. The cooling system must be maintained in the same manner as the engine oiling system, as each system is required to perform properly in order for the engine to operate efficiently for a long time.

Other Automobile Emission Sources

Before emission controls were mandated on the internal combustion engines, other sources of engine pollutants were discovered, along with the exhaust emission. It was determined the engine combustion exhaust produced 60% of the total emission pollutants, fuel evaporation from the fuel tank and carburetor vents produced 20%, with the another 20% being produced through the crankcase as a by-product of the combustion process.

CRANKCASE EMISSIONS

Crankcase emissions are made up of water, acids, unburned fuel, oil fumes and particulates. The emissions are classified as hydrocarbons (HC) and are formed by the small amount of unburned, compressed air/fuel mixture entering the crankcase from the combustion area during the compression and power strokes, between the cylinder walls and piston rings. The head of the compression and combustion help to form the remaining crankcase emissions.

Since the first engines, crankcase emissions were allowed to go into the air through a road draft tube, mounted on the lower side of the engine block. Fresh air came in through an open oil filler cap or breather. The air passed through the crankcase mixing with blow-by gases. The motion of the vehicle and the air blowing past the open end of the road draft tube caused a low pressure area at the end of the tube. Crankcase emissions were simply drawn out of the road draft tube into the air.

To control the crankcase emission, the road draft tube was deleted. A hose and/or tubing was routed from the crankcase to the intake manifold so the blow-by emission could be burned with the air/fuel mixture. However, it was found that intake manifold vacuum, used to draw the crankcase emissions into the manifold, would vary in strength at the wrong time and not allow the proper emission flow. A regulating type valve was needed to control the flow of air through the crankcase.

Testing, showed the removal of the blow-by gases from the crankcase as quickly as possible, was most important to the longevity of the engine. Should large accumulations of blow-by gases remain and condense, dilution of the engine oil would occur to form water, soots, resins, acids and lead salts, resulting in the formation of sludge and varnishes. This condensation of the blow-by gases occur more frequently on vehicles used in numerous starting and stopping conditions, excessive idling and when the engine is not allowed to attain normal operating temperature through short runs. The crankcase purge control or PCV system will be described in detail later in this section.

FUEL EVAPORATIVE EMISSIONS

Gasoline fuel is a major source of pollution, before and after it is burned in the automobile engine. From the time the fuel is refined, stored, pumped and transported, again stored until it is pumped into the fuel tank of the vehicle, the gasoline gives off unburned hydrocarbons (HC) into the atmosphere. Through redesigning of the storage areas and venting systems, the pollution factor has been diminished but not eliminated, from the refinery standpoint. However, the automobile still remained the primary source of vaporized, unburned hydrocarbon (HC) emissions.

Fuel pumped form an underground storage tank is cool but when exposed to a warmer ambient temperature, will expand. Before controls were mandated, an owner would fill the fuel tank with fuel from an underground storage tank and park the vehicle for some time in warm area, such as a parking lot. As the fuel would warm, it would expand and should no provisions or area be provided for the expansion, the fuel would spill out the filler neck and onto the ground, causing hydrocarbon (HC) pollution and creating a severe fire hazard. To correct this condition, the vehicle manufacturers added overflow plumbing and/or gasoline tanks with built in expansion areas or domes.

However, this did not control the fuel vapor emission from the fuel tank and the carburetor bowl. It was determined that most of the fuel evaporation occurred when the vehicle was stationary and the engine not operating. Most vehicles carry 5-25 gallons (19-95 liters) of gasoline. Should a large concentration of vehicles be parked in one area, such as a large parking lot, excessive fuel vapor emissions would take place, increasing as the temperature increases.

To prevent the vapor emission from escaping into the atmosphere, the fuel system is designed to trap the fuel vapors while the vehicle is stationary, by sealing the fuel system from the atmosphere. A storage system is used to collect and hold the fuel vapors from the carburetor and the fuel tank when the engine is not operating. When the engine is started, the storage system is then purged of the fuel vapors, which are drawn into the engine and burned with the air/fuel mixture.

The components of the fuel evaporative system will be described in detail later in this section.

VOLKSWAGEN EMISSION CONTROLS

General Information

Emission control functions are mostly handled by the engine management system through extremely precise air/fuel ratio control. There are 3 items that are not controlled by the engine management system; crankcase ventilation, fuel evaporative emissions and the catalytic converter. Vehicles sold in California and equipped with Motronic fuel injection are also equipped with an Exhaust Gas Recirculation (EGR) valve to help control NOx formations.

Crankcase Ventilation System

OPERATION

▶ **See Figure 1**

To send oil fumes and crankcase blow-by gasses into the engine for burning, all engines are equipped with some type of crankcase breather control valve. Volkswagen uses two different types; one is a simple restrictor and the other is a spring loaded diaphragm.

On 16V engines, a breather is mounted to the side of the engine block near the oil cooler. The breather contains a baffle plate that allows the oil to condense out of the blow-by gasses and drain back to the engine. The large hose connects to the air cleaner so filtered air can be drawn in as required. The small hose connecting to the intake manifold has a built-in restrictor orifice, creating a controlled vacuum leak to the intake manifold. When the throttle opening is small and manifold vacuum is high, crankcase oil fumes are drawn directly into the intake manifold. When the throttle opening is large and manifold vacuum low, some of the oil fumes flow through the large hose to the air cleaner.

The 8 valve engines are equipped with a diaphragm control valve mounted in the top of the cylinder head cover and connecting to the intake manifold. The spring and diaphragm maintain a constant balance against manifold vacuum, keeping blow-by vapor flow at a constant percentage of the total intake air volume. Another hose connecting to the air cleaner allows filtered air into the engine as required.

SERVICE

On both systems, there is no service required other than to check for damage that may cause vacuum leaks.

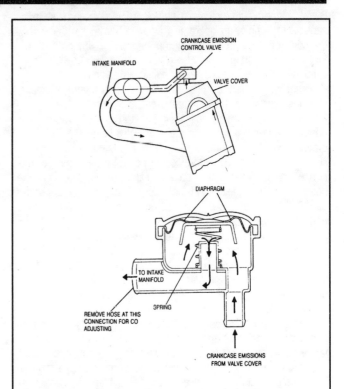

Fig. 1 Crankcase ventilation system on 8 valve engines uses a diaphragm valve mounted on top of the valve cover

Evaporative Emission Controls

OPERATION

▶ **See Figures 2 and 3**

This system prevents the escape of raw fuel vapors (unburned hydrocarbons, or HC) into the atmosphere. When the engine is not running, fuel vapors that build up in the tank flow through a hose to a carbon canister located in the inner fender below the air cleaner. When the engine is running, the vapors in the canister are carried to the intake manifold and burned in the engine.

On vehicles with a Digifant engine management system, the evaporative emission system is completely vacuum operated. The canister is purged of fuel vapors when a vacuum actuated valve is opened and fresh air is drawn into the open bottom of the canister. Vacuum for the valve is generated only at partial throttle openings. The purge air flows to the intake manifold through an orifice that limits the flow. These two features avoid radical air/fuel mixture changes when the canister is purged.

On vehicles with CIS-E fuel injection, the carbon canister is isolated from the intake manifold by a solenoid valve and a frequency valve. The solenoid valve is **ON** (open) whenever the engine is running. The frequency valve is cycled open and closed by the Motronic control unit to control flow rate depending on coolant temperature and engine speed/load conditions.

On both systems, the vacuum line to the canister connects to the vacuum vent valve. This valve is mounted near the fuel filler and allows vapors to flow to the canister but will close if the vehicle turns over to prevent a liquid fuel leak.

SERVICE

The system does not require any service under normal conditions other than to check for leaks. Check the hoses visually for cracks and check the seal on the gas tank filler cap. Replace the cap if the seal is split. If any hoses are in need of replacement, use only hoses marked EVAP, available from your local automotive supply store. If there is a strong smell of raw fuel from under the hood when the engine is not running, test the purge control valve.

TESTING

Motronic System

1. With the engine **OFF**, disconnect the hoses from both valves and connect a clean length of hose. It should be possible to blow through the frequency valve (normally open) but not the solenoid valve (normally closed).

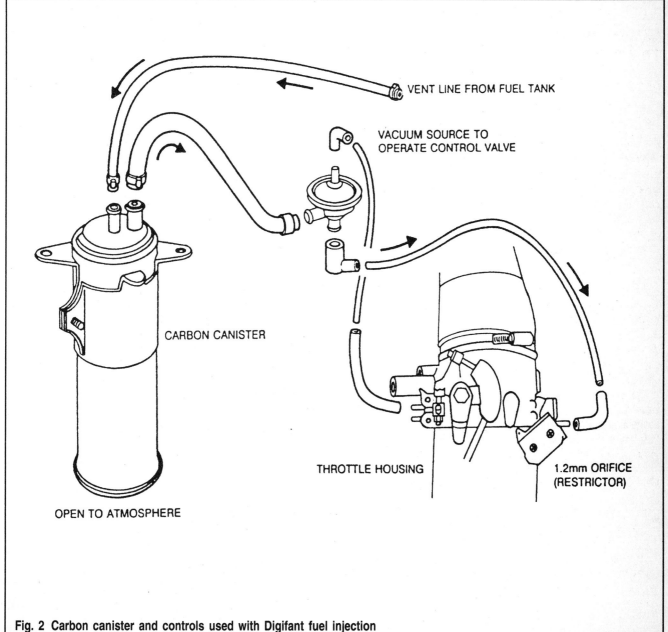

VENT LINE FROM FUEL TANK

VACUUM SOURCE TO OPERATE CONTROL VALVE

CARBON CANISTER

OPEN TO ATMOSPHERE

THROTTLE HOUSING

1.2mm ORIFICE (RESTRICTOR)

Fig. 2 Carbon canister and controls used with Digifant fuel injection

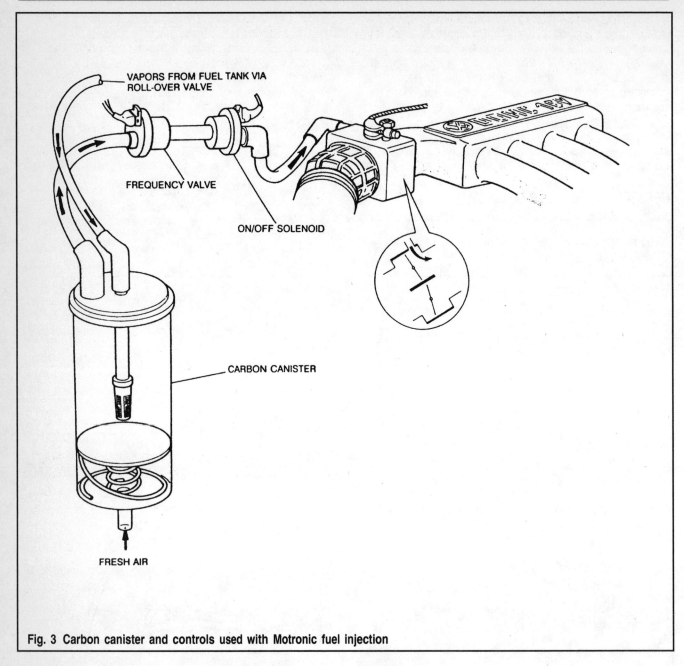

Fig. 3 Carbon canister and controls used with Motronic fuel injection

2. With the engine coolant less than 140°F (60°C), disconnect the purge hose from the canister to the frequency valve. With the engine at idle, there should be no vacuum.

3. As the engine warms to operating temperature, the solenoid valve should be **ON** and open. The frequency valve should begin to cycle **ON** and **OFF**, open and closed. There will be strong vacuum for about 30 seconds, then little or no vacuum for about 60 seconds.

4. If the system does not perform as described, pull back the connector boots so a voltmeter or test light can be connected with the wiring still connected to the valves. If voltage appears at the intervals described, 1 or both of the valves is faulty. If there is no voltage, the wiring or the engine control unit may be faulty.

Digifant System

1. Disconnect the top hose from the valve and connect a hand vacuum pump to the small port on top of the valve.

2. Disconnect the hose from the carbon canister to the control valve and run the engine at idle to provide vacuum to the bottom port.

3. Place a finger over the open port of the valve. When there is vacuum at the bottom port, you should not feel any vacuum at the open port.

4. Draw a vacuum on the small top port. The valve should open and you should feel vacuum at the open port.

Exhaust Gas Recirculation System

GENERAL INFORMATION

Vehicles sold in California with Motronic fuel injection are equipped with an EGR valve. To reduce oxides of nitrogen (NOx) emissions, metered amounts of exhaust gases are added to the air/fuel mixture to lower the peak flame temperature during combustion. The vacuum operated EGR valve controls the volume of exhaust gas flow into the intake manifold. Vacuum for the valve is controlled by coolant temperature and supplied through a vacuum amplifier. The EGR valve is closed when the engine is cold or at idle or full throttle. The valve is partially open just above idle and fully open at mid throttle settings.

TESTING

EGR Valve

▶ See Figure 4

1. With the engine at idle, connect a hand vacuum pump to the EGR valve and draw a vacuum. The engine should idle rough or even stall. This indicates the valve is opening and closing fully.
2. Reconnect the vacuum hose to the EGR valve, disconnect the vacuum supply hose at the thermoswitch and connect the hand pump. Draw a vacuum to make sure the thermoswitch operates. If the engine is cold, the idle should not change. If the coolant temperature is above about 120°F (49°C), the thermoswitch should open and allow vacuum to the EGR valve.
3. To test the vacuum amplifier, connect a tee fitting and vacuum gauge or mercury column to the amplifier input hose, between the throttle body and the amplifier. At idle, there should be about 0.3 inches (7.6mm) Hg vacuum.
4. Tee the gauge into the amplifier output hose, between the amplifier and the thermoswitch. At idle there should be about 1.9-3.5 inches (48-89mm) Hg vacuum.

REMOVAL & INSTALLATION

EGR Valve

1. Disconnect the vacuum hose from the EGR valve.
2. Unbolt the EGR line fitting on the opposite side of the valve.
3. Remove the two retaining bolts and lift the EGR valve from the intake manifold.
4. Installation is the reverse of removal. Use new gaskets and torque the bolts to 7 ft. lbs. (10 Nm).

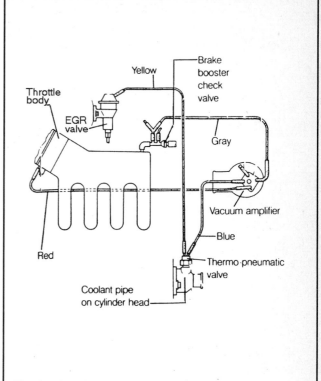

Fig. 4 EGR valve and control system on Motronic engines

Catalytic Converter

GENERAL INFORMATION

Gasoline Engine

The most obvious part of emission controls is the catalytic converter. It's function is to combine unburned hydrocarbons (HC) and carbon monoxide (CO) with oxygen to produce carbon dioxide (CO_2). It also helps to break down oxides of nitrogen (NOx). The catalyst operates in a very narrow range of exhaust gas oxygen concentration. Using signals from the oxygen sensor, the engine control unit constantly adjusts air/fuel ratio to provide the proper amount of oxygen to the catalyst.

All models use a 3-way catalyst for emissions control. It consists of a ceramic substrate that can handle the high temperatures generated inside. The substrate is coated with platinum-group metals that react with CO, HC and NOx. This is a totally passive device; there are no actuators or sensors and no additional air is required. It has no influence on the operation of the engine, unless it has melted and causes high exhaust backpressure. If this is suspected, the catalyst can be removed for inspection. By looking into the catalyst inlet, it should be possible to see through almost all of the passages in the honeycomb pattern ceramic blocks. If there is any melting which may cause high back pressure, it will be quite obvious. The most common cause of melting is raw fuel in the exhaust, such as when a failed spark plug is not replaced.

> ☀☀**CAUTION**
>
> **Catalytic converters operate at temperatures in excess of 1500°F. Do not park the vehicle in high grass or over combustible material. Do not remove the heat shields. Allow the vehicle to cool down before working on the exhaust system.**

Diesel Engine

The catalytic converter used on the ECO Diesel engine performs much the same way as in gasoline engines, however there are some differences. There is a different mix of catalyst metals, the ceramic substrate is designed for use with diesel engines and operating temperatures tend to be lower. The converter is used to reduce CO emissions and remove most of the odor of diesel exhaust. Like its gasoline counterpart, there are no controls or moving parts and no maintenance is required. If there is high exhaust backpressure and the catalytic converter is suspected of melting, it can be inspected by looking into the inlet with the unit removed.

Oxygen Sensor

GENERAL INFORMATION

This sensor is used to report the concentration of oxygen in the exhaust. It consists of a tube coated with platinum on the outside and zirconia on the inside. The tube is protected with a slotted outer shield. The platinum side is exposed only to exhaust gas. If there is any oxygen in the exhaust, a voltage is generated across the dissimilar metals that the engine control unit can read. The sensor operates only when it is above about 600°F. The sensor includes a built-in heater for faster response when the engine is started cold.

ELECTRONIC ENGINE CONTROLS

➡**Volkswagen uses two different engine management systems; Motronic and Digifant. These systems will be covered separately.**

Motronic System

GENERAL DESCRIPTION

▶ **See Figure 5**

The CIS-E Motronic system used on 16V engines is the latest development of the CIS-E fuel injection system. The system uses mechanical injectors, a fuel distributor, fuel pump and air flow sensor that are similar to those on earlier systems. Most of the electronic system controls are also the same. The major difference that the Electronic Control Unit

TESTING

➡**An exhaust gas analyzer is required to test the oxygen sensor.**

1. Disconnect the wiring at the sensor. If there is a brown wire, it is ground for the sensor heater. The green wire is for the sensor itself, the other wire is for voltage to the heater. On the wiring harness side of the connector, there should be 12 volts at the heater wire terminal with the ignition switch **ON**.

2. Turn the ignition switch **OFF** and connect an ohmmeter to the heater wire on the sensor connector. There should be 3-15 ohms resistance between the sensor heater and ground.

3. To test the sensor output, reconnect the wiring and warm the engine to normal operating temperature.

4. Remove the blue cap from the exhaust gas sample tap and insert the probe of an exhaust gas analyzer. With the engine at idle, disconnect the fuel pressure regulator vacuum hose from the intake manifold and plug the port. The CO reading should increase momentarily, then return to the original value. If it does not, the sensor or the engine control unit is faulty.

5. If the CO reading does not return to normal, Disconnect the sensor wiring and connect a jumper wire to the green wire terminal on the harness connector.

6. Touch the jumper wire to a flash light battery and ground the battery. This will send a 1.5 volt signal to the control unit.

7. Touch the wire alternately to the battery and to ground. If the CO reading changes, the engine control unit is functioning properly.

REMOVAL & INSTALLATION

The sensor is threaded into the catalytic converter or the exhaust pipe with an anti-seize compound on the threads. When replacing it, be careful not to get anti-seize in the slots of the outer shield. Torque to 37 ft. lbs. (50 Nm).

(ECU) now controls the ignition system as well as fuel injection. The new ECU is equipped with an adaptive learning program which allows it to learn and remember the normal operating range of the mixture control output signal. This gives the system the capability to compensate for changes in altitude, slight vacuum leaks or other changes due to things such as engine wear. Cold engine drivability and emissions are improved. The new ECU also is capable of cold start enrichment without the use of a thermo-time switch.

The fuel injector pressure is higher for better fuel atomization and residual pressure. The threads on the new injectors are different so they cannot be interchanged with older units. Some other components such as sensors are similar to those used on the Digifant engine management system. Some of the testing procedures are the same but the parts are not necessarily interchangeable.

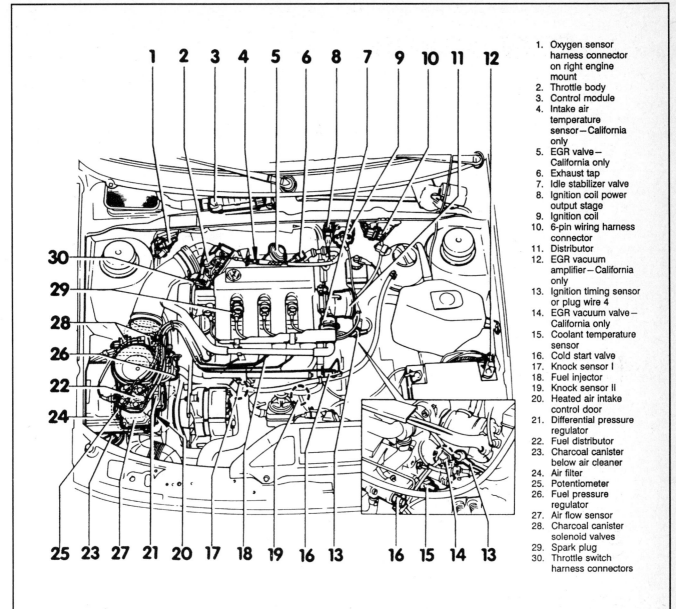

1. Oxygen sensor harness connector on right engine mount
2. Throttle body
3. Control module
4. Intake air temperature sensor—California only
5. EGR valve—California only
6. Exhaust tap
7. Idle stabilizer valve
8. Ignition coil power output stage
9. Ignition coil
10. 6-pin wiring harness connector
11. Distributor
12. EGR vacuum amplifier—California only
13. Ignition timing sensor or plug wire 4
14. EGR vacuum valve—California only
15. Coolant temperature sensor
16. Cold start valve
17. Knock sensor I
18. Fuel injector
19. Knock sensor II
20. Heated air intake control door
21. Differential pressure regulator
22. Fuel distributor
23. Charcoal canister below air cleaner
24. Air filter
25. Potentiometer
26. Fuel pressure regulator
27. Air flow sensor
28. Charcoal canister solenoid valves
29. Spark plug
30. Throttle switch harness connectors

Fig. 5 Schematic of CIS-E Motronic fuel injection system

Electronic Control Unit (ECU)

This unit is located above the firewall in the engine compartment. The ECU is supplied with an internal voltage regulator and operates at 8 volts to prevent control fluctuations when vehicle accessories are switched on. The ECU accepts the various input signals and calculates optimum fuel injection and ignition output control signals. The main output devices are the differential pressure regulator, ignition coil and the idle air stabilizer valve. The maximum engine speed is limited by the ECU through the differential pressure regulator. Above the tachometer 'red line', the lower chamber pressure is increased relative to the system pressure and the fuel supply to the injectors is interrupted.

The ECU is equipped with an adaptive learning program that learns the normal operating point of the air/fuel mixture. This information comes from the oxygen sensor and is only read when the charcoal canister frequency valve is in the **OFF** cycle. As the engine wears or is driven differently or with changes in altitude, control signals that the ECU considers 'normal' are modified to account for the deviations.

Fuel Distributor

▶ See Figure 6

The fuel distributor used in the Motronic system is very different from that used in earlier CIS systems. The unit is made of aluminum and is slightly smaller. The pressure relief valve and the frequency valve are no longer needed. Control plunger movement controls the amount of fuel supplied to the upper chamber. A differential pressure regulator mounted on the side controls the pressure in the lower chamber which ultimately controls the fuel flow to the injectors. When the engine is not running, the control plunger rests on an O-ring and there is some free-play between the plunger and air flow sensor arm. As before, the fuel distributor cannot be repaired, although the plunger O-ring can be replaced. When the fuel distributor is replaced, the plunger free-play must be adjusted. This adjustment affects hot start and fuel distributor sealing when the engine is not running. The adjustment procedure is provided with the removal and installation procedure in Section 5. Do not make any adjustments or remove the fuel distributor without checking system pressures first.

Air Flow Sensor and Position Sensor
▶ See Figure 8

The fuel distributor is mounted on top of a mechanical air flow sensor. Under the air duct boot is a venturi with a plate in the narrowest part of the bore. As the throttle opens and air flow increases, the plate is pushed farther up in the bore. This lifts a piston that uncovers slots in the fuel distributor to allow more fuel to the upper chamber.

The vertical position of the plate is measured with a potentiometer. A voltage is supplied to the position sensor and the portion of the signal returned to the ECU indicates the height of the sensor plate in the bore.

Idle Stabilizer Valve
▶ See Figure 9

The idle stabilizer is a motorized rotary valve that is operated by the ECU to control the amount of air that bypasses the throttle. This design allows very precise control of idle speed regardless of engine temperature or load. The valve is spring loaded towards the minimum opening position. The voltage that holds the valve open is applied in variable length pulses called a duty cycle. The duty cycle ranges from 5-95 percent. Because of this design, there is no idle speed adjustment.

Fuel Accumulator

The fuel accumulator is used to absorb variations in pump pressure that might effect pressure at the injectors. It also helps to maintain residual pressure when the engine is turned off. The accumulator is mounted next to the reservoir. There is no specific test for the accumulator and it cannot be repaired. If the fuel system cannot maintain residual pressure and the pressure fluctuates during the system pressure test, the fuel accumulator is faulty.

Fuel Pressure Regulators

The ECU controls the air/fuel ratio by adjusting the pressure in the lower chambers of the fuel distributor. The differential pressure regulator is attached to side of the fuel distributor. It consists of a plate with an electromagnet on either side. Resistance of the coils is 15-20 ohms. The ECU controls the current to the magnets, moving the plate side to side, which controls the size of the opening to the lower chamber. When the lower chamber pressure is high, the diaphragms are pushed up towards the outlets of the upper chamber, making the outlets smaller and reducing fuel flow. This provides for very fine adjustment of fuel flow to the injectors while maintaining the same pressure at the injectors. Pressure in the lower chambers ranges from 0-24 psi (0-1.6 BAR) lower than system pressure.

Also connected to the fuel distributor is the system pressure regulator. It is a simple spring and diaphragm type, with intake

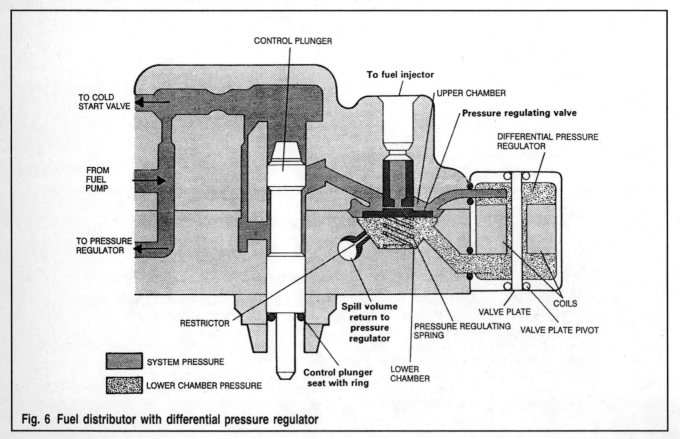

SYSTEM PRESSURE

LOWER CHAMBER PRESSURE

Fig. 6 Fuel distributor with differential pressure regulator

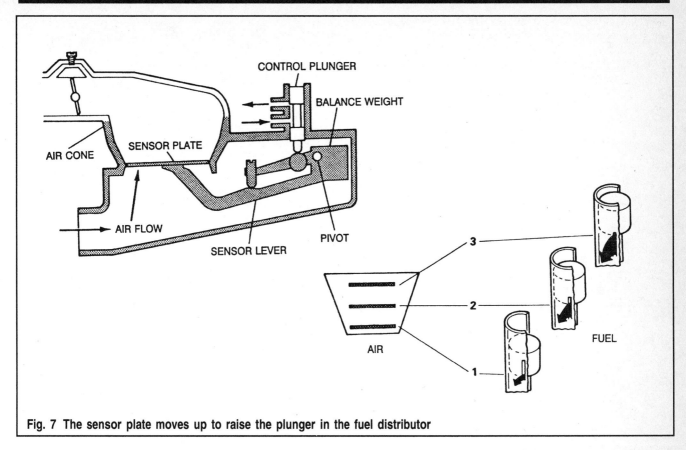

Fig. 7 The sensor plate moves up to raise the plunger in the fuel distributor

manifold vacuum connected to the diaphragm. As manifold vacuum changes with increasing engine load, the regulator adjusts system pressure to meet the increased fuel demand.

COMPONENT TESTING

Air Flow Sensor and Position Sensor

1. Remove the rubber boot from the top of the air flow sensor and lift the plate with pliers or a magnet. DO NOT not loosen the bolt. The plate should move up smoothly with some resistance and should drop when released. The plate rests on a spring which allows it to move down if the engine backfires.

2. To test the position sensor, make sure the ignition switch is **OFF** and unplug the connector. Check the resistance between terminals 1 and 2; it should be more than 4000

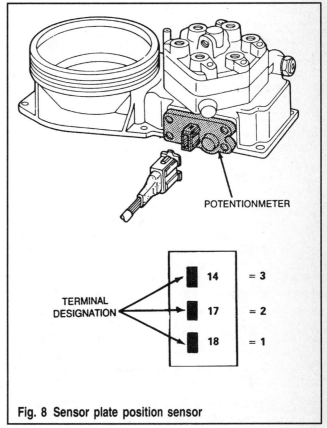

Fig. 8 Sensor plate position sensor

Fig. 9 Idle stabilizer valve is below the spark plug wire tray

ohms. Check the resistance between terminals 2 and 3; it should be less than 1000 ohms.

3. With the ohmmeter connected to terminals 2 and 3, move the plate up and down. The resistance should change smoothly to more than 4000 ohms at full travel.

4. Turn the ignition switch **ON**. Connect a voltmeter between terminals 1 and 3 of the wiring connector. There should be 4.5-5.5 volts from the ECU.

Idle Stabilizer Valve

1. With the valve installed, turn the ignition switch **ON** but do not start the engine. It should be possible to hear or feel the valve hum and/or vibrate.

2. Turn the ignition switch **OFF**. Unplug the connector from the idle stabilizer valve and connect an ohmmeter across the valve terminals. There should be 7-11 ohms resistance. Resistance may be higher on a warm engine.

3. Disable the ignition system so the engine will not start. Connect a voltmeter or an LED test lamp between terminal 1 of the connector and ground. When the starter is operated, there should be voltage at terminal 1.

4. Remove the valve and check for visual signs of scoring or binding on the rotating portion. Do not lubricate the valve. If it is receiving voltage but does not operate, it must be replaced.

FUEL PRESSURE TESTING

System and Differential Pressure
▶ See Figures 10, 11 and 12

❄❄CAUTION

The following procedure will produce fuel vapors. Make sure there is proper ventilation and take the appropriate fire safety precautions.

A special fuel pressure test gauge, small jumper wires and a multi-meter that reads milliamps are required to test the system. The gauge set is the standard VW1318 or an equivalent 0-140 psi (0-10 BAR) gauge with a tee fitting and a shut-off valve.

1. Disconnect the cold start injector line and connect the shut-off valve to the fuel distributor. Connect the other side of the tee to the lower chamber test point on the fuel distributor. This means that when the valve is open, the upper and lower chambers are connected by the test gauge lines. When the valve is closed, the gauge reads only lower chamber pressure. Connect the gauge to the third leg of the tee.

2. To test the differential pressure regulator, unplug the connector and connect the multi-meter to terminal 2 of the connector. Connect jumper wires so the meter will read the current draw when the regulator is operating. A special test harness is available to make these connections easier, VW tool no. 1315A/1.

➡**Do not let the jumper wires short together. If the wires touch when the ignition switch is ON, the ECU will be permanently damaged.**

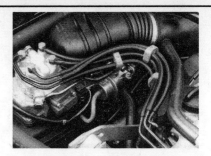

Fig. 10 The system pressure regulator is next to the differential pressure regulator. Disconnect the smaller fitting to the right to check flow rate.

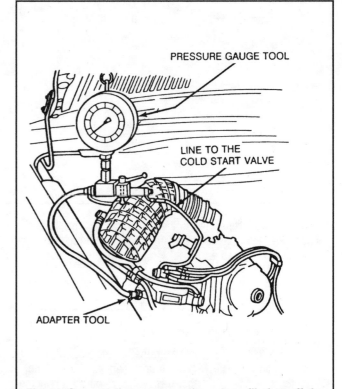

Fig. 11 Connect the gauge so the valve will shut off the upper chamber

3. On the fuse/relay panel under the dashboard, remove the fuel pump relay from the bottom right socket of the panel. A description of the panel appears in Section 6.

4. Connect a jumper wire with a switch to terminals **30** and **87** on the panel (they may be labeled 4 and 5). The fuel pump will run any time the switch is **ON**, even if the ignition switch is **OFF**.

5. With the ignition **OFF** and the test valve open, run the fuel pump to check system pressure; it should be 88-95 psi (6.1-6.6 BAR).

6. If the pressure is too high, there may be a blockage in the return line to the tank. If the system pressure is low, flow test the pump as described later.

7. If system pressure is correct, close the valve to read pressure in the lower chamber only and stop the pump. The

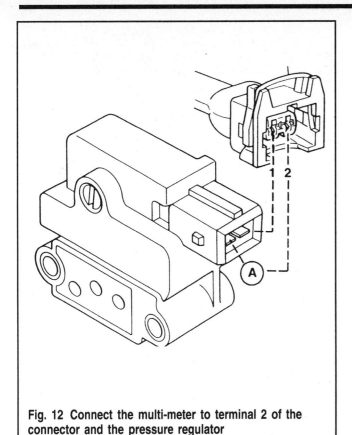

Fig. 12 Connect the multi-meter to terminal 2 of the connector and the pressure regulator

pressure should be about 4.5-7.5 psi (0.3 — 0.5 BAR) BELOW system pressure. If differential pressure is too low;

a. Disconnect the small fuel return line from the fuel distributor to the system pressure regulator and hold it in a container.

b. Run the pump for 1 minute and time the run carefully.

c. The flow should be 3.8-4.4 oz. (130-150cc). If the flow is correct but differential pressure is low, the differential pressure regulator may be faulty.

d. If the system pressure is correct but differential pressure and flow are both low, the fuel distributor is probably faulty.

8. To test differential pressure regulator current draw, stop the pump and turn the ignition switch **ON**. The multi-meter should read about 100 milliamps. With the fuel pump running, pressure in the lower chamber should stabilize at 19-23 psi (1.3-1.6 BAR).

9. If current draw and differential pressure are both incorrect, look for a bad connection or wiring problem between the regulator and the ECU. Check the resistance across the terminals on the differential pressure regulator; it should be 15-20 ohms. If no electrical problem is found, the differential pressure regulator is faulty.

Residual Pressure

1. If the engine has hot start problems, the system residual pressure may be leaking off. Connect the pressure gauge and test system pressure as described above.

2. Open the valve and run the pump with the ignition switch **OFF**. Stop the pump and note the pressure. After 10 minutes the pressure must not be lower than 48 psi (3.3 BAR). After 20 minutes, the pressure must be at least 46.5 psi (3.2 BAR).

3. If residual pressure is low, look for leaks at the fuel distributor O-ring under the plunger. This will appear as fuel dripping onto the air filter. Other possibilities are the fuel pump check valve, the fuel accumulator, a leaking injector, the fuel pressure regulator or improper free-play between the air flow sensor arm and the plunger in the fuel distributor. This is only likely if the fuel distributor has been removed.

FUEL PUMPS

▶ **See Figures 13, 14 and 15**

The Motronic system uses 2 fuel pumps, a small transfer pump inside the tank and the main pressure pump under the vehicle. The transfer pump is part of the fuel gauge sending unit but it can be replaced separately. It is accessed through a panel under the rear seat.

The main fuel pump is inside the reservoir in front of the rear axle beam. The pump incorporates a check valve to maintain pressure in the system when the pump is off to aid hot starts. The fuel filter is mounted to the side of the reservoir and is a 'lifetime' filter which only needs to be replaced if the fuel has been contaminated.

When the ignition switch is first turned **ON**, the pump will run for about 2 seconds and then stop if the ECU is not receiving an rpm signal from the Hall sender. The pump is operated by the ECU through a relay located on the main fuse/relay panel. The main relay terminals can be jumpered to run the pump for testing. A pump pressure test is described above.

Electrical Testing

1. With the engine cold, turn the ignition switch **ON** and listen to hear the fuel pumps run for about 2 seconds, then stop.

2. On the fuse/relay panel under the dashboard, remove the fuel pump relay from the bottom right socket of the panel. With the ignition switch **ON**, there should 12 volts at terminal 86. This is power for the relay coil that comes from the ignition switch.

3. The 2 largest terminals operate the fuel pump. With or without the ignition switch **ON**, there should be 12 volts at terminal 30.

4. When the large terminals are jumpered, the fuel pump will receive 12 volts even without the ignition. Use a jumper with a switch, such as a remote starter button, to check for voltage at the pump or to run the pump for pressure and flow testing.

5. When the jumper switch is **ON**, there should be 12 volts at the center and end terminals of the transfer pump connector. There should also be 12 volts at the main pump connector.

Fig. 13 Fuel pump, reservoir, filter and accumulator assembly

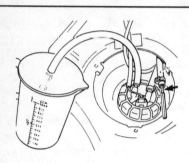

Fig. 14 Flow testing the transfer pump is the same on Motronic and Digifant systems

Flow Testing

✳✳CAUTION

The following procedures will produce fuel vapors. Make sure there is proper ventilation and take the appropriate fire safety precautions.

TRANSFER PUMP

1. Locate and remove the fuel pump relay and connect a jumper wire with a switch to the 2 largest terminals in the relay socket. Make sure the switch is **OFF**.

2. Disconnect the black fuel supply line from the transfer pump and plug the line. Connect a test line to the fitting and place the other end in a measuring container.

3. Remove the fuel filler cap and run the pump for 10 seconds. Time the run carefully.

4. The pump should deliver at least 10 oz. (300 cc) of fuel. If the flow is low, remove the pump see if the strainer is clogged. If not, the pump is faulty and must be replaced.

MAIN PUMP

1. Locate and remove the fuel pump relay and connect a jumper wire with a switch to the 2 largest terminals in the relay socket. Make sure the switch is **OFF**.

2. Disconnect the fuel return line at a point after the system pressure regulator in the engine compartment. Secure the line in a minimum 1 quart measuring container.

3. Use the switch to operate the fuel pump for 30 seconds. Time the operation carefully. The current draw will usually drop the voltage at the pump to about 2 volts less than battery voltage. Check the table below for flow rate.

FUEL INJECTORS

▶ **See Figures 16 and 17**

The CIS-E Motronic system uses air shrouded injectors. The injectors are mounted into inserts that are threaded into an air passage in the cylinder head. When the intake valve is open and air is flowing into the cylinder, a small amount of air also flows through the injector insert and swirls around the tip of the injector. This helps atomize the fuel spray for smoother and cleaner engine performance. The inserts and injectors used in the Motronic system are different from those used in earlier air shrouded injector systems and cannot be interchanged.

The injectors in all CIS systems are purely mechanical and open at a pre-determined pressure. All injectors are open when the engine is running, injecting fuel to the intake ports continuously. The spray pattern is critical to good atomization of the fuel, which will affect power and emissions. The injectors can be tested for spray pattern and leakage with tool US4480 or equivalent. This is a set of clear, graduated cylinders that allow viewing the spray pattern and measuring the fuel flow.

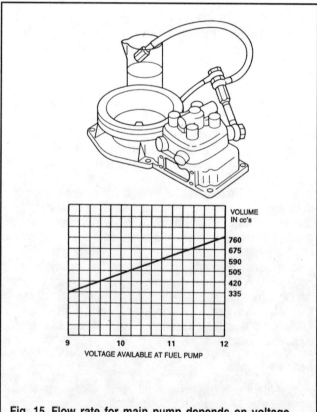

Fig. 15 Flow rate for main pump depends on voltage

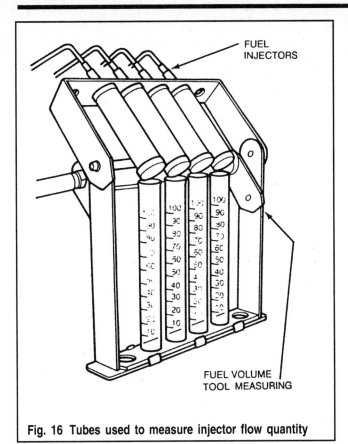

Fig. 16 Tubes used to measure injector flow quantity

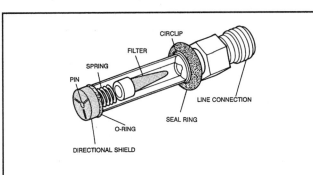

Fig. 17 Mechanical fuel injector on CIS-E Motronic system

Testing

1. Remove the injectors by prying them out of their rubber O-rings. If necessary, use a silicone spray to ease removal. Inspect the injectors for signs of leakage. They should not be wet.

2. Carefully route the fuel lines so the injectors can be inserted into the tubes.

3. Locate and remove the fuel pump relay on the main fuse panel and connect a jumper wire with a switch to terminals **30** and **87** on the panel. The fuel pump will run any time the switch is **ON**.

4. Remove the air flow sensor boot and insert a 0.020-0.040 inch (0.05-1.0mm) feeler gauge between the air flow sensor plate and the housing so the plate is slightly lifted.

5. Operate the fuel pump and observe the spray pattern. It should be a narrow conical pattern, even all the way around. Move the sensor plate up higher to see how the pattern changes. Any irregularity in the pattern indicates a partially clogged injector. Raising the sensor plate all the way may clear it.

6. After one tube has about 20cc, stop the fuel pump and observe the injectors. Note the quantity of fuel in each tube; they should all be within 2cc of each other.

7. Repeat the test with the sensor plate all the way up to flow about 80cc of fuel. The flows should all be within 8cc.

8. If an injector flows high or low, move it to another line and flow test them again. If the incorrect flow follows the injector, the injector is faulty. If the incorrect flow stays with the same fuel line, the line or the fuel distributor is faulty.

9. To leak test the injectors, remove the feeler gauge so the sensor plate is resting on its stop and run the fuel pump. There should be no fuel dripping from any injector. Any injector with a bad spray pattern, leak or incorrect flow quantity must be replaced.

COLD START INJECTOR

▶ **See Figure 18**

The cold start injector is supplied with system pressure whenever the pump is running. It is a simple solenoid valve with a spray nozzle on the end, operated directly by the ECU according to coolant temperature. The injector spray pattern can be tested by removing it from the intake manifold, however an assistant is required.

Testing

1. Disconnect the wiring to the cold start injector and connect a voltmeter or test light to the connector.

2. Disconnect the power output stage wiring from the coil so the engine will not start.

3. If the engine is not cold, disconnect the blue temperature sensor connector. Connect another coolant temperature sensor or a 15,000 ohm resistor across the wiring terminals to simulate a cold engine.

4. Have an assistant operate the starter with the key for about 10 seconds. There should be power to the injector connector for about 8 seconds.

5. To check spray pattern, remove the 2 screws to remove the injector but do not disconnect the fuel line. Reconnect the wiring.

6. Hold the injector over a container and have an assistant operate the starter for about 10 seconds. The injector should pulse fuel, making an even cone spray pattern, for about 8 seconds.

7. Release the ignition key and dry the end of the injector. The injector should not drip or become wet for at least 1 minute.

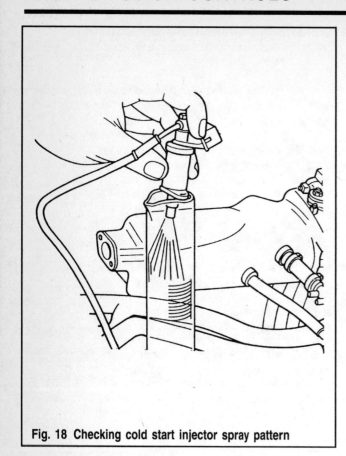

Fig. 18 Checking cold start injector spray pattern

TEMPERATURE SENSOR

There are two coolant temperature sensors mounted in the upper radiator hose-to-engine flange. The black connector is for the gauge on the instrument panel. The blue connector is for the ECU.

Testing

1. Disconnect the electrical connector at the sensor.
2. Using an ohmmeter, check the sensor resistance.
3. Compair obtained readings with the desired resistance values listed below. If obtained values differ from the desired reading, replace the sensor.
- 55°F (13°C) — 3000-3800 ohms
- 65°F (18°C) — 2200-3000 ohms
- 75°F (24°C) — 1800-2500 ohms
- 85°F (29°C) — 1500-2100 ohms
- 150°F (65°C) — 400-550 ohms
- 200°F (93°C) — 200-270 ohms

Digifant System

▶ See Figure 19

The Digifant system is all electronic, using electric injectors at a low injection pressure. All injectors are operated by the Electronic Control Unit (ECU) so injector timing and duration can be closely controlled for reduced emissions and improved fuel mileage. During deceleration above a specific rpm, the injectors are shut off to save fuel and reduce emissions. The air flow sensor uses an air vane that moves a potentiometer to signal its position to the ECU. The electric idle stabilizer a motorized rotary valve that controls the amount of air allowed to bypass the throttle plate. Very precise control is maintained over a wide range of idle loads and engine temperatures.

The ECU has the ability to store fault codes but codes and other self diagnostic functions can only be read with the VAG 1551 tester. Procedures described here are for testing without the VAG 1551.

ELECTRONIC CONTROL UNIT (ECU)

The ECU controls all fuel injection, idle speed and ignition functions and also acts as a rev limiter. Above the maximum rpm rating, the ECU will intermittently shut off the fuel injectors to prevent over-revving the engine. If an input or output device fault is detected and it is serious enough to cause engine control problems, the ECU will switch into a 'limp home' mode and the engine will be operated at a pre-set condition. The ECU is mounted in the tray above the fire wall.

AIR FLOW SENSOR

▶ See Figure 20

This unit converts air flow to a voltage signal. Air enters and moves a spring-loaded vane which moves a potentiometer. The potentiometer modulates a voltage sent from the ECU and the return signal represents the mass of air flowing to the intake manifold. Air temperature is also measured and reported to the ECU. The air/fuel mixture adjustment is also in this unit, which is an adjusting screw that allows a certain amount of air to bypass the vane and enter the engine unmeasured. More unmeasured air means a leaner mixture.

Testing

1. With the ignition **OFF**, unplug the sensor connector and measure the resistance across the end terminals of the sensor. These are for the air temperature sensor. At 60°F (15°C), there should be about 3000 ohms. At 80°F (27°C), there should be about 1900 ohms.
2. The resistance between terminals 3 and 4 should be 500-1000 ohms when the flap is in the rest position.
3. Connect the ohmmeter between the center terminals 2 and 3 and move the vane inside the sensor. The resistance should change smoothly and linearly as the vane is moved. There is a strong return spring on the flap but is should move smoothly with no binding.

THROTTLE POSITION SWITCHES

▶ See Figure 21

There are 2 switches on the throttle body, one above and one below. The lower switch signals the ECU when the throttle is at idle and the upper switch signals full throttle. This information is used to calculate fuel shut-off and ignition timing during deceleration, idle stabilizer valve operation and full throttle enrichment. If there is a problem with any of these functions, check these switches first.

1. Fuel pressure regulator
2. CO tap
3. Intake manifold
4. Fuel rail
5. Idle stabilizer valve
6. Full throttle switch
7. Idle speed set screw
8. Throttle support bracket
9. Idle switch
10. Intake air duct
11. Ignition coil
12. Hall sender control unit
13. Digifant ECU
14. 5-pin connector; power for ECU and injectors
15. Air cleaner
16. Air flow sensor with intake air temperature sensor
17. CO adjustment screw
18. Oxygen sensor connector
19. Distributor
20. Crankcase ventilation valve
21. Coolant temperature sensor (black)
22. Coolant temperature sensor (blue)
23. Knock sensor
24. Vacuum booster (automatic transaxle only)
25. Fuel injectors

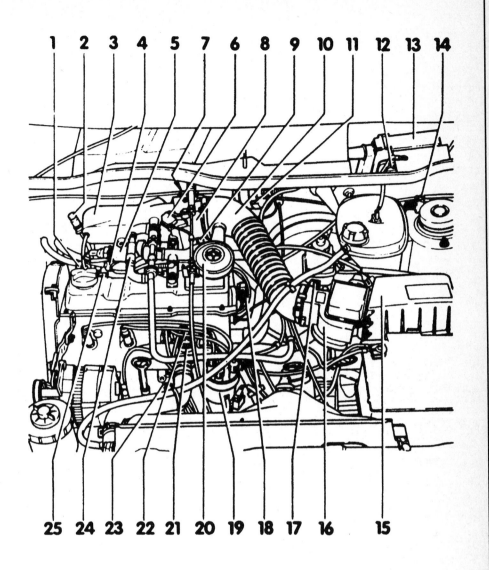

Fig. 19 Schematic of the Digifant fuel injection system — Cabriolet shown

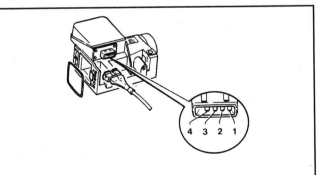

Fig. 20 Terminals for air flow and temperature sensors in the air flow sensor assembly

Testing

1. Locate the switches on the throttle body and unplug the connector.

2. Connect an ohmmeter to the idle switch and make sure it is closed when the throttle is against the stop. Open the throttle, position a 0.024 inch (0.60mm) feeler gauge against the stop and let the throttle close on the gauge. The switch must remain open. DO NOT adjust the throttle stop screw.

3. Connect the ohmmeter to the full throttle switch. Open the throttle all the way to the stop and make sure the switch closes. The switch should open when the throttle is allowed to close 10 degrees from the stop.

4. Turn the ignition switch **ON** and use a voltmeter to check for 5 volts at each switch connector. This signal comes directly from the ECU.

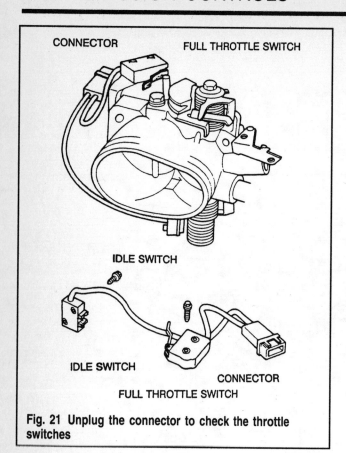

Fig. 21 Unplug the connector to check the throttle switches

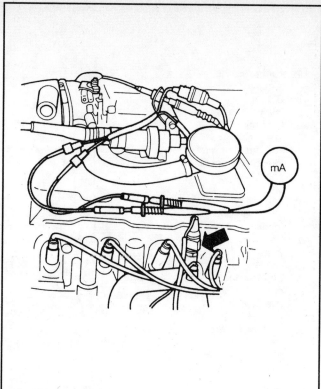

Fig. 22 A special adaptor is required to test the duty cycle of the idle stabilizer valve

IDLE STABILIZER VALVE

▶ See Figure 22

The idle stabilizer is a linear motor solenoid valve that is operated by the ECU. The linear motion moves a plunger to control an opening in the valve which controls the amount of air that bypasses the throttle. This design allows very precise control of idle speed regardless of engine temperature or load. The voltage supplied to the valve can't really be measured because it is not constant. To test the duty cycle of the valve in operation, a special adapter is required that allows connecting a multi-meter that reads milliamps while the wiring is connected to the valve.

Testing

1. With the ignition **ON** but the engine not running, the valve should vibrate to the touch. If not, make sure the idle switch on the throttle body is working properly and that the throttle is fully closed.

2. If there is no vibration at the valve, turn the ignition **OFF** and unplug the connector. Use an ohmmeter to check the resistance across the terminals on the valve. There should be about 2-10 ohms resistance.

3. Connect the adapter so a multi-meter can be connected. With the engine at operating temperature and idling, the current to the valve should fluctuate from 390-460 milliamps. With the blue temperature sensor wiring disconnected, the current should be steady.

4. If the current is not correct, remove the valve and check for visual signs of sticking. Do not lubricate the valve. If no

other problem is found, check the continuity of the wiring between the valve and the ECU with the ignition **OFF**.

5. If the idle stabilizer valve seems to work properly but engine idle is out of specification, check for a vacuum leak, a faulty coolant temperature sensor or some other problem with the engine control system.

FUEL PUMPS

▶ See Figure 23

The Digifant system uses 2 fuel pumps; a small transfer pump inside the tank and the main pressure pump under the vehicle. The transfer pump is part of the fuel gauge sending unit but it can be replaced separately. It is accessed through a panel under the rear seat. The transfer pump fills a reservoir and the main pump is partially immersed inside the reservoir. The pump incorporates a check valve to maintain pressure in the system when the pump is off to aid hot starts. The fuel filter is mounted to the side of the reservoir and is a 'lifetime' filter which only needs to be replaced if the fuel has been contaminated.

When the ignition switch is first turned **ON**, the pump will run for about 2 seconds and then stop if the ECU is not receiving an rpm signal. The pump is operated by the ECU through a relay located on the main fuse/relay panel. The main relay terminals can be jumpered to run the pump for testing. A pump pressure test is described in the pressure regulator test.

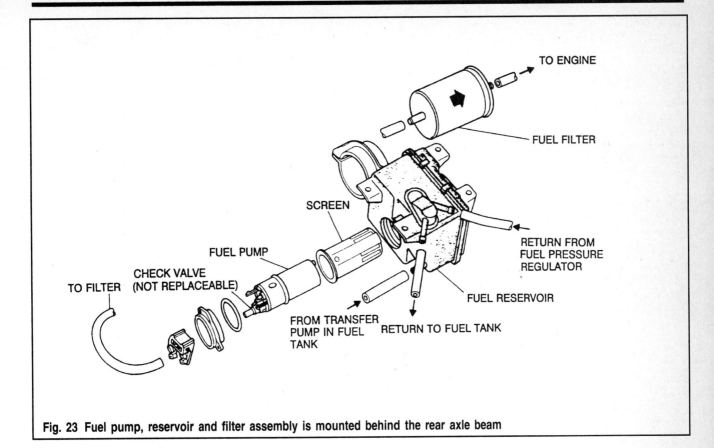

TO ENGINE

FUEL FILTER

SCREEN

RETURN FROM
FUEL PRESSURE
REGULATOR

FUEL PUMP

CHECK VALVE
(NOT REPLACEABLE)

TO FILTER

FUEL RESERVOIR

FROM TRANSFER
PUMP IN FUEL
TANK

RETURN TO FUEL TANK

Fig. 23 Fuel pump, reservoir and filter assembly is mounted behind the rear axle beam

Electrical Testing

1. With the engine cold, turn the ignition switch **ON** and listen to hear the fuel pumps run for about 2 seconds, then stop.

2. On the fuse/relay panel under the dashboard, remove the fuel pump relay. On Golf and Jetta, the relay is on the bottom right socket of the panel. On Cabriolet, the relay is second from the left, second row from the bottom.

3. With the ignition switch **ON**, there should 12 volts at terminal 86. This is power for the relay coil that comes from the ignition switch.

4. The 2 largest terminals operate the fuel pump. With or without the ignition switch **ON**, there should be 12 volts at one of the large terminals. Don't use the other terminal for voltmeter ground.

5. When the large terminals are jumpered, the fuel pump will receive 12 volts even without the ignition. Use a jumper with a switch, such as a remote starter button, to check for voltage at the pump or to run the pump for pressure and flow testing.

6. To check the transfer pump voltage, lift the rear seat and remove the access panel. With the ignition switch **OFF**, unplug the connector.

7. When the jumper switch is **ON**, there should be 12 volts at the center and end terminals of the connector. There should also be 12 volts across the main pump connector terminals under the vehicle.

Flow Testing

✳✳CAUTION

The following procedures will produce fuel vapors. Make sure there is proper ventilation and take the appropriate fire safety precautions.

TRANSFER PUMP

1. Locate and remove the fuel pump relay and connect a jumper wire with a switch to the 2 largest terminals in the relay socket. Make sure the switch is **OFF**.

2. Disconnect the black fuel supply line from the transfer pump and plug the line. Connect a test line to the fitting and place the other end in a measuring container.

3. Remove the fuel filler cap and run the pump for 10 seconds. Time the run carefully.

4. The pump should deliver at least 10 oz. (300 cc) of fuel. If the flow is low, remove the pump see if the strainer is clogged. If not, the pump is faulty and must be replaced.

MAIN PUMP

1. Locate and remove the fuel pump relay and connect a jumper wire with a switch to the 2 largest terminals in the relay socket. Make sure the switch is **OFF**.

2. Disconnect the fuel return line at a point after the system pressure regulator. The fuel return line at the reservoir is a good test point but remember to cap the open fitting on the reservoir. Secure the line in a minimum 1 quart measuring container.

3. Use the switch to operate the fuel pump for 30 seconds. Time the operation carefully. The pump should deliver at least 17 oz. (500 cc) of fuel.

FUEL INJECTORS

▶ **See Figure 24**

The electric injectors are secured in place by the fuel rail, which also houses the wiring. All injectors are wired together in parallel and are operated at the same time. Power is supplied to all injectors any time the ECU is receiving an rpm signal. The ECU operates the injectors by completing the ground circuit. Injectors can be tested electrically as an assembly or tested individually.

Testing

1. Unplug the connector on the end of the fuel rail and read the resistance across the terminals in the rail. A reading of 3.5-5.0 ohms indicates all injectors are good. A reading of 5.0-6.7 ohms indicates 1 bad injector; 7.5-10.0 ohms means 2 bad injectors; 15.0-20.0 ohms indicates 3 bad injectors.

2. If a high resistance is read, disconnect the wiring to all injectors and check each injector resistance individually; it should be 14-18 ohms each. If any injector is replaced, repeat the test in Step 1 to verify the wiring is correct.

3. To check the voltage to the injectors, connect a test light or voltmeter to the connector and operate the starter. The light will flicker and a voltmeter will show some voltage but probably not a full 12 volts. If there is no voltage, try the same test with one test lead connected to engine ground. If there is still no voltage, check the wiring between the ECU and injectors.

FUEL PRESSURE REGULATOR

This is a purely mechanical device, controlled by manifold vacuum. Fuel is supplied to the injectors through the common rail. The regulator controls the pressure in the rail by regulating the amount of fuel returned to the tank. It responds to manifold vacuum fluctuations and thereby compensates for engine load changes. When the engine is shut off, the regulator closes and seals to maintain residual fuel pressure in the injector lines for improved hot-start capability. The following test will also test overall system pressure.

Testing

1. With the engine **OFF**, remove the test connector plug from the service port on the end of the fuel rail.

✴✴CAUTION

A small amount of fuel will be released under pressure. Use a rag to shield and catch the spray and take appropriate fire safety precautions.

2. Attach a 0-60 psi (0-4.1 BAR) pressure gauge to the rail and start the engine. With the engine warm and at idle, the pressure should be about 36 psi (2.5 BAR). With the manifold vacuum hose disconnected, the pressure should increase to about 43 psi (3.0 BAR).

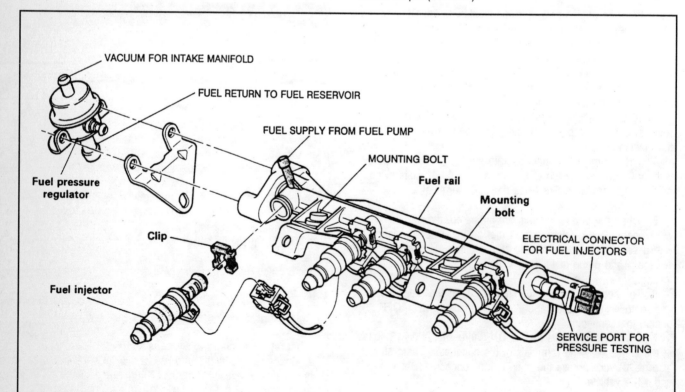

Fig. 24 Digifant fuel injector and rail assembly

3. Stop the engine and note the pressure. After about 10 minutes, the pressure should be no lower than 29 psi (2 BAR).

4. If the pressure has fallen below specification with the engine off, run the engine at idle to build the pressure again. Stop the engine and immediately crimp the fuel return line. If the pressure holds, the regulator is faulty. If the pressure falls, there is a leak somewhere else in the system, possibly the injectors or fuel pump check valve.

TEMPERATURE SENSOR

There are two coolant temperature sensors mounted in the upper radiator hose-to-engine flange. The black connector is for the gauge on the instrument panel. The blue connector is for the ECU.

There is also an air temperature sensor at the inlet end of the air flow sensor. Both temperature sensors operate with the same resistance values.

Testing

1. Unplug the sensor connector.
2. Using an ohmmeter, check the sensor resistance.
3. Compare the obtained values to the desired readings listed below. If resistance varies, replace the sensor.
   - 55°F (13°C) — 3000-3800 ohms
   - 65°F (18°C) — 2200-3000 ohms
   - 75°F (24°C) — 1800-2500 ohms
   - 85°F (29°C) — 1500-2100 ohms
   - 150°F (65°C) — 400-550 ohms
   - 200°F (93°C) — 200-270 ohms

DIAGNOSTIC CODES DATA

General Information

There are two basic engine management systems used, CIS-E Motronic and Digifant. The Motronic system, used on some Golf/Jetta models and all Passat models with the 16 valve 9A engine, is equipped with a self diagnostic program that will detect emissions related malfunctions and store fault codes in permanent memory. Certain output tests are also available in this program.

The newer fully electronic Digifant systems are used on all other engines. The Digifant I system, used on California models, is equipped with a self diagnostic program with a permanent memory for storing emissions related fault codes. Digifant II is basically the same system but is not equipped with a self diagnostic program. No fault codes are available on Digifant II systems, even with a diagnostic tester.

Vehicles equipped with anti-lock brakes and/or automatic transmission can store fault codes in those control units. Fault codes can be accessed through the same diagnostic connector under the shifter boot or console.

MOTRONIC CONTROL UNIT

The control unit operates all air/fuel mixture, idle speed and ignition timing functions. All the engine sensors and output devices are monitored by the self diagnostic program built into the control unit. The self diagnostic system can differentiate between intermittent and permanent faults and all fault codes are stored in permanent memory until intentionally erased. If an engine fault has not occurred within the last 50 engine starts, it is erased automatically. Codes can only be retrieved using the VAG 1551 Diagnostic Tester or equivalent. With the Diagnostic Tester, output signals can be generated to test certain output devices.

DIGIFANT I CONTROL UNIT

This system is used on California vehicles only. The control unit operates the fuel injectors, idle speed control actuator and ignition timing functions. All the engine sensors and output devices are monitored by the self diagnostic program built into the control unit. The self diagnostic system can differentiate between intermittent and permanent faults and all fault codes are stored in permanent memory until intentionally erased. If an engine fault has not occurred within the last 50 engine starts, it is erased automatically. When a permanent fault is detected, the ENGINE WARNING light on the instrument panel is turned ON until the fault is repaired and the memory cleared. Some codes can be retrieved by installing a jumper wire on the test connector and reading the flashes of the ENGINE WARNING light. The remaining codes can only be retrieved with the VAG 1551 Diagnostic Tester or equivalent. With the Diagnostic Tester, signals can be generated to test certain output devices.

AUTOMATIC TRANSMISSION CONTROL UNIT

The diagnostic program in electronically controlled transmissions is similar to the engine diagnostic program. If a permanent fault is detected, the transmission will operate only in third gear or reverse and the cruise control system will not operate. Appropriate fault codes will be stored in memory until repaired and erased. If the fault is intermittent and not present the next time the ignition switch is turned ON, the transmission will operate normally but the fault will remain in memory. The fault memory can be accessed only with the VAG 1551 Diagnostic Tester, or equivalent, at the diagnostic connector terminals under the shifter console.

ANTI-LOCK BRAKE SYSTEM CONTROL UNIT

Each time the engine is started, the control unit performs a self check while pressure is being built in the accumulator. If a serious fault is detected and the ABS light stays ON, the system will be turned OFF and only normal braking will be available. The self diagnostic program can differentiate between permanent and intermittent faults and will store the appropriate code in permanent memory. Fault codes are reported in order of priority, solenoid faults have the highest priority and intermittent faults the lowest. The fault memory can be accessed only with the VAG 1551 Diagnostic Tester, or equivalent, at the diagnostic connector terminals under the shifter boot or console.

Self-Diagnostics

SERVICE PRECAUTIONS

- Do not disconnect the battery or the control unit before reading the fault codes. On the Motronic system, fault code memory is erased when power is interrupted.
- Make sure the ignition switch is **OFF** before disconnecting any wiring.
- Before removing or installing a control unit, disconnect the negative battery cable. The unit receives power through the main connector at all times and will be permanently damaged if improperly powered up or down.
- Keep all parts and harnesses dry during service. Protect the control unit and all solid-state components from rough handling or extremes of temperature.

READING FAULT CODES

Engine Codes

1. Make sure the ignition switch is **OFF** and that all fuses are good. Make sure all ground connections under the hood are good, especially those for the control unit.
2. Remove the shifter knob and boot and connect the diagnostic tester to the black and white connectors towards the left or front of the vehicle.
3. Turn the tester **ON** to make sure it is receiving power. The screen will display 2 menu options; Rapid Data Transfer and Blink Code Output. Turn the ignition switch **ON**.
4. Select Rapid Data Transfer and Address Word 01, then press the Q button to enter the selection. The tester will display a control unit part number, the system it controls and an application (country) code.
   a. If the information is displayed and is correct, press the Run key to proceed: 'Select function XX' will be displayed.
   b. If 'Control unit does not answer' is displayed, use the Help key to display a list of possible causes. When the problem is repaired, return to Step 1 and start again.
5. When Function 02 is selected, the control unit will report fault codes to the tester.
6. When all codes have been reported, proceed to the Output Check Diagnosis or select Function 06 to exit the fault code memory without erasing the codes.

Transmission Codes

1. Make sure the ignition switch is **OFF** and that all fuses are good. Make sure all ground connections under the hood are good, especially those for the control unit.
2. Remove the shifter knob and boot and connect the diagnostic tester to the black and white connectors towards the left or front of the vehicle.

3. Turn the tester **ON** to make sure it is receiving power. The screen will display 2 menu options; Rapid Data Transfer and Blink Code Output. Turn the ignition switch **ON**.
4. Select Rapid Data Transfer and Address Word 02, then press the Q button to enter the selection. The tester will display a control unit part number, the system it controls and an application (country) code.
   a. If the information is displayed and is correct, press the Run key to proceed: 'Select function XX' will be displayed.
   b. If 'Control unit does not answer' is displayed, use the Help key to display a list of possible causes. When the problem is repaired, return to Step 1 and start again.
5. When Function 02 is selected, the control unit will report fault codes to the tester.
6. When all codes have been reported, proceed to the Output Check Diagnosis or select Function 06 to exit the fault code memory without erasing the codes.

ABS Codes

Fault codes for the ABS can only be retrieved with the VAG 1551 Diagnostic Tester or equivalent. All fuses and ground circuits must be good. If the ABS light on the instrument panel stays ON after the initial vehicle start-up test, there is at least one fault code stored in the control unit memory and the ABS system is switched OFF. If the light does not turn ON at all, check the wiring between the light and terminal 27 of the control unit. The control unit is mounted in the right rear of the luggage compartment.

1. Make sure the ignition switch is **OFF**. Remove the shifter knob and boot and connect the diagnostic tester to the black and white connectors towards the left or front of the vehicle.
2. Turn the tester **ON** to make sure it is receiving power. The screen will display 2 menu options; Rapid Data Transfer and Blink Code Output.
3. Select Blink Code Output, then press and hold the run button. When the 'Permanent ground' message is displayed, release the run button and turn the ignition switch **ON**. The ABS light should turn **ON** and when the run button is pressed and released, the first code should be displayed.
4. Each time the run button is pressed and released, the next code should be displayed. If the next code cannot be called up, the displayed fault must be repaired and the diagnostic procedure started again from the beginning.
5. If the message 'No blink code received' is displayed, check the wiring at terminals 26 and 27 of the control unit.
6. When the end of output message is displayed, turn the ignition switch **OFF**. When all faults have been repaired, the ABS light should turn OFF 4 seconds after the ignition switch is turned **ON**.
7. If the light stays ON, a fault may or may not still exist. Clear the fault code memory, turn the ignition switch **OFF** and **ON** again to see is the light will turn **OFF**. Read the fault code memory again if necessary.

OUTPUT CHECK DIAGNOSIS

Motronic System

Only the Motronic system is equipped with this program. It allows testing most of the engine output devices without running the engine. The program cannot be run without the

VAG 1551 Diagnostic Tester or equivalent. During the test, 4 output devices are activated in the following order:

Differential pressure regulator
Carbon canister frequency valve
Idle stabilizer valve
Cold start valve

Testing the differential pressure regulator requires a multimeter that will read milliamps. The other items can be checked with a voltmeter, test light or by listening and feeling for valve activation. The cold start valve is activated for a limited time to avoid flooding the engine.

1. Connect the diagnostic tester, turn the ignition switch **ON** and confirm that the tester will communicate with the control unit. See the procedure for retrieving fault codes.

2. Select Rapid Data Transfer and Function 03. When the test is started by pressing the Q button (enter), the first output signal is generated.

3. Each time the Run button is pressed, the tester will send an output signal to the next device on the list.

4. When the last item has been tested, select Function 06 to exit the program. To repeat the test, turn the ignition switch **OFF** and **ON** again.

CLEARING FAULT CODES

Engine

After all fault codes have been retrieved, select Function 05 and press the Q button to enter the selection. The memory will be erased only if all fault codes have been retrieved. Test drive the vehicle for at least 10 minutes, including at least 1 full throttle application above 3000 rpm. Check the fault code memory again to make sure all faults have been repaired.

Transmission

After all fault codes have been retrieved, select Function 05 and press the Q button to enter the selection. The memory will be erased only if all fault codes have been retrieved. Test drive the vehicle for at least 10 minutes and check the fault code memory again to make sure all faults have been repaired.

ABS Codes

When the ABS light turns OFF 4 seconds after starting the engine, drive the vehicle and reach a speed of at least 20 mph. If all faults have been repaired, the fault code memory will be erased.

Year — 1990
Model — Cabriolet
Body VIN — 15
Engine — 1.8L (1780cc)   **Cylinders** — 4
Fuel System — Digifant I
Engine Identifier — 2H

ENGINE CODES

Fault Code	Blink Code	Explanation
00000	4444	No faults in memory
00518	2212	Throttle position sensor
00522	2312	Coolant temperature sensor
00523	2322	Intake air temperature sensor
00525	2342	Oxygen sensor signal missing
00535	2141/2142	Knock sensor or control program
00537	2341	Oxygen sensor signal out of limit
00552	2323	Air flow sensor signal missing
01249	4411	Fuel injector circuit
65535	1111	Control unit defective
	0000	End of output

Year—1990
Model—Corrado
Body VIN—50
Engine—1.8L (1780cc)   **Cylinders**—4
Fuel System—Digifant I
Engine Identifier—PG

ENGINE CODES

Fault Code	Blink Code	Explanation
00000	4444	No faults in memory
00518	2212	Throttle position sensor
00519	2222	Manifold absolute pressure sensor
00521	2242	CO potentiometer
00522	2312	Coolant temperature sensor
00523	2322	Intake air temperature sensor
00525	2342	Oxygen sensor signal missing
00535	2141/2142	Knock sensor or control program
00537	2341	Oxygen sensor signal out of limit
01249	4411	Fuel injector circuit
65535	1111	Control unit defective
	0000	End of output

Year — 1990
Model — Golf GTi/Jetta GLi
Body VIN — 1G
Engine — 2.0L (1984cc)   **Cylinders** — 4
Fuel System — CIS-E Motronic
Engine Identifier — 9A

ENGINE CODES

Fault Code	Blink Code	Explanation
00000	4444	No faults in memory
65535	1111	Control unit defective
00281	1231	Vehicle speed sensor
00514	2112	Ignition reference sensor
00515	2113	Hall sender signal missing
00516	2121	Idle switch
00517	2123	Full throttle switch
00535	2141	Knock control program
00524	2142	Knock sensor 1 signal missing
00540	2144	Knock sensor 2 signal missing
00533	2231	Idle speed regulation out of limit
00520	2232	Air flow sensor signal missing
00522	2312	Coolant temperature sensor
00537	2341	Oxygen sensor signal out of limit
00525	2342	Oxygen sensor signal missing
00587	- -	Air/fuel mixture regulation
00560	2411	EGR temperature sensor signal out of limit
01257	4431	Idle stabilizer valve circuit
	0000	End of output

Year — 1991
Model — Cabriolet
Body VIN — 15
Engine — 1.8L (1780cc)   **Cylinders** — 4
Fuel System — Digifant I
Engine Identifier — 2H

ENGINE CODES

Fault Code	Blink Code	Explanation
00000	4444	No faults in memory
00518	2212	Throttle position sensor
00522	2312	Coolant temperature sensor
00523	2322	Intake air temperature sensor
00525	2342	Oxygen sensor signal missing
00535	2141/2142	Knock sensor or control program
00537	2341	Oxygen sensor signal out of limit
00552	2323	Air flow sensor signal missing
01249	4411	Fuel injector circuit
65535	1111	Control unit defective
	0000	End of output

Year – 1991
Model – Golf/Jetta
Body VIN – 16, 17
Engine – 1.8L (1780cc)   **Cylinders** – 4
Fuel System – Digifant I
Engine Identifier – RV

ENGINE CODES

Fault Code	Blink Code	Explanation
00000	4444	No faults in memory
00518	2212	Throttle position sensor
00522	2312	Coolant temperature sensor
00523	2322	Intake air temperature sensor
00525	2342	Oxygen sensor signal missing
00535	2141/2142	Knock sensor or control program
00537	2341	Oxygen sensor signal out of limit
00552	2323	Air flow sensor signal missing
01249	4411	Fuel injector circuit
65535	1111	Control unit defective
	0000	End of output

Year — 1991
Model — GTI/Jetta GLi
Body VIN — 1G
Engine — 2.0L (1984cc) **Cylinders** — 4
Fuel System — CIS-E Motronic
Engine Identifier — 9A

ENGINE CODES

Fault Code	Blink Code	Explanation
00000	4444	No faults in memory
65535	1111	Control unit defective
00281	1231	Vehicle speed sensor
00514	2112	Ignition reference sensor
00515	2113	Hall sender signal missing
00516	2121	Idle switch
00517	2123	Full throttle switch
00535	2141	Knock control program
00524	2142	Knock sensor 1 signal missing
00540	2144	Knock sensor 2 signal missing
00533	2231	Idle speed regulation out of limit
00520	2232	Air flow sensor signal missing
00522	2312	Coolant temperature sensor
00537	2341	Oxygen sensor signal out of limit
00525	2342	Oxygen sensor signal missing
00587	- -	Air/fuel mixture regulation
00560	2411	EGR temperature sensor signal out of limit
01257	4431	Idle stabilizer valve circuit
	0000	End of output

VACUUM DIAGRAMS

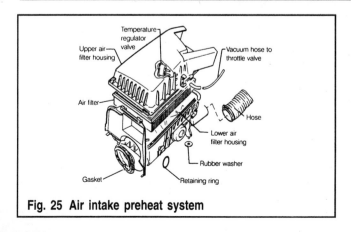

Fig. 25 Air intake preheat system

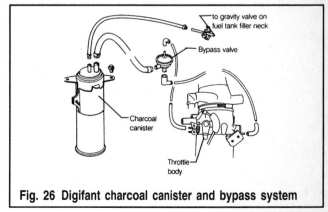

Fig. 26 Digifant charcoal canister and bypass system

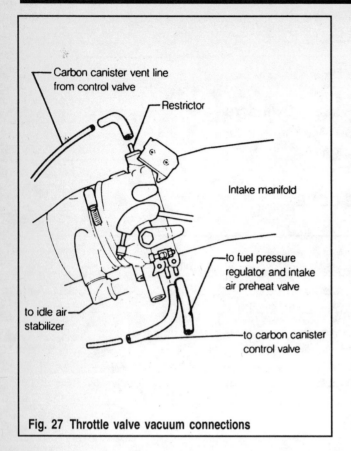

Fig. 27 Throttle valve vacuum connections

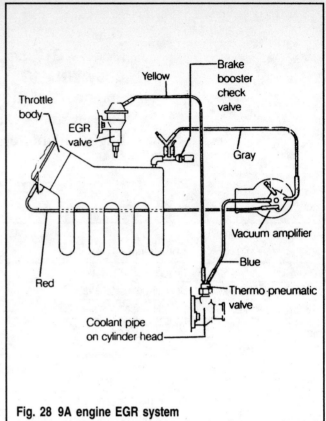

Fig. 28 9A engine EGR system

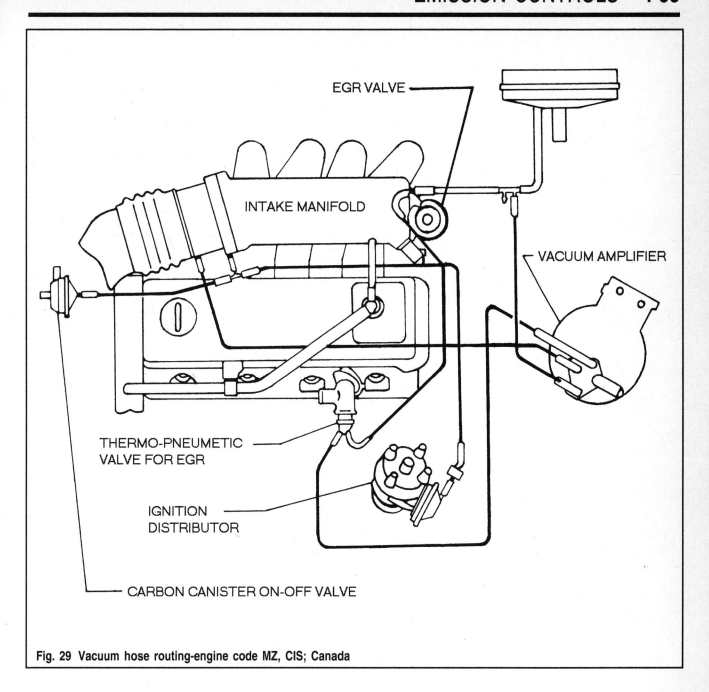

EGR VALVE

INTAKE MANIFOLD

VACUUM AMPLIFIER

THERMO-PNEUMETIC
VALVE FOR EGR

IGNITION
DISTRIBUTOR

CARBON CANISTER ON-OFF VALVE

Fig. 29 Vacuum hose routing-engine code MZ, CIS; Canada

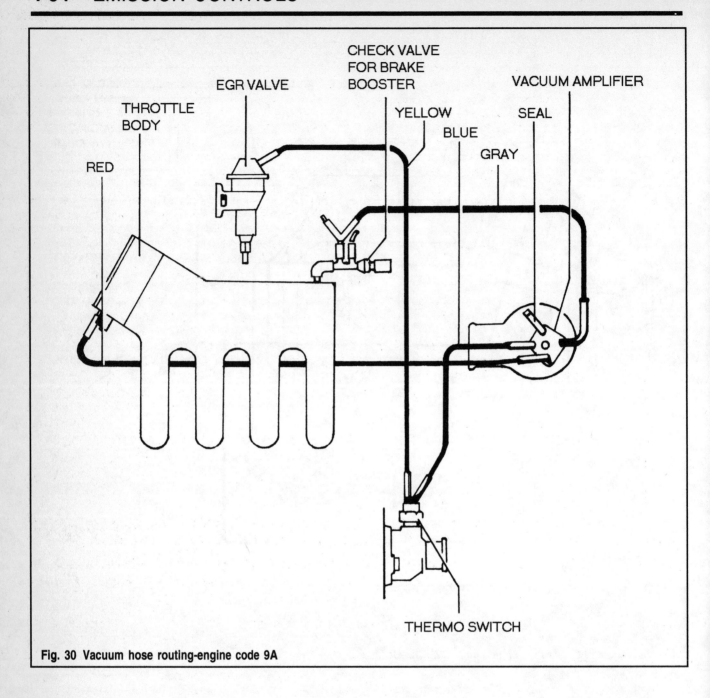

Fig. 30 Vacuum hose routing-engine code 9A

CIS-E MOTRONIC FUEL INJECTION SYSTEM
DIFFERENTIAL PRESSURE
  REGULATOR 5-5
FUEL DISTRIBUTOR 5-5
FUEL INJECTORS 5-3
FUEL PUMP 5-3
FUEL SYSTEM PRESSURE
  REGULATOR 5-3
GENERAL DESCRIPTION 5-2
OXYGEN SENSOR 5-5
DIESEL FUEL SYSTEM
DIESEL GLOW PLUGS 5-12
DIESEL INJECTION PUMP 5-11
DIESEL INJECTION TIMING 5-12

FUEL INJECTION LINES 5-10
FUEL INJECTOR 5-11
FUEL SUPPLY PUMP 5-11
FUEL SYSTEM SERVICE
  PRECAUTIONS 5-10
DIGIFANT FUEL INJECTION SYSTEM
AIR FLOW SENSOR 5-10
FUEL INJECTORS 5-8
FUEL PUMPS 5-7
GENERAL DESCRIPTION 5-7
PRESSURE REGULATOR 5-8
THROTTLE SWITCHES 5-10
FUEL TANK
FUEL TANK ASSEMBLY 5-13
SENDING UNIT 5-14

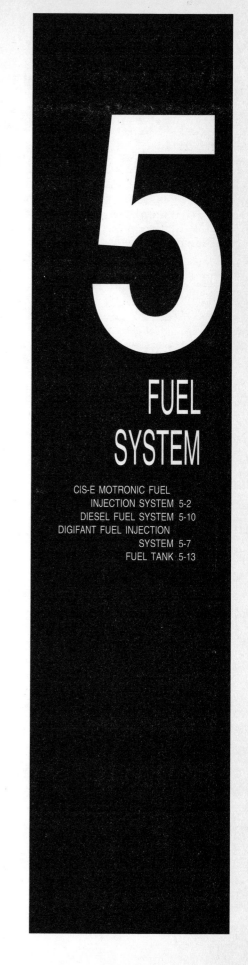

5

FUEL SYSTEM

CIS-E MOTRONIC FUEL
  INJECTION SYSTEM 5-2
DIESEL FUEL SYSTEM 5-10
DIGIFANT FUEL INJECTION
  SYSTEM 5-7
FUEL TANK 5-13

CIS-E MÔTRONIC FUEL INJECTION SYSTEM

General Description

▶ **See Figure 1**

The CIS-E Motronic system used on the 16V engine is a highly developed and electronically controlled version of the original Bosch Continuous Injection System (CIS). The mechanical fuel distributor, mechanical injectors and a high pressure fuel pump are the main components.

The fuel pump is mounted in a reservoir under the vehicle, along with the filter and fuel accumulator. The reservoir holds about 1 liter of fuel and is supplied by a small transfer pump in the fuel tank. The transfer pump is part of the fuel gauge sending unit assembly but it can be replaced separately.

The fuel distributor used in the Motronic system is very different from that used in earlier CIS systems. The unit is made of aluminum and is slightly smaller. It is still divided into an upper and a lower chamber but the pressure difference between chambers is not constant. A differential pressure regulator mounted on the side controls the pressure in the lower chamber which ultimately controls the fuel flow to the injectors. Control plunger movement controls the amount of fuel supplied to the upper chamber. When the engine is not running, the control plunger rests on an O-ring and there is some free-play between the plunger and air flow sensor arm. If the fuel distributor is replaced, the plunger free-play must be adjusted.

The fuel distributor is mounted on the mechanical air mass sensor. As air flows into the air cleaner and up through the sensor assembly, the air pushes the sensor plate up, which lifts up the fuel distributor plunger. When the engine is not running, the arm that the plate is bolted to rests on a spring. This allows some opposite movement of the plate if the engine back fires. There is no service procedure that requires disassembly of the air flow sensor. If the plate is removed, a special tool is required to center the plate in the bore.

The fuel injectors are purely mechanical and open at 54-70 psi (3.7-4.8 BAR) fuel line pressure. All injectors are open when the engine is running, injecting fuel to the intake ports continuously. They are mounted into plastic inserts that are threaded into the intake manifold. An O-ring is used to hold the injector in place and at the same time to seal the insert. Injectors can be removed from the insert without disconnecting the fuel line. The cold start injector is mounted at the flywheel end of the intake manifold. It is a simple solenoid valve with a spray nozzle tip. During starter operation, the control unit operates this injector when engine depending on coolant temperature is below 86°F (30°C).

Other components in the Motronic system include the oxygen sensor, a coolant temperature sensor, a position sensor in the air flow sensor, two throttle position switches, the idle air stabilizer valve, and the fuel system pressure regulator.

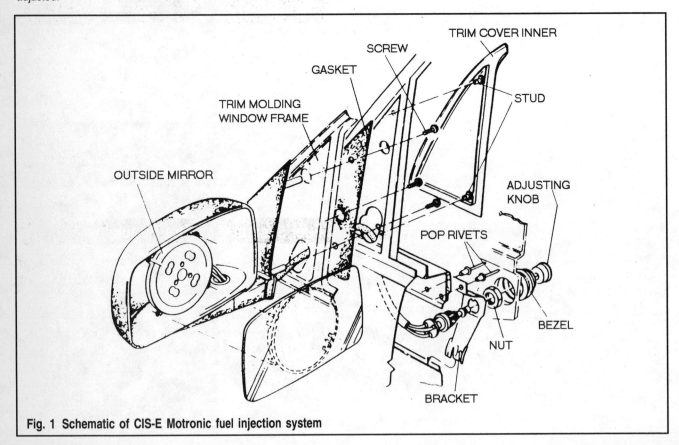

Fig. 1 Schematic of CIS-E Motronic fuel injection system

The function and testing of all these items is described in Section 4, Electronic Engine Controls.

✳✳CAUTION

Never smoke when working around gasoline! Avoid all sources of sparks or ignition. Gasoline vapors are EXTREMELY volatile! Most of the following procedures will produce fuel vapors. Make sure there is proper ventilation and take the appropriate fire safety precautions.

Before working on any components of the fuel system, any residual pressure should be relieved first to limit the possibility of injury or fire. This can be done by loosening any fitting in the system, but the cold start injector is easiest. Hold a rag at the fitting to catch the spray, loosen the fuel line bolt, then tighten it again. Do not over tighten the fitting or the copper sealing washer will split.

Fuel Pump

REMOVAL & INSTALLATION

▶ **See Figures 2 and 3**

Transfer Pump

1. Remove the rear seat and the access cover.
2. Disconnect the wiring and hoses and unscrew the lock ring.
3. Carefully lift out the pump and gauge sending unit assembly.
4. When installing the assembly, use a new seal.

Main Pump

1. Disconnect the negative battery cable.
2. Relieve the fuel system pressure.
3. Raise and safely support the rear or right side of the vehicle on jack stands.
4. Disconnect the wiring from the pump. Clean any dirt away from the fuel line fitting.
5. Use locking pliers to pinch off the fuel line from the transfer pump to the main pump. If the fuel line is metal, remove the rear seat and access panel and disconnect the line at the transfer pump.
6. Place a pan under the pump and disconnect the fuel line fitting from the pump.
7. Remove the retaining ring screws and slide the pump out of the reservoir.
   To install:
8. Moisten the pump O-ring with a little fuel and slide it into the reservoir. Install the retaining ring screws.
9. When connecting the fittings, use new copper washers and torque the fittings to 15 ft. lbs. (20 Nm).

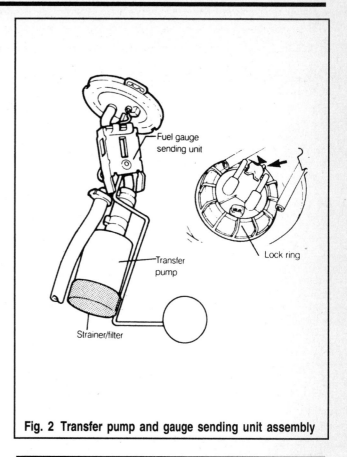

Fig. 2 Transfer pump and gauge sending unit assembly

Fuel Injectors

REMOVAL & INSTALLATION

1. Relieve the pressure from the system.
2. Using a fuel injector removal tool, pry the injectors up out of the head. A spray lubricant can help release stuck injectors.
3. Hold the fuel line fitting with a line wrench and unscrew the injector.
4. Installation is the reverse of removal. Lightly lubricate the rubber rings.

Fuel System Pressure Regulator

REMOVAL & INSTALLATION

▶ **See Figure 4**

1. Clean any dirt away from the fuel line fittings.
2. Disconnect the fittings and the vacuum line.
3. Remove the bolt to remove the regulator. Installation is the reverse of removal.

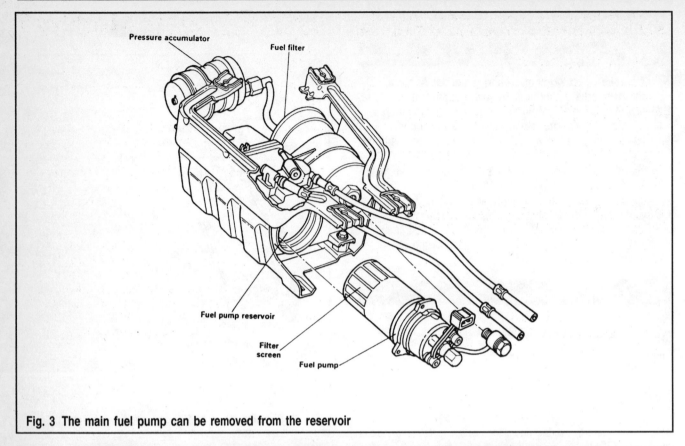

Fig. 3 The main fuel pump can be removed from the reservoir

Fig. 4 System fuel pressure regulator is mounted near the differential pressure regulator on the fuel distributor

Differential Pressure Regulator

REMOVAL & INSTALLATION

1. Disconnect the wiring.
2. Clean any dirt away from the fuel line fitting and remove the fitting.
3. Remove the 2 screws to remove the regulator. The screws are made of non-magnetic material. If the screws must be replaced, make sure they are non-magnetic.

Oxygen Sensor

REMOVAL & INSTALLATION

▶ **See Figure 5**

The sensor is threaded into the front of the catalytic converter with an anti-seize compound on the threads. When replacing it, be careful not to get anti-seize in the slots of the outer shield. Torque to 15 ft. lbs. (20 Nm).

Fuel Distributor

REMOVAL & INSTALLATION

▶ **See Figure 6**

1. Relieve the fuel system pressure.
2. Clean any dirt away from the fittings and disconnect the wiring from the differential pressure regulator.
3. Remove the fittings and disconnect the fuel lines from the fuel distributor.
4. Remove the screws to lift the distributor from the air flow sensor housing.
   To install:
5. If the distributor is being replaced, check plunger free-play adjustment. Install a new O-ring and fit the fuel distributor onto the air flow sensor. Install the screws.
6. Use new sealing washers and connect the fuel lines to the distributor. Torque the smaller fittings to 7 ft. lbs. (10 Nm). and the larger fittings to 15 ft. lbs. (20 Nm).

ADJUSTMENT

▶ **See Figures 7 and 8**

When the fuel distributor is replaced, the plunger free-play must be adjusted. This adjustment affects hot start and fuel distributor sealing when the engine is not running.

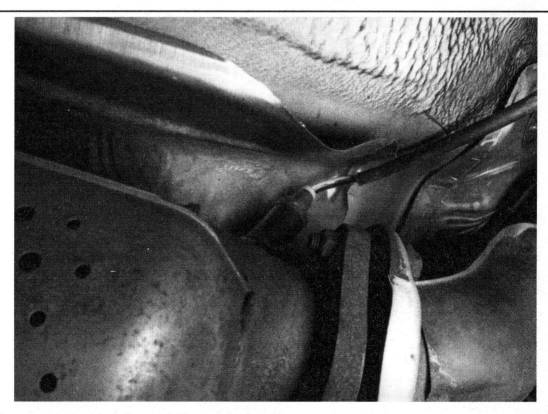

Fig. 5 The oxygen sensor is in the catalytic converter housing

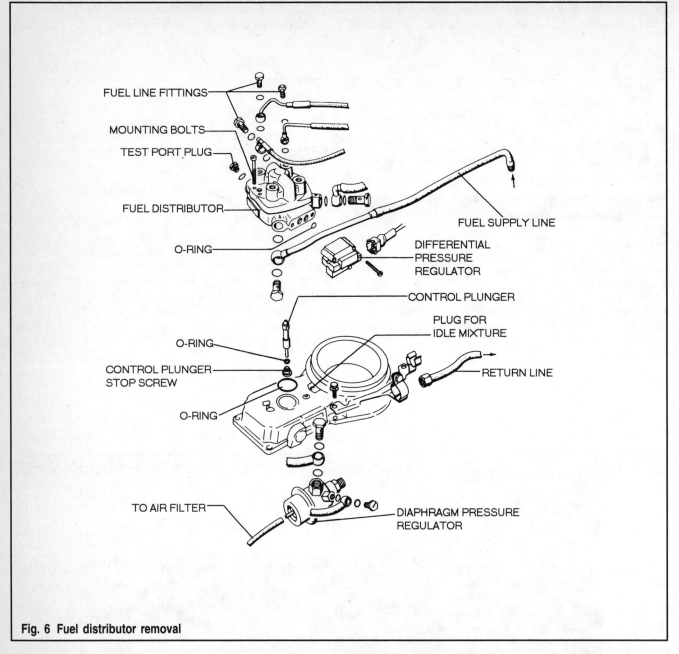

Fig. 6 Fuel distributor removal

Fuel Distributor Installed

1. Remove the air inlet boot from the sensor plate and operate the starter for about 10 seconds to build fuel system pressure. The engine will not start.

2. Measure the distance from the top of the air flow sensor housing to the sensor plate at the point nearest the fuel distributor.

3. Use a magnet on the sensor plate bolt to lift the plate until resistance is felt. The free-play movement should be 0.050-0.118 inches (1.3-3mm).

4. To adjust, remove the fuel distributor and follow the procedure outlined below.

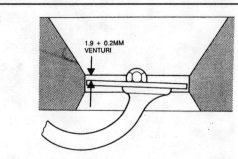

Fig. 7 Sensor plate free play can be measured to check plunger stop screw adjustment

Fuel Distributor Removed

1. Use a depth caliper to measure the distance from the shoulder of the gland nut to the stop screw. Distance **A** should be 0.024 inches (0.6mm).

2. Turn the stop screw in or out as required. Turning the screw in ¼ turn will increase the installed free-play by 0.050 inches. (1.3mm).

3. After adjusting plunger free-play, idle speed and CO must be checked.

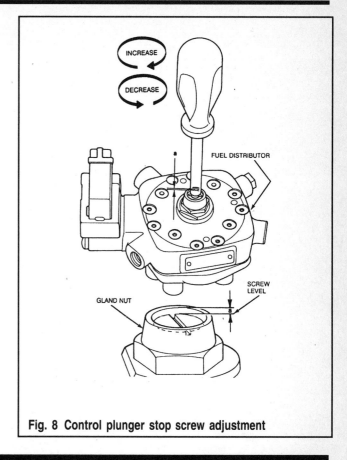

Fig. 8 Control plunger stop screw adjustment

DIGIFANT FUEL INJECTION SYSTEM

General Description

▶ **See Figure 9**

The Digifant system is all electronic, using electric injectors at a relatively low injection pressure. All injectors are operated by the Electronic Control Unit (ECU) so injector opening timing and duration can be closely controlled for reduced emissions and improved fuel mileage. During deceleration above about 1500 rpm, the injectors are shut off to save fuel and reduce emissions. The system uses an air vane and potentiometer type air flow sensor and an inlet air temperature sensor to calculate air flow into the engine. An idle stabilizer valve is used to control idle speed. This is a motorized rotary valve that controls the amount of air allowed to bypass the throttle plate.

The fuel pump is mounted in a reservoir under the vehicle along with the filter. The reservoir holds about 1 liter of fuel and is supplied by a small transfer pump in the fuel tank. The transfer pump is part of the fuel gauge sending unit assembly but it can be replaced separately.

The electric fuel injectors are secured in place by the fuel rail, which also houses the wiring. All injectors are wired together in parallel and are operated at the same time. Power is supplied to all injectors any time the ECU is receiving an rpm signal.

Other components in the Digifant system include the oxygen sensor, a coolant temperature sensor, a throttle position switch,

the idle air stabilizer valve, the fuel system pressure regulator and the ignition system. The function and testing of fuel system items is described in Section 4, Electronic Engine Controls.

✳✳CAUTION

Most of the following procedures will produce fuel vapors. Make sure there is proper ventilation and take the appropriate fire safety precautions.

Before working on any components of the fuel system, any residual pressure should be relieved first to limit the possibility of injury or fire. This can be done by loosening the service port bolt at the end of the fuel rail. Hold a rag at the fitting to catch the spray, loosen the fuel line bolt, then tighten it again. Do not over tighten the fitting or the copper sealing washer will split.

Fuel Pumps

REMOVAL & INSTALLATION

▶ **See Figure 10**

Transfer Pump

1. Remove the rear seat and the access cover.

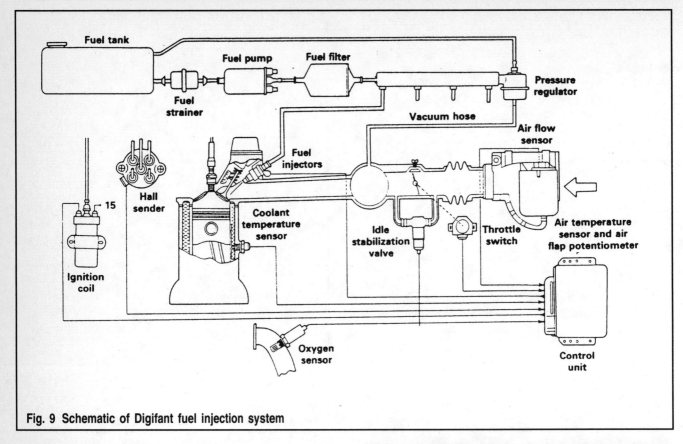

Fig. 9 Schematic of Digifant fuel injection system

2. Disconnect the wiring and hoses and unscrew the lock ring.

3. Carefully lift out the pump and gauge sending unit assembly.

4. When installing the assembly, use a new seal.

Main Pump

1. Disconnect the negative battery cable.
2. Relieve the fuel system pressure.
3. Raise and safely support the rear or right side of the vehicle on jack stands.
4. Disconnect the wiring from the pump. Clean any dirt away from the fuel line fitting.
5. Use locking pliers to pinch off the fuel line from the transfer pump to the main pump. If the fuel line is metal, remove the rear seat and access panel and disconnect the line at the transfer pump.
6. Place a pan under the pump and disconnect the fuel line fitting from the pump.
7. Remove the retaining ring screws and slide the pump out of the reservoir.

To install:
8. Moisten the pump O-ring with a little fuel and slide it into the reservoir. Install the retaining ring screws.
9. When connecting the fittings, use new copper washers and torque the fittings to 15 ft. lbs. (20 Nm).

Fuel Injectors

REMOVAL & INSTALLATION

▶ See Figure 11

1. Disconnect the negative battery cable and relieve the pressure from the fuel system.
2. Disconnect the fuel supply and return lines.
3. Dismount the idle stabilizer valve and lay it aside.
4. Unplug the wiring harness end connector and pry wiring guide away from the fuel distributor retainers.
5. Remove the fuel distributor retaining bolts and remove the rail, wiring guide, pressure regulator and injectors as an assembly.
6. Installation is the reverse of removal.

Pressure Regulator

REMOVAL & INSTALLATION

The regulator can be removed without removing the fuel rail assembly. When installing the regulator, use a new O-ring and hose clamp.

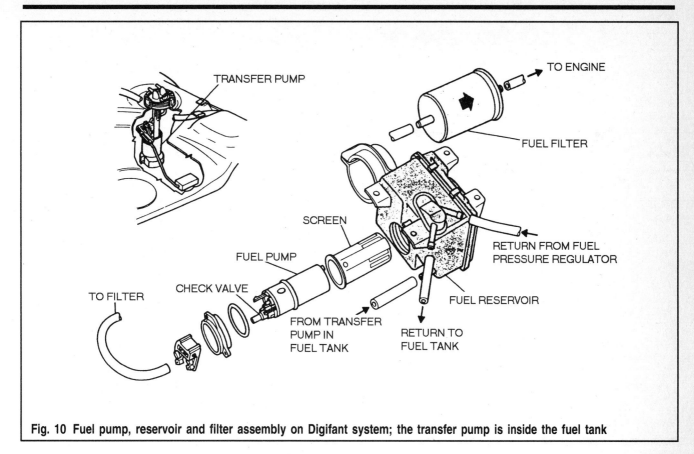

Fig. 10 Fuel pump, reservoir and filter assembly on Digifant system; the transfer pump is inside the fuel tank

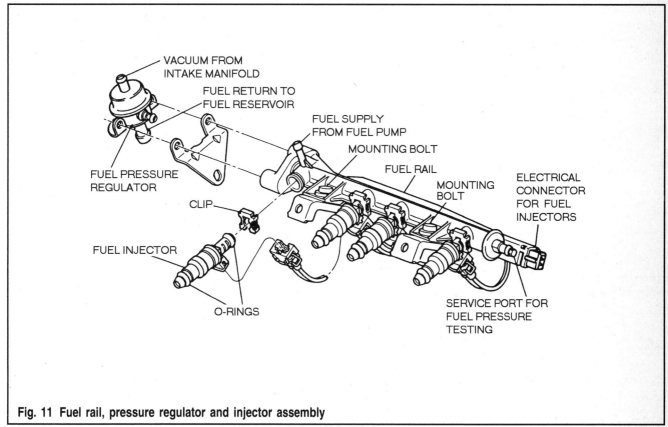

Fig. 11 Fuel rail, pressure regulator and injector assembly

Air Flow Sensor

REMOVAL & INSTALLATION

The air flow sensor is mounted either to the air cleaner housing or the air inlet duct. Make sure the ignition switch is **OFF** before disconnecting the wiring.

Throttle Switches

REMOVAL & INSTALLATION

▶ **See Figure 12**

The throttle switches are held in place with screws and are slotted for adjustment. Make sure the idle switch is closed when the throttle in in idle position. The full throttle switch should be closed for the last 10 degrees of throttle movement.

On California models, the throttle position sensor is mounted on the bottom of the throttle body. If the switch is replaced of disconnected, follow this procedure to reset the control unit:

1. With the engine not running, disconnect the crankcase breather hose at the top of the valve cover and plug the hose.

2. Run the engine at idle for 1 minute.

3. Disconnect the blue coolant temperature sensor and let the engine idle for 1 minute.

4. Stop the engine and reconnect the hose and wiring.

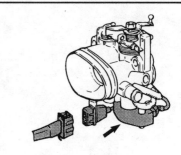

Fig. 12 Throttle position switch used on California models

DIESEL FUEL SYSTEM

In the 1991 model year, Volkswagen introduced the ECO Diesel engine in the Jetta. This is a standard diesel engine with a turbo charger and a catalytic converter. The turbo charger provides only about 6 psi boost but about a 40 percent increase in air flowing through the engine. This provides a modest power increase, but the objective is to greatly improve the engine's emissions performance. Since the system is designed for improved emissions rather than power, there is no fuel enrichment device on the injection pump.

Fuel System Service Precautions

• Do not allow fuel spray or fuel vapors to come into contact with a heating element or open flame. Do not smoke while working on the fuel system.

• To control fuel spills, place a shop towel around the fitting prior to loosening to catch the spray. Ensure that all fuel spillage is quickly wiped up and that fuel soaked rags are deposited into a fire safe container.

• Always use a backup wrench when loosening and tightening fuel line fittings. Always follow the proper torque specifications.

• Do not re-use fuel system gaskets and O-rings, replace with new ones. Do not substitute fuel hose where fuel pipe is installed.

• Cleanliness is absolutely essential. Clean all fittings before opening them and maintain a dust free work area while the system is open.

• Place removed parts on a clean surface and cover with paper or plastic to keep them clean. Do not cover with rags that can leave fuzz on the parts.

Fuel Injection Lines

REMOVAL & INSTALLATION

1. The lines should be removed as a set. Loosen the fittings at each injector.

2. Use a back-up wrench to loosen the lines from the injection pump.

3. Remove the lines as a set and cap the injectors and pump fittings immediately.

To install:

4. Make sure the flares on the lines are not split or flattened. If so, the line should be replaced. They can be purchased or made up separately but are usually replaced as a set.

5. Fit the lines into place and start all the nuts. Use a back-up wrench and torque the line nuts at the pump to 18 ft. lbs. (25 Nm). Do not over torque the nuts or the flares will split and the line will leak.

6. Torque the nuts at the nozzle end to 18 ft. lbs. (25 Nm).

Fuel Injector

REMOVAL & INSTALLATION

▶ **See Figures 13 and 14**

Faulty injectors can be located by loosening each line nut at the injector one at a time with the engine at a slightly fast idle. If the engine speed remains constant after loosening a line, that injector is faulty.

1. Remove the lines as a set and remove the spill tubes that connect the injectors.

2. Carefully remove the injectors using a clean 27mm deep socket.

3. With a magnet or small pick, remove the heat shields from the injector holes and discard them. New heat shields must be installed.

4. The injector can be disassembled if needed for cleaning and inspection. Clamp the upper body in a vise and loosen but do not remove the lower body.

5. Place the injector over a clean rag and unscrew the body. The parts can be cleaned with a brass wire brush if required but do not use any abrasive cleaning materials.

   To install:

6. Assemble the injector and torque the lower body to 51 ft. lbs. (70 Nm).

7. Install the new heat shield and torque the injectors to 51 ft. lbs. (70 Nm).

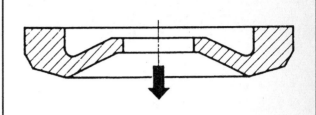

Fig. 14 Make sure the heat shield is installed with the dished side down

8. Install the spill tubes and injection lines. Torque the line nuts to 18 ft. lbs. (25 Nm). Do not over torque or the flares will split.

Fuel Supply Pump

REMOVAL & INSTALLATION

1. Remove the rear seat and the access cover.

2. Disconnect the wiring and hoses and unscrew the lock ring.

3. Carefully lift out the pump and gauge sending unit assembly.

4. When installing the assembly, use a new seal.

Diesel Injection Pump

REMOVAL & INSTALLATION

▶ **See Figure 15**

➡ **Special tools are required for injection pump installation. Do not remove the pump without these tools on hand.**

1. Disconnect the negative battery cable and remove the air cleaner, cylinder head cover and timing belt cover.

2. Turn the engine to TDC of No. 1 cylinder and insert a setting bar into the slot on the rear of the camshaft, VW tool 2065A or equivalent, to hold the camshaft in place. Remove the timing belt. Be careful to not turn the engine while the belt is removed.

3. Loosen the pump drive sprocket nut but don't remove it yet. Install a puller on the sprocket and apply moderate tension.

4. Rap the puller bolt with light hammer taps until the sprocket jumps off the tapered shaft, then remove the puller and sprocket. Be careful not to lose the Woodruff key.

5. Hold the pump fittings with a wrench and using a line wrench, remove the injection lines from the pump. Cap the pump fittings to keep dirt out. It may be easier to remove the lines from the injectors also and set them aside as an assembly. Cap the injector fittings to keep dirt out.

6. Disconnect the control cables, fuel solenoid wire and fuel supply and return lines.

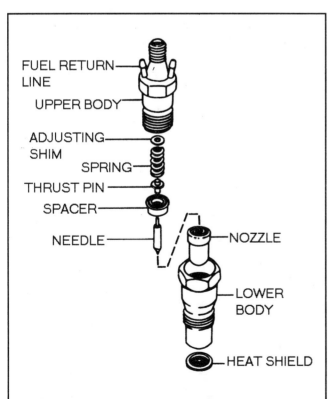

Fig. 13 The injector can be disassembled for cleaning and inspection

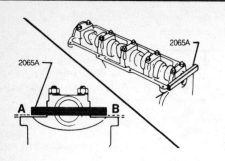

Fig. 15 Install the bar to hold the camshaft in position

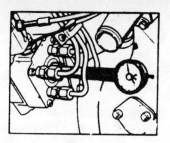

Fig. 16 Dial indicator installed for setting injection pump timing

7. Remove the pump mounting bolts and lift the pump from the vehicle.

To install:

8. When reinstalling, align the marks on the top of the mounting flange and the pump and torque the mounting bolts to 18 ft. lbs. (25 Nm).

9. Install the Woodruff key and sprocket and torque the nut to 33 ft. lbs. (45 Nm).

10. When reinstalling the supply and return lines, be sure the fitting marked OUT is used for the return line. This fitting has an orifice and must be in the correct place. Use new gaskets.

11. Turn the pump sprocket so the mark aligns with the mark on the side of the mounting flange and insert a pin through the hole in the sprocket to hold it in place.

12. Install the camshaft drive sprocket and belt and set the belt tension. Tension the drive belt by turning the tensioner pulley clockwise until belt can be flexed ½ in. (13mm) between the camshaft and the pump sprockets. Remove the pin.

13. Remove the camshaft holding bar. Turn the engine through 2 full turns, return to TDC of No. 1 cylinder and recheck the belt tension and camshaft timing.

14. Reinstall the injection lines, wiring and control cables. Torque the line nuts to 18 ft. lbs. (25 Nm).

Diesel Injection Timing

ADJUSTMENT

▶ **See Figure 16**

1. Turn the engine to TDC of No. 1 cylinder.

2. Make sure the pump control lever is fully against the low idle stop. If equipped with a manual cold start knob, make sure the knob is all the way in against the stop.

3. Remove the center plug on the pump head and install the adapter tool VW-2066 or equivalent, and a dial indicator. Preload the dial indicator to 2.5mm.

4. Slowly turn the engine counterclockwise until the dial gauge stops moving, then zero the dial indicator. This is the bottom of the pump stroke.

5. Turn the engine clockwise until the TDC mark on the flywheel aligns with the pointer on the bell housing.

6. The dial indicator should read 0.95-1.05mm (0.0374-0.0413 inches).

7. If adjustment is required, remove the timing belt cover and loosen the pump mounting bolts without turning the engine.

8. Turn the pump body to make the dial indicator read 1.00mm (0.0394 inches).

9. Torque the mounting bolts to 18 ft. lbs. (25 Nm) and turn the engine backwards about 1 turn. Turn the engine forwards to TDC of No. 1 cylinder and recheck the dial indicator.

10. When the correct setting is reached on the dial indicator, reinstall the belt cover and the center plug on the pump. Use a new copper gasket.

IDLE SPEED ADJUSTMENT

▶ **See Figure 17**

Diesel engines have both an idle speed and a maximum speed adjustment. The maximum speed adjustment is a high idle speed that prevents the engine from over-revving when the control lever is in the full speed position but there is no load on the engine. No increase in power is available through this adjustment. The control lever idle stop screw is no longer used for idle speed adjustment. The idle speed boost linkage includes an adjustment for basic idle speed.

1. If the vehicle has no tachometer, connect a suitable diesel engine tachometer as per the manufacturer's instructions.

2. Run the engine to normal operating temperature.

3. Make sure the manual cold start/idle speed boost knob is pushed in all the way.

4. Turn the linkage cap nut to adjust idle speed to 820-880 rpm, at a point where there is the least vibration.

5. Advance the control lever to full speed. The high idle speed is 5300-5400 rpm. Adjust as needed and secure the locknut with sealer.

Diesel Glow Plugs

▶ **See Figure 18**

DIAGNOSIS AND TESTING

1. Disconnect the engine temperature sensor.

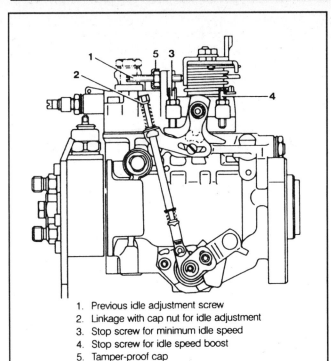

1. Previous idle adjustment screw
2. Linkage with cap nut for idle adjustment
3. Stop screw for minimum idle speed
4. Stop screw for idle speed boost
5. Tamper-proof cap

Fig. 17 Low idle speed adjustment is made at the linkage cap

2. Connect a test light between No. 4 cylinder glow plug and ground. The glow plugs are connected by a flat, coated busbar, located near the bottom of the cylinder head.

3. Turn the ignition key **ON**; the test light should light, then go out after 8-30 seconds.

4. If there is no voltage, go to Step 7.

5. To test each plug individually, disconnect the wire and remove the busbar from the glow plugs.

6. Connect an ohmmeter to each glow plug connection or use a test light. Each plug must have continuity to ground. The engine will probably start with one defective glow plug, but it will make a lot of smoke.

7. To test the glow plug control system, remove the glow plug relay from the bottom right socket of the main fuse/relay panel.

FUEL TANK

Fuel Tank Assembly

▶ **See Figure 19**

REMOVAL & INSTALLATION

1. Disconnect the negative battery cable. Remove the access panel under the rear seat or in the luggage compartment and disconnect the gauge sending unit wiring and hoses.

2. Raise and safely support the vehicle and drain the fuel tank.

8. With the ignition switch **OFF**, there should be 12 volts at terminal 30 on the socket in the panel. Terminal 85 should have continuity to ground.

9. Disconnect the stop solenoid wire from the pump so the engine will not start. With the ignition switch **ON**, there should be 12 volts at terminal 86. When the starter is operated with the ignition switch, there should be 12 volts at terminal 50.

10. Install the relay and disconnect and ground the temperature sensor wire. Connect a voltmeter or test light to the glow plug busbar.

11. With the stop solenoid wire still disconnected, operate the starter with the ignition switch. There should be power to the glow plugs.

12. If all voltages at the socket are correct but there is not power to the glow plugs, the relay is faulty and must be replaced.

REMOVAL & INSTALLATION

1. Remove the busbar connecting the glow plugs and determine which plugs need replacement.

2. Remove the defective plugs.

3. When installing new plugs, torque to 22 ft. lbs. (30 Nm).

➠**Diesel glow plugs have an air gap much like a spark plug to prevent overheating of the plug. Over-torquing the glow plug will close the gap and cause the plug to burn out.**

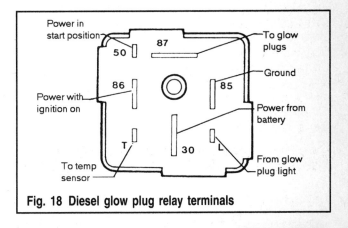

Fig. 18 Diesel glow plug relay terminals

3. On Cabriolet, remove the right rear inner fender and disconnect the breather hose from the filler. Remove but do not disconnect the gravity valve.

4. Detach the fuel pump bracket from the body and lower the pump enough to disconnect the fuel hoses from the tank.

5. On Cabriolet, the rear axle must be dropped out of the way.

   a. Disconnect the brake hydraulic hoses at both sides of the rear axle.

   b. Detach the rear axle from the body on both sides and let it hang on the parking brake cables.

6. Unhook the muffler supports and pull the large hose from the filler neck.

7. Support the tank, loosen the straps and carefully lower the tank out of the vehicle.

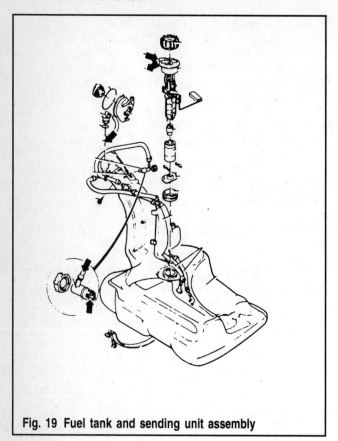

Fig. 19 Fuel tank and sending unit assembly

To install:

8. If a new tank is being installed, glue new foam strips to the tank in the same location as the old ones. Position the tank and secure it with the straps.

9. Connect the wiring and hoses to the sending unit.

10. Install the rear axle, connect the hydraulic lines and bleed the brakes.

Sending Unit

See Figure 19

REMOVAL & INSTALLATION

The sending unit can be reached through the access panel under the rear seat. Disconnect the wiring, unscrew the locking ring and lift the sending unit and transfer pump straight out. Before installing the unit, check the condition of the O-ring, replace it if necessary.

TORQUE SPECIFICATIONS

Component	US	Metric
Diesel fuel injection line nuts:	18 ft. lbs.	25 Nm
Diesel fuel injector:	51 ft. lbs.	70 Nm
Diesel fuel injector body:	51 ft. lbs.	70 Nm
Diesel glow plugs:	22 ft. lbs.	30 Nm
Diesel injection pump bolts:	18 ft. lbs.	25 Nm
Diesel injection pump sprocket nut:	33 ft. lbs.	45 Nm
Fuel distributor fittings		
Large fittings:	15 ft. lbs.	20 Nm
Small fittings:	7 ft. lbs.	10 Nm
Fuel pump fittings:	15 ft. lbs.	20 Nm
Oxygen sensor:	15 ft. lbs.	20 Nm

AIR CONDITIONING
COMPRESSOR 6-15
CONDENSER 6-16
CONTROL PANEL 6-16
EVAPORATOR CORE 6-16
EXPANSION VALVE 6-16
PRESSURE SWITCHES 6-18
RECEIVER/DRIER 6-17
REFRIGERANT LINES 6-18
CIRCUIT PROTECTION
FUSES 6-26
CRUISE CONTROL
CONNECTING ROD 6-19
CONTROL SWITCH 6-18
CONTROL UNIT 6-18
SPEED SENSOR 6-18
VACUUM SERVO 6-18
ENTERTAINMENT SYSTEM
RADIO 6-20
HEATER
BLOWER MOTOR 6-11
CONTROL HEAD AND CABLES 6-14
HEATER CORE 6-12
INSTRUMENTS AND SWITCHES
DYNAMIC OIL PRESSURE WARNING
SYSTEM 6-23
HEADLIGHT SWITCH 6-25
INSTRUMENT CLUSTER 6-23
VOLTAGE STABILIZER 6-23

WINDSHIELD WIPER SWITCH 6-24
LIGHTING
HEADLIGHTS 6-25
SIGNAL AND MARKER LIGHTS 6-25
**SUPPLEMENTAL RESTRAINT SYSTEM
(AIR BAG)**
GENERAL INFORMATION 6-9
SERVICE PRECAUTIONS 6-10
TRAILER WIRING 6-26
**UNDERSTANDING AND TROUBLE-
SHOOTING ELECTRICAL SYSTEMS**
MECHANICAL TEST EQUIPMENT 6-9
SAFETY PRECAUTIONS 6-2
SPECIAL TEST EQUIPMENT 6-6
TESTING AND EQUIPMENT 6-3
WIRING HARNESSES 6-7
WINDSHIELD WIPERS AND WASHERS
REAR WINDOW WASHER PUMP AND
FLUID RESERVOIR 6-23
REAR WINDOW WIPER MOTOR 6-22
REAR WIPER ARM 6-21
WINDSHIELD WASHER PUMP AND
FLUID RESERVOIR 6-22
WINDSHIELD WIPER MOTOR 6-21
WIPER ARM 6-21
WIPER LINKAGE 6-22
WIRING DIAGRAMS
SCHEMATICS 6-27
TERMINAL DESIGNATIONS 6-27

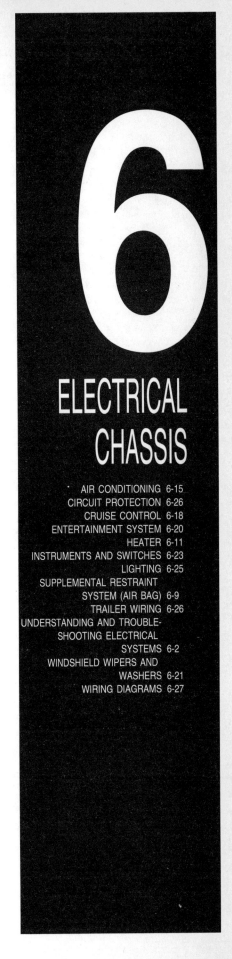

6

ELECTRICAL CHASSIS

AIR CONDITIONING 6-15
CIRCUIT PROTECTION 6-26
CRUISE CONTROL 6-18
ENTERTAINMENT SYSTEM 6-20
HEATER 6-11
INSTRUMENTS AND SWITCHES 6-23
LIGHTING 6-25
SUPPLEMENTAL RESTRAINT
SYSTEM (AIR BAG) 6-9
TRAILER WIRING 6-26
UNDERSTANDING AND TROUBLE-
SHOOTING ELECTRICAL
SYSTEMS 6-2
WINDSHIELD WIPERS AND
WASHERS 6-21
WIRING DIAGRAMS 6-27

UNDERSTANDING AND TROUBLE-SHOOTING ELECTRICAL SYSTEMS

Both import and domestic manufacturers are incorporating electronic control systems into their production lines. Most vehicles are equipped with one or more on-board computer, like the unit installed on your car. These electronic components (with no moving parts) should theoretically last the life of the vehicle, provided nothing external happens to damage the circuits or memory chips.

While it is true that electronic components should never wear out, in the real world malfunctions do occur. It is also true that any computer-based system is extremely sensitive to electrical voltages and cannot tolerate careless or haphazard testing or service procedures. An inexperienced individual can literally do major damage looking for a minor problem by using the wrong kind of test equipment or connecting test leads or connectors with the ignition switch ON. When selecting test equipment, make sure the manufacturers instructions state that the tester is compatible with whatever type of electronic control system is being serviced. Read all instructions carefully and double check all test points before installing probes or making any test connections.

The following section outlines basic diagnosis techniques for dealing with computerized automotive control systems. Along with a general explanation of the various types of test equipment available to aid in servicing modern electronic automotive systems, basic repair techniques for wiring harnesses and connectors is given. Read the basic information before attempting any repairs or testing on any computerized system, to provide the background of information necessary to avoid the most common and obvious mistakes that can cost both time and money. Although the replacement and testing procedures are simple in themselves, the systems are not, and unless one has a thorough understanding of all components and their function within a particular computerized control system, the logical test sequence these systems demand cannot be followed. Minor malfunctions can make a big difference, so it is important to know how each component affects the operation of the overall electronic system to find the ultimat e cause of a problem without replacing good components unnecessarily. It is not enough to use the correct test equipment; the test equipment must be used correctly.

Safety Precautions

✳✳CAUTION

Whenever working on or around any computer based microprocessor control system, always observe these general precautions to prevent the possibility of personal injury or damage to electronic components.

• Never install or remove battery cables with the key ON or the engine running. Jumper cables should be connected with the key OFF to avoid power surges that can damage electronic control units. Engines equipped with computer controlled systems should avoid both giving and getting jump starts due to the possibility of serious damage to components from arcing in the engine compartment when connections are made with the ignition ON.

• Always remove the battery cables before charging the battery. Never use a high output charger on an installed battery or attempt to use any type of 'hot shot' (24 volt) starting aid.

• Exercise care when inserting test probes into connectors to insure good connections without damaging the connector or spreading the pins. Always probe connectors from the rear (wire) side, NOT the pin side, to avoid accidental shorting of terminals during test procedures.

• Never remove or attach wiring harness connectors with the ignition switch ON, especially to an electronic control unit.

• Do not drop any components during service procedures and never apply 12 volts directly to any component (like a solenoid or relay) unless instructed specifically to do so. Some component electrical windings are designed to safely handle only 4 or 5 volts and can be destroyed in seconds if 12 volts are applied directly to the connector.

• Remove the electronic control unit if the vehicle is to be placed in an environment where temperatures exceed approximately 176°F (80°C), such as a paint spray booth or when arc or gas welding near the control unit location in the car.

ORGANIZED TROUBLESHOOTING

When diagnosing a specific problem, organized troubleshooting is a must. The complexity of a modern automobile demands that you approach any problem in a logical, organized manner. There are certain troubleshooting techniques that are standard:

1. Establish when the problem occurs. Does the problem appear only under certain conditions? Were there any noises, odors, or other unusual symptoms?

2. Isolate the problem area. To do this, make some simple tests and observations; then eliminate the systems that are working properly. Check for obvious problems such as broken wires, dirty connections or split or disconnected vacuum hoses. Always check the obvious before assuming something complicated is the cause.

3. Test for problems systematically to determine the cause once the problem area is isolated. Are all the components functioning properly? Is there power going to electrical switches and motors? Is there vacuum at vacuum switches and/or actuators? Is there a mechanical problem such as bent linkage or loose mounting screws? Doing careful, systematic checks will often turn up most causes on the first inspection without wasting time checking components that have little or no relationship to the problem.

4. Test all repairs after the work is done to make sure that the problem is fixed. Some causes can be traced to more than one component, so a careful verification of repair work is important to pick up additional malfunctions that may cause a problem to reappear or a different problem to arise. A blown fuse, for example, is a simple problem that may require more than another fuse to repair. If you don't look for a problem that caused a fuse to blow, for example, a shorted wire may go undetected.

Experience has shown that most problems tend to be the result of a fairly simple and obvious cause, such as loose or corroded connectors or air leaks in the intake system; making careful inspection of components during testing essential to quick and accurate troubleshooting. Special, hand held computerized testers designed specifically for diagnosing the system are available from a variety of aftermarket sources, as well as from the vehicle manufacturer, but care should be taken that any test equipment being used is designed to diagnose that particular computer controlled system accurately without damaging the control unit (ECU) or components being tested.

➡**Pinpointing the exact cause of trouble in an electrical system can sometimes only be accomplished by the use of special test equipment. The following describes commonly used test equipment and explains how to put it to best use in diagnosis. In addition to the information covered below, the manufacturer's instructions booklet provided with the tester should be read and clearly understood before attempting any test procedures.**

Testing and Equipment

INFORMATION

Jumper Wires

Jumper wires are simple, yet extremely valuable, pieces of test equipment. Jumper wires are merely wires that are used to bypass sections of a circuit. The simplest type of jumper wire is merely a length of multistrand wire with an alligator clip at each end. Jumper wires are usually fabricated from lengths of standard automotive wire and whatever type of connector (alligator clip, spade connector or pin connector) that is required for the particular vehicle being tested. The well equipped tool box will have several different styles of jumper wires in several different lengths. Some jumper wires are made with three or more terminals coming from a common splice for special purpose testing. In cramped, hard-to-reach areas it is advisable to have insulated boots over the jumper wire terminals in order to prevent accidental grounding, sparks, and possible fire, especially when testing fuel system components.

Jumper wires are used primarily to locate open electrical circuits, on either the ground (-) side of the circuit or on the hot (+) side. If an electrical component fails to operate, connect the jumper wire between the component and a good ground. If the component operates only with the jumper installed, the ground circuit is open. If the ground circuit is good, but the component does not operate, the circuit between the power feed and component is open. You can sometimes connect the jumper wire directly from the battery to the hot terminal of the component, but first make sure the component uses 12 volts in operation. Some electrical components, such as fuel injectors, are designed to operate on about 4 volts and running 12 volts directly to the injector terminals can burn out the wiring. By inserting an inline fuseholder between a set of test leads, a fused jumper wire can be used for bypassing open circuits. Use a 5 amp fuse to provide protection against voltage spikes. When in doubt, use a voltmeter to check the voltage input to the component and measure how much

voltage is being applied normally. By moving the jumper wire successively back from the lamp toward the power source, you can isolate the area of the circuit where the open is located. When the component stops functioning, or the power is cut off, the open is in the segment of wire between the jumper and the point previously tested.

✳✳CAUTION

Never use jumpers made from wire that is of lighter gauge than used in the circuit under test. If the jumper wire is of too small gauge, it may overheat and possibly melt. Never use jumpers to bypass high resistance loads (such as motors) in a circuit. Bypassing resistances, in effect, creates a short circuit which may, in turn, cause damage and fire. Never use a jumper for anything other than temporary bypassing of components in a circuit.

12 Volt Test Light

The 12 volt test light is used to check circuits and components while electrical current is flowing through them. It is used for voltage and ground tests. Twelve volt test lights come in different styles but all have three main parts; a ground clip, a probe, and a light. The most commonly used 12 volt test lights have pick-type probes. To use a 12 volt test light, connect the ground clip to a good ground and probe wherever necessary with the pick. The pick should be sharp so that it can penetrate wire insulation to make contact with the wire, without making a large hole in the insulation. The wrap-around light is handy in hard to reach areas or where it is difficult to support a wire to push a probe pick into it. To use the wrap around light, hook the wire to probed with the hook and pull the trigger. A small pick will be forced through the wire insulation into the wire core.

✳✳CAUTION

Do not use a test light to probe electronic ignition spark plug or coil wires. Never use a pick-type test light to probe wiring on computer controlled systems unless specifically instructed to do so. Any wire insulation that is pierced by the test light probe should be taped and sealed with silicone after testing.

Like the jumper wire, the 12 volt test light is used to isolate opens in circuits. But, whereas the jumper wire is used to bypass the open to operate the load, the 12 volt test light is used to locate the presence of voltage in a circuit. If the test light glows, you know that there is power up to that point; if the 12 volt test light does not glow when its probe is inserted into the wire or connector, you know that there is an open circuit (no power). Move the test light in successive steps back toward the power source until the light in the handle does glow. When it does glow, the open is between the probe and point previously probed.

➡**The test light does not detect that 12 volts (or any particular amount of voltage) is present; it only detects that some voltage is present. It is advisable before using the test light to touch its terminals across the battery posts to make sure the light is operating properly.**

Self-Powered Test Light

The self-powered test light usually contains a 1.5 volt penlight battery. One type of self-powered test light is similar in design to the 12 volt test light. This type has both the battery and the light in the handle and pick-type probe tip. The second type has the light toward the open tip, so that the light illuminates the contact point. The self-powered test light is dual purpose piece of test equipment. It can be used to test for either open or short circuits when power is isolated from the circuit (continuity test). A powered test light should not be used on any computer controlled system or component unless specifically instructed to do so. Many engine sensors can be destroyed by even this small amount of voltage applied directly to the terminals.

Open Circuit Testing

To use the self-powered test light to check for open circuits, first isolate the circuit from the vehicle's 12 volt power source by disconnecting the battery or wiring harness connector. Connect the test light ground clip to a good ground and probe sections of the circuit sequentially with the test light. (start from either end of the circuit). If the light is out, the open is between the probe and the circuit ground. If the light is on, the open is between the probe and end of the circuit toward the power source.

Short Circuit Testing

By isolating the circuit both from power and from ground, and using a self-powered test light, you can check for shorts to ground in the circuit. Isolate the circuit from power and ground. Connect the test light ground clip to a good ground and probe any easy-to-reach test point in the circuit. If the light comes on, there is a short somewhere in the circuit. To isolate the short, probe a test point at either end of the isolated circuit (the light should be on). Leave the test light probe connected and open connectors, switches, remove parts, etc., sequentially, until the light goes out. When the light goes out, the short is between the last circuit component opened and the previous circuit opened.

➡**The 1.5 volt battery in the test light does not provide much current. A weak battery may not provide enough power to illuminate the test light even when a complete circuit is made (especially if there are high resistances in the circuit). Always make sure that the test battery is strong. To check the battery, briefly touch the ground clip to the probe; if the light glows brightly the battery is strong enough for testing. Never use a self-powered test light to perform checks for opens or shorts when power is applied to the electrical system under test. The 12 volt vehicle power will quickly burn out the 1.5 volt light bulb in the test light.**

Voltmeter

A voltmeter is used to measure voltage at any point in a circuit, or to measure the voltage drop across any part of a circuit. It can also be used to check continuity in a wire or circuit by indicating current flow from one end to the other. Voltmeters usually have various scales on the meter dial and a selector switch to allow the selection of different voltages. The voltmeter has a positive and a negative lead. To avoid damage to the meter, always connect the negative lead to the negative (-) side of circuit (to ground or nearest the ground side of the circuit) and connect the positive lead to the positive (+) side of the circuit (to the power source or the nearest power source). Note that the negative voltmeter lead will always be black and that the positive voltmeter will always be some color other than black (usually red). Depending on how the voltmeter is connected into the circuit, it has several uses.

A voltmeter can be connected either in parallel or in series with a circuit and it has a very high resistance to current flow. When connected in parallel, only a small amount of current will flow through the voltmeter current path; the rest will flow through the normal circuit current path and the circuit will work normally. When the voltmeter is connected in series with a circuit, only a small amount of current can flow through the circuit. The circuit will not work properly, but the voltmeter reading will show if the circuit is complete or not.

Available Voltage Measurement

Set the voltmeter selector switch to the 20V position and connect the meter negative lead to the negative post of the battery. Connect the positive meter lead to the positive post of the battery and turn the ignition switch ON to provide a load. Read the voltage on the meter or digital display. A well charged battery should register over 12 volts. If the meter reads below 11.5 volts, the battery power may be insufficient to operate the electrical system properly. This test determines voltage available from the battery and should be the first step in any electrical trouble diagnosis procedure. Many electrical problems, especially on computer controlled systems, can be caused by a low state of charge in the battery. Excessive corrosion at the battery cable terminals can cause a poor contact that will prevent proper charging and full battery current flow.

Normal battery voltage is 12 volts when fully charged. When the battery is supplying current to one or more circuits it is said to be 'under load'. When everything is off the electrical system is under a 'no-load' condition. A fully charged battery may show about 12.5 volts at no load; will drop to 12 volts under medium load; and will drop even lower under heavy load. If the battery is partially discharged the voltage decrease under heavy load may be excessive, even though the battery shows 12 volts or more at no load. When allowed to discharge further, the battery's available voltage under load will decrease more severely. For this reason, it is important that the battery be fully charged during all testing procedures to avoid errors in diagnosis and incorrect test results.

Voltage Drop

When current flows through a resistance, the voltage beyond the resistance is reduced (the larger the current, the greater the reduction in voltage). When no current is flowing, there is no voltage drop because there is no current flow. All points in the circuit which are connected to the power source are at the same voltage as the power source. The total voltage drop always equals the total source voltage. In a long circuit with many connectors, a series of small, unwanted voltage drops due to corrosion at the connectors can add up to a total loss of voltage which impairs the operation of the normal loads in the circuit.

Indirect Computation of Voltage Drops

1. Set the voltmeter selector switch to the 20 volt position.
2. Connect the meter negative lead to a good ground.
3. Probe all resistances in the circuit with the positive meter lead.
4. Operate the circuit in all modes and observe the voltage readings.

Direct Measurement of Voltage Drops

1. Set the voltmeter switch to the 20 volt position.
2. Connect the voltmeter negative lead to the ground side of the resistance load to be measured.
3. Connect the positive lead to the positive side of the resistance or load to be measured.
4. Read the voltage drop directly on the 20 volt scale.

Too high a voltage indicates too high a resistance. If, for example, a blower motor runs too slowly, you can determine if there is too high a resistance in the resistor pack. By taking voltage drop readings in all parts of the circuit, you can isolate the problem. Too low a voltage drop indicates too low a resistance. If, for example, a blower motor runs too fast in the MED and/or LOW position, the problem can be isolated in the resistor pack by taking voltage drop readings in all parts of the circuit to locate a possibly shorted resistor. The maximum allowable voltage drop under load is critical, especially if there is more than one high resistance problem in a circuit because all voltage drops are cumulative. A small drop is normal due to the resistance of the conductors.

High Resistance Testing

1. Set the voltmeter selector switch to the 4 volt position.
2. Connect the voltmeter positive lead to the positive post of the battery.
3. Turn on the headlights and heater blower to provide a load.
4. Probe various points in the circuit with the negative voltmeter lead.
5. Read the voltage drop on the 4 volt scale. Some average maximum allowable voltage drops are:

> FUSE PANEL — 7 volts
> IGNITION SWITCH — 5volts
> HEADLIGHT SWITCH — 7 volts
> IGNITION COIL (+) — 5 volts
> ANY OTHER LOAD — 1.3 volts

➡ **Voltage drops are all measured while a load is operating; without current flow, there will be no voltage drop.**

Ohmmeter

The ohmmeter is designed to read resistance (ohms) in a circuit or component. Although there are several different styles of ohmmeters, all will usually have a selector switch which permits the measurement of different ranges of resistance (usually the selector switch allows the multiplication of the meter reading by 10, 100, 1000, and 10,000). A calibration knob allows the meter to be set at zero for accurate measurement. Since all ohmmeters are powered by an internal battery (usually 9 volts), the ohmmeter can be used as a self-powered test light. When the ohmmeter is connected, current from the ohmmeter flows through the circuit or component being tested. Since the ohmmeter's internal resistance and voltage are known values, the amount of current flow through the meter depends on the resistance of the circuit or component being tested.

The ohmmeter can be used to perform continuity test for opens or shorts (either by observation of the meter needle or as a self-powered test light), and to read actual resistance in a circuit. It should be noted that the ohmmeter is used to check the resistance of a component or wire while there is no voltage applied to the circuit. Current flow from an outside voltage source (such as the vehicle battery) can damage the ohmmeter, so the circuit or component should be isolated from the vehicle electrical system before any testing is done. Since the ohmmeter uses its own voltage source, either lead can be connected to any test point.

➡ **When checking diodes or other solid state components, the ohmmeter leads can only be connected one way in order to measure current flow in a single direction. Make sure the positive (+) and negative (-) terminal connections are as described in the test procedures to verify the one-way diode operation.**

In using the meter for making continuity checks, do not be concerned with the actual resistance readings. Zero resistance, or any resistance readings, indicate continuity in the circuit. Infinite resistance indicates an open in the circuit. A high resistance reading where there should be none indicates a problem in the circuit. Checks for short circuits are made in the same manner as checks for open circuits except that the circuit must be isolated from both power and normal ground. Infinite resistance indicates no continuity to ground, while zero resistance indicates a dead short to ground.

Resistance Measurement

The batteries in an ohmmeter will weaken with age and temperature, so the ohmmeter must be calibrated or 'zeroed' before taking measurements. To zero the meter, place the selector switch in its lowest range and touch the two ohmmeter leads together. Turn the calibration knob until the meter needle is exactly on zero.

➡ **All analog (needle) type ohmmeters must be zeroed before use, but some digital ohmmeter models are automatically calibrated when the switch is turned on. Self-calibrating digital ohmmeters do not have an adjusting knob, but its a good idea to check for a zero readout before use by touching the leads together. All computer controlled systems require the use of a digital ohmmeter with at least 10 megohms impedance for testing. Before any test procedures are attempted, make sure the ohmmeter used is compatible with the electrical system or damage to the on-board computer could result.**

To measure resistance, first isolate the circuit from the vehicle power source by disconnecting the battery cables or the harness connector. Make sure the key is OFF when disconnecting any components or the battery. Where necessary, also isolate at least one side of the circuit to be checked to avoid reading parallel resistances. Parallel circuit resistances will always give a lower reading than the actual resistance of either of the branches. When measuring the resistance of parallel circuits, the total resistance will always be lower than the smallest resistance in the circuit. Connect the meter leads to both sides of the circuit (wire or component) and read the actual measured ohms on the meter scale. Make sure the selector switch is set to the proper ohm scale for the circuit being tested to avoid misreading the ohmmeter test value.

✳✳CAUTION

Never use an ohmmeter with power applied to the circuit. Like the self-powered test light, the ohmmeter is designed to operate on its own power supply. The normal 12 volt automotive electrical system current could damage the meter.

Ammeters

An ammeter measures the amount of current flowing through a circuit in units called amperes or amps. Amperes are units of electron flow which indicate how fast the electrons are flowing through the circuit. Since Ohms Law dictates that current flow in a circuit is equal to the circuit voltage divided by the total circuit resistance, increasing voltage also increases the current level (amps). Likewise, any decrease in resistance will increase the amount of amps in a circuit. At normal operating voltage, most circuits have a characteristic amount of amperes, called 'current draw' which can be measured using an ammeter. By referring to a specified current draw rating, measuring the amperes, and comparing the two values, one can determine what is happening within the circuit to aid in diagnosis. An open circuit, for example, will not allow any current to flow so the ammeter reading will be zero. More current flows through a heavily loaded circuit or when the charging system is operating.

An ammeter is always connected in series with the circuit being tested. All of the current that normally flows through the circuit must also flow through the ammeter; if there is any other path for the current to follow, the ammeter reading will not be accurate. The ammeter itself has very little resistance to current flow and therefore will not affect the circuit, but it will measure current draw only when the circuit is closed and electricity is flowing. Excessive current draw can blow fuses and drain the battery, while a reduced current draw can cause motors to run slowly, lights to dim and other components to not operate properly. The ammeter can help diagnose these conditions by locating the cause of the high or low reading.

Multimeters

Different combinations of test meters can be built into a single unit designed for specific tests. Some of the more common combination test devices are known as Volt/Amp testers, Tach/Dwell meters, or Digital Multimeters. The Volt/Amp tester is used for charging system, starting system or battery tests and consists of a voltmeter, an ammeter and a variable resistance carbon pile. The voltmeter will usually have at least two ranges for use with 6, 12 and 24 volt systems. The ammeter also has more than one range for testing various levels of battery loads and starter current draw and the carbon pile can be adjusted to offer different amounts of resistance. The Volt/Amp tester has heavy leads to carry large amounts of current and many later models have an inductive ammeter pickup that clamps around the wire to simplify test connections. On some models, the ammeter also has a zero-center scale to allow testing of charging and starting systems without switching leads or polarity. A digital multimeter is a voltmeter, ammeter and ohmmeter combined in an instrument which gives a digital readout. These are often used when testing solid state circuits because of their high input impedance (usually 10 megohms or more).

The tach/dwell meter combines a tachometer and a dwell (cam angle) meter and is a specialized kind of voltmeter. The tachometer scale is marked to show engine speed in rpm and the dwell scale is marked to show degrees of distributor shaft rotation. In most electronic ignition systems, dwell is determined by the control unit, but the dwell meter can also be used to check the duty cycle (operation) of some electronic engine control systems. Some tach/dwell meters are powered by an internal battery, while others take their power from the car battery in use. The battery powered testers usually require calibration much like an ohmmeter before testing.

Special Test Equipment

A variety of diagnostic tools are available to help troubleshoot and repair computerized engine control systems. The most sophisticated of these devices are the console type engine analyzers that usually occupy a garage service bay, but there are several types of aftermarket electronic testers available that will allow quick circuit tests of the engine control system by plugging directly into a special connector located in the engine compartment or under the dashboard. Several tool and equipment manufacturers offer simple, hand held testers that measure various circuit voltage levels on command to check all system components for proper operation. Although these testers usually cost about $300-$500, consider that the average computer control unit (or ECM) can cost just as much and the money saved by not replacing perfectly good sensors or components in an attempt to correct a problem could justify the purchase price of a special diagnostic tester the first time it's used.

These computerized testers can allow quick and easy test measurements while the engine is operating or while the car is being driven. In addition, the on-board computer memory can be read to access any stored trouble codes; in effect allowing the computer to tell you where it hurts and aid trouble diagnosis by pinpointing exactly which circuit or component is malfunctioning. In the same manner, repairs can be tested to make sure the problem has been corrected. The biggest advantage these special testers have is their relatively easy hookups that minimize or eliminate the chances of making the wrong connections and getting false voltage readings or damaging the computer accidentally.

➡**It should be remembered that these testers check voltage levels in circuits; they don't detect mechanical problems or failed components if the circuit voltage falls within the preprogrammed limits stored in the tester PROM unit. Also, most of the hand held testers are designed to work only on one or two systems made by a specific manufacturer.**

A variety of aftermarket testers are available to help diagnose different computerized control systems. Owatonna Tool Company (OTC), for example, markets a device called the OTC Monitor which plugs directly into the assembly line diagnostic link (ALDL). The OTC tester makes diagnosis a simple matter of pressing the correct buttons and, by changing the internal PROM or inserting a different diagnosis cartridge, it will work on any model from full size to subcompact, over a wide range of years. An adapter is supplied with the tester to allow connection to all types of ALDL links, regardless of the number of pin terminals used. By inserting an updated PROM into the OTC tester, it can be easily updated to diagnose any new modifications of computerized control systems.

Wiring Harnesses

GENERAL INFORMATION

The average automobile contains about ½ mile of wiring, with hundreds of individual connections. To protect the many wires from damage and to keep them from becoming a confusing tangle, they are organized into bundles, enclosed in plastic or taped together and called wire harnesses. Different wiring harnesses serve different parts of the vehicle. Individual wires are color coded to help trace them through a harness where sections are hidden from view.

A loose or corroded connection or a replacement wire that is too small for the circuit will add extra resistance and an additional voltage drop to the circuit. A ten percent voltage drop can result in slow or erratic motor operation, for example, even though the circuit is complete. Automotive wiring or circuit conductors can be in any one of three forms:
1. Single strand wire
2. Multistrand wire
3. Printed circuitry

Single strand wire has a solid metal core and is usually used inside such components as alternators, motors, relays and other devices. Multistrand wire has a core made of many small strands of wire twisted together into a single conductor. Most of the wiring in an automotive electrical system is made up of multistrand wire, either as a single conductor or grouped together in a harness. All wiring is color coded on the insulator, either as a solid color or as a colored wire with an identification stripe. A printed circuit is a thin film of copper or other conductor that is printed on an insulator backing. Occasionally, a printed circuit is sandwiched between two sheets of plastic for more protection and flexibility. A complete printed circuit, consisting of conductors, insulating material and connectors for lamps or other components is called a printed circuit board. Printed circuitry is used in place of individual wires or harnesses in places where space is limited, such as behind instrument panel.

Wire Gauge

Since computer controlled automotive electrical systems are very sensitive to changes in resistance, the selection of properly sized wires is critical when systems are repaired. The wire gauge number is an expression of the cross section area of the conductor. The most common system for expressing wire size is the American Wire Gauge (AWG) system.

Wire cross section area is measured in circular mils. A mil is $\frac{1}{1000}$" (0.001"); a circular mil is the area of a circle one mil in diameter. For example, a conductor ¼" in diameter is 0.250 inches or 250 mils. The circular mil cross section area of the wire is 250 squared (250^2) or 62,500 circular mils. Imported car models usually use metric wire gauge designations, which is simply the cross section area of the conductor in square millimeters (mm^2).

Gauge numbers are assigned to conductors of various cross section areas. As gauge number increases, area decreases and the conductor becomes smaller. A 5 gauge conductor is smaller than a 1 gauge conductor and a 10 gauge is smaller than a 5 gauge. As the cross section area of a conductor decreases, resistance increases and so does the gauge number. A conductor with a higher gauge number will carry less current than a conductor with a lower gauge number.

➡ **Gauge wire size refers to the size of the conductor, not the size of the complete wire. It is possible to have two wires of the same gauge with different diameters because one may have thicker insulation than the other.**

12 volt automotive electrical systems generally use 10, 12, 14, 16 and 18 gauge wire. Main power distribution circuits and larger accessories usually use 10 and 12 gauge wire. Battery cables are usually 4 or 6 gauge, although 1 and 2 gauge wires are occasionally used. Wire length must also be considered when making repairs to a circuit. As conductor length increases, so does resistance. An 18 gauge wire, for example, can carry a 10 amp load for 10 feet without excessive voltage drop; however if a 15 foot wire is required for the same 10 amp load, it must be a 16 gauge wire.

An electrical schematic shows the electrical current paths when a circuit is operating properly. It is essential to understand how a circuit works before trying to figure out why it doesn't. Schematics break the entire electrical system down into individual circuits and show only one particular circuit. In a schematic, no attempt is made to represent wiring and components as they physically appear on the vehicle; switches and other components are shown as simply as possible. Face views of harness connectors show the cavity or terminal locations in all multi-pin connectors to help locate test points.

If you need to backprobe a connector while it is on the component, the order of the terminals must be mentally reversed. The wire color code can help in this situation, as well as a keyway, lock tab or other reference mark.

Wiring Repair

Soldering is a quick, efficient method of joining metals permanently. Everyone who has the occasion to make wiring repairs should know how to solder. Electrical connections that are soldered are far less likely to come apart and will conduct electricity much better than connections that are only 'pigtailed' together. The most popular (and preferred) method of soldering is with an electrical soldering gun. Soldering irons are available in many sizes and wattage ratings. Irons with higher wattage ratings deliver higher temperatures and recover lost heat faster. A small soldering iron rated for no more than 50 watts is recommended, especially on electrical systems where excess heat can damage the components being soldered.

There are three ingredients necessary for successful soldering; proper flux, good solder and sufficient heat. A soldering flux is necessary to clean the metal of tarnish, prepare it for soldering and to enable the solder to spread into tiny crevices. When soldering, always use a resin flux or resin core solder which is non-corrosive and will not attract moisture once the job is finished. Other types of flux (acid core) will leave a residue that will attract moisture and cause the wires to corrode. Tin is a unique metal with a low melting point. In a molten state, it dissolves and alloys easily with many metals. Solder is made by mixing tin with lead. The most common proportions are 40/60, 50/50 and 60/40, with the percentage of tin listed first. Low priced solders usually contain less tin, making them very difficult for a beginner to use because more heat is required to melt the solder. A common solder is 40/60 which is well suited for all-around general use, but 60/40 melts easier, has more tin f or a better joint and is preferred for electrical work.

Soldering Techniques

Successful soldering requires that the metals to be joined be heated to a temperature that will melt the solder — usually 360-460°F (182-238°C). Contrary to popular belief, the purpose of the soldering iron is not to melt the solder itself, but to heat the parts being soldered to a temperature high enough to melt the solder when it is touched to the work. Melting flux-cored solder on the soldering iron will usually destroy the effectiveness of the flux.

➡**Soldering tips are made of copper for good heat conductivity, but must be 'tinned' regularly for quick transference of heat to the project and to prevent the solder from sticking to the iron. To 'tin' the iron, simply heat it and touch the flux-cored solder to the tip; the solder will flow over the hot tip. Wipe the excess off with a clean rag, but be careful as the iron will be hot.**

After some use, the tip may become pitted. If so, simply dress the tip smooth with a smooth file and 'tin' the tip again. An old saying holds that 'metals well cleaned are half soldered.' Flux-cored solder will remove oxides but rust, bits of insulation and oil or grease must be removed with a wire brush or emery cloth. For maximum strength in soldered parts, the joint must start off clean and tight. Weak joints will result in gaps too wide for the solder to bridge.

If a separate soldering flux is used, it should be brushed or swabbed on only those areas that are to be soldered. Most solders contain a core of flux and separate fluxing is unnecessary. Hold the work to be soldered firmly. It is best to solder on a wooden board, because a metal vise will only rob the piece to be soldered of heat and make it difficult to melt the solder. Hold the soldering tip with the broadest face against the work to be soldered. Apply solder under the tip close to the work, using enough solder to give a heavy film between the iron and the piece being soldered, while moving slowly and making sure the solder melts properly. Keep the work level or the solder will run to the lowest part and favor the thicker parts, because these require more heat to melt the solder. If the soldering tip overheats (the solder coating on the face of the tip burns up), it should be retinned. Once the soldering is completed, let the soldered joint stand until cool. Tape and seal all soldered wire spli ces after the repair has cooled.

Wire Harness and Connectors

The on-board computer (ECM) wire harness electrically connects the control unit to the various solenoids, switches and sensors used by the control system. Most connectors in the engine compartment or otherwise exposed to the elements are protected against moisture and dirt which could create oxidation and deposits on the terminals. This protection is important because of the very low voltage and current levels used by the computer and sensors. All connectors have a lock which secures the male and female terminals together, with a secondary lock holding the seal and terminal into the connector. Both terminal locks must be released when disconnecting ECM connectors.

These special connectors are weather-proof and all repairs require the use of a special terminal and the tool required to service it. This tool is used to remove the pin and sleeve terminals. If removal is attempted with an ordinary pick, there is a good chance that the terminal will be bent or deformed. Unlike standard blade type terminals, these terminals cannot be straightened once they are bent. Make certain that the connectors are properly seated and all of the sealing rings in place when connecting leads. On some models, a hinge-type flap provides a backup or secondary locking feature for the terminals. Most secondary locks are used to improve the connector reliability by retaining the terminals if the small terminal lock tangs are not positioned properly.

Molded-on connectors require complete replacement of the connection. This means splicing a new connector assembly into the harness. All splices in on-board computer systems should be soldered to insure proper contact. Use care when probing the connections or replacing terminals in them as it is possible to short between opposite terminals. If this happens to the wrong terminal pair, it is possible to damage certain components. Always use jumper wires between connectors for circuit checking and never probe through weatherproof seals.

Open circuits are often difficult to locate by sight because corrosion or terminal misalignment are hidden by the connectors. Merely wiggling a connector on a sensor or in the wiring harness may correct the open circuit condition. This should always be considered when an open circuit or a failed sensor is indicated. Intermittent problems may also be caused by oxidized or loose connections. When using a circuit tester for diagnosis, always probe connections from the wire side. Be careful not to damage sealed connectors with test probes.

All wiring harnesses should be replaced with identical parts, using the same gauge wire and connectors. When signal wires are spliced into a harness, use wire with high temperature insulation only. With the low voltage and current levels found in the system, it is important that the best possible connection at all wire splices be made by soldering the splices together. It is seldom necessary to replace a complete harness. If replacement is necessary, pay close attention to insure proper harness routing. Secure the harness with suitable plastic wire clamps to prevent vibrations from causing the harness to wear in spots or contact any hot components.

➡**Weatherproof connectors cannot be replaced with standard connectors. Instructions are provided with replacement connector and terminal packages. Some wire harnesses have mounting indicators (usually pieces of colored tape) to mark where the harness is to be secured.**

In making wiring repairs, it's important that you always replace damaged wires with wires that are the same gauge as the wire being replaced. The heavier the wire, the smaller the gauge number. Wires are color-coded to aid in identification and whenever possible the same color coded wire should be used for replacement. A wire stripping and crimping tool is necessary to install solderless terminal connectors. Test all crimps by pulling on the wires; it should not be possible to pull the wires out of a good crimp.

Wires which are open, exposed or otherwise damaged are repaired by simple splicing. Where possible, if the wiring harness is accessible and the damaged place in the wire can be located, it is best to open the harness and check for all possible damage. In an inaccessible harness, the wire must be bypassed with a new insert, usually taped to the outside of the old harness.

When replacing fusible links, be sure to use fusible link wire, NOT ordinary automotive wire. Make sure the fusible segment is of the same gauge and construction as the one being replaced and double the stripped end when crimping the terminal connector for a good contact. The melted (open) fusible link segment of the wiring harness should be cut off as close to the harness as possible, then a new segment spliced in as described. In the case of a damaged fusible link that feeds two harness wires, the harness connections should be replaced with two fusible link wires so that each circuit will have its own separate protection.

➡ **Most of the problems caused in the wiring harness are due to bad ground connections. Always check all vehicle ground connections for corrosion or looseness before performing any power feed checks to eliminate the chance of a bad ground affecting the circuit.**

Repairing Hard Shell Connectors

Unlike molded connectors, the terminal contacts in hard shell connectors can be replaced. Weatherproof hard-shell connectors with the leads molded into the shell have non-replaceable terminal ends. Replacement usually involves the use of a special terminal removal tool that depress the locking tangs (barbs) on the connector terminal and allow the connector to be removed from the rear of the shell. The connector shell should be replaced if it shows any evidence of burning, melting, cracks, or breaks. Replace individual terminals that are burnt, corroded, distorted or loose.

➡ **The insulation crimp must be tight to prevent the insulation from sliding back on the wire when the wire is pulled. The insulation must be visibly compressed under the crimp tabs, and the ends of the crimp should be turned in for a firm grip on the insulation.**

The wire crimp must be made with all wire strands inside the crimp. The terminal must be fully compressed on the wire strands with the ends of the crimp tabs turned in to make a firm grip on the wire. Check all connections with an ohmmeter to insure a good contact. There should be no measurable resistance between the wire and the terminal when connected.

Mechanical Test Equipment

GENERAL INFORMATION

Vacuum Gauge

Most gauges are graduated in inches of mercury (in. Hg), although a device called a manometer reads vacuum in inches of water (in. H_2O). The normal vacuum reading usually varies between 18 and 22 in. Hg at sea level. To test engine vacuum, the vacuum gauge must be connected to a source of manifold vacuum. Many engines have a plug in the intake manifold which can be removed and replaced with an adapter fitting. Connect the vacuum gauge to the fitting with a suitable rubber hose or, if no manifold plug is available, connect the vacuum gauge to any device using manifold vacuum, such as EGR valves, etc. The vacuum gauge can be used to determine if enough vacuum is reaching a component to allow its actuation.

Hand Vacuum Pump

Small, hand-held vacuum pumps come in a variety of designs. Most have a built-in vacuum gauge and allow the component to be tested without removing it from the vehicle. Operate the pump lever or plunger to apply the correct amount of vacuum required for the test specified in the diagnosis routines. The level of vacuum in inches of Mercury (in. Hg) is indicated on the pump gauge. For some testing, an additional vacuum gauge may be necessary.

Intake manifold vacuum is used to operate various systems and devices on late model vehicles. To correctly diagnose and solve problems in vacuum control systems, a vacuum source is necessary for testing. In some cases, vacuum can be taken from the intake manifold when the engine is running, but vacuum is normally provided by a hand vacuum pump. These hand vacuum pumps have a built-in vacuum gauge that allow testing while the device is still attached to the component. For some tests, an additional vacuum gauge may be necessary.

SUPPLEMENTAL RESTRAINT SYSTEM (AIR BAG)

General Information

The air bag system used on Cabriolet is referred to as a Supplemental Restraint System (SRS). The SRS system is designed to provide additional protection for the driver in a forward collision by deploying an air bag from the steering column. It is not meant to replace the seat belt.

The Cabriolet equipped with the SRS uses a new design of front seat belt. There is an extra length or belt folded over and stitched together. The stitching is designed to separate gradually at a certain force, resulting in a more gradual deceleration of the occupants, subjecting them to a lesser force during a severe frontal impact.

The SRS incorporates 2 front deceleration sensors, a control unit with a safety sensor, air bag unit, spiral spring, knee bar, a control lamp and a warning lamp.

SYSTEM OPERATION

The diagnostic program in the control unit continuously monitors the readiness of the air bag unit, sensors and wiring. When the ignition switch is first turned ON, the air bag warning lamp will light up for approximately 5-8 seconds while the diagnostic program is running, then go out. If the light does not illuminate or stays on continuously, there is a fault in the system and the SRS will not function.

The SRS diagnostic module contains a safety sensor which is similar to the front crash sensors. Under normal circumstances, the air bag will be activated at an impact speed of more than 12 mph (20 km/h). The impact must in an area of 30 degrees longitudinal axis to the left and right of the vehicle; almost straight ahead. The safety sensor in the diagnostic unit and at least 1 of the front crash sensors must simultaneously make contact for the air bag to be activated. When this happens, the SRS control unit energizes the electrical circuit and the gas generators are ignited. This causes a sudden burning of a solid fuel mixture, which in turn completely inflates the air bag. Discharging takes place through holes on the side of the air bag facing away from the driver.

The SRS control unit incorporates a charge capacitor. When the ignition switch is turned to the **ON** position, the capacitor is charged to 35 volts. This energy remains stored while the vehicle is operating and can supply the air bag system if the vehicle's normal battery power is interrupted.

SYSTEM COMPONENTS

SRS Waring Light and Control Light

Both the warning light and control light, located in the instrument panel cluster, are used for the air bag system. The control light on the left is used to indicate the readiness of the system. When the ignition switch is first turned ON, the light must turn ON for 5-8 seconds, then turn OFF. If the light does not turn ON or stays ON, there is a fault in the system and the control unit will not activate the air bag.

Air Bag Unit

The air bag unit, folded up within the steering wheel, acts as a cushion between the driver and the steering wheel during a severe frontal impact. The unit includes an electrically activated gas generator which fills the air bag in about 2 tenths of a second.

Knee Bar

The knee bar, located beneath the instrument panel, is designed to prevent the front seat occupants from sliding out from under the air bag and seat belt.

Spiral Spring Assembly

The spiral spring assembly, located in the steering column, maintains electrical contact with the electrical system and air bag unit at all times.

Deceleration Sensor

The deceleration sensors, located in the right and left side plenum chamber, are used to activate the system. The sensor consists of a roller, mounted on a ramp and a spring band. The combination of the spring band and ramp allows the roller to move forward only after a predetermine deceleration is reached.

Air Bag Control Unit

The air bag control unit, located beneath the vehicle's center console, constantly monitors the air bag system. The SRS control unit consists of the following:
- A diagnostic unit with permanent fault memory
- A safety sensor to arm the system
- A capacitor to ignite the air bag in the event of a power interruption during an accident
- A step-up voltage transformer for igniting the gas generator
- System wiring harness

Service Precautions

❋❋CAUTION

Unintended deployment of the air bag inside or outside of the vehicle can cause serious or fatal injury. To avoid personal injury, all precautions must be strictly adhered to.

- Do not disassemble or tamper with the air bag assembly.
- Always store a removed air bag assembly with the pad surface upwards.
- Never install used air bag parts from another vehicle.
- Never treat SRS components with cleaning solutions or grease.
- Never subject the gas generators to temperatures above 212°F (100°C).
- If the SRS system was activated because of an accident, always replace all components, except the wiring.
- Never replace the original steering wheel with any other design, since it will make it impossible to properly install the air bag.
- Never install an air bag assembly that shows signs of being dropped or improperly handled, such as dents, cracks or deformation.
- Never alter or modified the air bag system wiring.
- Always wear gloves and safety glasses when handling a deployed air bag assembly. Wash hands with mild soap and water afterwards.
- Always store the air bag assembly on a secure flat surface, away from high heat source and free of oil, grease, detergent or water.

DISARMING THE SYSTEM

▶ **See Figure 1**

The back-up power supply for the air bag is in the control unit. It will drain down by itself after the battery is disconnected but this takes about 20 minutes. Do not use a computer memory saver device. It will keep the back-up power supply charged.

If it is necessary to remove the steering wheel, disconnect the negative battery cable and wait at least 20 minutes for the power supply to discharge. To remove the air bag unit, remove the Torx® screws on either side of the back of the steering wheel. The screws must be replaced when removed. Tilt the unit down and disconnect the wire. Place the air bag unit face up where it will not be disturbed and do not place anything on top of it.

ENABLING THE SYSTEM

If the air bag unit was removed, make sure the battery has been disconnected for more than 20 minutes before installing it. Connect the wire, fit the unit onto the steering wheel and

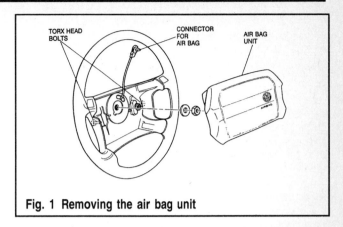

Fig. 1 Removing the air bag unit

install 2 new Torx® screws. Proper torque of the screws is critical to proper deployment of the air bag. Torque the screws to 7 ft. lbs. (10 Nm).

Make sure no one is in the vehicle, then connect the battery. Turn the ignition switch **ON** and verify that the left indicator light turns ON for 5-8 seconds, then goes out. If the light does not work properly, the air bag system must be serviced at the dealer.

HEATER

Blower Motor

REMOVAL & INSTALLATION

▶ **See Figures 2 and 3**

Golf and Jetta

The blower motor is located behind the glove box and it may be easier to remove the glove box to gain access to the motor. The series resistor is mounted on the motor.

1. Disconnect the wires at the blower motor.
2. At the blower motor flange near the cowl, disengage the retaining lug; pull down on the lug.
3. Turn the motor assembly clockwise to release it from it's mount, then remove it from the plenum.
4. The resistor can be checked by connecting an ohmmeter to terminal A and terminals 1 and 2. At terminal 1, resistance should be about 3.3 ohms. At terminal 2, resistance should be about 0.8 ohms.
5. Installation is the reverse of removal.

Cabriolet

The blower motor and series resistor are reached from under the hood, just in front of the windshield.

1. Disconnect the negative battery cable.
2. Remove the clips and gasket holding the water deflector in place and remove the deflector.
3. To remove the plastic cover that is now visible. Some vehicles have fasteners which are accessed from both under the hood and under the dash. If after removing all screws,

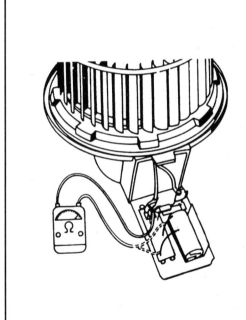

Fig. 2 Checking blower motor resistance on Golf and Jetta

bolts or clips visible from above, the cover still won't lift off, check under the dash for more screws.

4. On vehicles with air conditioning, disconnect the linkage for the air distribution flaps. Remove the remaining plastic cover.

5. The blower and series resistor are now accessible. Remove the screws and the motor.

6. Installation is the reverse of removal. Be sure the seal around the motor is properly reinstalled.

Heater Core

REMOVAL & INSTALLATION

▶ **See Figures 4 and 5**

Cabriolet

It is necessary to remove the instrument panel and to discharge the air conditioning system. If freon recovery equipment is not available, this job should be done at the dealer or a shop that has the proper equipment.

1. Disconnect the battery cable.

2. Remove the steering wheel. Tilt the shelf downward, remove the screws and remove the shelf.

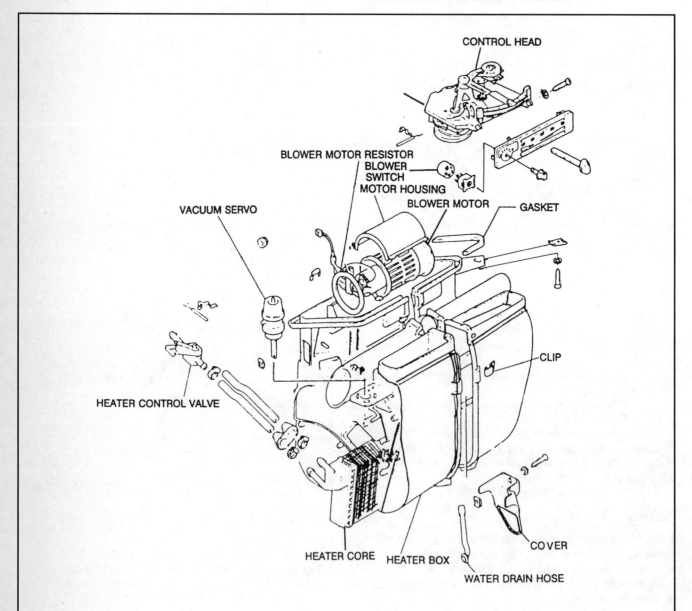

Fig. 3 Cabriolet heater assembly

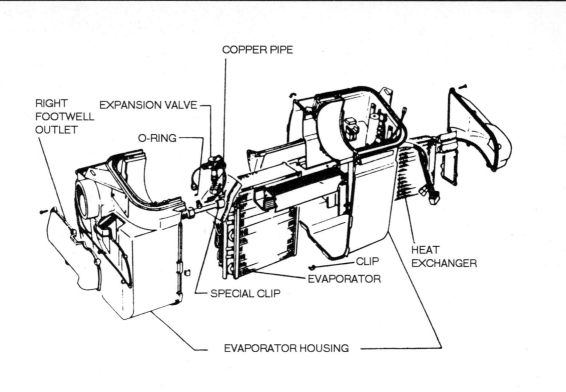

COPPER PIPE

RIGHT FOOTWELL OUTLET

EXPANSION VALVE

O-RING

HEAT EXCHANGER

CLIP

EVAPORATOR

SPECIAL CLIP

EVAPORATOR HOUSING

Fig. 4 Evaporator core removal — Cabriolet

3. From the driver's side, remove the instrument panel cover-to-instrument panel screws, pry out the clips and pull the cover downward.

4. Remove the shift knob and pull the boot out of the console.

5. From the driver's side, remove the instrument panel cover-to-instrument panel screws, pry out the clips and pull the cover downward.

6. From the passenger's side, remove the shelf-to-instrument panel screws and the shelf. Pry out the lower instrument panel cover-to-instrument panel clips and pull the cover from the guides.

7. At the console, remove the screws and pull the lower part of the console rearward.

8. From the heater/fresh air control, remove the knobs and trim.

9. From the upper part of the console, remove the screws and pull the upper part of the console out slightly. Disconnect the electrical connectors from the console and remove the upper console pan.

10. At the upper part of the instrument cluster, remove the instrument cluster trim screws and the trim. Remove the instrument cluster (center) screw and tip the cluster forward. Pull off the vacuum hose and multi-point connector from the instrument cluster. Disconnect the speedometer cable from the instrument cluster.

11. From the instrument panel, push the switch forward (out of the panel), pull the air ducts from the side vents.

12. Disconnect the electrical connectors from the ashtray housing and the wiring harness from the instrument panel.

13. Open the glove box and remove the screws from the center, left and right sides.

14. Pull out the heater/fresh air control, pry off the E-clip and disconnect the flap cable. Remove the control.

15. Remove the instrument panel-to-chassis screws and clips. Remove the instrument panel from the vehicle.

16. Drain the cooling system.

17. Disconnect the hoses from the heater core.

18. Discharge the air conditioning system into freon recovery equipment.

19. Disconnect the vacuum connectors from the fresh air box.

20. Disconnect the cables as required from the evaporator housing. Remove the retaining bolts, the heater core hoses, the evaporator inlet and outlet hoses and cap or plug the openings immediately.

21. Remove the heater assembly from the vehicle. Remove the screw and lift the heater core out of the housing.

To install:

22. Install the heater core into the housing and fit the housing into the vehicle. Connect the heater hoses and the air conditioner lines.

23. Position the instrument panel into the vehicle and install the screws and clips.

24. Install the heater/fresh air control, connect the flap control and the E-clip.

25. Install the glove box and secure with the screws.

26. Connect the wiring harness to the instrument panel.

27. Connect the speedometer cable, vacuum hose and multi-point connector to the instrument cluster. Install the instrument cluster and trim.

28. Install the upper console pan and connect the electrical connectors.

29. Install the heater controls, knobs and trim.

30. At the passenger's side, install the instrument panel cover and the shelf.

31. At the driver's side, install the instrument panel cover.

32. Install the shelf and tilt it upward. Install the steering wheel.

33. When the interior has been assembled, evacuate and recharge the air conditioner and fill and bleed the cooling system.

Golf an Jetta

It is necessary to remove the instrument panel and to discharge the air conditioning system. Procedures for discharging and servicing the air conditioning system are described in Section 1. If freon recovery equipment is not available, this job should be done at the dealer or a shop that has the proper equipment.

1. Disconnect the negative battery cable.

2. Drain the cooling system and disconnect the heater hoses from the firewall.

3. Properly discharge the air conditioning system using freon recovery equipment.

4. Remove the gear shift knob and boot and remove the center console.

5. Remove the steering wheel.

6. Remove the knee bar from below the dashboard.

7. Remove the steering column support bracket and lower the column.

8. Pull the knobs off the heater controls and remove the control assembly and the radio.

9. Remove the headlight switch and switch blanks to gain access to the screws. Remove the instrument cluster and trim panel around the cluster.

10. Remove the glove compartment.

11. At the firewall, remove the plastic tray and remove the 2 nuts holding the top of the dashboard.

12. Remove the main fuse panel and disconnect the plugs at the back. Disconnect the ground wires.

13. Disconnect any remaining wiring from the dashboard and remove the 4 last screws; 1 at each end and 1 at each end of the instrument cluster area. Remove the dashboard.

14. Disconnect the ducts and remove the heater housing. Remove the screws and slide the heater core out of the housing.

To install:

15. Install the heater core and make sure the housing seals and gaskets are in good condition. Replace as necessary.

16. With the heater housing properly installed, install the dashboard and connect the wiring. Install the steering column bracket bolts.

17. Install the fuse panel and connect the wiring.

18. Install the glove compartment, shift boot and knob and steering wheel.

19. When the interior has been assembled, evacuate and recharge the air conditioner and fill and bleed the cooling system.

Control Head and Cables

REMOVAL & INSTALLATION

1. Disconnect the negative battery cable.

2. Remove the bezel in order to gain access to the control head.

3. Remove the screws that fasten the control head to the instrument panel. Remove the control panel and disconnect the blower switch wiring.

4. Pry the cable clips free and disconnect the cables from the control levers to remove the control head.

5. Release the clips to disconnect the cables from the heater. Take note of the cable routing.

To install:

6. Fit the cables into place but don't install the retaining clips yet.

7. Connect the self-adjusting clip to the door crank and secure the cable.

8. Connect the upper end of the cable to the control head.

9. Place the temperature lever on the coolest side of its travel. Allowing the self-adjusting clip to slide on the cable, rotate the door counterclockwise by hand until it stops.

10. Cycle the lever back and forth a few times to make sure the cable moves freely.

ADJUSTMENT

1. Move the temperature control lever to the full cold position.

2. With the control cable attached to the air mix door link, pull the cable housing out and push the inner cable in the opposite direction.

3. Secure the cable in this position with the retaining clamp.

4. Operate the temperature control lever and check freedom of movement at full stroke range.

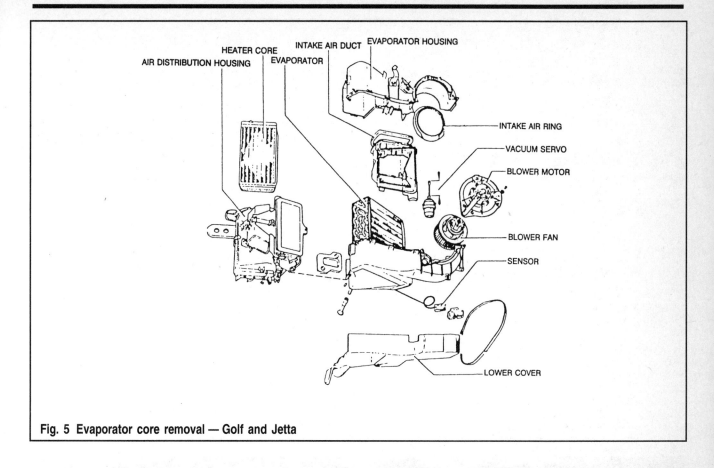

Fig. 5 Evaporator core removal — Golf and Jetta

AIR CONDITIONING

Compressor

REMOVAL & INSTALLATION

Gasoline Engine

◆ **See Figure 6**

Procedures for discharging and servicing the air conditioning system are described in Section 1. If freon recovery equipment is not available, this job should be done at the dealer or a shop that has the proper equipment.

1. Discharge the air conditioning system into freon recovery equipment.
2. Disconnect the wiring from the magnetic clutch on the compressor.
3. Disconnect the suction and the discharge lines from the compressor head. Cap or plug the openings in the compressor and the lines immediately.
4. Loosen the belt tension and disconnect the alternator wires. Remove the alternator.
5. Loosen the belt, remove the bolts and remove the compressor.
   To install:
6. Install the compressor to the bracket but do not tighten the bolts.
7. Connect the coolant lines to the compressor.

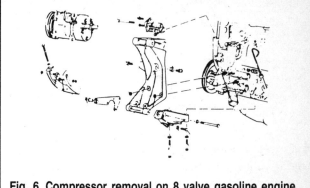

Fig. 6 Compressor removal on 8 valve gasoline engine

8. Install the alternator and all the drive belts. Adjust the belt tension.
9. Connect the wiring to the alternator and compressor.
10. Evacuate and recharge the air conditioning system.

Diesel Engine

◆ **See Figure 7**

The compressor removal procedure is the same as for gasoline engines except the injection pump must be removed first. Instructions for pump removal, installation and timing adjustment appear in Section 5.

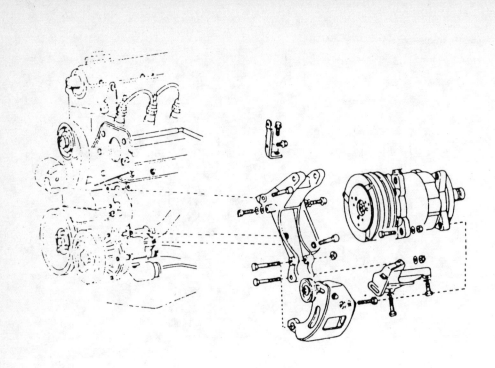

Fig. 7 Compressor removal on diesel engine

Condenser

REMOVAL & INSTALLATION

Procedures for discharging and servicing the air conditioning system are described in Section 1. If freon recovery equipment is not available, this job should be done at the dealer or a shop that has the proper equipment.

1. Disconnect the battery cables and remove the battery.
2. Drain the cooling system and remove the radiator.
3. Disconnect the inlet and outlet lines at the condenser. Cap or plug the openings immediately.
4. Remove the retaining brackets from the condenser and carefully lift the condenser from the front of the vehicle.
   To install:
5. Install the condenser and brackets.
6. Connect the inlet and outlet lines to the condenser.
7. Install the radiator and connect the hoses.
8. If the equipped with an automatic transmission, install the fluid cooling lines to the radiator.
9. Evacuate and charge the air conditioning system.

Evaporator Core

REMOVAL & INSTALLATION

This procedure is the same as removing the heater core. See Heater Core removal and installation earlier in this section.

Control Panel

REMOVAL & INSTALLATION

▶ See Figures 8 and 9

1. Pull the control knobs straight out to remove them.
2. Carefully pry the control panel off the dashboard.
3. Remove the screws and pull the control head out far enough to disconnect the vacuum lines and control cable.
4. Installation is the reverse of removal.

Expansion Valve

REMOVAL & INSTALLATION

The expansion valve is located within the evaporator housing assembly and is removed with the evaporator core.

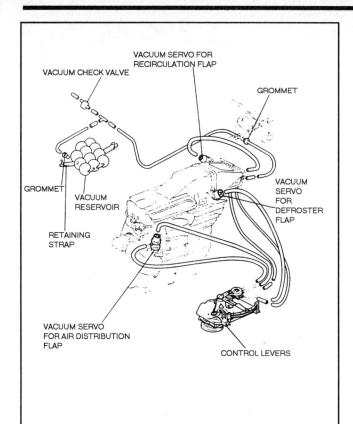

Fig. 8 Air conditioning control vacuum lines — Cabriolet

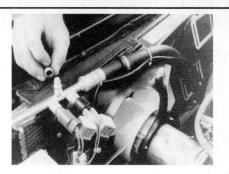

Fig. 10 System pressure switches are mounted near the high pressure service valve

Receiver/Drier

REMOVAL & INSTALLATION

1. Discharge the system using freon recovery equipment.
2. Disconnect the lines from the receiver/drier inlet and outlet fittings; be sure to plug or cap the openings.
3. Loosen the clamps and remove the receiver/drier from its mounting bracket.
4. Installation is the reverse of removal.

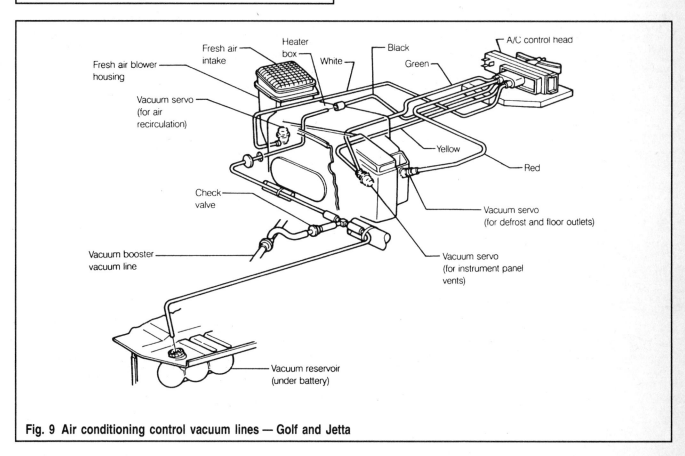

Fig. 9 Air conditioning control vacuum lines — Golf and Jetta

Refrigerant Lines

REMOVAL & INSTALLATION

1. Properly discharge the air conditioning system into freon recovery equipment.

2. Unscrew the desired line from its adjoining component. If the lines are connected with flare nuts, use a back-up wrench when disassembling. Cover the exposed ends of the lines to minimize contamination.

3. Remove the lines and discard the O-rings.

To install:

4. Coat the O-rings with refrigerant oil and connect the refrigerant lines. Use a back-up wrench to tighten the fittings.

5. Evacuate and recharge the air conditioning system.

CRUISE CONTROL

Control Switch

REMOVAL & INSTALLATION

▶ **See Figure 11**

1. Disconnect the negative battery cable.
2. Remove the horn pad.

➡**On Cabriolet, disarm the air bag system and remove the air bag unit.**

3. Mark the position of the steering wheel to the shaft and remove the wheel.

4. Remove the combination switch retaining screws. Carefully remove the switch from the steering column.

5. Remove the screws retaining the cruise control switch to combination switch and remove the cruise control switch.

To install:

6. Assemble the cruise control switch to the combination switch.

7. Install the combination switch and connect the wiring.

8. Align the marks made for the steering wheel-to-column position and install the steering wheel. Torque the nut to 30 ft. lbs. (40 Nm).

9. Install the horn pad. On Cabriolet, install the air bag unit and make sure no one is in the vehicle when connecting the battery.

Speed Sensor

REMOVAL & INSTALLATION

1. Disconnect the negative battery cable.
2. Remove the instrument cluster assembly.
3. From behind the cluster, disconnect the harness connector at the speedometer.

Pressure Switches

DESCRIPTION

▶ **See Figure 10**

There are two pressure switches near the high pressure service fitting. The lighter color switch is the low pressure limit switch. If pressure in the system falls below 25-33 psi (1.7-2.3 BAR), the compressor clutch will disengage. The switch will close again to allow compressor operation when system pressure is above 43 psi (3 BAR).

The darker switch operates the radiator fan. The fan runs at low speed as soon as the air conditioner is turned on. When pressure in the system is 200-220 psi (13.8-15.2 BAR), the switch closes and the fan will run at high speed. The switch will open again when pressure is about 174 psi (12 BAR).

4. Unscrew the sensor from the instrument cluster and remove it.

To install:

5. Position the sensor in place and screw it in securely.

6. Connect the wiring to the sensor and instruments and install the instrument cluster.

7. Connect the negative battery cable. Road test the vehicle and check the cruise control operation.

Control Unit

REMOVAL & INSTALLATION

1. Disconnect the negative battery cable.

2. On models with the 16V engine, the control unit is in the center console. On all other models, the control unit is under the right side of the dashboard.

3. Disconnect the electrical connector from the control unit.

4. Remove the bracket retaining screw and remove the control unit.

To install:

5. Plug in the electrical connector to the control unit.

6. Secure the control unit in place with the retaining screw.

7. Connect the negative battery cable. Road test the vehicle and check the cruise control operation.

Vacuum Servo

REMOVAL & INSTALLATION

1. Remove the air cleaner were applicable.

2. Disconnect the rod and the vacuum line from the servo.

3. Remove the nuts and remove the actuator from the engine.

4. Installation is the reverse of removal.

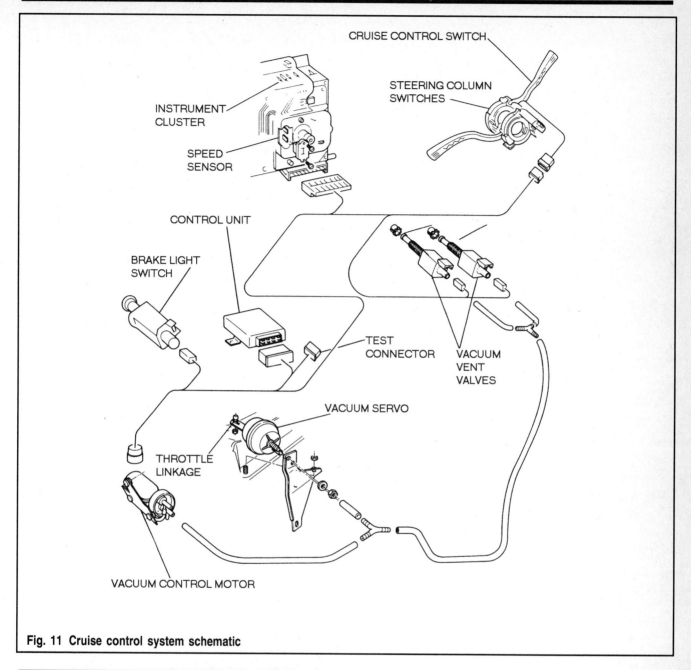

Fig. 11 Cruise control system schematic

Connecting Rod

ADJUSTMENT

▶ **See Figure 12**

1. Disconnect the connecting rod from the throttle lever ball socket.

2. Make sure the throttle is fully closed against the stop screw.

3. Adjust the length of the rod to fit exactly between the servo and the throttle, then turn the ball socket out one more turn to lengthen the rod.

4. Make sure the idle speed is correct and check the throttle for smooth movement.

Fig. 12 Control rod length should be 1 turn longer than an exact fit

ENTERTAINMENT SYSTEM

Radio

REMOVAL & INSTALLATION

1. On vehicles with a theft protected radio, obtain the security code.
2. Insert two removal pins into the sides of the face plate.
3. Push the tools away from each other to release the spring clips and pull the radio out far enough to unplug the wiring in the back.
   To install:
4. Connect the wiring and push the radio part way into the slot.
5. Enter the security code before pushing it in all the way.

ENTERING SECURITY CODE

Most vehicles are now equipped with Heidelberg V or VI radios that are equipped with a theft protection program. When the battery has been is disconnected or if the radio has been removed, the radio will lock-up electronically and cannot be operated until the security code is entered. On the Heidelberg V, if the proper code is not entered in six attempts, the radio will lock-up permanently and cannot be repaired. On the

Heidelberg VI, two incorrect attempts will lock the radio for about 1 hour.

The Heidelberg V may have a code assigned at the factory or a personal code created by the owner. The Hiedelberg VI has a code assigned at the factory and entered by the dealer during pre-delivery inspection. New radios come with the code printed on a sticker but not entered into memory. All codes are 4 digits. To code the radio:

Heidelberg V

1. Turn the radio **ON**. The radio should display the word SAF. DO NOT attempt to eject a cassette with the radio in this mode.
2. Push the AM/FM and SCAN buttons at the same time and hold them until the display changes, then release them immediately. The number 1000 will appear for about 3 seconds, then the display will go blank. Release the buttons then.

➡**If the buttons are held too long, the radio will interpret this as an attempt to enter an incorrect code.**

3. Use the first four station selector buttons to enter the code. The first digit of the code is always 1. Each time the other buttons are pushed, the number in that position will change.
4. When the code appears correctly in the display, push the AM/FM and SCAN buttons at the same time. When the radio plays and displays a frequency, release the buttons.

5. If the code was entered incorrectly three times, momentarily disconnect the battery and try again. If the code is entered incorrectly three more times, the radio cannot be coded and cannot be repaired.

Heidelberg VI

1. Turn the radio **ON**. The radio should display the word SAF. DO NOT attempt to eject a cassette with the radio in this mode.
2. Push the AM/FM and SCAN buttons at the same time and hold them until the display changes, then release them immediately. The number 1000 will appear and remain in the display.

➡**If the buttons are held too long, the radio will interpret this as an attempt to enter an incorrect code.**

3. Use the first four station selector buttons to enter the code. Each time a button is pushed, the number in that position will change.
4. When the code appears correctly in the display, push the AM/FM and SCAN buttons at the same time. When SAF appears in the display, release the buttons. The radio should play and display a frequency.
5. If the code was entered incorrectly two times, leave the radio **ON** for one hour and try again. This can be repeated as often as required.

WINDSHIELD WIPERS AND WASHERS

Wiper Arm

REMOVAL & INSTALLATION

▶ **See Figure 13**

1. Flip the cap up and pull it up to remove it.
2. Remove the nut to remove the arm.
3. When installing the arm, measure the distance between the center of the wiper blade and the base of the windshield:
    Golf and Jetta — 2.375 in. (60mm) from the base of the windshield.
    Cabriolet — 1.375 in. (35mm) on the driver's side and 2.5 in. (65mm) on the passenger side.
4. Torque the nut to 5 ft. lbs. (7 Nm). Do not over torque this nut or the linkage will bind.
5. Install the cap.

Rear Wiper Arm

REMOVAL & INSTALLATION

1. Flip the cap up and pull it up to remove it.
2. Remove the nut to remove the arm.

3. When installing the arm, the end of the wiper blade should be 0.375 in. (10mm) from the base of the window.
4. Torque the nut to 5 ft. lbs. (7 Nm). Do not over torque this nut or the linkage will bind.
5. Install the cap.

Windshield Wiper Motor

REMOVAL & INSTALLATION

▶ **See Figures 14, 15 and 16**

When removing the wiper motor, leave the mounting frame in place. If possible, do not remove the wiper drive crank from the motor shaft.

1. Disconnect the negative battery cable and remove the water shield at the base of the windshield.
2. Disconnect the relay rods from the wiper motor.
3. Note the position of the crank arm on the shaft. When the motor is in the parked position, the arm should be about 4 degrees up from horizontal.
4. Disconnect the wiring and remove the bolts to remove the motor from the frame.

To install:
5. Temporarily connect the wiring and run the motor. When the wiper switch is turned **OFF**, the motor will stop in the parked position.

Fig. 13 Lift the cap to remove the wiper arm

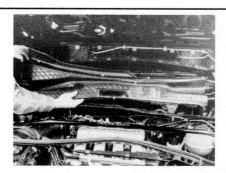

Fig. 14 Remove the rubber gasket to remove the water shield

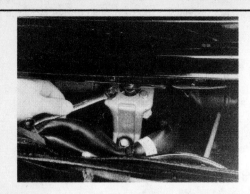

Fig. 15 Remove 2 bolts to remove the wiper motor

6. Install the motor and connect the linkage.

7. Run the motor again and make sure the arms and blades are properly positioned when the motor stops.

Rear Window Wiper Motor

REMOVAL & INSTALLATION

Golf and GTI

1. Remove the inside trim panel from the hatch.

2. Disconnect the relay rod from the drive crank on the motor.

3. Remove the 3 bolts securing the motor bracket to the body and move the assembly so the wiring can be disconnected.

4. Remove the assembly and separate the motor from the mounting bracket.

5. Installation is the reverse of removal. Before connecting the relay rod, run the motor for about 1 minute and turn the switch **OFF**. When the motor stops at the park position, install the relay rod and make sure the wiper arm is in the correct position.

Wiper Linkage

REMOVAL & INSTALLATION

1. Remove the wiper arms and the motor.

2. Remove the relay rods.

3. Remove the nut that secures the wiper shaft to the body and push it out of the frame.

4. Installation is the reverse of removal.

Windshield Washer Pump and Fluid Reservoir

REMOVAL & INSTALLATION

The reservoir is held in place with a single nut that can be reached with a long extension and socket. It may be easier to

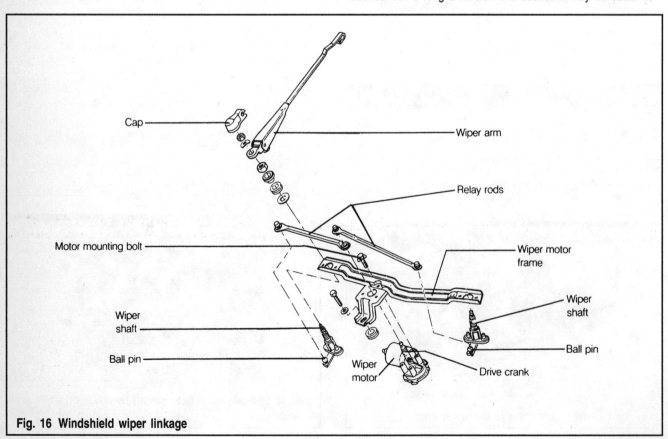

Fig. 16 Windshield wiper linkage

remove the nut and lift the reservoir out to disconnect the pump wiring and hose. The pump is held in place with a grommet and can be easily pulled out.

Rear Window Washer Pump and Fluid Reservoir

REMOVAL & INSTALLATION

The reservoir is behind the trim panel in the right side of the luggage compartment. Remove the 2 screws and pull the

INSTRUMENTS AND SWITCHES

Instrument Cluster

REMOVAL & INSTALLATION

▶ **See Figure 17**

1. Disconnect the negative battery cable. This job is easier with the steering wheel removed.
2. To disconnect the speedometer cable, reach behind the panel from below and squeeze the tabs of the plastic cable clip. Pull the cable out.
3. Remove the radio and the heater control knobs.
4. The switches are held in place with spring clips or barbs. Carefully pry the switches out of the dashboard and disconnect the wiring.
5. Remove the screws to remove the instrument trim panel.
6. Remove the screws and lay the instrument cluster down on the steering column. Disconnect the wiring and remove the cluster.
   To install:
7. Connect the wiring and fit the lower edge of the instrument cluster into place.
8. Lift the cluster into place and install the screws.
9. Install the trim panel and all the switches.
10. Before installing the radio, connect the battery and make sure all switches and instruments work properly.
11. Install the radio and heater controls. Enter the radio security code.

Voltage Stabilizer

TESTING

1. Connect the wiring to the instrument cluster.
2. Connect a voltmeter between terminals 1 and 2. Terminal 1 is positive.
3. Turn the ignition switch **ON**. The voltage should be 9.5-10.5 volts and stable. If not, replace the voltage stabilizer.

reservoir out to disconnect the wiring and hose. The pump is held to the reservoir with a grommet.

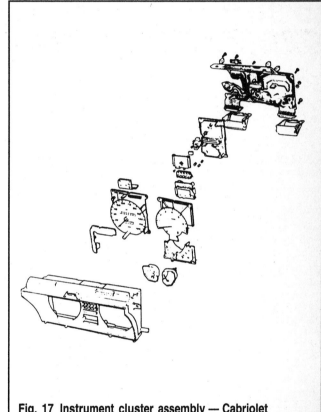

Fig. 17 Instrument cluster assembly — Cabriolet

Dynamic Oil Pressure Warning System

TESTING

The Cabriolet is equipped with a low oil pressure warning light and buzzer that are operated by the control unit in the instrument cluster. The control unit accepts signals from two different oil pressure switches and from the tachometer. If oil pressure drops below 0.3 BAR (4.4 psi) at idle or 1.8 BAR (26 psi) above 2000 rpm, the warning light will flash and the buzzer will sound. The 0.3 BAR switch is on the oil filter mounting base. On 8 valve engines, the 1.8 BAR switch is on

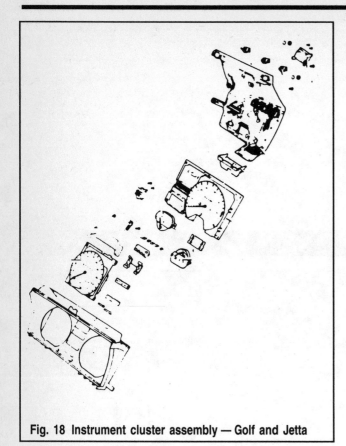

Fig. 18 Instrument cluster assembly — Golf and Jetta

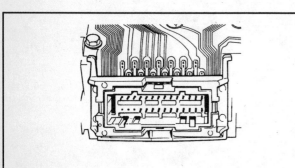

Fig. 19 Connector terminals on Golf and Jetta instrument cluster

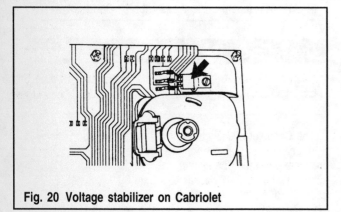

Fig. 20 Voltage stabilizer on Cabriolet

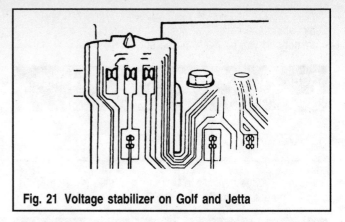

Fig. 21 Voltage stabilizer on Golf and Jetta

the flywheel end of the cylinder head. On 16V engines, both switches are on the oil filter mounting base.

1. Turn the ignition switch **ON**. The warning light should flash until the engine is started. If not, disconnect the wire from the 0.3 BAR switch and connect the wire to ground. If the light still does not flash, check the wiring and the control unit.

2. Connect an ohmmeter or powered test light to the switch terminal. There should be continuity to ground with the engine not running.

3. Remove the 0.3 BAR switch and connect a pressure gauge. The gauge should go up to at least 60 psi (4 BAR).

4. Start the engine. At idle the warning light should not flash unless the 0.3 BAR switch wire is grounded.

5. Raise the engine speed to 2000-2500 rpm. If oil pressure is above 1.8 BAR (26 psi) on gasoline engines or 1.4 BAR (20 psi) on diesel engines, the warning light should be **OFF**.

6. The 1.8 BAR switch terminal should have continuity to ground at idle and should be open above 2000 rpm.

Windshield Wiper Switch

REMOVAL & INSTALLATION

Golf and Jetta

1. Remove the horn pad from the steering wheel.
2. Make sure the front wheels are straight ahead and remove the nut and the steering wheel.
3. Remove the steering column covers and disconnect the wiring to the switches.
4. Remove the screws to remove the turn signal switch and the windshield wiper switch.
5. Installation is the reverse of removal. Torque the steering wheel nut to 30 ft. lbs. (40 Nm).

Cabriolet

1. Disarm the air bag system and remove the steering wheel as described in the beginning of this Section.
2. The air bag connects to the spiral spring behind the steering wheel. Note how the wheel fits into the spring assembly. Remove the 3 Phillips head screws to remove the spiral spring.

3. Remove the steering column covers and disconnect the wiring to the switches.

4. Remove the screws to remove the turn signal switch and the windshield wiper switch.

To install:

5. Install the wiper and turn signal switches and connect the wiring. Install the column covers.

6. Install the spiral spring. If the spring was turned while removed, it must be returned to its center position. Turn the spring all the way in one direction, then turn it back 4 full turns.

7. Install the spiral spring.

8. Install the steering wheel, making sure it fits into the spiral spring. Torque the nut to 30 ft. lbs. (40 Nm).

➡**If the battery was connected while the air bag unit was removed, disconnect the battery and wait at least 20 minutes for the back-up power supply to discharge before installing the air bag unit.**

9. With the battery disconnected, install the air bag unit with new Torx® screws and torque them to 7 ft. lbs. (10 Nm).

LIGHTING

Headlights

REMOVAL & INSTALLATION

▶ **See Figure 22**

1. Pull the connector off the bulb at the back of the headlight.

2. Push down on the clip to disengage it.

3. Pull the headlight bulb out of the housing. If it is difficult to remove, gently rock it up and down.

4. Be careful not to touch the glass part of the bulb. Any oil or dirt even from clean hands will cause a hot spot on the glass during operation and the bulb will break.

5. To ease installation, spray some silicone lubricant on your finger and rub it onto the rubber O-ring. Do not spray directly on the O-ring because it will also get on the bulb.

6. Install the bulb, snap the clip into place and connect the wiring.

Fig. 22 Be careful not to touch the glass on the headlight bulb

10. Make sure no one is in the vehicle when connecting the battery. Turn the ignition switch **ON** and make sure the warning light on the instrument panel stays **ON** for 5-8 seconds, then turns **OFF**.

Headlight Switch

REMOVAL & INSTALLATION

1. Disconnect the negative battery cable.

2. The headlight switch is held in place with spring clips or plastic barbs. The switch can be removed by carefully prying it out of the instrument panel. On Golf and Jetta, pry the top and bottom of the switch. On Cabriolet, pry the left and right sides.

3. Disconnect the wiring and remove the switch.

4. Installation is the reverse of removal.

AIMING

The procedure outlined here is intended to provide a basic adjustment only. Some states may have different aiming specifications or require the job be done by licensed technicians with specialized aiming equipment.

1. Park the vehicle on a level surface 25 feet from a vertical wall. There must be a horizontal reference point, such as a line on the pavement or another wall, at a right angle to the aiming wall. The fuel tank should be about 1/2 full, tire pressures must be correct and there must be a person in the driver's seat.

2. Measure the distance from the floor to the center of each headlight. Mark these heights on the wall and draw a line between them.

3. Measure the horizontal distance from the reference point to the center of each headlight. Make reference marks on the wall so that X marks the center of each headlight.

4. With the headlights on low beam, the high intensity zone of the light beam should be immediately below the line and about 2 inches to the right of the center of each headlight.

5. If adjustment is required, remove the grille and use a Phillips screw driver to move the headlights.

Signal and Marker Lights

REMOVAL & INSTALLATION

▶ **See Figure 23**

Front

On the front turn signal and side marker lights, the bulb can be removed after removing the lens. Inspect the condition of the lens seal and replace if required before installing the new bulb. Front turn signals bulbs are No.1034, side marker lights are bulb No.194.

Rear

The rear light bulbs can be reached from inside the luggage compartment. On Jetta and Cabriolet, the entire light bulb panel can be removed by squeezing the clips. On Golf and GTI, squeeze the spring clips and turn to remove the socket.

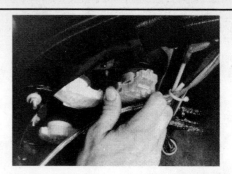

Fig. 23 On Golf, squeeze and turn to remove rear light socket

TRAILER WIRING

Wiring the car for towing is fairly easy. There are a number of good wiring kits available and these should be used, rather than trying to design your own. All trailers will need brake lights and turn signals as well as tail lights and side marker lights. Most states require extra marker lights for overwide trailers. Also, most states have recently required back-up lights for trailers, and most trailer manufacturers have been building trailers with back-up lights for several years. Additionally, some Class I, most Class II and just about all Class III trailers will have electric brakes. Add to this number an accessories wire, to operate trailer internal equipment or to charge the trailer's battery, and you can have as many as seven wires in the harness. Determine the equipment on your trailer and buy the wiring kit necessary. The kit will contain all the wires needed, plus a plug adapter set which included the female plug, mounted on the bumper or hitch, and the male plug, wired into, or plugged i nto the trailer harness. When installing the kit, follow the manufacturer's instructions. The color coding of the wires is standard throughout the industry. One point to note: some domestic vehicles, and most imported vehicles, have separate turn signals. On most domestic vehicles, the brake lights and rear turn signals operate with the same bulb. For those vehicles with separate turn signals, you can purchase an isolation unit so that the brake lights won't blink whenever the turn signals are operated, or, you can go to your local electronics supply house and buy four diodes to wire in series with the brake and turn signal bulbs. Diodes will isolate the brake and turn signals. The choice is yours. The isolation units are simple and quick to install, but far more expensive than the diodes. The diodes, however, require more work to install properly, since they require the cutting of each bulb's wire and soldering in place of the diode. One, final point, the best kits are those with a spring loaded cover on the vehicle mounted socket. This cover prevent dirt and moisture from corroding the terminals. Never let the vehicle socket hang loosely; always mount it securely to the bumper or hitch.

CIRCUIT PROTECTION

Fuses

REPLACEMENT

▶ See Figure 24

All fuses are in the main fuse/relay panel to the left of the steering column. The cover has a label to identify each fuse and the current rating of each fuse is printed on the fuse itself. A complete schematic of fuse and relay locations appears at the beginning of the main wiring diagrams for each model.

Fig. 24 All fuses are in the panel under the dashboard

WIRING DIAGRAMS

Terminal Designations

▶ **See Figure 25**

All European vehicle wiring diagrams use DIN Standard 72 552 Terminal Designations. This is a standardized system of labeling terminals according to their function, not their location. For example: terminal 15 is always voltage supplied by the ignition switch; terminal 30 is always voltage directly from the battery; terminal 56a is a headlight high beam connection, 56b is low beam. The following is a list of European standard terminal designations. Also included is a key showing the symbols used in all Volkswagen wiring diagrams.

Schematics

Term.	Definition
	Ignition coil, ignition distributor
1	Low voltage
	Ignition distributor with two separate electrical circuits
1 a	To ignition contact breaker I
1 b	To ignition contact breaker II
2	Short-circuit terminal (magneto ignition)
4	Ignition coil, ignition distributor, high voltage
	Ignition distributor with two separate electrical circuits
4 a	From ignition coil I, terminal 4
4 b	From ignition coil II, terminal 4
15	Plus (+) downstream of battery [output of ignition/driving switch]
15 a	Output at dropping resistor to ignition coil and starter
	Glow plug and starter switch
17	Start
19	Preheat
	Battery
30	Input from + battery terminal, direct
30 a	12/24 V series-parallel battery switch Input from + terminal of battery II
31	Return line to battery — battery terminal or ground, direct
31 b	Return line to negative battery terminal or ground, via switch or relay (switched negative)
	12/24 V series-parallel battery switch
31 a	Return line to – terminal of battery II
31 c	Return line to – terminal of battery I
	Electric Motors
32	Return line [1]
33	Main terminal connection [1]
33 a	Self-parking switch-off
33 b	Shunt field
33 f	For second lower-speed range
33 g	For third lower-speed range
33 h	For fourth lower-speed range
33 L	Counterclockwise rotation
33 R	Clockwise rotation
	Starter
45	Separate starter relay, output; starter, input (main current)
	Two-starter parallel operation Starting relay for engagement current
45 a	Output, starter I Input, starters I and II
45 b	Output, starter II
48	Terminal on starter and on start-repeating relay for monitoring starting procedure
	Turn-signal Flasher (pulse generator)
49	Input
49 a	Output
49 b	Output, second turn-signal circuit
49 c	Output, third turn-signal circuit
	Starter
50	Starter control (direct)
	Series-parallel battery switch
50 a	Output for starter control
50 b	Starter control with parallel operation of two starters with sequential control
	Starting relay for sequential control of the engagement current during parallel operation of two starters
50 c	Input at starting relay for starter I
50 d	Input at starting relay for starter II

Term.	Definition
	Start-locking relay
50 e	Input
50 f	Output
	Start-repeating relay
50 g	Input
50 h	Output
	[1]) Polarity reversal possible at terminals 32 – 33.
61	Alternator charge-indicator lamp
	Tone-sequence control device
71	Input
71 a	Output to horns 1 & 2, low
71 b	Output to horns 1 & 2, high
72	**Alarm switch** (rotating beacon)
75	**Radio, cigarette lighter**
76	Speaker
77	**Door-valve control**
	Switch Break-contact and changeover switches
81	Input
81 a	1st output, break side
81 b	2nd output, break side
	Make-contact switch
82	Input
82 a	1st output
82 b	2nd output
82 z	1st input
82 y	2nd input
	Multiple-position switch
83	Input
83 a	Output, position 1
83 b	Output, position 2
83 L	Output, left-hand position
83 R	Output, right-hand position
	Current relay
84	Input, actuator and relay contact
84 a	Output, actuator
84 b	Output, relay contact
	Switching relay
85	Output, actuator (end of winding to ground or negative) Input, actuator
86	Start of winding
86 a	Start of winding or 1st winding
86 b	Winding tap or 2nd winding
	Alternator
51	DC voltage at rectifier
51 e	DC voltage at rectifier with choke coil for daytime driving
	Trailer signals
52	Signals from trailer to towing vehicle, general
	Wiper motor, input (+)
53	
53 a	Wiper (+), self-parking switch-off
53 b	Wiper (shunt winding)
53 c	Electric windshield washer pump
53 e	Wiper (brake winding)
53 i	Wiper motor with permanent magnet and third brush (for higher speed)
	Stop lamp
54	For lamp combinations and trailer plug connections
	Trailer signal

Term.	Definition
54 g	Pneum. valve for additional retarding brake, electromagnetically actuated
55	**Fog lamp**
56	**Headlamp**
56 a	High beam, high-beam indicator lamp
56 b	Low beam
56 d	Headlamp-flasher contact
57	**Side-marker lamp: m-cycles, mopeds.** Abroad also cars, trucks, etc.
57 a	**Parking lamp**
57 L	Parking lamp, left
57 R	Parking lamp, right
58	**Side-marker lamps, tail lamps, license-plate lamps and instrument-panel lamps**
58 b	Tail-lamp changeover for single-axle tractors
58 c	Trailer plug-and-receptacle assembly for single-conductor tail-lamp cable with fuse in trailer
58 d	Variable-intensity instrument-panel lamp, tail-lamp and side-marker lamp
58 L	Left
58 R	Right, license-plate lamp
	Alternator (magneto generator)
59	AC voltage, output Rectifier, input
59 a	Charging armature, output
59 b	Tail-light armature, output
59 c	Stop-lamp armature, output
	Relay contact for break and changeover contacts
87	Input
87 a	1st output (break side)
87 b	2nd output
87 c	3rd output
87 z	1st input
87 y	2nd input
87 x	3rd input
	Relay contact for make contact
88	Input
	Relay contact for make and changeover contacts (make side)
88 a	1st output
88 b	2nd output
88 c	3rd output
	Relay contact for make contact
88 z	1st input
88 y	2nd input
88 x	3rd input

Generator and Generator Regulator

B +	Battery positive
B –	Battery negative
D +	Dynamo positive
D –	Dynamo negative
DF	Dynamo field
DF 1	Dynamo field 1
DF 2	Dynamo field 2
	Alternator
U, V, W	Alternator terminals

Directional Signals (Turn-Signal Flasher)

C	First indicator lamp
C0	Main terminal connection for separate indicator circuits actuated by the turn-signal switch
C2	Second indicator lamp
C3	Third indicator lamp (e.g. when towing two trailers)
L	Turn-signal lamps, left
R	Turn-signal lamps, right

Fig. 25 DIN Standard 72 552 Terminal Designations

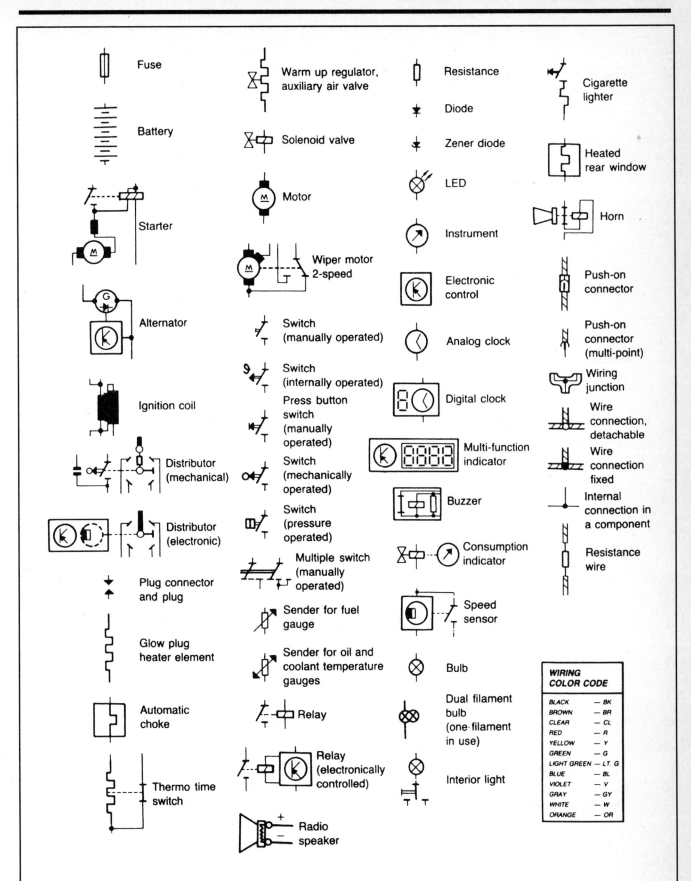

Fig. 26 Component symbols used in wiring diagrams

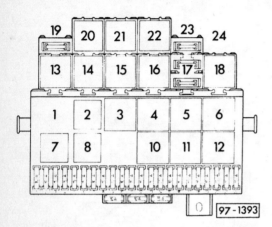

97-1393

Fuse arrangement

according to the numbers on fuse panel as seen from left to right:

		Amp
1	Radiator fan	30
2	Stop lights, cruise control	10
3	Cigarette lighter, radio, clock, interior lights	15
4	Emergency flasher system	15
5	Fuel pump, oxygen sensor heater	15
6	Open	
7	Tail, parking and side marker lights, left	10
8	Tail, parking and side marker lights, right	10
9	High beam right, high beam indicator light	10
10	High beam left	10
11	Wind. wipers and washer	15
12	Open	
13	Rear window defogger	15
14	Fresh air fan, glove compartment light	20
15	Back-up lights, shift console light (Auto. Transmission)	10
16	Horn	15
17	Power windows	10
18	Horn relay, oil temp. gauge, oil pressure gauge, voltmeter, seat belt warning light, coolant level and temperature warning light, cruise control	15
19	Turn signals	10
20	License plate lights, instrument panel lights	10
21	Low beam left	10
22	Low beam right	10

Separate fuses above fuse panel

17	— A/C	30
19	— Power Windows	20

Relay locations on fuse/relay panel

1 — Digifant control unit relay
2 — Fuel pump relay
3 — Seat belt warning system relay
4 — Open
5 — A/C relay
6 — Dual horn relay
7 — Open
8 — Load reduction relay
10 — Intermittent wiper relay
11 — Open
12 — Emergency flasher relay
13 — Open
14 — Radiator cooling fan afterrun control unit
15 — Open
16 — Open
17 — A/C thermofuse
18 — Coolant low level control unit
19 — Power window fuse
20 21 22 23 24 — Open

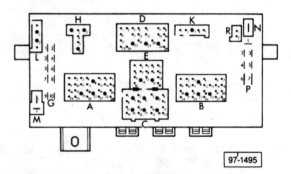

97-1495

Connections and plugs on fuse/relay panel

A — Instrument cluster wiring harness (blue)
B — Instrument cluster wiring harness (red)
C — Engine compartment wiring harness, left (yellow)
D — Engine compartment wiring harness, right (white)
E — Rear wiring harness (black)
G — Single connector
H — Air conditioner wiring harness (brown)
K — Seat belt warning system wiring harness (colorless)
L — Horn wiring harness (grey)
M — Headlight switch/terminal 56, headlight dimmer/flasher switch/terminal 56b
N — Single connector, to fuel injectors
P — Single connector, terminal 30
R — From Digifant control unit relay

Fig. 27 Main fuse and relay panel — Cabriolet

Description	Current track	Description	Current track	Description	Current track
Air flow sensor potentiometer, G19	27	**F**resh air blower series resistance, N23	157-158	**K**nock sensor, G61	25-27
Alternator, C	1-2	Fresh air control lever light, L16	99	License plate light, X	151, 153
Alternator warning light, K2	70	Fresh air fan, V2	159	Light switch, E1	142-149
Back-up light switch, F4	179	Fresh air fan switch, E9	157-159	Load reduction relay, J59	142-143
Back-up light, left, M16	171	Fuel gauge, G1	76	Luggage compartment light, W3	154
Back-up light, right, M17	180	Fuel gauge sending unit, G	51	Luggage compartment light switch, F5	154
Battery, A	4	Fuel pump, G6	50	**O**xygen sensor, G39	34-35
Brake and parking brake indicator light, K7	93	Fuel pump relay, J17	52-54	**P**arking brake warning light switch, F9	94
Brake fluid level warning contact, F34	98	Full throttle switch, F81	20	Parking light, left, M1	163
Brake light switch, F	173	Fuse, S1	236	Parking light, right, M3	166
Brake light, left, M9	173	Fuse, S2	173	**R**adiator cooling fan, V7	236-237
Brake light, right, M10	176	Fuse, S3	104	Radiator cooling fan after run control unit, J138	232-235
Cigarette lighter, U1	104	Fuse, S4	186	Radiator cooling fan thermoswitch, F87	232
Cigarette lighter light, L28	102	Fuse, S5	50	Radiator cooling fan thermoswitch, F18	236-238
Clock light, L8	82	Fuse, S6	155	Rear window defogger indicator light, K10	206-208
Coolant low level control unit, J120	58-59	Fuse, S7	162	Rear window defogger switch, E15	208
Coolant low level sender, G32	58	Fuse, S8	165	Rear window defogger switch light, L39	206
Coolant overheat warning light, K28	79	Fuse, S9	133	Rear window heater element, Z1	210
Coolant temperature gauge, G3	77	Fuse, S10	129	**S**eat belt switch, left, E24	91
Coolant temperature sender, G62	24	Fuse, S11	215	Seat belt warning light, K19	93
Coolant temperature sending unit, G2	57	Fuse, S12	229	Seat belt warning relay, J34	89-93
Digifant control unit, J169	20-38	Fuse, S13	208	Side marker lights, front, M11	162, 165
Digifant control unit relay, J176	37-38	Fuse, S14	157	Spark plug connectors, P	17-19
Digital clock, Y2	81	Fuse, S15	178	Spark plugs, Q	17-19
Door contact switch, left front, F2	88-89	Fuse, S16	199	Speed sensor, G54	77
Door contact switch, right front, F3	86	Fuse, S17	158	Starter, B	7-9
Emergency flasher relay, J2	187-189	Fuse, S17	34	**T**achometer, G5	71
Emergency flasher switch, E3	184-193	Fuse, S18	197	Tail light, left, M4	170
Emergency flasher warning light, K6	193	Fuse, S19	184	Tail light, right, M2	181
Engine oil pressure control unit, J114	65-67	Fuse, S20	154	Transfer fuel pump, G23	52
Engine oil pressure gauge, G11	116-117	Fuse, S21	130	Turn signal indicator light, K5	74
Engine oil pressure gauge light, L27	124	Fuse, S22	134	Turn signal light, left front, M5	164
Engine oil pressure sensor, G10	116	**H**all generator, G40	20-22	Turn signal light, left rear, M6	169
Engine oil pressure switch (0.3 bar), F22	61	Headlight dimmer flasher switch, E4	137-138	Turn signal light, right front, M7	167
Engine oil pressure switch (1.8 bar), F1	62	Headlight high beam warning light, K1	75	Turn signal light, right rear, M8	182
Engine oil pressure warning light, K3	63	Headlight switch light, L9	156	Turn signal switch, E2	190-191
Engine oil temperature gauge, G9	113-114	Headlight, left, L1	129, 130	**V**oltage regulator, C1	1-2
Engine oil temperature gauge light, L24	126	Headlight, right, L2	133, 134	Voltage stabilizer, J6	76
Engine oil temperature sensor, G8	113	Hi-mounted brake light, M25	174	Voltmeter, G14	119
		High-beam headlight, left, L13	127	Voltmeter light, L25	122
		High-beam headlight, right, L14	131	**W**asher wiper intermittent relay, J31	219-223
		Horn button, H	204	Windshield washer pump, V5	224
		Horn relay, J4	203-204	Windshield wiper motor, V	213-216
		Horns, H1	199, 201	Windshield-wiper intermittent switch, E22	219-223
		Idle speed stabilizer valve, N71	36-37		
		Idle switch, F60	23		
		Ignition coil, N	16-18		
		Ignition control unit, N41	17-20		
		Ignition distributor, O	17-19		
		Ignition starter switch, D	10-13		
		Injector, cyl. 1, N30	42		
		Injector, cyl. 2, N31	41		
		Injector, cyl. 3, N32	40		
		Injector, cyl. 4, N33	39		
		Instrument panel light, L10	83, 84		
		Instrument panel light dimmer switch, E20	149		
		Intake air temperature sensor, G42	26		
		Interior light, front, W	85-86		

Fig. 28 Current track index — Cabriolet

Wire connectors

T   — junction box, behind fuse/relay panel
T1a — single, near ignition coil
T1b — single, behind fuse/relay panel
T1c — single, behind fuse/relay panel
T1d — single, on firewall, right
T1e — single, behind fuse/relay panel
T1f — single, behind fuse/relay panel
T1g — single, behind fuse/relay panel
T1h — single, behind instrument panel
T1i — single, behind instrument panel
T1j — single, behind instrument panel, center
T1k — single, behind fuse/relay panel
T1m — single, behind fuse/relay panel
T1n — single, in luggage compartment, left
T1p — single, near left headlight
T1r — single, near right headlight
T1u — single, behind instrument panel
T1v — single, behind fuse/relay panel
T1w — single, in engine compartment, left front
T1x — single, in luggage compartment, left
T2a — double, behind fuse/relay panel
T2b — double, behind fuse/relay panel
T2c — double, behind instrument panel, center
T2d — double, near intake manifold
T2e — double, in engine compartment, left
T2f — double, behind fuse/relay panel
T2g — double, in luggage compartment, left
T2h — double, in luggage compartment
T2l — double, near left headlight
T3a — three-point, behind fuse/relay panel
T3b — three-point, behind instrument panel, center
T3c — three-point, behind center console
T3d — three-point, near right headlight
T3e — three-point, near left headlight
T3g — three-point, near starter
T3h — three-point, near valve cover
T4a — four-point, in engine compartment, rear
T5a — five-point, on firewall, left
T6 — six-point, on instrument cluster
T6a — six-point, behind fuse/relay panel
T8 — eight-point, on radio
T14 — fourteen-point, on instrument cluster

Ground connections

(1) — ground strap battery to body
(18) — on engine block
(30) — near fuse/relay panel
(42) — beside steering column
(50) — in luggage compartment, left
(51) — in luggage compartment, right
(81) — in instrument cluster wiring harness
(82) — in wiring harness, left front
(94) — in Digifant wiring harness
(108) — in wiring harness, left front

Welded wiring harness points

(A4) — plus connection (58b), in instrument cluster wiring harness
(G3) — plus connection, in fuel injector wiring harness
(G4) — wire connection, in fuel injector wiring harness

Fig. 29 Connector locations — Cabriolet

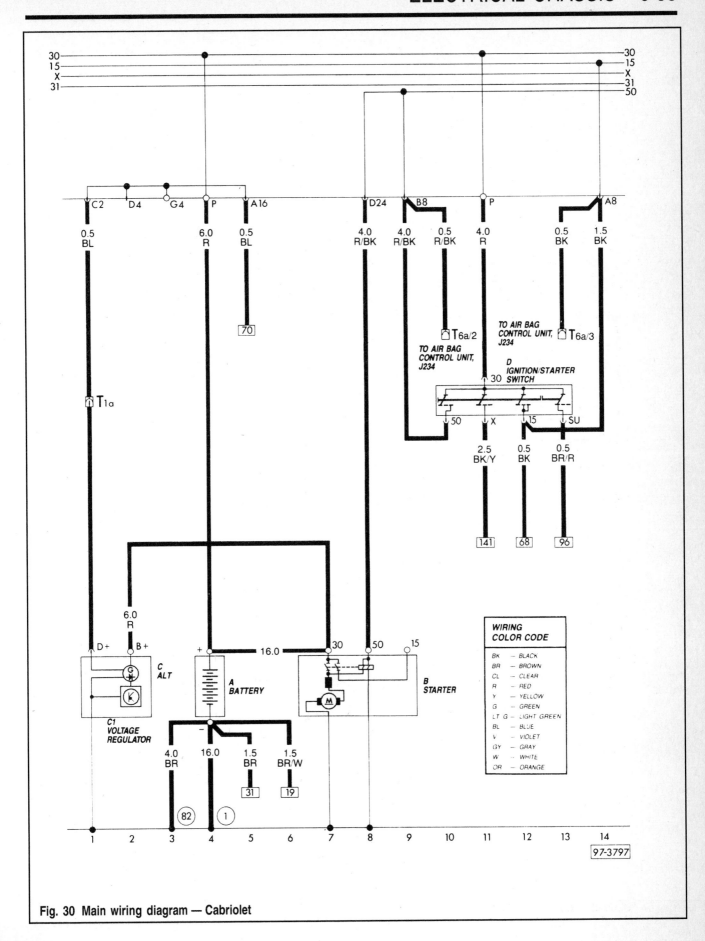

Fig. 30 Main wiring diagram — Cabriolet

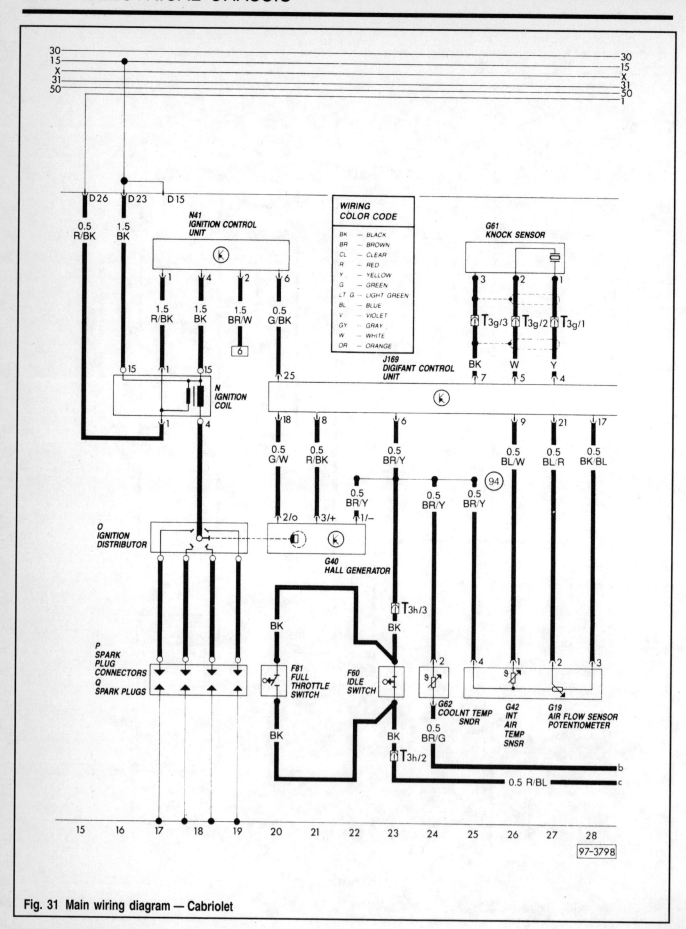

Fig. 31 Main wiring diagram — Cabriolet

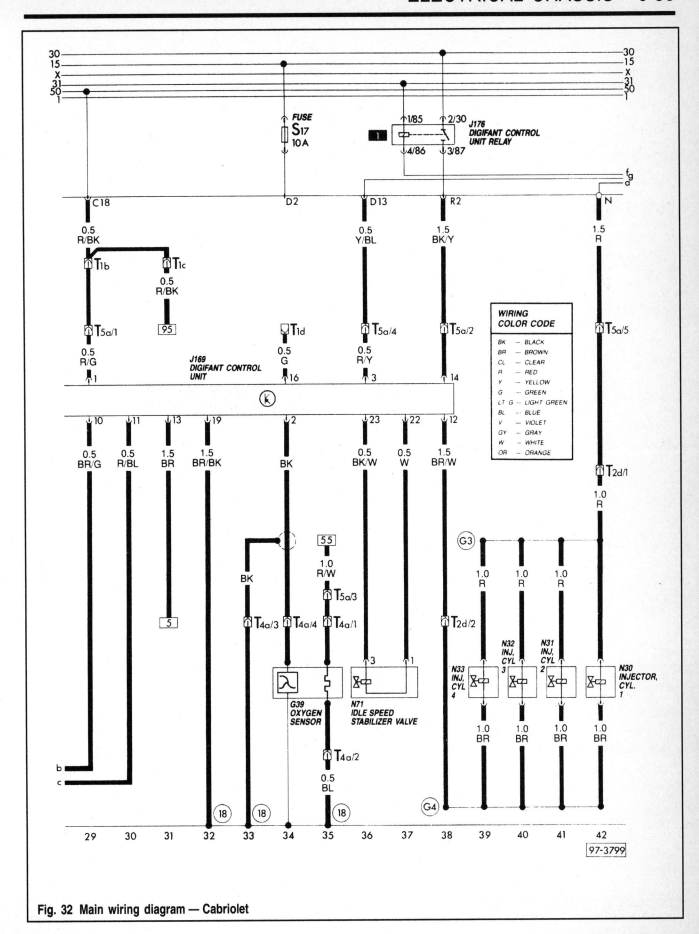

Fig. 32 Main wiring diagram — Cabriolet

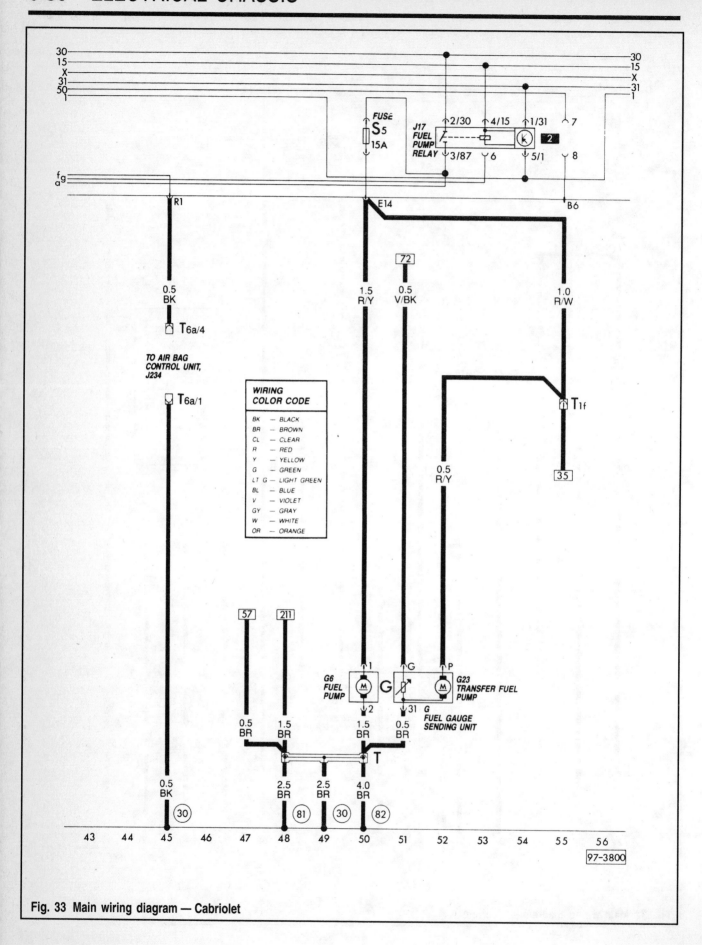

Fig. 33 Main wiring diagram — Cabriolet

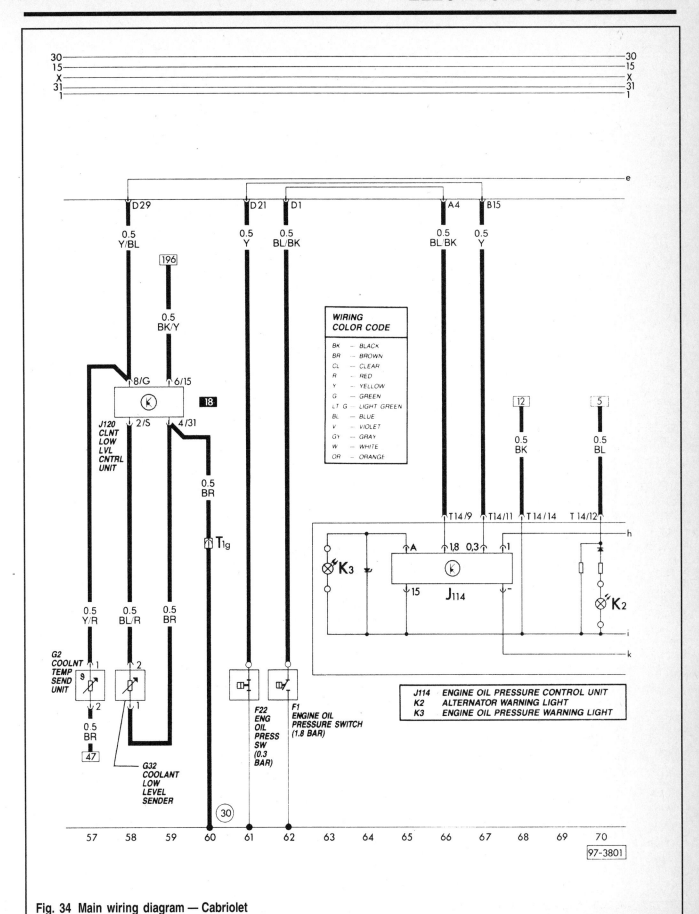

Fig. 34 Main wiring diagram — Cabriolet

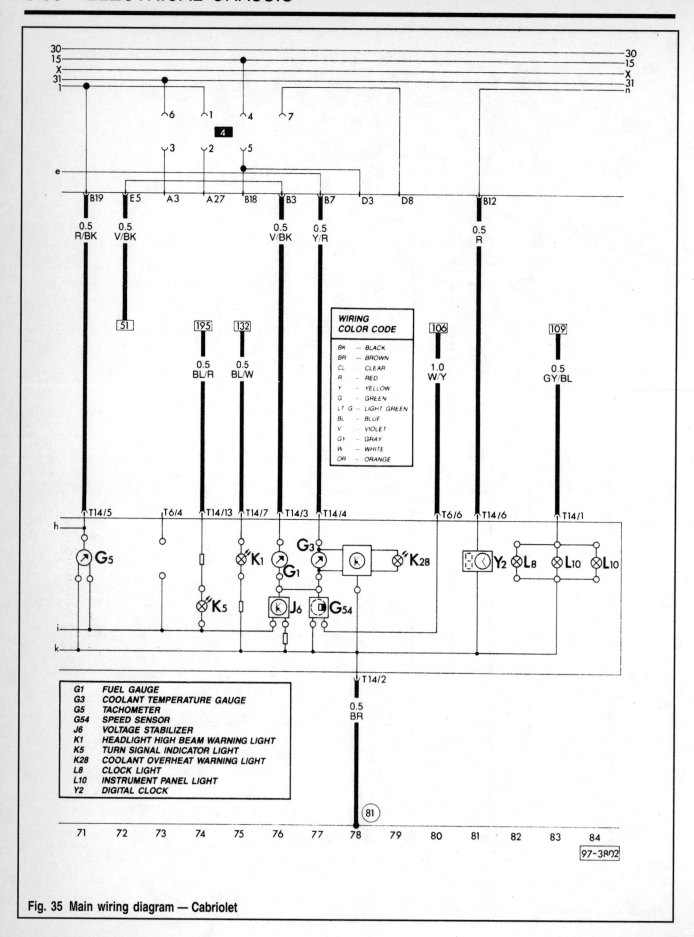

Fig. 35 Main wiring diagram — Cabriolet

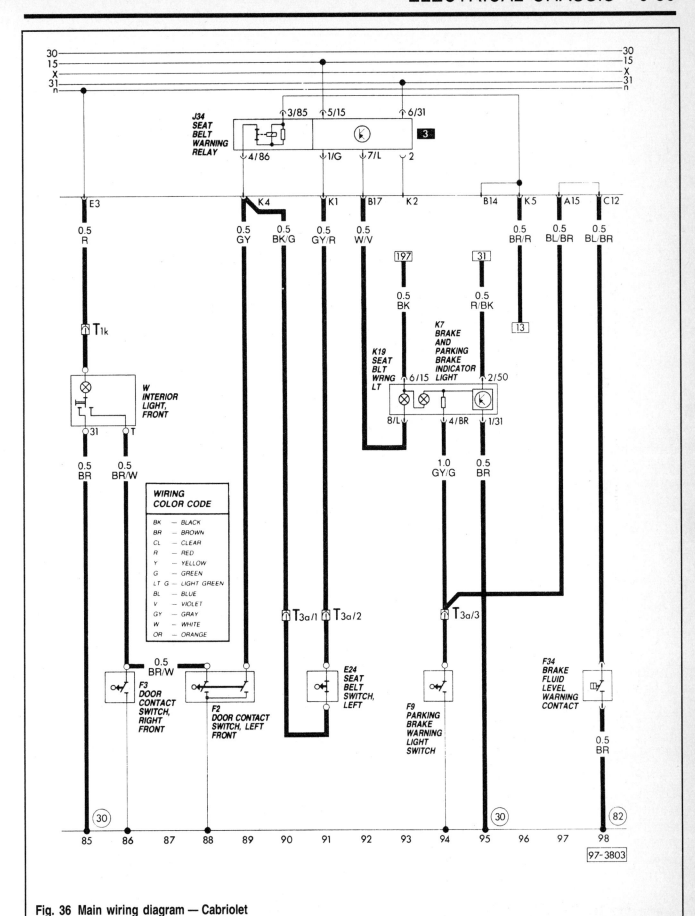

Fig. 36 Main wiring diagram — Cabriolet

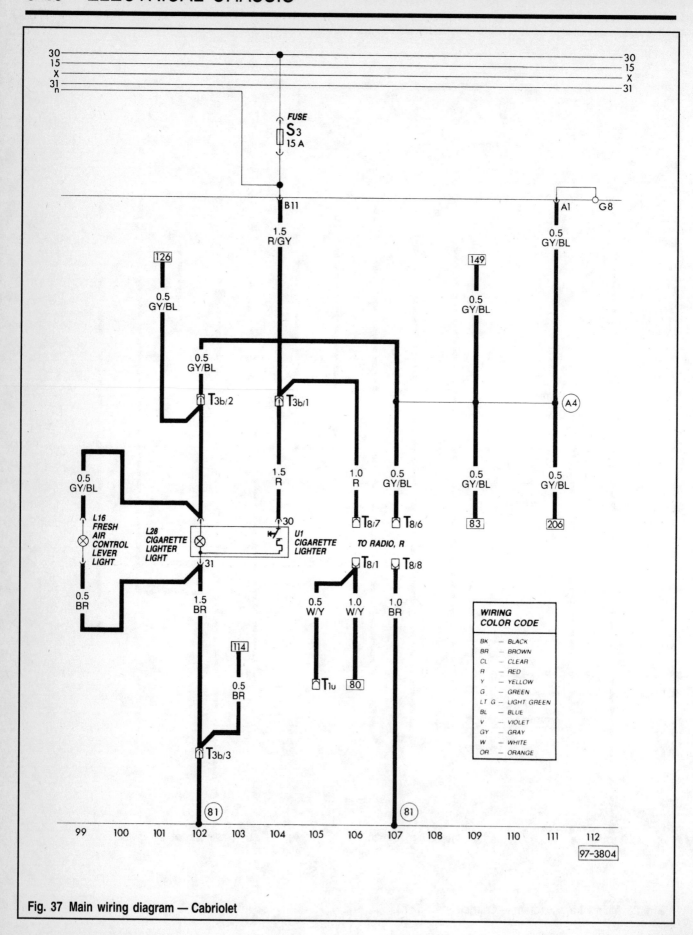

Fig. 37 Main wiring diagram — Cabriolet

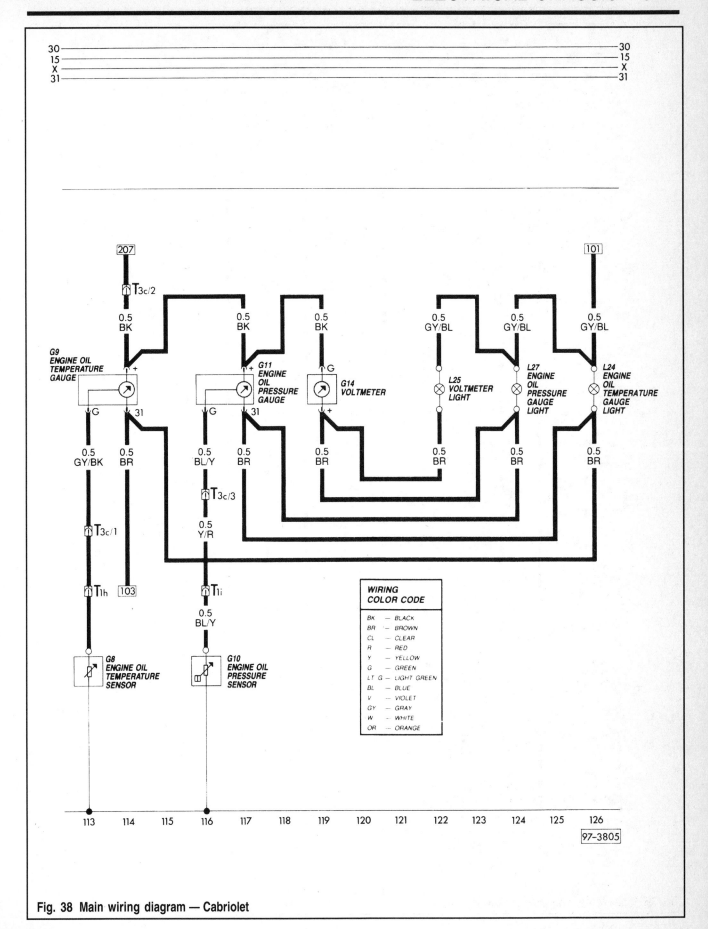

Fig. 38 Main wiring diagram — Cabriolet

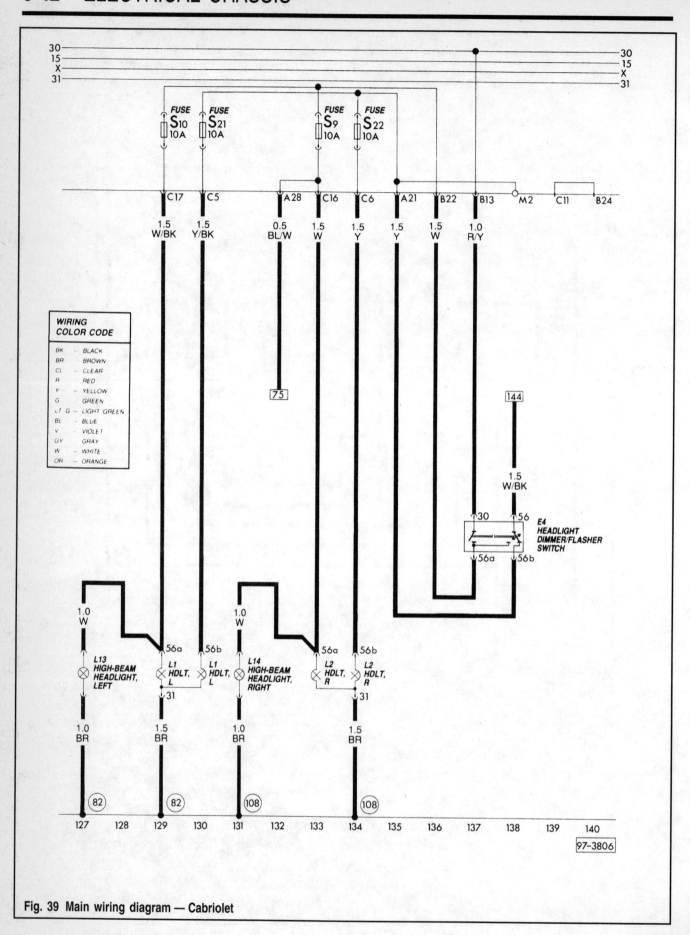

Fig. 39 Main wiring diagram — Cabriolet

97-3806

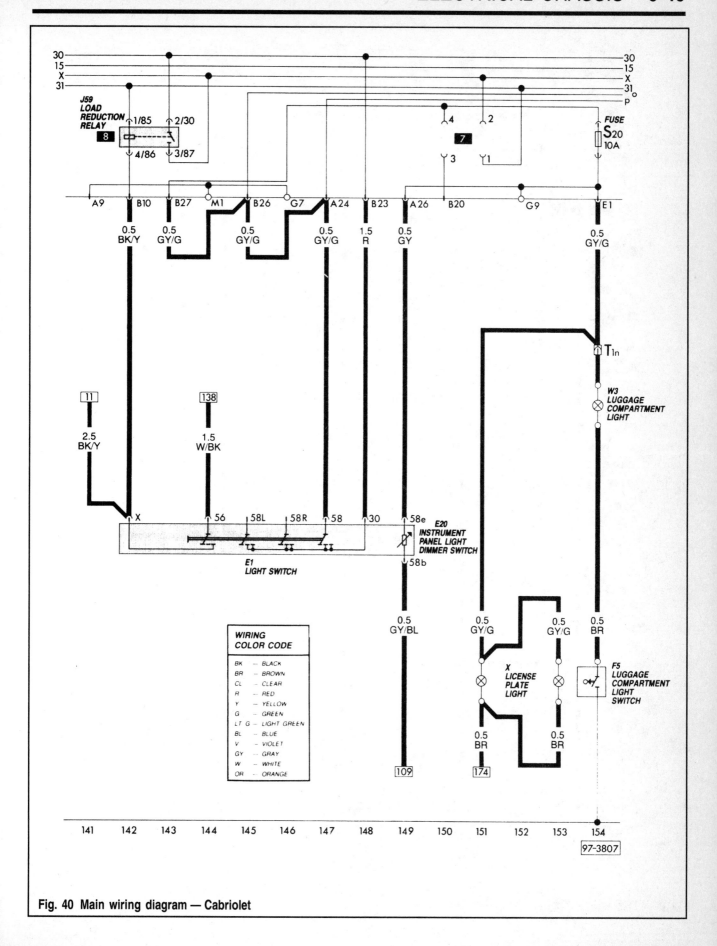

Fig. 40 Main wiring diagram — Cabriolet

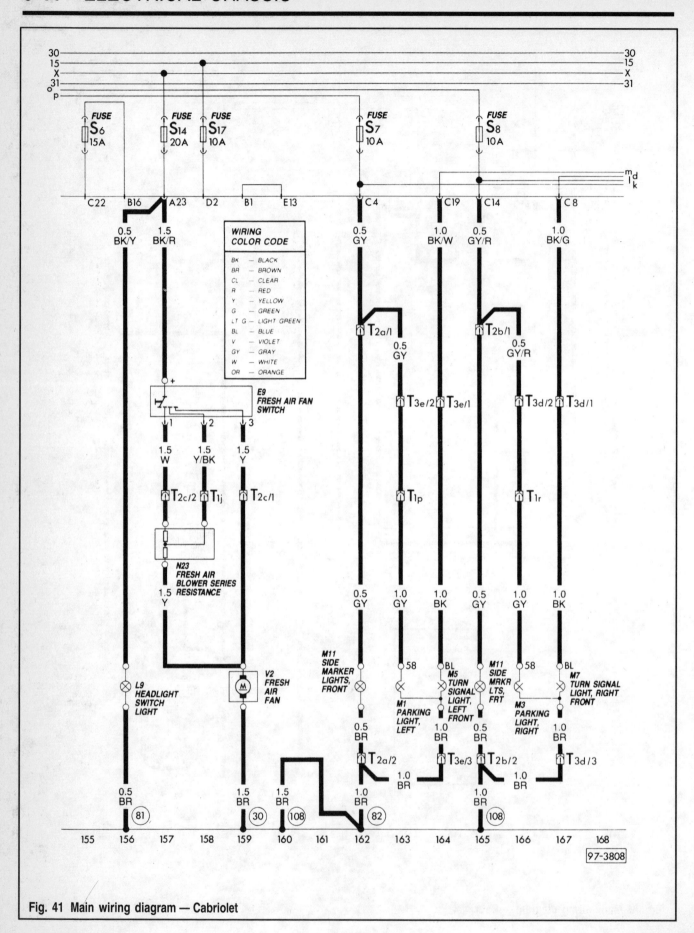

Fig. 41 Main wiring diagram — Cabriolet

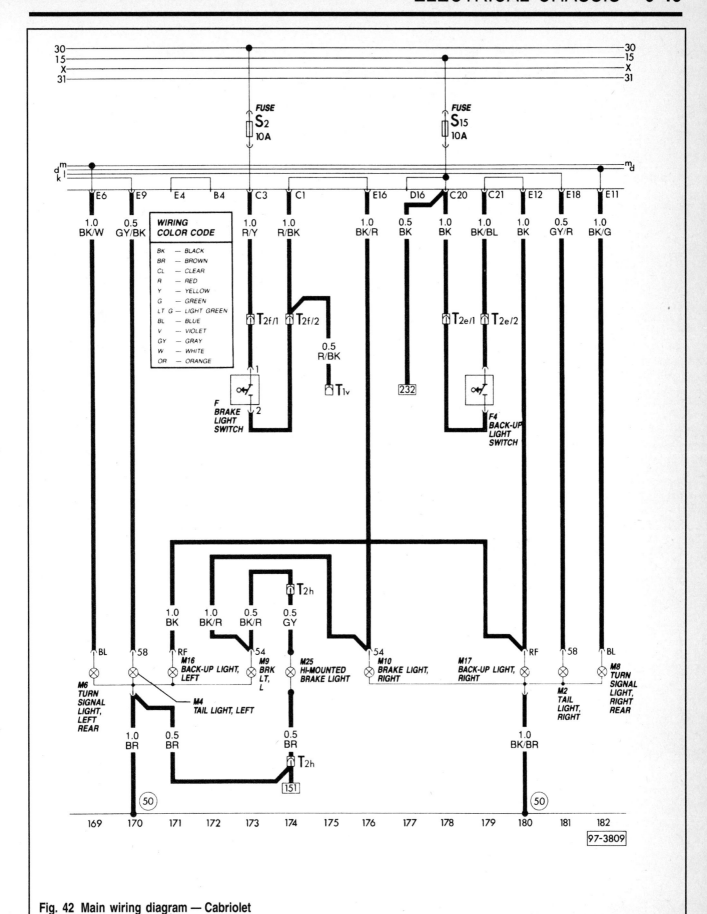

Fig. 42 Main wiring diagram — Cabriolet

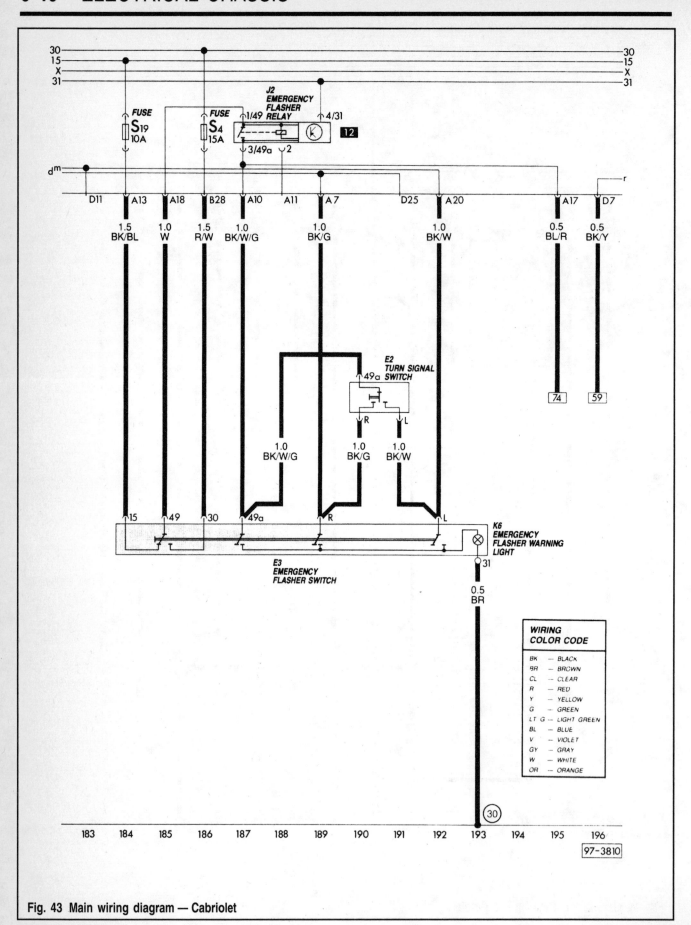

Fig. 43 Main wiring diagram — Cabriolet

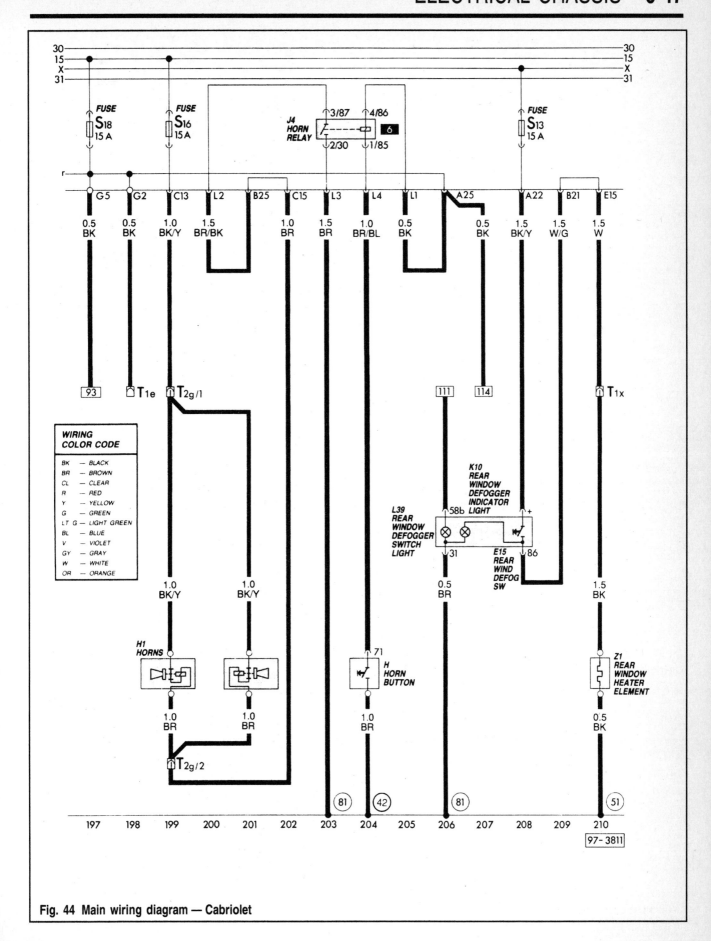

Fig. 44 Main wiring diagram — Cabriolet

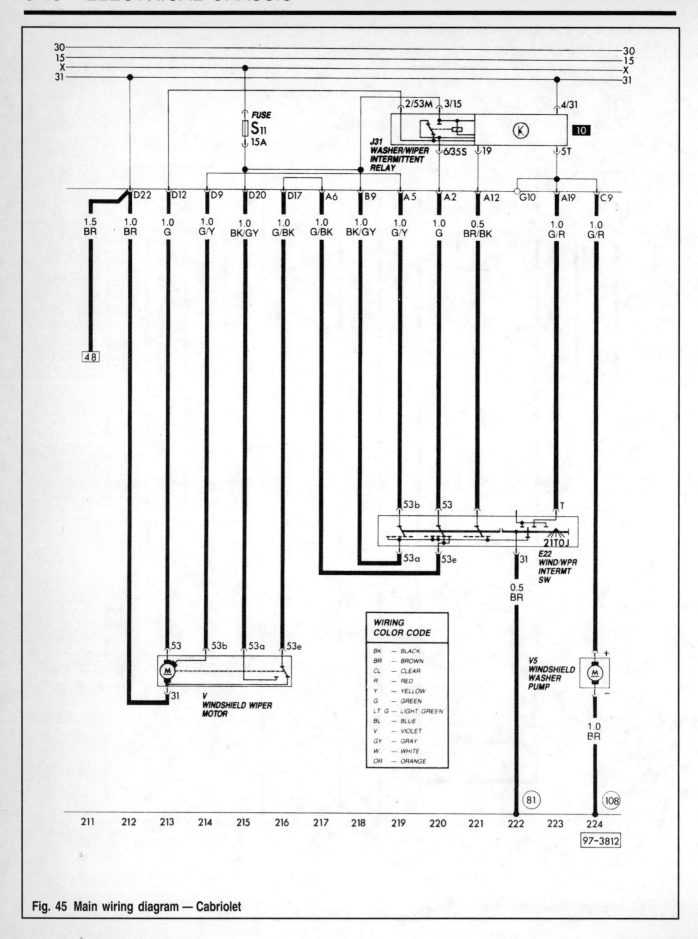

Fig. 45 Main wiring diagram — Cabriolet

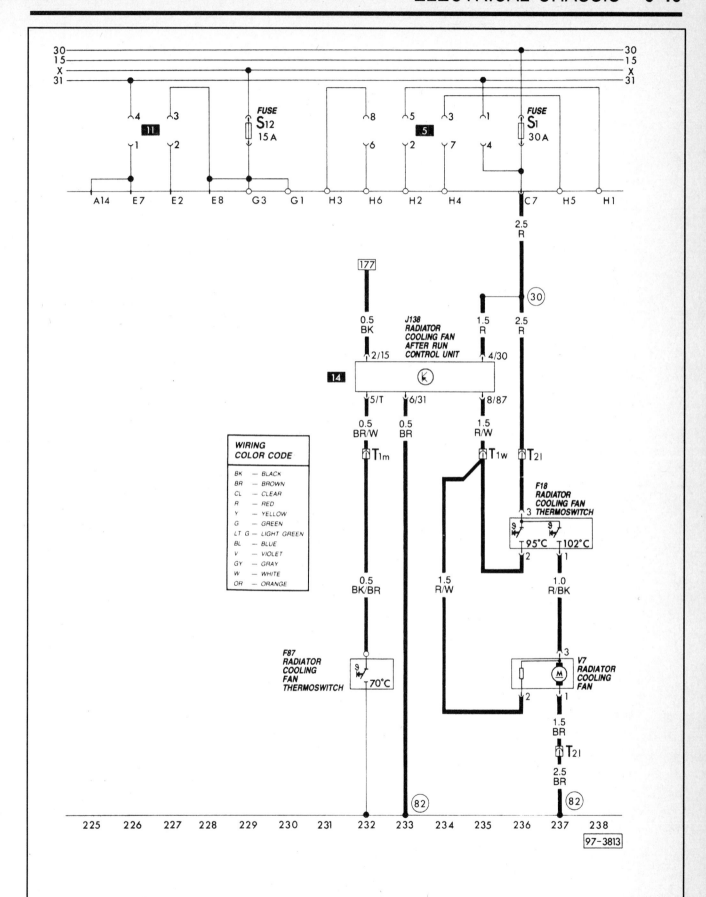

Fig. 46 Main wiring diagram — Cabriolet

Description	Current track
Air flow sensor potentiometer, G19	12
Brake and parking brake indicator light, K7	19
Coolant temperature sensor, G62	8
Digifant control unit, J169	5-26
Digifant control unit relay, J176	7-9
Fuel gauge sending unit, G	38
Fuel pump, G6	36
Fuel pump relay, J17	23-26
Fuse, S17	5
Fuse, S18	20
Fuse, S15	29
Fuse, S1	33
Fuse, S5	36
Hall generator, G40	5-7
Idle stabilizer valve, N71	21-22
Ignition coil, N152	1
Ignition coil power stage, N157	3-4
Ignition distributor, O	1-3
Injector, cyl. 1, N30	26
Injector, cyl. 2, N31	25
Injector, cyl. 3, N32	24
Injector, cyl. 4, N33	23
Intake air temperature sensor, G42	11
Knock sensor, G61	11-13
OBD fault warning light, K83	21
Oxygen sensor, G39	19-20
Radiator cooling fan, V7	34-35
Radiator cooling fan after run control unit, J138	29-32
Radiator cooling fan thermoswitch, F18	33-35
Radiator cooling fan thermoswitch, F87	29
Seat belt warning light, K19	20
Spark plug connectors, P	1-3
Spark plugs, Q	1-3
Throttle valve potentiometer, G69	15-16
Transfer fuel pump, G23	39

Wire connectors

T — junction box, behind fuse relay panel
T1 — single, behind fuse relay panel
T1a — single, behind fuse relay panel
T1b — single, behind fuse relay panel
T1d — single, behind fuse relay panel
T1f — single, behind fuse relay panel
T1k — single, behind fuse relay panel
T1m — single, behind fuse relay panel
T2 — double, behind fuse relay panel
T2l — double, near headlight, left
T2x — double, black, diagnostic connector, below transmission shift lever boot
T2z — double, white, diagnostic connector, below transmission shift lever boot
T3 — three-point, on ignition coil power stage
T3b — three-point, in engine compartment, rear
T3g — three-point, near starter
T4 — four-point, behind fuse/relay panel
T5a — five-point, near intake manifold
T5c — five-point, on firewall, left
T6 — six-point, behind fuse relay panel

Ground connections

(12) — in engine compartment, left
(18) — on engine block
(30) — beside fuse/relay panel
(82) — in left front wiring harness
(94) — in Digifant wiring harness

Welded wiring harness points

(C3) — plus connection (30), in left front wiring harness
(G1) — plus connection, in Digifant wiring harness
(G3) — plus connection, in injector wiring harness

Fig. 47 Digifant I engine management system — California Cabriolet

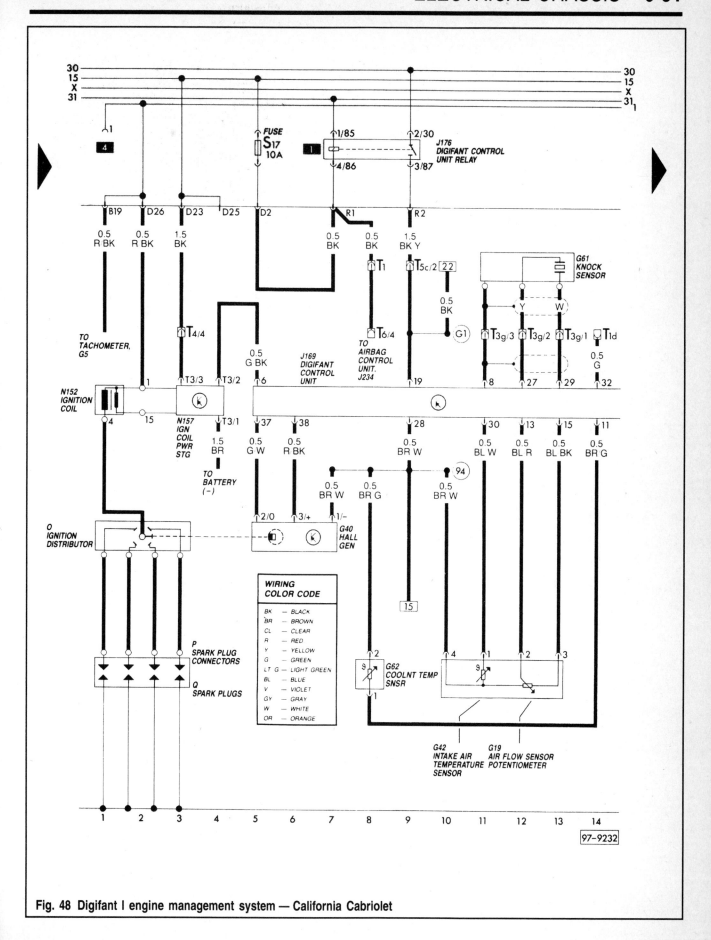

Fig. 48 Digifant I engine management system — California Cabriolet

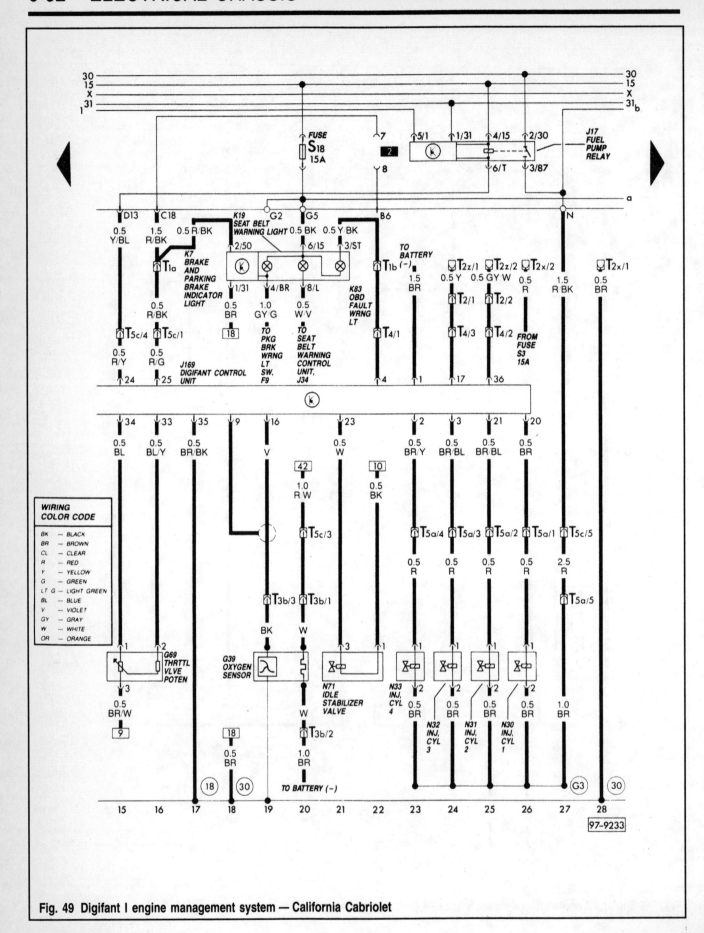

Fig. 49 Digifant I engine management system — California Cabriolet

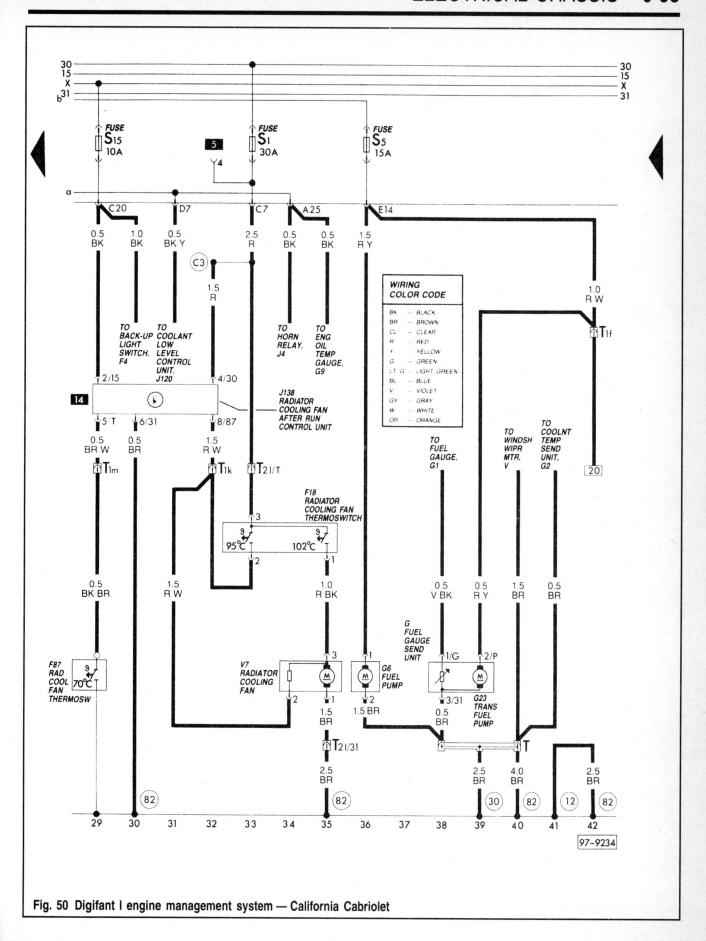

Fig. 50 Digifant I engine management system — California Cabriolet

Description	Current track
Contact, left, (cover installed), F155	3
Contact, right, (cover installed), F156	6
Convertible top circuit breaker, S68	8
Convertible top control unit, J256	3-11
Convertible top motor, V82	9
Convertible top switch, E137	3-5
Convertible top switch light, L72	2

Wire connectors

T1 — single, behind fuse/relay panel
T1a — single, behind fuse/relay panel
T2 — double, on convertible top motor
T5 — five-point, on convertible top switch
T17 — seventeen-point, in luggage compartment, left

Ground connections

(30) — beside fuse/relay panel

(50) — in luggage compartment, left

(51) — in luggage compartment, right

Welded wiring harness points

(A11) — plus connection, (58b) in instrument panel wiring harness

Fig. 51 Power convertible top — 1992 Cabriolet

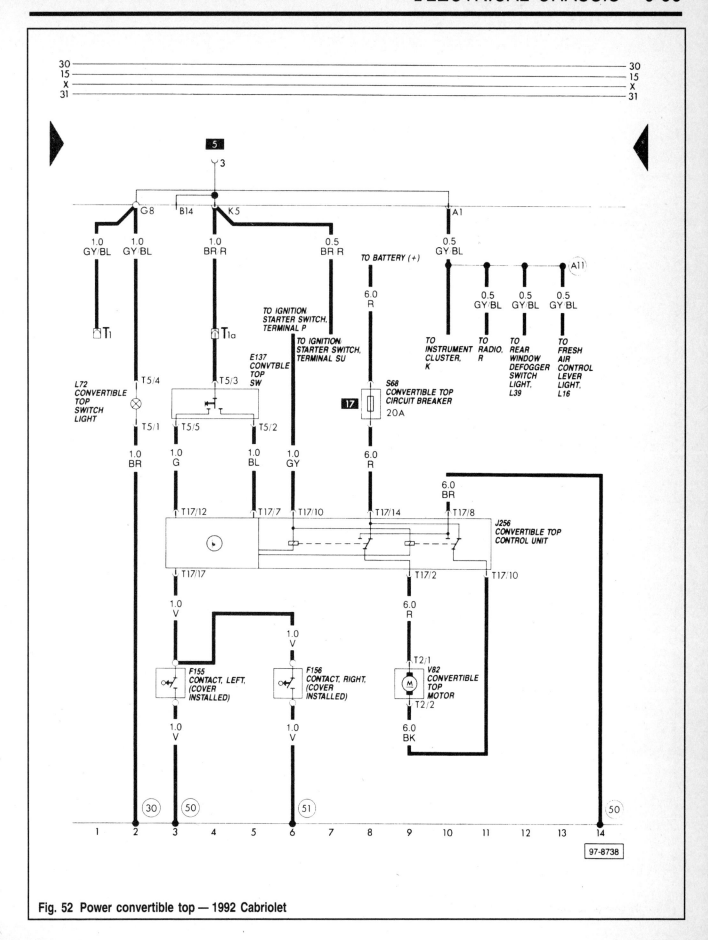

Fig. 52 Power convertible top — 1992 Cabriolet

Description	Current track
A/C compressor clutch, N25	6
A/C refrigerant high pressure switch, F23	10
A/C refrigerant low pressure switch, F73	6
A/C relay, J32	1-9
A/C switch, E35	5
A/C thermostat, E33	7
Fresh air blower series resistance, N23	2-4
Fresh air fan, V2	1
Fresh air fan switch, E9	2-4
Fuse, S14	12
Fuse, S1	14
Fuse, S23	4
Radiator cooling fan, V7	9-14
Radiator cooling fan relay, J26	12-14
Radiator cooling fan thermoswitch, F18	11-12

Wire connectors

T1d — single, on firewall, center
T1k — single, in engine compartment, left front
T2 — double, on A/C compressor
T2a — double, in engine compartment, left
T2b — double, in engine compartment, left
T5a — five-point, behind instrument panel
T5b — five-point, behind instrument panel

Ground connections

(18) — on engine block
(30) — near fuse/relay panel
(82) — in left front wiring harness

Fig. 53 Air conditioning — Cabriolet

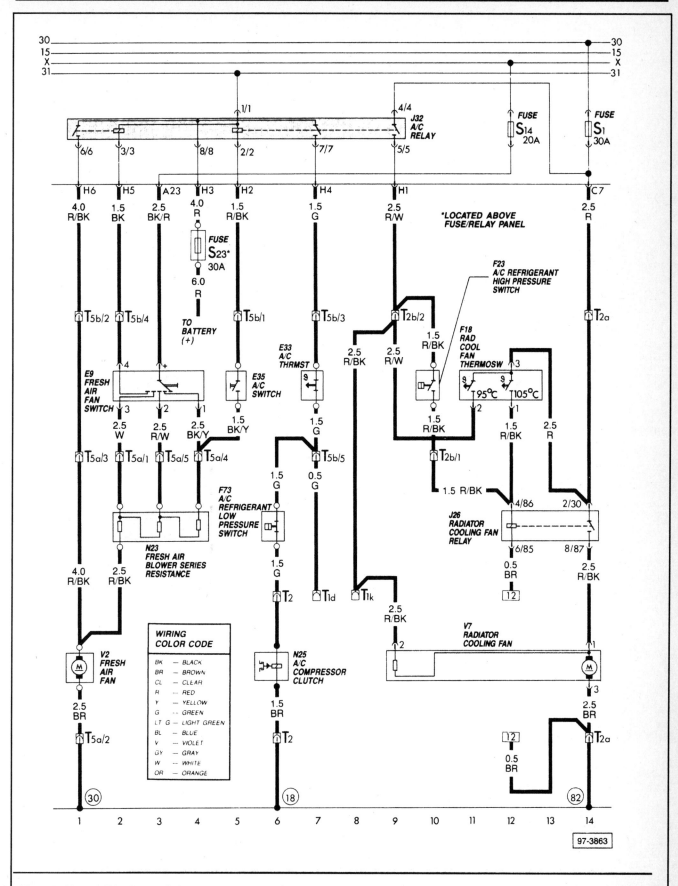

Fig. 54 Air conditioning — Cabriolet

Description	Current track
Automatic transmission console light, L19	7
Back-up light switch, F4	2
Back-up light, left, M16	4
Back-up light, right, M17	6
Fuse, S18	10
Fuse, S15	18
Radiator cooling fan after run control unit, J138	1
Shift lock control unit, J221	19-25
Shift lock solenoid, N110	19
Starter, B	34-35
Starter cut-out/back-up light switch, E17	8-14
Starting interlock relay, J207	31-38

Wire connectors

T1a — single, behind fuse/relay panel
T1b — single, behind fuse/relay panel
T1c — single, behind fuse/relay panel
T1d — single, behind fuse/relay panel
T1e — single, behind fuse/relay panel
T1f — single, behind fuse/relay panel
T1g — single, behind fuse/relay panel
T2 — double, behind fuse/relay panel
T2a — double, below transmission shift lever cover
T2e — double, in engine compartment, left
T2f — double, behind fuse/relay panel
T3 — three-point, below transmission shift lever cover
T4 — four-point, behind fuse/relay panel
T4a — four-point, near transmission shift lever
T6 — six-point, below transmission shift lever cover
T8 — eight-point, on radio
T9 — nine-point, on starting interlock relay

Ground connections

(30) — near fuse/relay panel
(54) — on rear apron
(63) — on tail light bulb holder, left
(64) — on tail light bulb holder, right
(102) — in automatic transmission wiring harness

Welded wiring harness points

(A4) — plus connection (58b), in instrument panel wiring harness
(U2) — plus connection (15), in automatic transmission wiring harness

Fig. 55 Automatic shift lock — Cabriolet

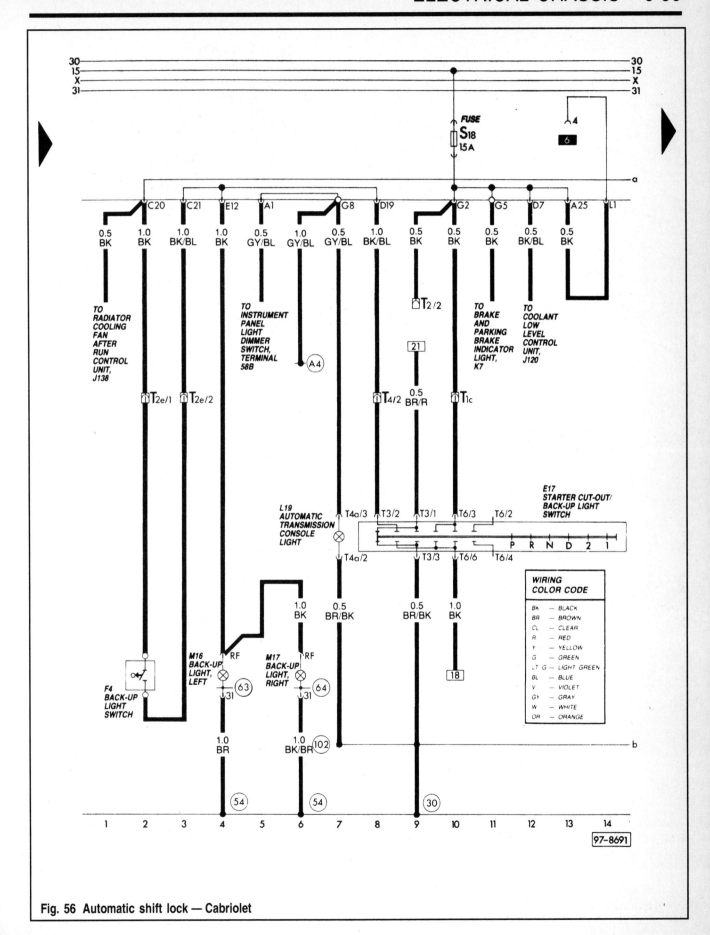

Fig. 56 Automatic shift lock — Cabriolet

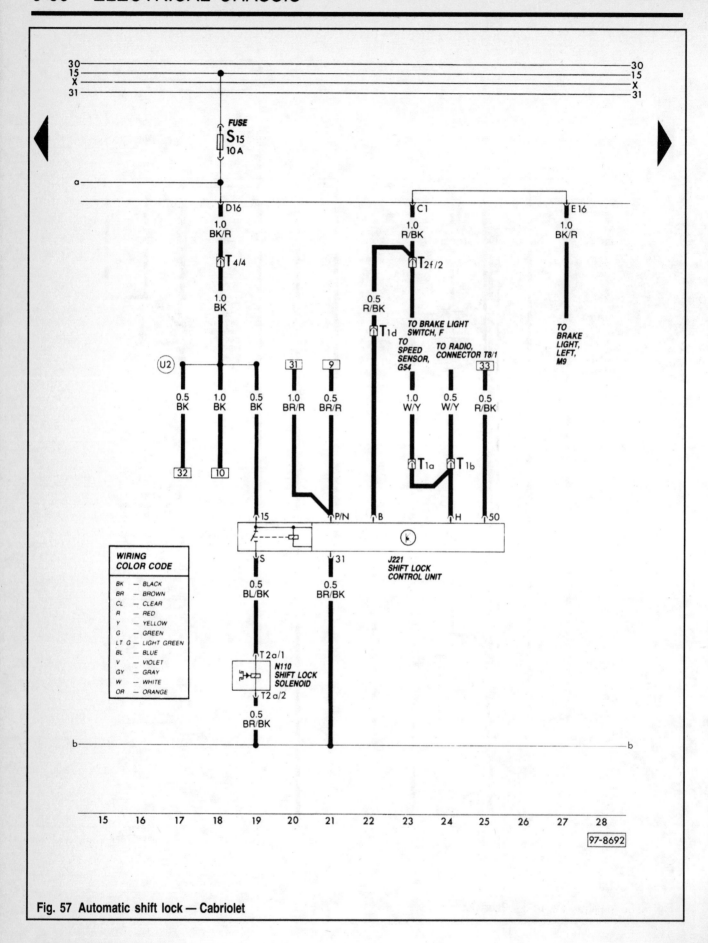

Fig. 57 Automatic shift lock — Cabriolet

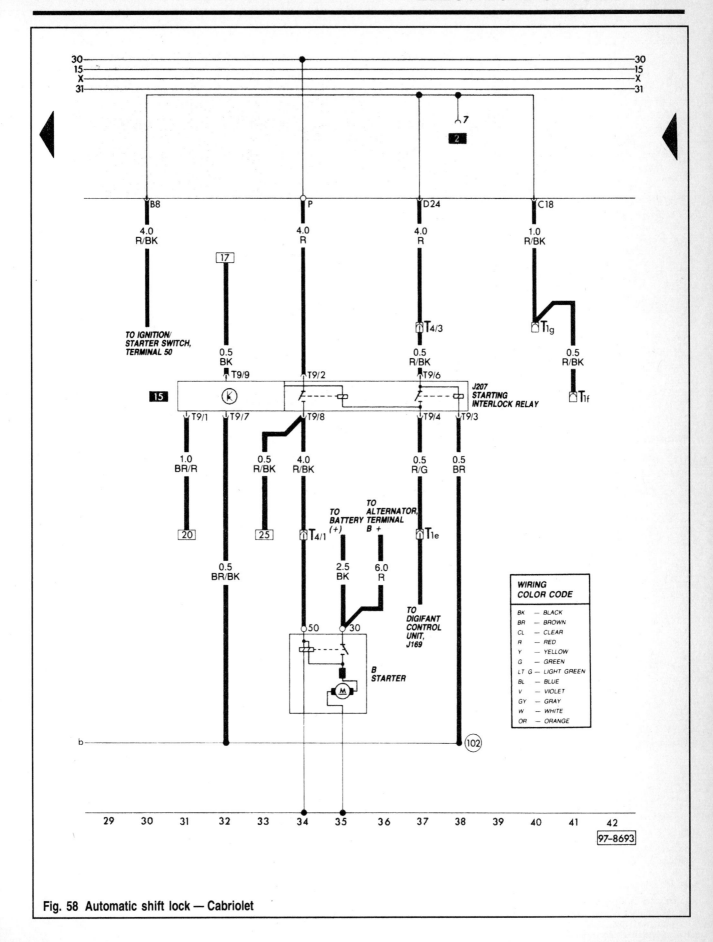

Fig. 58 Automatic shift lock — Cabriolet

Description	Current track
Door contact switch, left front, F2	12
Power window control unit, J139	1-15
Power window fuse, S37	11
Power window switch light, L53	4, 5
Window motor, left front door, V14	13
Window motor, right front door, V15	14
Window switch, left front, E40	1-4
Window switch, right front, E41	5-8

Wire connectors

T2a — double, in driver's door
T2b — double, in passenger's door
T8a — eight-point, on power window control unit
T8b — eight-point, on power window control unit
T8c — eight-point, on power window control unit

Ground connections

(40) — below rear seat, right

(89) — in power window wiring harness

Welded wiring harness points

(Q9) — plus connection, in power window wiring harness

(Q13) — plus connection, in power window wiring harness

(Q15) — plus connection, in power window wiring harness (left up)

(Q16) — plus connection, in power window wiring harness (left down)

Fig. 59 Power windows — Cabriolet

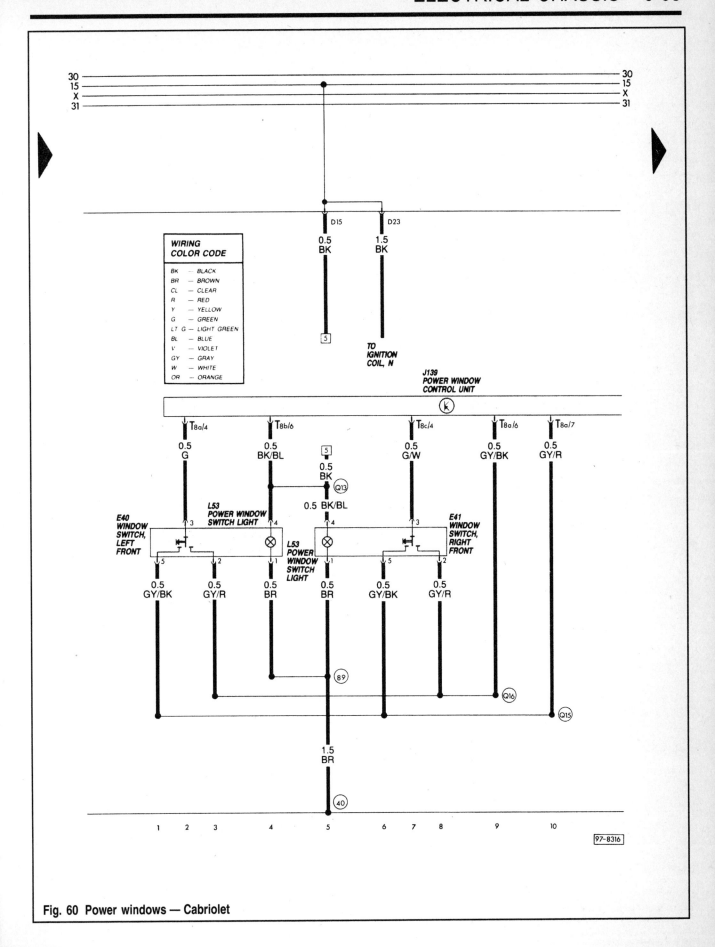

Fig. 60 Power windows — Cabriolet

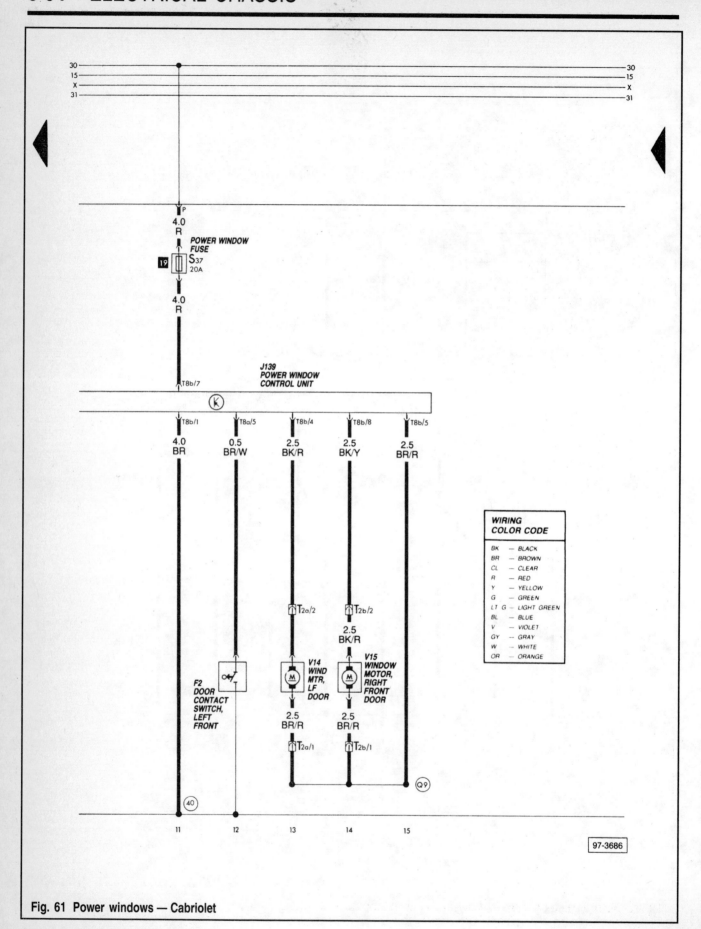

Fig. 61 Power windows — Cabriolet

Description	Current track
Daytime running light relay, J90	15-17
Daytime running lights resistor, N53	13
Fuse, S10	3
Fuse, S21	4
Fuse, S9	7
Fuse, S22	8
Fuse, S20	28
Fuse, S7	32
Fuse, S8	38
Headlight dimmer/flasher switch, E4	10-11
Headlight, left, L1	3, 4
Headlight, right, L2	7, 8
High-beam headlight, left, L13	1
High-beam headlight, right, L14	5
Instrument panel light dimmer switch, E20	23
License plate light, X	25, 27
Light switch, E1	16-23
Load reduction relay, J59	16-17
Luggage compartment light, W3	28
Luggage compartment light switch, F5	28
Parking light, left, M1	33
Parking light, right, M3	39
Side marker lights, front, M11	32, 38
Tail light, left, M4	29
Tail light, right, M2	37
Turn signal light, left front, M5	34
Turn signal light, right front, M7	40

Wire connectors

T1 — single, behind fuse/relay panel
T1a — single, behind instrument panel, left
T1b — single, behind instrument panel, left
T1c — single, behind instrument pnael, left
T1n — single, in luggage compartment, left
T1p — single, near headlight, right
T1r — single, near headlight, left
T2 — double, behind fuse/relay panel
T2a — double, behind fuse/relay panel
T2b — double, behind fuse/relay panel
T3d — three-point, near headlight, right
T3e — three-point, near headlight, left
T8 — eight-point, on radio
T14 — fourteen-point, on instrument cluster

Ground connections

(50) — in luggage compartment, left
(82) — in left front wiring harness
(108) — in left front wiring harness

Welded wiring harness points

(A4) — plus connection (58b), in instrument panel wiring harness

Fig. 62 Daytime running lights — Canadian model Cabriolet

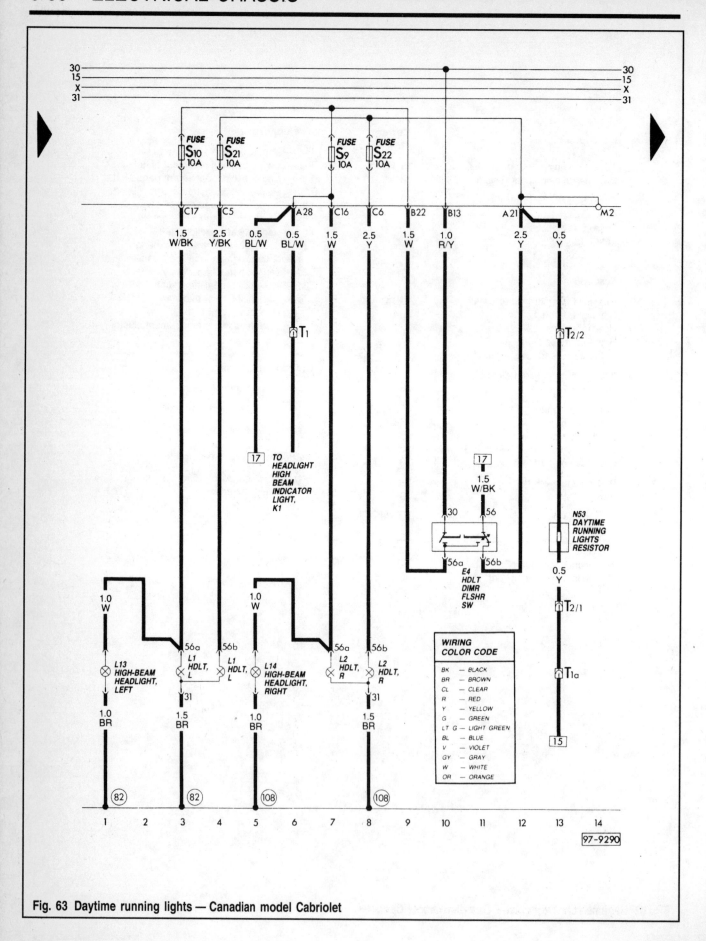

Fig. 63 Daytime running lights — Canadian model Cabriolet

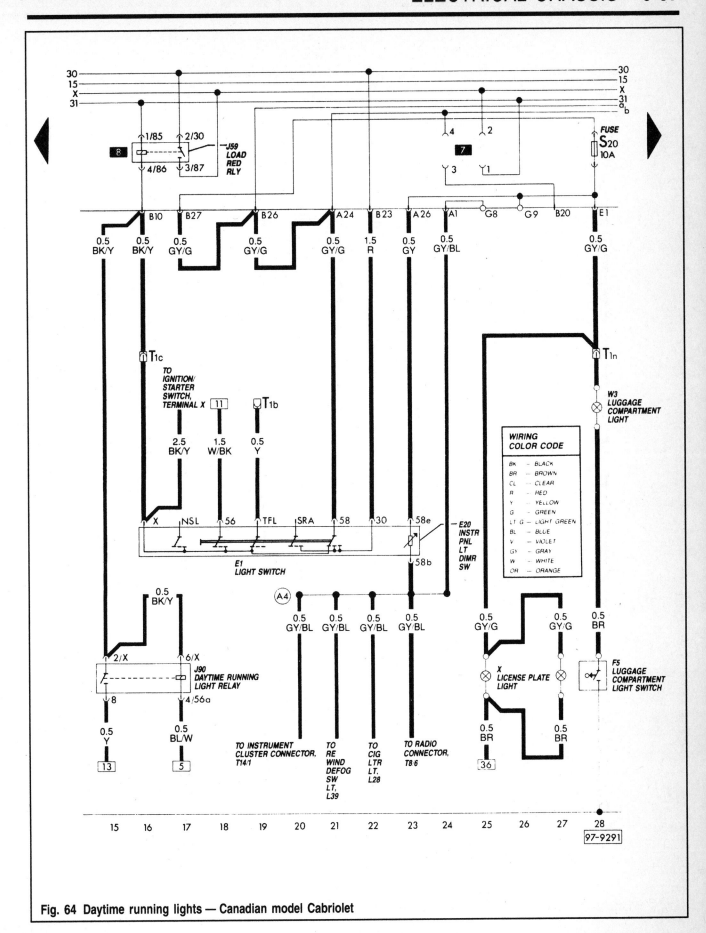

Fig. 64 Daytime running lights — Canadian model Cabriolet

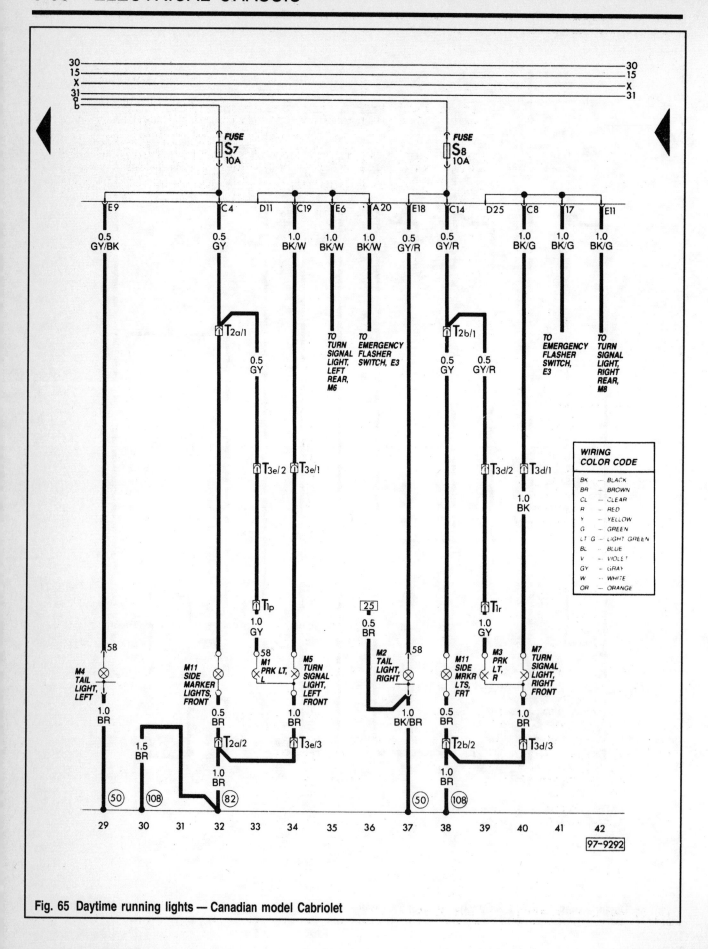

Fig. 65 Daytime running lights — Canadian model Cabriolet

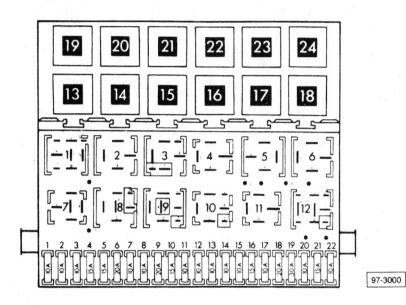

Fuse arrangement

according to the numbers on fuse panel from left to right:

                                          Amp.

		Amp.
1	Headlight, low beam, left	10
2	Headlight, low beam, right	10
3	Instrument panel lights, license plate lights	10
4	Glove box light, rear window wiper	15
5	Wiper/washer	15
6	Fresh air fan	20
7	Tail lights, side marker light, right	10
8	Tail lights, side marker light, left	10
9	Rear window defogger	20
10	Fog lights	15
11	Headlight, high beam, left, high beam indicator light	10
12	Headlight, high beam, right	10
13	Horn	10
14	Back-up lights, washer nozzle heaters	10
15	Open	
16	Dash warning lights	15
17	Emergency flasher switch, turn signals	10
18	Fuel pump, OXS heater	20
19	Radiator cooling fan, A/C	30
20	Brake lights, cruise control	10
21	Interior lights, digital clock	15
22	Radio, cigarette lighter	10

*Numbers in parentheses indicate production control number stamped on relay housing.

Relay location on fuse/relay panel

1	A/C relay
2	Rear window wiper/washer relay
3	Digifant control unit relay
4	Load reduction relay
5	Open
6	Emergency flasher relay
7	Fog light relay
8	Intermittent wiper relay
9	Seat belt warning system relay
10	Open
11	Horn relay
12	Fuel pump relay

Separate relays above fuse/relay panel

13	Radiator cooling fan after run control unit
14	Starting interlock relay (53)*
15	Open
16	Open
17	Open
18	Daytime driving light relay (Canada)
19	Automatic transmission relay
20	Open
21	Power window relay
22	Open
23	Fuse for A C, power seats
24	Power window fuse

Fig. 66 Main fuse and relay panel — Golf GL and GTI 8V

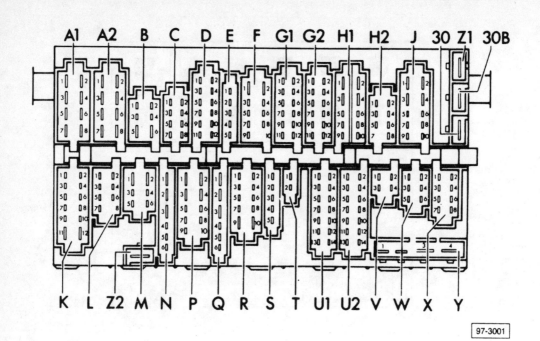

97-3001

Connections and plugs on fuse/relay panel

A1 — Headlight wiring harness (yellow)
A2 — Headlight wiring harness (yellow)
B — Open
C — Headlight wiring harness (yellow)
D — Optional equipment wiring harness (green)
E — Instrument wiring harness (green)
F — Engine compartment wiring harness, right (white)
G1 — Engine compartment wiring harness, right (white)
G2 — Engine compartment wiring harness, right (white)
H1 — Steering column switch wiring harness (red)
H2 — Steering column switch wiring harness (red)
J — Steering column switch wiring harness (red)
K — Rear wiring harness (black)
L — Rear wiring harness (black)
M — Rear wiring harness (black)
N — A/C wiring harness (green)
P — Rear window defroster wiring harness (blue)
Q — Instrument wiring harness (blue)
R — Light switch wiring harness (blue)
S — Engine compartment wiring harness, right (white)

T — Two-point connector (green)
U1 — Instrument cluster wiring harness (blue)
U2 — Instrument cluster wiring harness (blue)
V — Multi-function indicator wiring harness (green)
W — Six-point connector (green)
X — Warning lamp wiring harness (green)
Y — Single connector, terminal 30
Z1 — Single connector
Z2 — Single connector, terminal 31
30 — Single connector, terminal 30
30B — Single connector
31 — Single connector, terminal 31

Fig. 67 Fuse panel connectors — Golf GL and GTI 8V.

Description	Current track
Air flow sensor potentiometer, G19	69
Alternator, C	1-2
Alternator warning light, K2	98
Back-up light switch, F4	232
Back-up light, left, M16	202
Back-up light, right, M17	204
Battery, A	9
Brake and parking brake indicator light, K7	145
Brake fluid level warning contact, F34	140
Brake light switch, F	207
Brake light, left, M9	200
Brake light, right, M10	208
Cigarette lighter, U1	165
Cigarette lighter light, L28	164
Clock light, L8	104
Coolant low level sensor, G32	86
Coolant overheat warning light, K28	109
Coolant temperature gauge, G3	99
Coolant temperature sending unit, G2	87
Coolant temperature sensor, G62	66
Digifant control unit, J169	62-80
Digifant control unit relay, J176	79-80
Digital clock, Y2	105
Door contact switch, left front, F2	156-157
Door contact switch, left rear, F10	160
Door contact switch, right front, F3	159
Door contact switch, right rear, F11	161
Emergency flasher relay, J2	185-187
Emergency flasher switch, E3	184-187
Emergency flasher warning light, K6	188
Engine oil pressure switch (0.3 bar), F22	88
Engine oil pressure switch (1.8 bar), F1	89
Engine oil pressure warning light, K3	108
Fresh air control lever light, L16	242
Fresh air fan, V2	241
Fresh air fan series resistance, N23	245
Fresh air fan switch, E9	244-246
Fuel gauge, G1	100
Fuel gauge sending unit, G	36
Fuel pump, G23	39
Fuel pump relay, J17	34-36
Full throttle switch, F81	63
Fuse, S18	38
Fuse, S19	43
Fuse, S15	71
Fuse, S22	165
Fuse, S21	168
Fuse, S11	172
Fuse, S1	173
Fuse, S12	174
Fuse, S2	175
Fuse, S17	183

Description	Current track
Fuse, S8	199
Fuse, S20	207
Fuse, S7	209
Fuse, S3	218
Fuse, S10	231
Fuse, S14	232
Fuse, S6	245
Fuse, S9	257
Fuse, S13	265
Fuse, S5	270
Fuse, S4	291
Glove compartment light, W6	248
Hall generator, G40	62-64
Hall ignition control unit, N41	59-62
Headlight dimmer/flasher switch, E4	181
Headlight high beam indicator light, K1	103
Headlight switch light, L9	211
Headlight, left, L1	173
Headlight, right, L2	175
High-beam headlight, left, L13	172
High-beam headlight, right, L14	174
High-mount brake light, M25	205-207
Horn button, H	275
Horn relay, J4	262-264
Horns, H1	263, 265
Idle stabilizer valve, N71	78-79
Idle switch, F60	65
Ignition coil, N	58-60
Ignition distributor, O	59-61
Ignition starter switch, D	22-25
Injector, cyl. 1, N30	84
Injector, cyl. 2, N31	83
Injector, cyl. 3, N32	82
Injector, cyl. 4, N33	81
Instrument panel light dimmer switch, E20	218
Instrument panel light, L10	93-95
Intake air temperature sensor, G42	68
Interior light with delay switch, W15	159-160
Knock sensor, G61	67-69
License plate light, X	220, 223
Light switch, E1	214
Load reduction relay, J59	19
Luggage compartment light, W3	168
Luggage compartment light switch, F5	224
Make-up mirror light, right, W14	155
Oil pressure warning, coolant low level indicator and tachometer control unit, J243	104-120
Overheat fuse, S24	244
Oxygen sensor, G39	76-77
Parking brake warning light switch, F9	136
Parking light, left, M1	171
Parking light, right, M3	176

Description	Current track
Radiator cooling fan, V7	43-44
Radiator cooling fan after run control unit, J138	53-55
Radiator cooling fan thermoswitch, F18	43-46
Radiator cooling fan thermoswitch, F87	55
Rear window defogger indicator light, K10	256
Rear window defogger switch, E15	257
Rear window defogger switch light, L39	255
Rear window heater element, Z1	260
Rear window wiper/washer relay	285-287
Rear wiper motor	287-289
Seat belt switch, left, E24	151
Seat belt warning control unit, J34	147-151
Seat belt warning light, K19	144
Side marker lights, front, M11	169, 178
Spark plug connectors, P	59-61
Spark plugs, Q	59-61
Speed sensor, G54	100
Starter, B	12-14
Starting interlock relay	147, 148
Tachometer, G5	113-115
Tail light, left, M4	199
Tail light, right, M2	209
Transfer fuel pump, G6	37
Turn signal indicator light, K5	102
Turn signal light, left front, M5	170
Turn signal light, left rear, M6	198
Turn signal light, right front, M7	177
Turn signal light, right rear, M8	210
Turn signal switch, E2	190-192
Voltage regulator, C1	1-2
Voltage stabilizer, J6	99
Washer wiper intermittent relay, J31	276-280
Windshield and rear window washer pump	283
Windshield-wiper intermittent switch, E22	276-280

Fig. 68 Current track index — Golf GL and GTI 8V

Wire connectors

T1 — single, behind fuse/relay panel
T1a — single, above fuse/relay panel
T1b — single, in luggage compartment, left rear
T1f — single, near battery
T1h — single, behind fuse/relay panel
T1l — single, in luggage compartment
T1m — single, behind instrument panel, right
T1n — single, behind fuse/relay panel
T1r — single, in luggage compartment, left rear
T1x — single, near ignition coil
T2d — double, near intake manifold
T2e — double, behind instrument panel, right
T2h — double, near left headlight
T2i — double, near left headlight
T2k — double, near left headlight
T2l — double, on hood
T2m — double, on right firewall
T2p — double, in luggage compartment right
T2r — double, on upper right A-pillar
T2s — double, behind fuse/relay panel
T2t — double, on high mount brake light
T2u — double, near throttle valve housing
T2v — double, on fresh air blower series resistance
T2w — double, on hood
T3 — three-point, behind console
T3b — three-point, in engine compartment, rear
T3g — three-point, near starter
T4c — four-point, behind steering column switch cover
T4d — four-point, behind steering column switch cover
T5b — five-point, behind steering column switch cover
T5c — five-point, behind steering column switch cover
T5e — five-point, on fresh air blower series resistance
T6a — six-point, on left taillight
T6b — six-point, on right taillight
T6c — six-point, on left firewall
T7a — seven-point, behind steering column switch cover
T8 — eight-point, on radio
T28 — twenty eight-point, on instrument cluster

Ground connections

① — battery to body
② — transmission to body
⑮ — on cylinder head
⑱ — on engine block
㉚ — beside fuse/relay panel
㊹ — on lower left A-pillar
㊿ — in luggage compartment, left
(51) — in luggage compartment, right
(53) — in rear deck lid, right
(54) — on rear apron
(84) — engine block, in right front wiring harness
(94) — in Digifant wiring harness
(119) — in headlight wiring harness
(120) — in headlight wiring harness

Welded wiring harness points

(C1) — plus connection (58l), in front wiring harness, left
(C2) — plus connection (58r), in front wiring harness, left
(C3) — plus connection (30), in front wiring harness, left
(G3) — *plus connection, in injector wiring harness*
(G4) — plus connection, in injector wiring harness

Fig. 69 Connector locations — Golf GL and GTI 8V

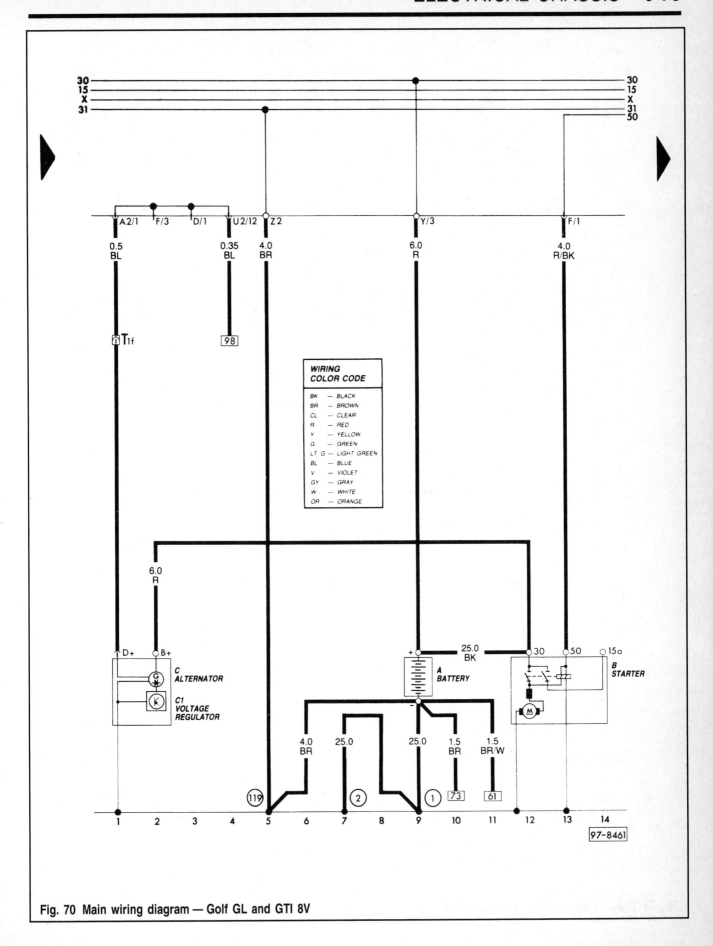

Fig. 70 Main wiring diagram — Golf GL and GTI 8V

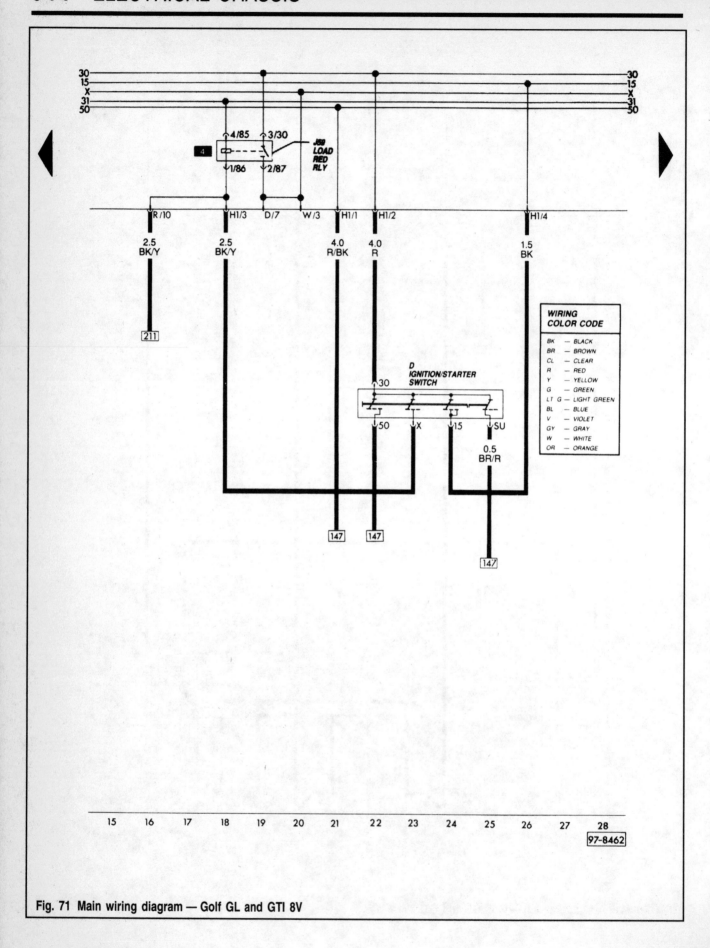

Fig. 71 Main wiring diagram — Golf GL and GTI 8V

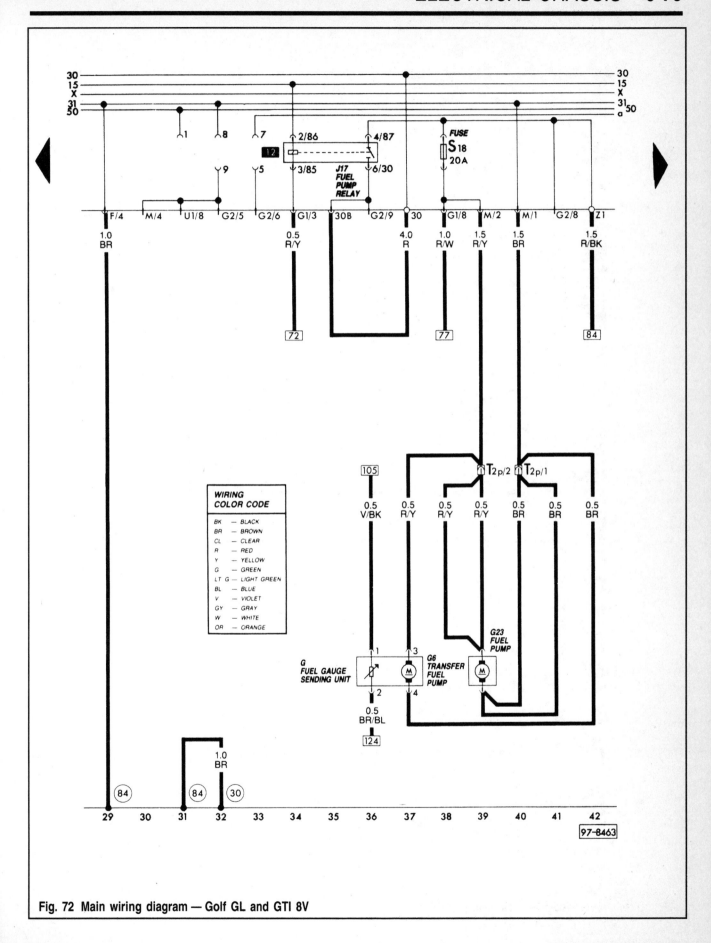

Fig. 72 Main wiring diagram — Golf GL and GTI 8V

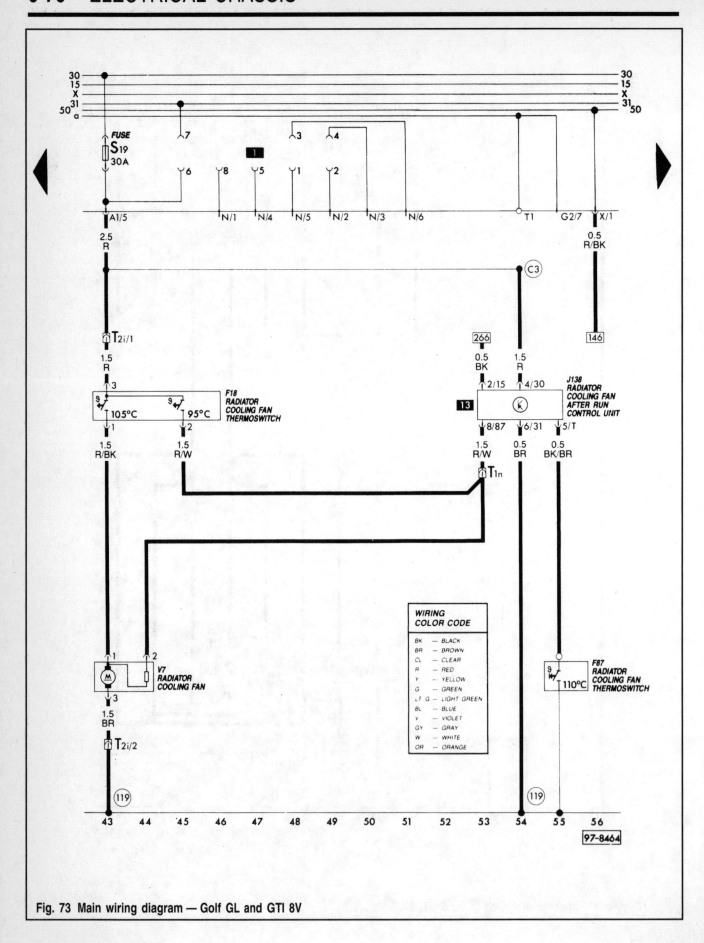

Fig. 73 Main wiring diagram — Golf GL and GTI 8V

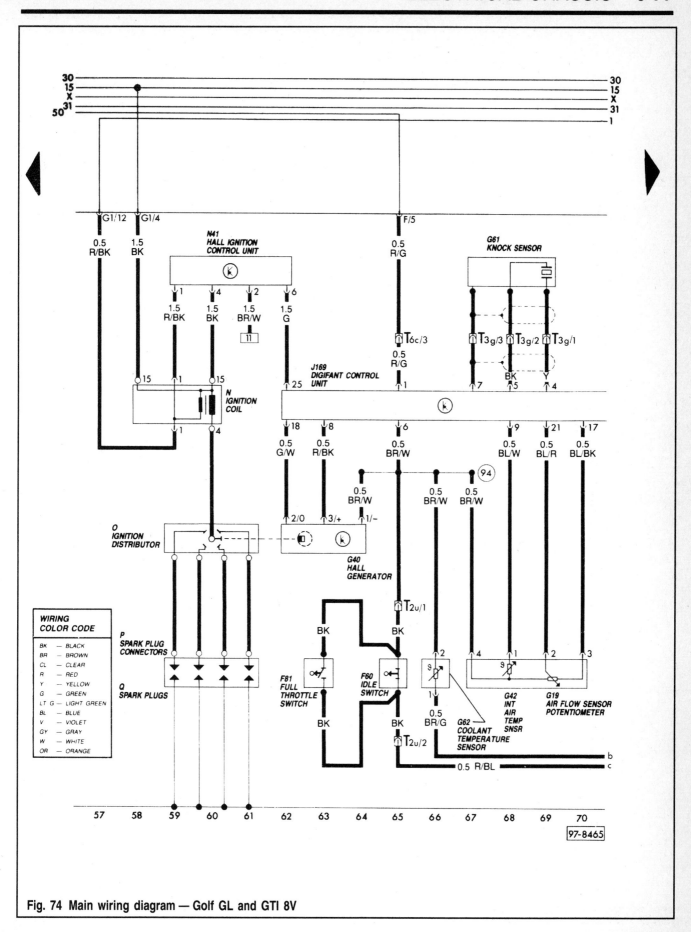

Fig. 74 Main wiring diagram — Golf GL and GTI 8V

97-8465

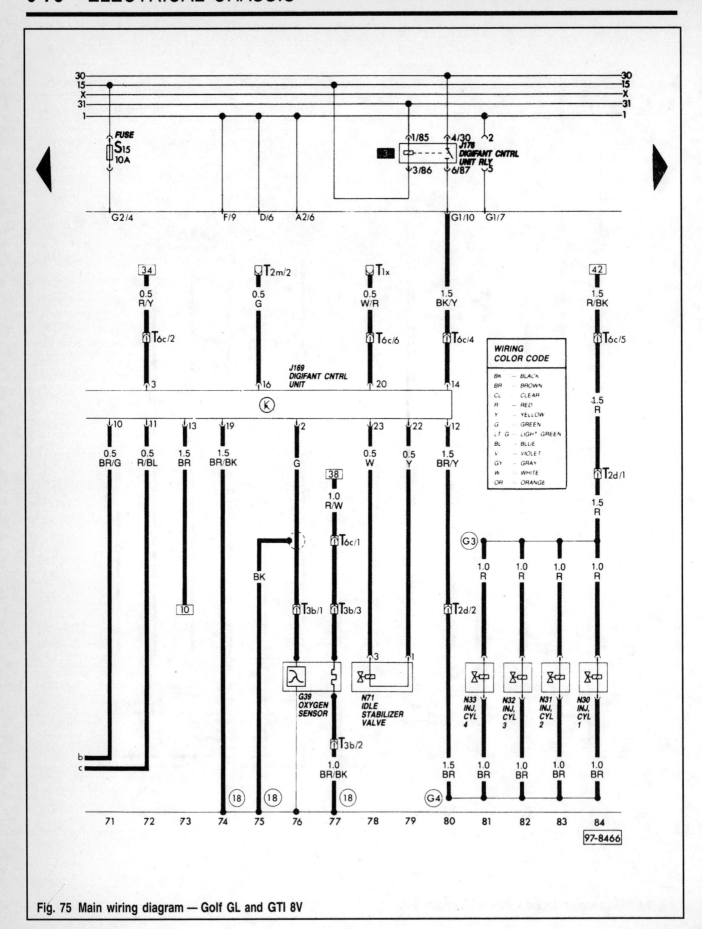

Fig. 75 Main wiring diagram — Golf GL and GTI 8V

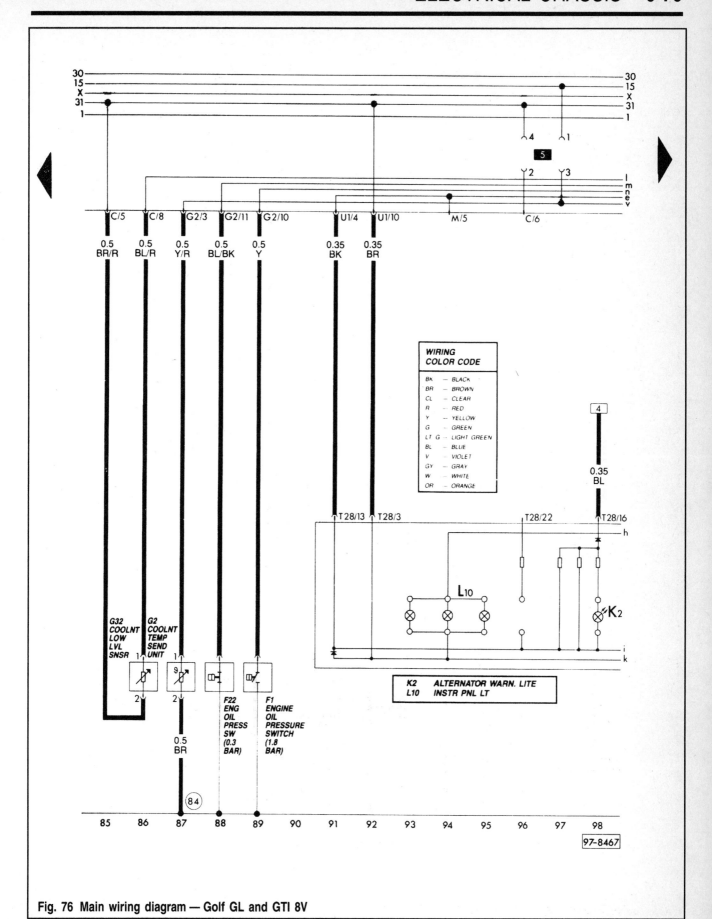

Fig. 76 Main wiring diagram — Golf GL and GTI 8V

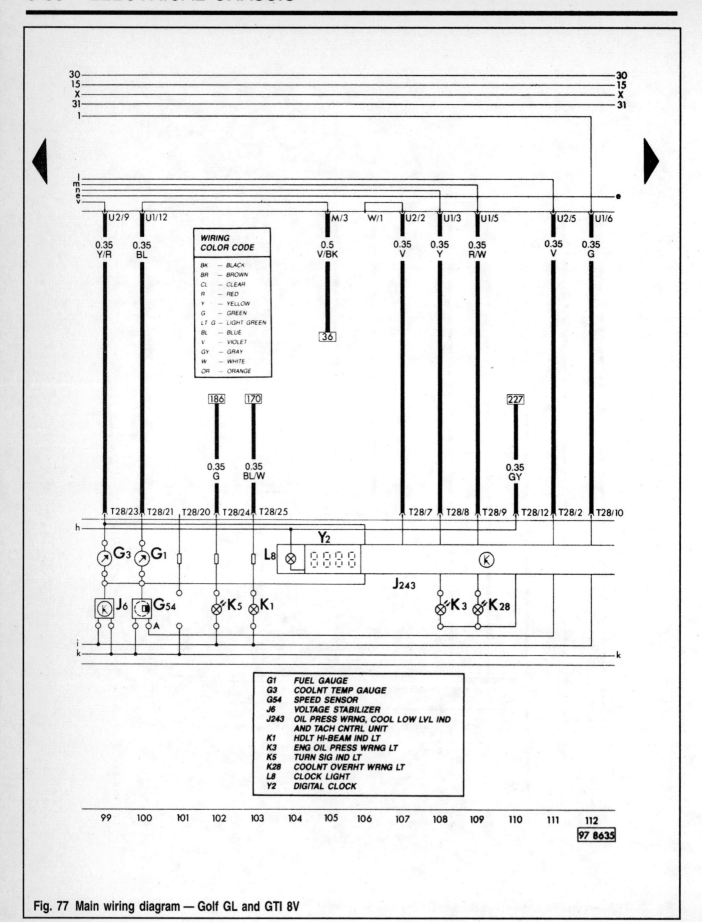

Fig. 77 Main wiring diagram — Golf GL and GTI 8V

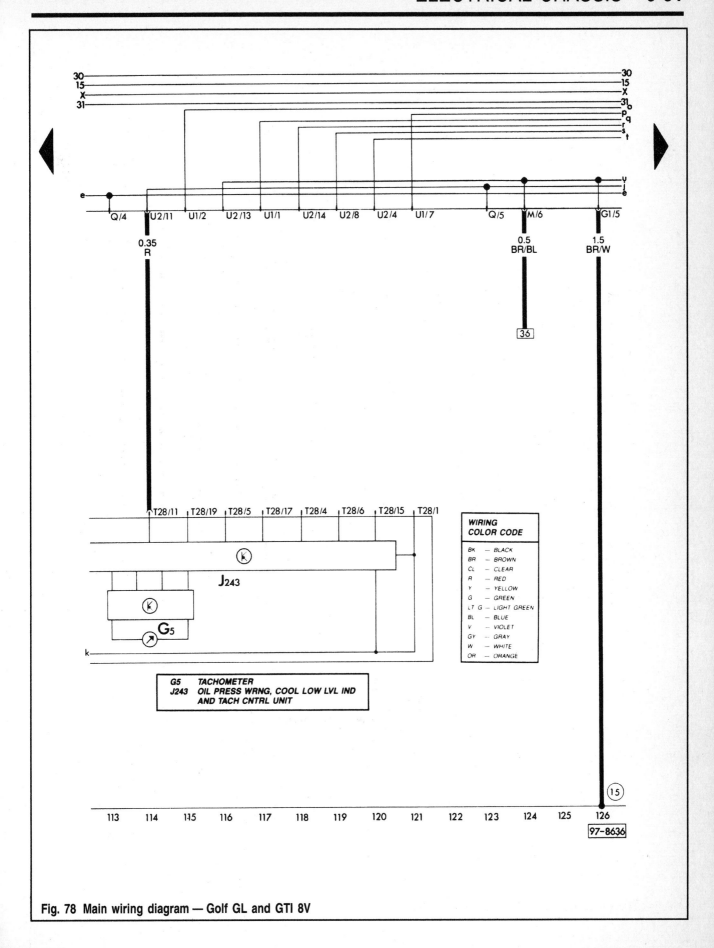

Fig. 78 Main wiring diagram — Golf GL and GTI 8V

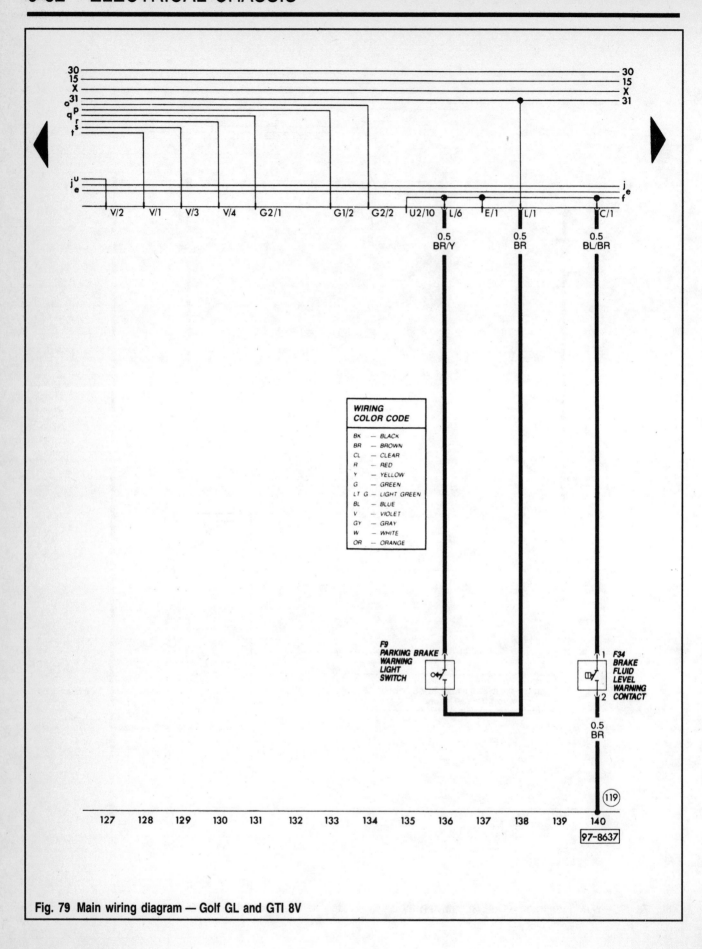

Fig. 79 Main wiring diagram — Golf GL and GTI 8V

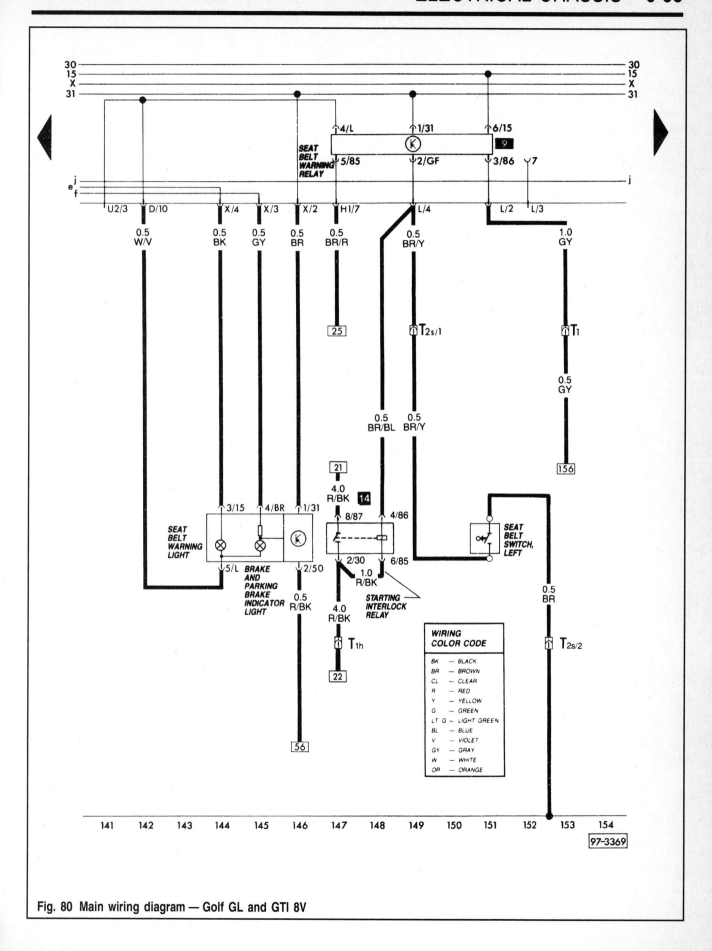

Fig. 80 Main wiring diagram — Golf GL and GTI 8V

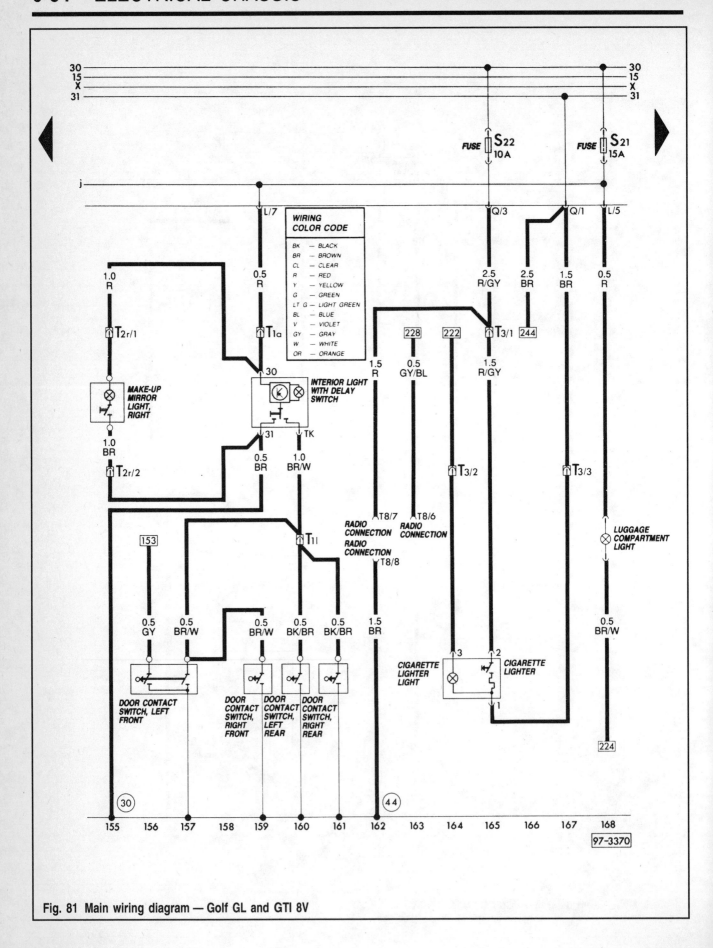

Fig. 81 Main wiring diagram — Golf GL and GTI 8V

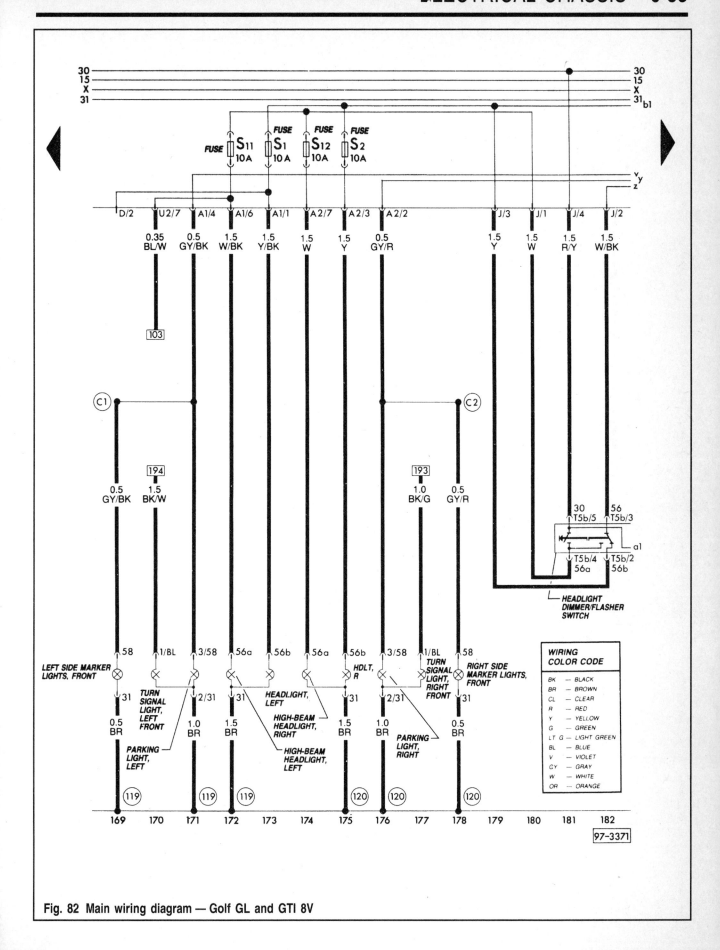

Fig. 82 Main wiring diagram — Golf GL and GTI 8V

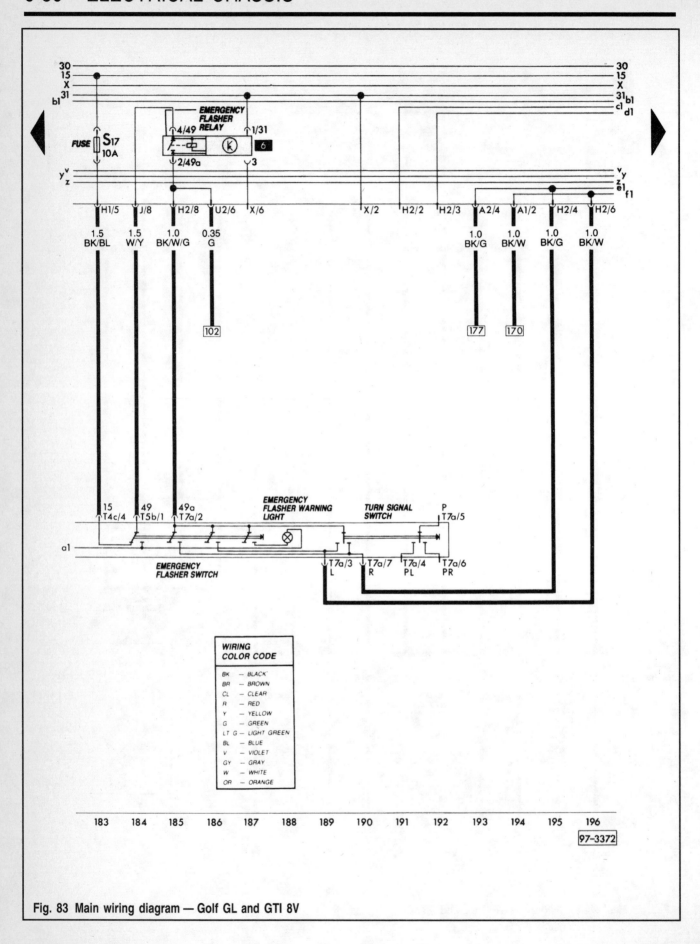

Fig. 83 Main wiring diagram — Golf GL and GTI 8V

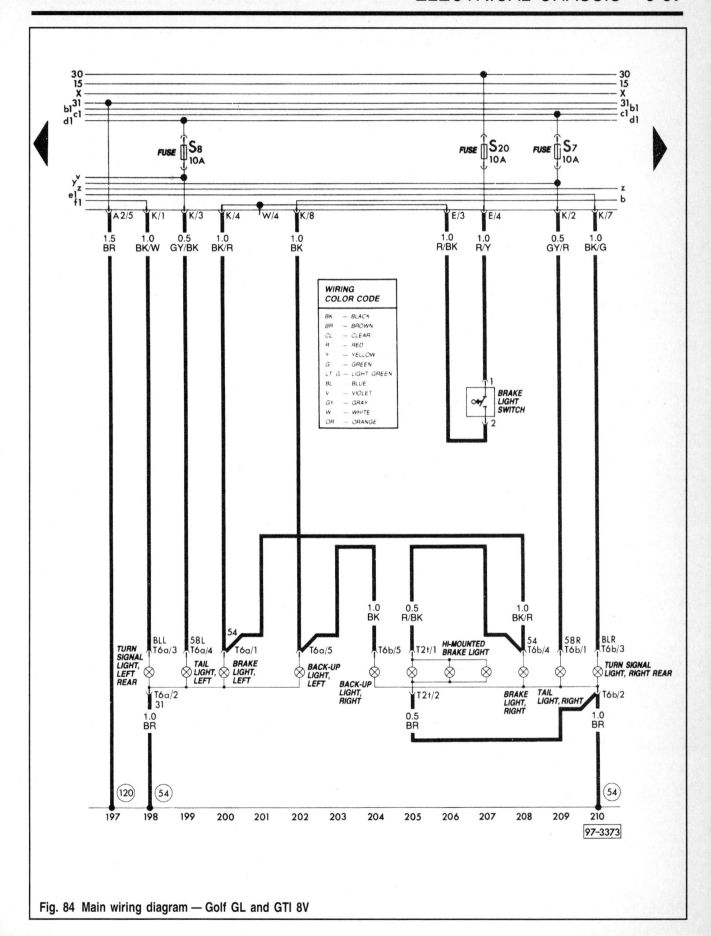

Fig. 84 Main wiring diagram — Golf GL and GTI 8V

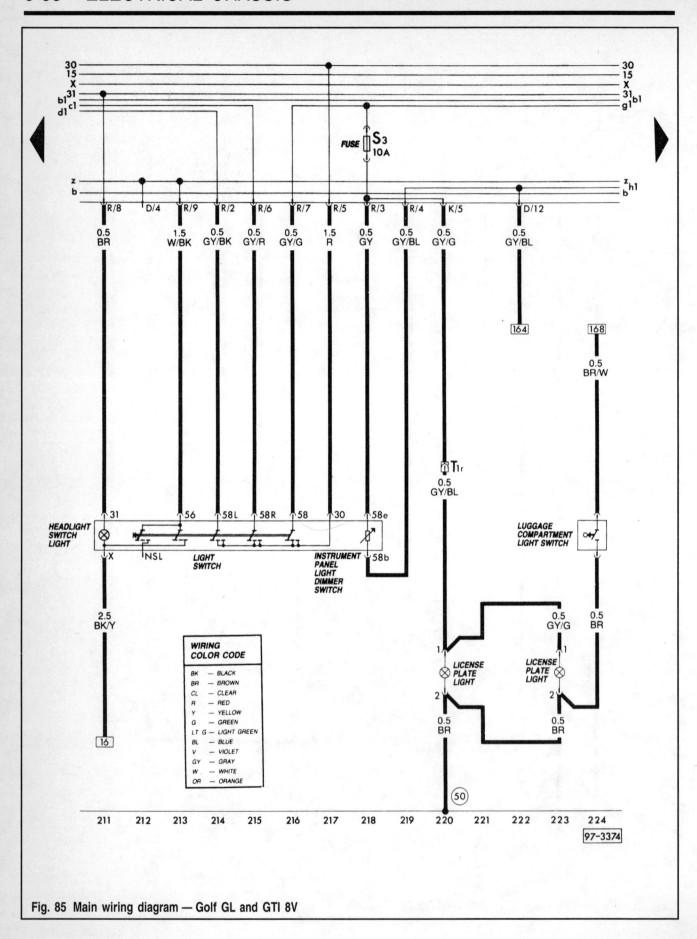

Fig. 85 Main wiring diagram — Golf GL and GTI 8V

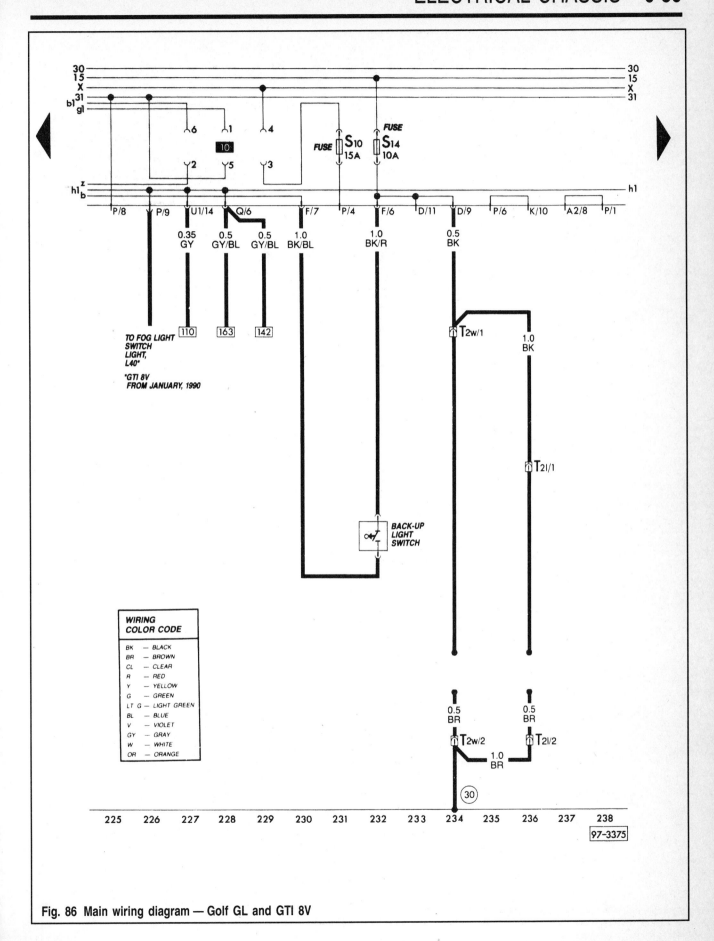

Fig. 86 Main wiring diagram — Golf GL and GTI 8V

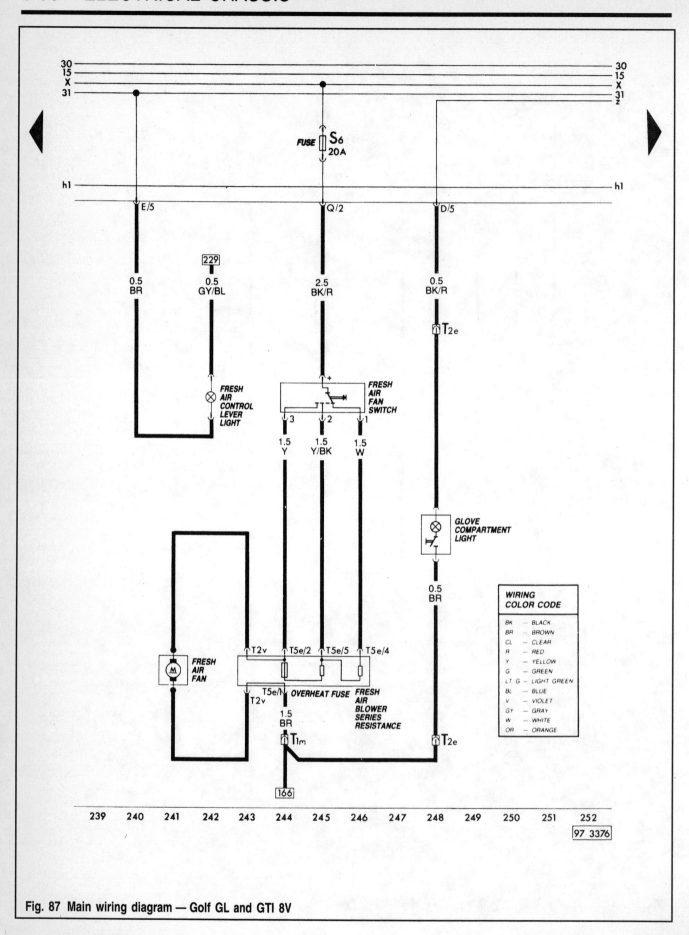

Fig. 87 Main wiring diagram — Golf GL and GTI 8V

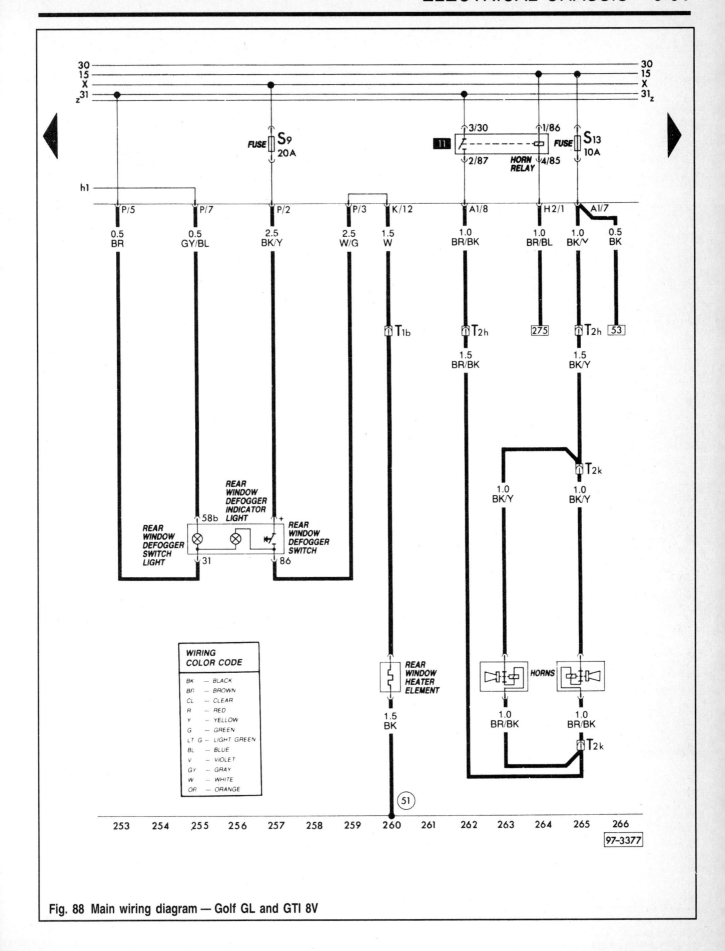

Fig. 88 Main wiring diagram — Golf GL and GTI 8V

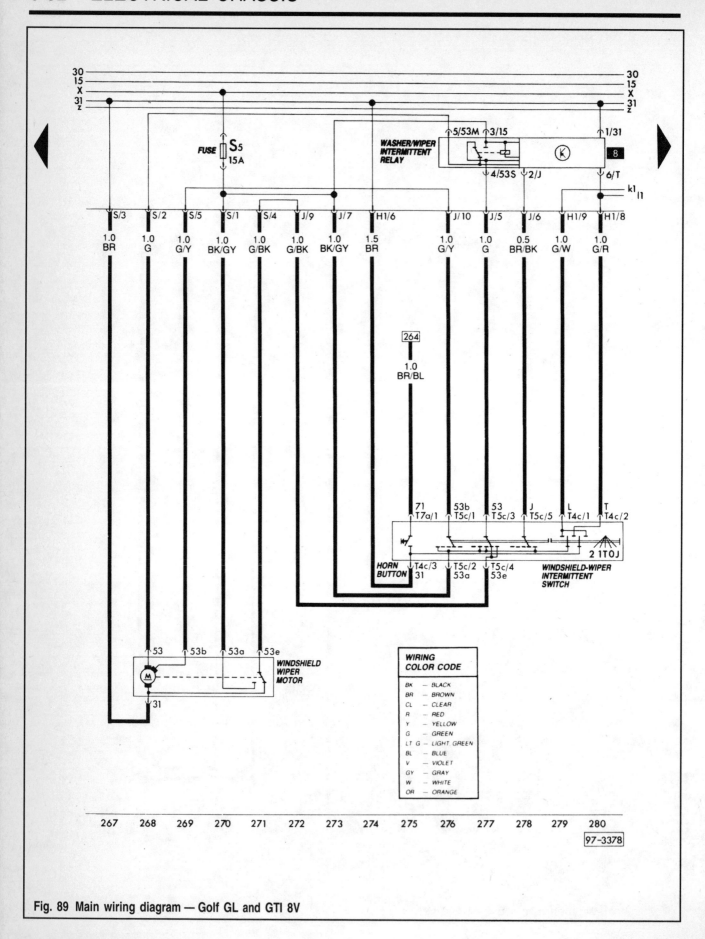

Fig. 89 Main wiring diagram — Golf GL and GTI 8V

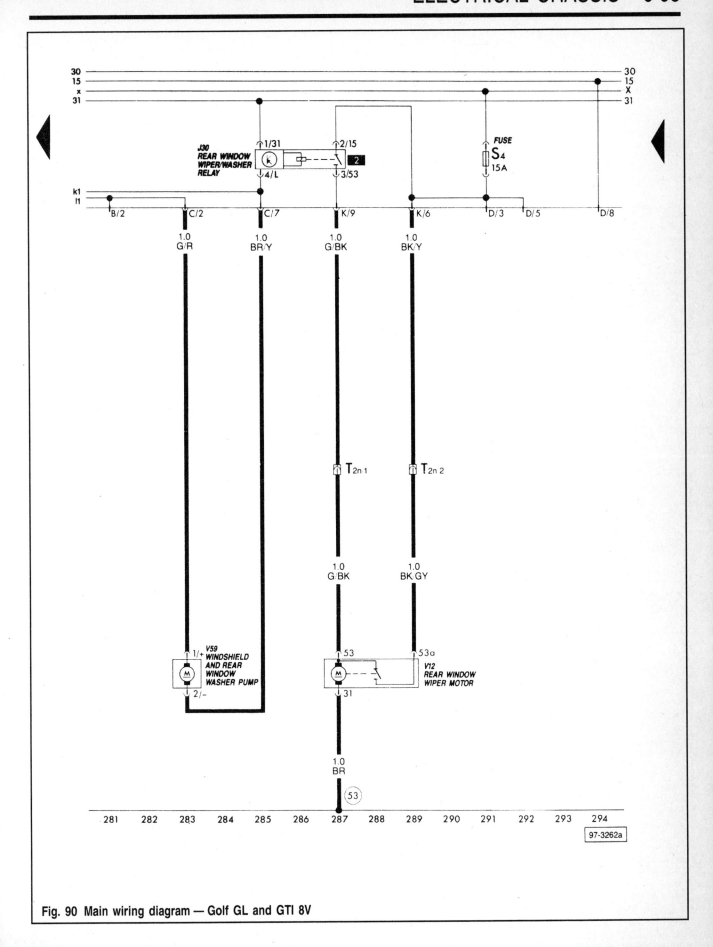

Fig. 90 Main wiring diagram — Golf GL and GTI 8V

Description	Current track
Air flow sensor potentiometer, G19	40
Alternator, C	1-2
Battery, A	9
Brake and parking brake indicator light, K7	47
Coolant temperature sensor, G62	36
Diagnostic connectors	53-56
Digifant control unit, J169	33-54
Digifant control unit relay, J176	38-39
Fuel gauge sending unit, G	17
Fuel pump, G6	24
Fuel pump relay, J17	20-21
Fuse, S18	25
Fuse, S16	48
Hall generator, G40	33-35
Idle stabilizer valve, N71	49-50
Ignition coil, N152	29
Ignition coil power stage, N157	31-32
Ignition distributor, O	29-31
Ignition, cyl. 1, N30	54
Injector, cyl. 2, N31	53
Injector, cyl. 3, N32	52
Injector, cyl. 4, N33	51
Intake air temperature sensor, G42	39
Knock sensor, G61	39-41
OBD fault warning light, K83	49
Oxygen sensor, G39	47-48
Seat belt warning light, K19	48
Spark plug connectors, P	29-31
Spark plugs, Q	29-31
Starter, B	13-14
Throttle valve potentiometer, G69	43-44
Transfer fuel pump, G23	19
Voltage regulator, C1	1-2

Wire connectors

T1f — single, near battery
T1x — single, behind fuse/relay panel
T2p — double, in luggage compartment, right
T2m— double, on firewall, right
T2x — double, black, diagnostic connector, under shift lever boot
T2z — double, white, diagnostic connector, under shift lever boot
T3 — three-point, on ignition coil power stage
T3b — three-point, in engine compartment, rear
T3g — three-point, near starter
T4 — four-point, on firewall, left
T5a — five-point, on firewall, left
T5c — five-point, on firewall, left

Ground connections

(1) — battery to body
(2) — transmission to body
(18) — on engine block
(30) — near fuse/relay panel
(94) — in Digifant wiring harness
(119) — in headlight wiring harness

Welded wiring harness points

(G1) — plus connection, in Digifant wiring harness
(G3) — plus connection, in injector valve wiring harness

Fig. 91 Digifant I engine management system — California Golf and GTI 8V

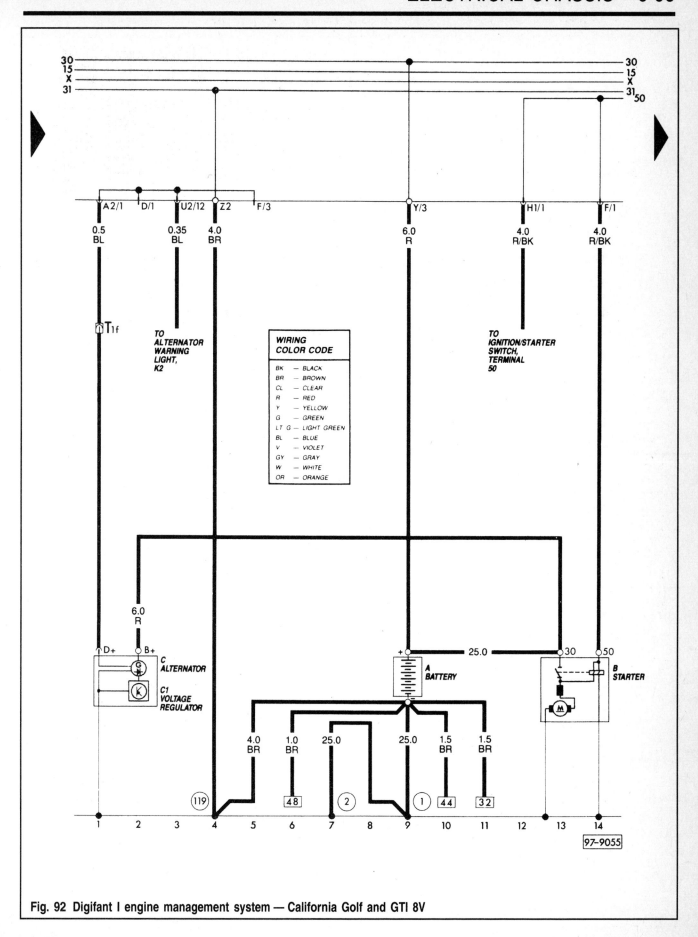

Fig. 92 Digifant I engine management system — California Golf and GTI 8V

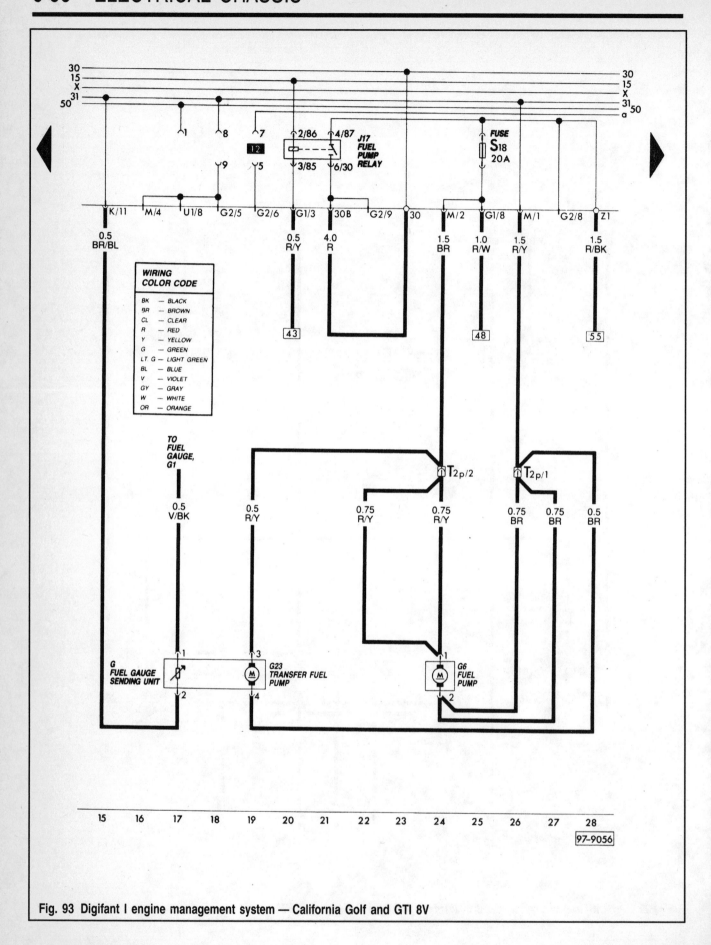

Fig. 93 Digifant I engine management system — California Golf and GTI 8V

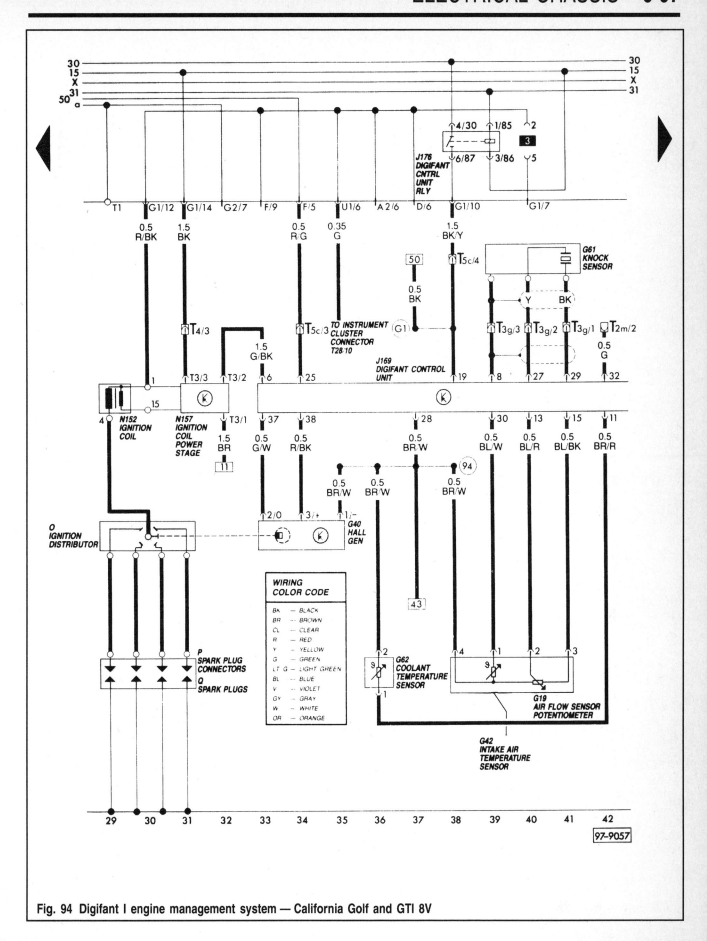

Fig. 94 Digifant I engine management system — California Golf and GTI 8V

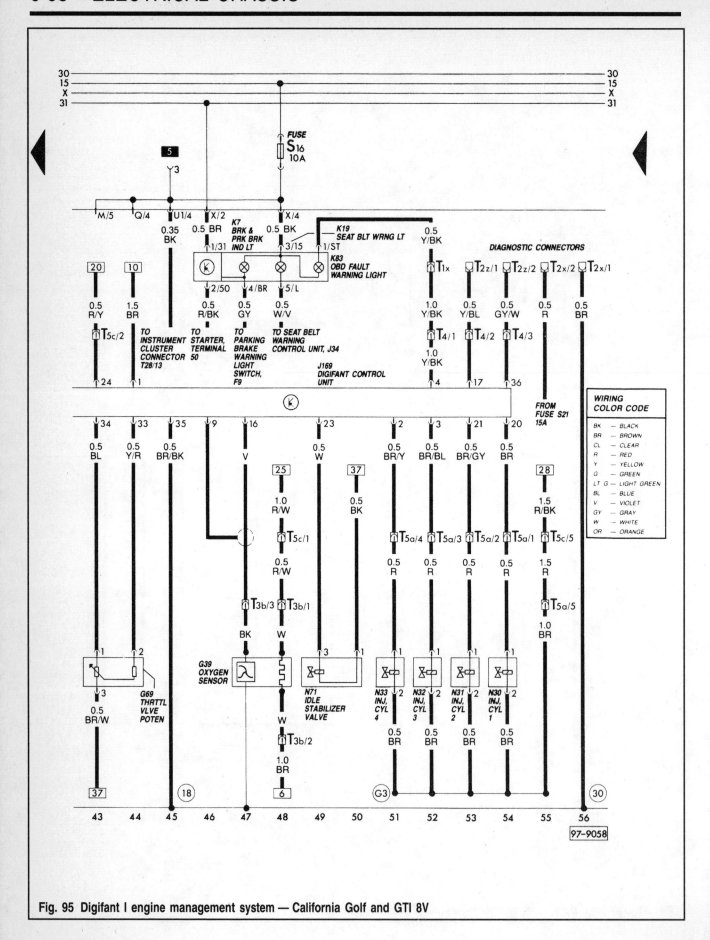

Fig. 95 Digifant I engine management system — California Golf and GTI 8V

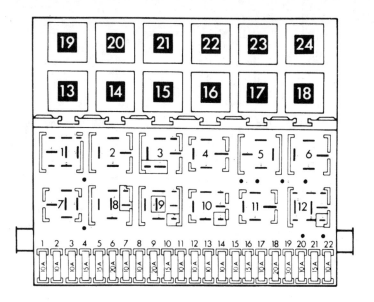

97-3000

Fuse arrangement

according to the numbers on fuse panel from left to right:

		Amp.
1	Headlight, low beam, left	10
2	Headlight, low beam, right	10
3	Instrument panel lights, license plate lights	10
4	Glove compartment light, rear window wiper	15
5	Windshield wiper/washer	15
6	Fresh air blower, A/C	20
7	Tail lights, side marker lights, right	10
8	Tail lights, side marker lights, left	10
9	Rear window defogger	20
10	Fog lights	15
11	Headlight, high beam, left, high beam indicator light	10
12	Headlight, high beam, right	10
13	Horn, radiator cooling fan	10
14	Back-up lights, washer nozzle heaters . .	10
15	Engine electronics, idle stabilizer valve, cold start valve	10
16	Dash warning lights, multi-function indicator	10
17	Emergency flashers, turn signals	10
18	Fuel pump, oxygen sensor	20
19	Radiator cooling fan, A/C	30
20	Brake lights, cruise control	10
21	Interior lights, luggage compartment lights, multi-function indicator	15
22	Radio, cigarette lighter	10

*Numbers in parentheses indicate production control number stamped on relay housing.

Relay location on fuse/relay panel

1 — A/C relay, J32 (13)*
2 — Rear window wiper/washer relay
3 — Open
4 — Load reduction relay, J59 (18)*
5 — Intermittent wiper relay, J31 (19)*
6 — Emergency flasher relay, J2 (21)*
7 — Fog light relay, J5
8 — Open
9 — Seat belt warning system control unit, J34 (4, 29)*
10 — Open
11 — Horn relay, J4 (53)*
12 — Fuel pump relay, J17 (80)*

Separate relays above fuse/relay panel

13 — Radiator cooling fan after run control unit, J138 (31)*
14 — Starter interlock relay, J207
15 — Open
16 — Open
17 — Power window relay (24)*
18 — Daytime running light relay (Canada)
19 — Open
20 — Open
21 — Open
22 — Open
23 — Fuse for A/C, heater
24 — Power window circuit breaker

Fig. 96 Main fuse and relay panel — GTI 16V

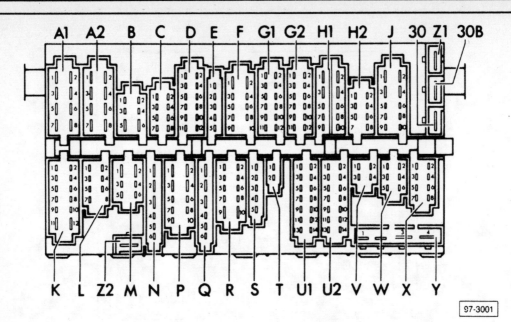

97-3001

Connections and plugs on fuse/relay panel

A1 — Headlight wiring harness (yellow), eight-point
A2 — Headlight wiring harness (yellow), eight-point
B — Open
C — Headlight wiring harness (yellow), eight-point
D — Optional equipment wiring harness (green), twelve-point
E — Instrument wiring harness (green), five-point
F — Engine compartment wiring harness, right (white), nine-point
G1 — Engine compartment wiring harness, right (white), twelve-point
G2 — Engine compartment wiring harness, right (white), twelve-point
H1 — Steering column switch wiring harness (red), ten-point
H2 — Steering column switch wiring harness (red), eight-point
J — Steering column switch wiring harness (red), ten-point
K — Rear wiring harness (black), twelve-point
L — Rear wiring harness (black), seven-point
M — Rear wiring harness (black), six-point
N — A/C wiring harness (green), six-point
P — Rear window defroster wiring harness (blue), nine-point
Q — Instrument wiring harness (blue), six-point
R — Light switch wiring harness (blue), ten-point
S — Engine compartment wiring harness, right (white), five-point

T — Two-point connector (green)
U1 — Instrument cluster wiring harness (blue), fourteen-point
U2 — Instrument cluster wiring harness (blue), fourteen point
V — Multi-function indicator wiring harness (green), four-point
W — Anti-lock brake system (ABS) wiring harness (green), six-point
X — Warning lamp wiring harness, ABS (green), eight-point
Y — Single connector, terminal 30
Z1 — Single connector
Z2 — Single connector, terminal 31
30 — Single connector, terminal 30
30B — Single connector

Wire Size

Wiring Diagrams identify wires by the metric wire size. Metric wires sizes indicate cross-sectional area in square millimeters (mm^2). The chart below lists metric wire sizes and their approximate equivalents in American Wire Gauge (AWG) sizes.

Metric size — cross section (mm^2)	American Wire Gauge Size (AWG)
0.35	22
0.5	20
0.75	18
1.0	16
1.5	14
2.5	12
4.0	10
6.0	8
16.0	4
25.0	2
35.0	2

Fig. 97 Fuse panel connectors — GTI 16V

Description	Current track	Description	Current track	Description	Current track
Air flow sensor potentiometer, G19	40-41	Full throttle switch, F81	27	Multi-function indicator vacuum sensor, G55	87-89
Alternator, C	1-2	Fuse, S18	19	Multifunction indicator (MFI), J119	74-92
Alternator warning light, K2	70	Fuse, S16	63		
Back-up light switch, F4	164	Fuse, S11	130	OBD fault warning light, K72	108
Back-up light, left, M16	159	Fuse, S1	131	Outside air temperature sensor, G17	102
Back-up light, right, M17	160	Fuse, S12	133	Overheat fuse, S24	208
Battery, A	5	Fuse, S2	134	Oxygen sensor, G39	24-25
Brake and parking brake indicator light, K7	109-111	Fuse, S8	157		
Brake fluid level warning contact, F34	106	Fuse, S20	161	Parking brake warning light switch, F9	104
Brake light switch, F	161	Fuse, S14	164	Parking light, left, M1	188
Brake light, left, M9	158	Fuse, S7	166	Parking light, right, M3	184
Brake light, right, M10	161	Fuse, S3	177	Radiator cooling fan, V7	197-198
Carbon canister on/off valve, N115	45	Fuse, S10	196	Radiator cooling fan after run control unit, J138	200-203
Carbon canister frequency valve, N80	46	Fuse, S9	214	Radiator cooling fan thermoswitch, F18	197-199
CIS-E Motronic Control Unit, J204	25-53	Fuse, S4	219	Radiator cooling fan thermoswitch, F87	202
Cigarette lighter, U1	242	Fuse, S13	221	Rear window defogger indicator light, K10	213
Cigarette lighter light, L28	241	Fuse, S5	228	Rear window defogger switch, E15	214
Clock light, L8	74	Fuse, S21	113	Rear window defogger switch light, L39	212
Cold start valve, N17	47	Fuse, S15	37	Rear window heater element, Z1	216
Coolant low level sensor, G32	58	Fuse, S17	141	Rear window wiper motor, V12	218-220
Coolant overheat warning light, K28	81	Fuse, S19	197	Rear window wiper washer relay, J30	222-223
Coolant temperature gauge, G3	71	Fuse, S6	208		
Coolant temperature sending unit, G2	59	Fuse, S22	242	Seat belt switch, left, E24	123
Coolant temperature sensor, G62	43	Glove compartment light, W6	204	Seat belt warning control unit, J34	114-118
Diagnostic connectors	29-34	Hall generator, G40	52-53	Seat belt warning light, K19	108-111
Differential pressure regulator, N73	39	Headlight dimmer flasher switch, E4	137-140	Side marker lights, front, M11	183
Digital clock, Y2	75-76	Headlight high beam indicator light, K1	65	Side marker lights, front, M11	187
Door contact switch, left front, F2	114-115	Headlight switch light, L9	170	Spark plug connectors, P	54-56
Door contact switch, right front, F3	117	Headlight, left, L1	131	Spark plugs, Q	54-56
		Headlight, right, L2	134	Speed sensor, G54	72
EGR temperature sensor, G98	42	High-beam headlight, left, L13	130	Starter, B	8-10
Emergency flasher relay, J2	143-145	High-beam headlight, right, L14	133	Starting interlock relay, J207	124-126
Emergency flasher switch, E3	141-148	High-mount brake light, M25	163-165		
Emergency flasher warning light, K6	146	Horn button, H	233	Tachometer, G5	83
Engine oil pressure switch (0.3 bar), F22	60	Horn relay, J4	217-218	Taillight, left, M4	157
Engine oil pressure switch (1.8 bar), F1	61	Horns, H1	219, 221	Taillight, right, M2	166
Engine oil pressure warning light, K3	80	Idle stabilizer valve, N71	48	Transfer fuel pump, G23	17
Engine oil temperature sensor, G8	100	Idle switch, F60	28	Turn signal indicator light, K5	66
Fresh air control lever light, L16	210	Ignition coil power stage, N70	54-56	Turn signal light, left front, M5	189
Fresh air blower, V2	205	Ignition distributor, O	54-56	Turn signal light, left rear, M6	156
Fresh air blower series resistance, N23	209	Ignition timing (reference) sensor, G4	50-51	Turn signal light, right front, M7	185
Fresh air blower switch, E9	207-209	Ignition starter switch, D	10-13	Turn signal light, right rear, M8	167
Fuel gauge, G1	72	Instrument panel light, L10	73-75	Turn signal switch, E2	148
Fuel gauge sending unit, G	16	Instrument panel light dimmer switch, E20	177	Voltage regulator, C1	1-2
Fuel pump, G6	19	Interior light with delay switch, W15	117-119	Voltage stabilizer, J6	71
Fuel pump relay, J17	26-27	Knock sensor, G61	30-32	Windshield and rear window washer pump, V59	224
		Knock sensor II, G66	34-36	Windshield wiper motor, V	226-229
		License plate light, X	177, 179	Windshield-wiper intermittent switch, E22	233-238
		Light switch, E1	170-177	Washer wiper intermittent relay, J31	234-238
		Load reduction relay, J59	11-12		
		Luggage compartment light, W3	113		
		Luggage compartment light switch, F5	181		
		Memory switch (multi-function ind.), E109	93-97		
		Multi-function indicator recall button, E86	93-97		

Fig. 98 Current track index — GTI 16V

Wire connectors

T1 — single, behind fuse/relay panel
T1a — single, above fuse/relay panel
T1b — single, above fuse/relay panel
T1c — single, in luggage compartment, left rear
T1d — single, behind fuse/relay panel
T1e — single, behind fuse/relay panel
T1f — single, near battery
T1g — single, in engine compartment, rear
T1h — single, behind instrument panel, right
T1i — single, behind fuse/relay panel
T1k — single, near left headlight
T1l — single, in luggage compartment
T1m— single, behind fuse/relay panel
T1o — single, near right headlight
T1p — single, near left headlight
T1r — single, in luggage compartment, left rear
T1s — single, behind fuse/relay panel
T2a — double, behind fuse/relay panel
T2b — double, behind fuse/relay panel
T2e — double, behind instrument panel, right
T2f — double, near left front suspension strut
T2g — double, behind fuse/relay panel
T2h — double, near left headlight
T2i — double, near left headlight
T2k — double, under driver's seat
T2l — double, in engine compartment, rear
T2n — double, in luggage compartment, left
T2p — double, in luggage compartment, right
T2v — double, on fresh air blower series resistance
T2x — double, black, diagnostic connector, under shift lever boot
T2y — double, white, diagnostic connector, under shift lever boot
T2z — double, blue, diagnostic connector, under shift lever boot
T3a — three-point, near starter
T3b — three-point, near starter
T3d — three-point, near right headlight
T3e — three-point, near left headlight
T3f — three-point, behind center console
T3g — three-point, behind instrument panel, center
T4c — four-point, behind steering column switch cover
T4d — four-point, behind steering column switch cover
T5b — five-point, behind steering column switch cover
T5c — five-point, behind steering column switch cover
T5e — five-point, on fresh air blower series resistance

Ground connections

T6a — six-point, behind fuse/relay panel
T6b — six-point, behind fuse/relay panel
T6c — six-point, on left taillight housing
T6d — six-point, on right taillight housing
T7a — seven-point, behind steering column switch cover
T9 — nine-point, on starter interlock relay
T28 — twenty eight-point, on instrument cluster

(1) — battery to body
(2) — transmission to body
(10) — on firewall, left
(15) — on cylinder head
(16) — on valve cover, right side
(18) — on engine block
(27) — on valve cover, right side
(29) — near cylinder head
(30) — beside fuse/relay panel
(38) — beside starter lock switch
(44) — on lower left A-pillar
(50) — in luggage compartment, left
(51) — in luggage compartment, right
(53) — in rear deck lid, right
(54) — on rear apron
(80) — in instrument panel wiring harness
(82) — in left front wiring harness
(84) — engine block, in right front wiring harness
(119) — in headlight wiring harness
(120) — in headlight wiring harness
(129) — in horn wiring harness
(138) — in CIS-E Motronic wiring harness
(139) — in CIS-E Motronic wiring harness

Welded wiring harness points

(C1) — plus connection (58l), in left front wiring harness
(C2) — plus connection (58r), in left front wiring harness
(C10) — plus connection (30), in headlight wiring harness
(C13) — plus connection, in horn wiring harness
(E6) — plus connection (15), in CIS-E Motronic wiring harness

Fig. 99 Connector locations — GTI 16V

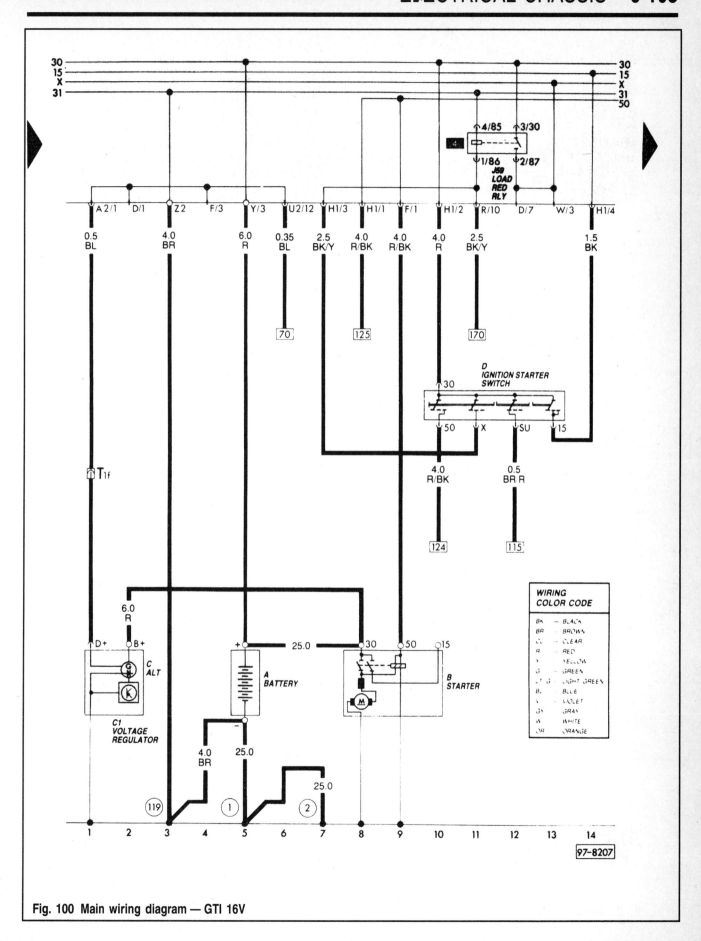

Fig. 100 Main wiring diagram — GTI 16V

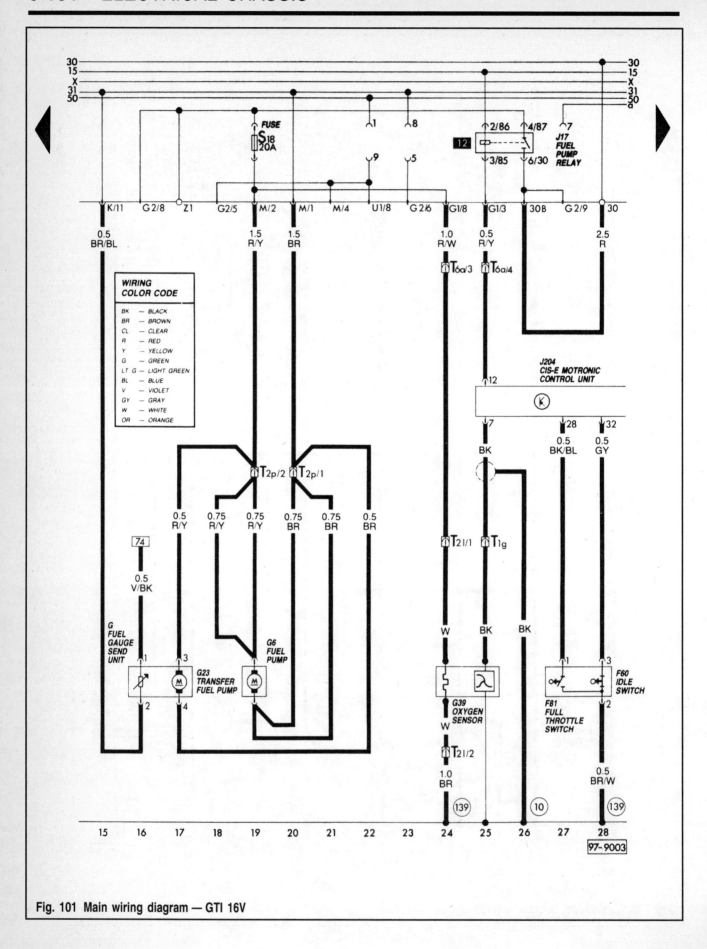

Fig. 101 Main wiring diagram — GTI 16V

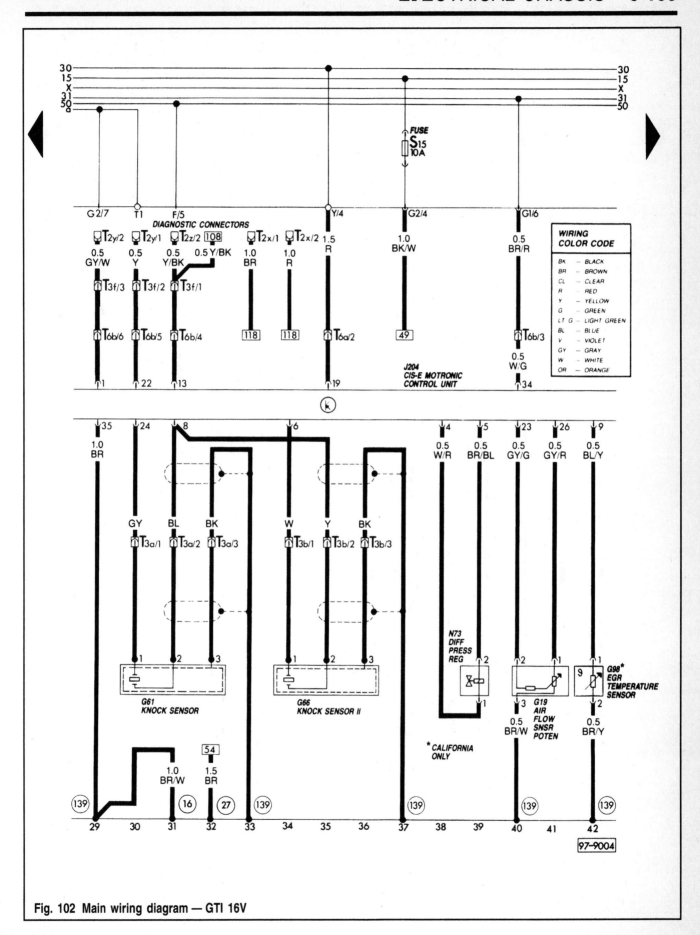

Fig. 102 Main wiring diagram — GTI 16V

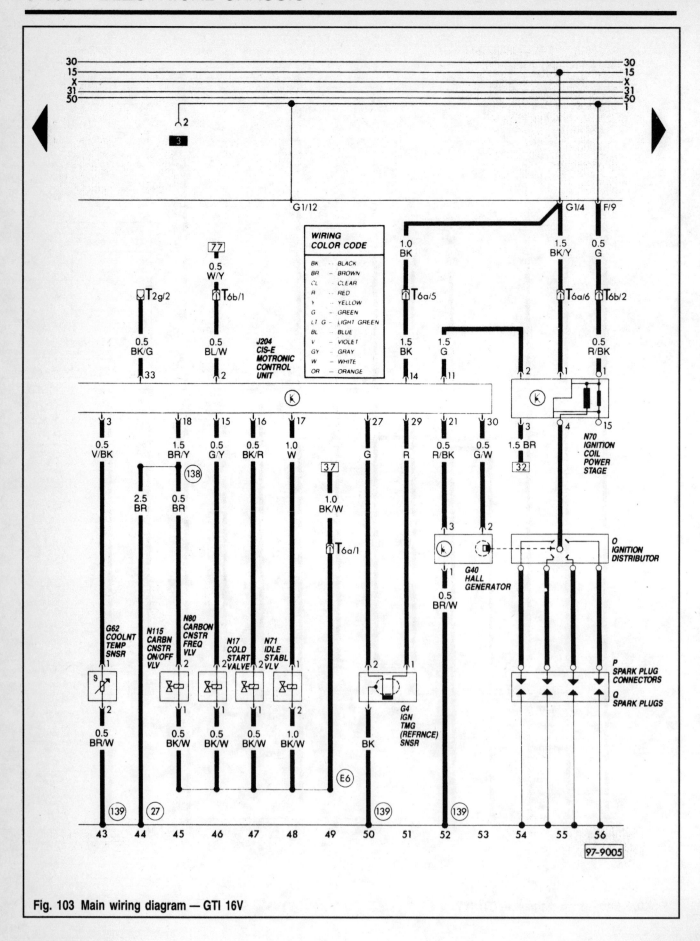

Fig. 103 Main wiring diagram — GTI 16V

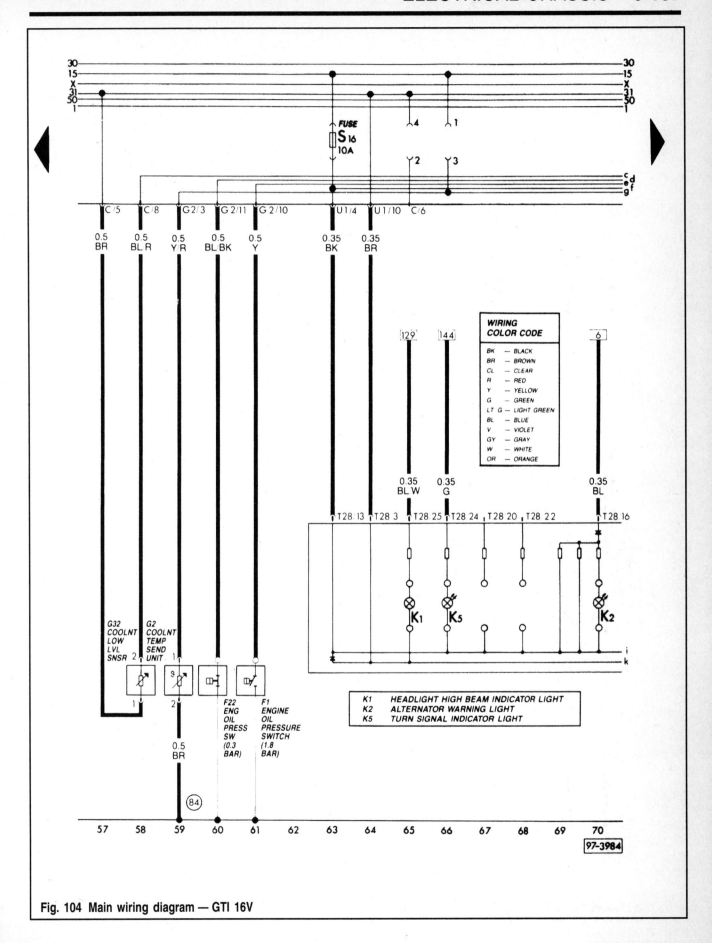

Fig. 104 Main wiring diagram — GTI 16V

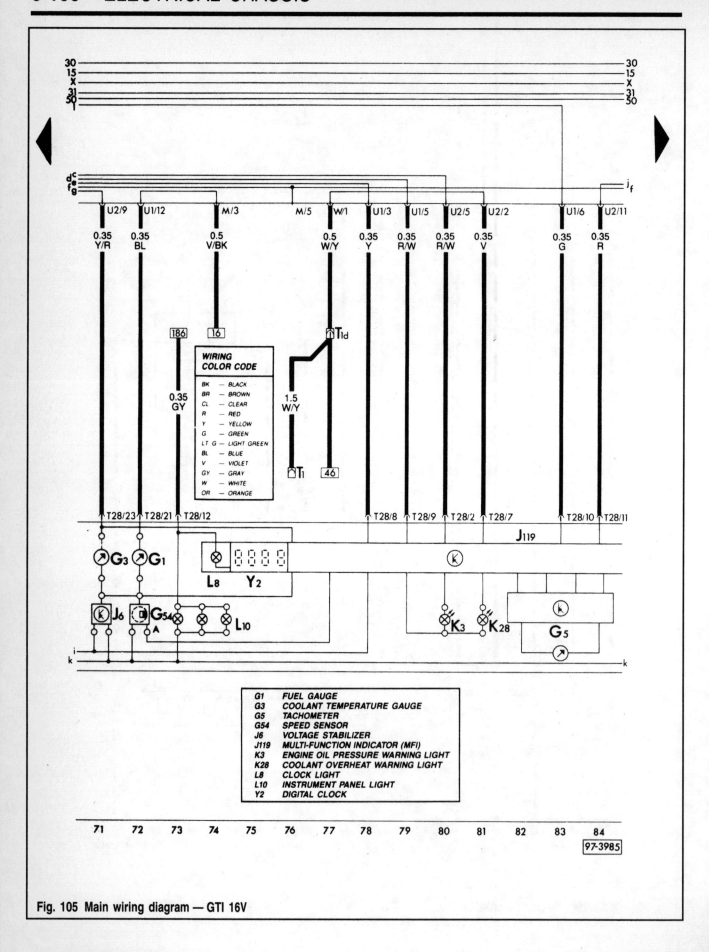

Fig. 105 Main wiring diagram — GTI 16V

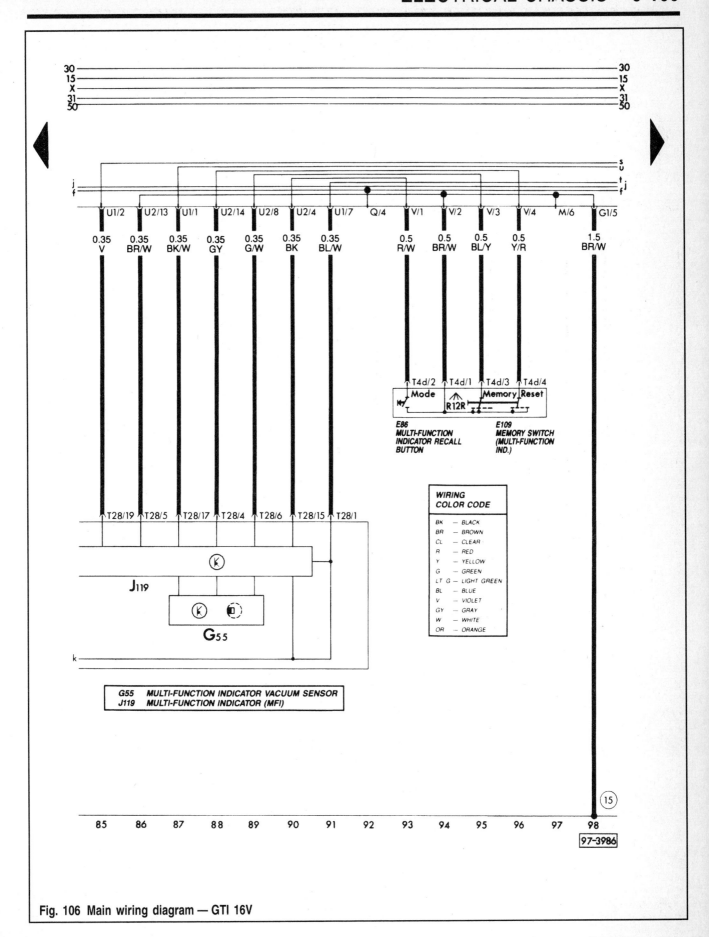

Fig. 106 Main wiring diagram — GTI 16V

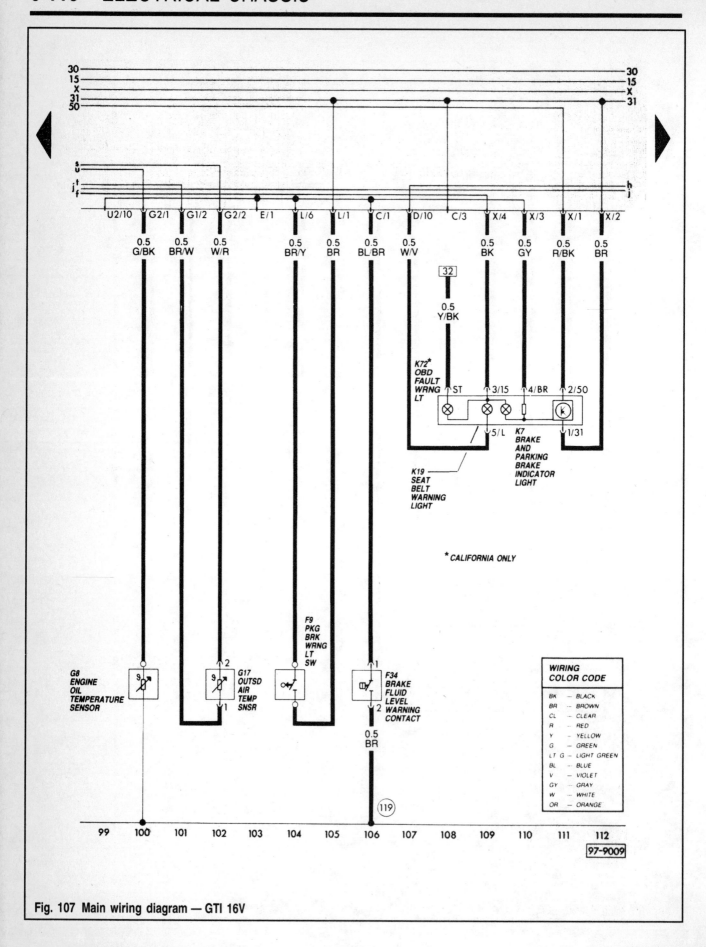

Fig. 107 Main wiring diagram — GTI 16V

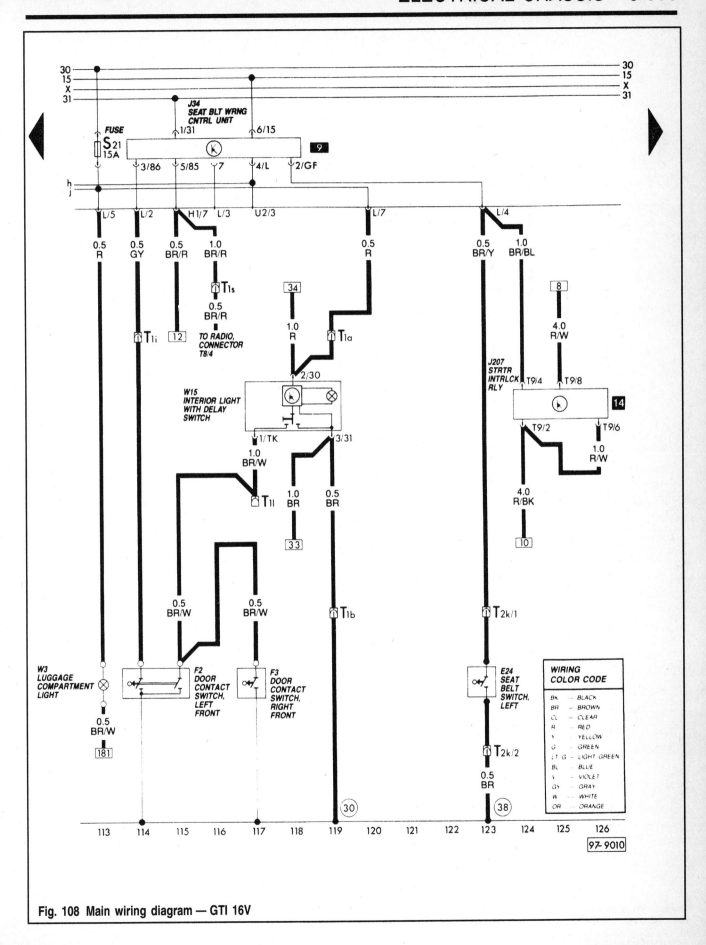

Fig. 108 Main wiring diagram — GTI 16V

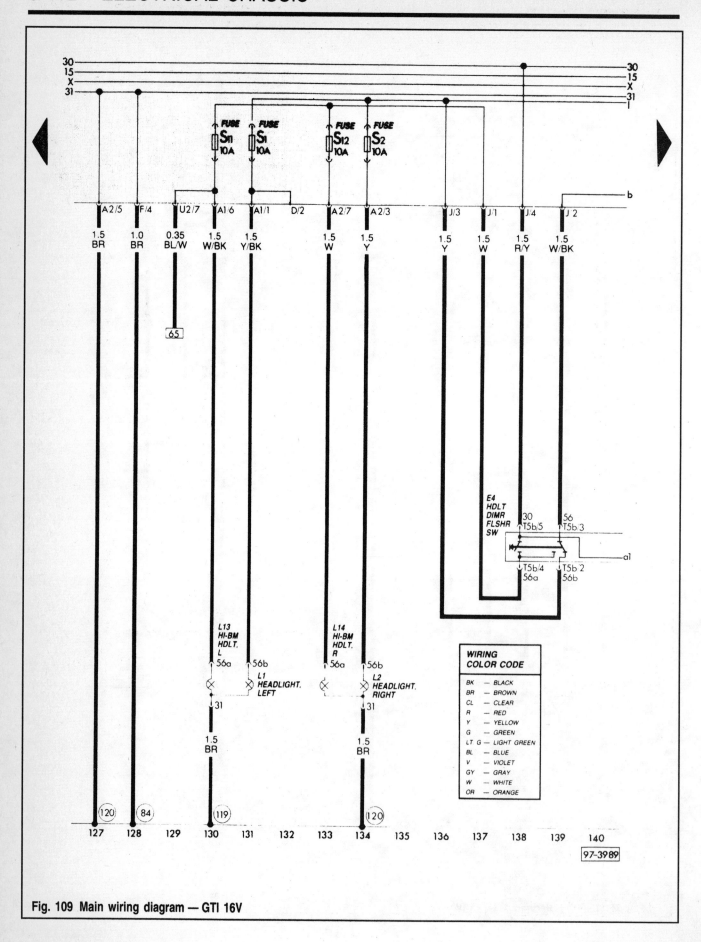

Fig. 109 Main wiring diagram — GTI 16V

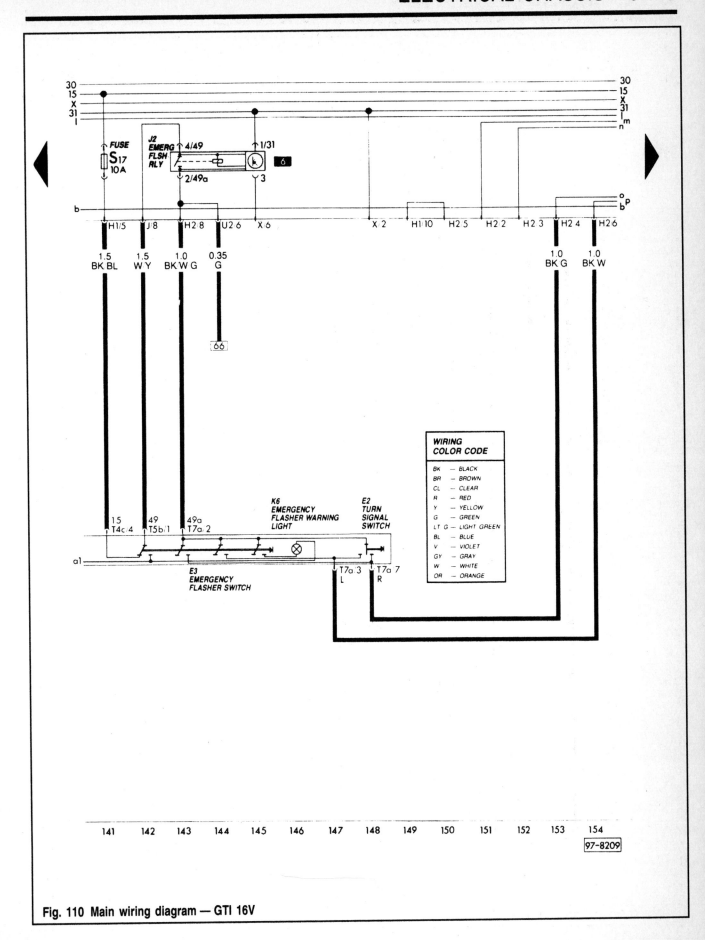

Fig. 110 Main wiring diagram — GTI 16V

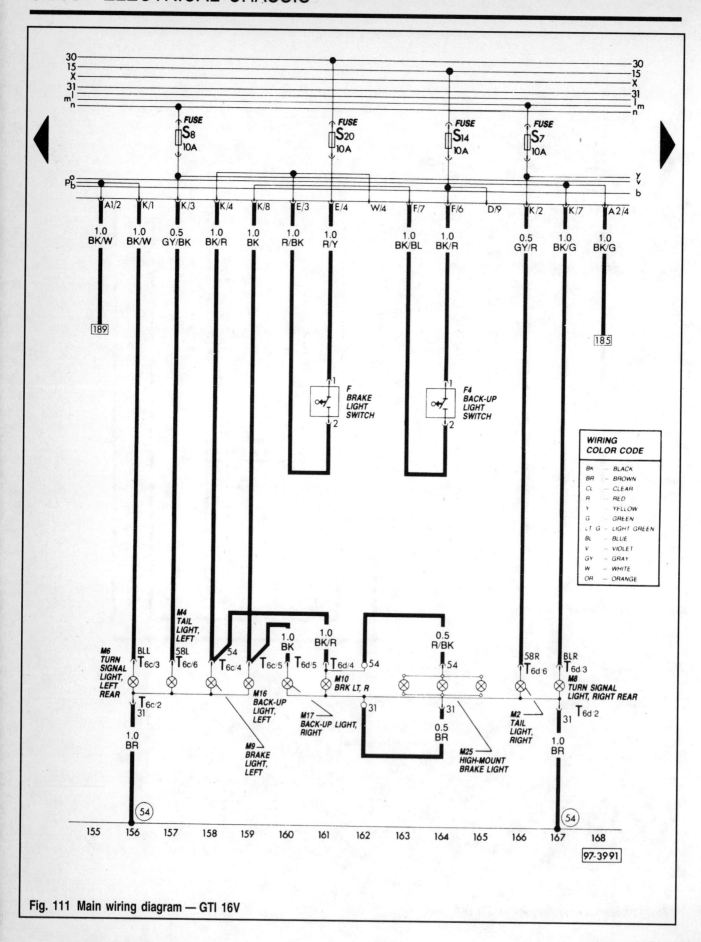

Fig. 111 Main wiring diagram — GTI 16V

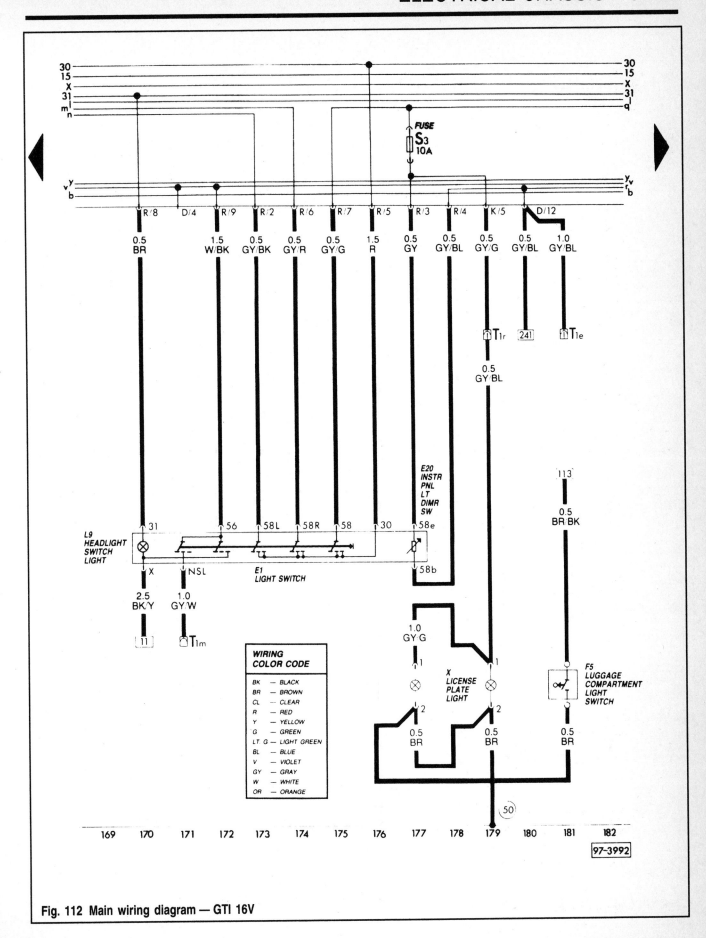

Fig. 112 Main wiring diagram — GTI 16V

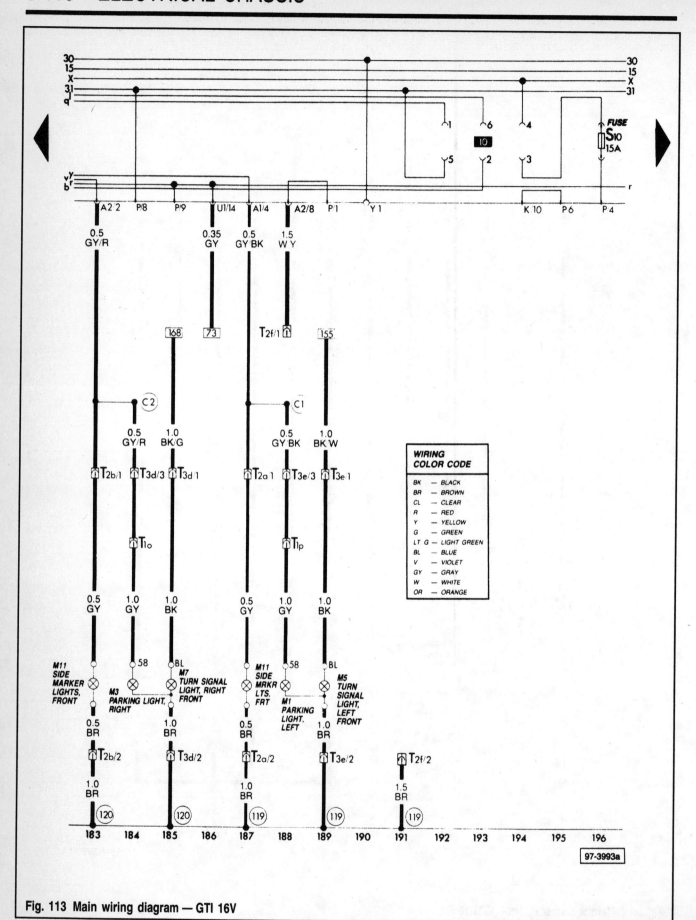

Fig. 113 Main wiring diagram — GTI 16V

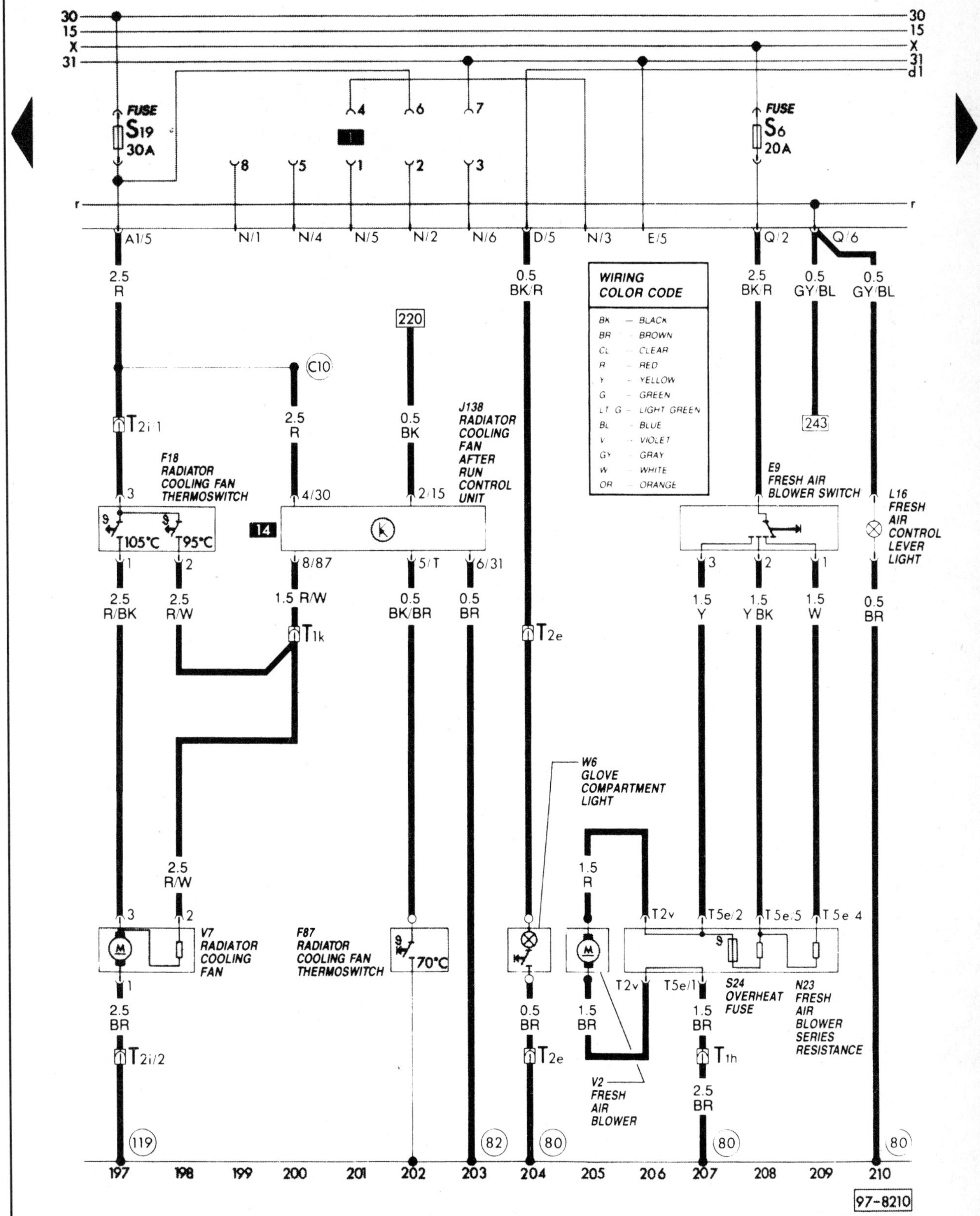

Fig. 114 Main wiring diagram — GTI 16V

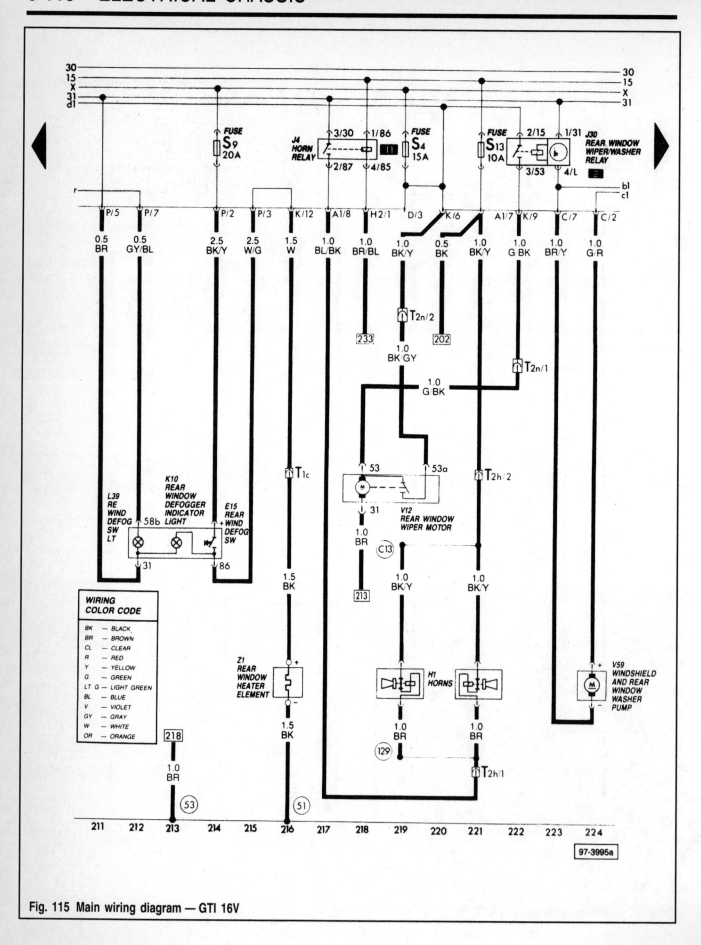

Fig. 115 Main wiring diagram — GTI 16V

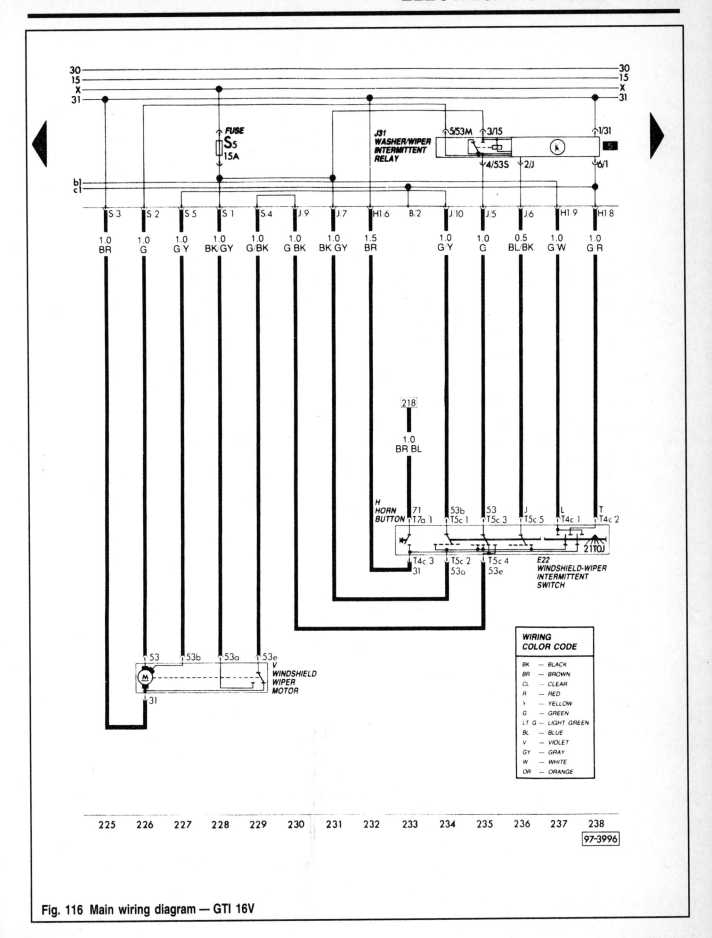

Fig. 116 Main wiring diagram — GTI 16V

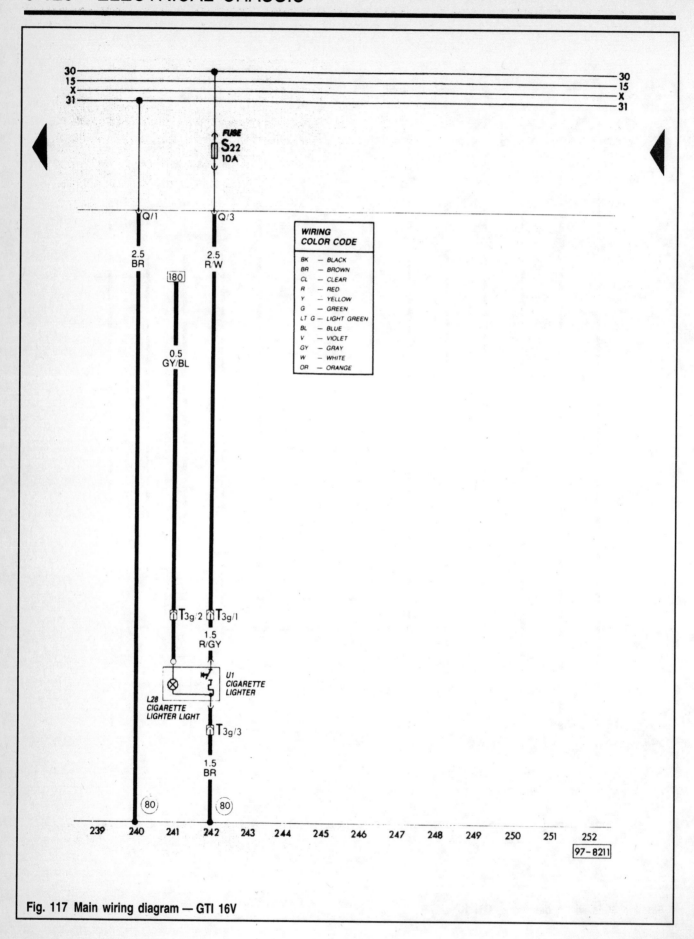

WIRING
COLOR CODE

BK	—	BLACK
BR	—	BROWN
CL	—	CLEAR
R	—	RED
Y	—	YELLOW
G	—	GREEN
LT G	—	LIGHT GREEN
BL	—	BLUE
V	—	VIOLET
GY	—	GRAY
W	—	WHITE
OR	—	ORANGE

Fig. 117 Main wiring diagram — GTI 16V

Description	Current track
Power window fuse	2
Power window relay	1-2
Power window switch light	4, 8, 12, 16, 21, 22, 27
Window lockout switch	13
Window motor, left front door	9
Window motor, left rear door	23
Window motor, right front door	5
Window motor, right rear door	18
Window switch, LR (in console)	23-27
Window switch, LR (in LR door)	22-25
Window switch, left front	8-11
Window switch, RR (in console)	16-20
Window switch, RR (in RR door)	18-21
Window switch, right front	4-7

Wire connectors

T2 — double, in passenger's door
T2c — double, in driver's door
T2d — double, in right rear door
T2e — double, in left rear door
T3 — three-point, on lower left B-pillar
T3a — three-point, on lower right B-pillar

Ground connections

(107) — in outside mirror wiring harness

Welded wiring harness points

(Q1) — plus connection (30), in power window wiring harness

(Q9) — in power window wiring harness

Fig. 118 Power windows — GTI 16V

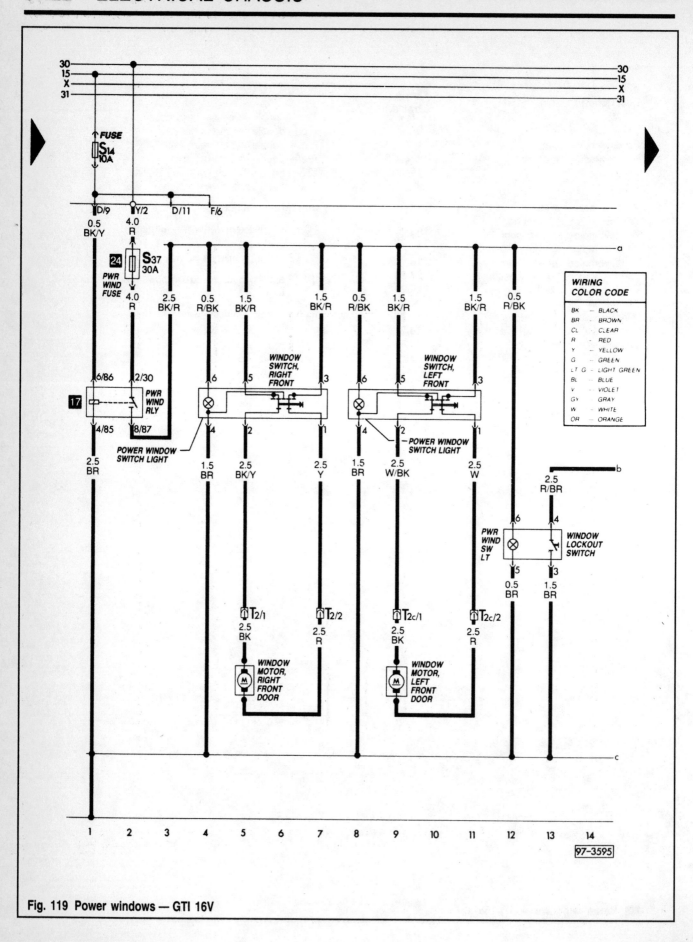

Fig. 119 Power windows—GTI 16V

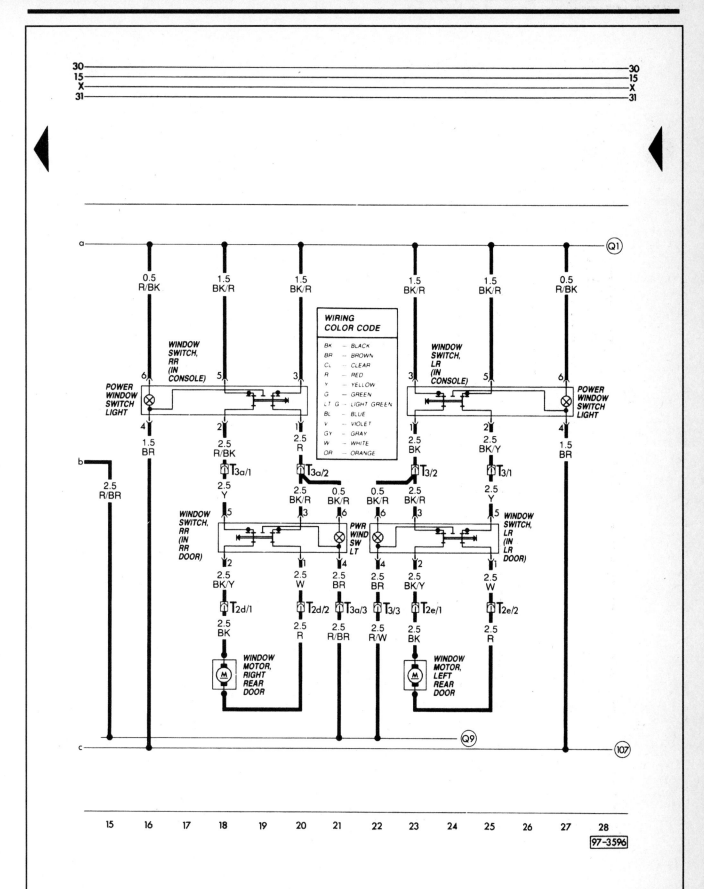

Fig. 120 Power windows — GTI 16V

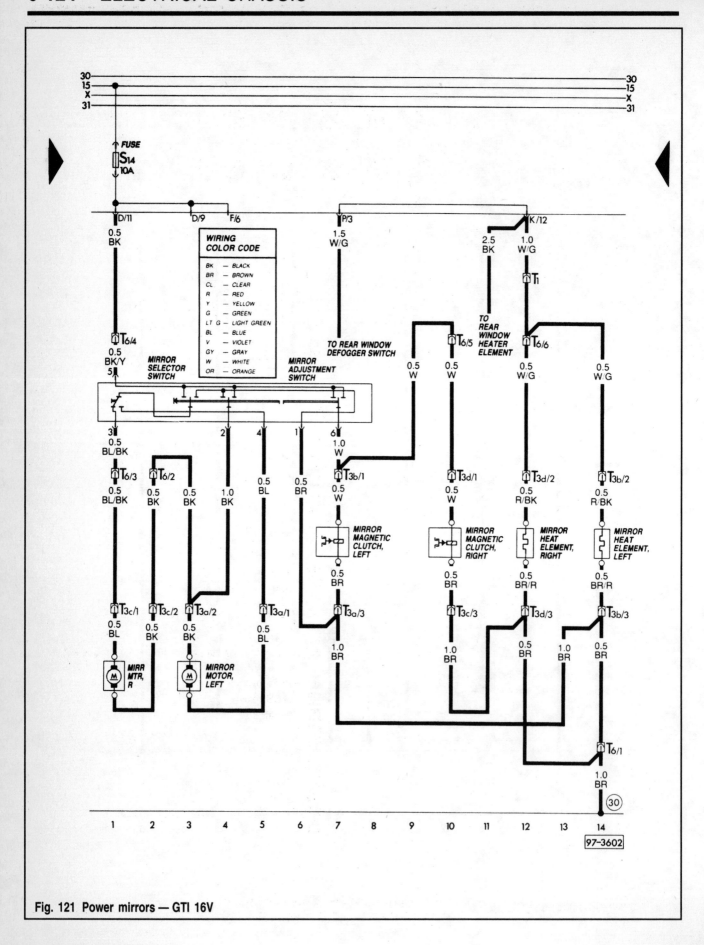

Fig. 121 Power mirrors — GTI 16V

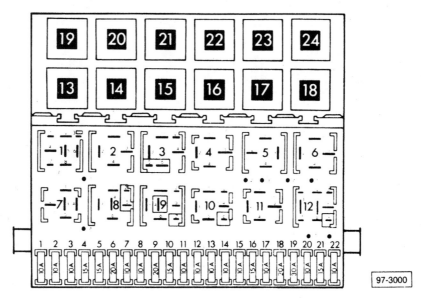

Fuse arrangement

according to the numbers on fuse panel from left to right:

		Amp.
1	Headlight, low beam, left	10
2	Headlight, low beam, right	10
3	Instrument panel lights, license plate lights	10
4	Glove box light	15
5	Wiper/washer	15
6	Fresh air fan	20
7	Tail lights, side marker light, right	10
8	Tail lights, side marker light, left	10
9	Rear window defogger	20
10	Open	
11	Headlight, high beam, left	10
12	Headlight, high beam, right	10
13	Horn	10
14	Back-up lights, washer nozzle heaters	10
15	Open	
16	Dash warning lights	15
17	Emergency flasher switch	10
18	Fuel pump, OXS heater	20
19	Radiator cooling fan, A/C	30
20	Brake lights	10
21	Interior lights, digital clock	15
22	Radio, cigarette lighter	10

*Numbers in parentheses indicate production control number stamped on relay housing.

Relay location on fuse/relay panel

- **1** — A/C relay
- **2** — Open
- **3** — Digifant control unit
- **4** — Load reduction relay
- **5** — Low coolant level control unit
- **6** — Emergency flasher relay
- **7** — Open
- **8** — Intermittent wiper relay
- **9** — Seat belt warning system relay
- **10** — Open
- **11** — Horn relay
- **12** — Fuel pump relay

Separate relays above fuse/relay panel

- **13** — Radiator cooling fan after run control unit
- **14** — Automatic transmission relay (53)* or Coolant temperature indicator relay (44)*
- **15** — ABS hydraulic pump relay
- **16** — ABS relay
- **17** — Heated seat control unit, driver
- **18** — Heated seat control unit, passenger
- **19** — Automatic transmission relay
- **20** — Open
- **21** — Power window relay
- **22** — ABS valves fuse
- **23** — Fuse for A/C, power seats
- **24** — Open

Fig. 122 Main fuse and relay panel — Jetta with Digifant II engine management system

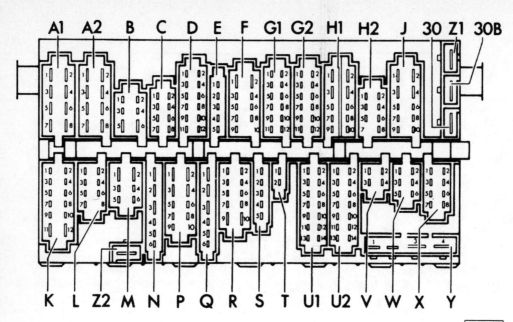

Connections and plugs on fuse/relay panel

A1 — Headlight wiring harness (yellow)
A2 — Headlight wiring harness (yellow)
B — Open
C — Headlight wiring harness (yellow)
D — Optional equipment wiring harness (green)
E — Instrument wiring harness (green)
F — Engine compartment wiring harness, right (white)
G1 — Engine compartment wiring harness, right (white)
G2 — Engine compartment wiring harness, right (white)
H1 — Steering column switch wiring harness (red)
H2 — Steering column switch wiring harness (red)
J — Steering column switch wiring harness (red)
K — Rear wiring harness (black)
L — Rear wiring harness (black)
M — Rear wiring harness (black)
N — A/C wiring harness (green)
P — Rear window defroster wiring harness (blue)
Q — Instrument wiring harness (blue)
R — Light switch wiring harness (blue)
S — Engine compartment wiring harness, right (white)

T — Two-point connector (green)
U1 — Instrument cluster wiring harness (blue)
U2 — Instrument cluster wiring harness (blue)
V — Multi-function indicator wiring harness (green)
W — Six-point connector (green)
X — Warning lamp wiring harness (green)
Y — Single connector, terminal 30
Z1 — Single connector
Z2 — Single connector, terminal 31
30 — Single connector, terminal 30
30B — Single connector
31 — Single connector, terminal 31

Fig. 123 Fuse panel connectors — Jetta with Digifant II

Description	Current track		Description	Current track		Description	Current track
Air flow sensor potentiometer	69		Headlight dimmer/flasher switch	181,182		Rear window defogger switch light	255
Air inlet temperature sender	68					Rear window heater element	260
Alternator	1,2		Headlight high beam warning light	103			
Alternator warning light	97		Headlight switch light	211		Seat belt switch, left	151
			Headlight, left	173		Seat belt warning light	144
Back-up light switch	232		Headlight, right	175		Seat belt warning relay	147-151
Back-up light, left	202		Hi-mounted brake light	205-207		Side marker lights, left	169
Back-up light, right	204		High-beam headlight, left	172		Side marker lights, right	178
Battery	9		High-beam headlight, right	174		Spark plug connectors	59-61
Brake and parking brake indicator light	144-146		Horn button	275		Spark plugs	59-61
			Horn relay	262-264		Speed sensor (for MFI and cruise control)	105
Brake fluid level warning contact	140		Horns	263,265		Starter	12-14
Brake light switch	207		Idle speed stabilizer valve	78,79			
Brake light, left	200		Idle switch	65		Tachometer	99
Brake light, right	208		Ignition coil	58-60		Tail light, left	199
			Ignition control unit	59-62		Tail light, right	209
Cigarette lighter	165		Ignition distributor	59-61		Transfer fuel pump	39
Cigarette lighter light	164		Ignition/starter switch	23-26		Turn signal indicator light	102
Clock light	113		Injector, cyl. 1	84		Turn signal light, left front	170
Coolant low level control unit	86,87		Injector, cyl. 2	83		Turn signal light, left rear	198
Coolant low level sender	86		Injector, cyl. 3	82		Turn signal light, right front	177
Coolant overheat warning light	107		Injector, cyl. 4	81		Turn signal light, right rear	210
Coolant temperature gauge	105		Instrument panel light	109-111		Turn signal switch	190-192
Coolant temperature sender	66		Instrument panel light dimmer switch	218			
Coolant temperature sending unit	87		Interior light with delay switch	159,160		Voltage regulator	1,2
						Voltage stabilizer	104
DIGIFANT control unit	62-80		Knock sensor	67-69			
DIGIFANT control unit relay	79,80					Washer nozzle heater, left	234
Digital clock	114,115		License plate light	220, 223		Washer nozzle heater, right	236
Door contact switch, left front	156,157		Light switch	211-218		Washer/wiper intermittent relay	276-280
Door contact switch, left rear	160		Load reduction relay	18,19		Windshield washer pump	287
Door contact switch, right front	159		Luggage compartment light	168		Windshield wiper motor	268-271
Door contact switch, right rear	161		Luggage compartment light switch	224		Windshield-wiper intermittent switch	275-280
Emergency flasher relay	185-187		Make-up mirror light, right	155			
Emergency flasher switch	183-187		Memory switch (multi-function ind.)	127-130			
Emergency flasher warning light	188		Multi-function indicator recall button	127-130			
Engine oil pressure control unit	91-93		Multifunction indicator (MFI)	116-123			
Engine oil pressure switch (0.3 bar)	88		Multifunction indicator pressure sender	117-119			
Engine oil pressure switch (1.8 bar)	89		Outside air temperature sensor	134			
Engine oil pressure warning light	90		Oxygen sensor	76,77			
Engine oil temperature sensor	131		Parking brake warning light switch	136			
Fresh air blower series resistance	243-246		Parking light, left	171			
Fresh air control lever light	242		Parking light, right	176			
Fresh air fan	241		Radiator cooling fan	43,44			
Fresh air fan switch	244-246		Radiator cooling fan after run control unit	53-55			
Fuel enrichment switch	63		Radiator cooling fan thermoswitch	43-46, 55			
Fuel gauge	104		Radio connection	162			
Fuel gauge sending unit	36		Rear window defogger indicator light	256			
Fuel pump	37		Rear window defogger switch	257			
Fuel pump relay	35,36						
Glove compartment light	248						
Hall generator	62-64						

Fig. 124 Current track index — Jetta with Digifant II

Wire connectors

T1 — single, behind fuse/relay panel
T1a — single, above relay panel
T1b — single, in luggage compartment, left rear
T1f — single, near battery
T1l — single, in luggage compartment
T1m — single, behind right dash
T1n — single, near left headlight
T1r — single, in luggage compartment, left rear
T2c — double, on left firewall
T2d — double, near intake manifold
T2e — double, behind right dash
T2h — double, near left headlight
T2i — double, near left headlight
T2k — double, near left headlight
T2l — double, on hood
T2m— double, on right firewall
T2p — double, in luggage compartment right
T2r — double, on upper right A-pillar
T2s — double, behind fuse/relay panel
T2t — double, on high mount brake light
T2u — double, near throttle valve housing
T2v — double, on fresh air blower series resistance
T2w— double, on hood
T3 — three-point, behind console
T3a — three-point, on left firewall
T3b — three-point, in engine compartment, rear
T3g — three-point, near starter
T4c — four-point, behind steering column switch
    cover
T4d — four-point, behind steering column switch
    cover
T5b — five-point, behind steering column switch
    cover
T5c — five-point, behind steering column switch
    cover
T5e — five-point, on fresh air blower series
    resistance
T6a — six-point, on left taillight
T6b — six-point, on right taillight
T7a — seven-point, behind steering column switch
    cover
T8 — eight-point, on radio
T16 — sixteen-point, on multi-function indicator
T28 — twenty eight-point, on instrument cluster

Ground connections

(1) — battery to body
(2) — transmission to body
(15) — on cylinder head
(18) — on engine block
(30) — beside fuse/relay panel
(44) — on lower left A-pillar
(50) — in luggage compartment, left
(51) — in luggage compartment, right
(54) — on rear apron
(84) — engine block, in right front wiring harness
(94) — in DIGIFANT wiring harness
(119) — in headlight wiring harness
(120) — in headlight wiring harness

Welded wiring harness points

(C1) — plus connection (58l), in front wiring harness, left
(C2) — plus connection (58r), in front wiring harness, left
(C3) — plus connection (30), in front wiring harness, left
(G3) — plus connection, in injector wiring harness
(G4) — plus connection, in injector wiring harness

Fig. 125 Connector locations — Jetta with Digifant II

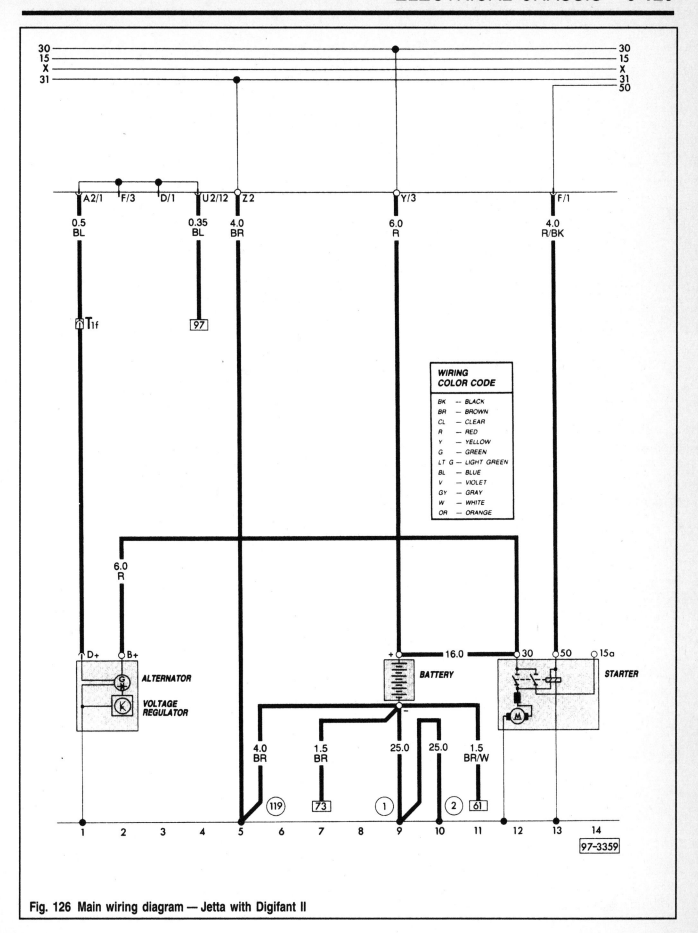

Fig. 126 Main wiring diagram — Jetta with Digifant II

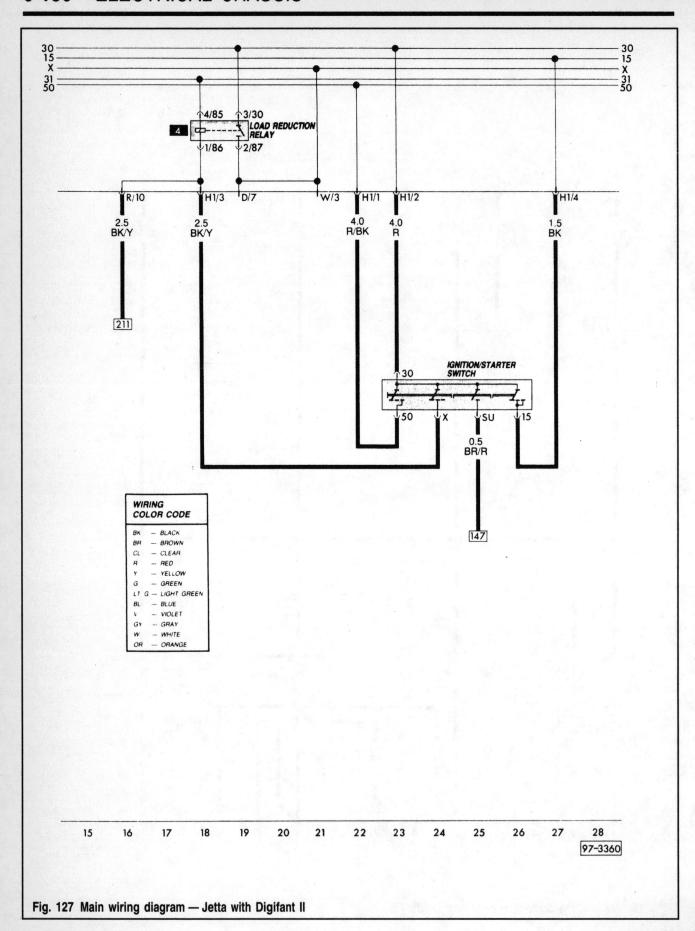

Fig. 127 Main wiring diagram — Jetta with Digifant II

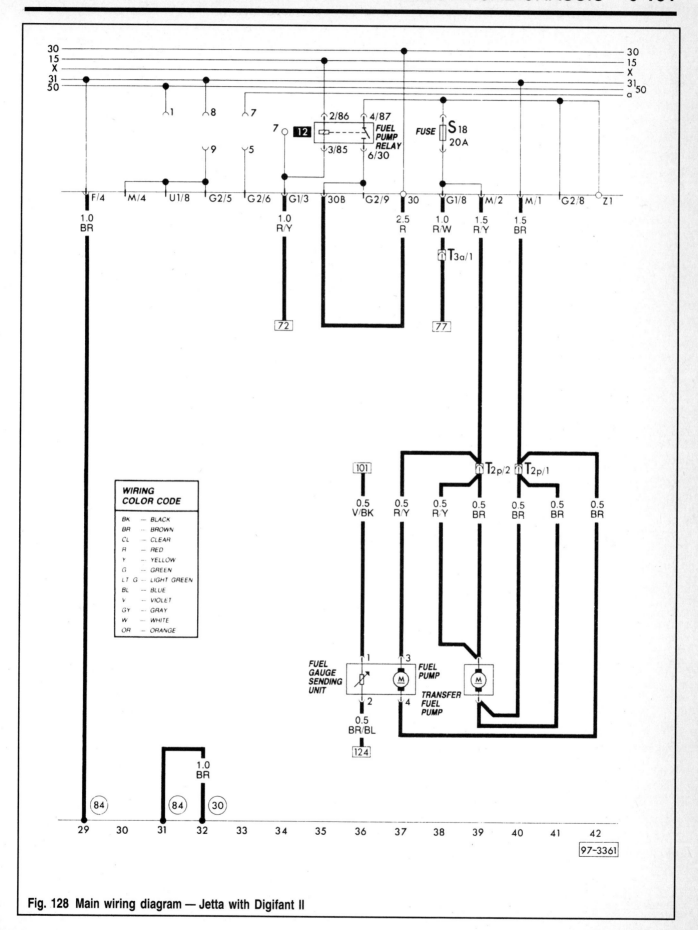

Fig. 128 Main wiring diagram — Jetta with Digifant II

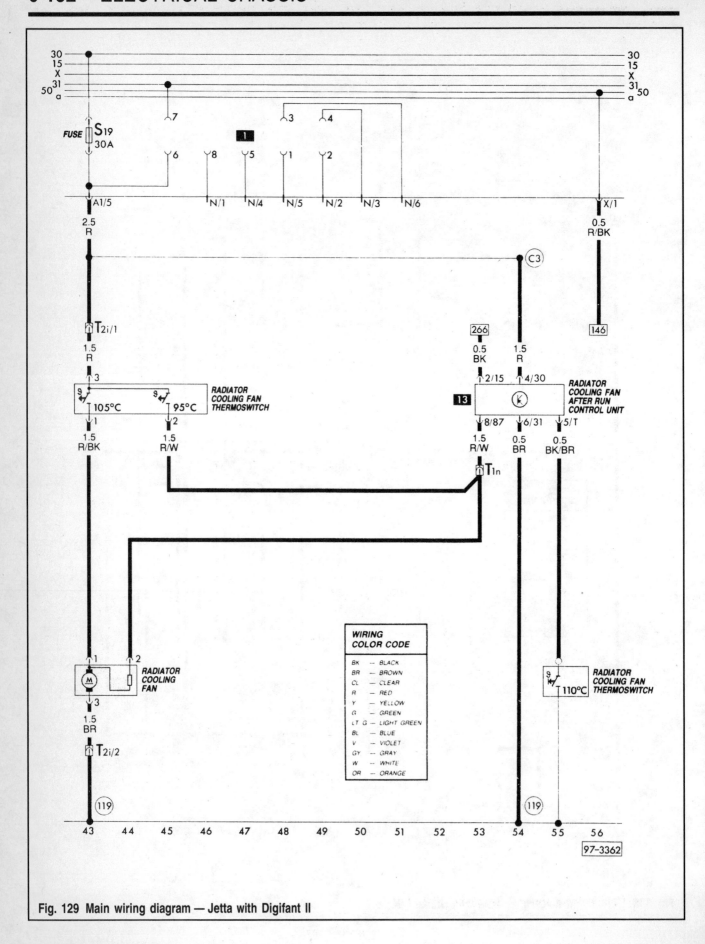

Fig. 129 Main wiring diagram — Jetta with Digifant II

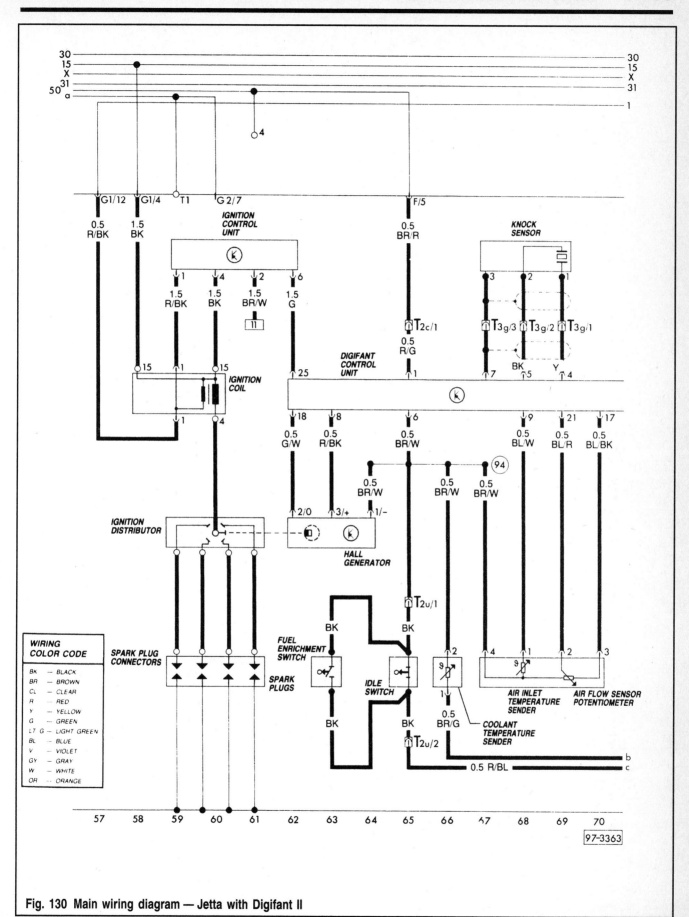

Fig. 130 Main wiring diagram — Jetta with Digifant II

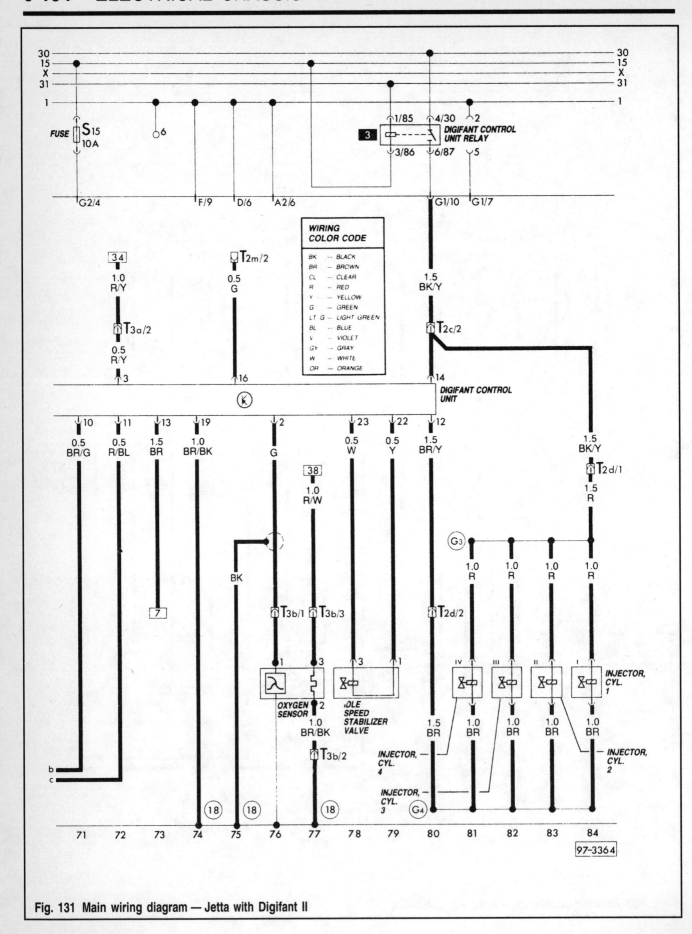

Fig. 131 Main wiring diagram — Jetta with Digifant II

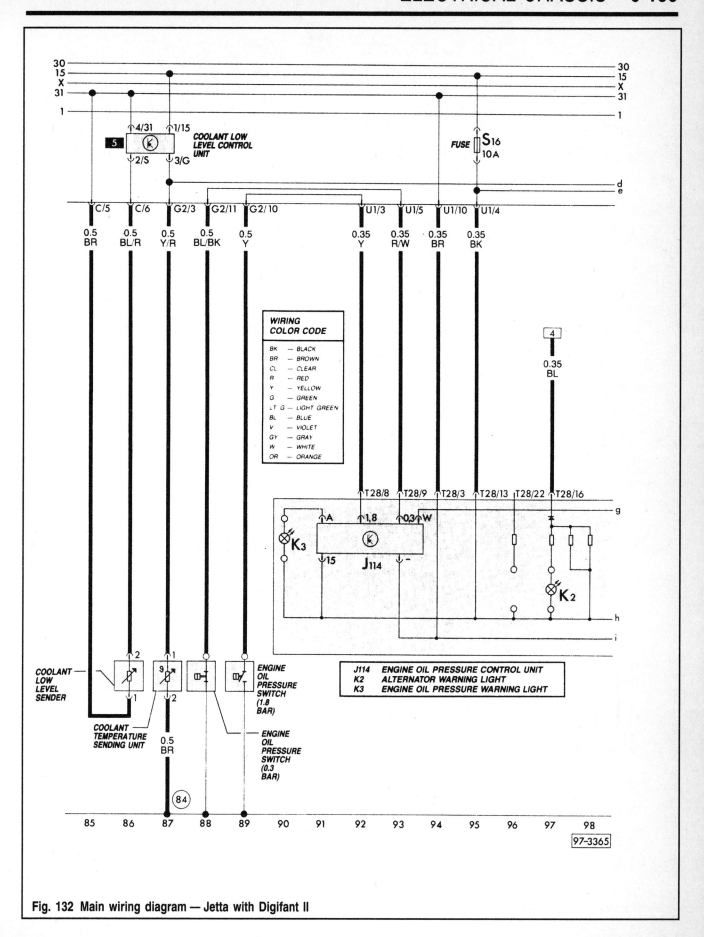

Fig. 132 Main wiring diagram — Jetta with Digifant II

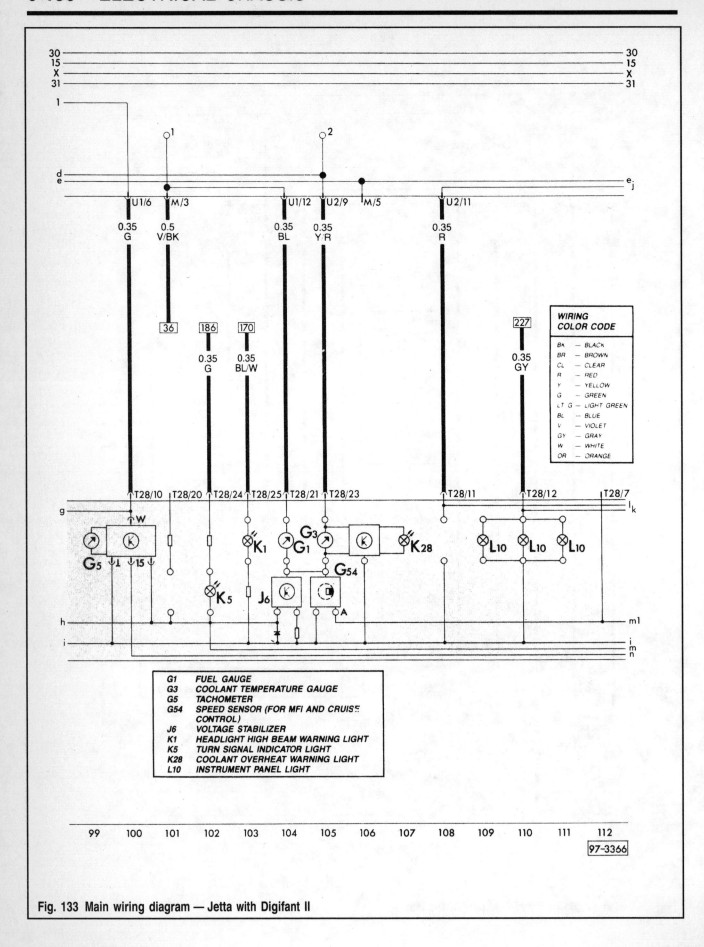

Fig. 133 Main wiring diagram — Jetta with Digifant II

WIRING COLOR CODE

BK — BLACK
BR — BROWN
CL — CLEAR
R — RED
Y — YELLOW
G — GREEN
LT G — LIGHT GREEN
BL — BLUE
V — VIOLET
GY — GRAY
W — WHITE
OR — ORANGE

G1 FUEL GAUGE
G3 COOLANT TEMPERATURE GAUGE
G5 TACHOMETER
G54 SPEED SENSOR (FOR MFI AND CRUISE CONTROL)
J6 VOLTAGE STABILIZER
K1 HEADLIGHT HIGH BEAM WARNING LIGHT
K5 TURN SIGNAL INDICATOR LIGHT
K28 COOLANT OVERHEAT WARNING LIGHT
L10 INSTRUMENT PANEL LIGHT

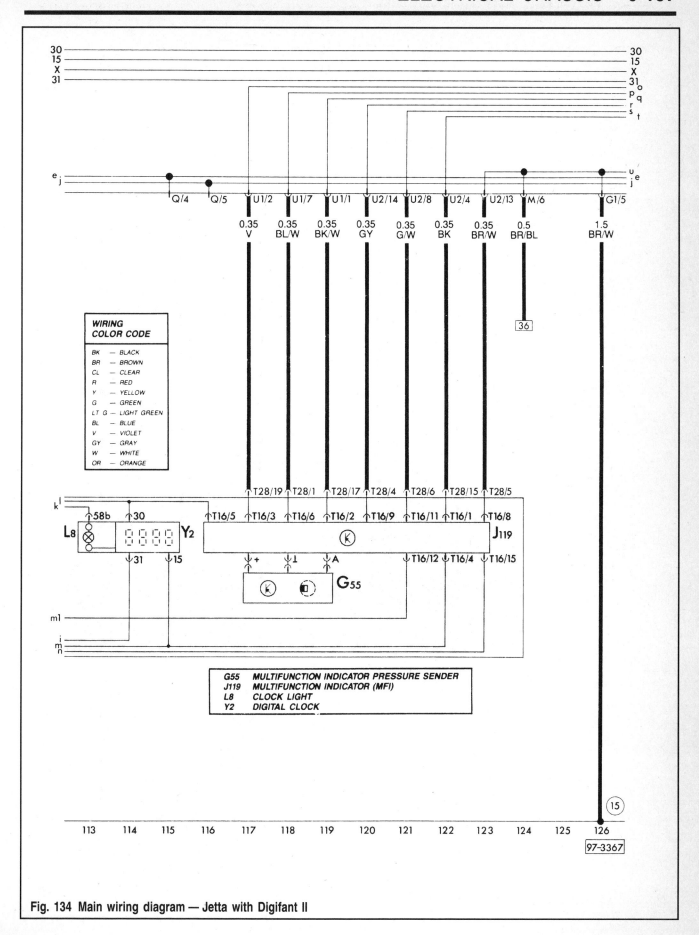

Fig. 134 Main wiring diagram — Jetta with Digifant II

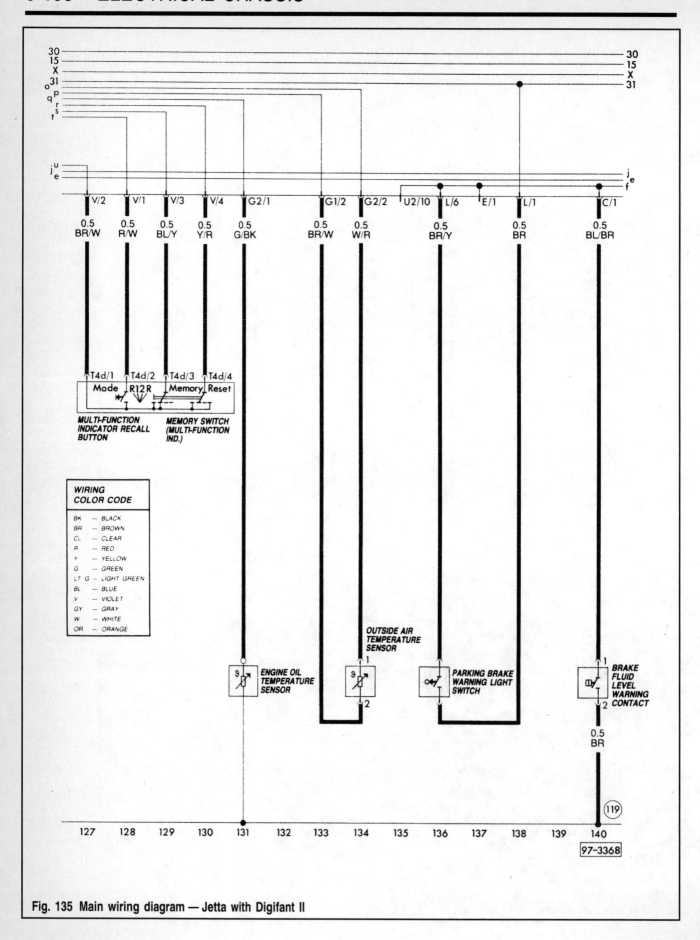

Fig. 135 Main wiring diagram — Jetta with Digifant II

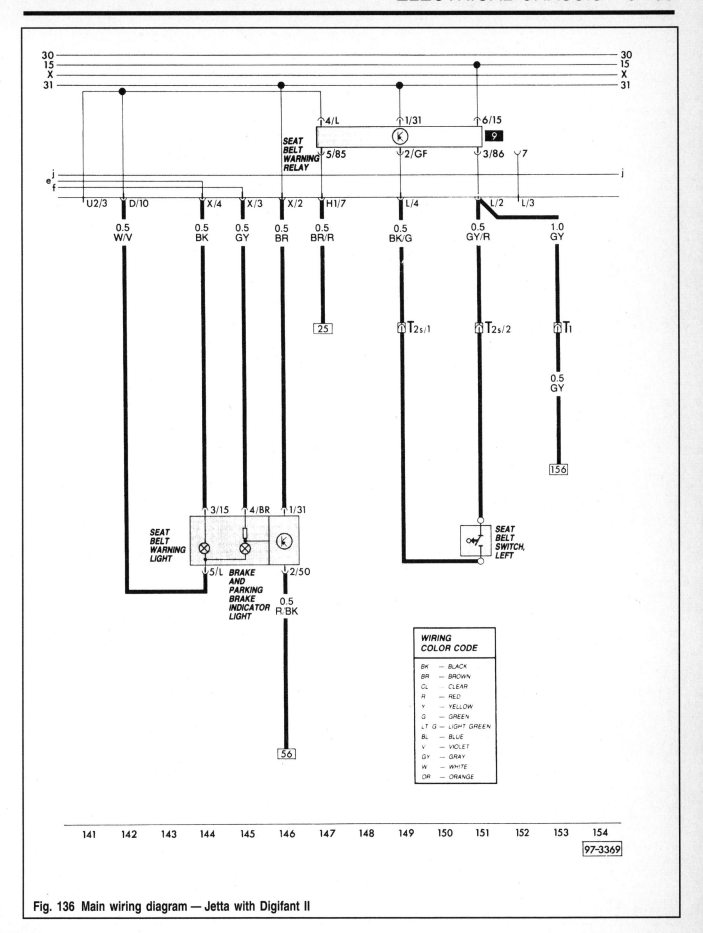

Fig. 136 Main wiring diagram — Jetta with Digifant II

97-3369

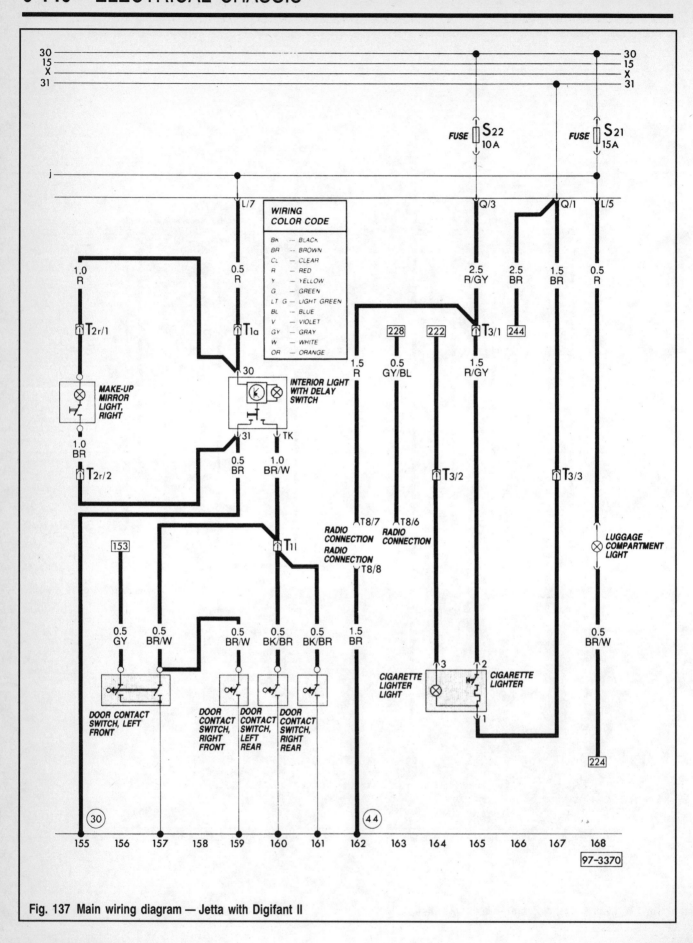

Fig. 137 Main wiring diagram — Jetta with Digifant II

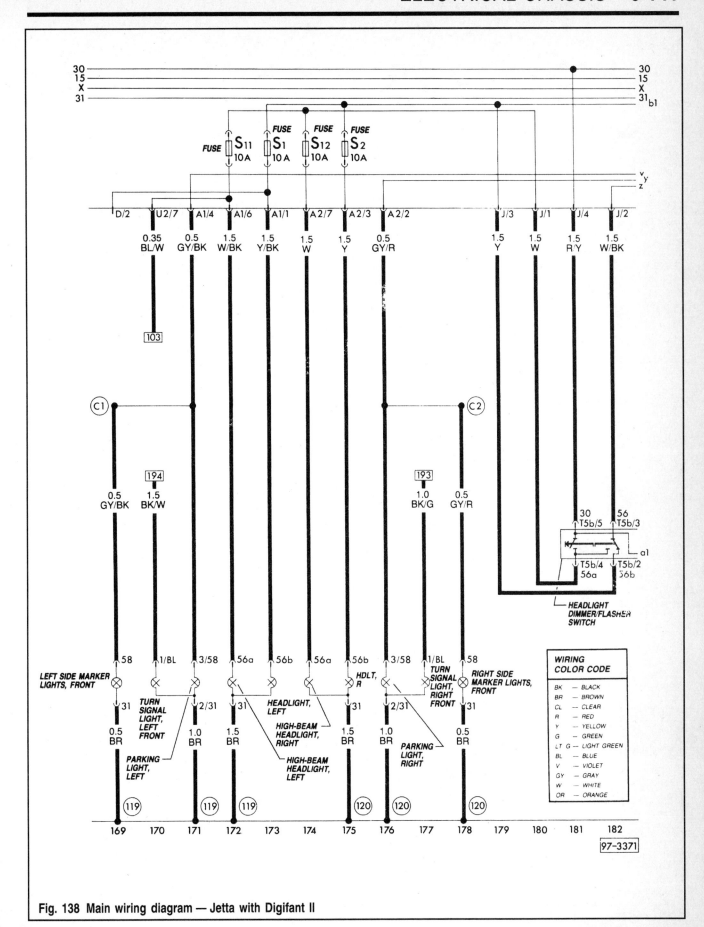

Fig. 138 Main wiring diagram — Jetta with Digifant II

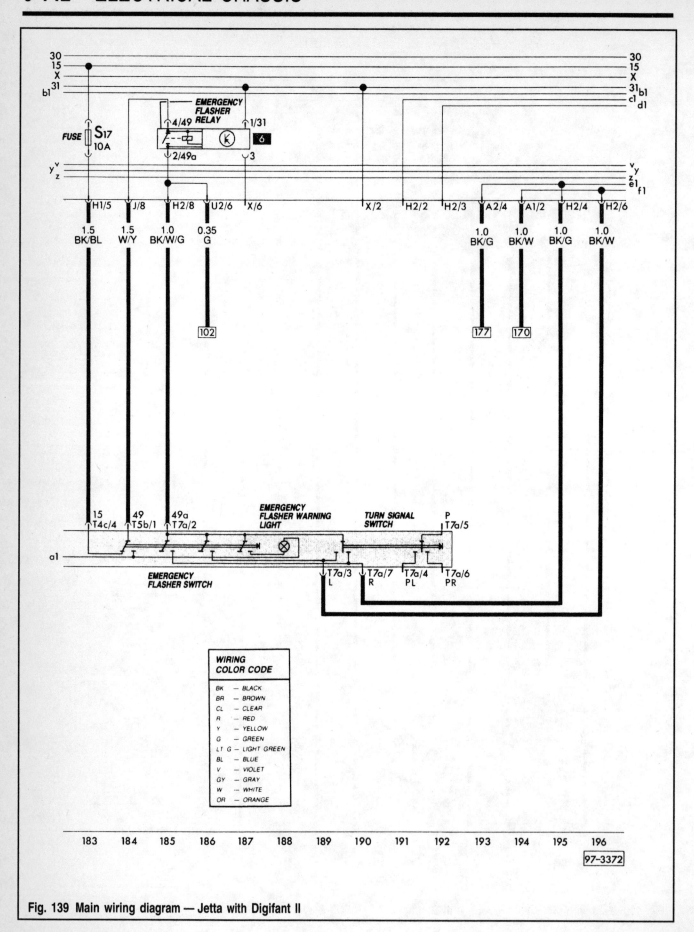

Fig. 139 Main wiring diagram — Jetta with Digifant II

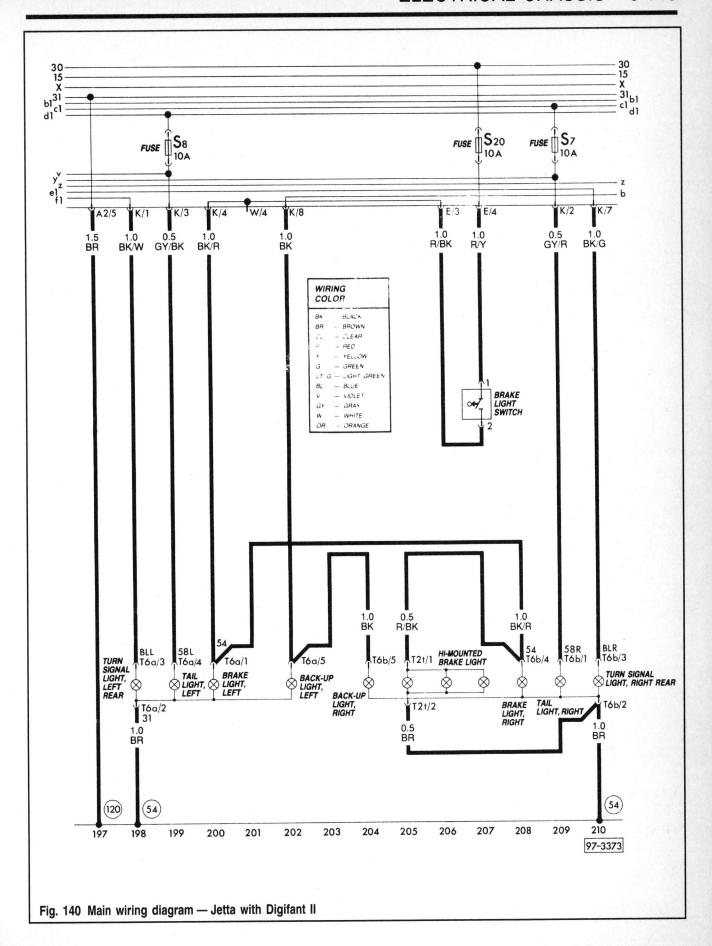

Fig. 140 Main wiring diagram — Jetta with Digifant II

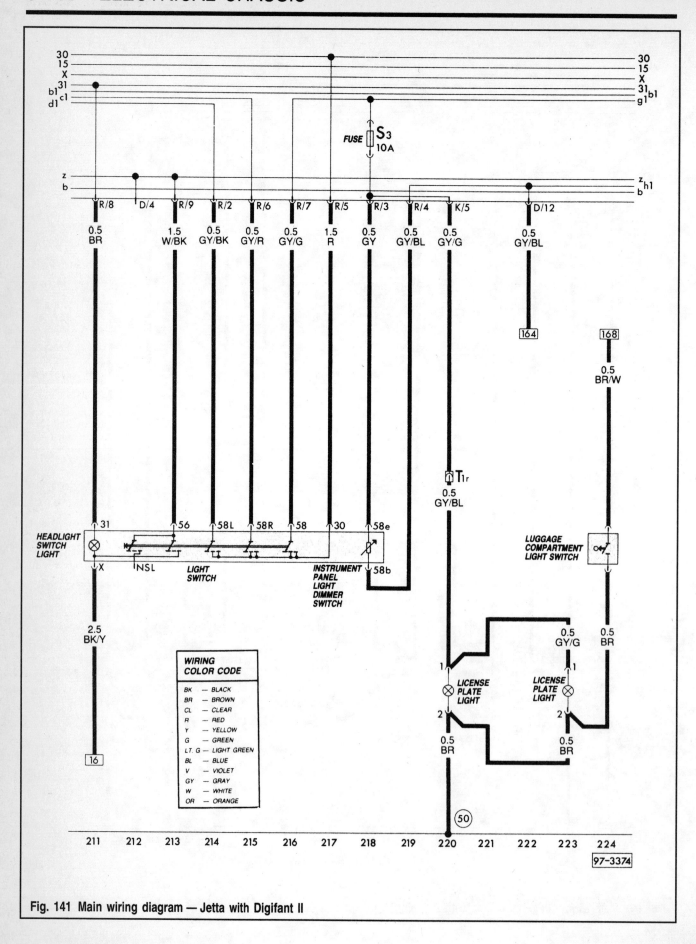

Fig. 141 Main wiring diagram — Jetta with Digifant II

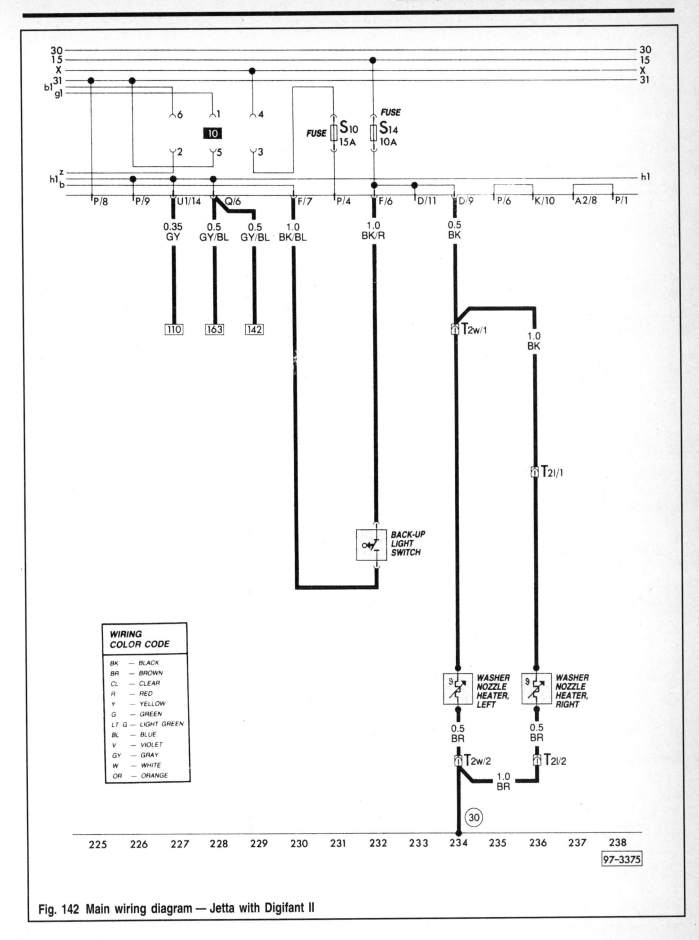

Fig. 142 Main wiring diagram — Jetta with Digifant II

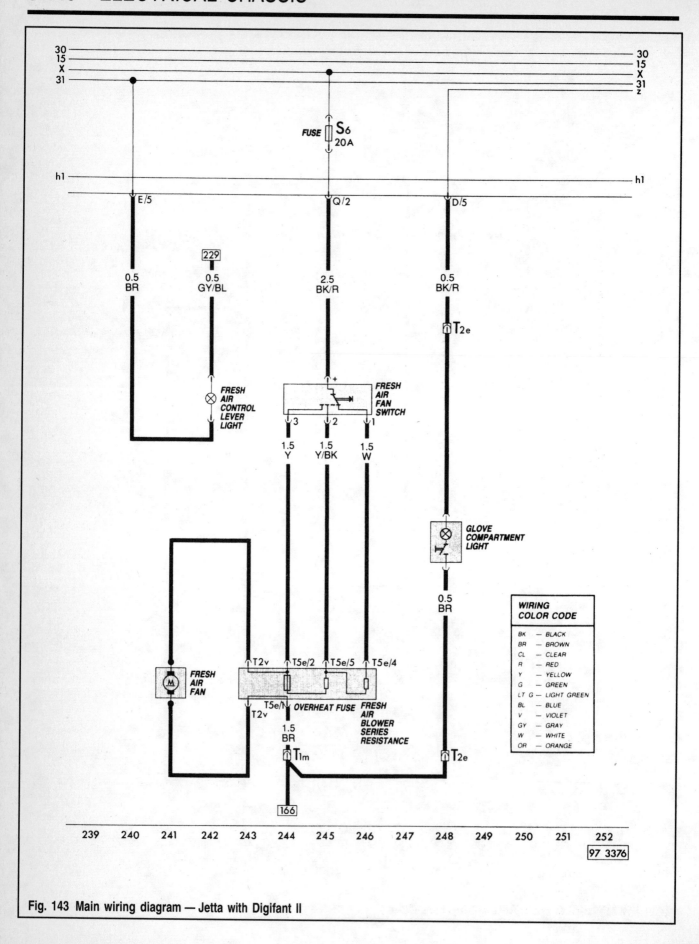

Fig. 143 Main wiring diagram — Jetta with Digifant II

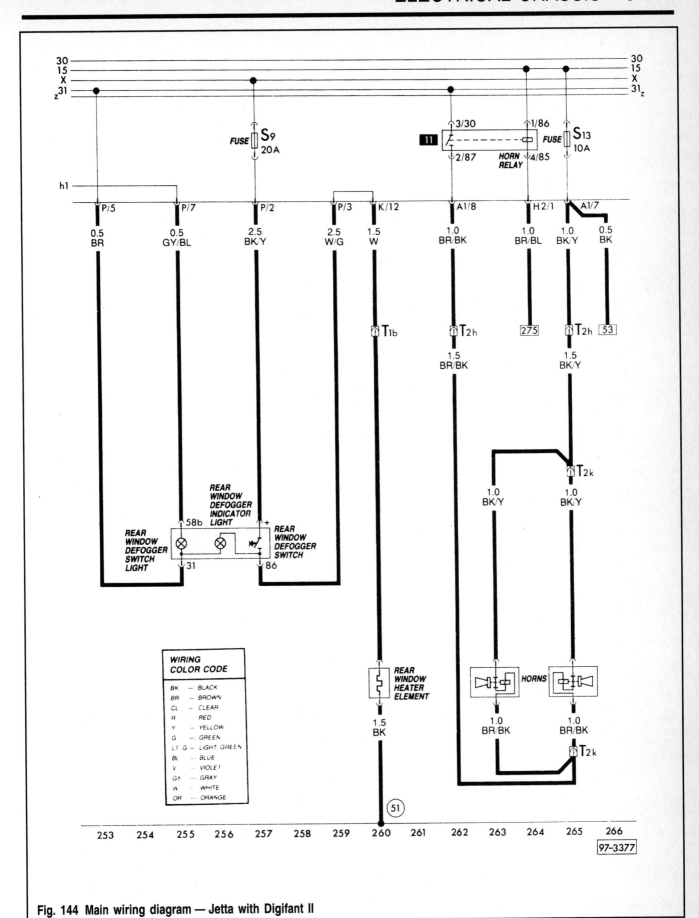

Fig. 144 Main wiring diagram — Jetta with Digifant II

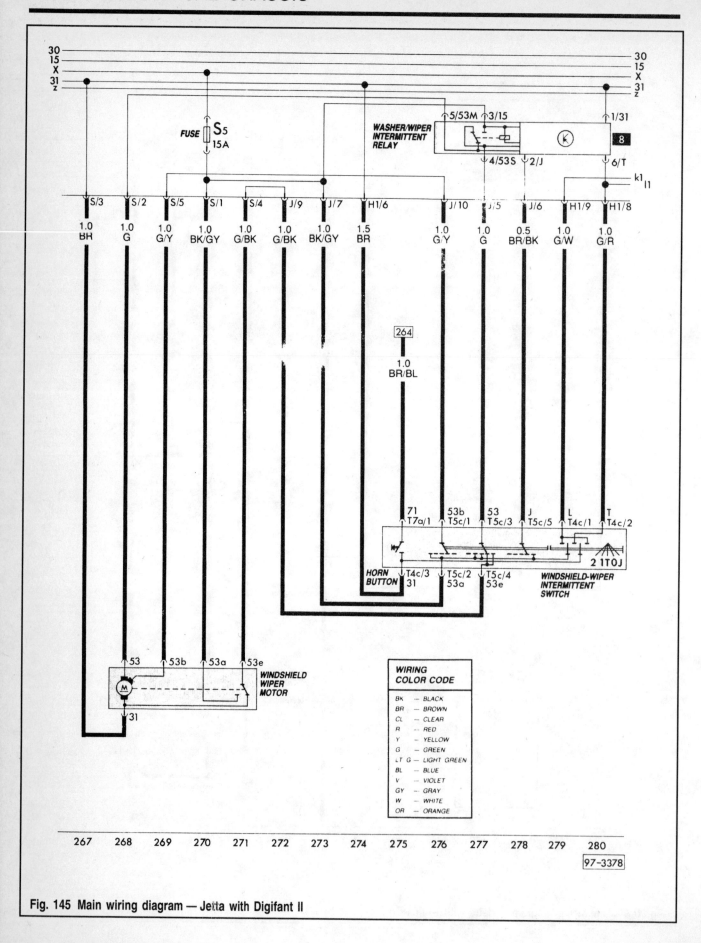

Fig. 145 Main wiring diagram — Jetta with Digifant II

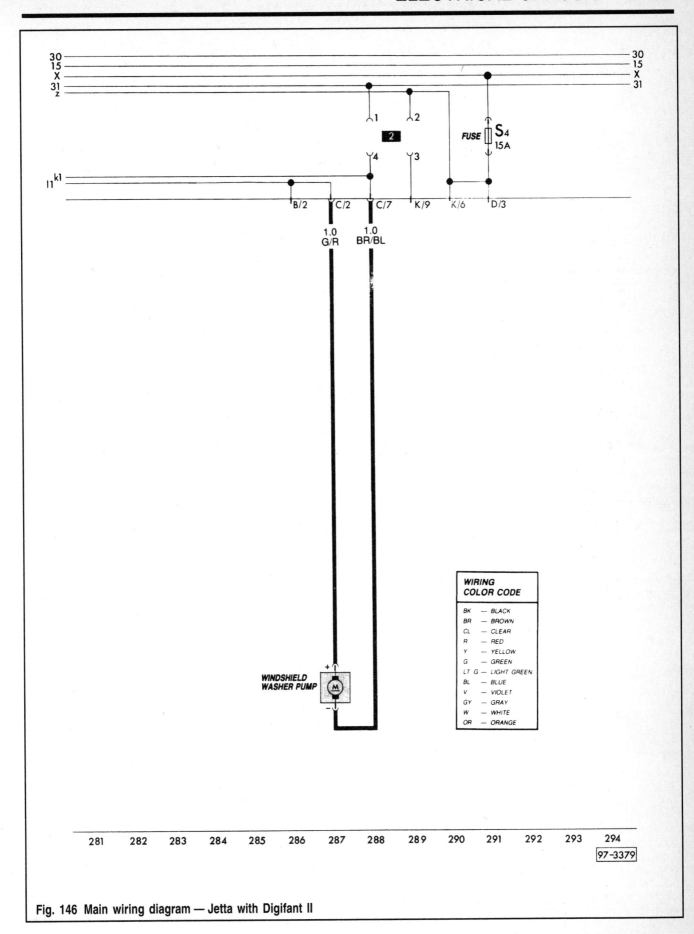

Fig. 146 Main wiring diagram — Jetta with Digifant II

Description	Current track
Air flow sensor potentiometer, G19	40
Alternator, C	1-2
Battery, A	9
Brake and parking brake indicator light, K7	47
Coolant temperature sensor, G62	36
Diagnostic connectors	53-56
Digifant control unit, J169	33-54
Digifant control unit relay, J176	38-39
Fuel gauge sending unit, G	17
Fuel pump, G6	24
Fuel pump relay, J17	20-21
Fuse, S18	25
Fuse, S16	48
Hall generator, G40	33-35
Idle stabilizer valve, N71	49-50
Ignition coil, N152	29
Ignition coil power stage, N157	31-32
Ignition distributor, O	29-31
Ignition, cyl. 1, N30	54
Injector, cyl. 2, N31	53
Injector, cyl. 3, N32	52
Injector, cyl. 4, N33	51
Intake air temperature sensor, G42	39
Knock sensor, G61	39-41
OBD fault warning light, K83	49
Oxygen sensor, G39	47-48
Seat belt warning light, K19	48
Spark plug connectors, P	29-31
Spark plugs, Q	29-31
Starter, B	13-14
Throttle valve potentiometer, G69	43-44
Transfer fuel pump, G23	19
Voltage regulator, C1	1-2

Wire connectors

T1f — single, near battery
T1x — single, behind fuse/relay panel
T2p — double, in luggage compartment, right
T2m— double, on firewall, right
T2x — double, black, diagnostic connector, under shift lever boot
T2z — double, white, diagnostic connector, under shift lever boot
T3 — three-point, on ignition coil power stage
T3b — three-point, in engine compartment, rear
T3g — three-point, near starter
T4 — four-point, on firewall, left
T5a — five-point, on firewall, left
T5c — five-point, on firewall, left

Ground connections

(1) — battery to body
(2) — transmission to body
(18) — on engine block
(30) — near fuse/relay panel
(94) — in Digifant wiring harness
(119) — in headlight wiring harness

Welded wiring harness points

(G1) — plus connection, in Digifant wiring harness
(G3) — plus connection, in injector valve wiring harness

Fig. 147 Digifant I engine management system — California Jetta

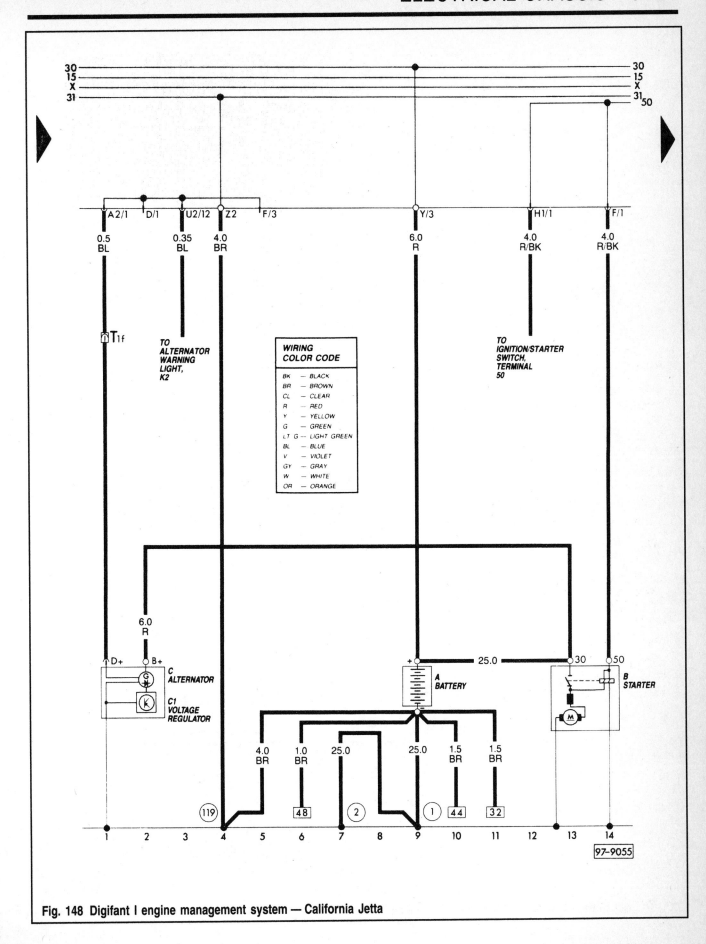

Fig. 148 Digifant I engine management system — California Jetta

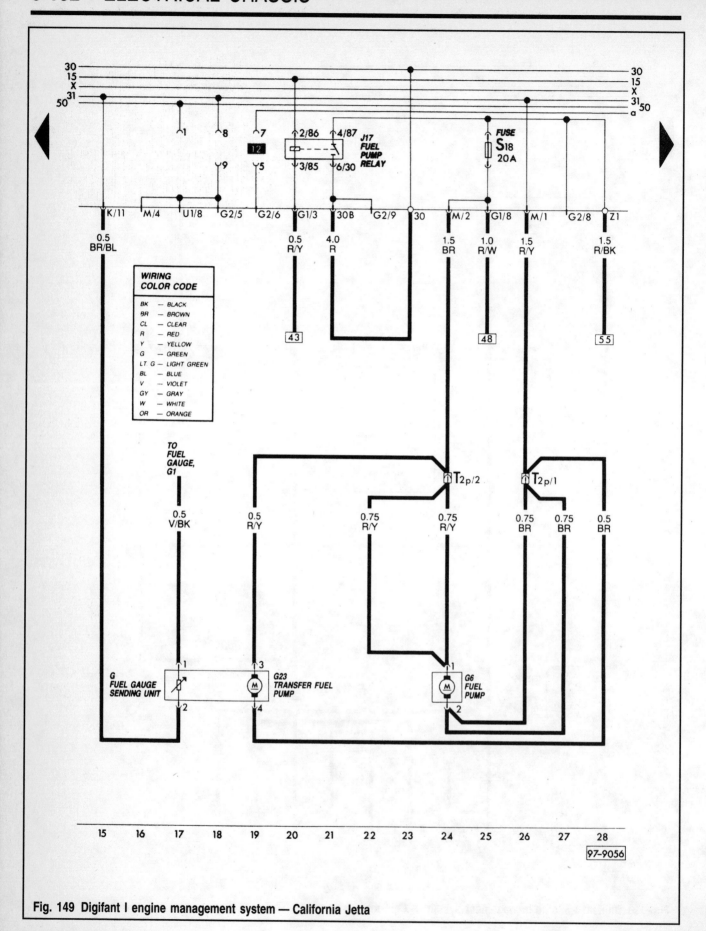

Fig. 149 Digifant I engine management cystem — California Jetta

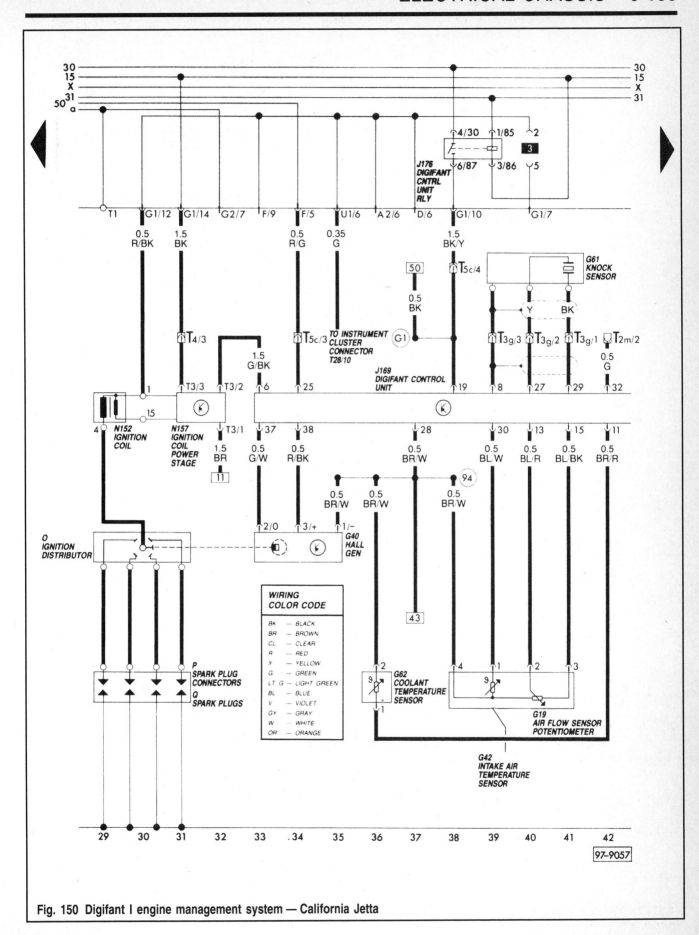

Fig. 150 Digifant I engine management system — California Jetta

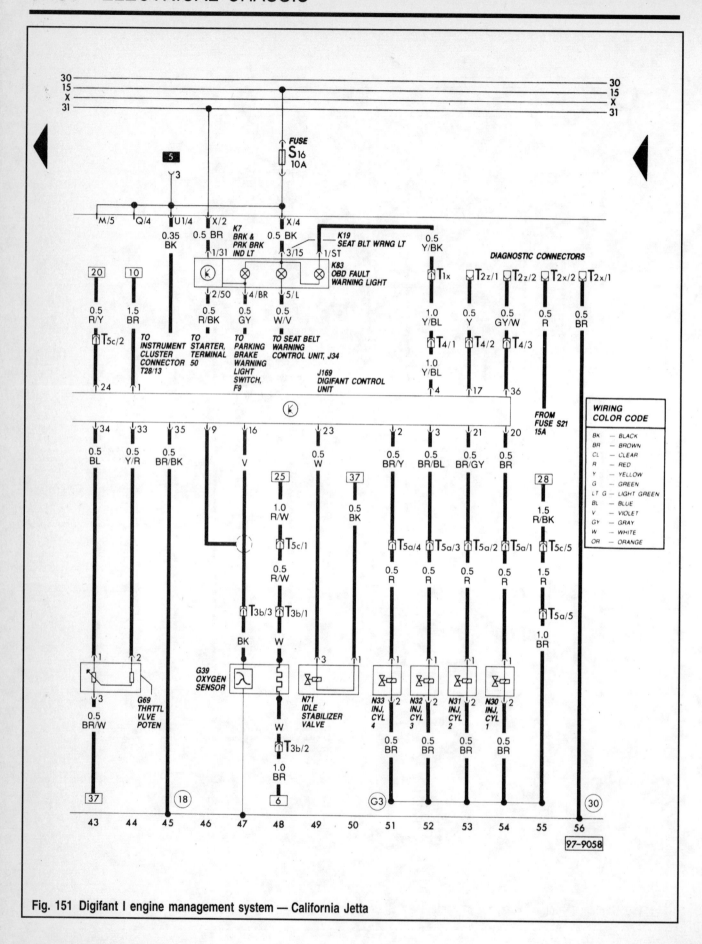

Fig. 151 Digifant I engine management system — California Jetta

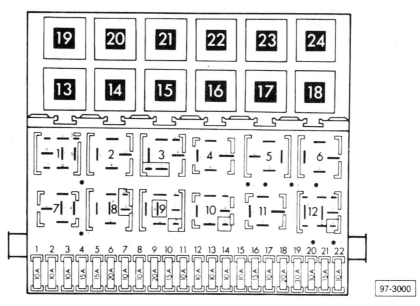

Fuse arrangement

According to the numbers on fuse panel from left to right:

		Amp
1	Headlight, low beam, left	10
2	Headlight, low beam, right	10
3	Instrument panel lights, license plate lights	10
4	Glove box light	15
5	Wiper/washer	15
6	Fresh air fan	20
7	Tail lights, side marker light, right	10
8	Tail lights, side marker light, left	10
9	Rear window defogger	20
10	Fog lights	15
11	Headlight, high beam, left	10
12	Headlight, high beam, right	10
13	Horn	10
14	Back-up lights, washer jet heaters	10
15	Open	
16	Dash warning lights	15
17	Emergency flasher switch	10
18	Fuel pump	20
19	Radiator cooling fan, A/C	30
20	Brake lights	10
21	Interior lights, digital clock	15
22	Radio, cigarette lighter	10

*Numbers in parentheses indicate production control number stamped on relay housing.

Relay location on fuse/relay panel

- **1** — A/C relay (13)*
- **2** — Open
- **3** — Open
- **4** — Load reduction relay (18)*
- **5** — Open
- **6** — Emergency flasher relay (21)*
- **7** — Open
- **8** — Intermittent wiper relay (19)*
- **9** — Seat belt warning system (4, 29)*
- **10** — Fog light relay (51, 53)*
- **11** — Horn relay (53)*
- **12** — Glow plug relay (60)*

Separate relays above fuse/relay panel

- **13** — Radiator cooling fan after run control unit (31)*
- **14** — Automatic transmission relay (53)* or Coolant temperature indicator relay (44)*
- **15** — ABS hydraulic pump relay (78)*
- **16** — ABS relay (79)*
- **17** — Heated seat control unit, driver (59)*
- **18** — Heated seat control unit, passenger (59)*
- **19** — Automatic transmission relay (53)*
- **20** — Open
- **21** — Power window relay (24)*
- **22** — ABS valves fuse
- **23** — Fuse for A/C power seats
- **24** — Power window fuse

Fig. 152 Main fuse and relay panel — Jetta Diesel

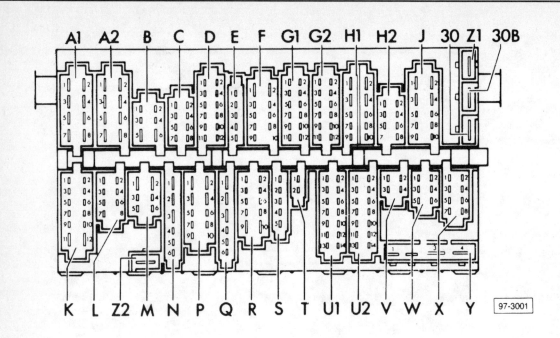

Connections and plugs on fuse/relay panel

A1 — Headlight wiring harness (yellow)
A2 — Headlight wiring harness (yellow)
B — Open
C — Headlight wiring harness (yellow)
D — Optional equipment wiring harness (green)
E — Instrument wiring harness (green)
F — Engine compartment wiring harness, right (white)
G1 — Engine compartment wiring harness, right (white)
G2 — Engine compartment wiring harness, right (white)
H1 — Steering column switch wiring harness (red)
H2 — Steering column switch wiring harness (red)
J — Steering column switch wiring harness (red)
K — Rear wiring harness (black)
L — Rear wiring harness (black)
M — Rear wiring harness (black)
N — A/C wiring harness (green)
P — Rear window defroster and fog light wiring harness (blue)
Q — Instrument wiring harness (blue)
R — Light switch wiring harness (blue)
S — Engine compartment wiring harness, right (white)
T — Two-point connector (green)
U1 — Instrument cluster wiring harness (blue)
U2 — Instrument cluster wiring harness (blue)
V — Multi-function indicator wiring harness (green)
W — Six-point connector (green)
X — Warning lamp wiring harness (green)
Y — Single connector, terminal 30

Z1 — Single connector
Z2 — Single connector, terminal 31
30 — Single connector, terminal 30
30B — Single connector
31 — Single connector, terminal 31

Fig. 153 Fuse panel connectors — Jetta Diesel

Description	Current track	Description	Current track	Description	Current track
Alternator, C	1-3	Fuse, S19	15	Make-up mirror light switch, right, F148	99
Alternator warning light, K2	56	Fuse, S6	21		
Altitude correction switch, F97	41	Fuse, S18	41	Make-up mirror light, right, W14	99-100
Altitude correction valve, N78	41	Fuse, S16	79		
		Fuse, S15	86	Oil pressure warning, coolant low level indicator and tachometer control unit, J243	64-77
Back-up light switch, F4	169	Fuse, S22	90		
Back-up light, left, M16	171	Fuse, S4	95		
Back-up light, right, M17	172	Fuse, S21	97	Overheat fuse, S24	22
Battery, A	4	Fuse, S11	116		
Brake and parking brake indicator light, K7	110	Fuse, S1	117	Parking brake warning light switch, F9	81
Brake fluid level warning contact, F34	83	Fuse, S12	119	Parking light, left, M1	142
		Fuse, S2	120	Parking light, right, M3	153
Brake light switch, F	183	Fuse, S17	127		
Brake light, left, M9	185	Fuse, S8	146	Radiator cooling fan, V7	15-16
Brake light, right, M10	187	Fuse, S7	149	Radiator cooling fan thermoswitch, F18	15-17
		Fuse, S3	162		
Cassette storage light, L66	85	Fuse, S9	175	Rear window defogger indicator light, K10	174
Cigarette lighter, U1	90	Fuse, S13	182		
Cigarette lighter light, L28	91	Fuse, S20	183	Rear window defogger switch, E15	175
Clock light, L8	62	Fuse, S10	191		
Coolant low level sensor, G32	44	Fuse, S14	193	Rear window defogger switch light, L39	173
Coolant overheat warning light, K28	67	Fuse, S5	200	Rear window heater element, Z1	177
Coolant temperature gauge, G3	57	Glove compartment light, W6	95	Seat belt switch, left, E24	107
		Glow plug, Q6	36-39	Seat belt warning control unit, J34	105-109
Coolant temperature sending unit, G2	45	Glow plug fuse strip, 50A, S39	39	Seat belt warning light, K19	109
		Glow plug indicator light, K29	59	Side marker lights, front, M11	143, 152
Digital clock, Y2	63	Glow plug relay, J52	34-37	Starter, B	6-7
Door contact switch, left front, F2	105-106				
		Headlight dimmer/flasher switch, E4	124-126	Tachometer, G5	73-75
Door contact switch, left rear, F10	102	Headlight high beam indicator light, connector T28/25, K1	61	Tail light, left, M4	146
Door contact switch, right front, F3	104	Headlight switch light, L9	156	Tail light, right, M2	149
		Headlight, left, L1	117	Turn signal indicator light, connector T28/24, K5	60
Door contact switch, right rear, F11	103	Headlight, right, L2	120	Turn signal light, left front, M5	141
		High-beam headlight, left, L13	116	Turn signal light, left rear, M6	145
Emergency flasher relay, J2	129-132	High-beam headlight, right, L14	119	Turn signal light, right front, M7	154
Emergency flasher switch, E3	127-131	High-mount brake light, M25	189-191		
Emergency flasher warning light, K6	132	Horn button, H	205	Turn signal light, right rear, M8	150
Engine oil pressure switch (0.3 bar), F22	46	Horn relay, J4	178-179	Turn signal switch, E2	133-134
		Horns, H1	180, 182		
Engine oil pressure switch (1.8 bar), F1	47	Ignition/starter switch, D	10-13	Voltage regulator, C1	1-3
		Instrument panel light dimmer switch, E20	162	Voltage stabilizer, J6	57
Engine oil pressure warning light, K3	66	Instrument panel light, connector T28/12, L10	52	Washer nozzle heater, left, Z20	193
Engine temperature sender (preheat system), G27	35	Interior light with delay switch, W15	101-102	Washer nozzle heater, right, Z21	192
Fresh air control lever light, L16	19	License plate light, X	167, 168	Washer/wiper intermittent relay, J31	206-210
Fresh air fan, V2	25	Light switch, E1	155-162	Water separator sender, G63	31-33
Fresh air fan series resistance, N23	21-24	Load reduction relay, J59	11-12	Windshield washer pump, V5	196
Fresh air fan switch, E9	21-23	Luggage compartment light, W3	165	Windshield wiper motor, V	198-201
Fuel cut-off valve, N43	42			Windshield-wiper intermittent switch, E22	206-210
Fuel gauge, G1	58	Luggage compartment light switch, F5	165		
Fuel gauge sending unit, G	30				

Fig. 154 Current track index — Jetta Diesel

Wire connectors

T1a — single, behind instrument panel, left
T1b — single, behind instrument panel, left
T1c — single, behind fuse/relay panel
T1d — single, above fuse/relay panel
T1e — single, in luggage compartment, left rear
T1f — single, in luggage compartment, left rear
T1g — single, in luggage compartment
T1h — single, in luggage compartment, left
T1i — single, behind fuse/relay panel
T1j — single, behind fuse/relay panel
T2a — double, near battery
T2b — double, near left headlight
T2c — double, behind instrument panel, right
T2d — double, on upper right "A" pillar
T2e — double, near left headlight
T2f — double, near left headlight
T2g — double, on hood
T2h — double, on hood
T2i — double, behind console
T2j — double, near right headlight
T2k — double, behind fuse/relay panel
T2l — double, near left headlight
T2m— double, on fresh air blower series resistance
T3a — three-point, behind console
T3b — three-point, near left headlight
T3c — three-point, near right headlight
T4c — four-point, behind steering column switch cover
T5a — five-point, on instrument panel, center
T5b — five-point, behind steering column switch cover
T5c — five-point, behind steering column switch cover
T5d — five-point, on fresh air blower series resistance
T6a — six-point, on left taillight
T6b — six-point, on right taillight
T7a — seven-point, behind steering column switch cover
T8 — eight-point, on radio
T28 — twenty eight-point, on instrument cluster

Ground connections

① — battery to body
② — transmission to body
⑫ — in engine compartment, left
㉚ — beside fuse/relay panel
㊹ — on lower A-pillar, left
㊿ — in luggage compartment, left
(51) — in luggage compartment, right
(54) — on rear apron
(63) — on left tail lamp housing
(64) — on right tail lamp housing
(80) — in instrument panel wiring harness
(84) — on engine block, in right front wiring harness
(85) — in engine compartment wiring harness
(119) — in headlight wiring harness
(120) — in headlight wiring harness

Welded wiring harness points

(C1) — plus connection 58l, in front wiring harness, left
(C2) — plus connection 58r, in front wiring harness, left

Fig. 155 Connector locations — Jetta Diesel

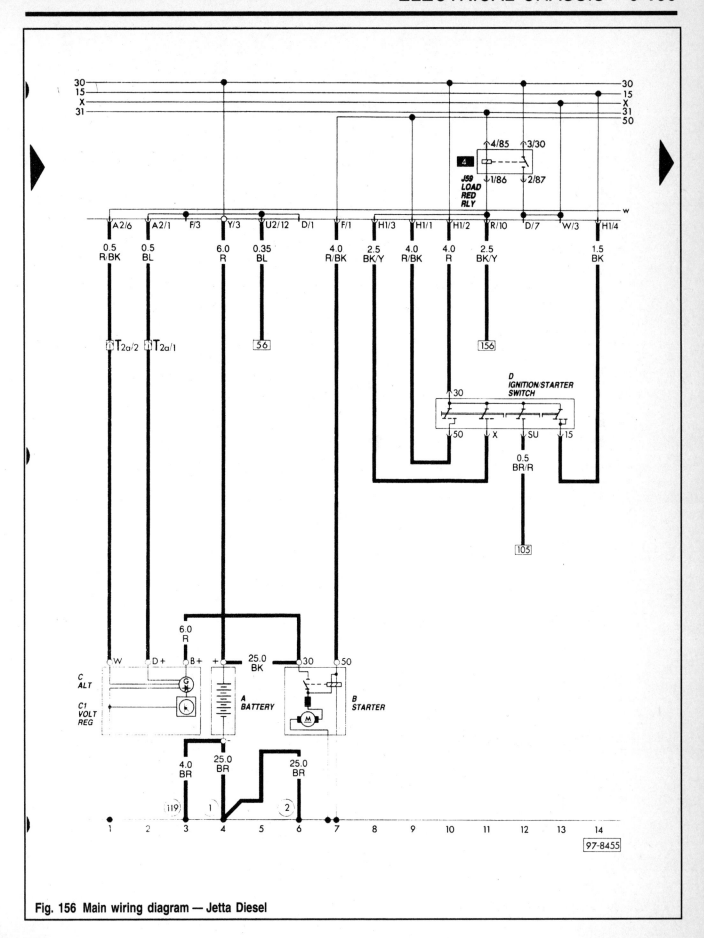

Fig. 156 Main wiring diagram — Jetta Diesel

97-8455

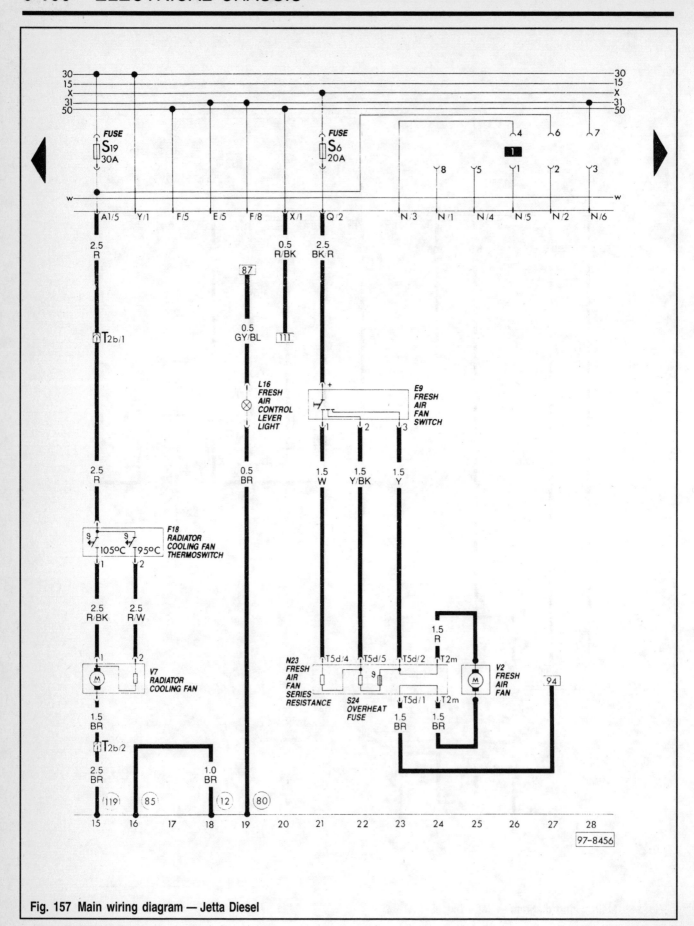

Fig. 157 Main wiring diagram — Jetta Diesel

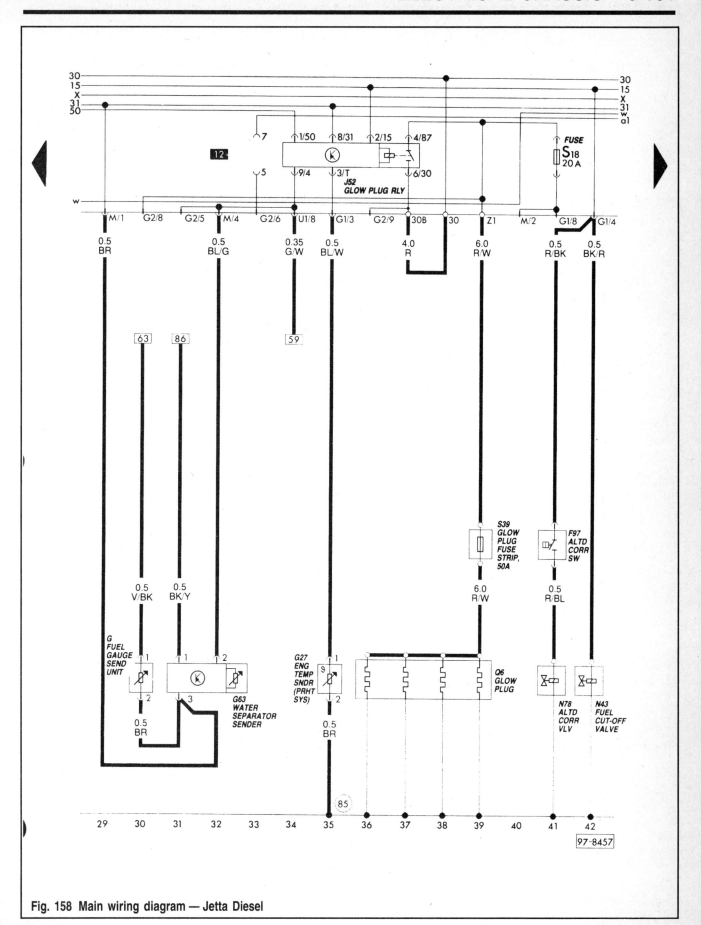

Fig. 158 Main wiring diagram — Jetta Diesel

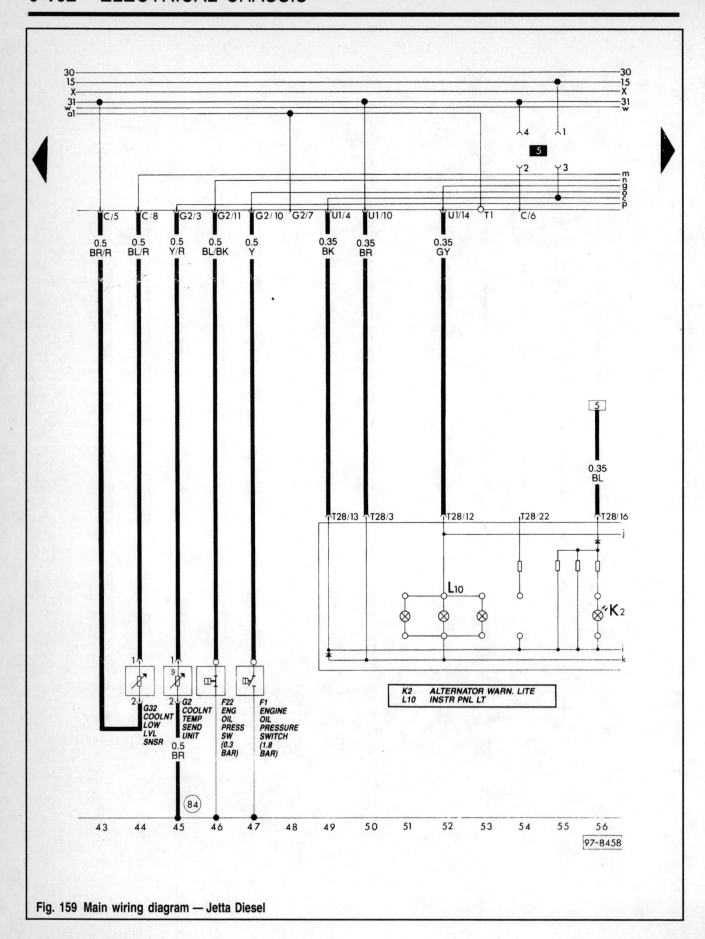

Fig. 159 Main wiring diagram — Jetta Diesel

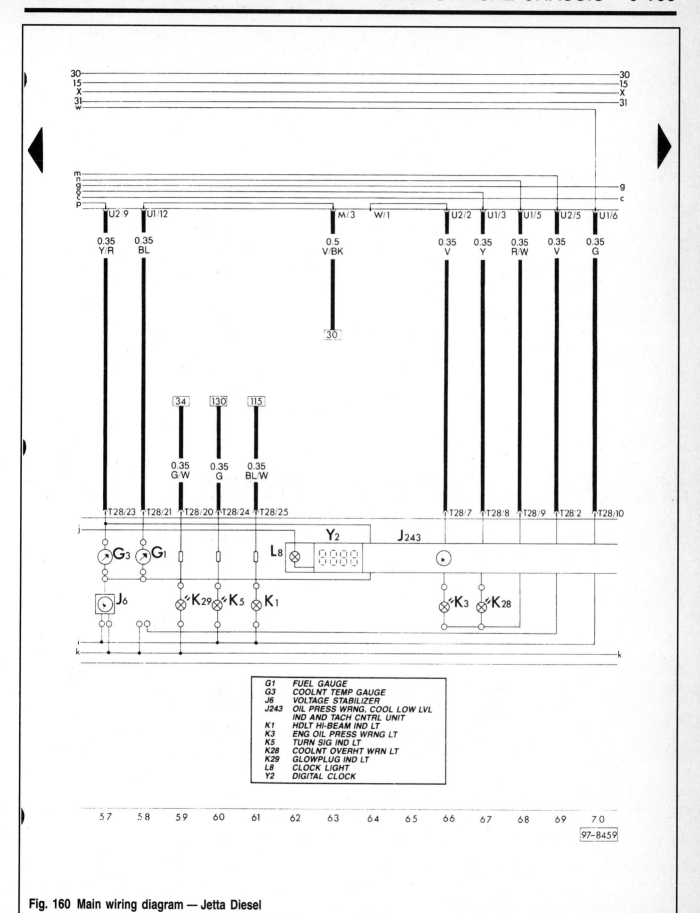

Fig. 160 Main wiring diagram — Jetta Diesel

G1	FUEL GAUGE	
G3	COOLNT TEMP GAUGE	
J6	VOLTAGE STABILIZER	
J243	OIL PRESS WRNG, COOL LOW LVL IND AND TACH CNTRL UNIT	
K1	HDLT HI-BEAM IND LT	
K3	ENG OIL PRESS WRNG LT	
K5	TURN SIG IND LT	
K28	COOLNT OVERHT WRN LT	
K29	GLOWPLUG IND LT	
L8	CLOCK LIGHT	
Y2	DIGITAL CLOCK	

97-8459

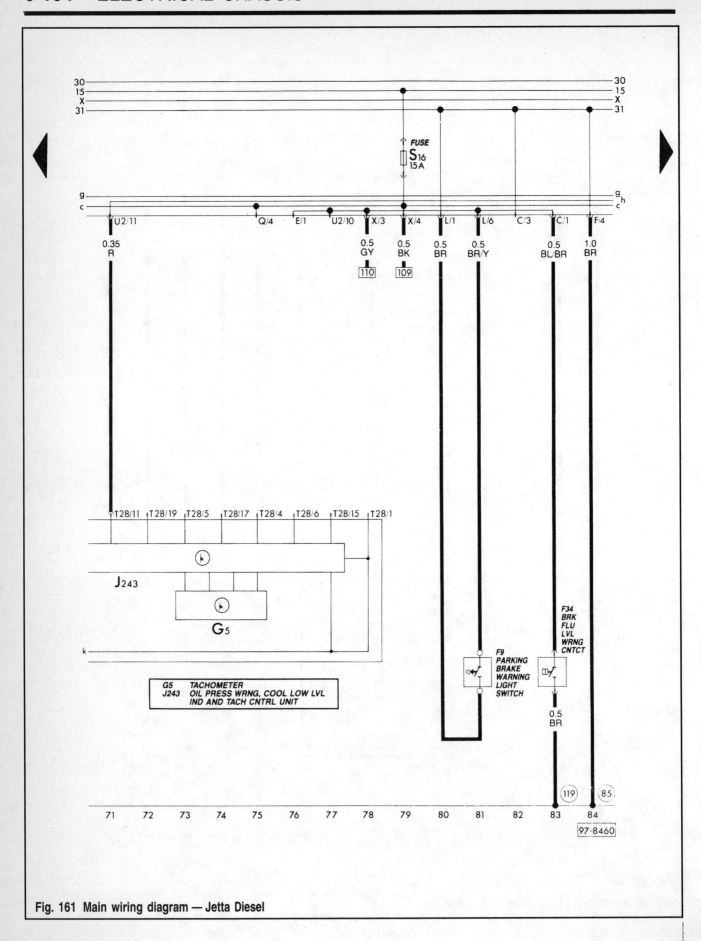

Fig. 161 Main wiring diagram — Jetta Diesel

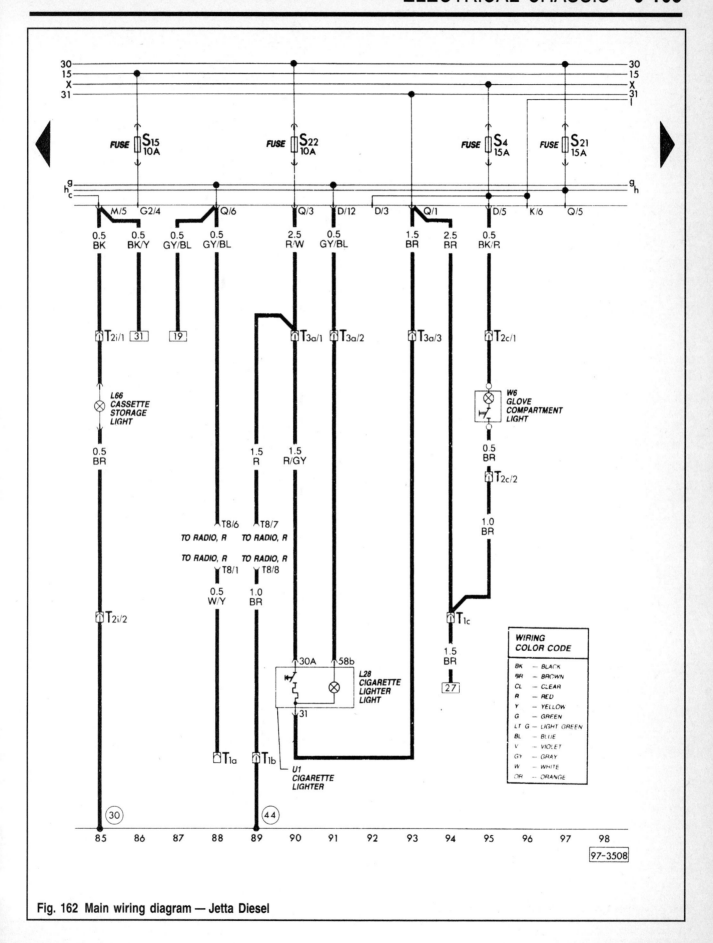

Fig. 162 Main wiring diagram — Jetta Diesel

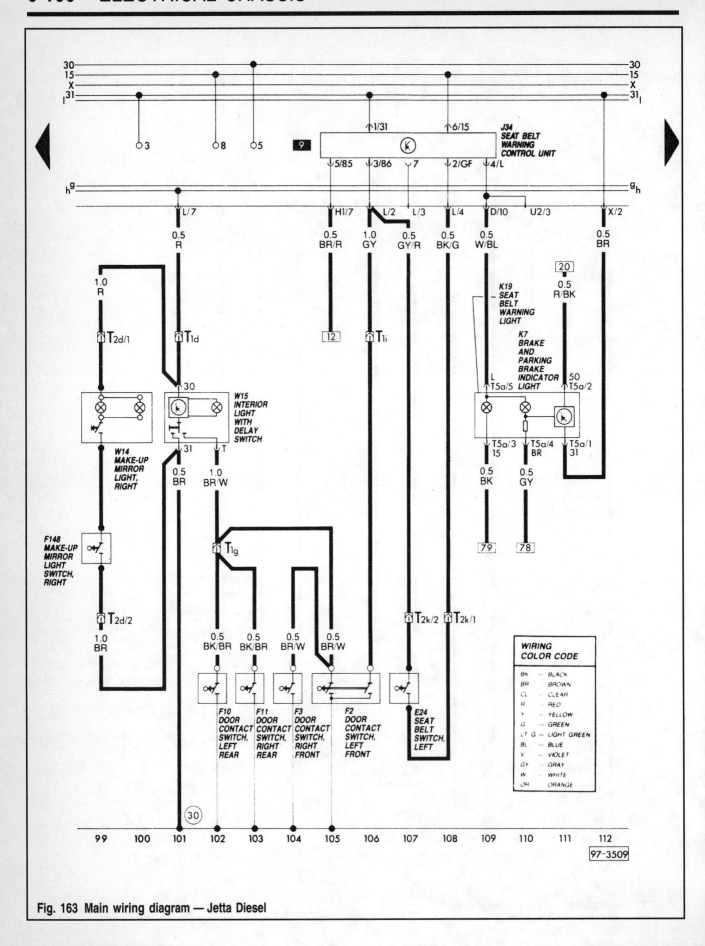

Fig. 163 Main wiring diagram — Jetta Diesel

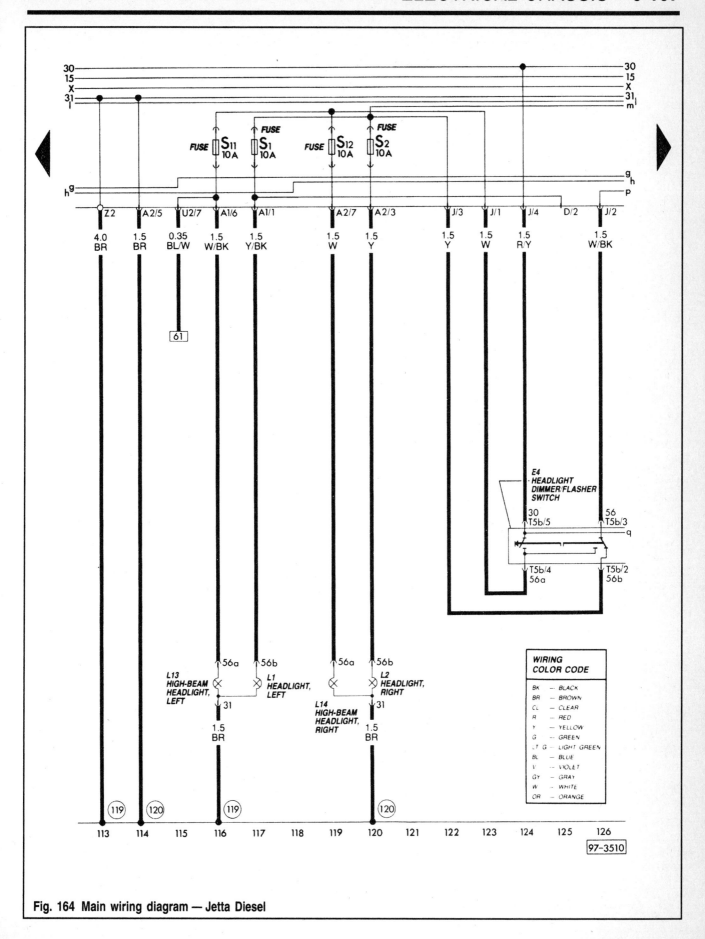

Fig. 164 Main wiring diagram — Jetta Diesel

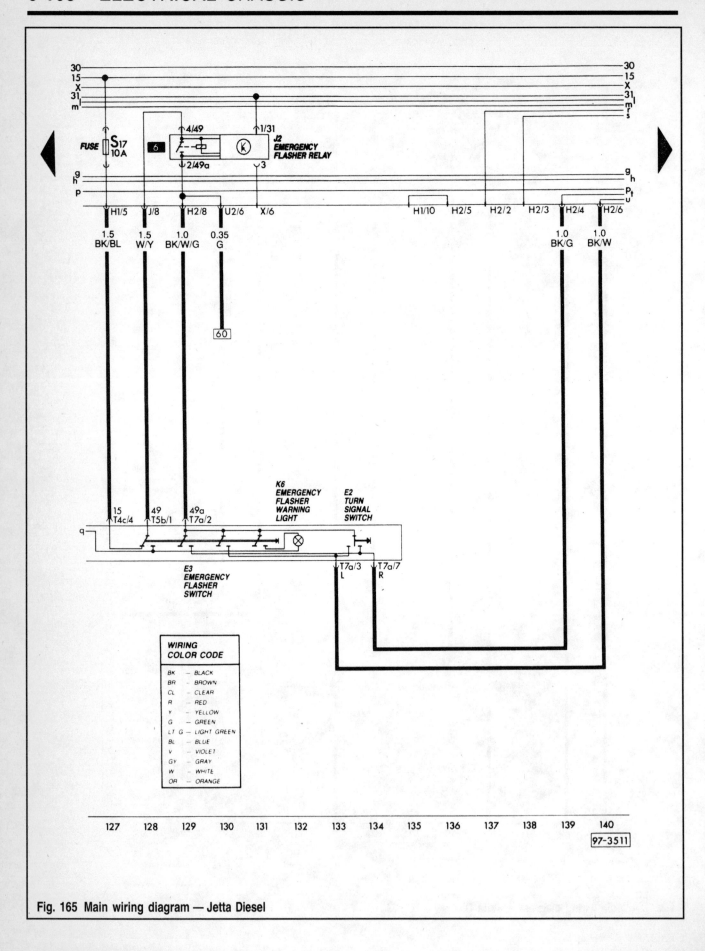

Fig. 165 Main wiring diagram — Jetta Diesel

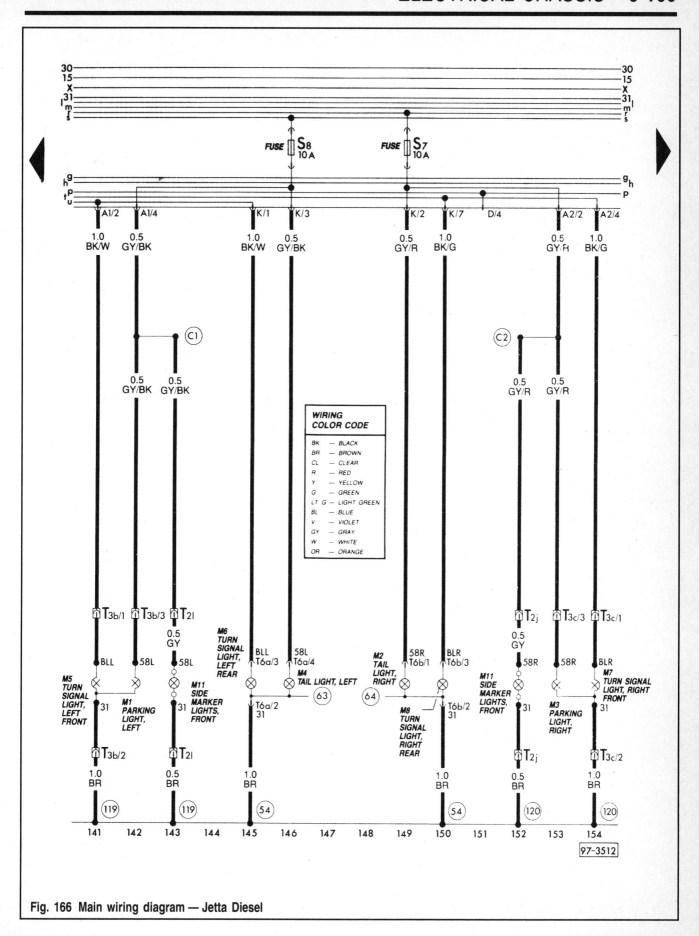

Fig. 166 Main wiring diagram — Jetta Diesel

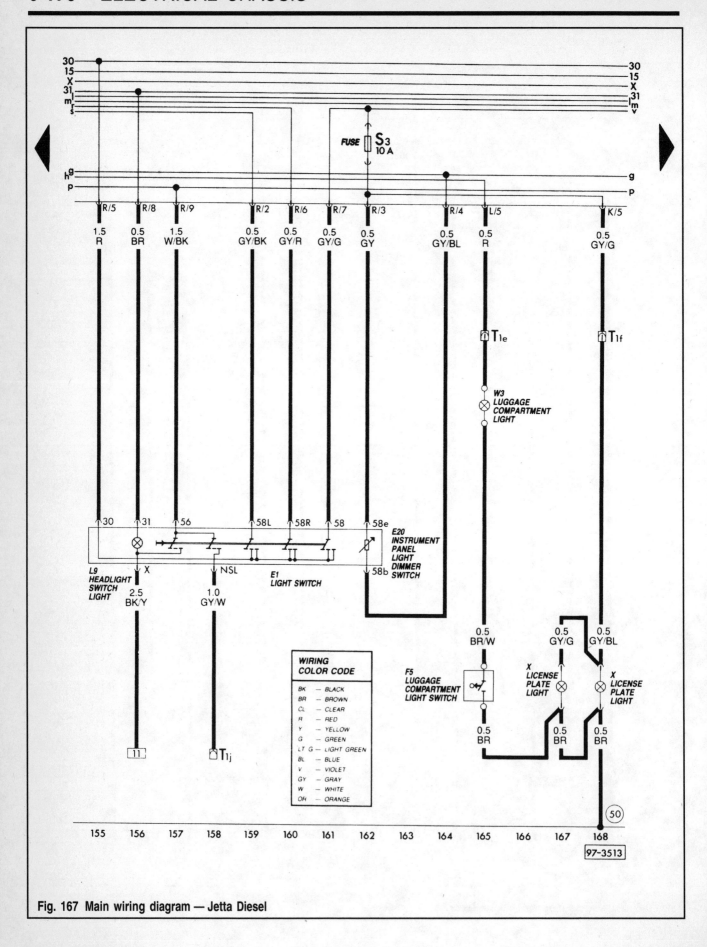

Fig. 167 Main wiring diagram — Jetta Diesel

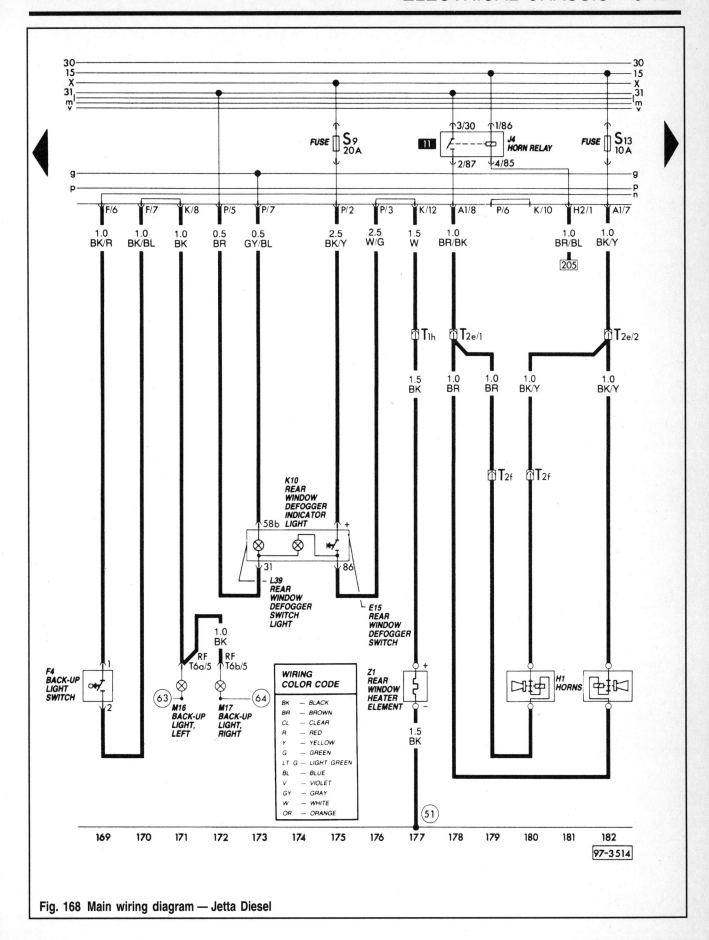

Fig. 168 Main wiring diagram — Jetta Diesel

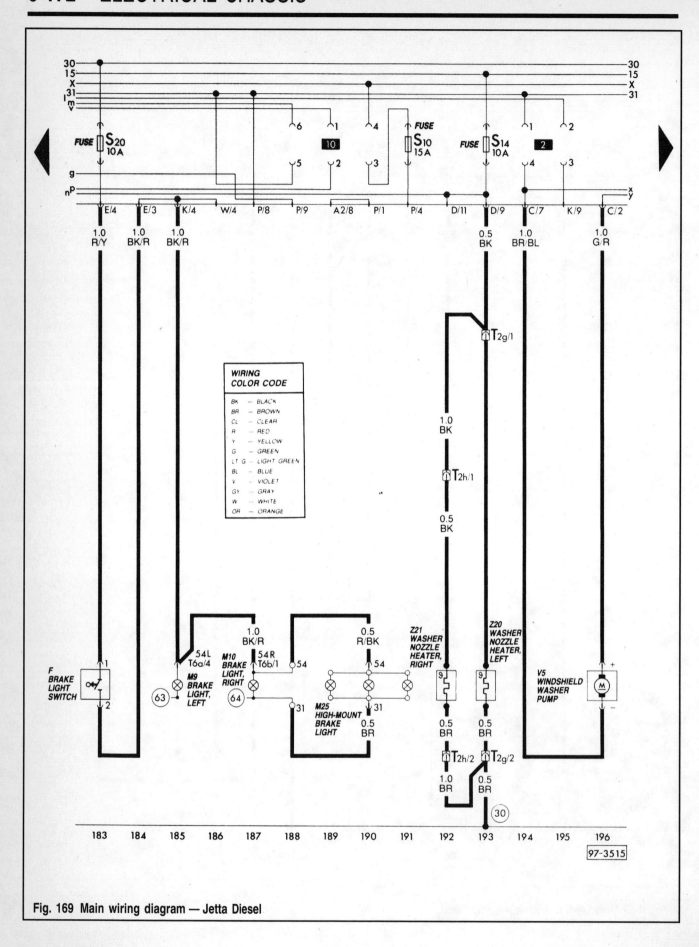

Fig. 169 Main wiring diagram — Jetta Diesel

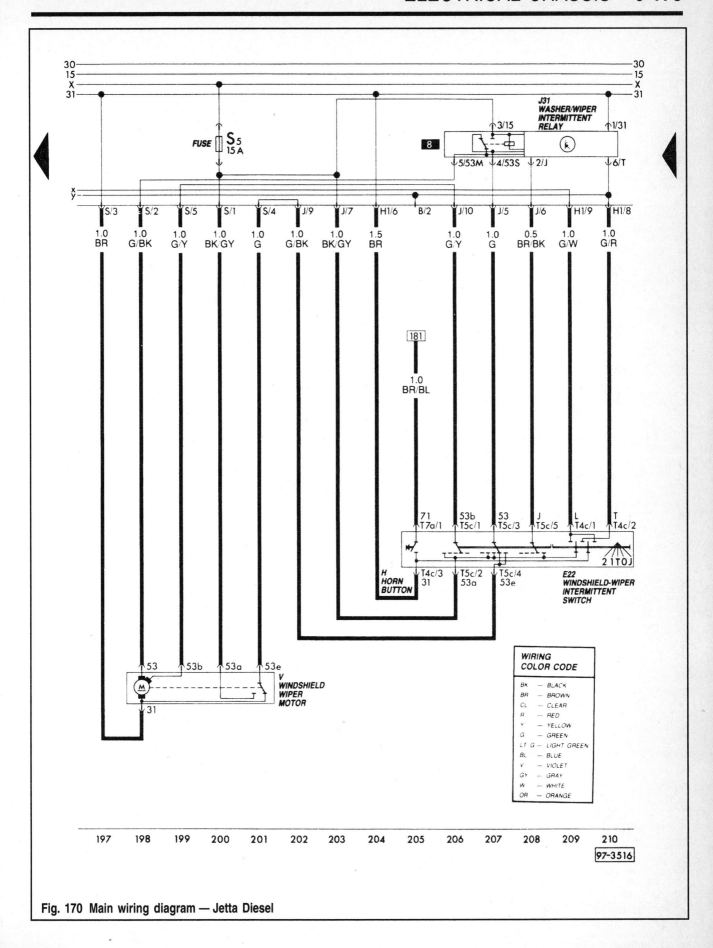

Fig. 170 Main wiring diagram — Jetta Diesel

Description	Current track
Automatic Transmission Console Light, L19	5
Back-Up Light, Left, M16	1
Back-Up Light, Right, M17	3
Fuse, S14	14
Park/Neutral Position (PNP) Switch, E17	7-13
Shift Lock Control Module, J221	19-26
Shift Lock Solenoid, N110	19
Starter, B	34-35
Starting Interlock Relay, J207	31-39

Wire connectors

T1 — single, behind fuse/relay panel
T1a — single, behind fuse/relay panel
T1b — single, behind fuse/relay panel
T1c — single, behind fuse/relay panel
T1d — single, behind fuse/relay panel
T1e — single, behind fuse/relay panel
T1f — single, behind fuse/relay panel
T1g — single, behind fuse/relay panel
T1h — single, behind fuse/relay panel
T1i — single, behind fuse/relay panel
T2 — double, below transmission shift lever cover
T2a — double, on automatic shiftlock solenoid
T3 — three-point, below transmission shift lever cover
T4 — four-point, behind fuse/relay panel
T6 — six-point, below transmission shift lever cover
T6a — six-point, on left taillight
T6b — six-point, on right taillight
T6c — six-point, near transmission selector lever
T8 — eight-point, on radio
T9 — nine-point, on starting interlock relay
T28 — twenty eight-point, on instrument cluster

Ground connections

- (30) — ground connection, -1-, near fuse/relay panel
- (54) — ground connection, on rear apron
- (63) — ground connection, on left taillight bulb holder
- (64) — ground connection, on right taillight bulb holder
- (102) — ground connection, in transmission wiring harness

Welded wiring harness points

- (U5) — wire connection -2- (15), in automatic transmission wiring harness

Fig. 171 Automatic shiftlock — Jetta

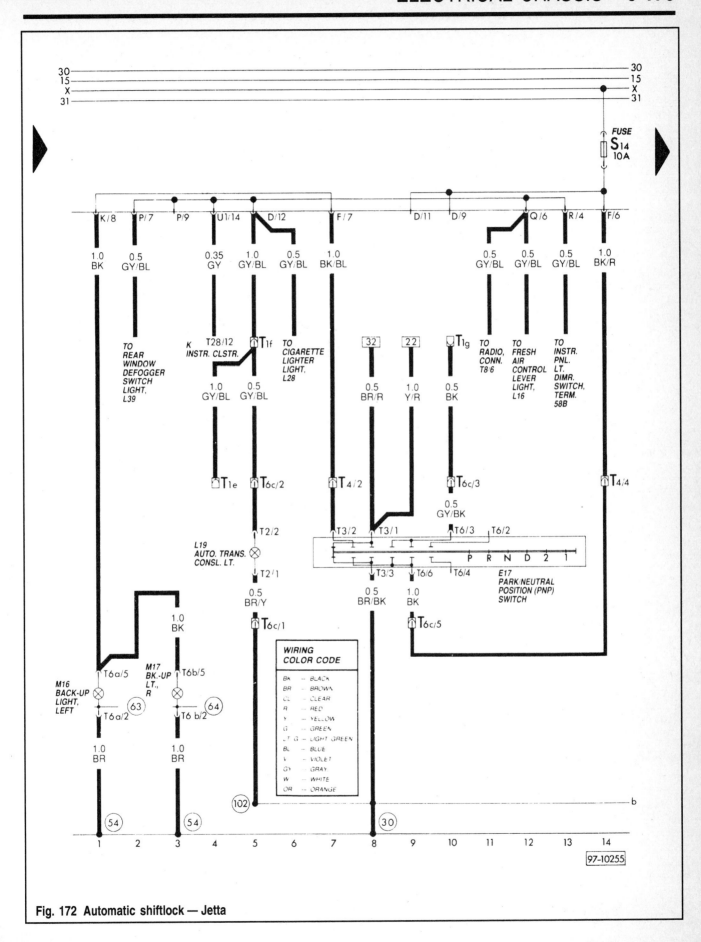

Fig. 172 Automatic shiftlock — Jetta

97-10255

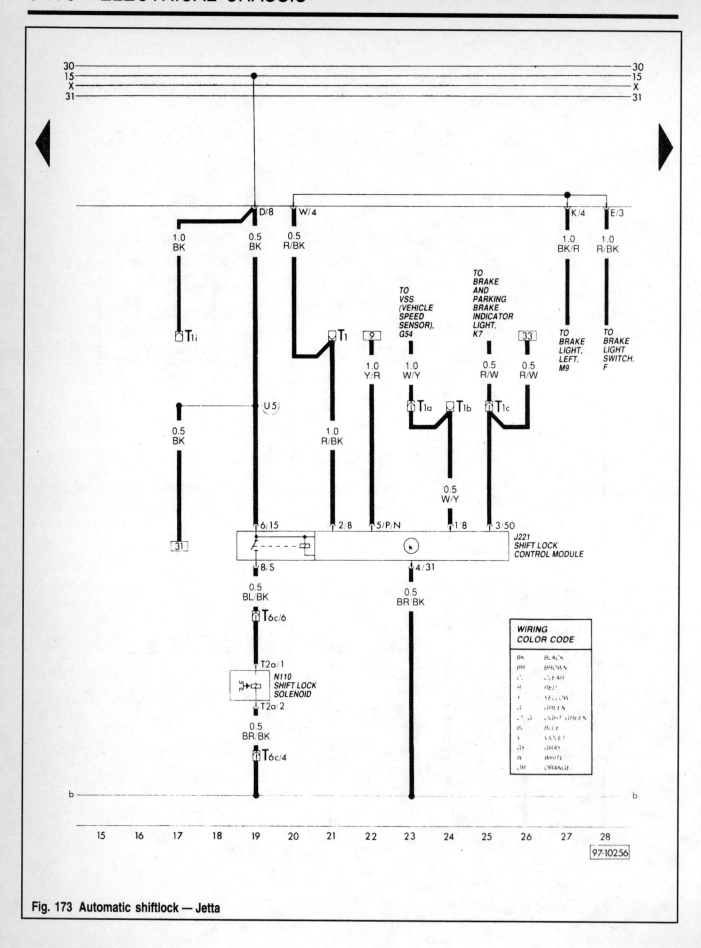

Fig. 173 Automatic shiftlock — Jetta

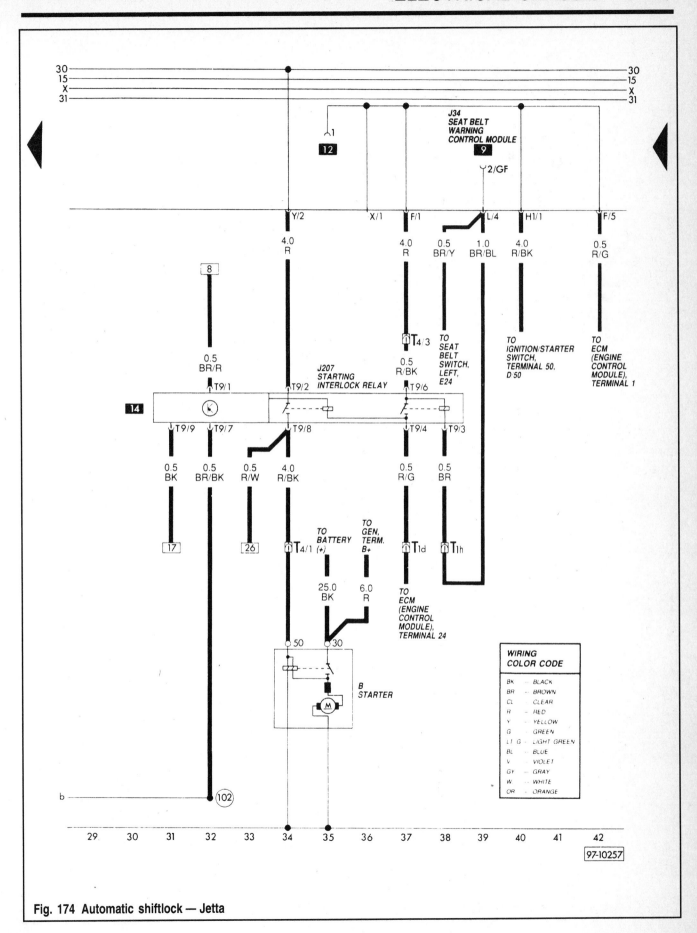

Fig. 174 Automatic shiftlock — Jetta

WIRING COLOR CODE

BK	—	BLACK
BR	—	BROWN
CL	—	CLEAR
R	—	RED
Y	—	YELLOW
G	—	GREEN
LT G	—	LIGHT GREEN
BL	—	BLUE
V	—	VIOLET
GY	—	GRAY
W	—	WHITE
OR	—	ORANGE

97-10257

Description	Current track
A/C compressor clutch, N25	41
A/C evaporator temperature switch, E33	11
A/C refrigerant high pressure switch, F23	27
A/C refrigerant low pressure switch, F73	41
A/C relay. J32	9-13
A/C switch, E35	2-6
A/C thermoswitch, F45	39-41
Coolant fan fuse. S42	25
Fresh air blower, V2	5
Fresh air blower series resistance. N23	2-5
Fresh air blower switch, E9	2-5
Fuse. S6	1
Fuse. S23	7
Fuse. S19	35
Overheat fuse. S24	5
Radiator cooling fan, V7	19-23
Radiator cooling fan relay, (2nd speed), J280	21-25
Radiator cooling fan relay, (3rd speed), J282	15-17
Radiator cooling fan thermoswitch, F18	33-36

Wire connectors

T1a — single, behind instrument panel
T1c — single, behind instrument panel
T2 — double, in engine compartment
T2a — double, behind instrument panel
T3 — three-point, on radiator fan shroud
T3a — three-point, behind instrument panel
T4 — four-point, on radiator fan shroud
T5a — five-point, behind instrument panel
T5b — five-point, behind instrument panel

Ground connections

(30) — near fuse/relay panel
(80) — in instrument panel wiring harness
(119) — in headlight wiring harness

Welded wiring harness points

(K20) — plus connection (30), in radiator fan wiring harness
(K21) — wire connection, in radiator fan wiring harness
(K22) — wire connection, in radiator fan wiring harness
(K24) — wire connection, in radiator fan wiring harness
(L9) — wire connection, in A/C wiring harness
(L10) — wire connection in A/C wiring harness

Fig. 175 Air conditioning — Jetta Diesel

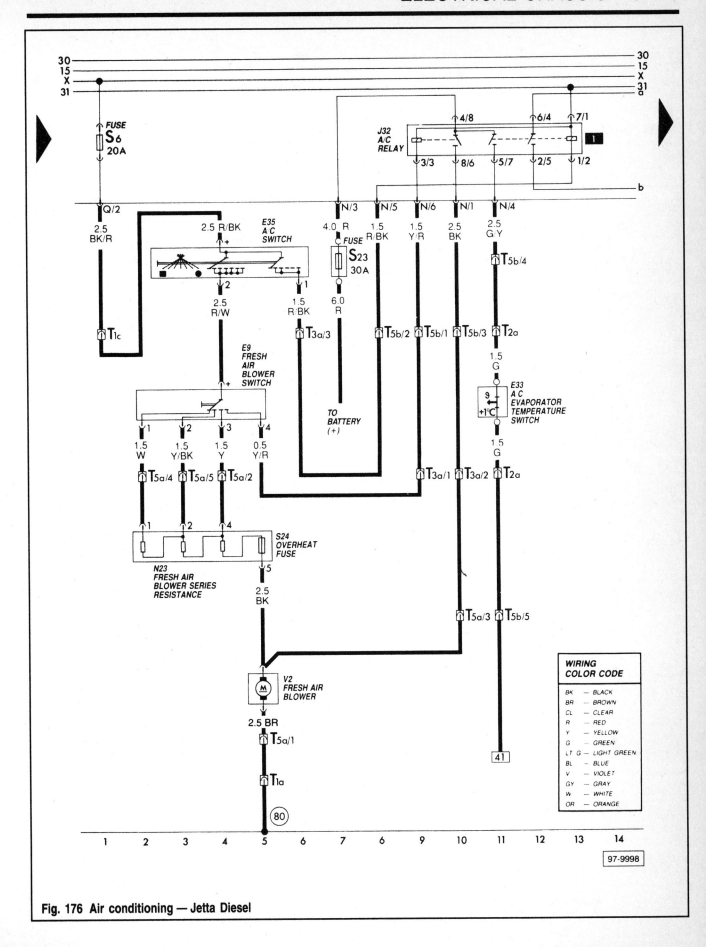

Fig. 176 Air conditioning — Jetta Diesel

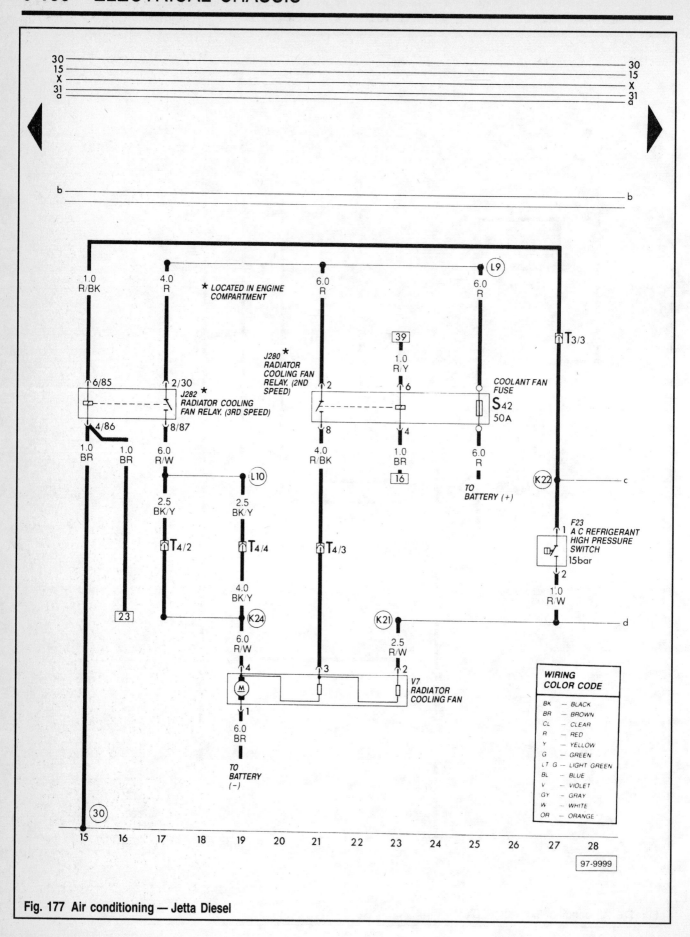

Fig. 177 Air conditioning — Jetta Diesel

AUTOMATIC TRANSAXLE
ADJUSTMENTS 7-14
AXLE SHAFT (HALFSHAFT) 7-17
FLUID PAN AND STRAINER 7-14
IDENTIFICATION 7-14
TRANSAXLE 7-16
CLUTCH
ADJUSTMENT 7-12
CLUTCH CABLE 7-12
CLUTCH PEDAL 7-12

DRIVEN DISC AND PRESSURE
PLATE 7-13
MANUAL TRANSAXLE
ADJUSTMENTS 7-2
AXLE SHAFT (HALFSHAFT) 7-11
BACK-UP LIGHT SWITCH 7-2
TRANSAXLE 7-3
TRANSAXLE 7-4
TRANSAXLE IDENTIFICATION 7-2

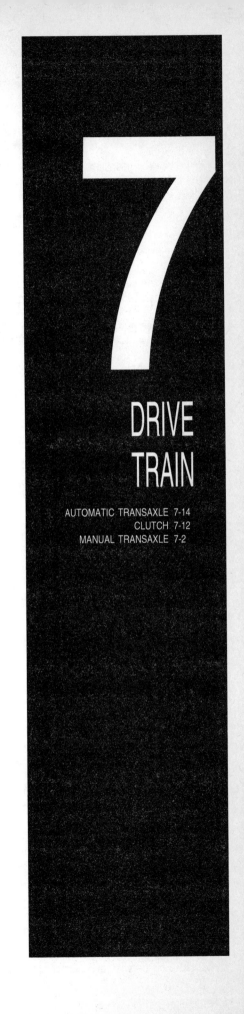

7

DRIVE TRAIN

AUTOMATIC TRANSAXLE 7-14
CLUTCH 7-12
MANUAL TRANSAXLE 7-2

MANUAL TRANSAXLE

Transaxle Identification

The transaxle is identified by a letter code that is stamped into the case near the top of the bellhousing. The first two or three digits are the transaxle code and the remaining numbers are the build date: day, month and year. The letter code indicates details about the transaxle such as the engine it goes with and the gear ratios. This code should also appear on the model identification label in the luggage compartment.

There is also a three digit type number stamped into the housing near the final drive output flange to identify the housing. All manual transaxles are type 020.

Adjustments

SHIFT LINKAGE

◆ **See Figures 1, 2, 4 and 5**

If the shift linkage has never been disconnected, adjustment may not be necessary. Check the condition of the engine/transaxle mounts and make sure the linkage fasteners are secure. If the linkage feels spongy or if it is difficult to put the transaxle into first or reverse, check the condition of the main rod bushing. This is a plastic bearing protected by a rubber boot just behind the shift rod clamp. On Cabriolet, there is a rubber boot around the bushing. Peel back the boot and make sure the nuts and bolts are still secure. If the bushing is broken or worn, it should be replaced. Lightly lubricate the bearing with a light silicone grease and fit the boot into place. Try shifting gears again before deciding to adjust the linkage.

Cabriolet

1. Remove the shift lever knob and the shifter boot.
2. There are 2 holes in the lever bearing plate that should be aligned with the holes in the mounting flange on the body. If necessary, loosen the bolts and move the bearing plate to align the holes.
3. If shifting is still spongy, put the transaxle in neutral and loosen the clamp on the shifter rod. Make sure the rod moves easily in the clamp.
4. Remove the boot protecting the bottom of the shift lever assembly.
5. Move the shift lever so the shift finger is centered in the lock-out plate.
6. Move the lever so the finger is 15mm (9/16 inch) from the plate, then tighten the clamp. If shifting is still difficult, reduce dimension A to 13mm (1/2 inch).

Golf and Jetta

A special alignment tool is made for adjusting the side-to-side position of the shift lever. On vehicles made after January

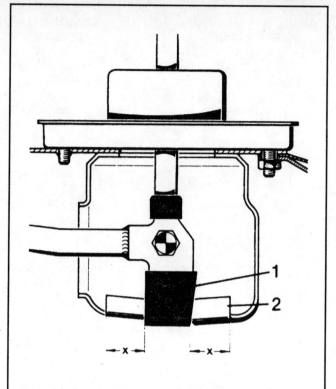

Fig. 1 Shift finger (1) should be centered in the lock-out plate (2) — Cabriolet

1991, the shift lever is equipped with an eccentric for fine adjustment.

1. Make sure the vehicle is on level ground and place the transaxle into neutral.
2. Under the vehicle, loosen the clamp on the shifter rod. Make sure the shifter lever moves freely on the shifter rod.
3. Remove the shifter knob and the boot.
4. Position the gauge alignment tool VW- 3104 on the shifting mechanism (lock it in place). Torque the clamp bolt to 19 ft. lbs. (25 Nm) and remove the tool.
5. When the shifter is in first gear, dimension **a** should be 1.0-1.5mm(0.040-0.060 inches) and the gears must engage smoothly when the engine is running.
6. If there is an eccentric adjustment, it can be used to make a fine adjustment of dimension **a** with the shifter in first gear.

Back-Up Light Switch

REMOVAL & INSTALLATION

The back-up light switch includes the fifth gear switch used by the up-shift light. It is mounted to the selector shaft housing on top of the transaxle, secured with 2 bolts and sealed with an O-ring.

1. Make sure the transaxle is in neutral.

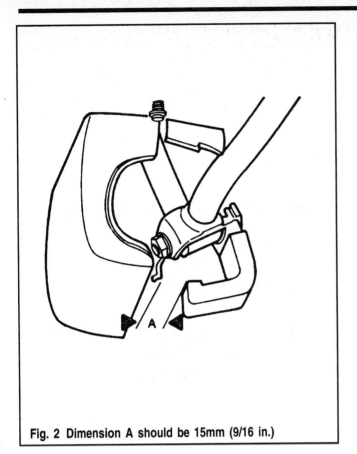

Fig. 2 Dimension A should be 15mm (9/16 in.)

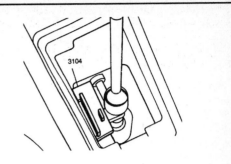

Fig. 4 Special tool used to adjust linkage — Golf and Jetta

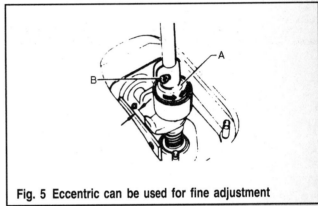

Fig. 5 Eccentric can be used for fine adjustment

2. Disconnect the wiring and remove the bolts to remove the switch. Be careful not to loose the O-ring or bolt bushings.

3. Fit the bushings and O-ring onto the switch and install it onto the transaxle. Torque the bolts to 7 ft. lbs. (10 Nm) and connect the wiring.

Transaxle

REMOVAL & INSTALLATION

Cabriolet

➡**If equipped with electronically theft-protected radio, obtain the security code before disconnecting the battery.**

1. Remove the battery.
2. Disconnect the backup light switch connector and the speedometer cable from the transaxle. Plug the speedometer cable hole.
3. Turn the crankshaft to align the timing marks to TDC.
4. To disconnect the shift linkage, pry open the ball joint ends and remove both selector rods. Remove the pin, disconnect the relay rod and put the pin back in the hole on the rod for safe keeping.
5. Raise and safely support the vehicle and remove the front wheels. Connect the engine sling tool VW-10-222A or equivalent, to the loop in the cylinder head and just take the

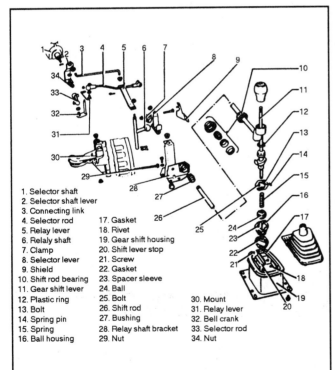

1. Selector shaft
2. Selector shaft lever
3. Connecting link
4. Selector rod
5. Relay lever
6. Relaly shaft
7. Clamp
8. Selector lever
9. Shield
10. Shift rod bearing
11. Gear shift lever
12. Plastic ring
13. Bolt
14. Spring pin
15. Spring
16. Ball housing
17. Gasket
18. Rivet
19. Gear shift housing
20. Shift lever stop
21. Screw
22. Gasket
23. Spacer sleeve
24. Ball
25. Bolt
26. Shift rod
27. Bushing
28. Relay shaft bracket
29. Nut
30. Mount
31. Relay lever
32. Bell crank
33. Selector rod
34. Nut

Fig. 3 Shift linkage assembly on Golf and Jetta, Cabriolet similar

weight of the engine off the mounts. Do not try to support the engine from below.

6. Remove the drain plug and drain the oil from the transaxle.

7. Detach the clutch cable from the linkage and remove it from the transaxle case.

8. Remove the starter and front engine mount. On 16V engines, remove the engine damper.

9. Remove the small cover behind the right halfshaft flange and remove the clutch cover plate.

10. Disconnect the halfshafts from the drive flanges and hang them up with wire. Do not let them hang by the outer CV-joint or the joint may come apart.

11. Remove the long center bolt from the left side transaxle mount.

12. Remove the entire rear mount assembly from the body and differential housing.

13. Lower the engine hoist enough to let the left mount free of the body and remove the mount from the transaxle.

14. Place a support jack under the transaxle, remove all the transaxle-to-engine bolts and carefully pry the transaxle away from the engine. Lower the transaxle from under the vehicle.

To install:

15. Coat the input shaft lightly with molybdenum grease and carefully fit the transaxle onto the engine. If necessary, put the transaxle in any gear and turn an output flange to align the input shaft spline with the clutch spline.

16. Install the engine-to-transaxle bolts and torque to 55 ft. lbs. (75 Nm).

17. When installing the mounts to the transaxle, torque the bolts to 33 ft. lbs. (45 Nm). Install but do not torque the bolts that go into the rubber mounts.

18. Install the starter and front mount.

19. With all mounts installed and the transaxle safely in the vehicle, allow some slack in the lifting equipment. With the vehicle safely supported, shake the engine/transaxle as a unit to settle it in the mounts. Torque all mounting bolts, starting at the rear and working forward. Torque the rubber mount bolts to 25 ft. lbs. (35 Nm). Torque the front mount bolts to 38 ft. lbs. (52 Nm).

20. Install the halfshafts and torque the bolts to 33 ft. lbs. (45 Nm). Install the clutch cover plates.

21. Connect the shift linkage and clutch cable and adjust as required.

22. Complete the remaining installation and refill the transaxle with oil.

Golf and Jetta

→**If equipped with electronically theft-protected radio, obtain the security code before disconnecting the battery.**

1. Remove the battery.

2. Disconnect the backup light switch connector and the speedometer cable from the transaxle; plug the speedometer cable hole.

3. Remove the upper engine-to-transaxle bolts.

4. Remove the 3 right side engine mount bolts, between the engine and firewall.

5. To disconnect the shift linkage, pry open the ball joint ends and remove the shift and relay shaft rods.

6. Remove the center bolt from the left transaxle mount.

7. Raise and safely support the vehicle and remove the front wheels. Connect the engine sling tool VW-10-222A or equivalent, to the loop in the cylinder head and just take the weight of the engine off the mounts. On the 16V engine, the idle stabilizer valve must be removed to attach the tool. Do not try to support the engine from below.

8. Remove the drain plug and drain the oil from the transaxle.

9. Remove the left inner fender liner.

10. Disconnect the halfshafts from the inner drive flanges and hang them from the body.

11. Remove the clutch cover plate and the small plate behind the right halfshaft flange.

12. Remove the starter and front engine mount.

13. Disconnect the clutch cable and remove it from the transaxle housing.

14. Place a jack under the transaxle and remove the last bolts holding it to the engine. Remove the remaining transaxle mount bolts and mounts.

15. Carefully pry the transaxle away from the engine and lower it from the vehicle.

To install:

16. Coat the input shaft lightly with molybdenum grease and carefully fit the transaxle in place. If necessary, put the transaxle in any gear and turn an output flange to align the input shaft spline with the clutch spline.

17. Install the engine-to-transaxle bolts and torque to 55 ft. lbs. (75 Nm).

18. When installing the mounts to the transaxle, torque the rear bracket-to-engine bolts and the transaxle support bolts to 18 ft. lbs. (25 Nm). Torque the left bracket-to-transaxle bolts to 25 ft. lbs. (35 Nm) and the remaining mounting bolts to 44 ft. lbs. (60 Nm). Install but do not torque the bolts that go into the rubber mounts.

19. Install the starter and front mount.

20. With all mounts installed and the transaxle safely in the vehicle, allow some slack in the lifting equipment. With the vehicle safely supported, shake the engine/transaxle as a unit to settle it in the mounts. Torque all mounting bolts, starting at the rear and working forward. Torque the bolts that go into the rubber mounts to 44 ft. lbs. (60 Nm).

21. Install the halfshafts and torque the bolts to 33 ft. lbs. (45 Nm). Install the clutch cover plates.

22. Connect the shift linkage and clutch cable and adjust as required.

23. Install the inner fender and complete the remaining installation. Refill the transaxle with oil.

Transaxle

OVERHAUL

Cleanliness is an important factor in the overhaul of the manual transaxle. Before opening up this unit, the entire outside of the transaxle assembly should be cleaned, preferably with a high pressure washer such as a car wash spray unit. Dirt entering the transaxle internal parts will negate all the time and effort spent on the overhaul. During inspection and reassembly, all parts should be thoroughly cleaned with solvent to aid inspection. Wiping cloths and rags should not be used to dry parts. Wheel bearing grease, long used to hold thrust washers and lube parts, should not be used. Lubricate seals with clean transaxle oil and use ordinary, unmedicated petroleum jelly to hold the thrust washers and to ease the assembly of seals, since it will not leave a harmful residue as grease often will. Do not use solvent on neoprene seals, if they are to be reused, or thrust washers. Before installing bolts into aluminum parts, oil or anti-seize compound can prevent bolts from galling the aluminum but pay attention to the application. Some bolts are secured in place with a thread locking compound such as Loctite®. Snaprings should be removed and installed with proper snapring tools to avoid distorting their shape. This will help insure proper seating when installed. Due to the large number of alloy parts used in this transaxle, torque specifications should be strictly observed. Care should be taken to reuse fasteners in their original locations.

Gear Case, Input Shaft and Pinion Shaft

DISASSEMBLY

▶ See Figures 6, 7, 8 and 9

➡The 5th gear synchronizer bolt and all circlips should be replaced any time they are removed. The 3rd gear circlip is used to adjust end play and comes in different thicknesses. The input shaft used with 8 valve engines is different from 16V engines and they cannot be interchanged.

1. Mount the transaxle assembly in a holding fixture.
2. Mount a bar with a bolt and spacer across the bellhousing to support the mainshaft.
3. Remove the cap from the drive flange and discard.
4. The left drive flange must be removed to disassemble the case. If the differential is to be removed, both drive flanges must be removed. There is a strong spring pushing the drive flange out against the circlip. If the special removal tool is not available:
   a. Locate a heavy bar that fits across the flange but leaves room around the side to access the circlip. Drill a 0.470 inch (12mm) hole through the center.
   b. Locate a long bolt or threaded rod that fits the M10 threads in the center of the output shaft.
   c. Use the bar and bolt to draw the flange down against the spring just enough to unload the circlip.
   d. Remove the circlip, then remove the bolt to remove the output flange.

➡The left and right drive flanges are different. Label them for proper assembly and keep them together with the tapered rings.

5. Remove the end cover and gasket. DO NOT remove the selector rod that has the small spring on the end. The selector assembly will fall apart inside the transaxle.
6. Remove the back-up light switch.
7. Remove the selector shaft detent plungers. Remove the cover, spring and selector shaft.

8. Use a screwdriver to move both front selector forks to engage 5th and reverse at the same time. This will lock the gear train so it cannot turn.
9. Remove the bolt from the center of the 5th gear synchro assembly. The bolt is very tight and is held in with thread locking compound. Make sure the transaxle is securely supported.
10. Pry the locking plate up and remove it. Unscrew the selector tube to remove the shift fork and synchro as an assembly. The tube does not move up or down, the shift fork will move up the tube. Be careful not to remove the selector rod.
11. Remove the circlip from 5th gear. On the 16V engine, 5th gear is secured with a plate. It may be necessary to use a puller to remove 5th gear.
12. Remove the reverse shaft fixing bolt from the side of the case.
13. Use an M6 12 point socket to remove the 4 bolts holding the input shaft bearing retainer to the rear of the case.
14. Remove the bolts holding the case halves together.
15. Secure a puller to the rear cover bolt holes so the bolt contacts the input shaft. Carefully press the housing off the rear bearing and lift the housing away from the transaxle. There may be a shim on top of the bearing.
16. To remove the shift forks, lift the selector rod slightly and remove the shift forks as an assembly.
17. To remove the input shaft, remove the 4th gear circlip. Lift out 4th gear and the input shaft together.
18. To remove the pinion shaft, the gears must be removed first. Remove the 3rd gear circlip and lift 3rd gear, 2nd gear, the bearings and the synchro assembly off the shaft. Be sure

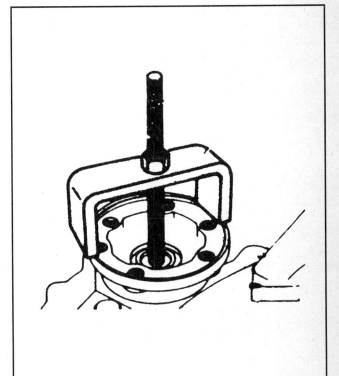

Fig. 6 The special tool for removing and installing the drive flange can be fabricated

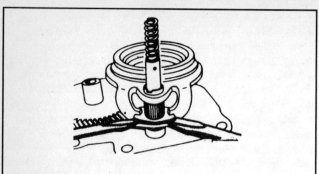

Fig. 7 Pry up the lock plate to unscrew the 5th gear shift fork

Fig. 8 The case must be pressed off the rear input shaft bearing

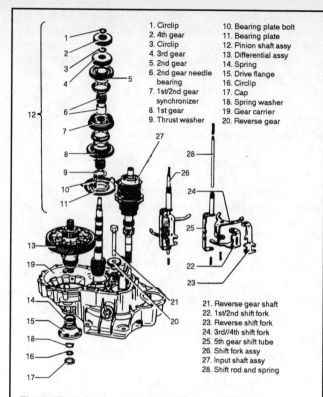

1. Circlip
2. 4th gear
3. Circlip
4. 3rd gear
5. 2nd gear
6. 2nd gear needle bearing
7. 1st/2nd gear synchronizer
8. 1st gear
9. Thrust washer
10. Bearing plate bolt
11. Bearing plate
12. Pinion shaft assy
13. Differential assy
14. Spring
15. Drive flange
16. Circlip
17. Cap
18. Spring washer
19. Gear carrier
20. Reverse gear
21. Reverse gear shaft
22. 1st/2nd shift fork
23. Reverse shift fork
24. 3rd//4th shift fork
25. 5th gear shift tube
26. Shift fork assy
27. Input shaft assy
28. Shift rod and spring

Fig. 9 The pinion shaft must be disassembled for removal

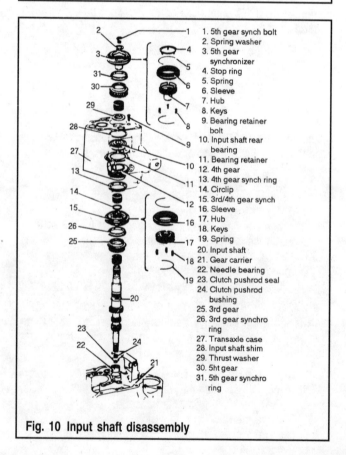

1. 5th gear synch bolt
2. Spring washer
3. 5th gear synchronizer
4. Stop ring
5. Spring
6. Sleeve
7. Hub
8. Keys
9. Bearing retainer bolt
10. Input shaft rear bearing
11. Bearing retainer
12. 4th gear
13. 4th gear synch ring
14. Circlip
15. 3rd/4th gear synch
16. Sleeve
17. Hub
18. Keys
19. Spring
20. Input shaft
21. Gear carrier
22. Needle bearing
23. Clutch pushrod seal
24. Clutch pushrod bushing
25. 3rd gear
26. 3rd gear synchro ring
27. Transaxle case
28. Input shaft shim
29. Thrust washer
30. 5ht gear
31. 5th gear synchro ring

Fig. 10 Input shaft disassembly

to place them on the bench in order, facing the same way, to ease correct assembly.

19. Remove the reverse gear and shaft.

20. Use a puller to remove the 1st gear and the 1st/2nd synchro together.

21. Remove the bolts to remove the bearing plate and the pinion shaft.

22. Third and 4th gear synchronizer must be pressed off the pinion shaft.

23. Before disassembling the synchronizers, measure the wear at dimension **a** with a feeler gauge. If the gap is 0.020 inches (0.5mm) or less, the synchronizer ring must be replaced.

24. The bearings can be removed from the shafts and the case with the appropriate pullers. If bearings are removed,

they should be replaced. Pay attention to any shims or spacers and make sure they are labeled for correct installation.

ASSEMBLY

▶ **See Figures 11, 12, 13, 14, 15, 16, 17 and 18**

➡**If the transaxle case, ring gear or the side bearings are replaced, adjust differential side bearing pre-load before assembling the transaxle.**

1. If none of these items is being replaced, go to Step 6. If new bearings are being installed, heat the bearing to about 212°F (100°C) and press it onto the shaft until it is fully seated. Be sure to replace the race in the housing.

2. Install a 0.65mm (0.025 inch) shim into the housing and temporarily install the bearing outer race. If this shim is not on hand, a thicker shim may be used but it must be small enough to allow some pinion shaft end play.

3. Set the pinion shaft into place. Do not oil the bearings or turn the shaft. Fit the outer race onto the smaller bearing, install the bearing plate and torque the bolts to 30 ft. lbs. (40 Nm).

4. Attach a dial indicator to the case and measure the end play of the shaft. Be careful not to turn the shaft or the bearings will settle and cause an incorrect reading.

5. The correct bearing shim size is obtained by adding the end-play measurement, the starting shim and a bearing pre-load of 0.20mm (0.008 inches). For example:

    Starting shim: 0.65mm (0.025 inches)
    End play: 0.30mm (0.012 inches)
    Pre-load: 0.20mm (0.008 inches)
    Correct shim: 15mm (0.045 inches)

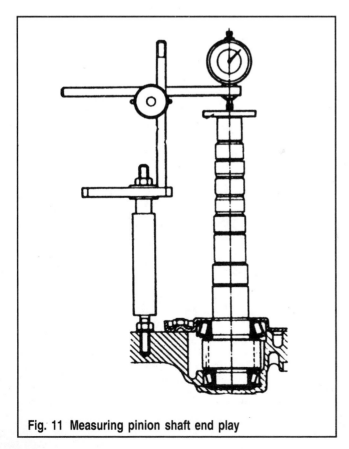

Fig. 11 Measuring pinion shaft end play

6. Shims are available in sizes from 0.65mm-1.40mm (0.025-0.055 in). Install the correct shim and oil the bearings before installing the pinion shaft.

7. Install the bearing plate and torque the bolts to 30 ft. lbs. (40 Nm). When the bearing pre-load is correct, it should require 5-13 inch lbs. to turn the shaft with new bearings or at least 3 inch lbs. with used bearings.

8. Install the 1st gear thrust washer with the shoulder facing the bearing plate.

9. If the synchronizer was disassembled:

    a. The original first gear synchronizer ring has a space with 3 teeth missing. The replacement ring has a full set of teeth and dimension **a** will be 0.042-0.066 inches (1.1-1.7mm).

    b. When assembling the 1st/2nd gear synchronizer, the groove in the hub must face first gear. The groove may be on the face or the edge of the teeth.

    c. The bent tab on the end of the key retainer spring must fit into one of the keys.

10. Install the needle bearing. The synchronizer hub should be heated to about 250°F (120°C) and must be pressed onto the shaft. Align the synchro ring grooves with the keys.

11. Install the reverse gear shaft and the gear.

12. If the 2nd gear needle bearing was removed, the race must be pressed or driven onto the shaft. Install the bearing, synchronizer assembly and 2nd and 3rd gears.

13. Install the 3rd gear circlip and make sure there is no gear end play. If the gear moves on the shaft or if the circlip cannot be installed, there are circlips available in thicknesses from 0.098-0.118 inches (2.5-3.0mm).

14. When assembling the input shaft, the new third gear synchronizer ring dimension **a** is 0.045-0.068 inches (1.15-1.75mm). The groove in the outer teeth must be towards fourth gear, the chamfer on the splines must be towards third gear.

15. If the input shaft has not been disassembled, remove the ball bearing with a puller that contacts only the inner race.

16. Install the input shaft assembly.

17. Install 4th gear and the circlip onto the pinion shaft.

18. Install the original ball bearing shim and press the bearing into the case. The wide shoulder on the inner race faces 4th gear.

19. Install the bearing retainer plate. Apply a thread locking compound to the bolts and torque them to 11 ft. lbs. (15 Nm).

20. Install the shift fork assembly.

21. Temporarily install the bolt into the reverse gear shaft. Turn the shaft so the bolt is evenly spaced between the case bolt holes, then remove the bolt.

22. Install a new gasket or apply a silicone sealer to the gear carrier.

23. Make sure the input shaft is supported at the bell housing. Slip the case onto the carrier and carefully drive the inner race of the ball bearing onto the input shaft.

24. Install a new gasket and start the bolt into the reverse gear shaft.

25. Install the case bolts and torque them to 18 ft. lbs. (25 Nm). Torque the reverse shaft bolt to 18 ft. lbs. (25 Nm).

26. Install the drive flange with a new circlip.

27. Heat 5th gear to about 212°F (100°C) and install it onto the shaft. Install the thrust washer and circlip.

28. Fit the synchronizer assembly onto the shaft and thread the tube up through the fork. The tube should project 0.197

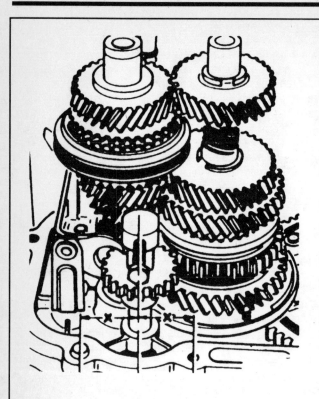

Fig. 12 The reverse shaft bolt must be evenly spaced between the case bolt holes

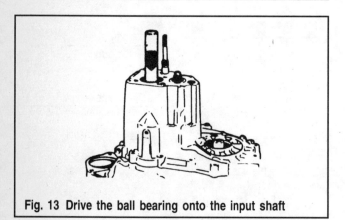

Fig. 13 Drive the ball bearing onto the input shaft

inches (5.0mm) above the fork. Don't install the locking plate yet.

29. Turn the input shaft at the input end and operate the shift forks to make sure the gears engage. DO NOT remove the shift rod from the tube or the fork assembly will fall apart inside the transaxle.

30. Shift the transaxle into 5th and reverse at the same time to lock it.

31. Apply a thread locking compound to a new synchronizer hub bolt, install the bolt and torque it to 111 ft. lbs. (150 Nm).

32. Install the selector shaft assembly, spring and cap. Torque the cap to 37 ft. lbs. (50 Nm).

33. Turn the input shaft while moving the selector shaft in and out, left and right to check engagement of all the gears.

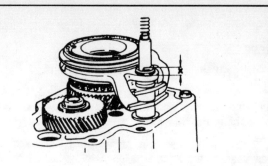

Fig. 14 The tube must project 0.197 in. (5mm) above the fork

34. Before installing the shift tube locking plate, check the gear alignment:

a. Pull the selector shaft out and turn to the left to select 5th gear.

b. Lift slightly on the shift fork to take up any free play in the sleeve.

c. Measure the overlap of the sleeve on 5th gear. The sleeve must be 0.039 inches (1.0mm) down over the gear. Adjust the sleeve position with the selector tube.

35. Slip 2 wrenches under the fork and press a new locking plate onto the tube.

36. Install the clutch pushrod.

37. Use a new gasket and install the end cover. Torque the bolts to 18 ft. lbs. (25 Nm).

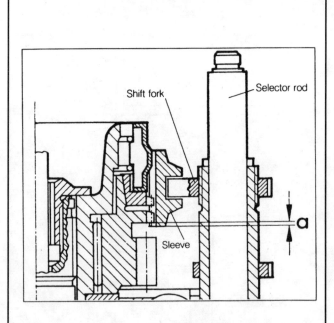

Fig. 15 The sleeve must be 0.039 in. (1.0mm) below the gear teeth

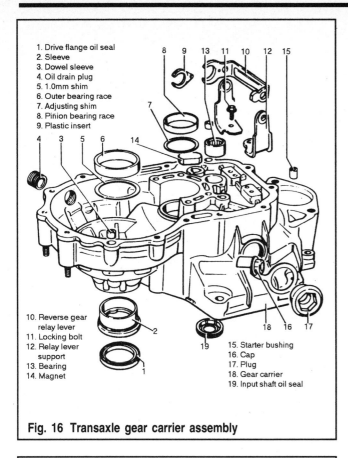

1. Drive flange oil seal
2. Sleeve
3. Dowel sleeve
4. Oil drain plug
5. 1.0mm shim
6. Outer bearing race
7. Adjusting shim
8. Pinion bearing race
9. Plastic insert
10. Reverse gear relay lever
11. Locking bolt
12. Relay lever support
13. Bearing
14. Magnet
15. Starter bushing
16. Cap
17. Plug
18. Gear carrier
19. Input shaft oil seal

Fig. 16 Transaxle gear carrier assembly

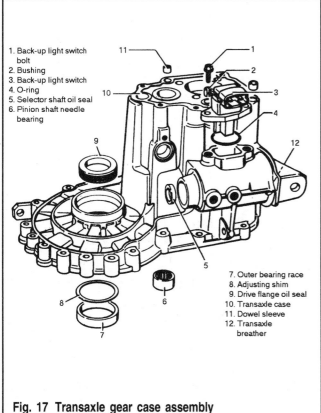

1. Back-up light switch bolt
2. Bushing
3. Back-up light switch
4. O-ring
5. Selector shaft oil seal
6. Pinion shaft needle bearing
7. Outer bearing race
8. Adjusting shim
9. Drive flange oil seal
10. Transaxle case
11. Dowel sleeve
12. Transaxle breather

Fig. 17 Transaxle gear case assembly

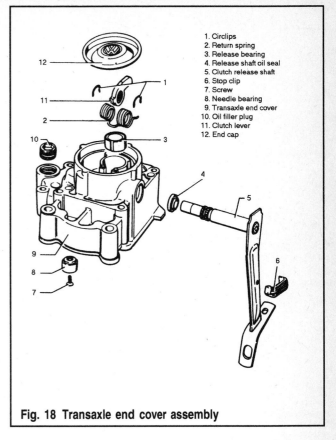

1. Circlips
2. Return spring
3. Release bearing
4. Release shaft oil seal
5. Clutch release shaft
6. Stop clip
7. Screw
8. Needle bearing
9. Transaxle end cover
10. Oil filler plug
11. Clutch lever
12. End cap

Fig. 18 Transaxle end cover assembly

Differential

DISASSEMBLY

▶ See Figure 19

➡If there are circlip grooves on the differential pinion shaft, install circlips even if the differential has not been disassembled.

1. To remove the differential, remove both drive flanges and the pinion shaft.
2. The differential pinion gears can be removed by removing the shafts. If there are cups holding the pinion shaft in place, use a hack saw to remove them.
3. If the ring gear must be removed, drill half way through the rivets with a 1/4 inch (6mm) drill bit. Use a 15/32 inch (12mm) bit to remove the rivet heads and drive the rivets out.
4. Press the ring gear off the differential housing.
5. The side bearings can be removed with a press or puller.

ASSEMBLY

1. Before installing the ring gear, press two of the new bolts into the differential housing to use a guides.
2. Heat the ring gear to about 212°F (100°C) and press it onto the differential housing.
3. Install the rest of the bolts and nuts and torque to 52 ft. lbs. (70 Nm).
4. Heat the side bearings to about 212°F (100°C) and press them onto the differential housing.

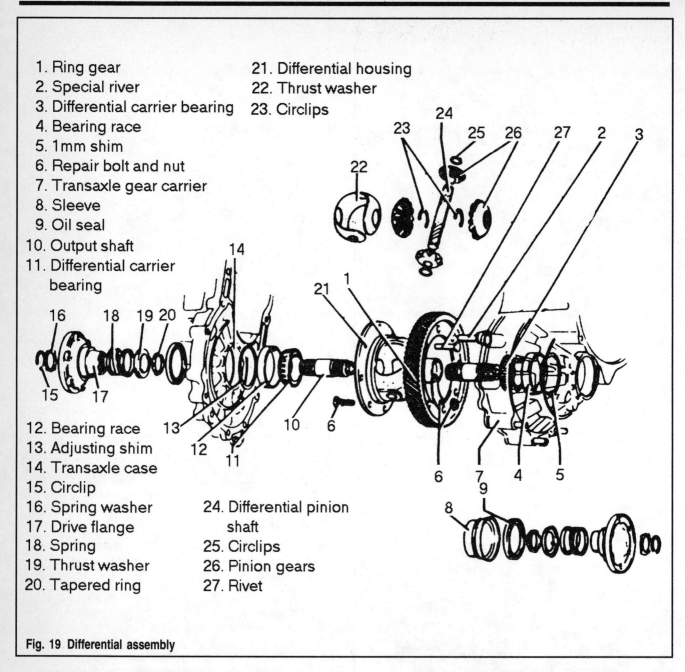

1. Ring gear
2. Special river
3. Differential carrier bearing
4. Bearing race
5. 1mm shim
6. Repair bolt and nut
7. Transaxle gear carrier
8. Sleeve
9. Oil seal
10. Output shaft
11. Differential carrier
    bearing
12. Bearing race
13. Adjusting shim
14. Transaxle case
15. Circlip
16. Spring washer
17. Drive flange
18. Spring
19. Thrust washer
20. Tapered ring
21. Differential housing
22. Thrust washer
23. Circlips
24. Differential pinion
    shaft
25. Circlips
26. Pinion gears
27. Rivet

Fig. 19 Differential assembly

5. Install the differential gears and pinion shaft and install the circlips.

ADJUSTMENT

The side bearing pre-load must be adjusted if the differential housing or side bearings have been replaced or if transaxle gear case or carrier have been replaced. If these items are all still the original components, differential adjustment is not necessary.

1. The shim under the outer bearing race in the gear carrier is always 1mm (0.039 inch) thick. Install the 1mm shim and the new outer race.

2. Install the outer race in the gear case without any shim.

3. Without lubricating the bearings or turning the differential, set the differential into the case.

4. Assemble the case, install 5 of the bolts and torque the bolts to 18 ft. lbs. (25 Nm). If a gasket is to be used for final assembly instead of silicone sealer, make sure there is a gasket installed now.

5. Secure a dial indicator to the case and pre-load it against the differential output shaft.

6. Lift the differential and measure the total free play in the case. Be sure not to turn the differential or the bearings will settle.

7. For proper bearing pre-load, the total bearing shim thickness must be 0.016 inches (0.40mm) greater than the dial indicator reading. Add the necessary shims under the bearing race in the transaxle case.

Axle Shaft (Halfshaft)

REMOVAL & INSTALLATION

▶ See Figures 20 and 21

❊❊CAUTION

The torque required to loosen the front axle nut is high enough to make the vehicle fall off of jack stands. Make sure the vehicle is on the ground when loosening or tightening the front axle nut.

1. With the vehicle on the ground, remove the front axle nut.
2. Raise and safely support vehicle and remove the front wheels.
3. Remove the ball joint clamping bolt and push the control arm down, away from the ball joint.
4. Remove the socket head bolts from the transaxle drive flange.
5. Remove the halfshaft from the drive flange and support it below the flange. Do not let it hang by the outer CV-joint or the joint may fall apart.
6. Push the halfshaft out of the hub. A wheel puller may be required.

To install:

7. Fit the halfshaft to the drive flange and install the bolts. It is not necessary to torque them yet.

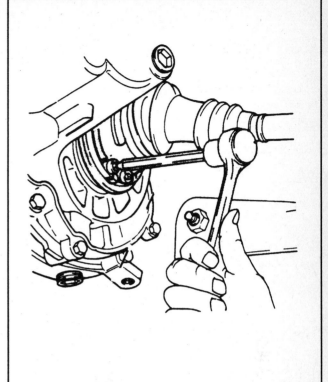

Fig. 21 A 6mm ball-end hex socket is available for removing the drive flange bolts

8. Apply a thread locking compound to the outer ¼ inch of the spline. Slip the spline through the hub and loosely install a new axle nut.
9. Assemble the ball joint and torque the nut and bolt to 37 ft. lbs. (50 Nm).
10. Install the wheel and hold it to keep the axle from turning. Torque the drive flange bolts to 33 ft. lbs. (45 Nm).
11. With the vehicle on the ground, torque the axle nut to 175 ft. lbs. (240 Nm) or Cabriolet or 195 ft. lbs. (265 Nm) on Golf and Jetta.

CV-JOINT AND BOOT OVERHAUL

▶ See Figure 22

The constant velocity joints (CV-joints) can be disassembled for cleaning and inspection but they cannot be repaired. All parts are machined to a matched tolerance and the entire CV-joint must be replaced as a unit. On Golf and Jetta, the CV-joints are different on the left and right sides and cannot be interchanged.

1. Raise and safely support the vehicle and remove the halfshaft.
2. Pry open and remove the boot clamps with a pair of wire cutters.
3. With the halfshaft securely clamped in a vise, the outer CV-joint can be removed by sharply rapping out on the joint with a plastic hammer. The joint will snap off of the circlip and slide off the axle.
4. To remove the inner joint, remove the circlip from the center and slide the joint off the axle.

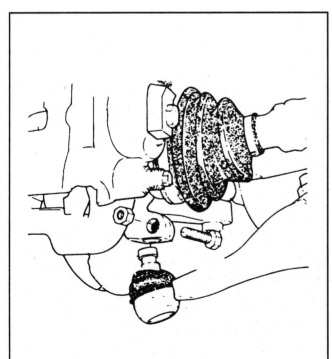

Fig. 20 Disconnect the lower ball joint to remove the halfshaft

5. Both boots can be removed after removing the CV-joint
To install:

6. Always replace both circlips and make sure the CV-joint is clean before installation. Wrap a piece of black electrical tape around the shaft splines and slip the inner clamp and the boot onto the shaft.

7. Remove the tape and install the dished washer with the concave side out so it acts as a spring pushing the CV-joint out. On the outer joint, install the thrust washer and a new circlip.

8. To install the outer joint, place it onto the spline and carefully tap straight in on the end with a plastic hammer. The joint will click into place over the circlip.

9. To install the inner joint, slide it onto the spline and push in enough to allow the circlip to fit into the groove in the axle shaft.

10. Pack the CV-joint with special CV-joint grease. DO NOT use any other type of grease.

11. Pack any remaining grease into the boot and install the clamps on the outer boot.

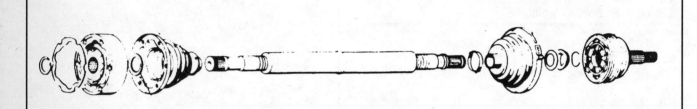

Fig. 22 CV-joint and halfshaft assembly

CLUTCH

❊❊CAUTION

The clutch driven disc contains asbestos, which has been determined to be a cancer causing agent. Never clean clutch surfaces with compressed air! Avoid inhaling dust from any clutch surface! When cleaning clutch surfaces, use a commercially available brake cleaning fluid.

Adjustment

All models are equipped with a self-adjusting clutch cable. The cable incorporates an adjustment mechanism at the transaxle end which automatically adjusts to compensate for normal clutch disc wear.

Clutch Cable

REMOVAL & INSTALLATION

➠If a new cable is being installed, the adjuster spring is retained by a strap. Remove the strap after cable installation.

1. This job requires 2 people. Depress the pedal and release several times.

2. Compress the spring located under the boot at the top of the adjuster mechanism and remove the cable at the release lever.

3. Unhook the eye from the clutch pedal and remove the cable.

4. Install the new cable onto the pedal. Compress the spring and have a helper pull the cable down and install it on the release lever.

5. Depress the clutch pedal several times to adjust the cable.

Clutch Pedal

REMOVAL & INSTALLATION

▸ See Figure 23

➠With turbo-diesel and 16V engines, the clutch pedal has an over-center spring. A special tool is required to hold the spring for removal and installation.

1. If only the over-center spring is to be removed, do not loosen the steering column. If the pedal is being removed, loosen the steering column and move it to the side.

2. Press the pedal and install the special retaining tool, 3113A.

3. Remove the clip to disconnect the cable from the pedal.

4. Remove the pin and remove the pedal from the bracket.

5. Installation is the reverse of removal. Remove the tool after installing the over-center spring.

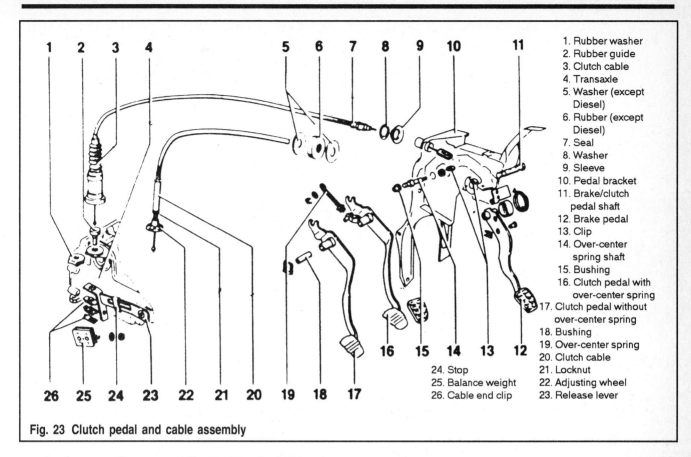

1. Rubber washer
2. Rubber guide
3. Clutch cable
4. Transaxle
5. Washer (except Diesel)
6. Rubber (except Diesel)
7. Seal
8. Washer
9. Sleeve
10. Pedal bracket
11. Brake/clutch pedal shaft
12. Brake pedal
13. Clip
14. Over-center spring shaft
15. Bushing
16. Clutch pedal with over-center spring
17. Clutch pedal without over-center spring
18. Bushing
19. Over-center spring
20. Clutch cable
21. Locknut
22. Adjusting wheel
23. Release lever
24. Stop
25. Balance weight
26. Cable end clip

Fig. 23 Clutch pedal and cable assembly

Driven Disc and Pressure Plate

REMOVAL & INSTALLATION

▶ See Figure 24

❈❈CAUTION

The clutch driven disc contains asbestos, which has been determined to be a cancer causing agent. Never clean clutch surfaces with compressed air! Avoid inhaling any dust from any clutch surface! When cleaning clutch surfaces, use a commercially available brake cleaning fluid.

This type of clutch is similar to a motorcycle clutch. The pressure plate is bolted to the crankshaft and the flywheel bolted to the pressure plate. The clutch release lever and bearing are in the left end of the transaxle. The clutch is actuated by a release rod which passes through a hollow transaxle shaft. The throwout bearing is in the transaxle and lubricated with transaxle oil.

➡NOTE: A special tool VW 547 is required to center the clutch disc.

1. Remove the transaxle.
2. Attach a toothed flywheel locking device and gradually loosen the flywheel to pressure plate bolts one or two turns at a time in a crisscross pattern to prevent distortion.
3. Remove the flywheel and the clutch disc.
4. Use a small pry bar to remove the release plate retaining ring. Remove the release plate.
5. Lock the pressure plate in place and unbolt it from the crankshaft. Loosen the bolts one or two turns at a time in a crisscross pattern to prevent distortion.
   To install:
6. Use new bolts to attach the pressure plate to the crankshaft. Use a thread locking compound and torque the bolts in a diagonal pattern to 22 ft. lbs. (30 Nm) plus 1/4 turn.
7. LIGHTLY lubricate the clutch disc splines, release plate contact surface, and pushrod socket with multipurpose grease. Install the release plate, retaining ring, and clutch disc.
8. Use special tool VW 547 or equivalent to center the clutch disc.
9. Install the flywheel, tightening the bolts one or two turns at a time in a crisscross pattern to prevent distortion. Torque the bolts to 15 ft. lbs. (20 Nm).
10. Install the transaxle.

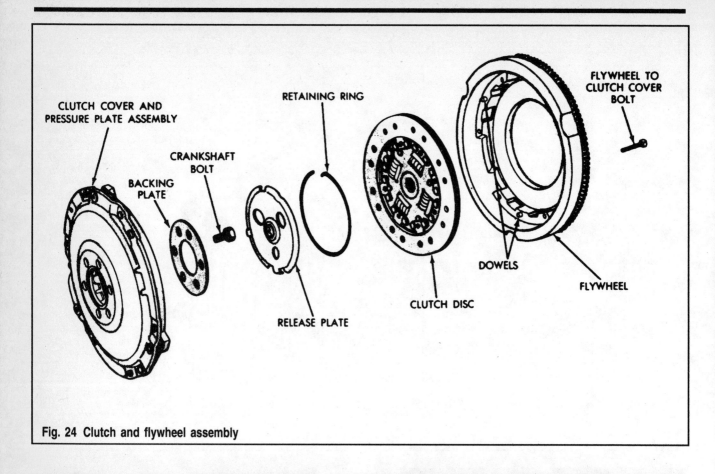

CLUTCH COVER AND PRESSURE PLATE ASSEMBLY

BACKING PLATE

CRANKSHAFT BOLT

RETAINING RING

RELEASE PLATE

CLUTCH DISC

DOWELS

FLYWHEEL

FLYWHEEL TO CLUTCH COVER BOLT

Fig. 24 Clutch and flywheel assembly

AUTOMATIC TRANSAXLE

Identification

All automatic transaxles are type 010 3-speed. If the transaxle is to be replaced, the first 2 or 3 letters on the number stamped into the torque converter housing are the transaxle code. This code describes the torque converter, gear ratios and valve body. The code also appears on the model identification label in the luggage compartment. While any type 010 automatic transaxle will fit into any model, the code describes the unit that is correct for that engine and body.

Fluid Pan and Strainer

REMOVAL & INSTALLATION

1. If equipped, remove the drain plug and let the fluid drain into a pan. If the pan has no drain plug, loosen the pan bolts until a corner of the pan can be lowered to drain the fluid.
2. Remove the pan bolts and take off the pan.
3. Discard the old gasket and clean the pan out. Be very careful not to get any threads or lint from rags into the pan.
4. The manufacturer recommends that the filter needn't be replaced unless the fluid is very dirty and burnt smelling. When replacing the strainer be careful, the specified torque for the strainer screws is only 24 inch lbs. (27 Nm).

5. Replace the pan with a new gasket and tighten the bolts, in a criss-cross pattern, to 15 ft. lbs. (20 Nm).
6. Using a long necked funnel, pour in 2 1/2 qts. (2.3L) of Dexron®II automatic transaxle fluid through the dipstick tube. Start the engine and shift through all the transaxle ranges with the car stationary. Check the level on the dipstick with the lever in Neutral. It should be up to the lower end of the dipstick. The difference between marks is 1 pint (0.23L). Add fluid as necessary, drive the car until it is warmed up and recheck the level.

Adjustments

CHECKING ADJUSTMENT

▶ See Figure 25

1. Run the engine at 1000-1200 rpm with the parking brake on and the wheels blocked.
2. Select the Reverse gear. A drop in engine speed should be noticed.
3. Select Park. Engine speed should increase. Pull the shift lever against the stop in the direction of Reverse. The engine speed should not drop (because reverse gear has not been engaged).
4. Move the shift lever to engage Reverse. Engine speed should drop as the gear engages.

5. Move the shift lever into Neutral. An increase in engine speed should be noticed.

6. Shift into Drive. A noticeable drop in engine speed should result.

7. Shift into 1. The lever must engage without having to overcome any resistance.

CABLE ADJUSTMENT

1. Warm up the engine and move the gearshift lever to Park.

2. To adjust the selector cable, loosen the cable clamp at the transaxle end and make sure the transaxle is really in Park. Tighten the clamp.

3. To adjust the throttle kick-down cable loosen the adjusting nuts and disconnect cable at the transaxle end.

4. Loosen the nuts holding the cable to the cylinder head cover. Make sure the throttle is fully closed.

5. Lightly pull the slack out of the cable without opening the throttle and tighten the adjusting against the bracket on the cylinder head cover. Tighten the locknut.

6. Connect the cable to the transaxle. With the accelerator pedal pressed to the floor, hold the transaxle lever against the kick-down stop and turn the cable adjuster to remove any slack from the cable housing.

7. Operate the accelerator several times to check for smooth movement.

NEUTRAL SAFETY/BACK-UP LIGHT SWITCH

The combination neutral start and backup light switch is mounted inside the shifter housing. The starter should operate

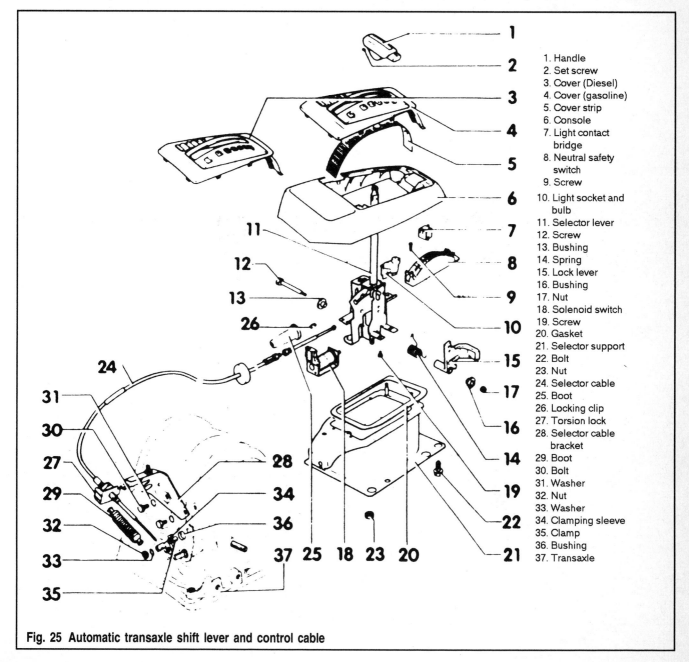

1. Handle
2. Set screw
3. Cover (Diesel)
4. Cover (gasoline)
5. Cover strip
6. Console
7. Light contact bridge
8. Neutral safety switch
9. Screw
10. Light socket and bulb
11. Selector lever
12. Screw
13. Bushing
14. Spring
15. Lock lever
16. Bushing
17. Nut
18. Solenoid switch
19. Screw
20. Gasket
21. Selector support
22. Bolt
23. Nut
24. Selector cable
25. Boot
26. Locking clip
27. Torsion lock
28. Selector cable bracket
29. Boot
30. Bolt
31. Washer
32. Nut
33. Washer
34. Clamping sleeve
35. Clamp
36. Bushing
37. Transaxle

Fig. 25 Automatic transaxle shift lever and control cable

in Park or Neutral only. Adjust the switch by moving it on its mounts. The back-up lights should only come on when the shift selector is in the Reverse position.

AUTOMATIC SHIFT LOCK SOLENOID

▶ **See Figures 26 and 27**

The shift lock solenoid prevents moving the selector lever out of Park unless the ignition switch is ON and the brake pedal is pressed. The solenoid is slotted on its mounting screws and can be adjusted by loosening the screws from under the vehicle. When the solenoid is released, the gap between the blocking piece and the blocking pin should be 0.012 inches (0.3mm).

Transaxle

REMOVAL & INSTALLATION

1. If equipped with electronically theft-protected radio, obtain the security code before disconnecting the battery.
2. Disconnect the battery and the speedometer drive and plug the hole in the transaxle.

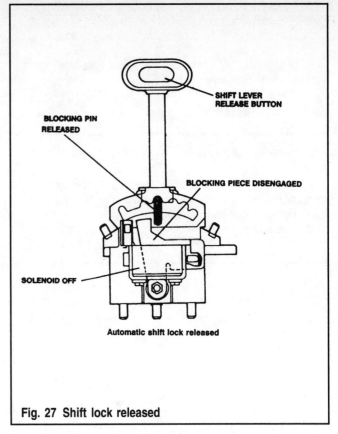

Fig. 27 Shift lock released

3. On Golf and Jetta, with the vehicle on the ground, remove the front axle nuts.

➡**When loosening or tightening an axle nut, make sure the vehicle is on the ground. Axle nut torque is high enough that loosen it with the vehicle on jack stands may cause the vehicle to fall.**

4. Raise and safely support the vehicle and remove the front wheels. Connect the engine sling tool VW-10-222A or equivalent, to the cylinder head and just take the weight of the engine off the mounts. On 16V engine, the idle stabilizer valve must be removed to attach the tool. Do not try to support the engine from below.
5. Remove the driver's side rear transaxle mount and support bracket.
6. On Golf and Jetta, remove the front mount bolts from the transaxle and from the body and remove the mount as a complete assembly.
7. Remove the selector and accelerator cables from the transaxle lever but leave them attached to the bracket. Remove the bracket assembly to save the adjustment.
8. Remove the halfshafts.
9. Remove the heat shield and brackets and remove the starter. On Cabriolet, the front mount comes off with the starter.
10. Remove the bellhousing lower cover and turn the engine as needed to remove the torque converter-to-flywheel bolts.
11. Remove the remaining transaxle mounts and, on Golf and Jetta, the subframe bolts and allow the subframe to hang free.

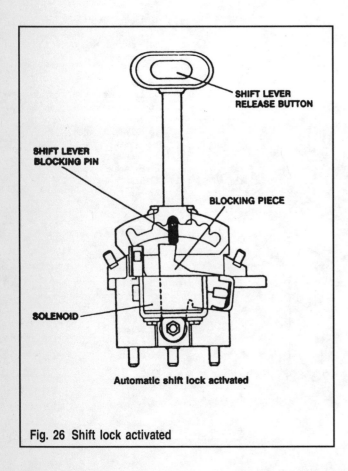

Fig. 26 Shift lock activated

12. Support the transaxle with a jack and remove the remaining engine-to-transaxle bolts. Be careful to secure the torque converter so it does not fall out of the transaxle.

13. Carefully lower the transaxle from the vehicle.

To install:

14. When reinstalling, make sure the torque converter is fully seated on the pump shaft splines. The converter should be recessed into the bell housing and turn by hand. Keep checking that it still turns while drawing the engine and transaxle together with the bolts.

15. Install the engine-to-transaxle bolts and torque to 55 ft. lbs. (75 Nm).

16. Install all mount and subframe bolts before tightening any on them. Tighten the bolts starting at the rear and work forward. Torque the smaller bolts to 25 ft. lbs. (34 Nm) and the larger bolts to 58 ft. lbs. (80 Nm). Remove the lifting equipment when all mounts are installed.

17. Install the torque converter-to-flywheel bolts and torque them to 26 ft. lbs. (35 Nm).

18. Install the starter and torque the bolts to 14 ft. lbs. (20 Nm). Install the heat shields.

19. Make sure the halfshaft splines are clean and apply a thread locking compound to the splines before sliding it into the hub. Connect the halfshafts to the drive flanges and torque the bolts to 33 ft. lbs. (45 Nm). Install new axle nuts but do not fully torque them until the vehicle is on the ground.

20. If removed, fit the ball joints to the control arm and torque the clamping bolt to 37 ft. lbs. (50 Nm).

21. Connect and adjust the shift linkage as required.

22. When assembly is complete and the vehicle is on its wheels, torque the axle nuts to 195 ft. lbs. (265 Nm) on Golf and Jetta or 175 ft. lbs. (240 Nm) on Cabriolet.

Axle Shaft (Halfshaft)

REMOVAL & INSTALLATION

❋❋CAUTION

NOTE:The torque required to loosen the front axle nut is high enough to make the vehicle fall off of jack stands. Make sure the vehicle is on the ground when loosening or tightening the front axle nut.

1. With the vehicle on the ground, remove the front axle nut.

2. Raise and safely support vehicle and remove the front wheels.

3. Remove the ball joint clamping bolt and push the control arm down, away from the ball joint.

4. Remove the socket head bolts from the transaxle drive flange.

5. Remove the halfshaft from the drive flange and support it below the flange. Do not let it hang by the outer CV-joint or the joint may fall apart.

6. Push the halfshaft out of the hub. A wheel puller may be required.

To install:

7. Fit the halfshaft to the drive flange and install the bolts. It is not necessary to torque them yet.

8. Apply a thread locking compound to the outer ¼ inch of the spline. Slip the spline through the hub and loosely install a new axle nut.

9. Assemble the ball joint and torque the nut and bolt to 37 ft. lbs. (50 Nm).

10. Install the wheel and hold it to keep the axle from turning. Torque the drive flange bolts to 33 ft. lbs. (45 Nm).

11. With the vehicle on the ground, torque the axle nut to 175 ft. lbs. (240 Nm) or Cabriolet or 195 ft. lbs. (265 Nm) on Golf and Jetta

CV-JOINT AND BOOT OVERHAUL

The constant velocity joints (CV-joints) can be disassembled for cleaning and inspection but they cannot be repaired. All parts are machined to a matched tolerance and the entire CV-joint must be replaced as a unit. On Golf and Jetta, the CV-joints are different on the left and right sides and cannot be interchanged.

1. Raise and safely support the vehicle and remove the halfshaft.

2. Pry open and remove the boot clamps with a pair of wire cutters.

3. With the halfshaft securely clamped in a vise, the outer CV-joint can be removed by sharply rapping out on the joint with a plastic hammer. The joint will snap off of the circlip and slide off the axle.

4. To remove the inner joint, remove the circlip from the center and slide the joint off the axle.

5. Both boots can be removed after removing the CV-joint.

To install:

6. Always replace both circlips and make sure the CV-joint is clean before installation. Wrap a piece of black electrical tape around the shaft splines and slip the inner clamp and the boot onto the shaft.

7. Remove the tape and install the dished washer with the concave side out so it acts as a spring pushing the CV-joint out. On the outer joint, install the thrust washer and a new circlip.

8. To install the outer joint, place it onto the spline and carefully tap straight in on the end with a plastic hammer. The joint will click into place over the circlip.

9. To install the inner joint, slide it onto the spline and push in enough to allow the circlip to fit into the groove in the axle shaft.

10. Pack the CV-joint with special CV-joint grease. DO NOT use any other type of grease.

11. Pack any remaining grease into the boot and install the clamps on the outer boot.

TORQUE SPECIFICATIONS

Component	US	Metric
Automatic transaxle pan:	15 ft. lbs.	20 Nm
Axle nut		
Cabriolet:	175 ft. lbs.	240 Nm
Golf and Jetta:	195 ft. lbs.	265 Nm
Back-up light switch:	7 ft. lbs.	10 Nm
Ball joint clamp bolt:	33 ft. lbs.	45 Nm
Halfshaft drive flange:	33 ft. lbs.	45 Nm
Engine-to-transaxle bolts:	55 ft. lbs.	75 Nm
Fifth gear synchronizer hub bolt:	111 ft. lbs.	150 Nm
Flywheel bolts:	15 ft. lbs.	20 Nm
Pinion shaft bearing plate:	30 ft. lbs.	40 Nm
Pressure plate–to–crankshaft:	22 ft. lbs.	(30 Nm) plus 1/4 turn
Ring gear bolts:	52 ft. lbs.	70 Nm
Selector shaft cap:	37 ft. lbs.	50 Nm
Shifter rod clamp bolt:	19 ft. lbs.	25 Nm
Starter bolts:	14 ft. lbs.	20 Nm
Torque converter–to–flywheel:	26 ft. lbs.	35 Nm
Transaxle case bolts:	18 ft. lbs.	25 Nm
Transaxle mount brackets:	33 ft. lbs.	45 Nm
Transaxle rubber mounts:	44 ft. lbs.	60 Nm

FRONT SUSPENSION
FRONT END ALIGNMENT 8-5
FRONT HUB AND WHEEL
 BEARING 8-4
FRONT STEERING KNUCKLE 8-4
LOWER BALL JOINT 8-3
LOWER CONTROL ARM 8-4
MACPHERSON STRUT 8-2
REAR SUSPENSION
REAR AXLE ASSEMBLY 8-9
REAR WHEEL BEARINGS 8-8
STRUT ASSEMBLY 8-8
STUB AXLE 8-9

STEERING
IGNITION LOCK CYLINDER 8-10
IGNITION SWITCH 8-10
MANUAL STEERING GEAR 8-12
POWER STEERING GEAR 8-12
POWER STEERING PUMP 8-12
STEERING COLUMN 8-10
STEERING LINKAGE 8-11
STEERING WHEEL 8-9
TURN SIGNAL AND WIPER
 SWITCHES 8-10
SUSPENSION AND STEERING
WHEELS 8-2

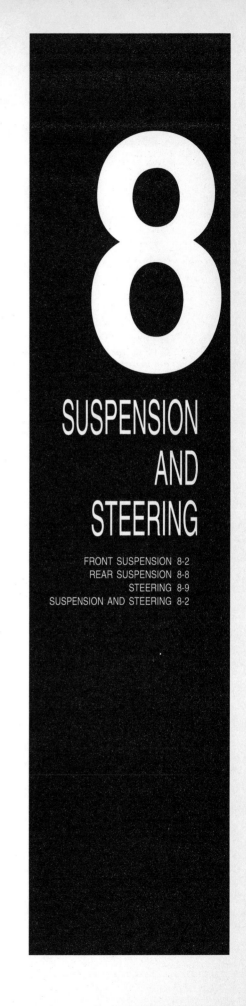

8

SUSPENSION AND STEERING

FRONT SUSPENSION 8-2
REAR SUSPENSION 8-8
STEERING 8-9
SUSPENSION AND STEERING 8-2

SUSPENSION AND STEERING

Wheels

REMOVAL & INSTALLATION

1. Loosen the lug bolts of the wheel to be removed. If they are seized, one or two heavy hammer blows directly on the end of the bolt head usually loosens the rust. Continued pounding will damage the brake drum or rotor.

2. Raise and safely support the vehicle on jack stands. There are small indentations in the rocker panels to indicate jacking points.

3. Remove the lug bolts and remove the wheel.

4. Installation is the reverse of removal. If desired, apply just a drop of oil to the threads to avoid seizing. DO NOT apply oil to the tapered head of the bolt or it will loosen when the vehicle is driven.

5. Torque the lug bolts to 81 ft. lbs. (110 Nm).

FRONT SUSPENSION

MacPherson Strut

REMOVAL & INSTALLATION

▶ **See Figures 1 and 2**

The upper strut-to-steering knuckle bolt may have an eccentric washer for adjusting wheel camber. Use a wire brush to clean the area and use a cold chisel to mark a fine line on the washer and the strut together. This matchmark may be enough to preserve the front wheel camber adjustment. It will at least be accurate enough to allow driving the vehicle to a shop for a proper front wheel alignment. If there is no eccentric washer, a new bolt and eccentric washer can be substituted. The parts are available through the dealer.

A special tool is required to remove the upper strut nut on Golf and Jetta. If necessary, it can be made by cutting away part of a 22mm socket.

1. Raise and safely support the vehicle and remove the front wheels.

2. Detach the brake line from the strut and remove the caliper. DO NOT let the caliper hang by the hydraulic line, hang it from the body with wire.

3. Clean and matchmark the position of the strut-to steering knuckle bolt.

4. Remove the bolts and push the steering knuckle down away from the strut. Support the knuckle so it is not hanging on the outer CV-joint.

5. On Cabriolet, remove the nuts holding the rubber strut bearing to the body and lower the strut from the vehicle.

6. On Golf and Jetta, use a hex wrench to hold the shock absorber rod and use the cut-away socket to remove the upper nut. Lower the strut from the vehicle.

INSPECTION

Alloy wheels with low profile, 50 series tires are somewhat fragile and tend to break or bend when hitting a pot hole. The damage usually occurs on the inside of the rim. If not too severe, the tire will still hold air but you'll probably feel a bump with each tire revolution. This type of damage makes the wheel unsafe for sustained highway driving, especially since the tire is usually also damaged. Some speciality shops have developed techniques for straightening alloy wheels, but success depends on sophisticated equipment as well as the degree of damage. If bent wheels are occurring frequently, you should probably consider a different wheel/tire combination. If less fragile steel wheels in the original size are installed, it will not be necessary to sacrifice the sharp handling qualities provided by 50 series tires.

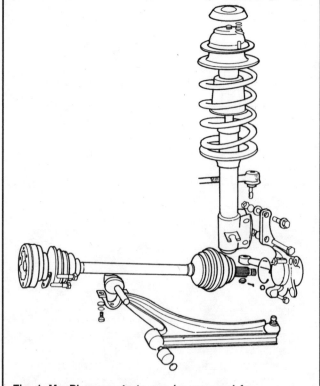

Fig. 1 MacPherson struts can be removed for disassembly

To install:

7. Place the strut into the fender and install the nuts. On Cabriolet, torque the 3 nuts to 14 ft. lbs. (20 Nm). On Golf and Jetta, install a new center nut and torque it to 44 ft. lbs. (60 Nm).

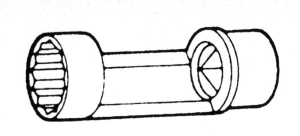

Fig. 2 Cut-away socket for removing upper strut nut on Golf and Jetta

8. Fit the knuckle into the strut and install the bolts. Make sure the matchmarks are aligned and install the nuts.

a. On Golf and Jetta, the strut-to-knuckle bolts are 2 different wrench sizes. Torque the 19mm bolts to 70 ft. lbs. (95 Nm) and the 18mm bolts to 59 ft. lbs. (80 Nm).

b. On Cabriolet, torque the strut-to-knuckle bolts to 70 ft. lbs. (95 Nm).

9. Install the brake caliper and torque the bolts to 44 ft. lbs. (60 Nm).

10. Install the wheel and align the front wheels.

STRUT OVERHAUL

▶ **See Figure 3**

Some special tools are required to disassemble the strut. First is a good quality spring compressor, usually available at larger parts stores. Also a special socket is needed to remove the upper strut nut. If necessary, it can be made by cutting away part of a 22mm socket. The same tool is required to remove the strut from Golf and Jetta.

✳✳CAUTION

The coil spring is very strong and under considerable pressure. If the correct tools and techniques are not available, do not attempt this job. Improper handling of coil springs can cause serious or fatal injury.

1. Remove the strut.

2. Anchor the strut in a vise so it cannot move and attach the spring compressor.

3. Compress the spring and remove the center nut at the top of the strut assembly. Remove the upper spring seat and spring. With the spring still in the compressor, place it where it will not be disturbed. The springs are color coded. When replacing, make sure both replacement springs have the same color code.

4. Use a pipe wrench to remove the threaded collar from the top of the strut. Remove the strut from the vice and pour the fluid into a drain pan.

5. Remove the strut rod and discard all the internal parts.

To install:

6. The new insert is probably a gas pressure shock absorber. Pour about 2 oz. of the old hydraulic oil into the strut and install the new insert. The fluid will help dissipate heat and extend the life of the insert.

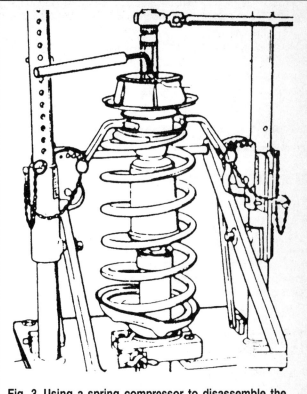

Fig. 3 Using a spring compressor to disassemble the front strut

7. Install the threaded collar and torque it to 30 ft. lbs. (40 Nm).

8. Fit the spring into place, install the upper seat and start the nut onto the rod. It may be easier to torque the nut before removing the spring compressor. Torque the nut to 44 ft. lbs. (60 Nm) and carefully remove the spring compressor.

Lower Ball Joint

INSPECTION

1. To check the ball joint, raise and safely support the vehicle. Let the front wheels hang free.

2. Insert a prybar between the control arm and the ball joint clamping bolt. Be careful to not damage the ball joint boot.

3. Measure the play between the bottom of the ball joint and the clamping bolt with a caliper. Total must not exceed 0.100 inch (2.5mm).

REMOVAL & INSTALLATION

1. Raise and safely support the vehicle, allowing the front wheels to hang. Remove the front wheels.

2. Remove the ball joint clamping bolt.

3. Pry the lower control arm down to remove the ball joint from the steering knuckle.

4. Remove the ball joint-to-lower control arm retaining nuts and bolts or drill out the rivets with a ¼ inch (6mm) drill. Remove the ball joint.

5. Install the new ball joint in the reverse order of removal. If no parts were installed other than the ball joint, no camber adjustment is necessary. Tighten the 2 control arm-to-ball joint bolts to 18 ft. lbs. (25 Nm) and the ball joint clamping bolt to 37 ft. lbs. (50 Nm).

Lower Control Arm

REMOVAL & INSTALLATION

➡**When removing the driver's side control arm on Cabriolet equipped with an automatic transaxle, it may be necessary to lift the engine/transaxle. First support the engine from above or below. Remove the front left engine mounting nut and bolt, remove the rear mount and raise the engine to expose the front control arm bolt.**

1. Raise and safely support the vehicle and remove the wheels.
2. Remove the ball joint clamping bolt and pry the control arm down.
3. Remove the rubber bushings to unfasten the stabilizer bar.
4. Remove the control arm mounting bolts and remove the control arm.
   To install:
5. Installation is the reverse of removal. Torque the following components:
   Cabriolet control arm bushing bolts — 50 ft. lbs. (68 Nm).
   Golf and Jetta front bushing bolts — 96 ft. lbs. (130 Nm), rear bolts — 59 ft. lbs. (80 Nm).
   Stabilizer bar link rods — 18 ft. lbs. (25 Nm).
   Stabilizer bar bushing clamp bolts — 32 ft. lbs. (43 Nm).
   Ball joint clamping bolt — 37 ft. lbs. (50 Nm).

Front Steering Knuckle

REMOVAL & INSTALLATION

✳✳CAUTION

The torque required to loosen the front axle nut is high enough to make the vehicle fall off of jack stands. Make sure the vehicle is on the ground when loosening or tightening the front axle nut.

1. With the vehicle on the ground, remove the front axle nut.
2. Raise and safely support the vehicle and remove the front wheels.
3. Detach the brake line from the strut and remove the caliper. Do not let the caliper hang by the hydraulic line, hang it from the body with wire.
4. Remove the caliper carrier and brake rotor.

5. Remove the cotter pin and nut and press out the tie rod end. A small puller is required.
6. Remove the ball joint clamp bolt and push the control arm down to disengage the ball joint.
7. Front wheel camber is set with eccentric washers on the bolts holding the bearing housing to the strut. Clean and mark the position of these washers so they can be reinstalled in the same position.
8. Remove the bolts and take the knuckle and bearing housing off the strut.
   To install:
9. Fit the knuckle to the strut and install the bolts. Align the marks and torque the nuts to 70 ft. lbs . (95 Nm).
10. Make sure the axle splines are clean and apply a bead of thread locking compound to the outer portion. Slid the axle into the hub and install a new axle nut. Do not torque it yet.
11. Fit the lower ball joint in place and install the clamp bolt. Torque it to 37 ft. lbs. (50 Nm).
12. Connect the tie rod and torque the nut to 26 ft. lbs. (35 Nm), then tighten as required to install a new cotter pin.
13. Install the brake disc and caliper. Torque the carrier bolts to 92 ft. lbs. (125 Nm) and the caliper guide bolts to 18 ft. lbs. (25 Nm). Secure the brake line in place.
14. With the wheel installed and the vehicle on the ground, torque the axle nut to 175 ft. lbs. (237 Nm) on Cabriolet or 195 ft. lbs. (265 Nm) on Golf and Jetta.

Front Hub and Wheel Bearing

REMOVAL & INSTALLATION

▶ **See Figures 4 and 5**

➡**The hub and bearing are pressed into the knuckle and the bearing cannot be reused once the hub has been removed.**

Without ABS

1. With the vehicle on the ground, remove the front axle nut. Raise and safely support the vehicle and remove the steering knuckle.
2. To remove the hub, support the knuckle assembly in an arbor press with the hub facing down.
3. Use a proper size arbor that will fit through the bearing and press the hub out.
4. If the inner bearing race stayed on the hub, clamp the hub in a vise and use a bearing puller to remove it.
5. On the knuckle, remove the splash shield and internal snaprings from the bearing housing.
6. With the knuckle in the same pressing position, press the bearing out.
7. Clean the bearing housing and hub with a wire brush and inspect all parts. Replace parts that have been distorted or discolored from heat. If the hub is not absolutely prefect where it contacts the inner bearing race, the new bearing will fail quickly.
   To install:
8. The new bearing is pressed in from the hub side. Install the snapring and support the steering knuckle on the press.

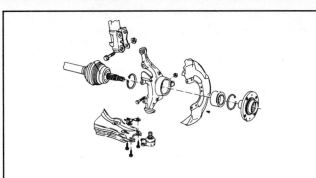

Fig. 4 Hub and bearing are pressed out of the steering knuckle

9. Using the old bearing as a press tool, press the new bearing into the housing up against the snapring. Make sure the press tool contacts only the outer race of the bearing.

10. Install the outer snapring and splash shield.

11. Support the inner race on the press and press the hub into the bearing. Make sure the inner race is supported or the bearing fail quickly.

12. Install the steering knuckle and be sure to torque the axle nut correctly before allowing the vehicle to roll.

With ABS

1. With the vehicle on the ground, remove the front axle nut. Raise and safely support the vehicle and remove the steering knuckle.

2. Clamp the upper knuckle-to-strut bolt boss in a vice.

3. Install the special press tool onto the hub as shown and press the hub out of the bearing.

4. If the inner bearing race stayed on the hub, clamp the hub in a vise and use a bearing puller to remove it.

5. On the knuckle, remove the splash shield and internal snaprings from the bearing housing.

6. After removing the snapring, the same press tool can be used to push the bearing out of the knuckle.

7. Clean the bearing housing and hub with a wire brush and inspect all parts. Replace parts that have been distorted or discolored from heat. If the hub is not absolutely prefect where it contacts the inner bearing race, the new bearing will fail quickly.

To install:

8. The new bearing is pressed in from the hub side using a regular arbor press. Install the snapring and support the steering knuckle on the press.

9. Using the old bearing as a press tool, press the new bearing into the housing up against the snapring. Make sure the press tool contacts only the outer race of the bearing.

10. Install the outer snapring and splash shield. If removed, install the speed sensor rotor onto the hub.

11. Support the inner race on the press and press the hub into the bearing. Make sure the inner race is supported or the bearing fail quickly.

12. Install the steering knuckle and be sure to torque the axle nut correctly before allowing the vehicle to roll.

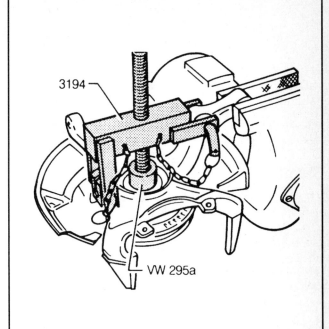

Fig. 5 If equipped with ABS, use the special press tool or equivalent bearing press to remove the hub and bearing

Front End Alignment

CASTOR

▶ **See Figure 6**

Wheel alignment is defined by three different adjustments in three planes. Looking at the vehicle from the side, castor angle describes the steering axis rather than a wheel angle. The steering knuckle is attached to the strut at the top and the control arm at the bottom. The wheel pivots around the line between these points to steer the vehicle. When the upper point is tilted back, this is described as positive castor. Positive castor tends to make the wheels self-centering, increasing directional stability. Excessive positive camber makes the wheels hard to steer and uneven castor will cause a pull to one side. On all Volkswagens, castor is not adjustable.

CAMBER

▶ **See Figure 7**

Looking at the wheels from the front of the vehicle, camber adjustment is the tilt of the wheel. When the wheel is tilted in at the top, this is negative camber. In a turn, a slight amount of negative camber helps maximize contact of the outside tire with the road. Too much negative camber makes the vehicle unstable in a straight line.

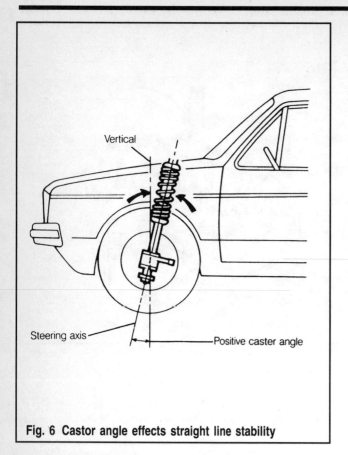

Fig. 6 Castor angle effects straight line stability

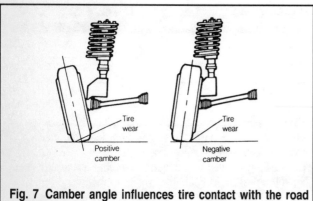

Fig. 7 Camber angle influences tire contact with the road

TOE-IN

▶ **See Figure 8**

Looking down at the wheels from above the vehicle, toe alignment is the distance between the front of the wheels relative to the distance between the back of the wheels. If the wheels are closer at the front, they are said to be toed-in or negative toe. A small amount of negative toe enhances directional stability and provides a smoother ride on the highway. On most front wheel drive vehicles, standard toe adjustment is either zero or slightly positive. When power is applied to the front wheels, they tend to toe in naturally.

If the tires are worn unevenly, if the vehicle is not stable on the highway or if the handling seems uneven in spirited driving, wheel alignment should be checked. If an alignment problem is suspected, first check tire inflation and look for other possible causes such as worn suspension and steering components, accident damage or unmatched tires. Repairs may be necessary before the wheels can be properly aligned. Wheel alignment requires sophisticated equipment and can only be done at a properly equipped shop.

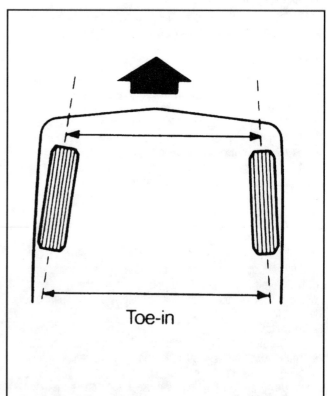

Fig. 8 Toe-in means the distance between the wheels is closer at the front

WHEEL ALIGNMENT

Year	Model	Caster Range (deg.)	Caster Preferred Setting (deg.)	Camber Range (deg.)	Camber Preferred Setting (deg.)	Toe-in (in.)	Steering Axis Inclination (deg.)
1990	Golf	±30'	1°30'	±20'	−35'	0°±10'	NA
	Jetta	±30'	1°30'	±20'	−35'	0°±10'	NA
	Cabriolet	±30'	1°50'	±30'	+20'	−5' to −30'	NA
1991	Golf	±30'	1°30'	±20'	−35'	0°±10'	NA
	Jetta	±30'	1°30'	±20'	−35'	0°±10'	NA
	Cabriolet	±30'	1°50'	±30'	+20'	−5' to −30'	NA
1992–93	Golf	±30'	1°30'	±20'	−35'	0°±10'	NA
	Jetta	±30'	1°30'	±20'	−35'	0°±10'	NA
	Cabriolet	±30'	1°50'	±30'	+20'	−5' to −30'	NA

NA—Not available

REAR SUSPENSION

The rear suspension consists of an axle beam which connects two trailing arms and a coil spring/shock absorber that are combined into a strut. The springs are relatively light and the strut can be disassembled without any special tools. The trailing arms mount to the body in rubber bushings. The rear strut cannot be overhauled and must be replaced as an assembly.

Strut Assembly

REMOVAL & INSTALLATION

▶ See Figure 9

➡ **Do not remove both suspension struts at the same time or the axle beam will be hanging on the brake lines.**

1. Working inside the vehicle, remove the cap from the top shock mount and remove the top nut, washer and rubber bushings.
2. Remove the second nut.
3. Slowly lift the vehicle and safely support it on jack stands. Do not place the stands under the axle beam.
4. Unbolt the strut from the axle and carefully remove the strut and spring from the vehicle. It may be necessary to press the axle down slightly.
5. Installation is the reverse of removal. Torque the strut-to-body nut to 23 ft. lbs. (31 Nm) on Cabriolet or 11 ft. lbs. (15

Nm) on Golf and Jetta. Torque the strut-to-axle bolts to 51 ft. lbs. (70 Nm).

Rear Wheel Bearings

REMOVAL & INSTALLATION

▶ See Figure 10

1. Raise and safely support the vehicle and remove the rear wheels.
2. On drum brakes, insert a small pry tool through a wheel bolt hole and push up on the adjusting wedge to slacken the rear brake adjustment.
3. On disc brakes, remove the caliper.
4. Remove the grease cap, cotter pin, locking ring, axle nut and thrust washer. Carefully remove the bearing and put all these parts where they will stay clean.
5. Remove the brake drum or rotor and pry out the inner seal to remove the inner bearing.
6. Clean all the grease off the bearings using solvent. If the bearings appear worn or damaged, they must be replaced.
7. To remove the bearing races, support the drum or rotor and carefully drive the race out with a long drift pin. They can also be removed on a press.
   To install:
8. Carefully press the new race into the drum or rotor. The old race can be used as a press tool but make sure it does not become stuck in the hub.
9. Pack the inner bearing with clean wheel bearing grease and fit it into the inner race. Press a new axle seal into place by hand.
10. Lightly coat the stub axle with grease and install the drum or rotor. Be careful not to damage the axle seal.
11. Pack the outer bearing and install the bearing, thrust washer and nut.
12. To adjust the bearing pre-load:
    a. Begin tightening the nut while turning the drum or rotor.
    b. When the nut is snug, try to move the thrust washer with a screwdriver.
    c. Back the nut off until the thrust washer can be moved without prying or twisting the screwdriver.

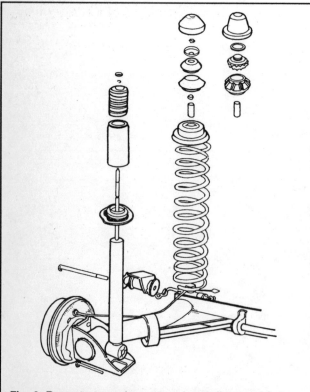

Fig. 9 Rear strut can be removed and disassembled without special tools

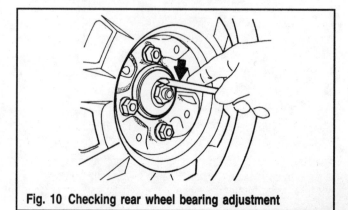

Fig. 10 Checking rear wheel bearing adjustment

13. Without turning the nut, install the locking ring so a new cotter pin can be installed through the hold in the stub axle. Bend the cotter pin.

14. Pack some grease into the cap and install it.

Stub Axle

REMOVAL & INSTALLATION

1. Raise and safely support the vehicle with jack stands and remove the rear wheels.

2. With disc brakes, remove the caliper and hang it from the spring with wire. Do not let the caliper hang by the hydraulic line.

3. Remove the brake drum or rotor.

4. With drum brakes, disconnect the brake line and plug it. Remove the brake backing plate complete with brake assembly.

5. Unbolt and remove the stub axle.

6. Installation is the reverse of removal. Make sure the axle mounting surface is clean and torque the nuts and bolts to 52 ft. lbs. (70 Nm). Torque the caliper mounting bolts to 48 ft. lbs. (65 Nm).

Rear Axle Assembly

REMOVAL & INSTALLATION

1. Raise and safely support the vehicle and remove the rear wheels.

2. Remove the rear brake caliper or drum.

3. Disconnect the brake line and remove the caliper or back plate (with brakes attached) from the vehicle.

4. Disconnect the other end of the brake line and unclip the brake line and parking brake cable from the axle. Unhook the brake pressure regulator spring from the bracket.

5. Support one side of the axle beam so it does not fall and remove the lower shock mount bolts from both sides.

6. Unless that is the part being repaired, avoid removing the axle bushing brackets. Removing these will mean aligning the rear bushings upon reassembly.

7. Remove the bolt from the center of each bushing and lower the axle from the vehicle.

To install:

8. Install the axle but do not torque the bushing bolts yet. They should be torqued with the vehicle on the ground to properly align the bushings.

9. Install the brakes, connect the hydraulic lines and bleed the brakes.

10. With the vehicle on the ground, torque the right side axle bushing bolt first, then pry the left side bushing slightly towards the center of the vehicle and torque the left side.

11. Torque the axle bushing bolts to 44 ft. lbs. (60 Nm) and the lower shock mount bolts to 52 ft. lbs. (70 Nm).

STEERING

Steering Wheel

REMOVAL & INSTALLATION

Golf and Jetta

1. Disconnect the horn wires or remove the horn fuse.

2. Carefully pry the center panel from the steering wheel. Disconnect the horn button wires.

3. Make sure the front wheels are straight ahead and remove the ignition key. Turn the wheel until it locks.

4. Remove the steering wheel nut. Matchmark the wheel to the column so it can be replaced in the same position and pull the wheel straight off the splines.

5. Installation is the reverse of removal. Torque the nut to 30 ft. lbs. (40 Nm).

Cabriolet

✳✳CAUTION

Accidental deployment of the air bag can result in serious or fatal injury. The air bag system is equipped with a back-up power supply. The battery must be disconnected for more than 20 minutes before the power supply is fully discharged and the system is considered disarmed. Do not use a memory saver power supply because it will keep the air bag power supply charged.

1. Disconnect battery, wait more than 20 minutes before beginning any repair procedure.

2. Remove the Torx® head screws at the back of the steering wheel.

3. Carefully detach the air bag unit from the wheel and disconnect the wire at the center.

4. Place unit in a safe place where it will not be disturbed with the horn pad up. Do not place anything on top of the unit.

5. Point the front wheels straight ahead, remove the ignition key to lock the steering column and remove the steering wheel nut and spring washer.

6. Mark the position of the wheel to the spline and pull the wheel straight off.

7. Installation is the reverse of removal. The gap between the wheel and the column should be 2-4mm (0.080-0.160 inches) and can be adjusted by pulling out or driving in the sleeve under the wheel. Torque the steering wheel nut to 30 ft. lbs. (40 Nm).

8. When installing the air bag, use new Torx® screws and tighten to 7.5 ft. lbs. (10 Nm.). Do not over torque or the air bag may not function properly. Make sure no one is in the vehicle when reconnecting the battery.

Turn Signal and Wiper Switches

REMOVAL & INSTALLATION

1. Disconnect the battery ground cable.
2. Remove the steering wheel. On Cabriolet with and air bag, remove the spiral spring assembly.
3. Remove the switch retaining screws and carefully pull the switch housing off the column.
4. Disconnect the electrical plugs at the back of the switch.
5. Installation is the reverse of removal. On Cabriolet, make sure the spiral spring is in the center position before installing the steering wheel. Total travel is 8 turns.

Ignition Switch

REMOVAL & INSTALLATION

The ignition switch is located at the bottom of the ignition key lock cylinder. The lock must be removed to remove the switch.

Ignition Lock Cylinder

REMOVAL & INSTALLATION

▶ See Figure 11

❊❊CAUTION

Accidental deployment of the air bag can result in serious or fatal injury. Disarm the air bag system prior to starting any repair procedure.

1. Disconnect the negative battery cable. On Cabriolet, remove the air bag unit and the serial spring.
2. Remove the steering wheel, steering column covers and the turn signal and wiper switches. Disconnect the ignition switch wiring.
3. Measure as shown and mark the cylinder housing with a center punch. Dimension **A** is 0.472 inches (12mm) and dimension **B** is 0.394 inches (10mm).
4. With a 1/8 inch (3.0mm) drill, carefully drill in about 1/8th inch (3.0mm) until the stop spring is visible.
5. Push the spring in to pull the cylinder out of the housing. If necessary, remove the bolt to slide the housing off the column.
To install:
6. Insert the lock cylinder into the housing with the key in the cylinder.
7. While gently turning the key side to side, press the cylinder in to the stop. It should click into place.

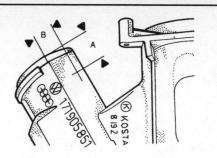

Fig. 11 Carefully measure and mark the intersection of dimensions A and B

8. Temporarily fit the steering wheel onto the splines and make sure the column locks and unlocks smoothly.
9. Install the switches, column covers, wiring and the steering wheel. On Cabriolet, make sure no one is in the vehicle when connecting the battery.

Steering Column

REMOVAL & INSTALLATION

▶ See Figures 12, 13 and 14

➡**The steering column shaft can be removed without removing the entire column assembly.**

1. Disconnect the negative battery cable.
2. On Cabriolet, remove the air bag unit as described previously. Don't forget to wait for the back-up power supply to discharge.
3. Remove the steering wheel, the turn signal and wiper switches.
4. Remove the ignition switch and the ignition lock housing.
5. To remove just the shaft, disconnect the shaft from the universal joint and pull it out of the column housing.
6. Remove the nuts or bolts as required and remove the steering column tube. On Cabriolet, pry out leaf spring at the base of the column tube.
To install:
7. Install the steering lock housing onto the column shaft.
8. Install the steering column tube.
9. Fit the shaft and lock housing onto the tube and connect the universal joint.
10. Install the switches, connect the wiring and test the switches before installing the steering wheel.
11. Install the steering wheel and torque the nut to 30 ft. lbs. (40 Nm).
12. On Cabriolet, disconnect the battery and wait at least 20 minutes before installing the air bag unit. Make sure no one is in the vehicle when connecting the battery.

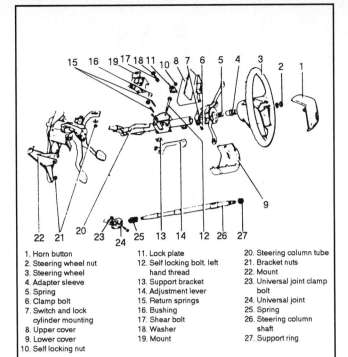

1. Horn button
2. Steering wheel nut
3. Steering wheel
4. Adapter sleeve
5. Spring
6. Clamp bolt
7. Switch and lock cylinder mounting
8. Upper cover
9. Lower cover
10. Self locking nut
11. Lock plate
12. Self locking bolt, left hand thread
13. Support bracket
14. Adjustment lever
15. Return springs
16. Bushing
17. Shear bolt
18. Washer
19. Mount
20. Steering column tube
21. Bracket nuts
22. Mount
23. Universal joint clamp bolt
24. Universal joint
25. Spring
26. Steering column shaft
27. Support ring

Fig. 12 Adjustable steering column on Golf and Jetta

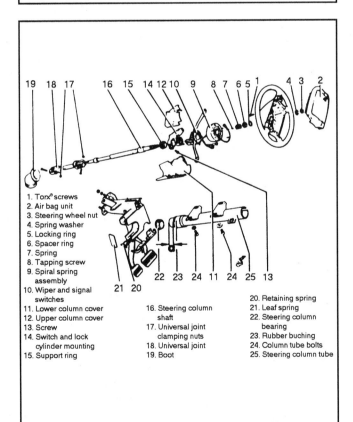

1. Torx® screws
2. Air bag unit
3. Steering wheel nut
4. Spring washer
5. Locking ring
6. Spacer ring
7. Spring
8. Tapping screw
9. Spiral spring assembly
10. Wiper and signal switches
11. Lower column cover
12. Upper column cover
13. Screw
14. Switch and lock cylinder mounting
15. Support ring
16. Steering column shaft
17. Universal joint clamping nuts
18. Universal joint
19. Boot
20. Retaining spring
21. Leaf spring
22. Steering column bearing
23. Rubber buching
24. Column tube bolts
25. Steering column tube

Fig. 13 Steering column for Cabriolet with air bag

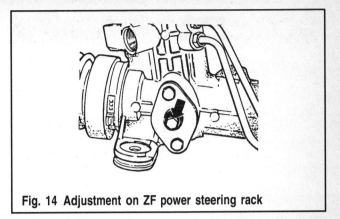

Fig. 14 Adjustment on ZF power steering rack

Steering Linkage

REMOVAL & INSTALLATION

Tie Rod Ends

➡On manual steering and TRW power steering gear, only the right side tie rod end is removable. The left tie rod must be replaced if the end joint is worn. On all vehicles, the front wheels must be aligned after steering gear repairs.

1. Raise and safely support the vehicle on jack stands and center the steering wheel.
2. Remove the cotter pin and use a ball joint press to disconnect the tie rod end from the steering knuckle. If a ball joint press is not available:
   a. Loosen but do not remove the nut from the tie rod end.
   b. Place a floor jack under the tie rod as close to the end as possible and raise it just enough to put pressure on the tie rod end. Do not lift the suspension.
   c. Where the tie rod end fits into the steering knuckle, rap sharply with a hammer directly on the end of the steering knuckle boss. The tie rod end should jump out of the tapered hole in the boss.
3. Mark or measure the length of the right tie rod so it can be installed with the correct toe adjustment.
4. On the right side tie rod, hold the rod with a wrench and loosen the lock nut. Count the number of turns required to remove the tie rod end.
5. To remove the left tie rod, disconnect the rubber boot from the end of the steering rack and turn the steering wheel all the way to the right.
6. Loosen the lock nut and unscrew the tie rod from the steering rack.
7. Installation is the reverse of removal. Make sure each tie rod is the original length before tightening the lock nuts.
8. After inserting the tie rod end into the steering knuckle, torque the nut to 26 ft. lbs. (35 Nm) and tighten as required to install a new cotter pin.

Manual Steering Gear

ADJUSTMENTS

The adjusting screw is on the rack housing and adjusts pinion gear-to-rack clearance. Turning the screw clockwise tightens the clearance. Turn the adjusting screw no more than 20 degrees and test drive the vehicle after each adjustment. If the adjustment does not improve steering response or feel, return the screw to its original position and look for worn or damaged steering or suspension parts.

REMOVAL & INSTALLATION

1. Raise and safely support the vehicle on jack stands and remove the ignition key to lock the steering wheel.
2. Remove the bolt from the steering shaft universal joint. Matchmark the universal joint to the pinion shaft.
3. Disconnect the tie rod ends from the steering knuckles.
4. Remove the mount nuts to remove the steering rack as an assembly.
5. Installation is the reverse of removal. Fit the pinion shaft into the universal joint while fitting the steering gear into place on the body.
6. Torque the steering gear mount nuts and the universal joint bolt to 22 ft. lbs. (30 Nm).
7. After inserting the tie rod ends into the steering knuckle, torque the nut to 26 ft. lbs. (35 Nm) and tighten as required to install a new cotter pin.

OVERHAUL

The steering rack and pinion assembly is not designed to be rebuilt and service parts are not available.

Power Steering Gear

ADJUSTMENT

▶ See Figures 13 and 15

ZF Steering Gear

1. This job requires 2 people. With the vehicle on the ground and the wheels straight ahead, turn the steering wheel back and forth about 30 degrees with the engine not running.
2. If the steering feels loose or makes noise, have an assistant turn the adjusting bolt clockwise until the noise stops. The noise may not stop completely so do not continue tightening the adjustment.

TRW Steering Gear

1. Remove the steering gear from the vehicle.
2. Loosen the lock nut and use the special pin wrench to turn the adjuster until the rack can be moved by hand without binding or excessive free play.

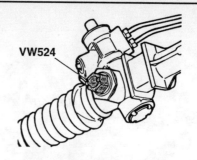

Fig. 15 Special pin wrench is required for adjusting the TRW power steering rack

3. Install the steering gear.

REMOVAL & INSTALLATION

1. Raise and safely support the vehicle on jack stands and remove the ignition key to lock the steering wheel.
2. Place a catch pan under the power steering gear to catch the fluid.
3. Disconnect the suction hose and the pressure lines and drain the fluid into the catch pan (discard the fluid).
4. Remove the bolt from the steering shaft universal joint. Matchmark the universal joint to the pinion shaft.
5. Disconnect the tie rod ends from the steering knuckles.
6. Remove the mount nuts to remove the steering rack as an assembly.

To install:
7. Fit the pinion shaft into the universal joint while fitting the steering gear into place on the body.
8. Torque the steering gear mount nuts and the universal joint bolt to 22 ft. lbs. (30 Nm).
9. After inserting the tie rod ends into the steering knuckle, torque the nut to 26 ft. lbs. (35 Nm) and tighten as required to install a new cotter pin.
10. Connect the hydraulic lines, refill the fluid reservoir and bleed the system as described later.

Power Steering Pump

REMOVAL & INSTALLATION

1. Place a catch pan under the power steering pump to catch the fluid.
2. Remove the suction hose and the pressure line from the pump, then drain the fluid into the catch pan (discard the fluid).
3. Loosen the tensioning bolt at the front of the tensioning bracket and remove the drive belt from the pump pulley.
4. Remove the pump mounting bolts and lift the pump from the vehicle.
5. To install, reverse the removal procedures. Torque the mounting bolts to 15 ft. lbs. (20 Nm) and adjust the drive belt. Fill the reservoir with approved power steering fluid and bleed the system.

BLEEDING

1. Fill the reservoir to the MAX level mark with approved power steering fluid.

2. With the engine idling, turn the wheels from the right to the left side as far as possible, several times.

3. Refill the reservoir to the MAX level and repeat the procedure until the level does not change.

TORQUE SPECIFICATIONS

Component	U.S.	Metric
Air bag unit mounting screws:	7.5 ft. lbs.	10 Nm
Ball joint bolts:	18 ft. lbs.	25 Nm
Ball joint clamping bolt:	37 ft. lbs.	50 Nm
Control arm bushing bolts:		
Cabriolet:	50 ft. lbs.	68 Nm
Golf and Jetta:		
Front bushing:	96 ft. lbs.	130 Nm
Rear bushing:	59 ft. lbs.	80 Nm
Front brake caliper carrier:	92 ft. lbs.	125 Nm
Front brake caliper guide bolts:	18 ft. lbs.	25 Nm
Front axle nut:		
Cabriolet:	175 ft. lbs.	237 Nm
Golf and Jetta:	195 ft. lbs.	265 Nm
Front strut collar nut:	30 ft. lbs.	40 Nm
Front strut-to-knuckle bolts:		
19mm bolts:	70 ft. lbs.	95 Nm
18mm bolts:	59 ft. lbs.	80 Nm
Rear axle bushing bolts:	44 ft. lbs.	60 Nm
Rear brake caliper:	48 ft. lbs.	65 Nm
Rear strut-to-body nut:	23 ft. lbs.	31 Nm
Rear strut-to-axle bolt:	51 ft. lbs.	70 Nm
Stabilizer bar links:	18 ft. lbs.	25 Nm
Stabilizer bar clamps:	32 ft. lbs.	43 Nm
Steering wheel nut:	30 ft. lbs.	40 Nm
Steering gear mount nuts:	22 ft. lbs.	30 Nm
Steering shaft universal joint bolt:	22 ft. lbs.	Nm
Steering pump mount bolts:	15 ft. lbs.	20 Nm
Stub axle bolts:	52 ft. lbs.	70 Nm
Tie rod nuts:	26 ft. lbs.	35 Nm
Upper strut nut:		
Cabriolet:	14 ft. lbs.:	20 Nm:
Golf and Jetta:	44 ft. lbs.	60 Nm
Wheel lug bolts:	81 ft. lbs.	110 Nm

ANTI-LOCK BRAKE SYSTEM
  CONTROL UNIT 9-20
  DESCRIPTION AND
    OPERATION 9-14
  FILLING AND BLEEDING 9-21
  MODULATOR ASSEMBLY 9-21
  RELIEVING ANTI-LOCK BRAKE
    SYSTEM PRESSURE 9-21
  TROUBLESHOOTING 9-15
  WHEEL SPEED SENSOR 9-20
BRAKE OPERATING SYSTEM
  ADJUSTMENTS 9-2
  BRAKE LIGHT SWITCH 9-3
  BRAKE LINES 9-4
  BRAKE PEDAL 9-3
  BRAKE SYSTEM BLEEDING 9-4
  DIESEL ENGINE VACUUM PUMP 9-3
  GENERAL DESCRIPTION 9-2
  MASTER CYLINDER 9-3

  POWER BRAKE BOOSTER 9-3
  PRESSURE REGULATING VALVE 9-4
FRONT DISC BRAKES
  BRAKE CALIPER 9-6
  BRAKE PADS 9-5
  BRAKE ROTOR 9-8
PARKING BRAKE
  CABLE 9-14
  PARKING BRAKE LEVER 9-14
REAR DISC BRAKES
  BRAKE CALIPER 9-12
  BRAKE PADS 9-11
  BRAKE ROTOR 9-13
REAR DRUM BRAKES
  BACK PLATE 9-11
  BRAKE DRUMS 9-9
  BRAKE SHOES 9-9
  WHEEL CYLINDER 9-10

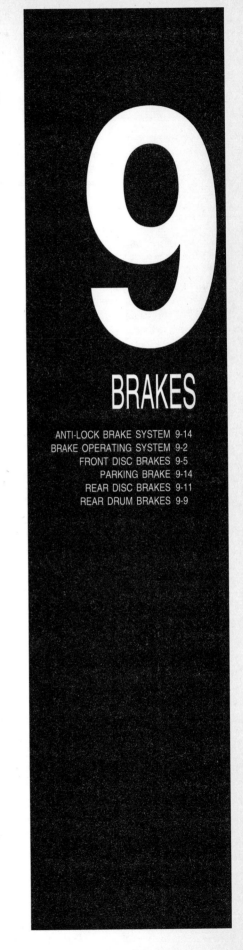

9

BRAKES

ANTI-LOCK BRAKE SYSTEM 9-14
BRAKE OPERATING SYSTEM 9-2
FRONT DISC BRAKES 9-5
PARKING BRAKE 9-14
REAR DISC BRAKES 9-11
REAR DRUM BRAKES 9-9

BRAKE OPERATING SYSTEM

General Description

All models are equipped with disc brakes on the front and either self adjusting drum brakes or self adjusting disc brakes on the rear. The brakes are hydraulically actuated through a dual circuit with a vacuum assist at the master cylinder. A rear pressure regulating valve is attached to the body and connected by a spring to the rear axle beam. The valve controls the hydraulic pressure available to the rear brakes as a function of the weight in the rear of the vehicle. The calipers are full floating single piston type. On rear disc brakes, the piston is threaded into the caliper and turns out automatically as required to maintain parking brake adjustment.

The Jetta is available with an Anti-Lock Brake System (ABS). The three-channel system includes a hydraulic modulator, a pressure accumulator, speed sensors at each wheel and an electronic control unit. The control unit is equipped with a self diagnostic program and is capable of storing fault codes. The code memory can only be accessed with the dealer's diagnostic equipment. The system operates at very high pressure and is capable of generating these pressures even when the engine is not running. Because of the need for special equipment and the dangerous pressures involved, owner service to the ABS braking is very limited.

Adjustments

PARKING BRAKE

Rear Drum Brakes

▶ **See Figure 1**

1. Raise and safely support the rear of the vehicle on jackstands so the rear wheels are free to turn.
2. With the parking brake handle down and the brake fully released, firmly apply the brake pedal once.
3. Pull the parking brake lever up 2-3 clicks. If the rear wheels cannot be turned by hand, no adjustment is required.
4. If adjustment is required, lower the lever and pull it up again only 2 clicks.
5. Remove the brake handle cover and loosen the locknuts.
6. Turn the adjusting nuts as required until the rear wheels cannot be turned in either direction by hand. If the wheels never lock up, there is a problem with the cables or the brakes and the drums should be removed for inspection.
7. Release the handle and make sure the wheels turn freely. If they do, tighten the locknuts.
8. If the wheels do not turn freely, back off the adjusting nuts as required. If brake handle travel is more than 3-4 clicks, there is a problem with the cables or the brakes and the drums should be removed for inspection.

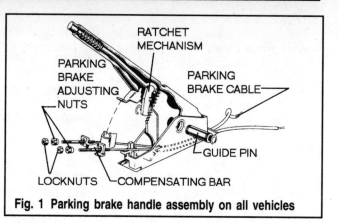

Fig. 1 Parking brake handle assembly on all vehicles

Rear Disc Brakes

▶ **See Figure 2**

➡**Parking brake adjustment is only necessary after replacing brake pads or other brake components. If the parking brake does not hold the vehicle, the rear calipers and brake pads must be removed for inspection.**

1. Raise and safely support the rear of the vehicle on jackstands and remove the rear wheels.
2. With the parking brake handle down and the brake fully released, firmly apply the brake pedal once.
3. Pull the parking brake lever up 2-3 clicks. If the rear wheels cannot be turned by hand, no adjustment is required.
4. If adjustment is required, loosen the locknuts and the adjusting nuts to just relieve the tension on the cables.
5. Hold the release button on the handle and move the handle up and down 3 or more times to seat the cables and make sure they move freely, then leave the handle down.
6. Tighten the cable adjusting nuts evenly until the actuating levers on the calipers just move off their stops. The gap must be less than 0.059 inch (1.5mm).
7. To check for correct adjustment:
   a. At the first click, the rotors should turn by hand with some drag.
   b. At the second click, the rotors should be difficult to turn.

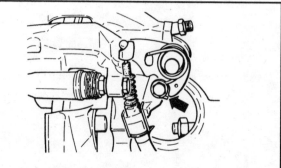

Fig. 2 The actuating lever gap on the rear caliper must be less than 0.059 in. (1.5mm)

c. At the third click, it should not be possible to turn the rotors by hand.

d. When the brake handle is released, the rotors should turn freely.

Brake Light Switch

REMOVAL & INSTALLATION

Golf and Jetta

The brake switch is mounted on the brake pedal support bracket. Disconnect and remove the switch by pulling the switch from the adjusting clip. To adjust it, depress the brake pedal and push in the switch as far as it will go. Pull the pedal back by hand as far as it will go. The switch is adjusted after no clicks are heard.

Cabriolet

1. Disconnect the wiring and unscrew the switch from the master cylinder.
2. Lubricate the threads of the new switch with brake fluid, install the switch and torque it to 18 ft. lbs. (25 Nm).
3. Connect the wires and bleed the brake system.

Brake Pedal

REMOVAL & INSTALLATION

1. Disconnect the clutch cable at the transaxle end.
2. Remove the clip and remove the brake/clutch pedal pivot pin.
3. Installation is the reverse of removal. Lightly lubricate the pin with white grease.

Master Cylinder

REMOVAL & INSTALLATION

Standard (Non-ABS) Brakes

1. To prevent brake fluid from spilling out and damaging the paint, place a protective cover over the fender.
2. Disconnect and cap the brake lines to keep dirt out.

3. Disconnect the wiring from the switches.
4. Remove the two master cylinder mounting nuts and pull the master cylinder away from the booster.
5. The reservoir is held into the master cylinder by a press fit into rubber sealing plugs and can easily be pulled off. To reinstall, moisten the plugs with brake fluid and press it on.

➡**Do not depress the brake pedal while the master cylinder is removed.**

To install:
6. Position the master cylinder and reservoir assembly onto the studs and install the washers and nuts. Torque the nuts to 15 ft. lbs. (20 Nm).
7. Remove the plugs and connect the brake lines.
8. Bleed the brake system.

OVERHAUL

Volkswagen does not recommend rebuilding master cylinders and service parts are not available from the dealer network.

Power Brake Booster

REMOVAL & INSTALLATION

Without ABS

1. Remove the master cylinder from the booster.
2. At the pedals, remove the clevis pin on the end of the booster pushrod by unclipping it and pulling it from the clevis.
3. Disconnect the vacuum hose from the booster.
4. Unbolt the booster; remove the 2 nuts under the dashboard or the 4 nuts holding the booster to its bracket. Remove the booster.
5. Installation is the reverse of removal. Install the master cylinder and bleed the system.

Diesel Engine Vacuum Pump

REMOVAL & INSTALLATION

1. Disconnect both vacuum lines from the pump.
2. Remove the hold-down clamp and remove the pump.
3. The diaphragm and valves inside the pump can be replaced. A pump rebuild kit is available through the dealer.
4. Installation is the reverse of removal. Torque the hold-down bolt to 15 ft. lbs. (20 Nm).

Pressure Regulating Valve

REMOVAL & INSTALLATION

▶ See Figure 3

✳✳CAUTION

The ABS hydraulic modulator is capable of self-pressurizing and can generate pressures above 3000 psi. any time the ignition switch is turned ON. Relieve the system pressure before testing or repairing the hydraulic system. Improper repair or test procedures can cause serious or fatal injury.

1. Raise and safely support the rear of the vehicle on jackstands.
2. If equipped with ABS, make sure the ignition switch stays **OFF** and pump the brake pedal 25-35 times to relieve the system pressure.
3. At the rear axle beam, disconnect the spring and relieve the pressure by pushing the lever towards the axle.
4. Using a line wrench, disconnect the lines from the valve.
5. Remove the retaining nuts and remove the valve from the frame.
6. Installation is the reverse of removal. Bleed the brake system.

Brake Lines

REMOVAL & INSTALLATION

Flexible Hoses

✳✳CAUTION

The ABS hydraulic modulator is capable of self-pressurizing and can generate pressures above 3000 psi. any time the ignition switch is turned ON. Relieve the

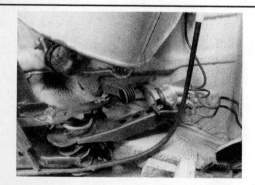

Fig. 3 Pressure regulating valve for rear brakes

system pressure before testing or repairing the hydraulic system. Improper repair or test procedures can cause serious or fatal injury.

➡When removing any brake line or hose, always use a flare nut wrench to prevent damage to the soft metal fittings.

1. If equipped with ABS, make sure the ignition switch stays **OFF** and pump the brake pedal 25-35 times to relieve the system pressure.
2. Using a flare nut wrench, remove and plug the brake hose from the caliper.
3. Remove the brake hose from the holding bracket on the strut.
4. Using a flare nut wrench to hold the steel brake line, remove the brake hose with a suitable flare nut wrench.
5. Plug the steel brake line after removal.
6. Installation is the reverse of removal. Torque the fittings to 20 ft. lbs. (27 Nm).

Steel Lines

Loosen the steel brake line fittings using flare nut wrenches only. If the steel line starts to twist, stop and lubricate with penetrating oil. Move the wrench back and forth until the fitting turns freely. A backup wrench should be used when loosening steel-to-rubber brake hoses. Steel brake lines can be repaired by installing a double flare after the damaged portion has been removed. The tools needed for this procedure may be purchased at a local hardware or auto parts store. Steel brake lines MUST be double flared.

Brake System Bleeding

Without ABS

➡Use only new DOT 3 or 4 brake fluid in all Volkswagen vehicles. Do not use silicone (DOT 5) fluid. Even the smallest traces can cause severe corrosion to the hydraulic system. All brake fluids are corrosive to paint.

1. The procedure described here is for non-ABS brakes only. Bleed the brakes with the engine off and booster vacuum discharged; pump the pedal with the bleeders closed about 20 times until the pedal effort gets stiff.
2. Fill the fluid reservoir.
3. On vehicles with a rear brake pressure regulator, press the lever towards the rear axle when bleeding the brakes.
4. Connect a clear plastic tube to the bleeder valve at the right rear wheel. Place the other end in a clean container.
5. Have an assistant pump the pedal to build pressure in the system, then hold pressure.
6. Open the bleeder slowly. When the pedal is all the way to the floor, close the bleeder before releasing the pedal.
7. Repeat this procedure until there are no air bubbles in the fluid stream. Be careful not to let the reservoir run out of brake fluid.

8. Repeat the procedure in sequence at the left rear, right front and left front: working farthest from the master cylinder to the nearest.

FRONT DISC BRAKES

✳✳CAUTION

Some brake pads contain asbestos, which has been determined to be a cancer causing agent. Never clean the brake surfaces with compressed air! Avoid inhaling any dust from any brake surface! When cleaning brake surfaces, use a commercially available brake cleaning fluid.

Two types of floating front caliper are used on models covered in this book. Vehicles with the 16V engine use a single piston, one piece caliper that is bolted to two guide pins that move in the pad carrier. As the brakes are applied, piston pushes the inner pad against the rotor and the caliper and guide pins move in the carrier to pull the outer pad against the rotor.

On other models, movement of the caliper is guided by sleeves and bushings that are in the caliper mounting holes but firmly bolted to the carrier. Anti-rattle springs are used to maintain a snug fit between the caliper and the carrier when the brakes are not in use.

Brake Pads

REMOVAL & INSTALLATION

Caliper with Guide Pins

▶ **See Figures 4 and 5**

✳✳CAUTION

The ABS hydraulic modulator is capable of self-pressurizing and can generate pressures above 3000 psi. any time the ignition switch is turned ON. Relieve the system pressure before testing or repairing the hydraulic system. Improper repair or test procedures can cause serious or fatal injury.

1. Raise and safely support the vehicle on jackstands and remove the front wheels.
2. If the brake fluid reservoir level is near the maximum line, siphon some brake fluid from the reservoir to prevent overflowing when the piston is retracted into the cylinder bore.
3. Hold the lower guide pin with an open wrench and remove the bolt securing the caliper to the guide pin. Do not remove the top bolt.
4. Pivot the caliper up on the upper guide pin and slide the pads straight out to remove them.

To install:
5. Place the old pad against the piston and use a C-clamp to push the piston all the way into the bore. If the rubber boot is split, if there is fluid leaking from the caliper or if the piston will not move in the bore, the caliper must be rebuilt or replaced.
6. Fit the new pads into the carrier and pivot the caliper into place.
7. The original bolts are micro-encapsulated with a thread locking compound. Install a new bolt or clean the old bolt and apply a thread locking compound.
8. When tightening the bolt, be sure to use a back-up wrench to hold the guide pin. Torque the bolt to 26 ft. lbs. (35 Nm).
9. Pump the brake pedal several times until the pedal is firm, then add new brake fluid as required.

Caliper with Sleeves and Bushings

▶ **See Figures 6, 7 and 8**

1. Raise and safely support the vehicle on jackstands and remove the front wheels.
2. If the brake fluid reservoir level is near the maximum line, siphon some brake fluid from the reservoir to prevent overflowing when the piston is pushed into the cylinder bore.
3. Put a large C-clamp around the caliper so it contacts the caliper body and the outer brake pad. Tighten the clamp to push the piston into the bore. Remove the clamp and push the caliper in and out to make sure the sleeves and bushings move freely.
4. With a 6mm Allen socket, remove the 2 bolts holding the caliper to the carrier. Push the caliper up and pivot the bottom of the caliper out of the carrier.
5. Hang the caliper from the front spring with a piece of wire. DO NOT let the caliper hang by the hydraulic line.
6. Remove the anti-rattle springs and the pads from the carrier and note their location.

To install:
7. Fit the anti-rattle springs into place and slide the new pads onto the carrier. The tang should be towards the inner pad.
8. Fit the caliper into place at the top and push up so it can be pivoted into place at the bottom. The tabs on the anti-rattle springs should be pushing against the inside of the caliper.
9. Make sure the caliper mounting bolts are clean. Install the bolts and torque them to 18 ft. lbs. (25 Nm).
10. Pump the brake pedal several times until the pedal is firm, then add new brake fluid as required.

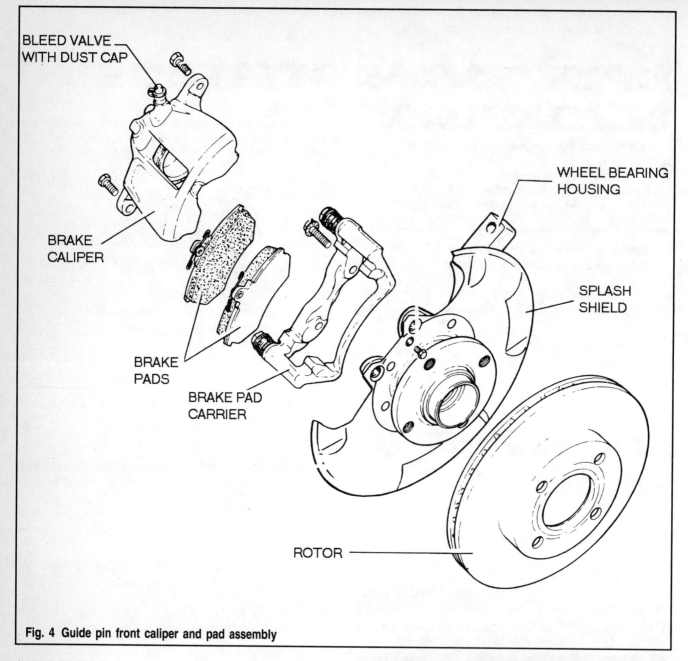

BLEED VALVE
WITH DUST CAP

WHEEL BEARING
HOUSING

BRAKE
CALIPER

SPLASH
SHIELD

BRAKE
PADS

BRAKE PAD
CARRIER

ROTOR

Fig. 4 Guide pin front caliper and pad assembly

INSPECTION

- The brake pad wear limit is 0.080 inches (2.0mm).
- If the pads show signs of heat cracks or if they are worn unevenly, check the caliper for a sticking piston or guides.
- Check the caliper for signs of fluid leakage or damage to the dust seal.
- Check the rotor for signs of heat cracks or discoloration.
- Minimum allowed thickness of solid brake rotors is 0.393 inches (10mm). Maximum allowed runout is 0.002 inches (0.06mm).
- Minimum allowed thickness of vented brake rotors is 0.708 inches (18mm). Maximum allowed runout is 0.002 inches (0.06mm).

Brake Caliper

REMOVAL & INSTALLATION

✳✳CAUTION

The ABS hydraulic modulator is capable of self-pressurizing and can generate pressures above 3000 psi. any time the ignition switch is turned ON. Relieve the system pressure before testing or repairing the hydraulic system. Make sure the ignition switch stays OFF and pump the brake pedal 25-35 times to relieve the system pressure. Improper repair or test procedures can cause serious or fatal injury.

Fig. 5 Hold the guide pin while removing or installing the caliper mounting bolts: rear caliper shown

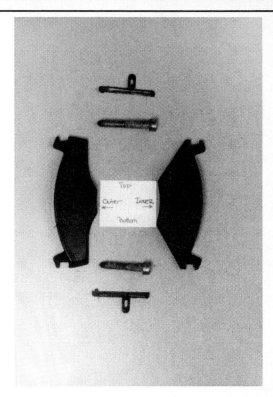

Fig. 7 The longer bolt goes at the top and the anti-rattle spring tang goes towards the inner pad

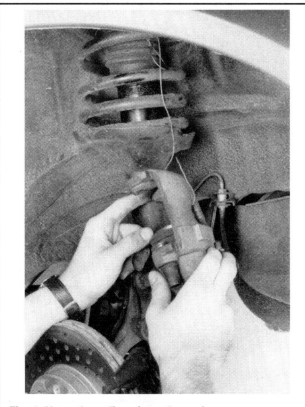

Fig. 6 Hang the caliper from the spring

Fig. 8 Hold the anti-rattle spring in place and install the pad

1. Raise and safely support the vehicle on jackstands and remove the wheels.

2. Loosen the hydraulic line at the caliper, then remove the caliper from the carrier. With guide pin calipers, be sure to hold the pin with a back-up wrench when removing the caliper bolts.

3. Remove the caliper from the hydraulic line and cap the line to prevent fluid leakage.

4. The carrier can be removed by removing the 2 bolts.

To install:

5. If removed, install the carrier. On standard brakes, torque the carrier bolts to 52 ft. lbs. (70 Nm). On ABS brakes, torque the carrier bolts to 92 ft. lbs. (125 Nm).

6. Thread the caliper onto the hydraulic line and hand-tighten it. Fit the caliper into place on the carrier.

7. On calipers with guide pins, torque the bolts to 25 ft. lbs. (35 Nm). On calipers with sleeves and bushings, torque the bolts to 18 ft. lbs. (25 Nm).

8. Tighten the hydraulic line and bleed the brakes.

OVERHAUL

▶ **See Figures 9 and 10**

1. Place the caliper in a vise or holding fixture.

2. Make sure the bleeder screw will loosen. If the screw breaks off, the caliper will have to replaced.

3. Remove the piston dust seal.

4. Place a wooden block in the caliper to prevent damage or injury to the piston. Carefully force the piston out by blowing compressed air into the hydraulic line fitting. Use only as much pressure as required and keep tools or fingers out of the way.

5. Remove the piston seal from the bore. Be careful not to damage the finished bore surface.

6. Clean all components with denatured alcohol that leaves no residue and dry with compressed air.

7. If the guide sleeves and bushings do not move freely, remove the dust seals and remove the sleeves. On calipers with guide pins, the pins are part of the carrier and usually not available separately.

8. Remove any rust or corrosion from the piston and bore with very fine emery paper and clean again. Excessive corrosion will cause the caliper to leak. Replace caliper if the corrosion can not be removed with fine emery paper.

9. Install the piston seal into the groove and make sure it is not twisted.

10. Lubricate the piston and bore with new brake fluid. Any thing else may cause damage to the rubber.

11. Install the piston and insert the inner lip of the dust seal into the groove in the brake caliper. The outer lip must slip into the groove in the piston. Make sure the dust seal is secure before installing the caliper.

Brake Rotor

REMOVAL & INSTALLATION

1. Raise and safely support vehicle and remove the wheel.
2. Remove the brake caliper, pads and the pad carrier.

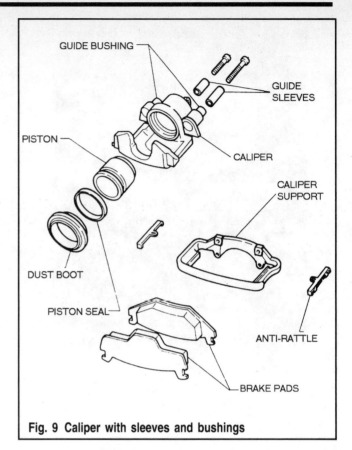

Fig. 9 Caliper with sleeves and bushings

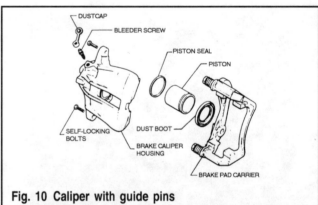

Fig. 10 Caliper with guide pins

3. With the wheel removed, the rotor is held in place only with a countersunk screw threaded into the hub. Remove the screw and slide the rotor off.

To install:

4. Install the rotor screw, clean the screw threads with a wire brush and install the screw. Torque the screw to 15 ft. lbs. (20 Nm).

5. Reinstall the caliper and pump the brake pedal several times to bring the pads into adjustment. Road test the vehicle.

INSPECTION

Brake rotors may be checked for lateral runout while installed on the car. This check will require a dial indicator gauge and stand to mount it on the caliper. VW has a special tool for this purpose which mounts the dial indicator to the caliper, but it can also be mounted on the shaft of a C-clamp attached to the outside of the caliper.

1. Remove the wheel and reinstall the wheel bolts (tightened to 65 ft. lbs.) to retain the rotor to the hub.

2. Mount the dial indicator securely to the caliper. The gauge stem should touch the rotor about 1/2 inch (13mm) from the outer edge.

3. Rotate the rotor and observe the gauge. Radial runout (wobble) must not exceed 0.002 inches (0.06mm). A rotor which exceeds this specification must be replaced or refinished.

REAR DRUM BRAKES

✳✳CAUTION

Some brake shoes contain asbestos, which has been determined to be a cancer causing agent. Never clean the brake surfaces with compressed air! Avoid inhaling any dust from any brake surface! When cleaning brake surfaces, use a commercially available brake cleaning fluid.

Brake Drums

REMOVAL & INSTALLATION

▶ **See Figure 11**

1. Raise and safely support vehicle and remove the rear wheels.

2. Insert a small pry tool through a wheel bolt hole and push up on the adjusting wedge to slacken the rear brake adjustment.

3. Remove the grease cap, cotter pin, locking ring, axle nut and thrust washer. Carefully remove the bearing and put all these parts where they will stay clean.

4. Carefully remove the drum.

5. Before installing, if any brake dust has fallen onto the axle, wipe off all the grease and apply a coat of new high

4. Brake rotors which have excessive radial runout, sharp ridges, or scoring can be refinished. First grinding must be done on both sides of the rotor to prevent squeaking and vibrating. Rotors which have only light grooves and are otherwise acceptable can be used without refinishing. The standard solid rotor is 12mm (0.472 inches) thick. It should not be ground to less than 10.5mm (0.413 inches). The standard vented rotor is 20mm (0.787 inches) thick and should be ground to no less than 18.5mm (0.728 inches).

temperature bearing grease. Install the parts in the reverse order of removal.

➡**When tightening the axle nut, the thrust washer must still be movable with a small screw driver. Spin the drum and check that the thrust washer can still be moved.**

6. When installing the locking ring, keep trying different positions of the ring on the nut until the cotter pin goes into the hole. Don't turn the nut to align the locking ring with the hole in the axle. Use a new cotter pin.

INSPECTION

- Check the drum for scoring or warping.
- Check for signs of heat cracking or discoloring.
- The maximum inside diameter after resurfacing must be no more than 7.106 inches (180.5mm).
- The maximum wear limit is 7.126 inches (181mm).

Brake Shoes

INSPECTION

- Check the shoes for contamination from brake fluid or axle grease.
- Minimum allowed lining thickness is 0.098 inches (2.5mm). This can be checked through the inspection plug on the back plate without removing the drum.

REMOVAL & INSTALLATION

▶ **See Figure 12**

1. Raise and safely support the vehicle and remove the rear wheels.

2. Remove the rear brake drum.

3. Remove the spring retainers by holding the pin behind the back plate, push in on the retainer and turn it ¼ turn.

4. Remove the shoes from the back plate by pulling first 1 shoe, then the other against the upper spring and from it's wheel cylinder slot. Detach the parking brake cable from the

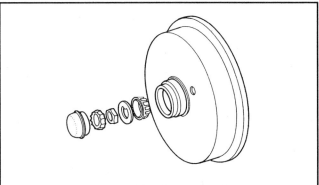

Fig. 11 Brake drum and bearing removal

brake lever. The entire shoe assembly should now be free of the vehicle.

5. Carefully note the position of each spring, as spring shapes and positions have varied from vehicle to vehicle and year to year.

6. Clamp the pushrod that holds the shoes apart at the top in a vise and begin removing the springs. Start with the lower return spring, adjusting wedge spring, upper return spring and then the tensioning spring and adjusting wedge.

7. On most vehicles, the parking brake lever must be removed from the old shoes and reused. When new parts are purchased, don't forget the clip that holds the parking brake lever pin in place.

To install:

8. Check the wheel cylinder for frozen pistons or leaks. If any defects are found, replace the wheel cylinder.

9. Inspect the springs. If the springs are damaged or show signs of overheating they should be replaced. Indications of overheated springs are discoloration and distortion.

10. Inspect the brake drum and recondition or replace as necessary.

11. Clean the back plate and lubricate the shoe contact points with a suitable brake lubricant.

12. With the push rod clamped in a vise, attach the front brake shoe and tensioning spring.

13. Insert the adjusting wedge between the front shoe and pushrod so its lug is pointing toward the backing plate.

14. Remove the parking brake lever from the old shoe and attach it onto the new rear brake shoe.

15. Put the rear brake shoe and parking brake lever assembly onto the pushrod and hook up the spring.

16. Connect the parking brake cable to the lever and place the whole assembly onto the backing plate.

17. Install the hold-down springs.

18. Install the upper and lower return springs.

19. Install the adjusting wedge spring.

20. Center the brake shoes on the backing plate, making sure the adjusting wedge is fully released (all the way up) before installing the drum.

21. Install the drum and wheel assembly.

22. Apply the brake pedal a few times to bring the brake shoe into adjustment.

23. If the wheel cylinder was replaced, bleed the system.

24. Road test the vehicle.

Wheel Cylinder

REMOVAL & INSTALLATION

1. Raise and safely support the vehicle and remove the wheel, drum and brake shoes.

2. Loosen the brake line on the rear of the cylinder but do not pull the line away from the cylinder or it may bend.

3. Remove the bolts and lockwashers that attach the wheel cylinder to the backing plate and remove the cylinder.

4. Position the new wheel cylinder on the backing plate and install the cylinder attaching bolts and lockwashers. Torque to 7.5 ft. lbs. (10 Nm).

5. Attach the brake line.

6. Install the brakes and bleed the system.

7. Road test the vehicle.

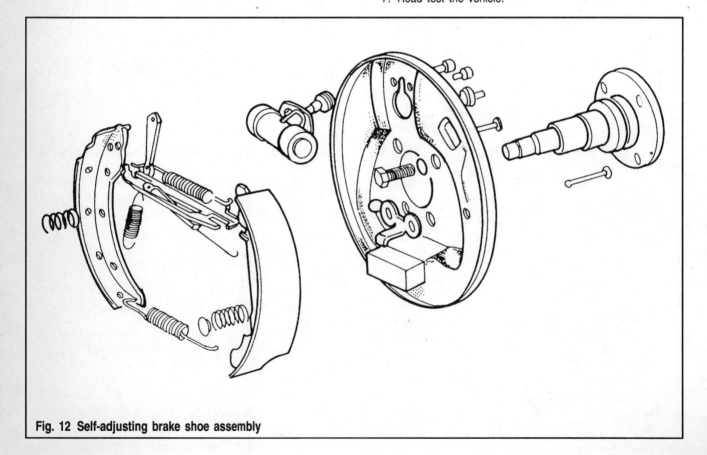

Fig. 12 Self-adjusting brake shoe assembly

Back Plate

REMOVAL & INSTALLATION

The same bolts hold the brake back plate and stub axle to the rear axle beam. The brake back plate can be removed with the brakes and wheel cylinder still attached. Disconnect the hydraulic line from the wheel cylinder and remove the 4 bolts to remove the back plate and stub axle. When installing, torque the bolts to 44 ft. lbs. (60 Nm).

REAR DISC BRAKES

※※CAUTION

Some brake pads contain asbestos, which has been determined to be a cancer causing agent. Never clean the brake surfaces with compressed air! Avoid inhaling any dust from any brake surface! When cleaning brake surfaces, use a commercially available brake cleaning fluid.

Brake Pads

REMOVAL & INSTALLATION

▶ See Figures 13 and 14

1. Raise and safely support the vehicle and remove the rear wheels.
2. Remove a sufficient quantity of brake fluid from the master cylinder reservoir to prevent it from over flowing when installing the pads. This is necessary as the caliper piston must be forced into the cylinder bore to provide sufficient clearance to install new pads.
3. Remove the parking brake cable clip from the caliper. Disconnect the parking brake cable.
4. Hold the guide pin with a back-up wrench and remove the upper mounting bolt from the brake caliper.
5. Swing the caliper downward and remove the brake pads.
6. Check the rotor for scoring and resurface or replace as necessary. Check the caliper for fluid leaks or a damaged dust seal. If any damage is found, the caliper will require overhauling or replacement.
   To install:
7. Retract the piston into the housing by rotating the piston clockwise.
8. Carefully clean the anchor plate and install the new brake pads onto the pad carrier.
9. Install the caliper to the pad carrier using a new self locking bolt or a thread locking compound and torque to 26 ft. lbs. (35 Nm).
10. Attach the hand brake cable to the caliper. It may be necessary to back off the adjustment nuts at the hand brake handle.
11. Fill the reservoir with brake fluid and pump the brake pedal about 40 times with the engine off to set the piston. Setting the piston with the power assist could cause the piston to jam.

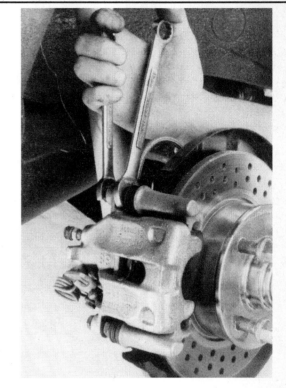

Fig. 13 Use a back-up wrench to remove the upper bolt from the guide pin

12. Check the parking brake operation, adjust the cable if necessary.
13. Road test the vehicle.

INSPECTION

- The brake pad wear limit is 0.080 inch (2.0mm).
- If the pads show signs of heat cracks or if they are worn unevenly, check the caliper for a sticking piston or guides.
- Check the caliper for signs of fluid leakage or damage to the dust seal.
- Check the rotor for signs of heat cracks or discoloration.
- Minimum allowed thickness of solid brake rotors is 0.393 inches (10mm). Maximum allowed runout is 0.002 inch (0.06mm).

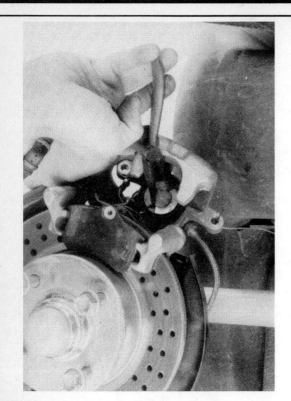

Fig. 14 Rotate the piston clockwise to retract it into the caliper

Brake Caliper

REMOVAL & INSTALLATION

✳✳CAUTION

The ABS hydraulic modulator is capable of self-pressurizing and can generate pressures above 3000 psi. any time the ignition switch is turned ON. Relieve the system pressure before testing or repairing the hydraulic system. Improper repair or test procedures can cause serious or fatal injury.

1. If equipped with ABS, make sure the ignition switch stays **OFF** and pump the brake pedal 25-35 times to relieve the system pressure.
2. Raise and safely support the vehicle on jackstands and remove the wheels.
3. Disconnect the parking brake cable.
4. Loosen the hydraulic line.
5. Use a back-up wrench to hold the guide pins and remove the caliper bolts.
6. Lift the caliper off the carrier and unscrew it from the hydraulic line.
7. Installation is the reverse of removal. Use new caliper mount bolts or clean the old bolts and apply a thread locking compound. Torque the bolts to 26 ft. lbs. (35 Nm).
8. Bleed the brakes.

OVERHAUL

▶ See Figure 15

1. Place the caliper in a vise or holding fixture.
2. Make sure the bleeder screw will loosen. If the screw breaks off, the caliper will have to replaced.
3. Remove the piston dust seal.
4. Unscrew the piston from the caliper. Do not attempt to blow the piston out with compressed air.
5. Remove the piston seal from the bore. Be careful not to damage the finished bore surface.
6. Clean all components with denatured alcohol that leaves no residue and dry with compressed air.
7. On calipers with guide pins, the pins are part of the carrier and usually not available separately.
7. Remove any rust or corrosion from the piston and bore with very fine emery paper and clean again. Excessive corrosion will cause the caliper to leak. Replace caliper if the corrosion can not be removed with fine emery paper.

➡**If the caliper is leaking at the parking brake lever, the caliper must be replaced.**

8. Install the piston seal into the groove and make sure it is not twisted.
9. Lubricate the piston and bore with new brake fluid. Any thing else may cause damage to the rubber.
10. Install the piston by screwing it onto the parking brake pushrod.
11. Insert the inner lip of the dust seal into the groove in the brake caliper. The outer lip must slip into the groove in the

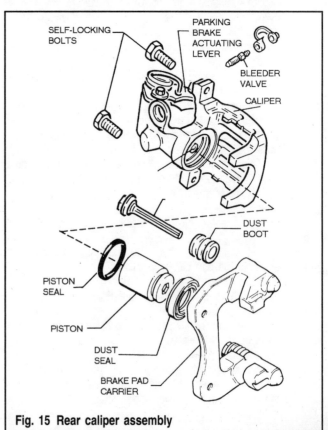

Fig. 15 Rear caliper assembly

piston. Make sure the dust seal is secure before installing the caliper.

Brake Rotor

REMOVAL & INSTALLATION

▶ **See Figure 16**

1. Raise and safely support vehicle and remove the rear wheels.

2. Remove the rear brake caliper and hang it from the rear spring with wire. Do not let the caliper hang by the hydraulic line.

3. Remove the grease cap, cotter pin, locking ring, axle nut and thrust washer. Carefully remove the bearing and put all these parts where they will stay clean.

4. Slip the rotor/hub off the axle.

To install:

5. Before installing, if any brake dust has fallen onto the axle, wipe off all the grease and apply a coat of new high temperature bearing grease. Install the parts in the reverse order of removal.

➡**When tightening the axle nut, the thrust washer must still be movable with a small screw driver. Spin the rotor and check that the thrust washer can still be moved.**

6. When installing the locking ring, keep trying different positions of the ring on the nut until the cotter pin goes into

the hole. Don't turn the nut to align the locking ring with the hole in the axle. Use a new cotter pin.

INSPECTION

Brake rotors may be checked for lateral runout while installed on the car. This check will require a dial indicator gauge and stand to mount it on the caliper. VW has a special tool for this purpose which mounts the dial indicator to the caliper, but it can also be mounted on the shaft of a C-clamp attached to the outside of the caliper.

1. Remove the wheel and reinstall the wheel bolts (tightened to 65 ft. lbs.) to retain the rotor to the hub.

2. Mount the dial indicator securely to the caliper. The gauge stem should touch the rotor about 1/2 inch (13mm) from the outer edge.

3. Rotate the rotor and observe the gauge. Radial runout (wobble) must not exceed 0.002 inch (0.06mm). A rotor which exceeds this specification must be replaced or refinished.

4. Brake rotors which have excessive radial runout, sharp ridges, or scoring can be refinished. First grinding must be done on both sides of the rotor to prevent squeaking and vibrating. Rotors which have only light grooves and are otherwise acceptable can be used without refinishing. The standard solid rotor is 12mm (0.472 inches) thick. It should not be ground to less than 10.5mm (0.413 inch).

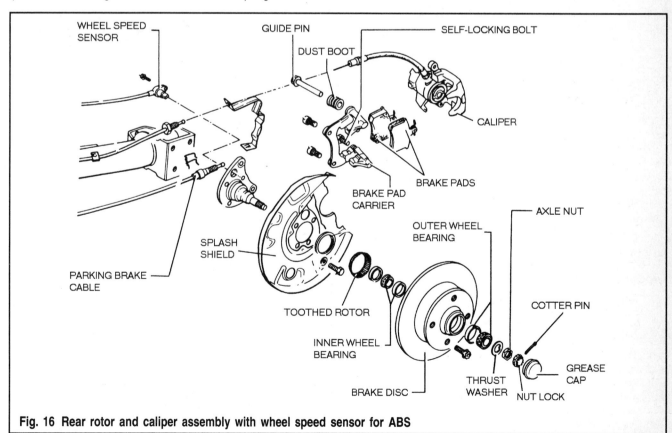

Fig. 16 Rear rotor and caliper assembly with wheel speed sensor for ABS

PARKING BRAKE

Cable

REMOVAL & INSTALLATION

Rear Drum Brakes

1. Block the front wheels and release the hand brake.
2. Raise and safely support the rear of the vehicle.
3. Remove the rear brake shoes.
4. Remove the brake cable assembly from the back plates.
5. Remove the cable adjusting nuts at the handle and detach the cable guides from the floor pan.
6. Pull the cables out from under the vehicle.
7. Installation is the reverse of removal. Adjust the parking brake and road test the vehicle.

Disc Brakes

1. Raise and safely support the vehicle.
2. Release the parking brake. It may be necessary to unscrew the adjusting nuts to provide slack in the brake cable.
3. At each rear wheel brake caliper, remove the spring clip retaining the parking brake cable to the caliper.

4. Lift the cable from the caliper mount and disengage it from the parking brake lever.
5. Pull the cables out from under the vehicle.
6. Installation is the reverse of removal. Adjust the parking brake as described at the beginning of this section.

ADJUSTMENT

➡️**Parking brake adjustment is at the beginning of this section.**

Parking Brake Lever

REMOVAL & INSTALLATION

1. Make sure the vehicle will not roll and remove the adjusting nuts from the brake cables under the parking brake handle.
2. Remove the spring clip from the guide pin and remove the pin. The lever will lift out when the button is pushed.
3. Installation is the reverse of removal. Push the button to fit the lever over the ratchet and insert the guide pin.
4. Adjust the parking brake as described at the beginning of this section.

ANTI-LOCK BRAKE SYSTEM

Description and Operation

Anti-lock Brake Systems (ABS) are designed to prevent locked-wheel skidding during hard braking or during braking on slippery surfaces. The front wheels of a vehicle cannot apply steering force if they are locked and sliding; the vehicle will continue in the previous direction of travel. The 4 wheel ABS system used on Volkswagen vehicles holds the wheels just below the point of locking, thereby allowing some steering response and preventing the rear of the vehicle from sliding sideways.

There are conditions for which the ABS system provides no benefit. Hydroplaning is possible when the tires ride on a film of water, losing contact with the paved surface. This renders the vehicle totally uncontrollable until road contact is regained. Extreme steering maneuvers at high speed or cornering beyond the limits of tire adhesion can result in skidding which is independent of vehicle braking. For this reason, the system is named anti-lock rather than anti-skid. Wheel spin during acceleration on slippery surfaces may also fool the system into detecting a system failure and entering the fail-safe mode.

Under normal conditions, the ABS system functions in the same manner as a standard brake system and is transparent to the operator. The system is a combination of electrical and hydraulic components, working together to control the flow of brake fluid to the wheels when necessary.

The Electronic Control Unit (ECU) is the electronic brain of the system, receiving and interpreting signals from the wheel speed sensors. The unit will enter anti-lock mode when it senses impending wheel lock at any wheel and immediately control the brake line pressures to the affected wheel(s) by issuing output signals to the hydraulic modulator assembly.

The hydraulic modulator contains solenoids which react to the signals from the ECU. Each solenoid controls brake fluid pressure to one wheel. The solenoids allow brake line pressure to build according to brake pedal pressure, hold (isolating the system from the pedal and maintaining current pressure) or decrease by isolating the pedal circuit and bleeding some fluid from the line.

The decisions regarding these functions are made very rapidly and each solenoid can be cycled up to 10 times per second. Volkswagen employs a 3-channel control system. The front wheels are controlled separately; the rears are controlled together, based on the signal of the wheel with the greatest locking tendency.

The operator may feel a pulsing in the brake pedal and/or hear popping or clicking noises when the system engages. These sensations are due to the valves cycling and the pressures being changed rapidly within the brake system. While completely normal and not a sign of system failure, these sensations can be disconcerting to an operator unfamiliar with the system.

Although the ABS system prevents wheel lock-up under hard braking, as brake pressure increases, wheel slip is allowed to increase as well. This slip will result in some tire chirp during ABS operation. The sound should not be interpreted as lock-up but rather as an indication of the system holding the wheel(s) just outside the locking point. Additionally, the final few feet of an ABS-engaged stop may be completed with the wheels locked; the system is inoperative below approximately 3 mph.

When the ignition is ON and vehicle speed is over 3 mph (5 kph), the ECU monitors the function of the system. Should a fault be noted, such a loss of signal from a sensor, the ABS system is immediately disabled by the ECU. The ANTI-LOCK dashboard warning lamp is illuminated to inform the operator. When the ABS system is disabled, the vehicle retains normal braking capacity without the benefits of anti-lock.

Troubleshooting

Vehicles with anti-lock brake systems (ABS) have an electronic fault memory and an indicator light on the instrument panel. When the engine is first started, the light will go on to indicate the system is pressurizing and performing a self diagnostic check. After the system is at full pressure, the light will go out. If it remains lit, there is a fault in the system.

The fault memory can only be accessed with the VW tester VAG 1551 or VAG 1598, or equivalent. If this diagnostic equipment is not available, most of the system can still be tested with a volt/ohmmeter. Service to the system is quite limited. Most components cannot be repaired, only replaced.

Before diagnosing an apparent ABS problem, make absolutely certain that the normal braking system is in correct working order. Many common brake problems (dragging parking brake, seepage, etc.) will affect the ABS system. A visual check of specific system components may reveal problems creating an apparent ABS malfunction. Performing this inspection may reveal a simple failure, thus eliminating extended diagnostic time.

1. Inspect the tire pressures; they must be approximately equal for the system to operate correctly.

2. Inspect the wheels and tires on the vehicle. They must be of the same size and type to generate accurate speed signals.

3. Inspect the brake fluid level in the reservoir.

4. Inspect brake lines, hoses, master cylinder assembly and brake calipers for leakage.

5. Visually check brake lines and hoses for excessive wear, heat damage, punctures, contact with other parts, missing clips or holders, blockage or crimping.

6. Check the calipers for rust or corrosion. Check for proper sliding action if applicable.

7. Check the calipers for freedom of motion during application and release.

8. Inspect the wheel speed sensors for proper mounting and connections.

9. Inspect the sensor wheels for broken teeth or poor mounting.

10. Certain driver induced faults, such as not releasing the parking brake fully, spinning the wheels under acceleration, sliding due to excessive cornering speed or driving on extremely rough surfaces may fool the system and trigger the dash warning light. These induced faults are not system failures but examples of vehicle performance outside the parameters of the control unit.

11. Many system shut-downs are due to loss of sensor signals to or from the controller. The most common cause is not a failed sensor but a loose, corroded or dirty connector. Check harness and component connectors carefully.

12. Check for correct battery voltage and inspect the condition of all ABS fuses.

SYSTEM TESTING

1. Make sure the ignition switch is **OFF** and unplug the control unit connector. The control unit is in the right rear of the trunk.

2. Use a volt/ohmmeter and the following charts to test the system. Start at the beginning and work all the way towards the end before removing any components.

3. After repairs, make sure the warning light on the instrument panel operates properly. It should light when the ignition is first turned **ON**, then go out after the vehicle starts moving. If not, the system is still not repaired.

✳✳CAUTION

The hydraulic modulator is capable of self-pressurizing and can generate pressures above 3000 psi. any time the ignition switch is turned ON. Relieve the system pressure before testing or repairing the hydraulic system. Improper repair or test procedures can cause serious or fatal injury.

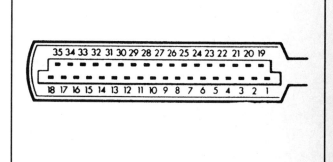

Fig. 17 ABS control unit connector

Test step	Connector terminals	Component to be tested	Testing requirements	Test results (specifications)	Additional steps (for test results NOT within specs)
1	2 + 1	ABS control unit (J104), voltage supply	• Switch ignition ON	Battery voltage (approximate) Note: Take reading on 20V scale	• Check wire from terminal 1 to ground • Check wire from terminal 2 to terminal D-7 (relay board)
2	3 + 1	ABS relay (J102), function	• Switch ignition ON • Remove fuse S16 • Bridge sockets 2 and 8 After testing: • Disconnect connections from sockets 2 and 8 • Install fuse S16	Battery voltage (approximate)	• Check wire from terminal 1 to ground • Check wire from terminal 3, via J102, to battery (+) • Perform Test step 9 • Perform Test step 24
3	12 + 1	Brake light switch, (F), function	• Switch ignition ON • Actuate brake pedal	Battery voltage (approximate)	• Check fuse S20 and brake light switch (F) • Check wire from terminal 1 to ground • Check wire from terminal 2 to terminal W-4 (relay board)
4	32 + 1	ABS relay for hydraulic pump (J185), function	• Switch ignition OFF • Pull plug terminal T2 from hydraulic pump (V64) • Press brake pedal to floor 20 times • Switch ignition ON After testing, reconnect plug terminal T2	Battery voltage (approximate)	• Check wire from terminal 1 to ground • Check wire from terminal 32, via J185 and fuse S53, to battery (+) • Perform Test step 12 • Perform Test step 32
5	4 + 22	Wheel speed sensor, right rear (G44), voltage	• Switch ignition OFF • Raise vehicle with hoist; support • Rotate right rear wheel, approximately 1 rotation per second	75 mV ac (minimum) Note: Take reading on 2V scale	• Check installation of sensor • Check plug type terminal T2 • Perform Test step 16 • Perform Test step 20
6	6 + 24	Wheel speed sensor, left rear (G46), voltage	• Switch ignition OFF • Raise vehicle with hoist; support • Rotate left rear wheel, approximately 1 rotation per second	75 mV ac (minimum)	• Check installation of sensor • Check plug type terminal T2 • Perform Test step 17 • Perform Test step 21
7	7 + 25	Wheel speed sensor, right front (G45), voltage	• Switch ignition OFF • Raise vehicle with hoist; support • Rotate right front wheel, approximately 1 rotation per second	75 mV ac (minimum)	• Check installation of sensor • Check plug type terminal T2 • Perform Test step 18 • Perform Test step 22

Test step	Connector terminals	Component to be tested	Testing requirements	Test results (specifications)	Additional steps (for test results NOT within specs)
8	5 + 23	Wheel speed sensor, left front (G47), voltage	• Switch ignition OFF • Raise vehicle with hoist; support • Rotate left front wheel, approximately 1 rotation per second	75 mV ac (minimum)	• Check installation of sensor • Check plug type terminal T2 • Perform Test step 19 • Perform Test step 23
9	1 + 3	ABS relay (J102), continuity	• Switch ignition OFF	1.5 Ohms (maximum) Note: Take reading on 200 Ohm scale	• Check circuit from terminal 3, via J102, to hydraulic unit ground • Check wire from terminal 1 to ground • If no open circuits exist, replace J102
10	1 + 20	ABS relay (J102), continuity	• Switch ignition OFF	1.5 Ohms (maximum)	• Check circuit from terminal 20, via J102, to hydraulic unit ground • Check wire from terminal 1 to ground • If no open circuits exist, replace J102
11	1 + 11	Inlet valve (N99), ground Outlet valve (N104), ground	• Switch ignition OFF	1.5 Ohms (maximum)	• Check circuit from terminal 11, via hydraulic unit to ground • Check wire from terminal 1 to ground
12	1 + 14	Hydraulic pump relay (J185), ground via high pressure switch (F109)	• switch ignition ON • press brake pedal to floor, 20 times	1.5 Ohms (maximum)	• Check circuit from terminal 14, to J185/186, and via F109, to ground • Check wire from terminal 1 to ground • Check continuity on F109
13	9 + 10.	Low pressure warning switch (F116), continuity Brake fluid level warning contact (F117), continuity	• Check for correct brake fluid level • Switch ignition ON • Wait until pump switches OFF (reservoir filled)	1.5 Ohms (maximum)	• Check circuit from terminal 9, via F117 and F116, to terminal 10 • Perform Test step 14 • Perform Test step 15
14	9 + 10	Low pressure warning switch (F116), continuity	• Check for correct brake fluid level • Switch ignition ON • Press brake pedal to floow, 20 times (reservoir filled)	100 K Ohms (minimum) Note: Take reading on 200 K Ohm scale	• Check if F116 has continuity between terminals 3 and 5, of hydraulic unit's 5-pin terminal. If YES, F116 is defective. Replace • Perform Test step 15
15	9 + 10	Brake fluid level warning contact (F117)	• Switch ignition ON • Wait until pump switches OFF (reservoir filled) • Switch ignition ON • Remove warning contact from reservoir	2 M Ohms (minimum), when warning contact float has been removed from fluid (simulating level below minimum)	• Check F117, when removed, for continuity. If YES, F117 is defective. Replace

Test step	Connector terminals	Component to be tested	Testing requirements	Test results (specifications)	Additional steps (for test results NOT within specs)
16	4 + 22	Wheel speed sensor, right rear (G44), resistance	• Switch ignition OFF	0.8–1.4 K Ohms Note: Take reading on 2 K Ohm scale	• Check plug connector T2 • Check speed sensor resistance (0.8–1.4 K Ohms) • Check wire to wheel speed sensor • Perform Test step 20
17	6 + 24	Wheel speed sensor, left rear (G46), resistance	• Switch ignition OFF	0.8–1.4 K Ohms	• Check plug connector T2 • Check speed sensor resistance (0.8–1.4 K Ohms) • Check wire to wheel speed sensor • Perform Test step 21
18	7 + 25	Wheel speed sensor, right rear (G45), resistance	• Switch ignition OFF	0.8–1.4 K Ohms	• Check plug connector T2 • Check speed sensor resistance (0.8–1.4 K Ohms) • Check wire to wheel speed sensor • Perform Test step 22
19	5 + 23	Wheel speed sensor, left front (G47), resistance	• Switch ignition OFF	0.8–1.4 K Ohms	• Check plug connector T2 • Check speed sensor resistance (0.8–1.4 K Ohms) • Check wire to wheel speed sensor • Perform Test step 23
20	1 + 4	Shielded wire to right rear wheel speed sensor (G44), insulator resistance	• Switch ignition OFF	2 M Ohms (minimum)	• Check wire for damaged insulation
21	1 + 6	Shielded wire to left rear wheel speed sensor (G46), insulator resistance	• Switch ignition OFF	2 M Ohms (minimum)	• Check wire for damaged insulation
22	1 + 7	Shielded wire to wheel speed sensor, right front (G45), insulator resistance	• Switch ignition OFF	2 M Ohms (minimum)	• Check wire for damaged insulation
23	1 + 5	Shielded wire to wheel speed sensor, left front (G47), insulator resistance	• Switch ignition OFF	2 M Ohms (minimum)	• Check wire for damaged insulation
24	1 + 8	ABS relay (J102), resistance	• Switch ignition OFF	50–100 Ohms Note: Take reading on 200 Ohm scale	• Check wire from terminal 8, via J102, to ground • Check coil resistance (50–100 Ohms). Replace J102, if necessary

Test step	Connector terminals	Component to be tested	Testing requirements	Test results (specifications)	Additional steps (for test results NOT within specs)
25	1 + 18	ABS main valve (N105), resistance	• Switch ignition OFF	2–5 Ohms	• Check wire from terminal 18, via N105, to ground • Check N105 coil resistance (2–5 Ohms). If defective, replace hydraulic unit • Perform Test step 33
26	11 + 17	Inlet valve, rear (N103), resistance	• Switch ignition OFF	5–7 Ohms	• Check wire from terminal 17, via N103, to ground • Test N103 resistance (5–7 Ohms). If defective, replace hydraulic unit
27	11 + 15	Inlet valve, right front (N99), resistance	• Switch ignition OFF	5–7 Ohms	• Check wire from terminal 15, via N99, to ground • Check N99 resistance (5–7 Ohms). If defective, replace hydraulic unit
28	11 + 35	Inlet valve, left front (N101), resistance	• Switch ignition OFF	5–7 Ohms	• Check wire from terminal 35, via N101, to ground • Check N101 resistance (5–7 Ohms). If defective, replace hydraulic unit
29	11 + 33	Outlet valve, rear (N104), resistance	• Switch ignition OFF	3–5 Ohms	• Check wire from terminal 33, via N104, to ground • Check N104 resistance (3–5 Ohms). If defective, replace hydraulic unit
30	11 + 34	Outlet valve, right front (N100), resistance	• Switch ignition OFF	3–5 Ohms	• Check wire from terminal 34, via N100, to ground • Check N100 resistance (3–5 Ohms). If defective, replace hydraulic unit
31	11 + 16	Outlet valve, left front (N102), resistance	• Switch ignition OFF	3–5 Ohms	• Check wire from terminal 16, via N102, to ground • Check N102 resistance (3–5 Ohms). If defective, replace hydraulic unit

Test step	Connector terminals	Component to be tested	Testing requirements	Test results (specifications)	Additional steps (for test results NOT within specs)
32	2 + 14	ABS hydraulic pump relay (J185), resistance	• Switch ignition OFF	50–100 Ohms	• Check wire from terminal 2, via J185, to contact 14 • Check coil resistance (50–100 Ohms). If necessary, replace J185
33	Bridge 2–18	ABS main valve (N105), function	• Switch ignition OFF • Press brake pedal to floor and hold • Switch ignition ON	Pulsation from brake pedal should be felt at foot	For defective N105 • Replace hydraulic unit
34	—	ABS hydraulic pump (V64), function	• Switch ignition OFF • Pump brake pedal 20 times to discharge reservoir • Mark fluid level on reservoir • Switch ignition ON	Fluid level in reservoir drops approximately 1.0 cm (0.4 in.)	• Check wire from battery (+), via fuse S53 and components J185 and V64, back to battery. If no opens exist, replace V64
35	Bridge 2-17-33	Inlet and outlet valve, rear (N103, N104), function	• Raise/support vehicle • Switch ignition OFF • Depress brake pedal	Rear wheels must lock	• Replace defective hydraulic unit
			• Switch ignition ON • Depress brake pedal	Rear wheels must rotate freely	
36	Bridge 2-15-34	Inlet and outlet valve, right front (N99, N100), function	• Raise/support vehicle • Switch ignition OFF • Depress brake pedal	Right front wheel must lock	• Replace defective hydraulic unit
			• Switch ignition ON • Depress brake pedal	Right front wheel must rotate freely	
37	Bridge 2-16-35	Inlet and outlet valve, left front (N101, N102), function	• Raise/support vehicle • Switch ignition OFF • Depress brake pedal	Left front wheel must lock	• Replace defective hydraulic unit
			• Switch ignition ON • Depress brake pedal	Left front wheel must rotate freely	

Control Unit

REMOVAL & INSTALLATION

1. Make sure the ignition switch is **OFF** and remove the right luggage compartment panel.
2. Remove the control unit and disconnect the wiring.
3. Installation is the reverse of removal. Make sure the warning light on the instrument panel goes out when the vehicle speed is above 3 mph.

Wheel Speed Sensor

REMOVAL & INSTALLATION

1. Raise and safely support the vehicle.
2. Remove the wheel and unbolt the sensor from the steering knuckle or stub axle.
3. The rotor portion of the sensor assembly is secured to the inside of the wheel hub. To remove the front rotor, the hub must be pressed out of the front wheel bearing.
4. On the rear wheels, the sensor is pressed into the brake rotor. To remove it:
   a. Remove the wheel bearing and the brake rotor.

b. Insert a drift pin through the wheel bolt holes and gently tap the speed sensor rotor out a little bit at each hole, much like removing an inner wheel bearing race.

To install:

5. When reinstalling, use a suitable sleeve to drive the speed sensor rotor into the brake rotor evenly. When the cover ring is installed, the distance from the ring to the splash shield should be 0.375 inch (9.5mm).

6. When reinstalling the sensor, use a dry lubricant on the sides of the sensor and torque the bolt to 7 ft. lbs. (10 Nm).

Relieving Anti-lock Brake System Pressure

With the ignition switch **OFF**, pump the brake pedal 25-35 times to depressurize the system. The system will recharge itself via the electric pump as soon as the ignition is turned **ON**. Disconnect the pump or the battery to prevent unintended pressurization. The system can then be serviced and bled normally.

Modulator Assembly

REMOVAL & INSTALLATION

▶ **See Figure ?**

1. Turn the ignition **OFF** and depress the brake pedal 25-35 times to depressurize the modulator assembly. Disconnect the pump or battery to prevent unintended pressurization.

2. Inside the vehicle near the right tail light, locate and disconnect the ABS control unit and the ground connection.

3. Remove the brake fluid from the reservoir with a suction pump.

4. Disconnect the brake lines from the modulator assembly and protect the connections from contamination with suitable plugs.

5. Working inside the vehicle, remove the left shelf under the dash to gain access to the brake pedal linkage. Remove the clevis bolt and disconnect the pedal.

6. Remove the locknuts and remove the pressure modulator.

7. Installation is the reverse of removal. Use new locknuts and torque to 18 ft. lbs. (25 Nm). Refill the reservoir with new brake fluid and bleed the system.

Filling and Bleeding

❊❊CAUTION

The hydraulic modulator is capable of self-pressurizing and can generate pressures above 3000 psi. any time the ignition switch is turned ON. Relieve the system pressure before servicing the hydraulic system. Improper repair or test procedures can cause serious or fatal injury.

FILLING THE SYSTEM

The reservoir on the hydraulic modulator is filled in the usual manner with no special procedures being necessary. Always wipe the cap and surrounding area clean of dirt and debris before opening the reservoir; the smallest bit of dirt may impair the operation of the system. When adding fluid, fill the reservoir only to the MAX line on the reservoir; do not overfill.

Only DOT 4 brake fluid must be used; silicone or DOT 5 fluid is specifically prohibited. Do not use any fluid which contains a petroleum base; these fluids will cause swelling and distortion of the rubber parts within the system. Do not use old or contaminated brake fluid. Do not reuse fluid which has been bled from the system.

BLEEDING THE SYSTEM

Bleeding may be performed using either a pressure bleeder or the manual method. In either case an assistant will be required to depress the brake pedal. Extreme cleanliness must be observed at all times. If using the manual method, the fluid reservoir must be filled to the upper edge before bleeding begins. Do not allow the fluid level to drop below the MIN mark at any time. Do not reuse fluid released during bleeding.

Front Brakes

1. Turn the ignition switch **OFF**.
2. Relieve the brake system pressure.
3. If using pressure bleeder equipment, connect it to the brake fluid reservoir and switch it on.
4. Connect a tight-fitting vinyl hose to the bleeder port of the caliper. If using pressure bleeding equipment, begin at the left front caliper. If using the manual method, begin on either side. Immerse the other end of the hose in a container of clean brake fluid.

➡ **Use of a cap or cover on the container is recommended. The brake fluid may bleed with enough force to splash out of an open container.**

5. Open the bleeder screw. Have an assistant depress the brake pedal slowly until the fluid flows without bubbles.
6. Close the bleeder screw before the pedal is released.
7. Remove the vinyl tube from the caliper. Inspect and top off the fluid supply in the reservoir if necessary.
8. Repeat the procedure at the opposite wheel.

Rear Brakes

▶ **See Figure 3**

1. Turn the ignition switch **OFF**.
2. Relieve the brake system pressure.
3. If using pressure bleeder equipment, connect it to the brake fluid reservoir and switch it on.

4. Connect a tight-fitting vinyl hose to the bleeder port of either caliper. Immerse the other end of the hose in a container of clean brake fluid.

➡**Use of a cap or cover on the container is recommended. The brake fluid may bleed with enough force to splash out of an open container.**

5. Open the bleeder screw. Have an assistant turn the ignition switch **ON**.

6. Press the lever of the proportioning valve towards the axle until brake fluid flows out without bubbles. Release the lever and close the bleeder screw.

➡**Running time of the ABS pump must not exceed 120 seconds at any one time. If this time is approached or exceeded, a minimum of 10 minutes cooling time is required before proceeding. Do not allow the fluid level to fall below the MIN line at any time.**

7. Switch the ignition **OFF** while transferring equipment. Remove the vinyl tube from the caliper. Inspect and top off the fluid supply in the reservoir if necessary.

8. Repeat the procedure at the opposite wheel.

9. Once both rear calipers are bled and the service equipment removed, switch the ignition **ON** until the pump shuts off.

10. Fill the brake fluid reservoir to the MAX line.

BRAKE SPECIFICATIONS

All measurements in inches unless noted.

Year	Model	Master Cylinder Bore	Brake Disc		Maximum Runout	Brake Drum Diameter			Minimum Lining Thickness	
			Original Thickness	Minimum Thickness		Original Inside Diameter	Max. Wear Limit	Maximum Machine Diameter	Front	Rear
1990	Jetta	0.820	①	②	0.002	7.087③	7.126	7.106④	0.276	0.098⑤
	Golf	0.820	①	②	0.002	7.087③	7.126	7.106④	0.276	0.098⑤
	Cabriolet	0.820	①	②	0.002	7.087③	7.126	7.106④	0.276	0.098⑤
1991	Jetta	0.820	①	②	0.002	7.087③	7.126	7.106④	0.276	0.098⑤
	Golf	0.820	①	②	0.002	7.087③	7.126	7.106④	0.276	0.098⑤
	Cabriolet	0.820	①	②	0.002	7.087③	7.126	7.106④	0.276	0.098⑤
1992–93	Jetta	0.820	①	②	0.002	7.087③	7.126	7.106④	0.276	0.098⑤
	Golf	0.820	①	②	0.002	7.087③	7.126	7.106④	0.276	0.098⑤
	Cabriolet	0.820	①	②	0.002	7.087③	7.126	7.106④	0.276	0.098⑤

① Solid disc—0.472
   Vented disc—0.787
② Solid disc—0.393
   Vented disc—0.708
③ Rear disc—0.394
④ Rear disc—0.319
⑤ Rear disc—0.276

EXTERIOR
ANTENNA 10-4
BUMPERS 10-3
CONVERTIBLE TOP 10-4
DOORS 10-2
FENDERS 10-4
GRILLE 10-3
HOOD 10-2
OUTSIDE MIRRORS 10-3
POWER TOP CYLINDERS 10-5
POWER TOP MOTOR 10-4
REAR HATCH 10-3
SUNROOF 10-8
TRUNK LID 10-2
INTERIOR
AIR CONDITIONER VENTS 10-9

CENTRAL LOCKING SYSTEM 10-9
DOOR GLASS AND
REGULATOR 10-10
DOOR PANELS 10-9
ELECTRIC WINDOW MOTOR 10-10
HEADLINER 10-9
INSIDE REAR VIEW MIRROR 10-13
INSTRUMENT PANEL 10-8
MANUAL DOOR LOCKS 10-9
REAR WINDOW OR HATCH
GLASS 10-13
SEAT BELTS 10-13
SEATS 10-13
SIDE QUARTER GLASS 10-13
WINDSHIELD 10-10

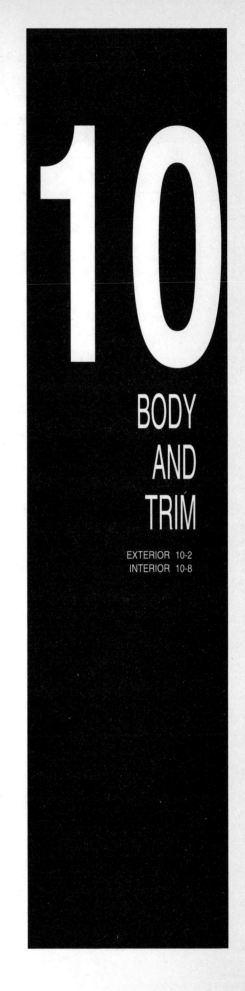

10

BODY AND TRIM

EXTERIOR 10-2
INTERIOR 10-8

EXTERIOR

Doors

REMOVAL & INSTALLATION

1. Open the door and support it securely with a floor jack or blocks. Remove the door check strap sleeve and remove the door check strap.
2. If necessary, remove the door panel to disconnect the wiring for speakers, electric windows, electric mirrors and the air line for power door locks.
3. Have an assistant steady the door and remove the hinge bolts to remove the door.
4. Installation is the reverse of removal.

ADJUSTMENT & ALIGNMENT

When checking door alignment, look carefully at each seam between the door and body. The gap should be even all the way around the door. Pay particular attention to the door seams at the corners farthest from the hinges; this is the area where errors will be most evident. Additionally, the door should push against the weatherstrip when latched to seal out wind and water. The contact should be even all the way around and the stripping should be about half compressed. The position of the door can be adjusted in three dimensions: fore and aft, up and down, in and out. The primary adjusting points are the hinge-to-body bolts.

1. Apply tape to the fender and door edges to protect the paint. Two layers of common masking tape works well.
2. Loosen the bolts just enough to allow the hinge to move. With the help of an assistant, position the door up and down as required and snug the bolts.
3. Inspect the door seams carefully and repeat the adjustment until correctly aligned.
4. Inspect the front door seal and determine how much it is being crushed. If there is little or no contact in this area, or if the door is recessed into the body at the front when closed, loosen the hinge-to-door bolts and adjust the door in or out as needed. Don't worry about the latch yet.
5. Make sure the door moves smoothly on the hinges without binding. When the door fits the opening correctly, tighten the bolts.
6. To adjust the latch, loosen the large cross-point screw holding the striker on the door jam on the body. These bolts will be very tight; an impact screwdriver is the best tool for this job. Make sure you are using the proper size bit.
7. With the bolts just loose enough to allow the striker to move if necessary, hold the outer door handle in the released position and close the door. The striker will move into the correct location to match the door latch. Open the door and tighten the mounting bolts. The striker may be adjusted towards or away from the center of the car, thereby tightening or loosening the door fit. The striker can be moved up and down to compensate for door position, but if the door is correctly mounted at the hinges this should not be necessary.

➡ **Do not attempt to correct height variations (sag) by adjusting the striker.**

8. After the striker bolts have been tightened, open and close the door several times. Observe the motion of the door as it engages the striker; it should continue its straight-in motion and not deflect up or down as it hits the striker.
9. Check the feel of the latch during opening and closing. It must be smooth and linear, without any trace of grinding or binding during engagement and release. It may be necessary to repeat the striker adjustment several times (and possibly re-adjust the hinges) before the correct door-to- body fit is achieved.

Hood

REMOVAL & INSTALLATION

1. Raise the hood and support it securely. Cover the painted areas of the body to protect the finish from being damaged. Scribe the hood hinge-to-hood locations for installation.
2. While an assistant holds the hood, remove the hinge-to-hood retaining bolts.
3. Remove the hood from the vehicle.
4. Installation is the reverse of removal. Align the hood with the scribe marks and torque the bolts to 15 ft. lbs. (20 Nm).

ALIGNMENT

Loosen the hinge to hood attaching bolts and move the hood from side to side until there is an equal amount of clearance on both sides of the hood and fender. Tighten the hood bolts.

Trunk Lid

REMOVAL & INSTALLATION

1. Open and support the trunk lid securely.
2. If necessary, remove the inner panel to disconnect any wiring or tubing.
3. Mark the position of the trunk lid hinge in relation to the trunk lid.
4. With an assistant, remove the two bolts attaching the hinge to the trunk lid. Remove the trunk lid from the vehicle.
5. Installation is the reverse of removal. Align the scribe marks and torque the bolts to 18 ft. lbs. (25 Nm).

ADJUSTMENT

To make the front-to-rear or side-to-side adjustment, loosen the trunk lid attaching bolts and move the trunk lid as necessary. Tighten the trunk lid attaching bolts. To make the up-and-down adjustment, loosen the hinge-to-hinge support attaching bolts and raise or lower the hinge as necessary. The trunk lid is at the correct height when it is flush with the trunk deck.

Rear Hatch

REMOVAL & INSTALLATION

1. Open the rear hatch fully and support it in place.
2. Carefully remove the trim fasteners with a flat screwdriver and remove the trim.
3. Disconnect the wiring and any tubing.
4. Remove the ball studs from both the upper and lower ends of the struts and remove them.

✳✳CAUTION

Never disassemble the support strut, as it is filled with high pressure gas. Do not turn the piston rod and the cylinder when the piston rod is extended. When discarding the strut, drill a 2-3mm (0.08-0.12 inch) hole in the bottom of the damper or use a hack saw to release the gas. Make sure to protect yourself against any metal particles that may be thrown into the air by the compressed gas during drilling.

5. Remove the rear hatch hinge bolts and remove the rear hatch.
6. Installation is the reverse of the removal procedure.

ALIGNMENT

1. To align the front-to-rear position of the hatch, loosen the hinge attaching bolts on both the hatch and the body.
2. Position the hatch so the gap is even all the way around the hatch.
3. To adjust the hatch closing position, loosen both the lock and striker bolts.

Bumpers

REMOVAL & INSTALLATION

Front

GOLF, GTI AND JETTA

1. Raise the vehicle and support with jackstands.
2. Remove the bracket on both body long members and bolts from underneath the vehicle.

3. Remove the small grille under the apron. Remove bumper bracket bolts and remove the bumper from the vehicle.
4. Install the bumper and torque the bolts to 59 ft. lbs. (83 Nm).

CABRIOLET

1. Raise the vehicle and support with jackstands.
2. Drill out the rivets holding the bumper cover to the body inside the front wheel well.
3. Disconnect the parking light wiring.
4. Remove the bolts and slide the bumper out of the brackets.
5. Installation is the reverse of removal. Torque the bolts to 66 ft. lbs. (90 Nm).

Rear

GOLF, GTI AND JETTA

1. Raise and support the vehicle with jackstands.
2. Working under the car, remove the bolts from both sides of the bumper.
3. Remove the bolts from each side of the luggage compartment.
4. Slide the bumper assembly away from the body.
5. Installation is the reverse of removal. Torque the inside bolts to 29 ft. lbs. (40 Nm) and the other four bolts to 51 ft. lbs. (70 Nm).

CABRIOLET

1. Raise the vehicle and support with jackstands.
2. Drill out the rivets holding the bumper cover to the body inside the rear wheel well.
3. Remove the bolts inside the luggage compartment and slide the bumper out of the brackets.
4. Installation is the reverse of removal. Torque the bolts to 66 ft. lbs. (90 Nm).

Grille

REMOVAL & INSTALLATION

Unclip the radiator grille at the lock carrier and remove upward. Check the rubber supports for damage.

Outside Mirrors

REMOVAL & INSTALLATION

▶ **See Figure 1**

1. On manual remote control mirrors, unscrew the adjusting knob. On electric remote mirrors, carefully pry the control out of the door and disconnect the wiring.
2. Remove the inside door panel.
3. Remove the cable control locknut or disconnect the wiring and remove the screws to remove the mirror from the door.
4. Installation is the reverse of removal.

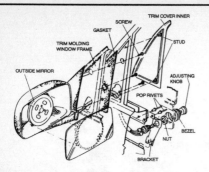

Fig. 1 Manual outside mirror removal; electric mirror similar

Antenna

REMOVAL & INSTALLATION

Fender Mount

1. Disconnect the negative battery cable.
2. Remove the radio and the instrument cluster.
3. Remove the drip tray above the firewall under the hood and pull the antenna cable from the foam tube. Note the routing for installation.
4. Remove the rubber grommet and unclip the antenna cable from the water tray.
5. Remove the inner wheelhouse liner.
6. Remove the mast retainer nut from the top of the fender.
7. Pull the assembly downward into the inner wheelhouse and remove the lower mounting bracket.
8. Install the antenna and route the wire through the vehicle. Keep the cable away from the heater control cables.
9. Tighten the mast nut.

Roof Mount

1. Remove the radio.
2. Remove the headliner as outlined later in this section.
3. Remove the antenna.
4. Installation is the reverse of removal.

Fenders

REMOVAL & INSTALLATION

Golf and Jetta

▶ See Figure 2

1. Use a heat gun and razor blade to soften and cut the PVC bead where the fender meets the A pillar. Be careful not to use too much heat.
2. Remove the front bumper cover.
3. Remove the bolts to remove the fender.
4. Installation is the reverse of removal. Be sure the zinc foil plates are in place at the bolt holes on the body. These prevent corrosion between the metal body parts.

Convertible Top

▶ See Figures 3 and 4

REMOVAL & INSTALLATION

Removing and installing the convertible top from the frame requires special tools and adhesives and also requires cutting the top fabric. The job is best left to a well equipped body shop with convertible top experience. The procedure described here is for removing the top and frame together as an assembly. Installation requires two people.

1. Open the top to release the tension but don't fold it back yet.
2. Bend open the metal tabs under the luggage compartment lining and pull the headliner off the tabs.
3. Pull the rear window defogger wiring out of the window seal.
4. Remove the window frame hinges and pull the cover off.
5. Remove the trim pieces at the rear corner of the rear windows.
6. On manual tops, remove the bolt to release the tension on the gas pressurized strut. Remove the clip at the other end and remove the strut.
7. If equipped with a power top, disconnect the cylinder from the top frame.
8. Disconnect the tensioning wire from its anchor on each side. A 4mm open end wrench can be used to prevent the wire from twisting.
9. Peel the top cover and tensioning wire out of the channels on the sides, then out of the rear channel.
10. Remove the headliner at the rear corners and remove the belt fastening bracket.
11. Remove the trim pieces covering the main bearing hinge. Remove the three bolts on each side and remove the top as an assembly.

To install:

12. Fit the top into place and start all the main bearing hinge bolts. When they are all started, tighten them.
13. Attach the belt at the rear corners.
14. Secure the tensioning wire to the anchors at each side and have a helper and top cover into the channel with a wooden drift.
15. Carefully align the beading and drive that into place with the drift.
16. Install the gas strut and try closing the top to make sure it fits properly and operates smoothly.
17. Install the rear window frame.
18. Attach the headliner and install the remaining trim pieces.

Power Top Motor

REMOVAL & INSTALLATION

➡**The top can be operated by hand if necessary by opening the valve on the pump. Turn the valve counterclockwise until it stops.**

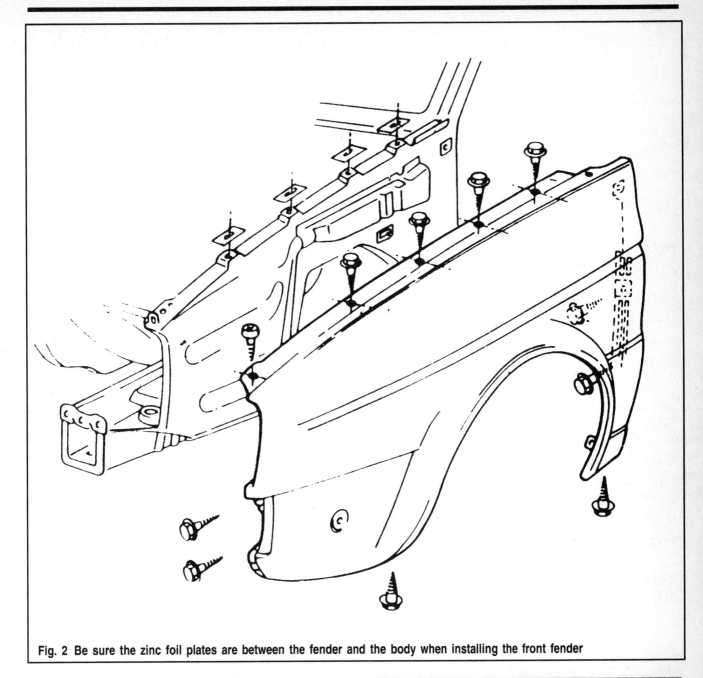

Fig. 2 Be sure the zinc foil plates are between the fender and the body when installing the front fender

1. Disconnect the negative battery cable.
2. Unclip and remove the left side luggage trim panel.
3. Disconnect the motor wiring.
4. Loosen the filler plug to relieve the pressure. Have a rag handy to catch any fluid that may spill.
5. Disconnect the hydraulic fittings that are accessible. Make sure the fittings are clean before disconnecting them and cover them with plastic or paper to keep dirt out. Do not use rags because the lint is enough to cause problems with the hydraulic system.
6. Remove the mount bolts and remove the pump and disconnect the remaining hydraulic fittings.
7. Installation is the reverse of removal. Fill and bleed the hydraulic system.

Power Top Cylinders

REMOVAL & INSTALLATION

▶ **See Figures 5, 6 and 7**

1. Unclip and remove the left side luggage compartment trim.
2. Bend the metal tabs and pull the top material up until the cylinders are visible.
3. Remove the lockring and pin to disengage the pushrod from the frame.
4. Remove the bracket nuts to remove the cylinder from the frame.

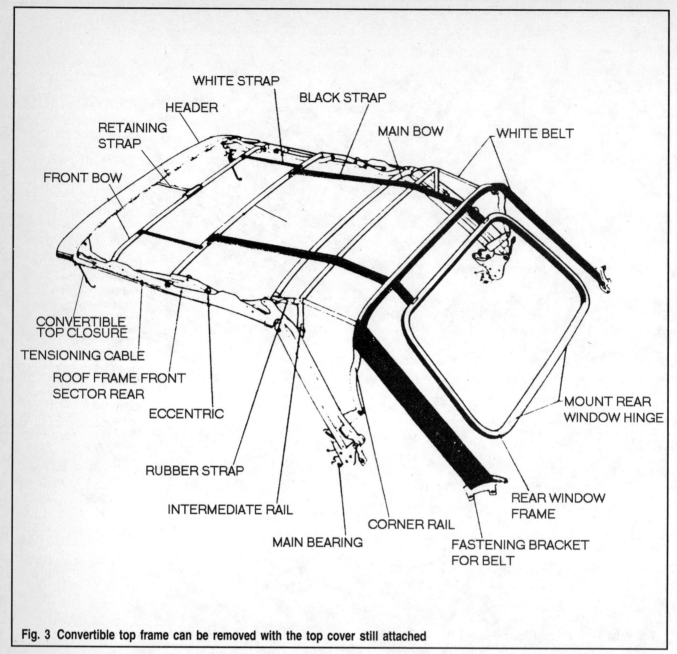

WHITE STRAP
HEADER
BLACK STRAP
RETAINING
STRAP
MAIN BOW
WHITE BELT
FRONT BOW

CONVERTIBLE
TOP CLOSURE
TENSIONING CABLE
ROOF FRAME FRONT
SECTOR REAR
ECCENTRIC
MOUNT REAR
WINDOW HINGE

RUBBER STRAP
INTERMEDIATE RAIL
REAR WINDOW
FRAME
MAIN BEARING
CORNER RAIL
FASTENING BRACKET
FOR BELT

Fig. 3 Convertible top frame can be removed with the top cover still attached

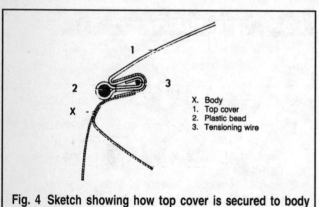

X. Body
1. Top cover
2. Plastic bead
3. Tensioning wire

Fig. 4 Sketch showing how top cover is secured to body

5. Disconnect the hydraulic line and remove the cylinder. Make sure no dirt or lint gets into the hydraulic system. Use plastic or paper covers to protect the fittings.

6. Installation is the reverse of removal. Fill and bleed the system.

BLEEDING THE SYSTEM

♦ See Figure 8

1. Remove the left side luggage compartment trim panel.
2. Turn the valve on the pump to the left (counterclockwise) until it stops.
3. Open and close the top by hand twice, then open the top and leave it open.
4. Close the valve (fully clockwise).

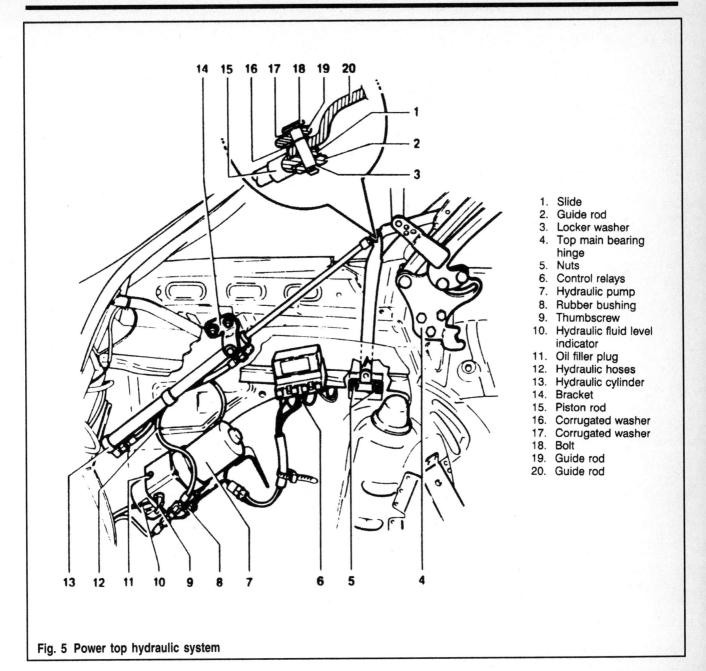

1. Slide
2. Guide rod
3. Locker washer
4. Top main bearing hinge
5. Nuts
6. Control relays
7. Hydraulic pump
8. Rubber bushing
9. Thumbscrew
10. Hydraulic fluid level indicator
11. Oil filler plug
12. Hydraulic hoses
13. Hydraulic cylinder
14. Bracket
15. Piston rod
16. Corrugated washer
17. Corrugated washer
18. Bolt
19. Guide rod
20. Guide rod

Fig. 5 Power top hydraulic system

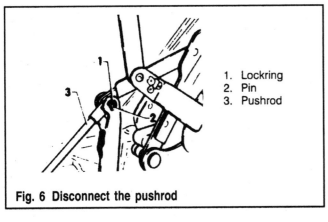

1. Lockring
2. Pin
3. Pushrod

Fig. 6 Disconnect the pushrod

Fig. 7 Remove the bracket to remove the cylinder

5. Remove the filler plug and add hydraulic fluid as needed. Do not over-fill.

➡ **The hydraulic fluid level must be checked with the top open. The level must be between the MIN and MAX marks.**

Sunroof

REMOVAL & INSTALLATION

♦ **See Figure 9**

1. Open the sunroof halfway and remove the steel clips at the front edge using a plastic wedge tool.
2. Close the sunroof and push the interior panel back all the way.
3. Remove both front guides from the outer panel.
4. Slide the springs at the rear guide in towards the center.

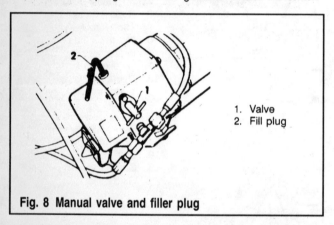

1. Valve
2. Fill plug

Fig. 8 Manual valve and filler plug

5. Remove the screws and remove the rear support plates in towards the center. Lift the sunroof cover out.
6. Installation is the reverse of removal.

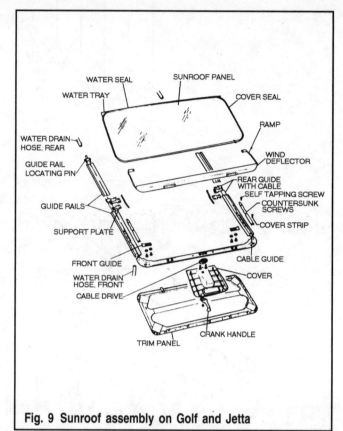

Fig. 9 Sunroof assembly on Golf and Jetta

INTERIOR

Instrument Panel

REMOVAL & INSTALLATION

✳✳CAUTION

On Cabriolet with an air bag, disconnect the negative battery cable and wait at least 20 minutes for the back-up power supply to discharge. Make sure no one is in the vehicle when connecting the battery. Unintended deployment of the air bag can cause serious or fatal injury.

1. Disconnect the negative battery cable.
2. Remove the gear shift knob and boot and remove the center console.
3. Remove the steering wheel.
4. Remove the knee bar from below the dashboard.
5. Remove the steering column support bracket and lower the column.
6. Pull the knobs off the heater controls and remove the control assembly and the radio.

7. Remove the headlight switch and switch blanks to gain access to the screws. Remove the instrument cluster and trim panel around the cluster.
8. Remove the glove compartment.
9. At the firewall, remove the plastic tray and remove the 2 nuts holding the top of the dashboard.
10. Remove the main fuse panel and disconnect the plugs at the back. Disconnect the ground wires.
11. Disconnect any remaining wiring from the dashboard and remove the 4 last screws; 1 at each end and 1 at each end of the instrument cluster area. Remove the dashboard.
   To install:
12. Fit the dashboard into place and start all 4 screws, then tighten them.
13. Install the fuse panel and connect the wiring.
14. Secure the steering column into place.
15. Install the switches and instrument cluster.
16. Install the heater controls and radio.
17. Install the console and connect all wiring.
18. Connect the battery to test the electrical system.
19. Install the steering wheel, knee bar and all remaining components.

Door Panels

REMOVAL & INSTALLATION

1. Remove the window regulator handle.
2. Remove the arm rest.
3. Remove the door lock knob.
4. Remove the inner door handle cover.
5. Using a flat screwdriver, gently separate the door trim panel clips from the door.
6. Lift the panel to remove it and disconnect the speaker or mirror wires as required.
7. Installation is the reverse of removal. Make sure the sheet of plastic behind the panel is properly sealed against the metal to keep drafts out of the interior.

Headliner

REMOVAL & INSTALLATION

1. Remove the inside rear view mirror and the sun visors.
2. Remove the screw from the center sun visor clip and turn the clip 90 degrees to remove it.
3. On Jetta, the side trim along the headliner is held with screws. Pry off the plastic caps and remove the screws to remove the trim.
4. On Golf, the side trim along the headliner is held with clips that can be pried out.
5. Pry open the screw covers and remove the screws to remove the assist handles.
6. Remove the screws from the windshield pillar trim and carefully pull the trim off the pillars.
7. Remove the side and rear pillar trim the same way.
8. Remove the end strip along the rear window.
9. Fully recline the seats, remove the center mounting clips and remove the headliner.
10. Installation is the reverse of removal. Do not use acetone or paint thinners to clean the headliner.

Air Conditioner Vents

REMOVAL & INSTALLATION

The ducts are held into the dashboard with barbed clips on the sides of the vent. They can be pried out and pushed in easily. Be careful not to damage the dashboard pad. Place a clean rag on the pad and pry carefully with a small screwdriver. If the pad is dented without breaking the 'skin', gently warm the pad with a heat gun and it should regain most of its original shape.

Manual Door Locks

REMOVAL & INSTALLATION

▶ See Figure 10

1. Remove the door panel.
2. Disconnect the linkage and remove the screws to remove the lock from the door.
3. When installing, hold lever A at a 90 degree angle and secure it with a screwdriver.
4. Insert the rod through the hole in the door and connect the lock linkage.
5. Remove the screwdriver, install the screws and connect the latch linkage.

Central Locking System

TESTING

▶ See Figures 11, 12 and 13

The heart of the pneumatic central locking system is the bi-pressure pump mounted in the luggage compartment. The pump runs both ways to provide vacuum or pressure as required for locking or unlocking. There are lock actuators at each door, the rear hatch or trunk and at the fuel filler door. The master actuator at the driver's door includes the switch that activates the pump. In normal operation, the pump runs for about 2 seconds and will build enough pressure or vacuum to operate all locks and activate an internal shut-off switch. If the pump runs for more than 5 seconds, a leak in the system is preventing shut-off switch operation and an automatic shut-off will occur in about 35 seconds. If the pump does not run at all, the problem is most likely electrical.

1. Open the luggage compartment and remove the left side interior trim. Unhook the strap, remove the pump cover and pull the pump out of the housing.
2. Install a small clamp on the hose before the first branching tee and turn the key in the driver's door lock. If the pump does not run at all, go to Step 7.
3. If the pump runs for more than 5 seconds, the shut-off switch inside is faulty and the pump must be replaced. If the

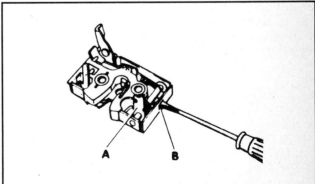

Fig. 10 Hold lever A in place to install the lock

pump stops in less than 5 seconds, the pump is good and there is a leak somewhere in the system.

4. Move the clamp to the upper branch of the tee and turn the driver's door lock again. If the pump runs too long, the leak is at the left rear door actuator or the hose.

5. If the pump stops in less than 5 seconds, move the clamp to the next hose junction at the right rear of the luggage compartment and test again. The hose that branches to the right supplies the fuel filler door and trunk or hatch actuator. The hose branching down supplies the right door actuators.

6. Continue moving the clamp towards the actuators until the pump does not stop within 5 seconds. This means the clamp is now past the leak and the previous section of hose or actuator is leaking.

7. If the pump does not run at all, disconnect the wiring and connect a voltmeter or test light to the center and right terminals on the connector. There should be 12 volts when the driver's door is unlocked.

8. Move the tester to the center and left terminals. There should be 12 volts when the driver's door is locked.

9. If the voltages appear as specified, the pump is faulty and must be replaced. If there is no voltage in either or both tests, the lock switch, wiring or fuse is faulty. The switch is part of the master actuator and cannot be replaced separately.

REMOVAL & INSTALLATION

1. To replace the pump, remove the left luggage compartment interior panel and remove the pump cover and the pump. Test the new pump before completing the installation.

2. To replace the actuator, remove the door panel. Follow the hose to the actuator and disconnect the hose and the linkage at the actuator. On the driver's door, disconnect the wiring.

3. Remove the screws and remove the actuator. Connect the hose to the new actuator and test the system before installing it.

Door Glass and Regulator

REMOVAL & INSTALLATION

▶ **See Figure 14**

Golf and Jetta

1. Lower the window glass and remove the door panel.
2. Carefully peel off the door screen so that it can be reused.
3. Raise the window enough to reach the regulator bolts, hold the glass underneath and unbolt the glass from the regulator.
4. To remove the glass, raise the glass by hand and tilt it as necessary to remove it from the track.
5. To remove the regulator, lower the glass carefully to the bottom of the door and remove the bolts to remove the regulator.
6. Installation is the reverse of removal. Torque all bolts to 61 inch lbs. (7 Nm).

Cabriolet

1. Lower the window glass and remove the door panel.
2. Carefully peel off the door screen so that it can be reused.
3. Raise the window enough to reach the regulator bolts, remove the bolts and lift the glass straight out.
4. To remove the regulator, remove the seven screws attaching the window regulator to the door and one screw from the winder.
5. Installation is the reverse of removal. Lubricate the sliding bracket on the regulator.

Electric Window Motor

REMOVAL & INSTALLATION

▶ **See Figure 15**

1. Remove the door panel.
2. Carefully peel off the door screen so that it can be reused.
3. Unbolt the window from the regulator and carefully lower it to the bottom of the door.
4. Disconnect the wiring and remove the motor mounting bolts.
5. Remove the 3 guide rail bolts and lower the motor and guide rail assembly out the bottom of the door.
6. Installation is the reverse of removal. The upper cable most be below the guide rail mounting bracket.

Windshield

➡**Bonded windshields require special tools and procedures. For this reason we recommend that all removal, installation and repair work be referred to a qualified technician or body shop.**

REMOVAL & INSTALLATION

Special tool set (431 898 099A) is required to perform this procedure. You will also need VW glass cutting tool 1351, double suction pad holders for holding the glass, and a caulking gun for applying the bonding and sealing compound.

1. Remove the rear view mirror, sun visors, front pillar trim, and front header trim.
2. Remove the wiper arms and cowl grille.
3. Remove the front window molding.
4. Remove the glass by separating the glass from the sealant using a commercial power or manually operated remover tool, or use the following procedure.

   a. Use an awl to make a hole in the sealant.

   b. Pass a piece of piano wire, about 3mm (1/8 inch) in diameter, through the hole, and attach wood bars to both ends.

   c. Two people should hold the bars, one inside and one outside the vehicle, and then "saw" the sealant from around the glass, cutting along the border between the glass and the sealant.

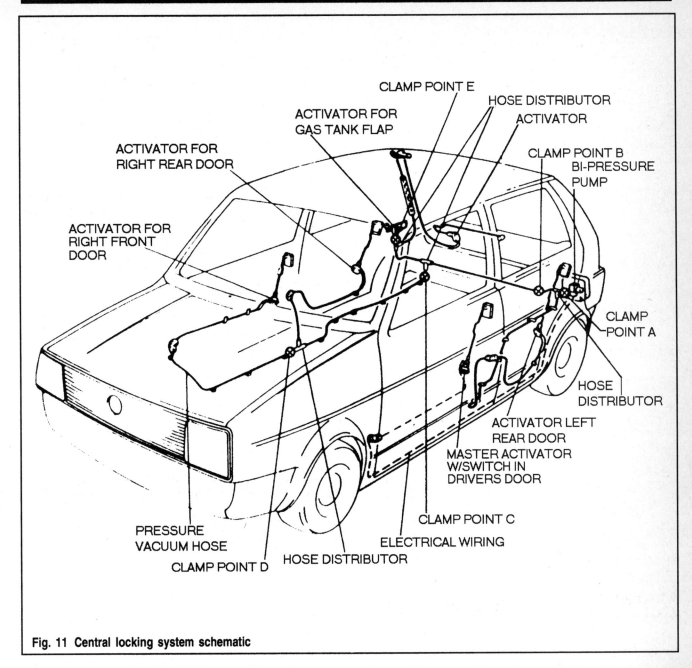

CLAMP POINT E

HOSE DISTRIBUTOR

ACTIVATOR FOR
GAS TANK FLAP

ACTIVATOR

ACTIVATOR FOR
RIGHT REAR DOOR

CLAMP POINT B
BI-PRESSURE
PUMP

ACTIVATOR FOR
RIGHT FRONT
DOOR

CLAMP
POINT A

HOSE
DISTRIBUTOR

ACTIVATOR LEFT
REAR DOOR

MASTER ACTIVATOR
W/SWITCH IN
DRIVERS DOOR

CLAMP POINT C

ELECTRICAL WIRING

PRESSURE
VACUUM HOSE

CLAMP POINT D

HOSE DISTRIBUTOR

Fig. 11 Central locking system schematic

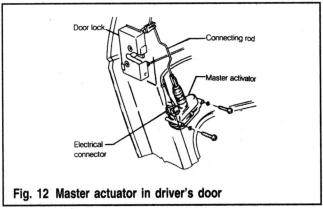

Door lock

Connecting rod

Master activator

Electrical
connector

Fig. 12 Master actuator in driver's door

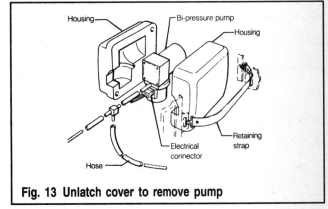

Housing

Bi-pressure pump

Housing

Electrical
connector

Retaining
strap

Hose

Fig. 13 Unlatch cover to remove pump

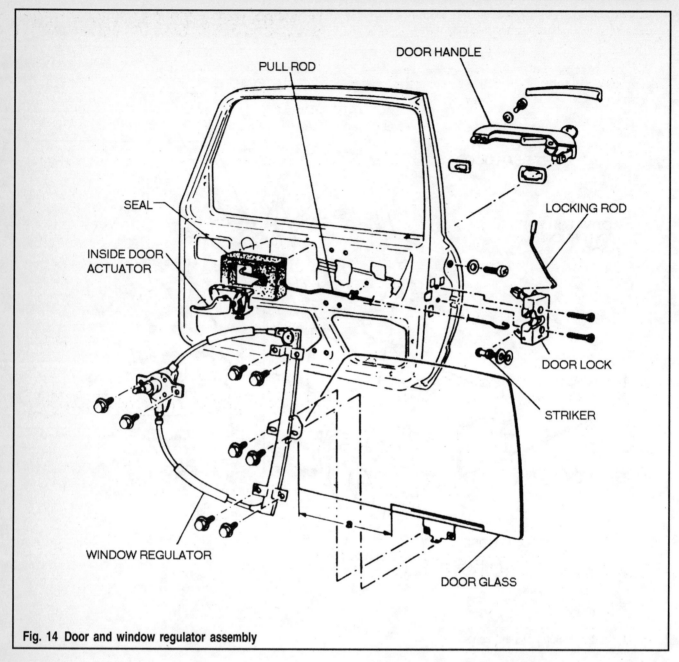

Fig. 14 Door and window regulator assembly

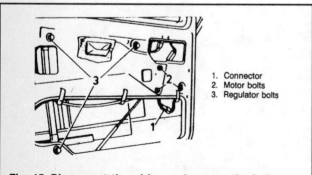

1. Connector
2. Motor bolts
3. Regulator bolts

Fig. 15 Disconnect the wiring and remove the bolts to remove the window motor and regulator together

d. With the help of an assistant, remove the glass from the vehicle. Make sure that no spacers or clips are lost during windshield removal.

To install:

5. Use a knife to smoothly trim the sealant on the body. Leave a layer about 1-2mm (0.04-0.08 inches) thick.

➡**If there are small gaps or flakes in the sealant use new sealant to patch it.**

6. Carefully clean and remove any dirt or grease from a 50mm (1.97 inch) wide area around the circumference of the glass and the remaining bond of the body.

7. Bond a dam along the circumference of the glass 5mm (0.20 inch) from the edge. Securely bond the dam and allow it to dry before proceeding to the next step.

8. Apply primer with a brush to the circumference of the glass and the body, and allow it to naturally dry for 20 to 30 minutes.

➡**Be sure not to allow dirt, water, oil, etc. to come in contact with the coated surfaces and do not touch it with your hand!**

9. Install the spacers.

10. When the primer has dried, apply an 11mm (0.43 inch) thick bead of repair seal, 7mm (0.28 inch) from the frame of the glass using a sealant gun. If necessary, smooth the repair seal to correct any irregularities.

11. Place the windshield into the frame. Fully lower the side windows to prevent any pressure from being exerted on the windshield should the doors be closed suddenly. Keep the door glass open until the repair seal dries.

12. Remove any access, or add repair seal where necessary.

13. Check the windshield for water leaks. If a leak is found, wipe off the water and add repair seal.

14. After checking water leakage, mount the pillar garnish, cowl panel, cowl grille, wipers, etc.

15. Attach the front header trim, sun visor, interior mirror, etc.

Rear Window or Hatch Glass

REMOVAL & INSTALLATION

The procedure for removing and installing the rear window glass is the same as the front windshield removal and installation procedures. Please refer to the front windshield removal and installation procedure as a guide when completing this repair.

Side Quarter Glass

REMOVAL & INSTALLATION

The procedure for removing and installing the stationary side windows is the same as the front windshield removal and installation procedures. Please refer to the front windshield removal and installation procedure as a guide when completing this repair.

Inside Rear View Mirror

REMOVAL & INSTALLATION

The break-away safety mirror can be removed by rotating the mounting stalk to the left or right.

Seats

REMOVAL & INSTALLATION

Front Seats

1. Slide the seat forward to the stop and remove the track cover beside the tunnel.

2. Remove the acorn nut, washer and bolt at the front of the center seat rail.

3. Pull the seat release handle and push the seat back and out of the tracks. Lift the seat out of the vehicle.

4. Installation is the reverse of removal.

Rear Seat

1. On Golf and Jetta, lift the seat cushion up and pull forward to remove it.

2. On Cabriolet, remove the two screws at the front of the seat cushion and pull forward and up.

3. Release the seat backrest and fold forward.

4. Release the locking lug in the mounting and pull the backrest out of the mounting.

5. Installation is the reverse of removal.

Seat Belts

REMOVAL & INSTALLATION

1. Disconnect the belt from the door mount and remove the front seat.

2. Remove the screw and bolt and release the spring loop to remove the belt retractor from the seat.

3. To remove the latch from the door, open the door and remove the 2 countersunk screws.

4. Installation is the reverse of removal. Torque the countersunk screws to 11 ft. lbs. (15 Nm) and the retractor bolt to 30 ft. lbs. (40 Nm).

AIR/FUEL RATIO: The ratio of air to gasoline by weight in the fuel mixture drawn into the engine.

AIR INJECTION: One method of reducing harmful exhaust emissions by injecting air into each of the exhaust ports of an engine. The fresh air entering the hot exhaust manifold causes any remaining fuel to be burned before it can exit the tailpipe.

ALTERNATOR: A device used for converting mechanical energy into electrical energy.

AMMETER: An instrument, calibrated in amperes, used to measure the flow of an electrical current in a circuit. Ammeters are always connected in series with the circuit being tested.

AMPERE: The rate of flow of electrical current present when one volt of electrical pressure is applied against one ohm of electrical resistance.

ANALOG COMPUTER: Any microprocessor that uses similar (analogous) electrical signals to make its calculations.

ARMATURE: A laminated, soft iron core wrapped by a wire that converts electrical energy to mechanical energy as in a motor or relay. When rotated in a magnetic field, it changes mechanical energy into electrical energy as in a generator.

ATMOSPHERIC PRESSURE: The pressure on the Earth's surface caused by the weight of the air in the atmosphere. At sea level, this pressure is 14.7 psi at 32{248}F (101 kPa at 0{248}C).

ATOMIZATION: The breaking down of a liquid into a fine mist that can be suspended in air.

AXIAL PLAY: Movement parallel to a shaft or bearing bore.

BACKFIRE: The sudden combustion of gases in the intake or exhaust system that results in a loud explosion.

BACKLASH: The clearance or play between two parts, such as meshed gears.

BACKPRESSURE: Restrictions in the exhaust system that slow the exit of exhaust gases from the combustion chamber.

BAKELITE: A heat resistant, plastic insulator material commonly used in printed circuit boards and transistorized components.

BALL BEARING: A bearing made up of hardened inner and outer races between which hardened steel balls roll.

BALLAST RESISTOR: A resistor in the primary ignition circuit that lowers voltage after the engine is started to reduce wear on ignition components.

BEARING: A friction reducing, supportive device usually located between a stationary part and a moving part.

BIMETAL TEMPERATURE SENSOR: Any sensor or switch made of two dissimilar types of metal that bend when heated or cooled due to the different expansion rates of the alloys. These types of sensors usually function as an on/off switch.

BLOWBY: Combustion gases, composed of water vapor and unburned fuel, that leak past the piston rings into the crankcase during normal engine operation. These gases are removed by the PCV system to prevent the buildup of harmful acids in the crankcase.

BRAKE PAD: A brake shoe and lining assembly used with disc brakes.

BRAKE SHOE: The backing for the brake lining. The term is, however, usually applied to the assembly of the brake backing and lining.

BUSHING: A liner, usually removable, for a bearing; an anti-friction liner used in place of a bearing.

CALIPER: A hydraulically activated device in a disc brake system, which is mounted straddling the brake rotor (disc). The caliper contains at least one piston and two brake pads. Hydraulic pressure on the piston(s) forces the pads against the rotor.

CAMSHAFT: A shaft in the engine on which are the lobes (cams) which operate the valves. The camshaft is driven by the crankshaft, via a belt, chain or gears, at one half the crankshaft speed.

CAPACITOR: A device which stores an electrical charge.

CARBON MONOXIDE (CO): A colorless, odorless gas given off as a normal byproduct of combustion. It is poisonous and extremely dangerous in confined areas, building up slowly to toxic levels without warning if adequate ventilation is not available.

CARBURETOR: A device, usually mounted on the intake manifold of an engine, which mixes the air and fuel in the proper proportion to allow even combustion.

CATALYTIC CONVERTER: A device installed in the exhaust system, like a muffler, that converts harmful byproducts of combustion into carbon dioxide and water vapor by means of a heat-producing chemical reaction.

CENTRIFUGAL ADVANCE: A mechanical method of advancing the spark timing by using flyweights in the distributor that react to centrifugal force generated by the distributor shaft rotation.

CHECK VALVE: Any one-way valve installed to permit the flow of air, fuel or vacuum in one direction only.

CHOKE: A device, usually a moveable valve, placed in the intake path of a carburetor to restrict the flow of air.

CIRCUIT: Any unbroken path through which an electrical current can flow. Also used to describe fuel flow in some instances.

CIRCUIT BREAKER: A switch which protects an electrical circuit from overload by opening the circuit when the current flow exceeds a predetermined level. Some circuit breakers must be reset manually, while most reset automatically

COIL (IGNITION): A transformer in the ignition circuit which steps up the voltage provided to the spark plugs.

COMBINATION MANIFOLD: An assembly which includes both the intake and exhaust manifolds in one casting.

COMBINATION VALVE: A device used in some fuel systems that routes fuel vapors to a charcoal storage canister instead of venting them into the atmosphere. The valve relieves fuel tank pressure and allows fresh air into the tank as the fuel level drops to prevent a vapor lock situation.

COMPRESSION RATIO: The comparison of the total volume of the cylinder and combustion chamber with the piston at BDC and the piston at TDC.

CONDENSER: 1. An electrical device which acts to store an electrical charge, preventing voltage surges.
2. A radiator-like device in the air conditioning system in which refrigerant gas condenses into a liquid, giving off heat.

CONDUCTOR: Any material through which an electrical current can be transmitted easily.

CONTINUITY: Continuous or complete circuit. Can be checked with an ohmmeter.

COUNTERSHAFT: An intermediate shaft which is rotated by a mainshaft and transmits, in turn, that rotation to a working part.

CRANKCASE: The lower part of an engine in which the crankshaft and related parts operate.

CRANKSHAFT: The main driving shaft of an engine which receives reciprocating motion from the pistons and converts it to rotary motion.

CYLINDER: In an engine, the round hole in the engine block in which the piston(s) ride.

CYLINDER BLOCK: The main structural member of an engine in which is found the cylinders, crankshaft and other principal parts.

CYLINDER HEAD: The detachable portion of the engine, fastened, usually, to the top of the cylinder block, containing all or most of the combustion chambers. On overhead valve engines, it contains the valves and their operating parts. On overhead cam engines, it contains the camshaft as well.

DEAD CENTER: The extreme top or bottom of the piston stroke.

DETONATION: An unwanted explosion of the air/fuel mixture in the combustion chamber caused by excess heat and compression, advanced timing, or an overly lean mixture. Also referred to as "ping".

DIAPHRAGM: A thin, flexible wall separating two cavities, such as in a vacuum advance unit.

DIESELING: A condition in which hot spots in the combustion chamber cause the engine to run on after the key is turned off.

DIFFERENTIAL: A geared assembly which allows the transmission of motion between drive axles, giving one axle the ability to turn faster than the other.

DIODE: An electrical device that will allow current to flow in one direction only.

DISC BRAKE: A hydraulic braking assembly consisting of a brake disc, or rotor, mounted on an axle, and a caliper assembly containing, usually two brake pads which are activated by hydraulic pressure. The pads are forced against the sides of the disc, creating friction which slows the vehicle.

DISTRIBUTOR: A mechanically driven device on an engine which is responsible for electrically firing the spark plug at a predetermined point of the piston stroke.

DOWEL PIN: A pin, inserted in mating holes in two different parts allowing those parts to maintain a fixed relationship.

DRUM BRAKE: A braking system which consists of two brake shoes and one or two wheel cylinders, mounted on a fixed backing plate, and a brake drum, mounted on an axle, which revolves around the assembly.

DWELL: The rate, measured in degrees of shaft rotation, at which an electrical circuit cycles on and off.

ELECTRONIC CONTROL UNIT (ECU): Ignition module, module, amplifier or igniter. See Module for definition.

ELECTRONIC IGNITION: A system in which the timing and firing of the spark plugs is controlled by an electronic control unit, usually called a module. These systems have no points or condenser.

ENDPLAY: The measured amount of axial movement in a shaft.

ENGINE: A device that converts heat into mechanical energy.

EXHAUST MANIFOLD: A set of cast passages or pipes which conduct exhaust gases from the engine.

FEELER GAUGE: A blade, usually metal, of precisely predetermined thickness, used to measure the clearance between two parts.

FIRING ORDER: The order in which combustion occurs in the cylinders of an engine. Also the order in which spark is distributed to the plugs by the distributor.

FLOODING: The presence of too much fuel in the intake manifold and combustion chamber which prevents the air/fuel mixture from firing, thereby causing a no-start situation.

FLYWHEEL: A disc shaped part bolted to the rear end of the crankshaft. Around the outer perimeter is affixed the ring gear. The starter drive engages the ring gear, turning the flywheel, which rotates the crankshaft, imparting the initial starting motion to the engine.

FOOT POUND (ft.lb. or sometimes, ft. lbs.): The amount of energy or work needed to raise an item weighing one pound, a distance of one foot.

FUSE: A protective device in a circuit which prevents circuit overload by breaking the circuit when a specific amperage is present. The device is constructed around a strip or wire of a lower amperage rating than the circuit it is designed to protect. When an amperage higher than that stamped on the fuse is present in the circuit, the strip or wire melts, opening the circuit.

GEAR RATIO: The ratio between the number of teeth on meshing gears.

GENERATOR: A device which converts mechanical energy into electrical energy.

HEAT RANGE: The measure of a spark plug's ability to dissipate heat from its firing end. The higher the heat range, the hotter the plug fires.

HUB: The center part of a wheel or gear.

HYDROCARBON (HC): Any chemical compound made up of hydrogen and carbon. A major pollutant formed by the engine as a byproduct of combustion.

HYDROMETER: An instrument used to measure the specific gravity of a solution.

INCH POUND (in.lb. or sometimes, in. lbs.): One twelfth of a foot pound.

INDUCTION: A means of transferring electrical energy in the form of a magnetic field. Principle used in the ignition coil to increase voltage.

INJECTOR: A device which receives metered fuel under relatively low pressure and is activated to inject the fuel into the engine under relatively high pressure at a predetermined time.

INPUT SHAFT: The shaft to which torque is applied, usually carrying the driving gear or gears.

INTAKE MANIFOLD: A casting of passages or pipes used to conduct air or a fuel/air mixture to the cylinders.

JOURNAL: The bearing surface within which a shaft operates.

KEY: A small block usually fitted in a notch between a shaft and a hub to prevent slippage of the two parts.

MANIFOLD: A casting of passages or set of pipes which connect the cylinders to an inlet or outlet source.

MANIFOLD VACUUM: Low pressure in an engine intake manifold formed just below the throttle plates. Manifold vacuum is highest at idle and drops under acceleration.

MASTER CYLINDER: The primary fluid pressurizing device in a hydraulic system. In automotive use, it is found in brake and hydraulic clutch systems and is pedal activated, either directly or, in a power brake system, through the power booster.

MODULE: Electronic control unit, amplifier or igniter of solid state or integrated design which controls the current flow in the ignition primary circuit based on input from the pick-up coil. When the module opens the primary circuit, the high secondary voltage is induced in the coil.

NEEDLE BEARING: A bearing which consists of a number (usually a large number) of long, thin rollers.

OHM:(Ω) The unit used to measure the resistance of conductor to electrical flow. One ohm is the amount of resistance that limits current flow to one ampere in a circuit with one volt of pressure.

OHMMETER: An instrument used for measuring the resistance, in ohms, in an electrical circuit.

OUTPUT SHAFT: The shaft which transmits torque from a device, such as a transmission.

OVERDRIVE: A gear assembly which produces more shaft revolutions than that transmitted to it.

OVERHEAD CAMSHAFT (OHC): An engine configuration in which the camshaft is mounted on top of the cylinder head and operates the valve either directly or by means of rocker arms.

OVERHEAD VALVE (OHV): An engine configuration in which all of the valves are located in the cylinder head and the camshaft is located in the cylinder block. The camshaft operates the valves via lifters and pushrods.

OXIDES OF NITROGEN (NOx): Chemical compounds of nitrogen produced as a byproduct of combustion. They combine with hydrocarbons to produce smog.

OXYGEN SENSOR: Used with the feedback system to sense the presence of oxygen in the exhaust gas and signal the computer which can reference the voltage signal to an air/fuel ratio.

PINION: The smaller of two meshing gears.

PISTON RING: An open ended ring which fits into a groove on the outer diameter of the piston. Its chief function is to form a seal between the piston and cylinder wall. Most automotive pistons have three rings: two for compression sealing; one for oil sealing.

PRELOAD: A predetermined load placed on a bearing during assembly or by adjustment.

PRIMARY CIRCUIT: Is the low voltage side of the ignition system which consists of the ignition switch, ballast resistor or resistance wire, bypass, coil, electronic control unit and pick-up coil as well as the connecting wires and harnesses.

PRESS FIT: The mating of two parts under pressure, due to the inner diameter of one being smaller than the outer diameter of the other, or vice versa; an interference fit.

RACE: The surface on the inner or outer ring of a bearing on which the balls, needles or rollers move.

REGULATOR: A device which maintains the amperage and/or voltage levels of a circuit at predetermined values.

RELAY: A switch which automatically opens and/or closes a circuit.

RESISTANCE: The opposition to the flow of current through a circuit or electrical device, and is measured in ohms. Resistance is equal to the voltage divided by the amperage.

RESISTOR: A device, usually made of wire, which offers a preset amount of resistance in an electrical circuit.

RING GEAR: The name given to a ring-shaped gear attached to a differential case, or affixed to a flywheel or as part a planetary gear set.

ROLLER BEARING: A bearing made up of hardened inner and outer races between which hardened steel rollers move.

ROTOR: 1. The disc-shaped part of a disc brake assembly, upon which the brake pads bear; also called, brake disc.
2. The device mounted atop the distributor shaft, which passes current to the distributor cap tower contacts.

SECONDARY CIRCUIT: The high voltage side of the ignition system, usually above 20,000 volts. The secondary includes the ignition coil, coil wire, distributor cap and rotor, spark plug wires and spark plugs.

SENDING UNIT: A mechanical, electrical, hydraulic or electromagnetic device which transmits information to a gauge.

SENSOR: Any device designed to measure engine operating conditions or ambient pressures and temperatures. Usually electronic in nature and designed to send a voltage signal to an on-board computer, some sensors may operate as a simple on/off switch or they may provide a variable voltage signal (like a potentiometer) as conditions or measured parameters change.

SHIM: Spacers of precise, predetermined thickness used between parts to establish a proper working relationship.

SLAVE CYLINDER: In automotive use, a device in the hydraulic clutch system which is activated by hydraulic force, disengaging the clutch.

SOLENOID: A coil used to produce a magnetic field, the effect of which is produce work.

SPARK PLUG: A device screwed into the combustion chamber of a spark ignition engine. The basic construction is a conductive core inside of a ceramic insulator, mounted in an outer conductive base. An electrical charge from the spark plug wire travels along the conductive core and jumps a preset air gap to a grounding point or points at the end of the conductive base. The resultant spark ignites the fuel/air mixture in the combustion chamber.

SPLINES: Ridges machined or cast onto the outer diameter of a shaft or inner diameter of a bore to enable parts to mate without rotation.

TACHOMETER: A device used to measure the rotary speed of an engine, shaft, gear, etc., usually in rotations per minute.

THERMOSTAT: A valve, located in the cooling system of an engine, which is closed when cold and opens gradually in response to engine heating, controlling the temperature of the coolant and rate of coolant flow.

TOP DEAD CENTER (TDC): The point at which the piston reaches the top of its travel on the compression stroke.

TORQUE: The twisting force applied to an object.

TORQUE CONVERTER: A turbine used to transmit power from a driving member to a driven member via hydraulic action, providing changes in drive ratio and torque. In automotive use, it links the driveplate at the rear of the engine to the automatic transmission.

TRANSDUCER: A device used to change a force into an electrical signal.

TRANSISTOR: A semi-conductor component which can be actuated by a small voltage to perform an electrical switching function.

TUNE-UP: A regular maintenance function, usually associated with the replacement and adjustment of parts and components in the electrical and fuel systems of a vehicle for the purpose of attaining optimum performance.

TURBOCHARGER: An exhaust driven pump which compresses intake air and forces it into the combustion chambers at higher than atmospheric pressures. The increased air pressure allows more fuel to be burned and results in increased horsepower being produced.

VACUUM ADVANCE: A device which advances the ignition timing in response to increased engine vacuum.

VACUUM GAUGE: An instrument used to measure the presence of vacuum in a chamber.

VALVE: A device which control the pressure, direction of flow or rate of flow of a liquid or gas.

VALVE CLEARANCE: The measured gap between the end of the valve stem and the rocker arm, cam lobe or follower that activates the valve.

VISCOSITY: The rating of a liquid's internal resistance to flow.

VOLTMETER: An instrument used for measuring electrical force in units called volts. Voltmeters are always connected parallel with the circuit being tested.

WHEEL CYLINDER: Found in the automotive drum brake assembly, it is a device, actuated by hydraulic pressure, which, through internal pistons, pushes the brake shoes outward against the drums.

2ENGINE PERFORMANCE AND TUNE-UPSPECIFICATIONS
   CHARTS 2-2
AIR CONDITIONING
  COMPRESSOR
    REMOVAL & INSTALLATION 6-15
  CONDENSER
    REMOVAL & INSTALLATION 6-16
  CONTROL PANEL
    REMOVAL & INSTALLATION 6-16
  EVAPORATOR CORE
    REMOVAL & INSTALLATION 6-16
  EXPANSION VALVE
    REMOVAL & INSTALLATION 6-16
  PRESSURE SWITCHES
    DESCRIPTION 6-18
  RECEIVER/DRIER
    REMOVAL & INSTALLATION 6-17
  REFRIGERANT LINES
    REMOVAL & INSTALLATION 6-18
AIR POLLUTION
  AUTOMOTIVE POLLUTANTS 4-2
  INDUSTRIAL POLLUTION 4-2
  INTERNAL COMBUSTION ENGINE POLLUTANTS
    HEAT TRANSFER 4-3
  NATURAL POLLUTANTS 4-2
  TEMPERATURE INVERSION 4-2
ANTI-LOCK BRAKE SYSTEM
  CONTROL UNIT
    REMOVAL & INSTALLATION 9-20
  DESCRIPTION AND OPERATION 9-14
  FILLING AND BLEEDING
    BLEEDING THE SYSTEM 9-21
    FILLING THE SYSTEM 9-21
    FRONT BRAKES 9-21
    REAR BRAKES 9-21
  MODULATOR ASSEMBLY
    REMOVAL & INSTALLATION 9-21
  RELIEVING ANTI-LOCK BRAKE SYSTEM PRESSURE 9-21
  TROUBLESHOOTING
    SYSTEM TESTING 9-15
  WHEEL SPEED SENSOR
    REMOVAL & INSTALLATION 9-20
AUTOMATIC TRANSAXLE
  ADJUSTMENTS
    AUTOMATIC SHIFT LOCK SOLENOID 7-16
    CABLE ADJUSTMENT 7-15
    CHECKING ADJUSTMENT 7-14
    NEUTRAL SAFETY/BACK-UP LIGHT SWITCH 7-15
  AXLE SHAFT (HALFSHAFT)
    CV-JOINT AND BOOT OVERHAUL 7-17
    REMOVAL & INSTALLATION 7-17
  FLUID PAN AND STRAINER
    REMOVAL & INSTALLATION 7-14
  IDENTIFICATION 7-14
  TRANSAXLE
    REMOVAL & INSTALLATION 7-16
BRAKE OPERATING SYSTEM
  ADJUSTMENTS
    PARKING BRAKE 9-2
    REAR DISC BRAKES 9-2
    REAR DRUM BRAKES 9-2
  BRAKE LIGHT SWITCH
    CABRIOLET 9-3
    GOLF AND JETTA 9-3
    REMOVAL & INSTALLATION 9-3
  BRAKE LINES
    FLEXIBLE HOSES 9-4
    REMOVAL & INSTALLATION 9-4
    STEEL LINES 9-4
  BRAKE PEDAL
    REMOVAL & INSTALLATION 9-3

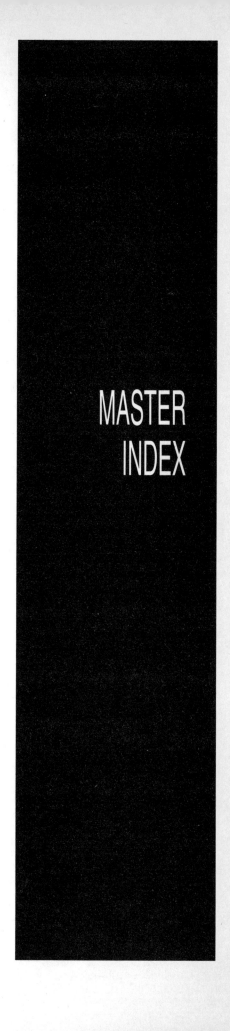

MASTER

INDEX

BRAKE SYSTEM BLEEDING
  WITHOUT ABS 9-4
DIESEL ENGINE VACUUM PUMP
  REMOVAL & INSTALLATION 9-3
GENERAL DESCRIPTION 9-2
MASTER CYLINDER
  OVERHAUL 9-3
  REMOVAL & INSTALLATION 9-3
  STANDARD (NON-ABS) BRAKES 9-3
POWER BRAKE BOOSTER
  REMOVAL & INSTALLATION 9-3
  WITHOUT ABS 9-3
PRESSURE REGULATING VALVE
  REMOVAL & INSTALLATION 9-4
CIRCUIT PROTECTION
FUSES
  REPLACEMENT 6-26
CIS-E MOTRONIC FUEL INJECTION SYSTEM
DIFFERENTIAL PRESSURE REGULATOR
  REMOVAL & INSTALLATION 5-5
FUEL DISTRIBUTOR
  ADJUSTMENT 5-5
  REMOVAL & INSTALLATION 5-5
FUEL INJECTORS
  REMOVAL & INSTALLATION 5-3
FUEL PUMP
  REMOVAL & INSTALLATION 5-3
FUEL SYSTEM PRESSURE REGULATOR
  REMOVAL & INSTALLATION 5-3
GENERAL DESCRIPTION 5-2
OXYGEN SENSOR
  REMOVAL & INSTALLATION 5-5
CLUTCH
ADJUSTMENT 7-12
CLUTCH CABLE
  REMOVAL & INSTALLATION 7-12
CLUTCH PEDAL
  REMOVAL & INSTALLATION 7-12
DRIVEN DISC AND PRESSURE PLATE
  REMOVAL & INSTALLATION 7-13
CRUISE CONTROL
CONNECTING ROD
  ADJUSTMENT 6-19
CONTROL SWITCH
  REMOVAL & INSTALLATION 6-18
CONTROL UNIT
  REMOVAL & INSTALLATION 6-18
SPEED SENSOR
  REMOVAL & INSTALLATION 6-18
VACUUM SERVO
  REMOVAL & INSTALLATION 6-18
DIAGNOSTIC CODES DATA
GENERAL INFORMATION
  ANTI-LOCK BRAKE SYSTEM CONTROL UNIT 4-23
  AUTOMATIC TRANSMISSION CONTROL UNIT 4-23
  DIGIFANT I CONTROL UNIT 4-23
  MOTRONIC CONTROL UNIT 4-23
SELF-DIAGNOSTICS
  CLEARING FAULT CODES 4-25
  OUTPUT CHECK DIAGNOSIS 4-24
  READING FAULT CODES 4-24
  SERVICE PRECAUTIONS 4-24

DIESEL ENGINE TUNE-UP PROCEDURES
DIESEL INJECTION TIMING
  ADJUSTMENT 2-12
FUEL SYSTEM SERVICE PRECAUTIONS 2-11
IDLE SPEED
  ADJUSTMENT 2-12
DIESEL FUEL SYSTEM
DIESEL GLOW PLUGS
  DIAGNOSIS AND TESTING 5-12
  REMOVAL & INSTALLATION 5-13
DIESEL INJECTION PUMP
  REMOVAL & INSTALLATION 5-11
DIESEL INJECTION TIMING
  ADJUSTMENT 5-12
  IDLE SPEED ADJUSTMENT 5-12
FUEL INJECTION LINES
  REMOVAL & INSTALLATION 5-10
FUEL INJECTOR
  REMOVAL & INSTALLATION 5-11
FUEL SUPPLY PUMP
  REMOVAL & INSTALLATION 5-11
FUEL SYSTEM SERVICE PRECAUTIONS 5-10
DIGIFANT FUEL INJECTION SYSTEM
AIR FLOW SENSOR
  REMOVAL & INSTALLATION 5-10
FUEL INJECTORS
  REMOVAL & INSTALLATION 5-8
FUEL PUMPS
  REMOVAL & INSTALLATION 5-7
GENERAL DESCRIPTION 5-7
PRESSURE REGULATOR
  REMOVAL & INSTALLATION 5-8
THROTTLE SWITCHES
  REMOVAL & INSTALLATION 5-10
ELECTRONIC ENGINE CONTROLS
DIGIFANT SYSTEM
  AIR FLOW SENSOR 4-18
  ELECTRONIC CONTROL UNIT (ECU) 4-18
  FUEL INJECTORS 4-22
  FUEL PRESSURE REGULATOR 4-22
  FUEL PUMPS 4-20
  IDLE STABILIZER VALVE 4-20
  TEMPERATURE SENSOR 4-23
  THROTTLE POSITION SWITCHES 4-18
MOTRONIC SYSTEM
  COLD START INJECTOR 4-17
  COMPONENT TESTING 4-13
  FUEL INJECTORS 4-16
  FUEL PRESSURE TESTING 4-14
  FUEL PUMPS 4-15
  GENERAL DESCRIPTION 4-10
  TEMPERATURE SENSOR 4-18
ELECTRONIC IGNITION
DESCRIPTION AND OPERATION 2-4
DIAGNOSIS AND TESTING
  DISTRIBUTOR CAP AND ROTOR 2-8
  HALL SENDER 2-4
  IGNITION COIL 2-8
  IGNITION CONTROL UNIT 2-5
  IGNITION WIRES 2-8
  KNOCK SENSOR 2-6
  POWER OUTPUT STAGE 2-5

ENGINE ELECTRICAL
ALTERNATOR
  ALTERNATOR PRECAUTIONS 3-6
  REMOVAL & INSTALLATION 3-6
BATTERY
  REMOVAL & INSTALLATION 3-6
DIESEL GLOW PLUGS
  REMOVAL & INSTALLATION 3-5
  TESTING 3-5
DISTRIBUTOR CAP AND ROTOR
  DIGIFANT 3-5
  IGNITION WIRES 3-5
  MOTRONIC 3-5
  TESTING 3-4
DISTRIBUTOR
  REMOVAL & INSTALLATION 3-4
HALL SENDER
  REMOVAL & INSTALLATION 3-2
IGNITION COIL
  DIGIFANT SYSTEM 3-2
  MOTRONIC SYSTEM 3-2
  REMOVAL & INSTALLATION 3-2
  TESTING 3-2
IGNITION SYSTEM PRECAUTIONS 3-2
STARTER
  REMOVAL & INSTALLATION 3-7
  SOLENOID REPLACEMENT 3-7
  TESTING 3-7
VOLTAGE REGULATOR 3-6
ENGINE MECHANICAL
CAMSHAFT (VALVE) COVER
  16V ENGINE 3-18
  EXCEPT 16V ENGINE 3-18
  REMOVAL & INSTALLATION 3-18
CAMSHAFT(S) AND BEARINGS
  16V ENGINES 3-32
  8 VALVE ENGINE 3-31
  INSPECTION 3-33
  REMOVAL & INSTALLATION 3-31
CRANKSHAFT AND MAIN BEARINGS
  BEARING OIL CLEARANCE 3-39
  CRANKSHAFT END-PLAY/CONNECTING ROD SIDE PLAY 3-40
  CRANKSHAFT REPAIRS 3-40
  REMOVAL & INSTALLATION 3-38
CYLINDER HEAD
  CLEANING AND INSPECTION 3-25
  DIESEL ENGINE 3-23
  GASOLINE ENGINE 3-22
  REMOVAL & INSTALLATION 3-22
  RESURFACING 3-25
DESCRIPTION
  DIESEL ENGINE 3-7
  GASOLINE ENGINES 3-7
ENGINE MOUNTS
  ADJUSTMENT 3-18
ENGINE OVERHAUL TIPS 3-8
ENGINE
  DIESEL ENGINE 3-17
  GASOLINE ENGINE 3-14
  REMOVAL & INSTALLATION 3-14
EXHAUST MANIFOLD
  GASOLINE ENGINE 3-19
  REMOVAL & INSTALLATION 3-19
FLYWHEEL
  REMOVAL & INSTALLATION 3-40
INSPECTION TECHNIQUES 3-8
INTAKE MANIFOLD
  DIESEL ENGINE 3-19

GASOLINE ENGINES 3-19
  REMOVAL & INSTALLATION 3-18
INTERMEDIATE SHAFT
  REMOVAL & INSTALLATION 3-33
MAIN OIL SEALS
  REMOVAL & INSTALLATION 3-38
OIL COOLER
  REMOVAL & INSTALLATION 3-20
OIL PAN
  REMOVAL & INSTALLATION 3-28
OIL PUMP
  INSPECTION 3-29
  INSTALLATION 3-29
  REMOVAL 3-29
OVERHAUL TIPS 3-8
PISTONS AND CONNECTING RODS
  CLEANING AND INSPECTION 3-34
  CYLINDER BORE 3-34
  CYLINDER HONING 3-36
  DIESEL PISTONS 3-37
  PISTON RINGS 3-37
  REMOVAL & INSTALLATION 3-33
RADIATOR AND FAN
  REMOVAL & INSTALLATION 3-20
REPAIRING DAMAGED THREADS
  CHECKING ENGINE COMPRESSION 3-9
  DIESEL ENGINES 3-11
  GASOLINE ENGINES 3-9
THERMOSTAT
  REMOVAL & INSTALLATION 3-18
TIMING BELT COVER
  REMOVAL & INSTALLATION 3-29
TIMING BELT
  DIESEL ENGINES 3-30
  GASOLINE ENGINES 3-29
  REMOVAL & INSTALLATION 3-29
TIMING SPROCKETS
  REMOVAL & INSTALLATION 3-31
TOOLS 3-8
TURBOCHARGER
  DIESEL ENGINE 3-20
  REMOVAL & INSTALLATION 3-20
VALVE GUIDES
  REMOVAL & INSTALLATION 3-28
VALVE LIFTERS 3-28
VALVE SEATS
  RECONDITIONING 3-28
VALVE SPRINGS
  INSPECTION 3-28
  REMOVAL & INSTALLATION 3-27
VALVE STEM SEALS
  CYLINDER HEAD INSTALLED 3-27
  CYLINDER HEAD REMOVED 3-27
  REPLACEMENT 3-27
VALVES
  INSPECTION 3-26
  REFACING VALVES 3-26
  REMOVAL & INSTALLATION 3-26
WATER PUMP
  REMOVAL & INSTALLATION 3-20
ENTERTAINMENT SYSTEM
RADIO
  ENTERING SECURITY CODE 6-20
  REMOVAL & INSTALLATION 6-20
EXHAUST EMISSIONS
COMPOSITION OF THE EXHAUST GASES
  CARBON MONOXIDE 4-4
  HYDROCARBONS 4-3

NITROGEN 4-4
OXIDES OF SULFUR 4-4
OZONE 4-4
PARTICULATE MATTER 4-4
OTHER AUTOMOBILE EMISSION SOURCES
CRANKCASE EMISSIONS 4-5
FUEL EVAPORATIVE EMISSIONS 4-5
EXHAUST SYSTEM
EXHAUST PIPE
16 VALVE ENGINE 3-42
8 VALVE ENGINE 3-41
REMOVAL & INSTALLATION 3-41
GENERAL DESCRIPTION 3-40
REAR SECTION
REMOVAL & INSTALLATION 3-43
EXTERIOR
ANTENNA
REMOVAL & INSTALLATION 10-4
BUMPERS
REMOVAL & INSTALLATION 10-3
CONVERTIBLE TOP
REMOVAL & INSTALLATION 10-4
DOORS
ADJUSTMENT & ALIGNMENT 10-2
REMOVAL & INSTALLATION 10-2
FENDERS
REMOVAL & INSTALLATION 10-4
GRILLE
REMOVAL & INSTALLATION 10-3
HOOD
ALIGNMENT 10-2
REMOVAL & INSTALLATION 10-2
OUTSIDE MIRRORS
REMOVAL & INSTALLATION 10-3
POWER TOP CYLINDERS
BLEEDING THE SYSTEM 10-6
REMOVAL & INSTALLATION 10-5
POWER TOP MOTOR
REMOVAL & INSTALLATION 10-4
REAR HATCH
ALIGNMENT 10-3
REMOVAL & INSTALLATION 10-3
SUNROOF
REMOVAL & INSTALLATION 10-8
TRUNK LID
ADJUSTMENT 10-3
REMOVAL & INSTALLATION 10-2
FIRING ORDERS 2-3
FLUIDS AND LUBRICANTS
AUTOMATIC TRANSAXLE
DRAIN AND REFILL 1-23
FLUID RECOMMENDATIONS 1-23
LEVEL CHECK 1-23
PAN AND FILTER SERVICE 1-24
BODY LUBRICATION 1-26
CHASSIS GREASING 1-25
CLUTCH MASTER CYLINDER
FLUID RECOMMENDATIONS 1-25
COOLING SYSTEM
DRAIN AND REFILL 1-24
FLUID RECOMMENDATIONS 1-24
FLUSHING AND CLEANING THE SYSTEM 1-25
LEVEL CHECK 1-24
DIFFERENTIAL
FLUID RECOMMENDATIONS 1-24
LEVEL CHECK 1-24
ENGINE OIL RECOMMENDATIONS
CHECKING ENGINE OIL LEVEL 1-21

DIESEL ENGINES 1-21
GASOLINE ENGINES 1-21
OIL AND FILTER CHANGE 1-22
FLUID DISPOSAL 1-20
FUEL REQUIREMENTS
DIESEL ENGINES 1-21
GASOLINE ENGINES 1-20
MANUAL TRANSAXLE
DRAIN AND REFILL 1-23
FLUID RECOMMENDATIONS 1-23
LEVEL CHECK 1-23
MASTER CYLINDER
FLUID RECOMMENDATIONS 1-25
LEVEL CHECK 1-25
POWER STEERING PUMP
FLUID RECOMMENDATIONS 1-25
LEVEL CHECK 1-25
REAR WHEEL BEARINGS
ADJUSTMENT 1-26
REMOVAL, PACKING & INSTALLATION 1-26
STEERING GEAR 1-25
FRONT DISC BRAKES
BRAKE CALIPER
OVERHAUL 9-8
REMOVAL & INSTALLATION 9-6
BRAKE PADS
CALIPER WITH GUIDE PINS 9-5
CALIPER WITH SLEEVES AND BUSHINGS 9-5
INSPECTION 9-6
REMOVAL & INSTALLATION 9-5
BRAKE ROTOR
INSPECTION 9-8
REMOVAL & INSTALLATION 9-8
FRONT SUSPENSION
FRONT END ALIGNMENT
CAMBER 8-5
CASTOR 8-5
TOE-IN 8-6
FRONT HUB AND WHEEL BEARING
REMOVAL & INSTALLATION 8-4
FRONT STEERING KNUCKLE
REMOVAL & INSTALLATION 8-4
LOWER BALL JOINT
INSPECTION 8-3
REMOVAL & INSTALLATION 8-3
LOWER CONTROL ARM
REMOVAL & INSTALLATION 8-4
MACPHERSON STRUT
REMOVAL & INSTALLATION 8-2
STRUT OVERHAUL 8-3
FUEL TANK
FUEL TANK ASSEMBLY
REMOVAL & INSTALLATION 5-13
SENDING UNIT
REMOVAL & INSTALLATION 5-14
GASOLINE ENGINE TUNE-UP PROCEDURES
SPARK PLUG WIRES
REMOVAL & INSTALLATION 2-3
SPARK PLUGS
REMOVAL & INSTALLATION 2-2
SELECTION 2-2
HEATER
BLOWER MOTOR
REMOVAL & INSTALLATION 6-11
CONTROL HEAD AND CABLES
ADJUSTMENT 6-14
REMOVAL & INSTALLATION 6-14

HEATER CORE
REMOVAL & INSTALLATION 6-12
HISTORY 1-6
HOW TO USE THIS BOOK 1-2
IDLE SPEED AND AIR/FUEL MIXTURE
GENERAL INFORMATION
INSPECTION PROCEDURE 2-10
IGNITION TIMING
IGNITION TIMING
ADJUSTMENT 2-9
TIMING MARK LOCATIONS 2-8
INSTRUMENTS AND SWITCHES
DYNAMIC OIL PRESSURE WARNING SYSTEM
TESTING 6-23
HEADLIGHT SWITCH
REMOVAL & INSTALLATION 6-25
INSTRUMENT CLUSTER
REMOVAL & INSTALLATION 6-23
VOLTAGE STABILIZER
TESTING 6-23
WINDSHIELD WIPER SWITCH
REMOVAL & INSTALLATION 6-24
INTERIOR
AIR CONDITIONER VENTS
REMOVAL & INSTALLATION 10-9
CENTRAL LOCKING SYSTEM
REMOVAL & INSTALLATION 10-10
TESTING 10-9
DOOR GLASS AND REGULATOR
REMOVAL & INSTALLATION 10-10
DOOR PANELS
REMOVAL & INSTALLATION 10-9
ELECTRIC WINDOW MOTOR
REMOVAL & INSTALLATION 10-10
HEADLINER
REMOVAL & INSTALLATION 10-9
INSIDE REAR VIEW MIRROR
REMOVAL & INSTALLATION 10-13
INSTRUMENT PANEL
REMOVAL & INSTALLATION 10-8
MANUAL DOOR LOCKS
REMOVAL & INSTALLATION 10-9
REAR WINDOW OR HATCH GLASS
REMOVAL & INSTALLATION 10-13
SEAT BELTS
REMOVAL & INSTALLATION 10-13
SEATS
REMOVAL & INSTALLATION 10-13
SIDE QUARTER GLASS
REMOVAL & INSTALLATION 10-13
WINDSHIELD
REMOVAL & INSTALLATION 10-10
JACKING 1-28
LIGHTING
HEADLIGHTS
AIMING 6-25
REMOVAL & INSTALLATION 6-25
SIGNAL AND MARKER LIGHTS
REMOVAL & INSTALLATION 6-25
MANUAL TRANSAXLE
ADJUSTMENTS
CABRIOLET 7-2
GOLF AND JETTA 7-2
SHIFT LINKAGE 7-2
AXLE SHAFT (HALFSHAFT)
CV-JOINT AND BOOT OVERHAUL 7-11
REMOVAL & INSTALLATION 7-11

BACK-UP LIGHT SWITCH
REMOVAL & INSTALLATION 7-2
TRANSAXLE IDENTIFICATION 7-2
TRANSAXLE
CABRIOLET 7-3
DIFFERENTIAL 7-9
GEAR CASE, INPUT SHAFT AND PINION SHAFT 7-5
GOLF AND JETTA 7-4
OVERHAUL 7-4
REMOVAL & INSTALLATION 7-3
MODEL IDENTIFICATION 1-6
PARKING BRAKE
CABLE
ADJUSTMENT 9-14
DISC BRAKES 9-14
REAR DRUM BRAKES 9-14
REMOVAL & INSTALLATION 9-14
PARKING BRAKE LEVER
REMOVAL & INSTALLATION 9-14
PUSH-STARTING AND TOWING 1-28
REAR DISC BRAKES
BRAKE CALIPER
OVERHAUL 9-12
REMOVAL & INSTALLATION 9-12
BRAKE PADS
INSPECTION 9-11
REMOVAL & INSTALLATION 9-11
BRAKE ROTOR
INSPECTION 9-13
REMOVAL & INSTALLATION 9-13
REAR DRUM BRAKES
BACK PLATE
REMOVAL & INSTALLATION 9-11
BRAKE DRUMS
INSPECTION 9-9
REMOVAL & INSTALLATION 9-9
BRAKE SHOES
INSPECTION 9-9
REMOVAL & INSTALLATION 9-9
WHEEL CYLINDER
REMOVAL & INSTALLATION 9-10
REAR SUSPENSION
REAR AXLE ASSEMBLY
REMOVAL & INSTALLATION 8-9
REAR WHEEL BEARINGS
REMOVAL & INSTALLATION 8-8
STRUT ASSEMBLY
REMOVAL & INSTALLATION 8-8
STUB AXLE
REMOVAL & INSTALLATION 8-9
ROUTINE MAINTENANCE
AIR CLEANER
REMOVAL & INSTALLATION 1-9
AIR CONDITIONING SYSTEM
CHARGING THE SYSTEM 1-18
DISCHARGING THE SYSTEM 1-18
EVACUATING THE SYSTEM 1-18
GAUGE SETS 1-17
LEAK TESTING 1-19
REFRIGERANT LEVEL CHECK 1-17
SAFETY WARNINGS 1-16
SYSTEM INSPECTION 1-16
BATTERY
CABLES AND CLAMPS 1-14
FLUID LEVEL INSPECTION 1-13
GENERAL MAINTENANCE 1-12
REPLACEMENT 1-15
TESTING SPECIFIC GRAVITY 1-14

BELTS
  CHECKING TENSION AND ADJUSTMENT 1-15
  REPLACEMENT 1-15
CRANKCASE VENTILATION SYSTEM 1-11
EVAPORATIVE CANISTER
  SERVICING 1-12
FUEL FILTER
  REMOVAL & INSTALLATION 1-10
FUEL/WATER SEPARATOR
  DRAINING WATER 1-11
HOSES
  REMOVAL & INSTALLATION 1-16
SERVICE INTERVALS
  15,000 MILE SERVICE 1-9
  30,000 MILE SERVICE 1-9
  60,000 MILE SERVICE 1-9
  7500 MILE SERVICE 1-9
  EVERY 2 YEARS 1-9
TIRES AND WHEELS
  INFLATION PRESSURE 1-20
  STORAGE 1-20
  TIRE DESIGN 1-20
  TIRE ROTATION 1-19
  TREAD DEPTH 1-20
WINDSHIELD WIPERS
  REMOVAL & INSTALLATION 1-19
SERIAL NUMBER IDENTIFICATION
  ENGINE 1-8
  TRANSAXLE 1-8
  VEHICLE 1-6
SERVICING YOUR VEHICLE SAFELY
  DO'S 1-5
  DON'TS 1-5
STEERING
  IGNITION LOCK CYLINDER
    REMOVAL & INSTALLATION 8-10
  IGNITION SWITCH
    REMOVAL & INSTALLATION 8-10
  MANUAL STEERING GEAR
    ADJUSTMENTS 8-12
    OVERHAUL 8-12
    REMOVAL & INSTALLATION 8-12
  POWER STEERING GEAR
    ADJUSTMENT 8-12
    REMOVAL & INSTALLATION 8-12
  POWER STEERING PUMP
    BLEEDING 8-13
    REMOVAL & INSTALLATION 8-12
  STEERING COLUMN
    REMOVAL & INSTALLATION 8-10
  STEERING LINKAGE
    REMOVAL & INSTALLATION 8-11
  STEERING WHEEL
    REMOVAL & INSTALLATION 8-9
  TURN SIGNAL AND WIPER SWITCHES
    REMOVAL & INSTALLATION 8-10
SUPPLEMENTAL RESTRAINT SYSTEM (AIR BAG)
  GENERAL INFORMATION
    SYSTEM COMPONENTS 6-10
    SYSTEM OPERATION 6-10
  SERVICE PRECAUTIONS
    DISARMING THE SYSTEM 6-11
    ENABLING THE SYSTEM 6-11

SUSPENSION AND STEERING
  WHEELS
    INSPECTION 8-2
    REMOVAL & INSTALLATION 8-2
TOOLS AND EQUIPMENT
  SPECIAL TOOLS 1-3
TRAILER TOWING
  ENGINE COOLING 1-27
  HITCH WEIGHT 1-27
  TRAILER WEIGHT 1-27
  WIRING 1-27
TRAILER WIRING 6-26
UNDERSTANDING AND TROUBLE-SHOOTING ELECTRICAL
  SYSTEMS
  MECHANICAL TEST EQUIPMENT
    GENERAL INFORMATION 6-9
  SAFETY PRECAUTIONS
    ORGANIZED TROUBLESHOOTING 6-2
  SPECIAL TEST EQUIPMENT 6-6
  TESTING AND EQUIPMENT
    INFORMATION 6-3
  WIRING HARNESSES
    GENERAL INFORMATION 6-7
VACUUM DIAGRAMS 4-31
VALVE LASH 2-10
VOLKSWAGEN EMISSION CONTROLS
  CATALYTIC CONVERTER
    GENERAL INFORMATION 4-9
  CRANKCASE VENTILATION SYSTEM
    OPERATION 4-6
    SERVICE 4-6
  EVAPORATIVE EMISSION CONTROLS
    OPERATION 4-6
    SERVICE 4-7
    TESTING 4-7
  EXHAUST GAS RECIRCULATION SYSTEM
    GENERAL INFORMATION 4-9
    REMOVAL & INSTALLATION 4-9
    TESTING 4-9
  GENERAL INFORMATION 4-6
  OXYGEN SENSOR
    GENERAL INFORMATION 4-10
    REMOVAL & INSTALLATION 4-10
    TESTING 4-10
WINDSHIELD WIPERS AND WASHERS
  REAR WINDOW WASHER PUMP AND FLUID RESERVOIR
    REMOVAL & INSTALLATION 6-23
  REAR WINDOW WIPER MOTOR
    REMOVAL & INSTALLATION 6-22
  REAR WIPER ARM
    REMOVAL & INSTALLATION 6-21
  WINDSHIELD WASHER PUMP AND FLUID RESERVOIR
    REMOVAL & INSTALLATION 6-22
  WINDSHIELD WIPER MOTOR
    REMOVAL & INSTALLATION 6-21
  WIPER ARM
    REMOVAL & INSTALLATION 6-21
  WIPER LINKAGE
    REMOVAL & INSTALLATION 6-22
WIRING DIAGRAMS
  SCHEMATICS 6-27
  TERMINAL DESIGNATIONS 6-27